The Scrappy Evangelist

ISBN: 978-1-5051-1023-4

ACS Books is an imprint of TAN Books
PO Box 410487
Charlotte, NC 28241
www.TANBooks.com

Printed and bound in the United States of America.

The Scrappy Evangelist

Chesterton and a
New Apologetics
for Today

Fr. Paul Rowan

ACS BOOKS

Preface

BY DALE AHLQUIST

President of the American Chesterton Society

A THEISM IS NOT NEW. Doubt and denial have been around as long as faith. But just as religion goes through periods of decline and revival, so does irreligion. Though the same basic truths collide with the same basic errors across the ages, they always have a different look to them and a different urgency. We have lately seen the rise of something called the New Atheism, with celebrity spokesmen who are basically apologists for a scientific materialism that sneers and snarls at religion in general and Christianity in particular. But while only a tiny percentage of the population actually professes atheism, an expanding mass of people effectively think and live atheistically. God is not part of their thinking or part of their day, not even part of their week, as they have stopped going to church. They are a long way off from the comprehensive theology of the Catholic Church, either knowing only enough about it to reject it, or not knowing enough to care.

Thus, the need for a New Apologetic to address both the active and passive unbelievers of today. The era known as the Modern Age is not only past its prime, it is hobbling with age. It has had to step aside for an unwieldy label known as The

Post-Modern, as if we have already sped past ourselves. Is there anyone who can get us to stand still long enough to see the truth?

Enter Chesterton. Or rather, Re-Enter Chesterton. Immensely popular in his time, G.K. Chesterton died over eighty years ago and was forgotten. Then, for some reason, people started to read him again. One of those people was a young boxer from Liverpool who became a Roman Catholic priest: Paul Rowan.

Father Rowan here presents Chesterton's life and thought and sense of wonder, and then brings him to bear on the question at hand. Is the witty journalist and poet who tossed off dozens of books on various subjects, who was once named by Pope Pius XI as a Defender of the Faith, still worthy of the title?

Whatever ties Chesterton to the time in which he wrote, only adorns him. It does not define him. This colorful character transcends his time and speaks to the post-modern audience, anticipating their objections to the faith, their broken thinking and their broken lives. Timeless writers tend to be timely.

. Although this is a scholarly work, Father Rowan invokes a fighter's term, which was also Chesterton's term: scrappy. Chesterton is a fighter, and he takes on post-modern doubt and disbelief with its own methods, which are indeed scrappy. But Chesterton, who fights in the heavy-weight division, is fluid in his movement, intuitive in his strategy, has a counter-punch for anything his opponents offer, and rains devastating blows of logic and common sense. Father Rowan gives us a ringside seat.

G.K. Chesterton says, "The Catholic Church will always be attacked because it is Catholic, and it will always be defended because it is Catholic."

Foreword

BY RT. REV. PHILIP EGAN BA, STL, PHD

Bishop of Portsmouth, England

"If I am asked, purely as an intellectual question, why I believe in Christianity, I can only answer 'For the same reason an intelligent agnostic disbelieves in Christianity'. I believe in it quite rationally upon the evidence. But the evidence in my case, as in that of the intelligent agnostic, is not really in this or that alleged demonstration; it is in an enormous accumulation of small but unanimous facts"
(G. K. Chesterton *Orthodoxy*).

APOLOGETICS (from Gk. *apologeomai* 'to make a defence of oneself' and 'to make a case for') is a branch of Christian theology that seeks to defend the Christian faith from criticism and to present compelling arguments for its truth-claims. Apologetics has been around since New Testament times and has taken different forms and approaches in different eras. St. Peter once said: "Always be prepared to make a defence to any one who calls you to account for the hope that is in you. Yet do it with gentleness and reverence; and keep your conscience clear, so that, when you are abused, those who revile your good behaviour in Christ may be put to shame" (1 Peter 3: 14-6). An early example of this in practice was St. Paul addressing the Council of the Areopagus, arguing that the Unknown God already familiar to the Athenians was the One he had come to preach (Acts 17:22-34).

As a literary form, apologetics developed once Christianity began to win converts amongst the educated classes of the Roman Empire. In the mid 2nd century, St. Justin Martyr (d. 165), Tatian (d. 180) and, Irenaeus (d. 202), the Bishop of Lyons, each in their own way presented the case for Christianity. They defended the concept of monotheism and the divinity of Christ against the Roman and Greek *panthea* and, developing the approach of the evangelist St. Matthew, demonstrated for Jewish believers how Christ fulfilled the prophecies of the Old Testament. They also defended the Church against pagan charges of cannibalism, incest, misanthropy and atheism. In the 3rd century, Clement of Alexandria (d. 215) and Origen (d. 254) brought Christian beliefs into dialogue with the Middle Platonism of the day, defending Christian orthodoxy against the errors of Gnosticism. Other writers of the Early Church, who were also apologists, included Eusebius of Caesarea (d. 339) and the great Augustine of Hippo (d. 430).

Two of the most notable mediaeval apologists were St. John Damascene (d. 749), who defended the use of sacred images during the Iconoclastic Controversy, and St. Anselm of Canterbury, who proposed the noteworthy 'Ontological Argument' for God's existence, a demonstration from logic and metaphysics in contrast to arguments based on cosmology. The thirteenth century was a time of new thinking and cross-currents, thanks to the recovery of Aristotle's metaphysics, with new intellectual movements, including Aristotle's habit of science based on empirical observation. These were taken up by St. Albert the Great (d. 1280) and his protégé, St. Thomas Aquinas (d. 1274). Aquinas authored two important works, which in different ways are apologetical. His *Summa Contra Gentiles* (literally "Against the Pagans", or more properly "The Truth of the Catholic Faith against the Errors of Unbelievers") offered a synthesis of theology to assist missionaries in presenting the Christian faith to non-believers. In it, Aquinas seeks to show how human nature is naturally oriented towards knowing and loving God, a demonstration with a remarkably modern ring. The other work was his famous *Summa Theologiae*, in which he outlines 'Five Ways' (change, causality, contingency, excellence and teleology) to show, on the basis of human experience, that it is not unreasonable to assert the existence of God.

After the Reformation, both Catholic and Reformed apologetics became polemical and vehemently controversialist. For Catholics, the point at issue was the manner in which Revelation is transmitted, by Scripture alone or by both Scripture and the Church's Tradition. The Dominican theologian Thomas Cajetan (d. 1534) and the Jesuit Cardinal, St. Robert Bellarmine (d. 1621) sought to defend Catholic doctrine on the nature of the Church, on the papacy, on the seven sacraments, on Purgatory and the intercession of the saints. This strongly anti-Protestant stance marked all Catholic apologetics (and theology) until recent times.

In the Enlightenment period, challenges to the Christian faith came from the various new movements in philosophy, scholarship and science, many of which were atheistic, agnostic or indifferentist. In the eighteenth century, revelation became contested, in the nineteenth, the relationship between faith and reason, and in the twentieth, the role of religion in the public square. Thus Deist thinkers, whilst asserting His existence, portrayed God as a 'Divine Clockmaker', little concerned with current human affairs, and human morality as founded not on revelation but right reason. Eighteenth century Anglican thinkers such as Bishop Joseph Butler (d. 1752) in response sought to defend Christianity as a revealed religion. Catholic apologetics meanwhile adopted the traditional three-fold demonstration of the existence of God by natural theology, the divinity of Christ, shown by miracles and the Resurrection, and the truth-claims of the Roman Church, shown by its four marks (unity, holiness, catholicity and apostolicity).

A number of nineteenth century movements in art, music and literature, four in particular, challenged the relationship of faith and reason. At the risk of simplification, romanticism, with its emphasis on intuition and affectivity, espoused the 'turn to the subject.' Liberalism underlined the freedom of the individual and gave rise to what John Henry Cardinal Newman (d. 1890) called the 'anti-dogmatic principle.' Rationalism submitted religious truth-claims to human reason and modernism submitted them to personal experience. Apologetical arguments responded with a renewed consideration of the innate structures of the human person. Blessed Antonio Rosmini (d. 1855) and Ambrose Gardeil (d. 1931) argued that God was transcendentally intended within the act of human knowing. Maurice Blondell (d. 1949) saw action for good as the answer to the human quest for meaning, whilst Newman in his *Grammar of Assent* saw all knowledge as having a fiduciary character, certainty being reached through the convergence of probabilities. This, meanwhile, was the era of Charles Darwin (d. 1882), in which a growing collision, real or apparent, took place between science and religion, together with the emergence of modern historical scholarship and forms of biblical exegesis that seemed to challenge many of the presuppositions of Christian doctrine.

The twentieth century raised the issue of the general relevance of religion and its role in the public square. The rise of secularism, the political and economic philosophy of Marxism and the challenges raised by Freudianism and other forms of psychology, meant that Christianity and its cultural patrimony became increasingly eclipsed and overlaid in Western European nations. This process accelerated after the 1960s, with its sexual and social revolutions leading to the demise of the traditional family. In response, an outstanding series of Christian apologists arose, of whom G. K. Chesterton here is the best-known, along with Hilaire Belloc (d. 1953), Clive Staples Lewis (d. 1963), and Michael Sheehan (d. 1945). The *Nouvelle Théologie* of the inter-war years sought to overcome the limits of the prevailing Neo-Scholasticism by returning to biblical, patristic and medi-aeval sources, and these new lines of thought were vindicated at the Second Vatican Council (1962-5). Thus, the Lutheran theologian Paul Tillich (d. 1965) and Karl Rahner (d. 1984), the most significant figure in post-conciliar Catholic theolo-gy, sought to show that in the deep structures of their being, humans are oriented towards divine. Hans Kung (b. 1928) has endeavoured to propose Christianity as a most perfect form of religion, Peter Kreeft (b. 1937) that classical wisdom continues to have much to say to contemporary moral and social life, and René Latourelle (b. 1918) that Jesus Christ is the answer to all human problems.

Today, post-modern currents of thought challenge traditional and Christian anthropology: What is the meaning of being hu-man? What is the human person? How can a person attain true happiness? Contradictory and opposed anthropologies compete for dominance. Are humans just higher animals, biological ma-chines, objects to be manipulated for pleasure, gain and power? Or are humans radically other, persons to be respected, crea-tures with limits, people with dignity and vocation? Advances in medical science combine with revolutions in personal and social *mores* to raise controverted issues around abortion, eugenics, euthanasia and gender identity. Contemporary apologetics, typi-fied by the lead of Pope St. John Paul II (d. 2005), Pope Benedict XVI (b. 1927) and Pope Francis (b. 1936), has thus taken an anthropological turn, seeking to uphold the immeasurable dignity and value of the human person, solidarity and communion, truth and mercy, truth and freedom.

Meanwhile, in today's context, it must be admitted that apologetics has undergone a decline, even an eclipse, thanks to the fluid and confusing situation within Western culture and within the Christian Church itself. Fr. Rowan tackles some of the issues in Chapter Six of this book. Many argue that a Northern and European idiom cannot speak effectively to the whole Church of every land or place. They contest the very possibility of apologetics as a rational demonstration. In the past, the aim was to demonstrate the intellectual coherence and truth of doctrine, whereas today the issue is about meaning. What convinces is not argument, they aver, but image over word, authenticity, holiness of life, a grand gesture, a good example, a personal approach, practical help and aid-work. Apologetics in the past has often been combative; arguably the need today is for conversation and dialogue. Because of the atavistic individualism of much Western culture, a bespoke approach is required. Arguments from history – that, for instance, Christ's identity is proven by His miracles - or from authority – that, once the papacy is shown as grounded on Matthew 16: 18, everything else follows on - are now discredited, thanks to the renewal of theology and biblical exegesis. Indeed, the key issue for a modern apologetics, it might be argued, is the addressee. In the past, the addressee was a non-Catholic Christian or an unbeliever, a person of good will and common sense not belonging to the Church. But today, who is the addressee? Many Christians do not practice faith and those that do, raise the same searching questions as non-believers. A new apologetics therefore needs clearly to identify its ground, its purpose and its scope.

I warmly commend this scholarly work on the great and saintly English writer, journalist, poet and Christian apologist, G. K. Chesterton, his life, his thought, his writings. Fr. Rowan's book is an important contribution to Chesterton studies. But the question he asks in *Towards a New Apologetics* is also an important question about apologetics for Christians today: What can be learnt from Chesterton, the great and unsurpassedly eloquent master of the early twentieth century? How can Chesterton help contemporary Christians to articulate and defend their faith in the complex and materialistic secular culture of the twenty-first century with all the intellectual, moral and spiritual confusion it engenders?

Recent popes have summoned Christians to an evangelisation "new in its ardour, new in its methods and new in its expression" (Pope St. John Paul II). This is exactly where the inspiring figure and personality of G. K. Chesterton, together with his writings and *bon mots*, can assist Christians both in their own growth and in their witness to others. Fr. Rowan draws from Chesterton elements that can assist an apologetics for today: the need to dialogue with unbelievers, attention to the *preambula fidei*, the sense of fellowship on life's journey, the mystery of the universe, the necessity for a dialogue between faith and culture, human freedom and self-transcendence, the centrality of the Person of Jesus Christ and the role of conversion, especially of heart and will. Of course, as Chesterton himself insists, Christian faith must always be performative. Fr. Rowan is thus able to conclude that a "renewed apologetics needs to recognise .. that the most dangerous sort of unbelief is to be found not in explicit formulations about the meaning of human existence in the cosmos, but in the concrete refusal to love here and now in that cosmos."

Acknowledgments

(and a Little Note about Popes and Projects)

"You cannot love a thing without wanting to fight for it."

"I believe in getting into hot water. I think it keeps you clean."

"The issue is now clear. It is between light and darkness and everyone must choose his side."

—*G. K. Chesterton*

"WHAT YOU GONNA SAY NOW, HUH? 'He can't go one round!' 'He'll get him in two!' 'He pulls his head back!' 'He holds his hands too low!' Well I'm still pretty!" Cassius Clay (later Muhamad Ali), after winning the World Heavyweight Title against Sonny Liston on 25th February 1964 (a fight in which most people thought he would be annihilated, and which took place some three years before he was sent into exile for refusing to be drafted for the Vietnam War)

Chesterton says that when it comes to life, the critical thing is whether you take things for granted or take them with gratitude. Deepest (and not always expressed) gratitude goes to my parents, Mal and Mike, for giving me the rudiments of the Catholic vision, as well as the space and freedom to discern and explore God's call to love. Special thanks to Dad for his nuanced wisdom about the Church, the truth of which I see ever more clearly, the older I get. He taught me to respect authority, but he also drummed it into me never to be afraid to speak truth to power, since power is an attribute of the Omnipotent God and those who exercise it are answerable to Him. I salute my two sisters, Michele and Elaine, for treating both my achievements and disasters with the same degree of (ultimate) disinterest, and for remaining, throughout the rough and tumble of family co-existence, wonderful people and steadfast friends.

The Scriptures distinguish in more than one place between apparent and real friends, and Ecclesiasticus 6:14 reminds us that a faithful friend is a sturdy shelter and a treasure. With some of the following people I have enjoyed years (even decades) of true companionship, precious and lasting bonds forged through good times and bad, as we lived, laughed and fought battles about justice and injustice, truth and falsehood, substance and spin, genuine love and self-service carried out in the name of God. Some of the other people listed I have not known anywhere near as long, but they quickly became friends because they shared similar instincts about which side they were on in such scraps. Some simply said the right thing at the right time and provided essential etrength and focus. I would like to thank (in alphabetical order): Christopher Beirne; Fr. Gerry Devlin; Michael and Eveline Dodd; Bishop Philip Egan; Fr. Rob Esdaile; Monsignor Nicholas France; Fr. Paul Murray OP; Richard Pitkethly; William Quinton; Archbishop Arthur Roche; Archbishop Charles Scicluna; Sr. Gemma Simmonds, CJ; Moya St. Leger; Dr. Anthony Towey; Monsignor Anthony Wilcox.

For the immediate publication of this book, not to mention its punchy, pugilistic preface, as well as for several years of friendship rooted in faith, love of G. K. Chesterton and wine, my heartfelt gratitude goes to Dale Ahlquist, President of the American Chesterton Society and the world's foremost Chestertonian. I thank Don Flanagan, Editor at ACS Books, for serving this project wonderfully with his patience, generosity, many talents and keen eye. And I thank Ted Schluenderfritz for his amazing work as Graphic Designer. These three gentlemen managed to Americanize an Englishman's script without horrifying him in the slightest, and were also crystal clear on those occasions when this punch-drunk old has-been had (according to Dale) fallen flat on his face and was making no sense in the script! All mistakes are mine, therefore, and may all blessings be theirs.

I am indebted to Fr. Paul Murray OP, Archbishop Charles Scicluna and Bishop Philip Egan for finding time in their crazy schedules to prepare some words of commendation for this project (Bishop Egan in a wonderfully crafted foreword). These three men, each in his own way, provide models of humble discipleship, placing considerable intelligence, generosity and authority at the service of the diocesan, national, international and Roman Church. To all who occupy, whether lay or ordained, positions of power and authority in the evangelising mission of the Church, these men are a reminder of something Pope Francis often refers to: that there is an eschatologically vital distinction to be made between Christian love and the featherbedding of one's own agenda in the name of Christ.

I would like to make a public record of my appreciation of the role in my life of Fr. Michael Paul Gallagher SJ, former Professor of Fundamental Theology at the Pontifical Gregorian University Rome, and my tutor for the doctoral thesis on which this book is based. For a quarter of a century, until his untimely death in November 2015, Michael Paul's inspiration, friendship and support kept me going, through three periods of study and ministry in Rome and beyond. He was the best of teachers – firm and sure in his critical evaluation, but always somehow gentle and encouraging in his tone. Like his father Ignatius, 'MPG' got me to recognize that God is always at work in the midst of all things, both in our success and our mess, and that God really uses our life, our work, our writing, our preaching and our teaching to touch the hearts of others during our brief sojourn in this world. This book is published with gratitude in his memory.

Chesterton says that we cannot love a thing without wanting to scrap for it. He also said that a real soldier does not fight because he hates what is in front of him, but because he loves what is behind him. In a fallen world and a sinful Church (of which we are all part), sometimes one has to fight against people if one is to do the thing that is loving, truthful and just. People have fought for me and I have fought for them. It is to Laura, as a sign of my love for all those I love, that I dedicate this book.

A Last Little Note: In the sixth and final chapter of this book, I talk of how Pope Benedict XVI called for the Church to open up a "Court of the Gentiles" in order to dialogue with those who do not share the Church's faith: to put the wisdom of the Church in conversation with the aspirations and movements of a western culture; to put Peter in dialogue with Pan. The reader will notice that Pope Benedict is mentioned several times this book, but not Pope Francis, because the book is based on a thesis that was defended in Rome three months before Francis' election. I suspect that Chesterton would have loved both Benedict and Francis for different reasons. To this next project I hope to turn soon.

Contents

CHAPTER III

Wonder, Paradox, and Contingency. 173

CHAPTER IV

Community and Church in the Search for God. 297

Introduction

THE SECOND VATICAN COUNCIL provided the occasion for the first serious engagement with atheism in the history of the Church. *Gaudium et spes* 19 says:

> The dignity of man rests above all on the fact that he is called to communion with God. The invitation to converse with God is addressed to man as soon as he comes into being. For if man exists it is because God has created him through love, and through love continues to hold him in existence. He cannot live fully according to truth unless he freely acknowledges that love and entrusts himself to his creator. Many however of our contemporaries either do not at all perceive, or else explicitly reject, this intimate and vital bond of man to God. Atheism must therefore be regarded as one of the most serious problems of our time, and one that deserves more thorough treatment.

No longer was atheism to be seen merely as an error in the interpretation of the meaning of existence, or the official philosophy of hostile communistic political regimes, or the sinful attitude of a proud and arrogant mind. Rather, atheism was to be understood as an existential and pastoral problem, as many of the Church's contemporaries were unable to recognize an invitation that had been extended to them to enter into relationship with the Creator whose love was the origin, daily sustenance, and ultimate resting place of their very being.

As we shall see in Chapter II, one of the most distinctive features of of G. K. Chesterton's was his way of seeing, of recognizing: Chesterton saw differently and thereby recognized certain things about the cosmos. He looked out upon life with eyes that wondered at the sheer gift of existence, and this wonder then became the occasion for joyful gratitude for the gift. Chesterton's own journey toward God started through wonder and joyful gratitude, but it was a wonder that had to be rediscovered after it had been lost. He would have agreed—because of personal lived experience—with *Gaudium et spes* that the inability to believe in God is more a question of unrecognized relationship, rather than a theoretical rejection (though, of course, the latter can be a product of the former). Although Chesterton's own deep sense of wonder had been something instinctive to him in his childhood, it had become eclipsed by the crises that accompanied the onset of adolescence and young adulthood in a late Victorian English culture. As we shall see, during the crisis of his time as a student at the Slade School of Art, Chesterton became unable to perceive the richness of the full range of human experiences. After he emerged from this crisis he was able to say that he "hung on to the remains of religion by one thin thread of thanks. I thanked whatever gods might be, not like Swinburne, because no life lived for ever, but because any life lived at all."[1]

In this book, we shall ask if there are lessons to be learned from Chesterton for all those who are trying to help people make sense of faith in twenty-first century postmodern culture. How can Chesterton help these apologists to help others in their struggles to flourish, discover meaning, and live life? How can he help others make sense of the possibility of God?

---

[1] *Autobiography*, 91.

1. Origins of the Book

The idea of undertaking a book on this particular topic was born as a result of two strands of my experience as a student, pastor, and teacher.

Firstly, for over two decades I have been fascinated by the person and works of G. K. Chesterton (1874-1936). The initial attraction was because he seemed to offer to my youthful need for certainty and spiritual identity some rather definite and confidently expressed Christian and Catholic answers. However, as the years went by and my own spiritual journey unfolded, I began to perceive that there were elements in the life and works of Chesterton that I had not fully appreciated: that his path to the Christian faith and to the Catholic Church in particular had taken a rather circuitous route and that, while his answers were confident, they were offered with a humility that was totally respectful of and charitable toward those who disagreed with them, because Chesterton was a man full of sympathy toward those who were struggling to make sense of existence.

Secondly, over the years of my pastoral ministry and teaching, I have been asked again and again why I always seem to have a slight leaning toward or preference for the secular, and for people who struggle to make sense of issues of faith, or who are un-churched. In seeking an answer to this question, I have come to realize that if many people in our secular Western culture feel disconnected, unmoved, untouched and apathetic toward the language, images and treasures of our Christian tradition, the fault is not always theirs. In a complex and increasingly secular world there is a different climate and context for religious faith today, in which the cultural supports for faith are no longer there. Consequently it is no longer so easy to inherit a religious faith—from one's parents, or from any of the institutions that have traditionally handed on the Christian message. One need not accept all the claims of a Western culture that is a strange mix of modernity and postmodernity to see clearly that people have been shaped by persuasive forces that can often be superficial and hostile toward tradition, authority and universal claims to meaning and truth. At the same time, the Church must also bear some degree of responsibility for the decline in faith. If there is a failure in communication, then responsibility for this can lie, to a greater or lesser degree, in one or both parties. Therefore it is legitimate to ponder whether or not the Church has proclaimed the treasures of its tradition with as much creativity, imagination and pastoral wisdom as it might. The desire to seek new ways of translating the Christian heritage for the many different contexts in which people find themselves today has always been a vital part of my ministry.

It would be misleading to say that the secular culture offers no hope for the possibilities of faith. There are encouraging signs: since the desire for God is written in the heart of humanity,[2] therefore the search for meaning, for a foundation for living and for love and community abide. People still experience their hungers and hopes for what the Catholic tradition calls the presence of God. Part of the mission of the Church at the beginning of the twenty-first century is to invite the people of our culture who feel distant from the Church to bring their questions, longings, yearnings, hopes, aspirations, searching, hurts, sin, beauty, color and energy into the Christian community, to contribute to and shape that community, and to be shaped by it.

---

[2] *Catechism of the Catholic Church*, 27.

Apologetics has been a long-standing field of theology with a rich tradition, starting with the New Testament itself, and moving through some of the Church Fathers, Augustine of Hippo, Aquinas, Pascal, Newman, Blondel and other great figures. It is intimately connected with the proclamation of the Gospel, even if not strictly part of it. Addressing both unbelievers in their doubts and believers in their struggles, apologetics seeks to spell out, in a systematic way, why there are good grounds for considering the Christian proclamation to be true. Though it is neither necessary nor sufficient for Christian faith, and though it can never amount to a compelling proof for the claims of faith, apologetics aims to show that it is reasonable and not unintelligent to believe the Gospel. It seeks to organize the signs or bits of evidence for the claims of the Gospel, such that they can lead a person to take personal responsibility for her faith.

For various reasons, which will be briefly sketched out in the sixth chapter of this book, apologetics has fallen into difficulties in more recent times, and seems to some people to be overly defensive of Christian claims, superficially rationalist or neglectful of the utterly unique nature of Christian revelation. As cultural factors change, theological fashions can also change of course, and there has been a renewed emphasis in the last thirty years or so, right across the spectrum of Christian churches, including the Catholic Church, on the value of apologetics in spreading the Gospel in a secular culture. The challenges to apologetics today come primarily because the tone of unbelief of many people is not so much that of the confident rationalist rejection of God that is embodied in the "New Atheism" of Dawkins et al. The new addressee of the Christian apologist is the relatively comfortable Westerner living within the social structures of a culture in which God seems unnecessary, and faith appears unreal and irrelevant. The new preambles of credibility need to address the fact that today's unbelief has more of a flavour of having been culturally induced, rather than "thought out" or existing because of explicitly held ideas and ideologies.

Today's apologetics, therefore, has to contain both an existential and cultural dimension and an intellectual and rational dimension. It has to have a more pastoral tone that can help people to become liberated enough to re-imagine themselves and rethink some of the assumptions of the dominant culture. It has to be generous enough to recognize what exists within the culture that is in harmony with the aspirations of the Gospel and seek to dialogue with it, and at the same time courageous and rigorously intelligent enough to critique the irrational, dehumanizing and anti-Gospel elements of the culture. After all, the New Atheists have not merely hugged people into unbelief.

Given that G. K. Chesterton wrote for a wide secular readership and debated and lectured in halls at the height of the world's enthrallment with modernity, this book asks what Chesterton can contribute to this new agenda for apologetics. Chesterton believed that, "if Christianity should happen to be true—then defending it may mean talking about anything or everything"[3] and, consequently, he went on to defend a Christian perspective in so much of what he published. His wisdom and insight into countless topics is as fresh and pertinent today as the day he wrote it. Many of his works have never been out of print, and many have come back into print as new generations have discovered the relevance of his genius for their own day.

---

[3] G. K. Chesterton, *Daily News*, 12th December 1903, cited in D. Ahlquist, *G. K. Chesterton: The Apostle of Common Sense*, 19.

2. METHOD, LIMITS, AND
SOURCES OF THE RESEARCH

The main focus of this book is a critical analysis and evaluation of the life and writings of the English journalist and author, G. K. Chesterton (1874-1936). On one level it is possible to begin anywhere with Chesterton and find something useful for apologetics. However, because Chesterton wrote over a hundred books, penned contributions to two hundred other books, and because he wrote novels, short stories, detective fiction, poems, plays, newspaper essays, pieces on art and literary criticism, social and cultural criticism, politics, history, economics, philosophy, and theology, it follows that any book which uses his work for its sources will, of necessity, find it essential to set limits very quickly. To this end, and though several other sources in the vast Chestertonian corpus will occasionally be used, this book will draw primarily on (in order of date of publication) *Heretics* (1905), *Orthodoxy* (1908), *St. Francis of Assisi* (1923), *The Everlasting Man* (1925), *The Catholic Church and Conversion* (1927), *The Thing: Why I Am A Catholic* (1929), *Saint Thomas Aquinas: The Dumb Ox* (1933) and *Autobiography* (1936). These works form the main sources of research and determine the parameters of our study because they are the works that, in my judgment, contain the insights and passages that are most explicitly relevant to our topic. It is important to note that special attention will be paid to *Orthodoxy*, one of the Christian masterpieces of the twentieth century, regarded by Chesterton himself as "a sort of slovenly autobiography,"[4] and a work that describes the spiritual and intellectual journey which led him to embrace the Christian creed.

---

[4] *Orthodoxy*, 215.

3. Aim of the Book

This book aims to answer the question: What can the life and works of G. K. Chesterton contribute to the forging of a new agenda for apologetics in today's postmodern cultural context?

4. Structure of the Book

The book consists of this present introduction, six chapters and a conclusion. The chapters are as follows: Chapter One: A Biographical Sketch; Chapter Two: The Submerged Sunrise of Wonder; Chapter Three: Wonder, Paradox, and Contingency; Chapter 4: Community and Church in the Search for God; Chapter 5: Doing the Truth in the Romance of the Ordinary; Chapter 6: Scrappy Evidence for a Postmodern World.

The first chapter offers an overview of the life of Chesterton and explores more fully his early development. A movement is traced from his childhood, which provided him with a (not idyllic) happiness that he treasured all his life, through the crisis that shook him during the solipsistic, possibly even suicidal years of his adolescence and young adulthood, from which he eventually emerged, in his own words, thanks to the "mystical minimum of gratitude" for being—for the fact that anything exists at all. The intellectual, imaginative, and spiritual maturation that took place in Chesterton during this time of crisis, and which is most cogently expressed in his 1908 work *Orthodoxy*, laid the imaginative and intellectual foundations of his hope-filled view of the cosmos, and it remained the foundation on which the rest of his prodigious literary and apologetic output was erected.

The second chapter examines how Chesterton's life and works show that so often, before setting out on the journey toward

God, the first step that is often required is a liberation at the level of disposition. Once he had got free of the reigning materialistic and pessimistic worldview of the Aesthetes, Chesterton's wonder, humility, and joyful gratitude in the face of existence followed. Sometimes people need to be free from certain things in order to be free for the journey of faith. Spiritual hungers and a sense of intelligent wonder may be blocked by the cultural assumptions and the self-images that these induce in people. Therefore apologetics today has to retain its traditional identity and yet become more anthropological, humbly placing itself in dialogue with spirituality, evangelization, and other ecclesial and secular disciplines, in order to help people get in touch with their hungers and hopes, which remain in spite of the difficulties and pressures of twenty-first century living.

Although Chesterton certainly believed in employing the mind to the full in the quest for God, the second chapter of the book points out that he believed that a human being was more than a cool, logical, rationalistic processor of concepts. Adopting the latter as an approach to understanding the cosmos can often be accompanied by an attitude that sees knowledge about this world and the big questions of reality as ways of asserting one's intellectual superiority and winning arguments. This is a superficial disposition and not especially helpful as a stance from which to discuss anything truly worthwhile, since the most evident thing about the cosmos is that the key to its mystery is not obvious. For Chesterton, then, a personal decision is required if we are to see accurately. If we make that decision, if we take that step, the cosmos opens up before us and we begin to see the paradoxical nature of the mystery of reality.

The third chapter goes on to explore the notion of paradox that was central to so much of Chesterton's work, and which allowed him to argue for a broad apologetics: one which admitted evidence for the existence of God from a variety of areas of the human experience of life in the cosmos. He believed in starting from anywhere in making the case for God, and was utterly opposed to reducing faith to a few singular perspectives, themes, or agendas (to do which would be to bow before false gods). More specifically, this chapter looks at Chesterton's "Ethics of Elfland" (Chapter 4 of *Orthodoxy*) and Chesterton's exploration of both contingency and "the doctrine of conditional joy" (the moral law and its relationship to human flourishing). The chapter ends with an exploration of the importance of art in the thought of Chesterton (who trained as an artist before making his career as a journalist). For Chesterton, fallen human beings have a habit of forgetting their greatness and the lessons of Elfland, and it was for this reason that he contended that so much of modern art had become divorced from the search for the transcendent and eternal, in favor of the ephemeral, transient, and new. The artistic faculty (which Chesterton believed could be expressed in many ways: for example, through painting, writing, planting a garden, bringing up children, teaching, coaching a sport) is a uniquely human quality that allows human beings a share in the creativity of God. It reminds us of our divine nature and points to the divine, and is born when the temporary touches the eternal.

The fourth chapter outlines how Christian faith is a journey undertaken with others. A brief perusal of some of the friendships in Chesterton's life enables us to understand how community is built up and necessary for the journey toward God. We also discover there some valuable lessons for the apologist. It will be noted how a refusal or an inability to pledge oneself to relationships with others will make the face of God less easy to discern. With this in mind, the chapter will explore the Church as the place par excellence where faith is born and where people find nourishment and community for the adventure of moving toward God. The chapter will look to articulate the importance and relevance of the graced, struggling, and sinful Church in a postmodern culture that does not always make such an apologetics an easy task.

The Church claims to be the sign and sacrament of the very concrete and definitive self-giving of God in Jesus of Nazareth, a definiteness that can be another cause of nervousness and hostility for the postmodern person. The long history of God's self-revelation to humanity, which culminates in the Everlasting Man, and the translation of that revelation for the many and varied situations in which people find themselves in the numerous cultures and movements of history down to our own day, constitute the tradition of the Church's theological reflection. The chapter explores the need for Peter to be in constant dialogue with Pan if he is to mediate God's meaning for a new generation of searchers. The Church can discern where the Spirit of God is already at work in the hungers, yearnings, and quests of a culture, and help the people of that culture to see that the Spirit who is active within their lives leads to Christ. The Spirit can gently help them see that their quest could become lonely and fruitless without the nourishing wisdom of a community that has behind it a long history of reflecting on human and divine realities.

In the fifth chapter we discover how for Chesterton, gratitude for the double gift of a cosmos and a life by which to enjoy that cosmos is the seedbed of all virtue. To be humble enough to recognize the blessing of one's creatureliness and to be thankful for this "infinite debt" is the fuel that drives us toward the love of one's fellow creatures by sharing with them the gift of the cosmos in accordance with the will of the Creator. Humility consists of maintaining in harmony two truths: the fact that we are nothing and yet everything—contingent creature and beloved child of God. Humility causes us to become aware of our lack, need, and inner poverty before the fullness that is Christ. Humor is its cognate and a uniquely human characteristic that points to God.

This chapter also explores how God is not a deistic landlord who has gone missing from human existence, but the God of the ordinary and the everyday. Christ promises us another advocate to be with us, to shape and mold us in the drama of daily choices. The notion of the abiding presence of the Spirit, leading us ever more deeply into humility and the religious conversion toward truth and love, is the immanent presence of the God who is also transcendent. The costly conversion that constitutes the fundamental religious call to love is that which builds up community. We see, then, that Christianity is not merely something that exists to make us feel good about ourselves and our world. If we are aware that life and the cosmos are a gift that comes to us out of the generous love of God, we are to slowly learn also that with that gift comes the burden of caring for others, especially the weak and wounded of our world. If we are loved, we must rise out of our comfort zone in order to show a gritty love to others. This willingness to enter into the vulnerabilities of others by becoming vulnerable in love ourselves makes us more able to discern the face of God.

The sixth and final chapter offers a brief historical context for the status of apologetics today—describing how it fell out of fashion in the recent past, but also how it has re-emerged toward the end of the twentieth century and at the turn of the new millennium as a strong and fruitful theological discipline in a postmodern world. This is underlined by a consideration of Pope Benedict XVI's call for the Church to open up a Court of the Gentiles in order to dialogue with those who do not share the Church's faith: to put the wisdom of the Church in conversation with the aspirations and movements of a western culture or, as Chesterton might have put it, to put Peter in dialogue with Pan. In *Orthodoxy* Chesterton noted that "scrappy" bits of evidence for the existence of God, coming from various sources (referred to as the Book, Battle, Landscape, and Old Friend, which give this present book its title), have a more convincing overall effect. This chapter therefore proceeds to explore some of the "scrappy" bits of evidence discovered in a study of Chesterton, clues which might, when taken together rather than in isolation, generate a cumulative persuasiveness that appeals in a holistic way to the whole person in a postmodern culture.

5. Original Contribution and Further Research

It goes without saying that the vast corpus of G. K. Chesterton's works constitutes a rich resource for research. Nevertheless, so far as I can ascertain, no systematic study of his life and work has been undertaken in the field of fundamental theology, which seeks to gather together insights that might prove useful for the reformulation of an apologetics that is able to meet the challenges of twenty-first century postmodern culture.

It is my hope that this book can offer a solid platform for others to build on in their own research, serving as an impetus for further discussion about the nature of contemporary apologetics and its overlap with other disciplines in the Church's evangelizing mission in a complex world. It is further hoped that this book may also contribute to the ever-increasing body of knowledge about the person, life, work, and contemporary relevance of G. K. Chesterton.

CHAPTER I

A Biographical Sketch

Once a man is dead, if it be only yesterday, the newcomer must piece him together from descriptions really as much at random as if he were describing Caesar or Henry II.[1]

I think there never was a time when your heart was not a catholic heart. You were an 'anima naturaliter catholica.'[2]

T HIS FIRST CHAPTER offers an overview of the life of G. K Chesterton and explores his early development. The biographical sketch traces his movement from a childhood which provided a happiness that he treasured all his life (though it was not idyllic) and through the crisis that shook him during the solipsistic and possibly suicidal years of his adolescence and young adulthood—a terrible period from which he eventually emerged, in his own words, thanks

---

[1] G. K. Chesterton, *Charles Dickens*, 106.

[2] Father Vincent McNabb's comment (a rephrasing of Tertullian) to Chesterton, in F. Valentine, *Father Vincent McNabb, O.P.: the portrait of a great Dominican*, 271.

to the "mystical minimum of gratitude" for being, for the fact that anything exists at all. The intellectual, imaginative, and spiritual maturation that took place in Chesterton during this time of crisis is most cogently captured in *Orthodoxy*. In the final part of this first chapter we turn to this work, which laid the rock-solid imaginative and intellectual foundations of Chesterton's hope-filled view of the cosmos.

Five works in particular were of enormous assistance in putting together this biographical overview: firstly and most obviously, Chesterton's *Autobiography*[3]; secondly, the classic biography penned by Maisie Ward;[4] then the much more recent works by Joseph Pearce[5] and, in particular, William Oddie, which are fine examples of the studies of Chesterton which are being created for a new generation[6]; and finally the biographical beginning to economist Russell Sparkes' anthology of Chesterton,[7] with whose astute analysis of certain seminal moments in the life of Chesterton it is impossible not to concur. The excellent new biography produced in 2011 by Ian Ker[8] was published too late to influence the writing of this chapter, but its contributions to the later chapters of this book have been acknowledged in the appropriate places.

[3] G. K. Chesterton, *Autobiography*.

[4] M. Ward, *Gilbert Keith Chesterton*. Hereafter, *GKC*.

[5] J. Pearce, *Wisdom and Innocence: A Life of G. K. Chesterton*. Hereafter, *Wisdom and Innocence*.

[6] W. Oddie, *Chesterton and the Romance of Orthodoxy: The Making of GKC 1874-1908*. Hereafter, *CRO*.

[7] R. Sparkes, *Prophet of Orthodoxy: The Wisdom of G. K. Chesterton*, 1-96.

[8] I. Ker, *G. K. Chesterton: A Biography*, Oxford: Oxford University Press, 2011. Hereafter *GKC*.

1. A Brief Biographical Overview of Chesterton's Life

Gilbert Keith Chesterton was born in Kensington in London on May 29, 1874, the son of Edward Chesterton and Marie Grosjean. His parents were nominal Unitarians who embraced liberal politics. For the sake of social respectability they had their son baptized into the Church of England. Chesterton had a sister, Beatrice, five years his senior, who died when he was three years old, and a brother, Cecil, five years younger. Despite the death of his older sibling, the deep joy of Chesterton's childhood was to mark him indelibly for the rest of his life. He believed that it was natural to human beings to be joyful and to seek the true source of this deep-seated joy, and these were beliefs that marked his writings and apologetics.

Chesterton's formal education took place in London at the Colet Court Preparatory School, Saint Paul's School, and the Slade School of Art at University College. As a young man he was particularly influenced by the contemporary worldview of the Aesthetes, and he experienced a period of what he described as "madness," passing through agnosticism, scepticism, pessimism, depression, despair, and possibly suicidal tendencies, before dabbling with paganism, the occult, and spiritualism. This long, lonely meandering through various philosophies and worldviews left him with both a deep hostility toward scepticism and pessimism and a tender empathy for all who are lost in the jungles of those outlooks. The absent-minded Chesterton never found the discipline of institutional learning easy, and he left the Slade without a degree in the summer of 1895 to enter the world of work. He had had a poem called "The Song of Labour" published in *The Speaker* in 1892, and one entitled

"Easter Sunday" published in 1895, and this had convinced him that his vocation lay not in art, but in writing. In September 1895, therefore, Chesterton went to work for a small London publishing company that specialized in works of the occult. He did not stay long, leaving six months later for a larger group, Fisher Unwin, also of London, where he remained until 1901.

Although hopelessly disorganized and untidy in his professional life, Chesterton's passion for literature and incredible capacity for absorbing and remembering things made him an invaluable asset at Unwin's. He had been occasionally asked to write art and literary reviews for *The Bookman* during this period, but in the autumn of 1899 Chesterton received the unexpected opportunity that was to be the springboard to a long and fruitful literary career. This same publication asked him to write a longer review of the work of the artist Poussin. Although art criticism was in its infancy, Chesterton beautifully grasped the heart of Poussin's work, and his piece paved the way for his literary career. For the rest of his life Chesterton believed that the way in which one expresses what one has to say radically affects whether or not it is heard. Creative expression and a way of communicating that can take hold of the imagination of the addressee are vital for any apologetics in a secular culture whose imagination has become tired, cynical, pragmatic, and reduced in its capacities.

By 1900 Chesterton had published his first books, both of them collections of poetry, and hence this year saw the real beginning of his public life. The first work was entitled *Greybeards at Play*, but Chesterton was not happy with it and does not refer to it in his autobiography, instead listing the second work, *The Wild Knight and other Poems*, as his bow on the literary stage. Chesterton now began to find himself in regular demand as a writer and journalist, as he wrote columns for various newspapers such as *The Speaker*. Some of these were published in book form in 1901, the year in which he found sufficient work as a writer to justify leaving Unwin's. This was also the year in which the *Daily News* began to commission work from him. He was to write a regular Saturday column for this newspaper until his dismissal in 1913 by the newspaper's owner, George Cadbury, who took exception to Chesterton's criticisms of both his own commercial policies and those of English society. By 1905 the *Illustrated London News* had also asked him to write a weekly column, which he did until his death in 1936.

In 1896 Chesterton met Frances Blogg, a practicing Anglo-Catholic lady whom he married in 1901 and who was to be the unseen influence on Chesterton for the rest of his life. In 1900 he met another figure who was to exert a profound influence on the direction of his life: the Roman Catholic writer, historian, and political activist Hilaire Belloc. As we shall see shortly, both of these meetings were to influence Chesterton decisively toward Christian orthodoxy. Eight years after their first meeting Chesterton was to join forces with Belloc against George Bernard Shaw and Herbert George Wells in a debate that was conducted in the radical journal *New Age* and in debating halls throughout the whole of 1908 and which concluded with a lampoon from Shaw, called "The Chesterbelloc."[9] While it might be argued that this was the first time that the general public had first been aware of the relationship between Shaw and Chesterton, the point of Shaw's satire was that Chesterton and Belloc were so united in the general public's perception that they were almost like a pantomime elephant. Whether or not this was true, the mythical Chesterbelloc was born and from that moment on, right down to our own day, many people believed

---

[9] Published in *New Age*, 15 February 1908.

(understandably, but erroneously) that Belloc and Chesterton were both mere toys dancing before the public gallery in the hands of the puppet master known as the Chesterbelloc. More will be said about this public perception in Chapter IV, but for now let it be said that it is far too simplistic an understanding of the friendship between Chesterton and Belloc.

What is beyond dispute is that the influence of both Belloc and Frances nudged Chesterton in the direction of an orthodox Christian worldview, which found expression in the writing that he gradually began to produce on a more regular basis in the early years of the twentieth century. For example, Chesterton supported *The Speaker's* unpopular, and therefore very brave, stance against Britain's invasion of the tiny Boer Republic of South Africa. One might speculate that a largely (practically, if not theoretically) agnostic or atheistic late Victorian Britain worshipped at the shrine of imperialist patriotism, so Chesterton was taking a great risk. He was nothing if not frank in his written pieces, arguing that what was really at stake in such campaigns was not the noble effort to bring civilization to native, less fortunate peoples (patronizingly referred to as the "white man's burden" from the poem by Kipling), but the coveting of other people's natural assets (gold, in the case of the Boer republic). He questioned the moral status of both the war and the means for winning it, given that the occupation forces interned women and children in concentration camps that resulted (though not intentionally) in thousands of deaths. Even if some of Chesterton's language immediately strikes our own contemporary sensibilities as rather offensive, one can well imagine how much more offended, and for entirely different reasons, the average English gentleman might be reading the newspapers at the breakfast table.

"My country right or wrong" is a thing which no patriot would think of saying except in a desperate case. It is like saying, "My mother

drunk or sober"....What have we done, and where have we wandered,
that we should talk as if we have never done anything more intelligent
than found colonies and kick niggers? We are the children of light,
and it is we who sit in darkness.[10]

Here we see an early example of Chesterton's willingness to criticize the enthroned systems of thought that shape the popular
mindset and give it its dominant self-images or self-understanding. One of the perennial tasks of a healthy apologetics
is to be countercultural in a way that is carefully discerning,
forthright, and yet, at the same time, that seeks the good of the
culture it criticizes, such that it does not descend to the level of
mere anger or complaint.

As stated above, the powerful but silent presence that exerted
the greatest influence on Chesterton throughout his life was
that of his wife. They married in 1901 at Kensington Anglican
Church since, much to Chesterton's amazement, Frances
was a practicing Anglo-Catholic. As Chesterton says in his
autobiography:

> ...she actually practised a religion. This was something utterly un-
> accountable both to me and to the whole fussy culture in which we
> lived. Any number of people proclaimed religions, chiefly oriental
> religions, analysed or argued about them; but that anybody could
> regard religion as a practical thing like gardening was something
> quite new to me and, to her neighbours, new and incomprehensible.
> She had been, by an accident, brought up in the school of an Anglo-
> Catholic convent; and, to all that agnostic or mystic world, practising
> a religion was much more puzzling than professing it.[11]

The sheer inability of many Victorians to comprehend the practicing of a religion meant that Chesterton was fascinated by
his wife, and her prayer life taught him a lot about liturgy and

---

[10] G. K. Chesterton, *The Defendant*, 73, 125.

[11] G. K. Chesterton, *Autobiography*, 153.

public worship. Chesterton later described his wife as the first Christian he had ever met who was happy. These two facets of their life together give a hint of the enormous, life-changing part Frances was to play in his life. She witnessed to the truth of Christianity in her whole person. After she came into his life he was much more sympathetic to the notion of institutional Christianity and clergy, and his Christian faith deepened. By 1911, ten years after their wedding day, Chesterton dedicated *The Ballad of the White Horse* (his epic poem on Ethandune and Alfred the Great, considered by many to be his finest piece, replete with religious themes) to his wife with the words "I bring these rhymes to you/Who brought the cross to me."[12]

Together they faced the joys and trials of life: among the latter can be included the depression and suicide of Frances's brother in 1906 and her consequent devastation and dabbling with spiritualism; Frances's own bouts of depressive illness; Cecil's trial, conviction, and sentencing on the charge of criminal libel in 1913, after he used his journal The New Witness to make allegations of insider trading in Marconi shares at the highest levels of government; Cecil's death in a field hospital in France at the end of the First World War; and, perhaps the greatest sadness of all, the fact that Frances, in spite of surgery, was unable to bear children. Their bond and their faith gave them the strength to survive such tragedies and a resolute ability to live lives full of gratitude, hope, joy, and laughter.

Gilbert and Frances Chesterton were inseparable and, when Frances died only two years after her husband, George Bernard Shaw wondered if she had died of widowhood[13]—died of a broken heart, as the saying goes. Their mortal remains lie in

---

[12] *Ballad of the White Horse*, xli.

[13] M. Ward, *GKC*, 406.

the same grave in the Roman Catholic parish of St. Teresa, Beaconsfield, England. The significance of Chesterton's relationship with his wife, as the lens through which he saw everything else in life and his most basic experience of life in community, is a subject to which we shall return in Chapter IV.

Rooted in the love he shared with Frances, Chesterton rapidly acquired fame as a journalist and author, building a worldwide reputation as one of the wisest and most prolific writers in history. He wrote over a hundred books, contributed to two hundred other books, wrote novels, short stories, detective fiction (including the much-loved Father Brown priest-detective series), poems, plays, and thousands of newspaper essays. He wrote pieces on art and literary criticism, social and cultural criticism, politics, history, economics, philosophy, and theology. In all of these various genres Chesterton sought to uncover the multiple layers of meaning that are to be found in the rich mystery that is life in the cosmos and the transcendent source of that meaning.

Churning out thousands of words every week, Chesterton's enormous engine was powered by vast amounts of food and drink, especially of the alcoholic variety. Standing at six feet four inches, weighing over three hundred pounds, smoking a cigar and wearing a cloak and hat and with glasses on the end of his nose, Chesterton was an imposing, if slightly eccentric figure. The burden of his workload and lifestyle led to serious health complications. In November 1914, shortly after the outbreak of war, he fell desperately ill, slipping into a coma on Christmas Eve. Frances went through a couple of months of considerable turmoil, not least because she wondered if she should contact her husband's friend, Father John O'Connor, to receive Chesterton into the Church of Rome before he died, which seemed highly likely. Converting to Catholicism was a painful subject for Frances, but it was something that she and her husband had discussed several times. After a terrible period for Frances, in which Chesterton did indeed almost die, mid-January saw the beginnings of signs of hope and a period of convalescence. By Easter 1915 the threat had passed, and Chesterton began working again in May.

Chesterton's brother Cecil was in the trenches in 1916, and so the editorship of *The New Witness* passed to Chesterton. After Cecil's death in 1918, Chesterton continued the editorship for the rest of his life, reluctantly accepting the advice of friends and letting the publication trade on his fame by being re-named as *G. K.'s Weekly*. The burden of this editorship was considerable. The sense of duty he felt toward his deceased brother's memory exacted a high price both financially and emotionally. The distinguished Chesterton scholar Aidan Mackey, however, says that things could not be otherwise, and not merely because the journal was Cecil's creation:

> Some people have deplored this burden, saying that without it he could have written many more books, such as the studies he planned of Shakespeare, Napoleon and Savonarola. This seems to me to be a mistaken view, because the paper was central to his thinking and provided a platform from which some of his best thinking issued. He cared nothing for fame either in his time or in the future. He was a propagandist; an agitator standing in the market-place and reaching out to the ordinary men and women he so unaffectedly loved. To ask him to change course and reign as a purely literary celebrity would amount to asking him not to be Gilbert Keith Chesterton.[14]

This passage displays, I believe, something very important at the heart of Chesterton's writing: he saw his work as a vocation, a ministry that he performed with untiring devotion and imagination, in order to serve God and other people. As

---

[14] *G. K. Chesterton: A Prophet for the 21st Century*, 7.

we shall see in Chapters III and V in our exploration of the Ethics of Elfland and Chesterton's notion of service of the other as the secret of life, Chesterton believed that all goods, including talents, wealth, popularity, and fame, were gifts that were given in order that human beings could love their fellow human beings.

In the early years of the twentieth century Chesterton had shaken off the doubts and agnosticism of his adolescence and early adulthood in order to embrace Christianity, a journey chronicled in *Orthodoxy*. This work explains how he had worked out the fundamentals of the orthodox Christian worldview for himself and had come to embrace them. In this publication he presented a lucid description of why his cosmic philosophy was filled with hope, based as it was on a deep sense of wonder at the goodness of existence and of gratitude for the fact that life is a sheer, unmerited free gift—a gratitude that was to be expressed by embracing and enjoying the gift.

This hope-filled philosophy of life was, he contended, being eroded by the excesses of modern thought. Consequently much of his work was a lively, though amiable and humorous, critique of anything related to the exaggerations of modernity, which he perceived as constituting an attack on the goodness of life and human flourishing (which we can call the humanum). Although modernity has provided many opportunities for the deepening of Christian faith, its imbalances are often characterized by hostility toward religion in general and Christianity in particular. It is small wonder, then, that much of what Chesterton wrote was concerned with defending Christian principles and the Church. We shall return in Chapter II to the way Chesterton perceived culture as affecting the possibilities for faith and the need to have a healthy suspicion of the regnant ideologies that compete with the Kingdom of God.

So, Chesterton's gradual move toward the Christian creed was in no small part due to the influence of Belloc and the daily blessing of living in union with Frances. However, when in 1922 Chesterton became a Roman Catholic (a fact which surprised many people familiar with his work, as they had always supposed him to be one already[15]) Frances was deeply saddened. She knew that it was something her husband simply had to do, and she felt relieved that he had finally come to a decision about a matter with which he had struggled for years, but she felt unable to follow him. Their utter devotion to each other and their many years of worshipping together on Sundays, as well as Chesterton's deep reluctance to upset his friends and a vague suspicion that the Catholic Church would impair his spiritual freedom, had kept him from entering the fullness of communion with Rome for years.

After the First World War his ideas changed, and he became increasingly convinced that the Anglican Church, for which he always held great affection, could no longer stand up to the ideologies of the hour. He wrote to his mother, who was still grieving the recent loss of Chesterton's father, explaining,

> I have thought about you, and all that I owe to you and my father, not only in the way of affection, but of the ideals of honour and freedom and charity and all other good things you always taught me: and I am not conscious of the smallest break or difference in those ideals; but only of a new and necessary way of fighting for them...the fight for the family and the free citizen and everything decent must now be waged by [the] one fighting form of Christianity...I believe it is the truth.[16]

---

[15] See the epigraph from Vincent McNabb, OP, at the beginning of this chapter: Chesterton's beliefs and writings were largely Catholic in nature, even if he had not yet embraced full communion with Rome when he expressed them.

[16] M. Ward, *GKC*, 297-8.

Chesterton knew that this news would cause his mother pain, and she was not alone in her sorrow. Although Frances was later to follow her husband into the Catholic Church, she cried tears on the day of his reception into full communion with Rome. It is important to note here that Chesterton, speaking with those who do not share his own position, gives all apologists some valuable pointers for constructing an agenda for apologetics in any age: he states his views carefully and as reasonably as possible; he recognizes the many good and valuable things that lie outside the position he is now embracing; he states how he sees these values as being completed, not denied, by his new position; and, as far as is humanly possible, he tries to avoid giving offence to those with whom he is communicating, without thereby compromising the truth.

After becoming a Catholic, Chesterton spent the last fourteen years of his life writing, traveling, lecturing, and debating in the United States, in Canada, Poland, Palestine, Spain, Italy, and several other countries. Although he was never naïve enough to bow down and blindly worship anything where there was some element of human involvement—the Catholic Church included, as we shall see in Chapter IV—as he grew in his faith his concerns about spiritual freedom were dissipated and he began to see Catholicism, when at its best, as the best guarantor of spiritual and intellectual freedom against the narrow and dehumanizing ideological forces of the day. He saw Rome as the guardian of his deeply held conviction that all parts of the cosmos are connected and inter-related, a community of beings coming from the hand of the same Creator, and not so much a movement as "a meeting place; the trysting-place of all the truths in the world."[17]

---

[17] *The Thing: Why I Am a Catholic, Collected Works* Vol. 3, 132.

In the 1930s he made an impressive debut for the BBC in the emerging medium of radio broadcasting. Though an imposing figure, the tone with which he communicated in public matched the style with which he wrote: full of humility, humor, paradox, surprise, wonder, gratitude, and joy. He had an incredibly attractive personality and talent for friendship and, though he took on the leading intellectuals of his day—figures such as George Bernard Shaw, H. G. Wells, Bertrand Russell, and Clarence Darrow—and neither sought nor gave intellectual quarter, those who disagreed with him most were often the ones who most adored him. Before and after he became a Catholic, he developed deep friendships with Protestants, Catholics, and members of all God's other peoples, including agnostics and atheists. Since he was one of the leading literary figures of the day, politicians, writers, ecclesiastics, and other famous figures sought his company and opinions.

He died in Beaconsfield on the morning of Sunday 14th June 1936 and was buried in his home parish of St. Teresa (named for St. Thérèse of Lisieux), in a grave whose headstone was carved by Eric Gill. Cardinal Hinsley of Westminster and Monsignor Fulton J. Sheen were in attendance. At a Requiem Mass in Westminster Cathedral two weeks later, the former read out a telegram of condolence from Cardinal Eugenio Pacelli on behalf of Pope Pius XI:

> Holy Father deeply grieved death of Mr Gilbert Keith Chesterton devoted son Holy Church gifted Defender of the Catholic Faith. His Holiness offers paternal sympathy people of England assures prayers dear departed, bestows Apostolic benediction.[18]

Although he never saw human beings as a faceless agglomeration of individuals, Chesterton's work reached the masses and

---

[18] M. Ward, *GKC*, 405.

was written for the ordinary citizen, rather than for academics. He always saw himself first and foremost as a journalist who was trying to communicate a message that was crucial to human flourishing and happiness. Although he had a great eye for detail and deeply appreciated the manifold wonders of life, he was much more interested in the fundamentals that underpin life in this cosmos. To some critics, therefore, his work may at times seem repetitive and irritatingly ill-disciplined. Eamon Duffy notes that some people have contended that Chesterton was too much of a Christian or Catholic propagandist, especially in later years, citing George Orwell's complaint that, "Every book that he [Chesterton] wrote...had to demonstrate beyond possibility of mistake the superiority of the Catholic over the Protestant or the pagan."[19] However, all Chesterton's works contain profound insights and a breadth of vision that are communicated with wit, humor, and imagination. As Duffy says:

> If Chesterton is repetitive, and can be sectarian, Orwell was mistaken in dismissing the last twenty years of Chesterton's output. Even the worst of Chesterton's books show flashes of the old brilliance. [While writing of Dickens Chesterton commented, "The best of his work can be found in the worst of his works."] Mutatis mutandis, that applies as much to Chesterton himself as to Dickens: his verse apart, literary form was of less interest to Chesterton than the core ideas to which his writing so often returned.[20]

It is arguable that Chesterton could indeed be repetitive but, beyond the immediate irritation that this may cause for some people, it need not be a major distraction, unless the reader's chief concern is to be entertained rather than stimulated to seek wisdom: certain elements that are foundational to the quest

---

[19] Ed. K. L. Morris, *The Truest Fairy Tale: An Anthology of the Religious Writings of G. K. Chesterton* (hereafter *TTFT*), 10.

[20] Ibid.

for wisdom need to be repeated again and again, no matter how irksome this may seem. As Hugh Kenner put it, "There is a penultimate stage of disillusion in the study of Chesterton wherein he seems to be saying the same thing over and over again; the ultimate stage is to realize that he says it so often because it can never really be said; in fact, because there is nothing else to say."[21]

For the first third of the twentieth century Chesterton was regarded as possibly the most gifted and most important literary-religious figure, a man recognized wherever he went. Although Chesterton is today regarded by some as an outmoded eccentric, there has been an enormous resurgence of interest in the man and his writings. There will never be universal agreement on the merits and demerits of his work, but no less a figure than Etienne Gilson called Chesterton "one of the deepest thinkers who ever existed,"[22] and figures as disparate as C. S. Lewis, Michael Collins, Mohandas Gandhi, Ernest Hemingway, Graham Greene, Evelyn Waugh, George Bernard Shaw, H. G. Wells, Agatha Christie, Dorothy Sayers, Dorothy Day, E. F. Schumacher, Hilaire Belloc, Orson Welles, Paul Claudel, W. H. Auden, Kingsley Amis, and Sigrid Undset have acknowledged their debt to Chesterton.

Perhaps such a wide variety of people recognized wisdom in Chesterton because he was able to show them various glimmers of the truth, beauty, and goodness that are to be found at the heart of ordinary existence. He believed that if we look at ordinary, everyday things nine hundred and ninety-nine times, then we are safe; but if we look at them for a thousandth time, we are suddenly in a position where we may see them properly

---

[21] *Paradox in Chesterton*, 9.

[22] M. Ward, *GKC*, 382.

for the first time.[23] As we shall see, that is why he often wrote in such a paradoxical way: he believed that the truth sometimes has to come as a surprise, because that is the only way we will recognize and appreciate it, so accustomed have our eyes become to taking things for granted.

At the risk of sliding into hagiography, it may also be possible that Chesterton's self-conception as a jobbing journalist, rather than an academic, gave him the necessary freedom from pride not to be excessively interested in what the critics thought of him. His writings communicated the sense that what makes us great is not where we stand out from one another, but where we are the same as each other, and therefore connected to each other: his work communicated the fact of our contingency, our radical dependence on a great love and providence outside us, and the consequent truth of our radical inter-relatedness and communion.

2. Chesterton's Childhood

Chesterton refers to his birth in 1874 with the wit and wisdom for which he became famous, making light of the gullibility and credulousness of which he was accused for becoming a Roman Catholic by a modern mindset that was enthralled with the sort of empirical proof provided by the method of the natural sciences:

> Bowing down in blind credulity, as is my custom, before mere authority and the tradition of the elders, superstitiously swallowing a story I could not test at the time by experiment or private judgment, I am firmly of the opinion that I was born on the 29th of May, 1874, on Campden Hill, Kensington...[24]

---

[23] G. K. Chesterton, *The Napoleon of Notting Hill, Collected Works* Vol. 6, 227.

[24] *Autobiography*, 5.

We have already noted how the death of Beatrice was the dark shadow over an otherwise unblemished and sunny childhood. His grief was possibly made worse by the reaction of his father, who turned her picture to the wall, removed her belongings from the house and asked that her name not be mentioned. Chesterton said of the subject of his sister, "I have little to go on; for she was the only subject about which my father did not talk."[25] It is clear that Chesterton regrets never being able to discuss the death of his sister with his father, and that it was an event he remembered often in the lonely wondering of his adolescence.

It was also an event that made him live in fear of losing his brother, too, some day. It is also a sign of what Joseph Pearce refers to as the "ever-elusive but all-pervasive power of child-hood."[26] When in conversation with someone, the apologist must never forget that this is a person with dignity, with a child-hood, adolescence, and pivotal events in their life story, and the apologist must always be willing to situate the person and their beliefs and pronouncements in the light of this broader horizon. As we shall see in Chapter IV, Chesterton himself was able to do this in his dealings with Shaw.

The all-pervasiveness of Chesterton's childhood is evidenced by the fact that Chesterton refers consistently to the sense of wonder which filled his boyhood and which became the fertile experiential soil in which his writing flourished. He saw this nursery period as time spent in the magical Fairyland or Elfland. The toy theatre in which he and Cecil staged plays with miniature characters is the thing which he most vividly recalls:

> The first thing I can remember seeing with my own eyes was a young man walking across a bridge. He had a curly moustache and an

---

[25] Ibid.

[26] *Wisdom and Innocence*, 7.

attitude of confidence verging on a swagger. He carried in his hand a disproportionately large key of a shining yellow metal and wore a large golden or gilded crown...To those who may object that such a scene is rare in the home life of house-agents living immediately to the north of Kensington High Street, in the later seventies of the last century, I shall be compelled to admit, not that the scene was unreal, but that I saw it through a window more wonderful than the window in the tower; through the proscenium of a toy theatre constructed by my father; and that (if I am really to be pestered about such irrelevant details) the young man in the crowd was about six inches high and proved on investigation to be made of cardboard...The scene has to me a sort of aboriginal authenticity impossible to describe.[27]

This love of the dramatic and the creative, the world of the vivid image, the power of imagination, and the sheer inability to see the ordinary and the everyday as anything other than extraordinary, never left Chesterton. As we shall see in Chapter III, the humdrum everyday was for him itself a theatre, the arena in which the encounter with God takes place in an infinite and wonderful variety of ways. The ordinary and the everyday is Elfland, the place of magical fairy tales. For Chesterton this cosmos is the magical gift given to us all and, therefore, exploration of this gift is the necessary starting point for any apologetics, and indeed offers any number of entry points at which we can join the pathway to God. The need to engage the imagination in order to help people understand themselves and their place in the cosmos was also fundamental to his way of writing.

From fairy tales, especially George McDonald's *The Princess and the Goblin*, Chesterton was to learn some of the lessons in life which he considered most fundamentally important: that ordinary, everyday life is a wild and exciting place, an adventure; that human beings are simultaneously capable of the greatest good and the most atrocious evils; that there is a price

---

[27] Ibid., 27-28, 46.

to be paid for enjoying this world (a price which consists in obedience to the inherent rules of the adventure—a subject he referred to as the "fairy godmother philosophy" in "The Ethics of Elfland."[28] Life is often harsh before it delivers happiness; and we face a life of incredible loneliness if we travel without friends as companions on the journey. We shall see later that when in *Orthodoxy* Chesterton wrote about his discovery of orthodox Christian faith, he said that it confirmed what he had already learned in the nursery from the ethics of Elfland.

Despite the impossibility of speaking with his father about Beatrice's death, there can be no question that Chesterton loved both his parents and believed them to be enormously positive formative influences on his life. Chesterton therefore feels he must apologize to those who might wish to explain him by drawing on psychological theories that see nothing but the seeds of adult ruination in childhood:

> I am sorry if the landscape or the people appear disappointingly respectable and even reasonable, and deficient in all those unpleasant qualities that make a biography really popular. I regret that I have no gloomy and savage father to offer to the public gaze as the true cause of all my tragic heritage; no pale-faced and partially poisoned mother whose suicidal instincts have cursed me with the temptations of the artistic temperament. I regret that there was nothing in the range of our family much more racy than a remote and mildly impecunious uncle; and that I cannot do my duty as a true modern, by cursing everybody who made me whatever I am.[29]

On the contrary, he wishes to distance himself from those psychoanalysts who hold that,

> our minds are merely manufactured by accidental conditions, and therefore have no ultimate relation to truth at all. With all possible

---

[28] Chapter IV of *Orthodoxy*.

[29] *Autobiography*, 26.

apologies to the freethinkers, I still propose to hold myself free to think. And anybody who will think for two minutes will see that this thought is the end of all thinking. It is useless to argue at all, if all our conclusions are warped by our conditions. Nobody can correct anybody's bias, if all mind is all bias.[30]

Here we have two paragraphs that reveal a recurring phenomenon in Chesterton's life and work: the use of his imaginative capacities to critique what he considered to be the pseudo-scientific approach of many intellectuals of his day. He saw it as his duty to critique those who used a little knowledge to blind people of lesser academic training. He saw it as part of his journalistic vocation and part of any apologist's vocation to restore sight to the latter, to be their defender, to speak up for those who could not speak for themselves and to reassure them that the instinctive common-sense approach that they had to the world was indeed well-founded and not under real threat from the purveyors of such pseudo-intellectualism.

Responding to the criticism that he was something akin to an overgrown child who had never really grown up and faced the real world, Chesterton never apologized for the sense of wonder and gratitude he had known since being a child. "…I believe in prolonging childhood…I can only say that this nursery note is necessary if all the rest [of his autobiography] is to be anything but nonsense; and not even nursery nonsense." He then points out that he knows plenty of "the real world":

In the chapters that follow, I shall pass to what are called real happenings, though they are far less real. Without giving myself any airs of the adventurer or the globetrotter, I may say I have seen something of the world; I have traveled in interesting places and talked to interesting men; I have been in political quarrels often turning into faction fights; I have talked to statesmen in the hour of the destiny

---

of States; I have met most of the great poets and prose writers of my time;…I have seen the fanatical Arabs come up from the desert to attack the Jews in Jerusalem. There are many journalists who have seen more of such things than I; but I have been a journalist and I have seen such things.[31]

However, even if he can claim to be a man of the world, for Chesterton these many worldly experiences were not so much a glimpse into reality as was that afforded to him in his childhood:

> [All of these adult experiences] will be unmeaning, if nobody understands that they still mean less to me than Punch and Judy on Campden Hill…In a word, I have never lost the sense that [childhood] was my real life; the real beginning of what should have been a more real life; a lost experience in the land of the living…It is only the grown man who lives a life of make-believe and pretending; and it is he who has his head in a cloud.[32]

For Chesterton there was a fundamental difference between knowledge and wisdom, between sophistication and the wisdom that lies beyond sophistication, which is a return to the simple grasp of the mysterious nature of reality that one first knows in childhood. The apologist who addresses a secular culture, which prides itself on its complex sophistication and on the manifold branches of knowledge that modernity has afforded us, must indeed acknowledge the goodness of such sophisticated knowledge. However, at the same time he must point out that the mere acquisition of knowledge, in and of itself, is not enough. It is one thing to know many things, but it is quite another to know what such knowledge is for and how it contributes to the overall task of human flourishing.

One of the tasks of the Christian apologist today is to point out that, while uncritical naivety is not a good thing, and

---

[31] Ibid., 50-51.

[32] Ibid.

therefore a mature Christian faith must always permit itself to be informed by modernity and to be in dialogue with other perspectives, nevertheless postmodernity has something to teach us too. While we may never reject the goodness of modernity and become pre-modern, we must also listen to one of the tenets of the postmodern view, which says we must move beyond the arrogance of thinking we know all there is to know, transcending the modern cynicism which our culture often displays about the things of faith or the realms of the spiritual; we must recover that post-sophisticated innocence of heart, found in abundance in Chesterton, which realizes that, beyond the many insights and benefits won for us through the modern project, a deep-seated wonder before a reality that is sheer gift is still the wisest of human responses.

3. The Slade Experience

Though as a boy Chesterton went to the famous cathedral school of St. Paul's, it seems that the mammoth intellect that he later displayed was seldom to be witnessed in the early days of his schooling. In time, however, the sense of community that was built through friendships with Edmund Clerihew Bentley, Lucian Oldershaw, and other members of a group which they formed and named the Junior Debating Club, helped him to grow in confidence. Chesterton began to flourish, finding expression in debate, written presentations, articles, and poems. The masters at St. Paul's began to notice the change in him, such that Frederick Walker, the High Master, was able to award him the Milton Prize for poetry for his submission on St. Francis Xavier in the summer term of 1892. His success inspired him to think more and more of poetry, and he was to write poetry for friends, loved ones, and the general public for the rest of his life. Two years later, Walker told Mrs. Chesterton that her son was "six foot of genius" to be cherished.[33]

In 1892, at the age of eighteen, and as a reward for these prize-winning efforts, Gilbert's father took him abroad for the first time, to France. The trip may have occasioned spiritual explorations for Chesterton, because for the next year religious themes are to be found in his poetry. However, late Victorian England was largely agnostic and Chesterton was not a Christian. By the time he had started to write religious poetry, between the ages of eighteen and nineteen, Chesterton had not formulated a definite view on any religious theme.

Although he wrote in *Orthodoxy* (in 1908) that, "I was a pagan at the age of twelve, and a complete agnostic at the age of sixteen,"[34] it might be nearer the mark to say that at this stage he was still searching, exploring, asking questions and wrestling with the great questions of existence, with crumbs of Protestantism, Catholicism, paganism, agnosticism, socialism, liberalism, and spiritualism all contributing to his philosophical diet. The spiritualism in the above list is what Chesterton referred to as "knowing the devil":

> I am not proud of believing in the Devil. To put it more correctly, I am not proud of knowing the Devil. I made his acquaintance by my own fault; and followed it up along lines which, had they been followed further, might have led to devil-worship or the devil knows what.[35]

This took place during a period when Chesterton was drifting, rootless, restless, and unfocused. Instead of going to university with his friends in 1892, Chesterton had decided to enter the

---

[33] M. Ward, *GKC*, 33.

[34] *Orthodoxy*, 288.

[35] *Autobiography*, 78.

Slade Art School of University College, London, in the hope of pursuing an artistic career.

The Slade is an important focus in Oddie's seminal work[36] whose importance to Chesterton studies will possibly resonate for decades to come. In this work the author explores Chesterton's imaginative and spiritual development, from his happy, if not idyllic childhood, through his schooldays and youth, to his emergence onto the London literary scene and the period of intellectual maturity that is expressed in the 1908 work, *Orthodoxy*. This publication laid down the imaginative and intellectual foundations on which the remainder of his life's prodigious, if unsystematic, literary output was to be built. Oddie sees his emergence in the first decade of the twentieth century as one of the finest journalists of the age in the context of the fin de siècle and the Edwardian cultural crisis.

Oddie is correct in locating the heart of Chesterton's vision, as expounded in *Orthodoxy*, in the formative experiences of this period. The greatness of Chesterton lies not in any one genre of writing, but in the depth of thought that is to be found in all of his work. The view of the cosmos that fills his writing was forged in the crisis he lived through at the Slade and in his subsequent reflection on that crisis, and he used a rhetorical and imaginative style to draw his reader's attention back to this foundational worldview again and again.

Although it is sometimes argued that Chesterton's work was so disparate and uneven that an academic philosopher or theologian might better use his time exploring the mind of a more systematic thinker, such as Augustine, Aquinas, Lonergan, Rahner, or Ratzinger, the author of this book has to side with Randall Paine who notes:

---

[36] W. Oddie, *CRO*.

The great value of Chesterton is precisely his fusion of the philosophical with the rhetorical, the imaginative and even the charitable.
Perhaps the fullness of these harmonized endowments could best be
expressed by saying that he possesses an Augustinian imagination, a
Thomistic intellect and a Franciscan heart.[37]

For Paine, Chesterton's wisdom has a prophetic nature to
it, calling us back to "the lost art of a fully incarnate human
reflection."[38] Chesterton learned painful lessons at the Slade
about the dangers of an overly rationalist, scientific, and ce-
rebral approach to human living. And he protested against
such a truncated understanding of knowledge for the rest of
his life. An awareness of these same dangers is also part of the
postmodern mindset. Though an avowed believer in truth and
in overarching narratives (to use this postmodern term anach-
ronistically), Chesterton seems to anticipate some aspects of
postmodern criticism by his way of writing, which is born of a
perception that human nature is complex and so much more
than the merely rational. For Chesterton, human beings are
holistic creatures: rational certainly, but also imaginative, free,
spiritual, affective, loving, hating, and much more besides.

For Chesterton, then, to be human is to find oneself in an
adventure, a complex and multi-layered cosmic drama. He
learned this lesson in the crucible of human experience and in
the midst of crisis. All that he was to become was forged out of
being lost for a while, as he wandered aimlessly onto the terrain
of the scepticism which he later referred to as "the thought that
stops all thought"[39] and, in the clutches of the solipsistic depression that ensued, he entertained certain unspecified moral
temptations.

---

[37] *The Universe and Mr. Chesterton*, 7.

[38] Ibid., 8.

[39] *Orthodoxy*, 236.

Reeling from this experience, and linking the insights that emerged from it with the vital lessons of his childhood, he emerged at the age of twenty to gaze on the cosmos for the rest of his life with radically different eyes. It might be argued that Chesterton's entering into full communion with the Church of Rome at the age of forty-eight, while clearly a momentous milestone on his spiritual journey, was really a flowering of this youthful, post-Slade moment, when he chose to embrace the goodness, color, and complexity of the gift of life. The important thing to grasp is that Chesterton's life's work was the fruit of the basic vision of life formed through the combination of the momentous experience of the Slade years with his childhood intuitions.

It is necessary to set the Slade experience in a context. The cultural movement known as Aestheticism was at its most influential from 1890–1895 (the year in which it collapsed, with Oscar Wilde's imprisonment). During this period Chesterton grew from being a sixteen-year-old adolescent to a man recently come of age. Oddie notes that, "references to the decadents made by Chesterton during the first decade of the new century reflect a still raw and passionate loathing."[40] Chesterton's brother says that what Gilbert "describes as 'the decadent school,' which then dominated 'advanced literature' had, I am certain, a more powerful effect on the development of Chesterton's thought than we have yet fully recognized."[41]

Oddie argues that it was not merely the homosexual nature of Wilde's philosophy of life that alarmed Chesterton, but its subversive nature.[42] Writing in his *Autobiography* some forty

---

[40] *CRO*, 111.

[41] Ibid.

[42] Ibid.

years or so after the events, Chesterton could say of the mood that descended on him during his time at the Slade, "something may have been due to the atmosphere of the Decadents, and their perpetual hints of the luxurious horrors of paganism; but I am not disposed to dwell much on that defence."[43] Oddie interprets this less passionate surmise as being because, "by the 1930s, the memory of his revulsion at the implications of 'the green carnation' [Wilde] had dimmed, perhaps."[44] As we shall see, Chesterton was indeed able to display a more compassionate understanding of Wilde later in life than in the earlier years of his career.

So what are the key elements of the Slade crisis, which was to prove such a turning point in the life of Chesterton? His Autobiography contains a chapter called "How to be a Lunatic," which is vital if we are to understand his mature thought and how it emerged from this experience. There we are told that the crisis was both intellectual and moral in nature:

> At a very early age I had thought my way back to thought itself. It is a very dreadful thing to do; for it may lead to thinking that there is nothing but thought. At this time I did not distinguish between dreaming and waking; not only as a mood, but as a metaphysical doubt, I felt as if everything might be a dream. It was as if I had myself projected the universe from within, with all its trees and stars; and that is manifestly even nearer to going mad.[45]

Here it is evident that while at the Slade Chesterton was tinkering with solipsism. As well as this philosophical element, there was also an ethical element to the crisis, as Chesterton was struggling to find some code by which to conduct his behavior:

---

[43] *Autobiography*, 90.

[44] *CRO*, 111.

[45] *Autobiography*, 89.

And as with mental, so with moral extremes. There is something truly menacing in the thought of how quickly I could imagine the maddest, when I had never committed the mildest crime…There was a time when I had reached that moral anarchy within, in which a man says, in the words of Wilde, that "Atys with the blood-stained knife were better than the thing I am."[46]

So he was tempted by "a very negative and even nihilistic philosophy,"[47] and it cast a shadow of depression over his mind during his time at the Slade.

Chesterton was later able to recount the experience to the friend who had walked with him during those days, E. C. Bentley. He dedicated *The Man Who Was Thursday* to Bentley, in gratitude for their friendship, with a poem called "A Cloud Was On the Mind of Men":

This is a tale of those old fears, even of those emptied hells,
And none but you shall understand the true thing that it tells…
Oh, who shall understand but you; yea, who shall understand?
The doubts that drove us through the night as we two talked amain,
And day had broken on the streets e'er it broke upon the brain.
Between us, by the peace of God, such truth can now be told;
Yea, there is strength in striking root and good in growing old.
We have found common things at last and marriage and a creed,
And I may safely write it now, and you may safely read.[48]

The poem describes the difficulties of the period, how this desolation did not last and how now, looking back, Chesterton wishes to thank Bentley for the sense of solidarity and community that he found in their friendship and conversation, which helped him to survive. It also relates how the bonds of commitment within community and institutional living, which become

---

[46] Ibid., 90.

[47] Ibid., 88.

[48] *The Man Who Was Thursday*, 21.

part of the lives of most people as they mature, are things that are truly native to human beings.[49]

The desire of the decadent spirit to be set free to drink in all manner of experience went hand in hand with a moral relativism that set itself against all cultural norms of ethical behavior (attitudes which, as we shall see in our final chapter, are also to be found among postmodern sensibilities). "The decay of society was praised by artists as the decay of a corpse is praised by worms. The aesthete was all receptiveness, like the flea. His only affair in this world was to feed on its facts and colours, like a parasite on blood."[50]

In Chapter II we shall see that Chesterton believed that the movements and characteristics of a culture can capture the imagination of the people who dwell in that culture, as they swim in the ocean of its influences. This will, in turn, affect the capacities for faith of these people, as the images with which they interpret themselves, the world, their place within it and its overall meaning become shaped, often unconsciously, by the messages of the cultural constructs that surround them.

It seems that Chesterton was influenced by the culture of decadence and flirted with its ideas. How did he emerge from the sadness and depression that this dalliance brought upon him? In Chesterton's *Autobiography* he describes how he "hung on to religion by one thin thread of thanks," explaining that:

> ...no man knows how much he is an optimist, even when he calls himself a pessimist, because he has not really measured the depths

---

[49] The Decadents cherished values which permitted human beings to escape, however transiently, the human condition, by means of posing, artifice, and evil, all of which, because unnatural, were superior to nature in their view. Ties, institutions and maturity, as traditional values that had arisen from centuries of human experience, were regarded with contempt. Though not a perfect mirroring, it is, as has been said above, interesting to note how some of these same tensions exist today in a postmodern culture.

[50] G. K. Chesterton, *George Bernard Shaw*, 78.

of his debt to whatever created him and enabled him to call himself anything. At the back of our brains, so to speak, there was a forgotten blaze or burst of astonishment at our own existence. The object of the artistic and spiritual life was to dig for this submerged sunrise of wonder; so that a man might suddenly understand that he was alive, and be happy.[51]

What Chesterton expresses here is also captured in a letter he had written some four decades earlier to Bentley:

> Inwardly speaking I have had a funny time. A meaningless fit of depression, taking the form of certain absurd psychological worries, came upon me, and instead of dismissing it and talking to people, I had it out and went very far into the abysses indeed. The result was that I found that things, when examined, necessarily spelt such a mystically satisfactory state of things, that without getting back to earth, I saw lots that made me certain it is all right. The vision is fading into common day now, and I am glad. It is embarrassing talking to God face to face, as a man speaketh to a friend.[52]

Wonder, joy, and gratitude for the gift of the ordinary and the everyday were the deeply human experiences that led him out of solipsism, despair, and despondency. Oddie notes:

> The particular virtue that lay behind Chesterton's recovery of optimism was the virtue of gratitude: and if we seek for a corresponding doctrinal element in his recovery of some kind of religious belief, it was his discovery of the fundamental necessity of the doctrine of creation.[53]

Chesterton did indeed travel into the depths of the abyss, only to rediscover the submerged sunrise of wonder, and knew that all would be well. He spent the rest of his life writing for others that it would be "all right": he lived the vocation of an

---

[51] *Autobiography*, 92.

[52] W. Oddie, *CRO*, 124.

[53] Ibid, 123.

apologist for existence, life, color, energy, joy, and the Creator
who underpinned all of these. He became a Christian apologist
with a career dedicated to expanding on the goodness of the
common things of life, as captured by the dedication he penned
for Bentley in *The Man Who Was Thursday* (it's worth quoting
again):

> Between us, by the peace of God, such truth can now be told;
> Yea, there is strength in striking root and good in growing old.
> We have found common things at last and marriage and a creed,
> And I may safely write it now, and you may safely read.[54]

So again, *Orthodoxy* was the intellectual and spiritual autobiography that captures the mature worldview which he sought
to share with others for the rest of his life. This masterpiece
explains how it required several years of further spiritual exploration before he realized that the hope-filled personal vision of
reality at which he had arrived after the Slade experience was
in fact the one espoused and set forth in the Apostles' Creed;
but the starting point for his whole literary output was what he
had lived through at the Slade, and it stayed with him all his
life. Having found his way out of the pit of despair, he never
forgot the lessons of those dark days and, like C. S. Lewis a few
decades later, he became a safe guide for all who lose their way.
As he says when commenting on a man who claimed he knew
several people who were saved from madness by Chesterton's
novel *The Man Who Was Thursday*: "He must have been rather
generously exaggerative; he may have been mad himself, of
course; but then so was I. But I confess it flatters me to think
that, in this period of lunacy, I may have been a little useful to
other lunatics."[55]

---

[54] *The Man Who Was Thursday*, 21.

[55] *Autobiography*, 101.

This period of decadence and despair left scars that, with time and thoughtful reflection became sources of wisdom that provided healing for others. In the personal trials and sorrows he faced in life, evil was a reality that Chesterton knew from personal experience, and it was a reality which made him think that some of the most popular leading modern thinkers of the day, such as Shaw and Wells, were hopelessly naïve in their philosophies of unrestrained evolutionary progressivism.

It might be argued that the Second World War and other events of the twentieth century proved Chesterton right in thinking that an unbridled modernity ignores the Christian notion of fallen human nature at its peril, but Chesterton would also be the first to remind us that evil need not be, that human nature is not irredeemably fallen, that there is indeed a redemption for us and that the Spirit of the Redeemer is at work in human history. The world has to be loved because it is God's world, secularization has to be seen as a complex reality with all sorts of hues and tones, and the Christian theologian has to live in the world with a hope-filled realism and always resist the world-weary cynicism that makes unlikely bedfellows of the post-Second World War agnostic-atheistic existentialists and some of the late twentieth-century religious veterans of the Culture Wars. To these essential features of a culturally attuned twenty-first-century apologetics we shall return.

---

4. Fleet Street and Heretics: *Journalistic Apologist for the Ordinary and the Everyday*

So marked was Chesterton by the sheer joy and gratitude for ordinary things and humdrum living after coming through the Slade years that he wished to share that joy with others, and he began to discern a vocation as a poet, journalist, and writer who could help people to see, or remember, the goodness of life and their own inherent greatness.

> Religion has had to provide that longest and strangest telescope—the telescope through which we could see the star upon which we dwelt. For the mind and eyes of the average man this world is as lost as Eden and as sunken as Atlantis. There runs a strange law through the length of human history—that men are continually tending to undervalue their environment, to undervalue their happiness, to undervalue themselves. The great sin of mankind, the sin typified by the fall of Adam, is the tendency, not towards pride, but towards this weird and horrible humility. This is the great fall, the fall by which the fish forgets the sea, the ox forgets the meadow, the clerk forgets the city, every man forgets his environment and, in the fullest and most literal sense, forgets himself. This is the real fall of Adam, and it is a spiritual fall. It is a strange thing that many truly spiritual men, such as General Gordon, have actually spent some hours in speculating upon the precise location of the Garden of Eden. Most probably we are in Eden still. It is only our eyes that have changed.[56]

This passage is worth quoting at length because the notion that human beings have forgotten who they are is central to the Chestertonian vision. At the Slade he had forgotten the primordial sense of the goodness of existence, which he had instinctively grasped in childhood. The importance of being present to the richness and goodness of everyday experience, so often forgotten amidst the daily pressures of living, was constantly emphasized by Chesterton. The truths that Chesterton discovered during the foundational experience at the Slade would more properly be termed "re-discoveries" of things he had already known as a child:

> I was subconsciously certain then [in childhood], as I am consciously certain now, that there was the white and solid road and the worthy beginning of the life of man; and that it is man who afterwards

---

[56] *The Defendant*, 9-10.

darkens it with dreams or goes astray from it in self-deception. It is only the grown man who has a life of make-believe and pretending; and it is he who has his head in a cloud.[57]

He had been filled with a sense of wonder and gratitude at the marvels that lay all around in him in childhood:

> Mere existence, reduced to its most primary limits, was extraordinary enough to be exciting. Anything was magnificent as compared with nothing…At the back of our brains, so to speak, there was a forgotten blaze or burst of astonishment at our own existence. The object of the artistic and spiritual life was to dig for this submerged sunrise of wonder.[58]

Toward the end of his life he looked back upon life with the gratitude of one who had received an undeserved gift, a gift which still seemed wonderful to him:

> I had in childhood, and have partly preserved out of childhood, a certain romance of receptiveness, which has not been killed by sin or even by sorrow; for though I have not had great troubles, I have had many. A man does not grow old without being bothered; but I have grown old without being bored. Existence is still a strange thing to me; and as a stranger I give it welcome.[59]

Again we discern here that for Chesterton, even after a life full of achievements and replete with the experiences of life, the abiding attitude he has toward life is that of a deep sense of awe, wonder, and gratitude. This is the beginning of Chestertonian wisdom.

Because he had himself forgotten and rediscovered the vision of his childhood, he was sympathetic toward those who had also lost their way. So, despite forcefully attacking the

---

[57] *Autobiography*, 51.

[58] Ibid., 91-2.

[59] Ibid, 352.

Aesthetes in the early twentieth century, in time Chesterton's tone toward Oscar Wilde changed. Wilde "was so fond of being many-sided that among his sides he even admitted the right side. He loved so much to multiply his souls that he had among them one soul at least that was saved. He desired all beautiful things—even God."[60]

Several of the bored "refugees from the Age of Dorian" eventually joined the Catholic Church, among them Wilde's lover, the poet John Gray, who became a much-loved parish priest in Scotland. (To say nothing of the reported deathbed conversion of Wilde himself.) In that light, it has been asked, "Was this the reason that Chesterton did not persist in his angry denunciations of the 'green carnation'?"[61]

As we see from the main characters in Chesterton's novel *The Ball and the Cross*—the naive, and rather humorless young Catholic, McIan, and the fiery atheist Turnbull—Chesterton did not hesitate to depict both believers and unbelievers as heroes and people who possess admirable qualities. Gentleness of tone, charitableness in argumentation and in the attribution of motives, and an ability to see the strengths, truth, beauty, and goodness in the positions of those with whom he was in dialogue and disputation were, as we shall see, hallmarks of Chesterton's writing and debating. They are fundamental qualities that must mark any agenda for apologetics in a secular and pluralistic world.

It would be a mistake, however, to think that Chesterton's kindness and understanding meant that he was slow to point out what he perceived as error. He survived his experimentation with decadence because of a lot of soul-searching, as he

---

[60] "Oscar Wilde," *A Handful of Authors*, ed. D. Collins, 146.

[61] W. Oddie, *CRO*, 124.

struggled to find the antidote to the poisoned philosophical and moral foundations of his life. The various fashionable ideas and worldviews with which he had toyed at the turn of the century, such as theosophies or ethical societies, did not convince him in the end because, ultimately, they viewed truth as a simple thing.

For Chesterton reality and the truth about reality were paradoxical, manifestly complex, multi-layered and multi-colored. He viewed the chief problem with so many of the ideas of the period—Kipling's imperialism, the socialist worldview of Shaw and Wells, unbridled capitalism, the belief in relentless human progress, materialism and the Darwinian survival of the fittest— as reductionist in their views of the world, reducing reality to their own favorite bits of the truth, while leaving out so much else. By refusing to acknowledge the paradoxical and multi-faceted nature of reality they were, in a word, manipulating reality. In Chapter III we shall return to the centrality of paradox and non-reductionism in Chesterton.

Chesterton wrote several articles and essays criticizing such reductionist modern opinions. In 1903, for example, after Robert Blatchford had declared in his newspaper, The Clarion, that materialistic evolutionary theory had proved that science was the only route to progress in the modern world, that the foundations of religious worldviews were in tatters and that human beings would be better off trying to create a religion of philanthropy and alleviating poverty in the slums by the surrendering of personal freedom to government officials and social engineers, Chesterton entered into an amiable but frank correspondence with Blatchford through a series of articles in the same paper.

> There is a liberty that has made men happy in dungeons, as it may make them happy in slums. It is the liberty of the mind, that is to say, it is the one liberty on which Mr. Blatchford makes war...

[When human beings claim to be free] "No, No," says the face of Mr. Blatchford, suddenly appearing at the window, "your thoughts are the inevitable result of heredity and environment. Your thoughts are as material as your dungeons. Your thoughts are as mechanical as the guillotine."…[If this ever came to pass] Man, the machine, will stand up in these flowery meadows and cry aloud, "Was there not once a thing, a church, that taught us that we were free in our souls?"[62]

It is evident from this passage that by this stage of his life Chesterton had come to see that the Christian creed was the defender of all that was truly human and that by attacking this creed, its opponents were also attacking ordinary human things and human flourishing:

What I was defending seemed to me a plain matter of ordinary human morals. Indeed it seemed to me to raise the question of the very possibility of morals…It was not that I began by believing in supernatural things. It was that the unbelievers began by disbelieving even in normal things.[63]

The other articles he wrote at this time, directed against such vociferous opponents as Shaw and Wells, in addition to Blatchford, were later revised and published in book form in *Heretics* in 1905. In this book Chesterton says that, whether we acknowledge it or not, each of us has a general view of existence, a philosophy of life, a worldview that is based on our ultimate understanding of things, and that this affects everything that we say and do: ideas have consequences. There is no outlook that we hold on life that does not translate into concrete consequences in our daily lives. We all hold dogmas and translate them into action, whether or not we acknowledge that we hold these dogmas:

---

[62] *The Blatchford Controversies, Collected Works* Vol. 1, 394-5.

[63] *Autobiography*, 181-2.

The human brain is a machine for coming to conclusions; if it cannot come to conclusions it is rusty. When we hear of a man too clever to believe…it is like hearing of a nail that was too good to hold down a carpet; or a bolt that was too strong to keep a door shut…Man can be defined as an animal that makes dogmas. As he piles doctrine on doctrine and conclusion on conclusion in the formation of some… philosophy or religion, he is…becoming more and more human. When he drops one doctrine after another in a refined scepticism, when he declines to tie himself to a system, when he says that he has outgrown definitions…holding no form of creed but contemplating all, then he is by that very process sinking slowly backwards into the vagueness of the vagrant animals and the unconsciousness of the grass. Trees have no dogmas. Turnips are singularly broad-minded.[64]

We see in this passage an instance of Chesterton's desire to distinguish the uniqueness of the human species against the dominant Darwinian notion that human beings are just one more species of the animal kingdom, a theme which was to recur almost two decades later in *The Everlasting Man*.

It is often thought that *Heretics* contains the negative, more critical side of Chesterton's arguments, whereas *Orthodoxy* later sets down more positively his own distinctive worldview. While it is correct to see *Heretics* as very important in its role as a prologue and complement to *Orthodoxy*, both historically and philosophically, it is also in its own right, as leading Chesterton scholar Dale Ahlquist says, "one of Chesterton's most import-ant books."[65] Although the very title of the book may have a rather frightening ring to it for some people today, Ahlquist maintains that it is important to bear in mind that the book concerns itself much more with defending good things rather than attacking bad things: "Chesterton's book is not an attack

---

[64] *Heretics, Collected Works* Vol. 1, 196-7.

[65] *G. K. Chesterton: The Apostle of Common Sense*, 34.

but a defense,"[66] a defense of the ancient truths of common sense that are forever under attack. "We who are Christians never knew the great philosophic common sense which inheres in that mystery until the anti-Christian writers pointed it out to us."[67] For Chesterton, then, Christianity contains common sense, while the great heresies often display a lack of common sense. Any apologetics must aim, therefore, to preserve all that is good, true, and beautiful and be conducive to human flourishing, and to critique and resist all that is bad and untrue, and that leads to the ugliness of dehumanization.

The word heresy comes from the Greek αἵρεσις, *hairesis*, which in turn comes from *haireomai*, meaning "to choose." The heresy is a choice made, a choice that results in isolating and exaggerating a fragment of the truth at the expense of the totality of truth. It is at best a half-truth, or, perhaps better, a truth that is held so close to the eye that it blocks out the other truths that are also part of the truth. Christ is fully God, but that does not mean that Christ is not fully human. Christ is fully human, but that does not mean that Christ is not fully God. The ancient Christological heresies held either of these two truths so close to the eye that they blocked out the counter-balancing truth necessary for the fuller vision of orthodox truth.

So a heresy is not so much a false truth as an incomplete truth. A heresy takes part of the truth and proposes it as the whole truth, thereby either rejecting or not being aware of the other constituent elements of truth. A heresy is, for example, a doctrine that says that since sobriety is good, alcohol must be bad, or since alcohol is good, sobriety must be bad; or since chastity is good, sex must be bad, or since sex is good,

---

[66] Ibid., 35.

[67] G. K. Chesterton, *Heretics*, 206.

chastity must be bad. This notion of truth is just one instance of the common sense with which *Heretics* is filled and which can be used both to defend the orthodox Christian position and to challenge an excessively narrow understanding of that position.

Chesterton engages with the heretics in this book with his customary charity and forthrightness. They all take some truth, some good, such as science or health or progress, and hold it too close to the eye, thereby blocking out larger or at least complementary truths, such as philosophical assumptions, or the holistic nature of the person, or the priority of the individual over the state machine. He uses one of his favorite literary devices, and one to be repeated some forty years later by C. S. Lewis,[68] by asking us to consider observing the earth by looking at modern society as a man from Mars might do.

If we did so, we would notice that all previous revolutions in history claimed to be restoring truth, claiming the orthodox high ground, and denouncing all previous authorities as heretical. It was only the leading intellectual voices of the twentieth century that actually boasted of being heretical, boasted that it does not matter what opinion anyone held or boasted that, as Shaw put it: "The golden rule is that there are no golden rules."[69]

> But there is one thing that is infinitely more absurd and unpractical than burning a man for his philosophy. This is the habit of saying that his philosophy does not matter, and this is done universally in the twentieth century…A man's opinion…on Botticelli matters; his opinion on all things does not matter.[70]

---

[68] C. S. Lewis, *Mere Christianity*, 86-7. Here, in Book III, Chapter 5, "Sexual Morality," Lewis explores the human phenomenon of striptease from the hypothetical perspective of a person from another world.

[69] G. B. Shaw, *Man and Superman: a Comedy and a Philosophy*, 181.

[70] *Heretics*, 40.

Opposing with great courage and confidence the leading and loudest intellectual, cultural, and political voices of the day, Chesterton claimed that literature, thought, and communication that did not even pretend to impart meaning and put us in contact with reality, was pure fiction, little more than a series of games to divert and entertain the specialist intellectual elites. By making such a claim Chesterton had ruffled feathers. People felt aggrieved that Chesterton had meted out criticisms of other people's philosophies of life, without stating his own. Taking up the gauntlet, therefore, he wrote *Orthodoxy*.

---

5. ORTHODOXY

Orthodoxy is often thought of as "the book in which Chesterton first fully declared himself unmistakably."[71] As Chesterton himself said, in the book's first chapter, it "is a kind of slovenly autobiography"[72] and, according to Oddie,

> It was both the conclusion of a process of self-discovery and the key document (for there were others) in which, at this pivotal moment in his life, he assessed not only where it was that he now stood, but how it was that his journey had followed the course that it did.[73]

It is the crystallization of a worldview, out of which all his other thoughts and works grow. If it is "slovenly" it is also, in his own words, a kind of "intellectual journey"[74] of a man whose childhood, adolescence, early adulthood, and early professional life provided milestones which were occasions of real growth and maturity. Seasons of pain and darkness became catalysts

---

[71] W. Oddie, *CRO*, 4.

[72] *Orthodoxy*, 215.

[73] W. Oddie, *op.cit.*, 4.

[74] *Orthodoxy*, 218.

for the development of a philosophy of life characterized by hope and joy.

In the preface, Chesterton writes that *Orthodoxy* is meant to be read as a companion to *Heretics*. Whereas the earlier work critiqued several of the worldviews on offer among the intellectuals of the day, the later work was more positive in its intent, expressing its author's own worldview. He says in the first chapter that it is written as "an answer to a challenge" since, as intimated above, one man targeted by Chesterton in *Heretics* had pointed out, "I will begin to worry about my philosophy... when Mr. Chesterton has given us his."[75] Chesterton says that he faces the same difficulty that Newman faced in writing the *Apologia*: in order to be sincere, he has to be autobiographical. Dermot Lane writes that,

> The question of God...is about the possibility of experiencing God in the world. Where do we experience God in this life? At what point(s) in human existence does the reality of God impinge on human experience? What are the basic ingredients of an experience of God? The mystery of God is not some kind of theorem to be proved; it is rather, an experience to be lived.[76]

It might be argued, then, that all theology and all apologetics are, to some degree, autobiographical. To write his autobiographical account is what really interests Chesterton, not whether *Orthodoxy* actually succeeds as apologetic:

> It is the purpose of the writer to attempt an explanation, not of whether the Christian Faith can be believed, but of how he personally has come to believe it. The book is therefore arranged upon the positive principle of a riddle and its answer. It deals first with all the writer's

---

[75] *Orthodoxy*, 211. Chesterton is paraphrasing George Slythe Street, a journalist writing a review in the *Outlook* of 17th June 1905, and his actual words were, "I shall not begin to worry about my philosophy of life until Mr. Chesterton discloses his."

[76] D. A. Lane, *The Experience of God: An Invitation to Do Theology*, vi.

own solitary and sincere speculations and then with all the star-
tling style in which they were all suddenly satisfied by the Christian
Theology. The writer regards it as amounting to a convincing creed.
But if it is not that it is at least a repeated and surprising coincidence.[77]

The vision of life that was forged in the crucible of the Slade
had become central to Chesterton. When challenged to state
his worldview, he wrote down how he had arrived at it and how
he had been surprised to find that it had been discovered and
written down before, in the Christian creed. *Orthodoxy* is a
theological appreciation of a concrete, particular, ordinary, everyday, and contingent world, and it maintains that we can find
God in all things. The vision expounded in this key work was
the source from which all other insights of Chesterton came.

In the opening chapter Chesterton says that he will be seeking, "in a vague and personal way, in a set of mental pictures
rather than in a series of deductions, to state the philosophy in
which I have come to believe. I will not call it my philosophy;
for I did not make it. God and humanity made it; and it made
me."[78] Chesterton uses the classical literary image of the journey
or odyssey:

> I have often had a fancy for writing a romance about an English
> yachtsman who slightly miscalculated his course and discovered
> England under the impression that it was a new island in the South
> Seas...[He planted] the British flag on that barbaric temple which
> turned out to be the Pavilion at Brighton, [and] felt rather a fool. I am
> not here concerned to deny that he looked a fool. But if you imagine
> that he felt a fool, or at any rate that the sense of folly was his sole
> or his dominant emotion, then you have not studied with sufficient

---

[77] The Preface to the work is not included in the English edition of the work in 1908, but it
does appear in an American edition of the same year. The Ignatius Press edition that I have
used for all references in this book does not contain the Preface, but it is included in another
edition listed in the Bibliography, on pp. 15-16.

[78] *Orthodoxy*, 211.

delicacy the rich romantic nature of the hero of this tale. His mistake was really a most enviable mistake; and he knew it, if he was the man I take him for. What could be more delightful than to have in the same few minutes all the fascinating terrors of going abroad combined with all the humane security of coming home again?[79]

Here we see a key Christian theme, which the apologist does well always to bear in mind: the journey toward the God who created the cosmos and all within it is precisely that—a journey, an odyssey, a voyage of discovery that lasts a lifetime, and it will often be an adventure filled with wrong turns and errors. Chesterton also re-emphasizes that the worldview which he had discovered was precisely that: a discovery, and not a creation of his own:

How can we contrive to be at once astonished at the world and yet at home in it? How can this queer cosmic town, with its many-legged citizens, with its monstrous and ancient lamps, how can this world give us at once the fascination of a strange town and the comfort and honour of being our own town?...When I fancied that I stood alone I was really in the ridiculous position of being backed up by all Christendom. It may be, Heaven forgive me, that I did try to be original; but I only succeeded in inventing all by myself an inferior copy of the existing traditions of civilized religion. The man from the yacht thought he was the first to find England; I thought I was the first to find Europe. I did try to found a heresy of my own; and when I had put the last touches to it, I discovered that it was orthodoxy.[80]

The apologist must be aware that he can never live the journey for the people with whom he is in dialogue, never force them to see what they cannot see for themselves, and must always encourage the spirit of adventure in them and teach them to relish and stay with their questions on their journey in order that in the end they be more free to see. At the same time he

---

[79] Ibid., 211-2.

[80] Ibid., 212, 214.

must always be unafraid of shedding light on the quests of his addressees, since several people have struggled with the same issues and questions and made the same wrong turns in the past. As we shall see in Chapter IV, the Church has a long tradition of thinking based on the real, concrete experiences of people who have undertaken the journey of life in this cosmos.

The purpose in writing *Orthodoxy* was to show how its author, finding himself alive in a cosmos, had felt both an instinct of wonder and a need for security and comfort. This double instinct, to the author's great surprise, was satisfied by Christianity. Chesterton does not believe it possible to offer a complete justification of Christian faith, but instead chooses "to follow one path of argument."[81] He assumes that his reader is neither apathetic nor cynical, neither bored with life nor sneering at the value of life:

> "If a man says that extinction is better than existence or blank existence better than variety and adventure, then he is not one of the ordinary people to whom I am talking. If a man prefers nothing I can give him nothing."[82]

The apologist needs a dialogue partner who is at least interested enough in life to discuss it, if conversations are to be in any way helpful; perhaps an important matter for consideration today is how the apologist rouses the interest of people, how he awakens the hunger for God that is native to human beings. Of course, there are seasons in life when the cares and anxieties of daily living may place on us burdens that are so heavy that the face of God may seem, for a time at least, imperceptible; or else there will be cultural pressures which eclipse the face of God. It is then that the creative imagination of the apologist

---

[81] Ibid., 212.

[82] Ibid.

is called into play, in order that she may forge new ways of making God more accessible. Chesterton points out that his argument for God and the Christian creed demonstrates how Christianity answered a double spiritual need which he felt: "the need for that mixture of the familiar and the unfamiliar which Christendom has rightly named romance."[83]

> ...nearly all people I have ever met in this western society in which I live would agree to the general proposition that we need this life of practical romance; the combination of something that is strange with something that is secure. We need so to view the world as to combine an idea of wonder and an idea of welcome. We need to be happy in this wonderland without once being merely comfortable. It is this achievement of my creed that I shall chiefly pursue in these pages.[84]

Chesterton did not discover Christianity so much as he discovered a correspondence between his ordinary, everyday, common-sense convictions and Christianity. Common sense posits the world that we experience, and Christianity addresses that world.

Summarizing the main points of the first chapter of *Orthodoxy*, which sets the scene for the vision that will unfold, we can say that: Chesterton's experiences did not help him to create a philosophy of life, but to discover what had already been discovered before him by Christian thinkers; he had felt a deep sense of wonder at the world, and yet a deep sense of being at home in the world, as though it were both a strange place and yet his world, his home; the need to explain this double instinct of unfamiliarity with familiarity was met by the Christian notion of romance (a term which he explains later, as we shall see); and he discovered that his other common-sense convictions (which we shall also explore in later chapters) were

---

[83] Ibid., 212.

[84] Ibid., 213.

also addressed by Christianity, a fact that he found convincing, or at the very least a repeated and surprising coincidence.

In the second chapter of *Orthodoxy* Chesterton writes that "the man who begins to think without the proper first principles goes mad; he begins to think at the wrong end. As for the rest of these pages we have to try and discover what is the right end."[85] One of Chesterton's main criticisms of modern philosophy is that it debates where thought begins. In this writer's opinion, then, though it is a highly theological work, *Orthodoxy* is not in the first instance a work of Christian apologetics; rather, it is first of all a work about the philosophical issue of first principles (and where they lead), and secondly, and rather surprisingly for Chesterton, how these find a home and nourishment in the Christian faith. This element of surprise has significance for the purposes of a book seeking a renewed agenda for apologetics today, a significance to which we shall return: in what ways can the apologist surprise and delight her addressees as she seeks to link their ordinary, everyday lives, questions, and explorations with the treasures of the Christian tradition?

Chapters 2 and 3 of *Orthodoxy*, entitled "The Maniac" and "The Suicide of Thought" respectively, take up Chesterton's criticisms of modern thought and are described by Chesterton as a "preliminary negative sketch" of habits of modern thought that lead to the dead ends he had known personally at the Slade. The first habit is the one possessed by the Maniac, the solipsist who attempts to reason his way to the first principles of thought, a path that will, according to Chesterton, lead him to madness if followed consistently right through to the bitter end.

The second is that of the Sceptic, who doubts that there are any principles at all. To read *Orthodoxy* at all, Dale Ahlquist

---

[85] Ibid., 230.

says, "we have to be prepared to go on Chesterton's journey with him" and "the first steps are the most important ones. It means the difference between getting home and getting lost."[86] In words that are reminiscent of the formative experiences of Chesterton's childhood, adolescence, and young adulthood, Chesterton tells how these steps are first to accept the reality of sin and then to accept both the limits of reason and the importance of the imagination. Given that it was not possible to assume that everyone recognized the fact of sin, another approach had to be taken:

> But though moderns deny the existence of sin, I do not think that they have yet denied the existence of a lunatic asylum. We all agree still that there is a collapse of the intellect as unmistakable as a falling house…as all thoughts and theories were once judged by whether they tended to make a man lose his soul, so for our present purpose all modern thoughts and theories may be judged by whether they tend to make a man lose his wits.[87]

One of the important things about this passage is that Chesterton shows the need to find some common ground on which the apologist can stand with his interlocutor. On what do we agree, before we begin the discussion about our disagreements? Although sin, because a theological concept, may not have been universally recognized as a reality in Edwardian culture, human sanity and insanity were still important benchmarks for the acceptability of a theory or philosophical outlook. The effects on Chesterton of his flirtation with solipsism that had taken place some fifteen or so years before now bear fruit for others in these chapters. Chesterton, ever the defender of reason in all his writings, here points out the limits of reason. "The madman is not the man who has lost his reason. The

---

[86] *G. K. Chesterton: The Apostle of Common Sense*, 23.

[87] *Orthodoxy*, 217-8.

madman is the man who has lost everything except his reason."[88] Though human beings are rational creatures, it is unhealthy to neglect the other dimensions that constitute a human being.

> Poetry is sane because it floats easily in an infinite sea; reason seeks to cross the infinite sea and so make it finite…The poet only asks to get his head into the heavens. It is the logician who seeks to get the heavens into his head. And it is his head that splits.[89]

Art, freedom, affectivity, and so many other elements are needed for a balanced and healthy epistemology and for human existence.

There is a difference, then, between being reasonable and being a rationalist (in the sense of believing that reason alone is sufficient for interpreting the world). Reason is a wonderful gift in coming to understand reality, but it can only take us so far in this task and has to be supplemented by creative imagination and faith (captured by Chesterton in the word "poetry"). For Chesterton, the problem with "the madman" is that his view of the cosmos, his philosophy of life, is not broad enough. His vision makes perfect rational sense to him, but he is nevertheless wrong:

> [The madman's error lies in the fact that] his mind moves in a perfect but narrow circle. A small circle is quite as infinite as a large circle; but though it is quite as infinite, it is not so large. In the same way the insane explanation is quite as complete as the sane one, but is not so large. A bullet is quite as round as the world, but it is not the world. There is such a thing as a narrow universality; there is such a thing as a small and cramped eternity…The lunatic's theory explains a large number of things, but it does not explain them in a large way."[90]

---

[88] Ibid., 222.

[89] Ibid., 220.

[90] Ibid., 222.

Chesterton is fighting against the imperialism of the rationalistic and scientistic[91] outlook of his day, where what was real was reduced to the physical, the empirically measured or the logically grounded. As it was put by Charles Dickens, through the voice of Gradgrind:

> Now what I want is, Facts. Teach these boys and girls nothing but Facts. Facts alone are wanted in life. Plant nothing else, and root out everything else. You can only form the minds of reasoning animals upon Facts: nothing else will ever be of any service to them.[92]

Dickens was rebelling against a superficial view of reality and advocating a vision of the cosmos that was much more poetic, deep, multi-layered, and saturated with beauty than could ever be entertained by the merely scientific imagination. The latter type of imagination is that of a person who lives with "...a horrible clarity of detail... but [is] not hampered by a sense of humor or charity, or by the dumb certainties of experience." Such people dwell "in the clean and well-lit prison of one idea;...sharpened to one painful point...without healthy hesitation and healthy complexity...the combination of an expansive and exhaustive reason with a contracted common sense."[93]

Of course Chesterton's critique of scientism is as valid today as it was a century ago. It should also be apparent, however, that Chesterton's wonderful images of narrow universalities, cramped eternities, spiritual contractions, logical completeness, well-lit prisons of one idea, and a lack of humor and charity, can be present in many of the participants, religious or otherwise,

---

[91] Although to place the word in Chesterton's mouth would be anachronistic, the reality which the word "scientism" denotes was very much part of Edwardian culture.

[92] *Hard Times*, London: Penguin, 1995, 9.

[93] *Orthodoxy*, 221, 225.

who engage in so many of the discussions in our postmodern world. Jim Wallis has written that,

> It is time for left and the right to admit that they have run out of imagination, that the categories of liberal and conservative are dysfunctional and that what is needed is a radicalism that takes us beyond the selective sympathies of both the right and the left. Such a radicalism can be found only in the gospel which is neither liberal nor conservative but fully compassionate.[94]

Chesterton's *Orthodoxy* would agree with Wallis that Christianity challenges us to move beyond our "single issue" viewpoint of the complex cosmos in which we live. We should recognize what is true, good, and beautiful in the position of the interlocutor who stands before us. However, we should not then be afraid to say in addition,

> Oh, I admit that you have your case and have it by heart, and that many things do fit into other things as you say. I admit that your explanation explains a great deal; but what a great deal it leaves out! Are there no other stories in the world except yours; and are all men busy with your business?[95]

The apologist, then, has to stay in relationship with the person with whom he finds himself in dialogue, not to push him away, not to make a caricature of his position, not to dismiss him out of hand; but to listen to him, learn something from him (even if, ultimately, he can't agree with everything stated in that position) and not deliberately misunderstand or ridicule. For Chesterton we must not let what's worst in each other eclipse what's best in each other, and continue to trust in our common task of seeking wisdom, truth, beauty, goodness and

---

[94] Cited by Ronald Rolheiser, *http://www.ronrolheiser.com/columnarchive/?id=321*, [last accessed 3rd January 2011].

[95] *Orthodoxy*, 223.

living together. Once we operate on a wavelength that enables us to listen, then we can speak; once we are open to learning, then we can teach:

> ...How much larger your life would be if your self could become smaller in it; if you could look at other men with common curiosity and pleasure...You would break out of this tiny and tawdry theatre in which your own little plot is always being played, and you would find yourself under a freer sky, in a street full of splendid strangers."[96]

Chesterton, recalling the lessons he learned at the Slade, believes that all who participate in conversations about the nature of the cosmos we share need to remove themselves from the center of the universe if they are truly to begin to see the world as it really is, and discover its true beauty and goodness. The desire and willingness to dialogue is central.

It might be argued that today, over a hundred years after the publication of *Orthodoxy*, one sees more than ever that Chesterton's words are not simplistically pious, but blunt, realistic, and astutely political. Until people who disagree with each other religiously, politically, philosophically, and ideologically on the world stage, in the boardroom, in the classroom, and in the family home learn to listen to each other, there can be no peace, no justice, no security, no living together, no joy, and no growth in real learning and wisdom. Without the principles enunciated here by Chesterton, all interlocutors will remain immature thinkers and truncated human beings, too closed to perceive that the richness of reality always transcends what we know.

Chapter 2 of *Orthodoxy* closes with Chesterton offering us two images that symbolize the two types of thought he has tried to describe in the preceding pages: the circle, exemplified by a serpent eating its tail, is the symbol of the narrow,

---

[96] Ibid.

cramped habit of mind of the solipsist; and the cross, which is symbolic of an epistemological approach that remains ever open to learning more and more about the cosmos. If the use of reason alone is what makes for an unbalanced and ultimately insane person whose philosophy is too narrow, then here, in the word "paradox," and its links with what Chesterton terms "mysticism," we get a hint of what restores sanity. "Mysticism keeps men sane."[97]

One may wonder, given its specific connotations in the Christian tradition to which Chesterton now saw himself as belonging, whether mysticism was really the best term to use. However, he uses this word to denote the person who draws nearer to the truth, to penetrate the riddles of the cosmos, by embracing paradox. We shall explore the notions of solipsism, scepticism, and paradox more fully in Chapter III. For now let us note that, for Chesterton, there is at the heart of reality, at the heart of all things, a contradiction that the logical cannot explain away. It is a mystery, a knot that cannot be untied.

> The ordinary man has always been sane because the ordinary man has always been a mystic. He has permitted the twilight. He has always had one foot in earth and the other in fairyland. He has always left himself free to doubt his gods; but (unlike the agnostic of today) free also to believe in them. He has always cared more for truth than for consistency. If he saw two truths that seemed to contradict each other, he would take the two truths and the contradiction along with them. His spiritual sight is stereoscopic, like his physical sight: he sees two different pictures at once and yet sees all the better for that…[98]

For Chesterton paradox is the truth inherent in a contradiction, in which two strands of truth become inextricably tied up in a knot, but if we try to untie the knot we miss something. "The

---

[97] Ibid., 230.

[98] Ibid., 230-1.

whole secret of mysticism is this: that man can understand everything by the help of what he does not understand." The impatient person who seeks consistency and uniformity claims to have untied the knot by his narrow, reductionist philosophy. "The morbid logician seeks to make everything lucid, and succeeds in making everything mysterious," whereas the mystic "allows one thing to be mysterious, and everything else becomes lucid."[99]

> Chesterton is not encouraging lazy thinking, but he is trying to show that insoluble mystery lies at the heart of reality, and that only by permitting this element of mystery will everything else become lucid. Although reason has its place, its starting point is not reasonable but, as he said earlier, is rooted in an assumption of faith. As he says elsewhere, "You can never prove your first statement or it would not be your first statement."[100] Logic is a process that relies on assumptions, and so for Chesterton, truth can be found with logic, but only if we have first found truth without logic.[101]

The mystic is the sane person and all thinking, including sound theological thinking and apologetics, has to remain humble before the immense and complex paradoxical mysteries of the cosmos and God. We can never claim to have "understood" or "to know" these mysteries. As we shall see later, the fourth chapter of *Orthodoxy* makes more explicit the fact that the universe is a datum, a given, the gift of the Creator to be received and enjoyed, and not a problem to be solved. The mystic, Chesterton's "common man," the person with the common sense vision of reality, is the one who sees the universe correctly and who has the basic attitude in which all wisdom can grow and flourish. In his very first book of essays, Chesterton said that, "the most

---

[99] Ibid., 231.

[100] *Daily News*, 22nd June 1907, private collection of D. Ahlquist.

[101] *Daily News*, 25th February 1905, private collection of D. Ahlquist.

unfathomable schools and sages have never attained to the gravity which dwells in the eyes of a baby three months old. It is the gravity of astonishment at the universe…a transcendent common sense."[102]

It is a theme that he returns to again and again. "I think there is a mystical minimum in human history and experience, which is at once too obscure to be explained and too obvious to be explained away."[103] His whole career is a plea not to take the cosmos and human life for granted, but to receive it as a gift, a miraculous gift. To exist in this world in the correct manner, one has to accept it as a precious, unnecessary, unfathomable, and precarious gift.

The refusal to submit to gift and mystery means that we end up frantically searching for understanding and control. We miss the whole point, "the impossible universe which stares us in the face."[104]

> The real trouble with this world of ours is not that it is an unreasonable world, nor even that it is a reasonable one. The commonest kind of trouble is that it is nearly reasonable, but not quite. Life is not an illogicality; yet it is a trap for logicians. It looks just a little more mathematical and regular than it is; its exactitude is obvious, but its inexactitude is hidden.[105]

The beauty, richness, and complexity of the cosmos will always escape the rationalist's attempts to subjugate and control it with categories of thought that ignore paradox. As we shall see in Chapter III, one of the things that Chesterton discovered about the cosmos is that, because it is paradoxical, it raises lots of

---

[102] *The Defendant*, 65.

[103] *Uses of Diversity*, 13.

[104] *Heretics*, 207.

[105] *Orthodoxy*, 285.

questions. Questions seem to be part and parcel of the human life that participates in the great drama of reality. Chesterton also noted that Christianity not only answers questions, but also raises them. Here we find another of Chesterton's surprising harmonies between Christianity and the world. The answers of the Christian creed do not eliminate mystery and questions—rather, they deepen the former and produce more of the latter. The world and the Church are both truly playgrounds in which the intellect and all else that properly belongs to the humanum can rejoice.

Of course, there is so much more to *Orthodoxy* than is contained in its first two chapters, which I have tried to cover in these few brief pages. It has so much to contribute to the creation of a new agenda for apologetics, and so we shall return to it repeatedly in the remaining chapters of this book, especially Chapter III, in order to explore more of its penetrating wisdom. In this short introduction I have sought merely to show how those early chapters were the autobiographical fruit of Chesterton's intellectual and spiritual journey, the distillation of a worldview formed by the dramas of Chesterton's childhood, adolescence, and young adulthood, and the foundations on which his other ideas and works were built.

6. Concluding Reflections

This opening chapter has offered a biographical summary of the life of G. K. Chesterton, highlighting some of the major events and milestones on his journey, which helped to shape the man and the worldview that he expressed so imaginatively in his writing and other forms of communication. It also called attention in a preliminary way to some factors that were deemed helpful for the forging of an agenda for apologetics today, elements that will be revisited and deepened later in this book. It has placed a special emphasis on the formative experiences of Chesterton's childhood and his years of study at the Slade school of Art, arguing that these culminated in the crystallization of a philosophy of life that is typically Chestertonian and finds its best and mature expression in the 1908 work of *Orthodoxy*.

We have seen that Chesterton had had a mostly happy childhood, and that this had led him to believe that deep-seated joy was the natural human disposition, and unhappiness an unnatural disposition. Pointing out that he had lived many of the experiences which are commonly thought to make a person knowledgeable and sophisticated in the ways of the world, Chesterton maintained that none of these were as "real" as the experience of joy and gratitude for the sheer gift of existence—the gift of Elfland—which he had known in his childhood. Exploration of the gift of the cosmos is the starting point for any apologetics, since it offers any number of entry points at which we can join the path that leads to the God who is the giver of the gift of the cosmos.

The crisis period of the Slade was a time when Chesterton, touched by the Aestheticism of the Decadents, which was in the cultural ascendancy, experienced solipsistic depression, joylessness, tedium, and moral temptations. Writing forty years later, he stated that he managed to hold on to religion by the thin thread of thanks for the gift of existence that had been inculcated in him during childhood. For Chesterton there is an enormous difference between knowledge and wisdom.

While pre-critical naivety is not a good thing, such that the Church will always be in need of the healthy insights of modernity, still postmodernity also has something to contribute to the task of human flourishing: it reminds us that we are more than the sum of our knowledge; that a fuller conception of what it is to be human implies much more than materialistic scientism would have us believe; and that the wisest posture before reality remains the humble, grateful, and post-sophisticated innocence of heart that was found in Chesterton, and not the proud, arrogant posture of some more virulent strands of modernity. Each of us needs to remove ourselves from the center of the cosmos and to stand in solidarity with each other, cognizant of the fact that we are in communion with one another and connected to one another because we are contingent beings, radically dependent on a love outside of us who gave each of us the cosmos and existence in that cosmos, and who is the true source and center of that cosmos.

For Chesterton, real wisdom does not consist in the desire to grasp, control, and manipulate the world as if it were some sort of possession, but in the ability to receive with gratitude and share with generosity the gift that the world is. Having learned these lessons the hard way, Chesterton saw it as his journalistic vocation to help others who were in danger of getting lost in life, and he sought to defend especially those who were powerless as governments, intellectuals, and other cultural agents of the reigning ideologies attempted to manipulate them in some way. Because of his own bitter experiences, Chesterton knew that unbalanced distortions of the modern project (which is good in itself) led to an attack on the humanum, and this led him to confront head-on, albeit humorously and in a kindly manner, the major thinkers who espoused such views.

We shall see in the chapters ahead that at all times Chesterton attempted to state his own position reasonably, while attempting to discern all that was true and of value in the position of those with whom he was in dialogue. As far as was humanly possible he tried to avoid giving offense to those whom he was debating. He looked to discern the issues on which he could agree with his dialogue partner, before working out what they must discuss and debate. Nevertheless, he neither sought nor gave intellectual quarter, and he spoke the truth plainly as he saw it, pointing out to those moderns who considered themselves to be the sole proponents of reason—over against the superstition and tradition of the pre-moderns—that, though reason is a wonderful gift given to us to help us know reality, it can only take us so far in this task, and has to be aided by creative imagination and faith (of which reason itself is an example). He criticized all reductionisms, all attempts to reduce the beauty and complexity of reality to being less than it truly is, and for this reason he became the great champion of paradox against the rationalists.

By the early years of the twentieth century, having met and married Frances, who was to be the great woman behind the great man, and having developed a close friendship with Belloc, he had become certain that Christianity was the guarantor of the human joy that he had known as a child, and he believed that attacks on the faith were attacks on human flourishing and on all that made life worth living, views which he expressed in many different forms in his 1905 work *Heretics*. Having riled people with his criticisms in this work, he was challenged to state his own philosophy of life, and he did so in the 1908 work *Orthodoxy*. This book gave him the opportunity to take stock, assessing where he now stood and how he had reached that position. It was the expression of a worldview distilled from the experiences of his childhood and the Slade years, and the fundamental autobiographical standpoint out of which all his later ideas and works grew.

In *Orthodoxy* he looked to dialogue with a partner who shares at least a minimal interest in life. He pointed out that he had always felt a double instinct about his life in the cosmos: a sense of wonder at the world, and yet a sense of feeling of being at home in the world; a sense of unfamiliarity combined with familiarity. He later discovered that this same double intuition had been experienced before him by Christian thinkers and was explained by the Christian creed. He went on to notice how several other instincts and lessons that he had learned for himself in life, especially by means of the experiences of childhood and nihilistic solipsism, were also surprisingly confirmed by the teachings of Christianity. When he thought that he had unearthed a brand new philosophy of life that could help him to chart a course through the cosmos, he learned that it had been discovered a long time before his own existence in that cosmos. *Orthodoxy* is, then, a description of how the philosophical issue of first principles, which Chesterton thought he had discovered for himself, led, much to his surprise, to the Christian faith that had long been their home and the source of their nourishment. The book challenges us to ask how the apologist can surprise and delight his addressees as he seeks to link their ordinary, everyday lives and questions with the treasures of the Christian tradition. It asks the apologist to use her imagination in order to reach the imaginations of others, to help them appreciate the wonderful complexity of what it is to be a human being in the cosmos, to invite them to reflect on the adventure of their struggles and to learn to listen to and recognize reality in a new way. It invites people in a secular culture to re-imagine their humanity.

Having survived the Slade, Chesterton knew in a deeper way the joy he had known in childhood. As we shall see, his wisdom can be used to help set people free from the culturally induced images to which they have become accustomed, so that they can imagine their lives and their place in the cosmos in a different way. If we accept his invitation to journey deeper than the surface of the ways in which we normally think of ourselves, we may find ourselves on the threshold of accepting an invitation into something that may not always have made sense to us. Chesterton can prepare us for the surprise of what is revealed in Christ by helping us to explore the surprises of our own depths. He teaches us that, in a world full of richness and paradox, Christian faith sheds light on mystery, but does not eliminate mystery. For those of us who seek to translate human explorations into theologies and apologetics, who look to offer good reasons why faith in God is reasonable and not unintelligent, and who seek to bring together human quests and the answer given to us by God in Christ, Chesterton has much to contribute—not least of all a reminder that our work is never done and that we must remain imaginative in our theology and apologetics, and humble before the divine mystery.

The Submerged Sunrise of Wonder

At the back of our brains, so to speak, there was a forgotten blaze or burst of astonishment at our own existence. The object of the artistic and spiritual life was to dig for this submerged sunrise of wonder; so that a man might suddenly understand that he was alive, and be happy.[1]

Religion has had to provide that longest and strangest telescope—the telescope through which we could see the star upon which we dwelt. For the mind and eyes of the average man this world is as lost as Eden and as sunken as Atlantis. There runs a strange law through the length of human history—that men are continually tending to undervalue their environment, to undervalue their happiness, to undervalue themselves…Most probably we are in Eden still. It is only our eyes that have changed.[2]

CHESTERTON STROVE to defend the ordinary, everyday life of men and women, because he believed that through such little things people find their way home to the God who is both their divine source and final resting

---

[1] G. K. Chesterton, *Autobiography*, 92.

[2] G. K. Chesterton, *The Defendant*, 9-10.

place. He believed that all people were created in order to enjoy the good things of a cosmos in which they were intended to flourish and fashion their eternal destiny.

From the very beginning of his journalistic career Chesterton was aware that new cultural forces threatened the ability of people to flourish and live the good life. That a religious perspective is necessary to safeguard human values such as freedom was the very point he made when he first became a prominent public figure. As we have seen, in 1903 Robert Blatchford, a socialist journalist and author, announced in his newspaper the Clarion that the astonishing scientific advances in human knowledge had done away forever with the need for religion. Theology was to be consigned to the dustbin of history, and a new type of trust in philanthropy was to be established, one which expended its energy on improving this world, rather than on splitting fine scholastic hairs about another world which probably did not exist. If government-appointed specialists, scientific experts, and social engineers were given permission to apply the latest scientific findings to the problems of society and the state-granted control over the freedom of individuals, then the amelioration and eventual cure of society's ills would rapidly ensue. Genetic and environmental manipulation by scientists would resolve the problematic issues, according to Blatchford.

Blatchford and Chesterton penned a series of articles on their divergent viewpoints on such matters, praising each other's virtues, but also expressing their core disagreements. As we have already seen, in concluding the exchange Chesterton wrote:

> There is a liberty that has made men happy in dungeons, as it may make them happy in slums. It is the liberty of the mind, that is to say, it is the one liberty on which Mr. Blatchford makes war…"No, No," says the face of Mr. Blatchford…"your thoughts are the inevitable

gift of existence, and gratitude led to a sense of humility before something much bigger than him, and from this came joy. By unpacking the further implications of this, we shall see that Chesterton arrived at the conclusion that there is a God.

We have already noted that wonder, gratitude, and joy were among the chief characteristics of Chesterton's childhood, during which he looked upon the world in the light of an eternal morning that "had a sort of wonder in it as if the world were as new as myself."[7] Looking back from the vantage point of the end of his life, Chesterton could write that his childhood revealed to him that he lived in a cosmic setting which he shared with the rest of creation. It was "real life; the real beginnings of what should have been a more real life; a lost experience in the land of the living."[8] Almost anything that Chesterton remembers from his childhood gave him this sense of primordial wonder:

> What was wonderful about childhood is that anything in it was a wonder. It was not merely a world full of miracles; it was a miraculous world. What gives me this shock is almost anything I recall; not the things that I should think most worth recalling.[9]

This sense of the magical nature of human existence, the sense that the world is Elfland or Fairyland, is not for Chesterton something strange and abnormal, a privileged moment of existence, an exception to the rule of normal living from which we later become detached as we grow older and more familiar with "reality"; rather, the attitude of the child toward existence itself remains reality, the proper criterion for judging adult attitudes toward life. The child's sense of the magical nature of existence,

---

[7] Ibid., 45.

[8] Ibid., 51.

[9] Ibid., 34.

what Jacques Maritain referred to as the "intuition of being,"[10] of the world as gift leading to a sense of wondering joy, is something instinctive and given with consciousness itself. One of the tasks of living, of growing up into adulthood, is to unpack the consequences of this gift. This unpacking led Chesterton to experience a deep sense of humility and joy before the reality of the gift of existence and the Ultimate Giver of the gift.

The important point at this juncture for the purposes of our book is that Chesterton's journey to God started through wonder. Are there lessons here for all those who, in our own culture, seek the face of God? Is a sense of wonder the first crucial step, the sine qua non, for the human adventure into Christian faith? Do human eyes first have to be opened to something before people can truly begin the spiritual journey? How do people start out on this spiritual adventure? What first gets them under way? What awakens human wonder and hope?

In seeking to answer these questions it is worth underlining once again that Chesterton's own deep sense of wonder had been something instinctive to him in his childhood, but that this had then been eclipsed by the mixture of rhythms and crises that accompanied the onset of adolescence and young adulthood in late Victorian England. We shall return to a fuller exploration of the role that darkness, doubts, and cultural forces can play in the journey to faith later in this chapter, but here it is worth saying that the pain of the Slade years acted almost as a rouser, something that awoke in Chesterton an urgent need to explore his experience. There was a deep sadness in Chesterton, possibly the beginnings of a depression,

---

[10] For an excellent summary of this and some of the other main themes in Maritain's work, see Michael Novak, "A Salute to Jacques Maritain," *The Catholic Writer: The Proceedings of the Wethersfield Institute* 2 (1989), 65-82, http://www.catholiceducation.org/articles/arts/al0066.html [accessed 14th May 2010].

as he struggled with the solipsistic and pessimistic demons within. Almost like a negative magnifying glass being held over the pages of a human life, pain can cause some of the lines or zones of life to become enlarged and some to become smaller, such that a distortion takes place, and the full tale of human experience is not recounted and the full richness of human experience left unperceived.

As we saw in our first chapter, after his own youthful period of darkness and struggle, Chesterton penned a poem to E. C. Bentley as a mark of gratitude to his friend, in recognition of the comradeship provided by him during those trying times. During his moments of doubt, despair, and suffering, Chesterton had found friendship and a sense of togetherness in the company of Bentley and his other friends in the Junior Debating Club.[11] One can only speculate on the specific contents of their conversations, but if this poem and the contents of Chesterton's notebook are taken at face value, it seems logical to suppose that Chesterton found a space within which he could speak of his own doubts and fears with honesty. Is it possible to suggest that this might have prepared the ground for a breakthrough of liberating grace?

The degree to which community is an essential facet of the search for the face of God is discussed more fully in Chapter IV. Here we can say that when an opportunity to share life with others is afforded to a person, new possibilities to perceive the goodness of self, others, and life are discovered. A distorted picture of reality gives way to a fuller vision. Negatives can prepare the way for tentative positives, as new hope emerges. Perhaps the conversations with Bentley paved the way for

---

[11] For more detailed accounts of the interactions between Chesterton and his friends in the JDC and the mutual affection they held for each other, see Ward, *GKC*, 36-38.

Chesterton to move from various prisons of doubt and despair to a liberating recollection of the goodness and trustworthiness of self, others, and reality. Such honest conversations can reveal that hurts and disappointments are no longer the burdens of a lonely self, but are gently shared and, in that sharing, the self learns to trust that there are other, hitherto unrecognized or forgotten, dimensions to reality and dimensions of goodness. There emerges a new awareness of spiritual hungers and other dimensions of the self and of others, and a new humility which recognizes a mysterious and multi-faceted complexity to the world.

Chesterton learned that the journey to God begins with the journey from lack of freedom to greater freedom. Finding himself unfree, held fast in solipsistic chains of doubt about the worth of himself, human beings, and the extra-mental world, Chesterton found himself in thick fogs about the meaning of existence. He was unable to trust the goodness of life, knowing something of the experience of the student to whom he later referred as "the Diabolist," a man whom he described as "a pessimist, which is something more atheistic than an atheist; he was a fundamental sceptic, that is a man without fundamentals. He was one who disbelieved in man much more than he did in God."[12] The inability to find worth in oneself or other human beings seriously impedes the search for God.

For Chesterton, solipsism was an existential threat and not merely a theoretical philosophy, "the alternative where, in the absence of a cosmos, thought itself was reduced to nullity."[13] Despite the validity of some of their insights (we shall see in his study of Aquinas that Chesterton did not believe that human

---

[12] *Autobiography*, 146.

[13] S. Jaki, *Chesterton: A Seer of Science*, 95.

beings merely drink in and process data from an external world in order to come to knowledge of reality), Chesterton believed that Kant and post-Kantian philosophers, if read uncritically, could lead people into solipsism, which "may lead to thinking that there is nothing but thought."[14] One of the dangerous consequences of this, for Chesterton, is moral in nature. Knowing in his own life the temptations that come from a worldview that doubts the reality of anything but the ego, he calls solipsism a "panegoistic extreme of thought."[15] He criticizes those writers and artists affected by this philosophy for trying to "impress their own personalities" on the world,[16] instead of using their gifts to give life to others.

Chesterton knew all too well that the wounds inflicted upon us in life can tempt us not to trust our deepest selves, others, or life itself, such that we perceive only shadow in those places. "Man knows that there is…that within which can never be hated too much." However, if we are awakened by life to the light of our own goodness and awakened to the goodness of others and reality, this can often lead to a more explicitly spiritual journey of faith. Being aware that there is also within us something "that can never be valued too highly…a philosophy which emphasizes both [the human capacity for goodness and badness], violently and simultaneously, [enables us to] restore the balance to the brain."[17]

The fostering of an attitude of trust, the nurturing of faith in self, others, and life, can often heal the wounds that have

---

[14] *Autobiography*, 89

[15] *Orthodoxy*, 229.

[16] Ibid.

[17] "The Spirit of the Age in Literature," *Sidelights on New London and Newer York*, cited in *TTFT*, 58.

come to us from our experience. Fostering "faith" (lower case 'f') in these things brought about the possibility of religious "Faith" (upper case 'F') later for Chesterton. The wonder at the miraculous gift of life which Chesterton had known as a child had been eclipsed, but once he began to perceive again a sense of wonder, he was able to set out on the journey of faith in God. What Bernard Lonergan refers to as conversion took place. Lonergan states that authentic objectivity, contact with the real, is a function of properly constituted subjectivity (the converted mind). The poorly operating mind is one that is preoccupied with self and thereby loses contact with the external world.[18] Because smaller lights were switched on for Chesterton, a bigger Light became possible. He experienced the keenest sense of wonder and the most intense gratitude for and delight in the things which life has to offer. Not to experience a sense of wonder and gratitude for at least something at some point in life would probably be highly unusual for a human life, but perhaps equally unusual is the frequency with which Chesterton, post-Slade, displayed his thankfulness.

> You say grace before meals.
> All right.
> But I say grace before the play and the opera,
> And grace before the concert and pantomime,
> And grace before I open a book,
> And grace before sketching, painting,
> Swimming, fencing, boxing, walking, playing, dancing;
> And grace before I dip the pen in the ink.[19]

Chesterton's rediscovery of gratitude, humility, and joy had been born in the crucible of the pain and darkness of the Slade

---

[18] See "Understanding and Being," *The Collected Works of Bernard Lonergan*, vol. 5, Toronto: University of Toronto Press, 1990, 173-4.

[19] From the *Notebooks,* cited in Ward, *GKC,* 47.

experience, through which he had been helped by the presence of his friends. There had been a battle of moods going on in Chesterton during this period. He had known feelings of sadness, pessimism, despair, and negativity on the one hand, and feelings of wonder, gratitude, and joy on the other. In Ignatian terms, Chesterton had known both desolation and consolation. He had emerged from this battle of moods rediscovering the consolation of his childhood and believing that consolation is the natural state of the human person. He knew that desolation had come when he had experienced himself as a lonely self, imprisoned within a solipsistic vision of the cosmos. Consolation had come when he had experienced himself as being in community of life with others, who were gifts in a cosmos full of gifts, a cosmos that was itself gift.

The struggle that had taken place had been between two understandings of himself. He realized that sin follows from making oneself the center of the universe, thereby attempting to take the primacy that belongs to God alone. When we do this we deny our nature, our true state in the cosmos as child of God. To sin is to forget who we are,[20] and so authentic self-knowledge is essential in order to live joyfully and to open up the possibility for God.

> To [Victor Hugo] delight in himself was the first condition of all optimism, and faith in himself the first condition of all faith. If a man does not enjoy himself whom he has seen, how shall he enjoy God whom he has not seen? To the great poet, as to the child, there is no hard-and-fast line drawn between the ego and the Cosmos.[21]

The battle of self-images is at the heart of Ignatian spirituality, which contends that (just as it was for Chesterton) awareness

---

[20] The Greek for sin is *Hamartia*, from *hamartanein*, to miss the mark/target, to err.

[21] "Victor Hugo," in *A Handful of Authors*, cited in *TTFT*, 148.

of this struggle of images and moods is the first step in becoming free for further exploration, wonder, and judgments about life. Chesterton's spiritual journey became a foundation for his later explicit theology. Chesterton had been awakened to the angels and demons within by this struggle of self-images. As he was later to discover with Frances's (and her brother's) struggles with depression, a desolation that is more permanent can be destructive. Tragic as this condition is, however, it is not the default position for human beings. Certainly the flow of ordinary, everyday experience will inevitably entail an alternation of moods, but Chesterton realized that consolation is the natural state. Once he had returned to that position, his life became one that flowed outwards in love and goodness toward the world, and this was expressed through a creativity which was the fruit of his passion for recognizing goodness, beauty, and truth wherever he found them.

It was the feeling of sadness brought on by solipsism and the boredom that came from flirting with moral temptations which roused Chesterton from his desolation. He was aware of drifting through existence in sadness, rather than living with enthusiasm. He knew the dissatisfaction of a life lived in lonely solipsistic pessimism and, wondering about what was going on within him, he started to wonder also about what was in front of him. A deeper call from the negativity within occasioned the call to look without, and he began to move away from the immature outlook that had followed his flirtation with Aestheticism and solipsistic rationalism. This immature half-life or mere existence was shaken by sadness and boredom and provided a window to look upon new possibilities of self and cosmos. The cramped and imprisoned false self emerged into the fuller freedom of the true self through the gift of wonder, but only after the whole process was occasioned by sadness, boredom, and moral temptation. The short-lived desolation proved useful and fruitful.

Chesterton's experience during his time at the Slade holds much importance for apologetics in our 21st-century culture. Chesterton's experience of the "sad self" and his emergence into the "wonder-filled self," his experience of desolation and consolation, reveal that the journey toward God often begins with some discovery or rediscovery of wonder, and this often only happens when a person is woken up to move toward that through pain, dissatisfaction, or unexpected joy. The true self can become eclipsed by the false self, and the false self can drift through life ignoring or suppressing the hungers and spiritual layers of the deeper self. Pain or unexpected joy renews wonder and leads to new images of possibility for self, others, world, and God.

That there are more layers of the self and the cosmos than there at first appear to be is something that Chesterton discussed in chapters 2 and 3 of *Orthodoxy*. Though he was the great advocate of reason, Chesterton knew that there was more to the human person than the merely rational, and not to recognize this was to court danger. "The madman is not the man who has lost his reason. The madman is the man who has lost everything except his reason."[22] The human person is much more than the rational, left-brain, logical information-processor; she is also right-brain, intuitive, creative, poetic, or what Chesterton calls "mystical." To ignore or underplay the value of these more neglected dimensions of the human person is to shrink and be diminished. It is also to miss out on the wonders of the cosmos. This distinction is worth quoting again:

---

[22] *Orthodoxy*, 222.

> Poetry is sane because it floats easily in an infinite sea; reason seeks to cross the infinite sea and so make it finite....The poet only asks to get his head into the heavens. It is the logician who seeks to get the heavens into his head. And it is his head that splits.[23]

The beauty, richness, and complexity of the cosmos will always escape the rationalist's attempts to subjugate and control it with categories of thought, for the world is much richer and more mysterious than the rationalist's worldview permits.

> The real trouble with this world of ours is not that it is an unreasonable world, nor even that it is a reasonable one. The commonest kind of trouble is that it is nearly reasonable, but not quite. Life is not an illogicality; yet it is a trap for logicians. It looks just a little more mathematical and regular than it is; its exactitude is obvious, but its inexactitude is hidden; its wildness lies in wait.[24]

However, once Chesterton had come through the Slade battles, he knew that for the rest of his life there would be dimensions of reality that were forever opened up for exploration.

> The whole secret of mysticism is this: that man can understand everything by the help of what he does not understand. The morbid logician seeks to make everything lucid, and succeeds in making everything mysterious. The mystic allows one thing to be mysterious, and everything else becomes lucid.[25]

By recognizing that there were zones of his own humanity that were not mapped by strictly rational categories—from which emerge the poetic, the imaginative, which are part of what he refers to as the mystical—Chesterton was filled with humility and wonder before the gift of a cosmos.

---

[23] Ibid., 220.

[24] Ibid., 285.

[25] Ibid., 231.

Once he had had his own sense of wonder rekindled, he was able to write, "the world will never starve for want of wonders; but only for want of wonder."[26] His rediscovered wonder caused him to have a keen interest in things. The world is so full of interesting things that he decided to explore them, and so ended up feeling an intense gratitude and joy. He wrote that he never found any subject or person that was uninteresting,[27] although his own personal experience had taught him that various factors in daily living can cause us to overlook the wonders that are all around us. Daily living can make the world seem tired and jaded, and from this other problems arise:

> The effect of this staleness is the same everywhere; it is seen in all drug-taking and dram-drinking and every form of the tendency to increase the dose. Men seek stranger sins or more startling obscenities as stimulants to their jaded senses…They try to stab their nerves to life…They are walking in their sleep and try to wake themselves up with nightmares.[28]

He knew from dabbling in the worldview of the Aesthetes that increasing the dosage leads to boredom and dissatisfaction, and then one is unable to feel what he was later to feel for the rest of his life: "a fierce pleasure in things being themselves…the wetness of water, the fieriness of fire, the steeliness of steel, the unutterable muddiness of mud."[29]

Having rediscovered this keen sense of the reality of things, he felt compelled to share it with others: he had found his vocation as a writer. Having been aroused to see the world in its fullness, he wished to awaken in others the sense of wonder.

---

[26] *Tremendous Trifles*, 5.

[27] *Illustrated London News*, 11th January 1913, *Collected Works* Vol. 29, 419.

[28] *The Everlasting Man*, 159.

[29] Letter to Frances, cited in Ward, *GKC*, 79.

At the back of our brains, so to speak, there was a forgotten blaze or burst of astonishment at our own existence. The object of the artistic and spiritual life was to dig for this submerged sunrise of wonder; so that a man might suddenly understand that he was alive, and be happy.[30]

Using his gifts as a literary artist, he hoped to be able to paint images with words in order to help reawaken in others a sense of wonder that had become dulled by daily living. He wanted to "to provide that longest and strangest telescope—the telescope through which we could see the star upon which we dwelt," for he was aware that "Most probably we are in Eden still. It is only our eyes that have changed."[31] Tired, adult eyes are weary of the repetitive and find it monotonous. As we shall see in our next chapter, Chesterton believed that art can help renew our eyesight. "The success of any work of art is achieved when we say of any subject, a tree or a cloud or a human character, 'I have seen that a thousand times and I never saw it before.'"[32] Imagination needs to be engaged in order to help people to really perceive what is before them and really live life:

The whole object of real art, of real romance—and, above all, of real religion—is to prevent people from losing the humility and gratitude which are thankful for daylight and daily bread; to prevent them from regarding daily life as dull or domestic life as narrow; to teach them to feel in sunlight the song of Apollo and in the bread the epic of the plough. What is now needed most is intensive imagination. I mean the power to turn our imagination inwards, on the things we already have, and to make those things live…really learning how to experience our experiences…learning how to enjoy our enjoyments.[33]

---

[30] *Autobiography*, 92.

[31] *The Defendant*, 9-10.

[32] *The Thing: Why I Am A Catholic*, 173.

[33] *Illustrated London News*, 20th October 1924, *Collected Works* Vol. 33, 411.

It is interesting that Chesterton, who remained suspicious of the Catholic Modernists,[34] here places a lot of emphasis on the more positive role that imagination can play in helping a person come to religious faith through inspection of their daily experience. We shall have occasion to return to the importance of Chesterton's appreciation of imagination later, but it is evident that he believes that if a person, in a spirit of reverence born of wonder, gratitude, and humility, honors fully what he encounters each day, he will find it soaked in a magic that comes from another world.

Out of hundreds of examples that could be offered to illustrate this last point of Chesterton's, I will take just one, from *Tremendous Trifles*, a book which contains some of the essays he wrote in the *Daily News* between 1901 and 1909. On 4th November 1905, Chesterton wrote a column entitled "On a Piece of Chalk."[35] The piece describes how he set out to do some drawing with chalks, only to find that he did not possess a piece of white chalk. He goes on to describe white as a distinct color, a positive thing, rather than a negative absence of color. He goes on to say that virtue (such as chastity) is also a positive human quality, and not merely the absence of vices or the avoidance of moral dangers (since chastity is a positive way to live a life of love, and not merely the "abstention from sexual wrong"). Unable to find a piece of white chalk, he "suddenly stood up and roared with laughter...[for he] was sitting on an immense warehouse of white chalk. The landscape was made entirely of white chalk...this southern England...is a piece of chalk."[36]

---

[34] See I. Boyd, "Chesterton's Anglican Reaction to Modernism," in A. Nichols, ed., *Chesterton and the Modernist Crisis*, Saskatoon: The Chesterton Review Press, 1990, 5-36.

[35] *Tremendous Trifles*, 5-8.

[36] Ibid., 8.

In this essay, as in so many other instances of his work, apart from using everyday objects to convey some deep philosophical or theological truth (like the analogous natures of the color white and virtue), Chesterton also puts before us the ordinary, everyday things with which we have become over-familiar (the landscape of southern England), and asks us to see how extraordinary and miraculous they actually are, and how what we are desperately seeking is often there before our very eyes, unperceived. To underline this, the same book of essays tells of the objects in his pocket, the people we meet every day on the street, the things we come across in railway stations: Chesterton is awakening us to the fact that the things in our life that appear to be mere trifles are actually tremendous.

> Whatever it is that we are all looking for, I fancy that it is really quite close…Always the kingdom of Heaven is "at hand"…so I for one should never be astonished if the next twist of a street led me to the heart of that maze in which all the mystics are lost.[37]

The things of daily living which appear to us to be humdrum have the potential to lead us to God. They are sacramental. As we shall see in our next chapter, when we look at "The Ethics of Elfland," once Chesterton had grasped in wonder the essential nature of reality as gift and not necessity, he began to see everything as a sign or symbol: everything pointed somewhere, signifying something from another world. "It is impossible for anything to signify nothing."[38] He then wanted to use his enormous powers of imagination to help others to wonder at the meaning that is inherent in everything in the cosmos. "The function of imagination is not to make strange things settled,

---

[37] "A Glimpse of My Country," *Tremendous Trifles*, 105.

[38] *A Handful of Authors*, New York: Sheed & Ward, 1953, 40.

so much as to make settled things strange; not so much to make wonders facts as to make facts wonders."[39]

Elfland, reality, life in this cosmos, teach us that existence itself, as utterly non-necessary and magical, is the first cause of wonder. Existence "has a value wholly inexpressible,"[40] but it is the writer's (as artist) task to express it. It was Chesterton's vocation to awaken people to their true existential situation in a world that stands before us full of richness. People are not always aware of that richness, because their eyes have become tired and things have become over-familiar. He wrote that, "our cynical indifference is an illusion; it is the greatest of all illusions; the illusion of familiarity."[41] One of his main ambitions was to help people realize that they should learn to look at things with which they had become familiar until they looked unfamiliar again.

Having awoken to the realization that human beings can live only a half-life, a mere existence in which they remain unaware of anything other than the surface dimensions of their humanity, Chesterton wanted to rouse others from the slumbers of mere existence. The cataracts had fallen from his own eyes after experiencing the boredom, moral temptation, and unhappiness which can ensue from not trusting the goodness of self, others, and reality, and from the ever-present danger of egocentric solipsism. The potential of pain to rouse us from half-life, the power of deprivation or loss to help us perceive the as-yet unperceived depths of both self and the cosmos became a recurrent theme in his writing. In Elfland everything—even a deficiency, an illness, or a sprained foot—points to something, signifies something, and can teach us something.

---

[39] *The Defendant*, 37.

[40] *Robert Browning*, Teddington: Echo Library, 2006, 83.

[41] *The Everlasting Man*, 154.

I feel grateful for the slight sprain which has introduced this mysterious and fascinating relationship between one of my feet and the other. The way to love anything is to realize that it might be lost. In one of my feet I can feel how strong and splendid a foot is; in the other I can realize how very much otherwise it might have been. The moral of the thing is wholly exhilarating. This world and all our powers in it are far more awful and beautiful than even we know until some accident reminds us.[42]

In this passage we are reminded again to look at reality as gift. Everything we have we might not have had. To live in this world is to live in a contingent, utterly non-necessary world. All that exists is gift. "If you wish to realize how fearfully and wonderfully God's image is made, stand on one leg. If you want to realize the splendid vision of all visible things—wink the other eye."[43] The contingency of life challenges human beings to wonder to what extent they appreciate the gifts in their lives. Do they love and appreciate what they have? Do they take it for granted?

This appreciation of the ordinary and the everyday is something that is at the heart of one of Chesterton's favorite stories, *Robinson Crusoe*. Crusoe, washed up from a shipwreck onto a desert island, manages to rescue a few things from the sea:

...the best thing in the book is simply the list of things saved from the wreck. The greatest of poems is an inventory. Every kitchen tool becomes ideal because Crusoe might have dropped it in the sea. It is a good exercise, in empty or ugly hours of the day, to look at anything, the coal-scuttle or the bookcase, and think how happy one could be to have brought it out of the sinking ship on to the solitary island. But it is a better exercise still to remember how all things have had this hair-breadth escape: everything has been saved from a wreck."[44]

[42] "The Advantages of Having One Leg," *Tremendous Trifles*, 22-23.

[43] Ibid.

[44] *Orthodoxy*, 267.

The great wreck from which all things in Elfland have been rescued is the wreck of non-being. "Men spoke much in my boyhood of restricted or ruined men of genius: and it was common to say that many a man was a Great Might-Have-Been. To me it is a more solid and startling fact that any man in the street is a Great Might-Not-Have-Been."[45] Becoming aware of our own contingency and of the contingency of all that we have is a great step toward looking upon all that we have with new eyes of grateful appreciation. Then we can begin to live life more fully.

What enables us to live with greater gratitude is humility. "Humility is a grand, a stirring thing, the exalting paradox of Christianity, and the sad want of it in our own time is, we believe, what really makes us think life dull, like a cynic, instead of marvellous, like a child."[46] There needs to be a change in the perceiver of the cosmos, not the cosmos perceived:

> Humility is perpetually putting us back in the primal darkness. There all light is lightning, startling and instantaneous. Until we understand that original dark, in which we have neither sight nor expectation, we can give no hearty and childlike praise to the splendid sensationalism of things.[47]

The child has not grown old like the adults, and

> ...kicks his legs rhythmically through excess, not absence, of life. Because children have abounding vitality, because they are in spirit fierce and free, therefore they want things repeated and unchanged. They always say, "Do it again"; and the grown-up person does it again until he is nearly dead. For grown-up people are not strong enough to exult in monotony.

---

[45] Ibid.

[46] From the *Notebook*, cited in Ward, *GKC*, 59.

[47] *Heretics*, 128

Chesterton remembers that it is to the child that the Kingdom of Heaven belongs. There is something divine in the child, for "...perhaps God is strong enough to exult in monotony...It may be that He has the eternal appetite of infancy; for we [adults] have sinned and grown old, and our Father is younger than we."[48]

At the Slade Chesterton had known the depths of despair and a sense of being only half-alive, because of the pessimism that makes the ego the center of reality, to such a degree that the ego is left sceptical of the possibility that there is any reality other than self. Humility, recognizing that we are not in fact the center of reality, that we are not self-sufficient beings, but contingent beings, dependent on the source of being and inter-dependent with all other contingent beings in the cosmos, is the way out of despair and into a fuller life in which everything appears as wonder, as it does to the child. Humility means knowing our true place in reality: knowing that we are nothing because utterly dependent on God for our being; and yet everything, because called into being by God, or, as Shakespeare puts it, through the mouth of Hamlet: "how infinite in faculty...this quintessence of dust."[49] Humility is the virtue that enables us to feel both small enough to sense our unworthiness before the greatness of everything of which we are part, and yet privileged enough to enjoy it as gift.

Humility is neither self-exaltation nor self-deprecation, for we are neither the center of the cosmos nor an unimportant part of the cosmos. We are not independent, but dependent and inter-dependent; we are not God, but we are a child of God, and called to live with other children of God in the gift of God's cosmos, and we are called to contribute the gift of self

[48] *Orthodoxy*, 263-4.

[49] *Hamlet: Prince of Denmark*, Act II, Scene II

for the life of others. Indeed, we remember from *Orthodoxy* that, since Elfland is gift, utterly unsolicited and unmerited, we show our gratitude for the gift by living life with humility and self-control in the face of the limits of Elfland, thereby giving our obedience to the Person who is the source of Elfland: "we should thank God for beer and Burgundy by not drinking too much of them."[50] The next chapter explores more fully these connections among creation, morality, and human flourishing.

The fact that there is anything at all, that there is such a thing as Elfland, is utter surprise, utter unmerited gift. The realization of this surprise gift leads to joy, which in turn leads Chesterton to posit the existence of God. Aidan Nichols[51] points out that, in Chesterton's poem *The Ballad of the White Horse*, when the Virgin Mary asks King Alfred at the lowest point of his battle with the Danes, "do you have joy without a cause...?"[52] Chesterton "indicates a kind of aperture in experience: via this aperture we are open to the transcendent realm that is God." Nichols maintains that by characterizing joy as uncaused, Chesterton does not intend to depict it as:

> ...a random or chance occurrence, ontologically rootless. On the contrary, precisely because, for him, joy is neither empirically bounded nor ethically relevant, its foundation must be sought at a deeper level, where the finite opens onto the infinite. Were joy a reaction to empirically specific states or situations, it could be regarded as determined by those states or situations. Were it ethical in content, it could be seen as a reflection of a self-constituted human meaning. But since, as Chesterton indicates, it is neither of these things, its raison d'être must be sought at a point which may be called metaphysical: on the finite-infinite frontier.[53]

---

[50] *Orthodoxy*, 268.

[51] Nichols, A., *A Grammar of Consent: The Existence of God in Christian Tradition*, 166.

[52] *The Ballad of the White Horse*, Book I "The Vision of the King" p.17.

[53] *A Grammar of Consent*, 166-7.

Joy, then, is being distinguished from happiness. Happiness, whose root is "hap," meaning "chance" or "fortune," is very much dependent on whether things are going well for a person outwardly: relationships, job, money, and so on. Happiness is the great feeling one has when things are progressing well. Joy, on the other hand, is an inner state that comes with wisdom and virtue and which survives the vicissitudes of external circumstances. Ultimately joy is one of the fruits of the Spirit,[54] a gift from the personal source of all that exists. As Nichols says, for Chesterton,

> Joy…lies deeper than happiness or unhappiness, pleasure or pain. All of these are reactions to particular conditions or events within existence, whereas joy is the reaction to the fact that there should be such a thing as existence at all. Intimately related to wonder before the fact of being, joy is an implicit affirmation of the doctrine of creation and hence of the truth of theism.[55]

Just as Paul, when writing to the Church in Galatia, knew from his own life that joy can survive in spite of one's personal circumstances, so Chesterton described Charles Dickens as a man who had whitewashed the universe in a blacking factory.[56] This, of course, echoed Chesterton's own experience: doubts and darkness do indeed come as a result of a variety of burdens in a human life, but these need not damage permanently one's capacity for joy at the gift of existence. "Man is more himself, man is more manlike, when joy is the fundamental thing in him and grief the superficial…by [Christianity's] creed joy becomes something gigantic and sadness becomes something special

---

[54] Galatians 5: 22-23.

[55] *G. K. Chesterton: Theologian*, 108-9.

[56] *Charles Dickens*, 21.

and small."[57] As we shall see in Chapters IV and VI, because life is ultimately meaningful and not absurd, the cosmos is ultimately a joyful place.

Chesterton experienced a wondrous and joyful surprise at existence, and felt humbled to be granted the gift of being part of something that was so much greater than him. With that came deep gratitude for what he could only describe as gift:

> Man is a creature; all his happiness consists in being a creature; or, as the Great Voice commanded us, in being a child. All his fun is in having a gift or present; which the child, with profound understanding, values because it is a "surprise." But surprise implies that a thing comes from outside ourselves; and gratitude that it comes from someone other than ourselves. It is thrust through the letter-box; it is thrown in at the window; it is thrown over the wall. Those limits are the lines of the very plan of human pleasure.[58]

Joy comes from recognizing the surprise gift of whatever stands before us in our daily existence, an existence into which we were thrown without prior consultation and in the midst of which we already find ourselves when we first learn to use our capacities for rational thinking. However, true rationality leads us to see the need for a divine Giver of the gift, protestations to the contrary notwithstanding. If Chesterton knew from his own life that daily experience can submerge the sense of wonder, nevertheless, if someone asks, "What nonsense is all this; do you mean that a poet cannot be thankful for grass and wild flowers without connecting it with theology; let alone your theology?" Chesterton's life had taught him to reply:

> "Yes; I mean he cannot do it without connecting it with theology, unless he can do it without connecting it with thought. If he can manage to be thankful when there is nobody to be thankful to, and

---

[57] *Orthodoxy*, 364-5.

[58] *The Poet and the Lunatics*, 86.

no good intentions to be thankful for, then he is simply taking refuge in being thoughtless in order to avoid being thankless."[59]

The sense of wonder and joyful gratitude, rooted in humility, for the surprise gift of a cosmos necessarily leads to ultimate questions about the source and goal of that cosmos.

For Chesterton, wonder at the gift of the cosmos leads us to the virtue of humility, which, as the Latin etymology of the word suggests,[60] means being grounded or rooted in the truth of the human condition. One of its cognates is humor, and in Chapter IV we shall return to the importance of humor, its connection with humility, and the relative positions of humor and humility in Paganism and Christianity. Here we may recall what we noted above—that humility means holding in tension two truths about human beings: that in one sense we are nothing, as we are completely dependent in our being, utterly contingent and not ipsum esse subsistens, self-sufficient Being, or God; and in an equally real sense we are everything, because we are called into being by God, along with the other beings in the cosmos.

For Chesterton, true humility (as distinct from the false humility of a self-deprecation that ignores one half of this pair of truths in tension) means bending the knee in respect for and obedience to a reality that is richer than one's own ego. Such a person no longer considers himself the center of the cosmos and so is free from the tyranny of the ego and the need to manipulate others and all reality in order to achieve his own goals. He sees other people and the world as ends in themselves and not merely the means to his own narcissistic goals. To live in this way is to love: others, the cosmos, and God. To live in

---

[59] Autobiography, 348.

[60] Humus is the Latin word for "soil".

this way is to conform one's freedom to the truth, which is to be truly free, a state that brings joy.

Francis of Assisi's sheer joy in the face of existence came from the fact that the creation was his sister, both of them having come from the same creative Hand, *ex nihilo*. "In a fashion [Francis] endures and answers even the earthquake irony of the Book of Job; in some sense he is there when the foundations of the world are laid, with the morning stars singing together and sons of God shouting for joy."[61] In the same way, Chesterton felt the need for God because of the goodness of existence. His conversion to Christian theism came not from a frantic Feuerbachian search for a reason to ground happiness in the face of unhappiness, but from an overflowing joy at the goodness of Elfland—dragons, witches, and poisoned apples notwithstanding:

> The important matter was this, that it entirely reversed the reason for optimism. And the instant the reversal was made it felt like the abrupt ease when a bone is put back in the socket...all the optimism of the age had been false and disheartening for this reason, that it had always been trying to prove that we fit in to the world. The Christian optimism is based on the fact that we do not fit in to the world.[62]

We may note here the contrast between the states of mind and heart which Chesterton experienced when considering the materialistic and Christian interpretations of life in the world. "The modern philosopher had told me again and again that I was in the right place, and I had still felt depressed even in acquiescence. But I had heard that I was in the wrong place, and my soul sang for joy, like a bird in spring."[63] There is an

---

[61] *Saint Francis of Assisi*, 69-70.

[62] *Orthodoxy*, 283.

[63] Ibid., 284.

Augustinian wavelength here: Chesterton's sense of lacking or needing something became the springboard or impetus for him to see life positively, as being ultimately rooted in the good. A sense of wonder and gratitude had teleological consequences for Chesterton: what is the *telos*, the final end, of human beings? The wonderful things of this cosmos do not satiate his desire, but stir it up and cause him to conclude that the human person has somehow got lost and "been a tramp since Eden." He contends that, "Man has always been looking for that home....[but under the cultural influence of scepticism]. For the first time in history he begins to really doubt the object of his wanderings on the earth. He has always lost his way; but now he has lost his address."[64]

Chesterton wrote those words fifteen centuries after Augustine had penned in prayer, "...thou hast created us for thyself, and our heart knows no rest, until it may repose in thee."[65] It is a common human experience to seek answers to the question of why we are here and why we never feel totally at home in the world; to seek where we can find lasting peace and joy; to wonder how we can live with the restlessness that our desires bring; to recognize that we have to engage in a lifelong struggle in order to find some peace; and also to recognize that there is no enduring rest in this world.

At the same time Christian tradition has long seen this universal human hunger, this strange weariness or restlessness of heart, as a starting point for the journey toward faith and (as we shall see in the fourth chapter) toward finding a way of living that can express our creativity and satisfy (albeit never fully, this side of the grave) our capacity for joy. This universal

---

[64] *What's Wrong with the World?* 53.

[65] *Confessions*, Book I, Chapter 1, 31.

human longing is not a proof for the existence of God, but it is a pointer toward the possibility of God. Almost like a pulley that dragged Chesterton's spirit down on one side, his inability to feel at home in the world was the impetus that simultaneously lifted his spirit toward new possibilities of faith. He felt a sense of awe-filled wonder as he sensed that he was in relationship with something bigger, something beyond himself. Chesterton's belief in another world was a result of his belief in the goodness of life and not because, *pace* Feuerbach, he was an escapist seeking to avoid the despair and absurdity of this world. What he sought was the ultimate foundation of the hope that filled him.

2. SURVIVING ONE'S MOODS:
Darkness and Doubts

Summarizing Chesterton's journey from the Slade to the Christian faith, one could say that, finding himself deeply unhappy and wary of trusting self, others, and reality itself, the pain, loneliness, and deep dissatisfaction which he experienced had been a springboard, an awakening, an arousal to adventure. In that adventure (or romance, as he often called it), Chesterton explored his experience more attentively, reflected on it, came to his conclusions and then built his life on the foundations of those conclusions. He then spent the rest of his life telling others of his story, in an effort to rouse them to their own adventure. New images of himself, others, and the world emerged to replace the formerly enthroned images, and Chesterton came to rediscover the wonder he had known as a child.

This experience consisted of wonder at the surprise that anything existed at all, and he felt humble and grateful before the sheer greatness of existence in a cosmos that possessed the quality of all surprises: that of gift. With the sense that existence was a gift came the notion that there was a God: a Giver who provides the gift. Thus Chesterton had survived moments of bleak darkness that had threatened to engulf him and had come out on the other side believing in a personal God who had created the cosmos and who sustains it in being at every moment of its existence.

In a piece entitled "The *Orthodoxy* of Hamlet,"[66] Chesterton quotes Shakespeare's Hamlet. The eponymous character knows the struggles of darkness and despairing moods, yet he is able to say:

> ...and indeed it goes so heavily with my disposition that this goodly frame, the earth, seems to me a sterile promontory, this most excellent canopy, the air, look you, this brave o'erhanging firmament, this majestical roof fretted with golden fire, why, it appears no other thing to me than a foul and pestilent congregation of vapours. What a piece of work is a man! How noble in reason! How infinite in faculty!...And yet, to me, what is this quintessence of dust? Man delights not me: no, nor woman neither, though by your smiling you seem to say so.[67]

In this passage Hamlet describes how, although he cannot perceive the world as good or human beings as created in the image of anything good, yet nevertheless he believes them to be so. Chesterton sees in this passage a key quality of faith:

> It is, perhaps, the most optimistic passage in all human literature... The modern, like the modern conception of Hamlet, believes only

---

[66] "The Orthodoxy of Hamlet" *Lunacy and Letters*, http://209.236.72.127/wordpress/?page_id=1124. Hereafter, OH.

[67] Act II, scene 2, lines 305-317, cited in *Lunacy and Letters*.

in mood. But the real Hamlet, like the Catholic Church, believes in reason. Many fine optimists have praised man when they felt like praising him. Only Hamlet has praised man when he felt like kicking him as a monkey of the mud…This is the definition of a faith. A faith is that which is able to survive a mood.[68]

Faith, for Chesterton, is the ability to survive one's moods. That wise insight is one that has found confirmation in the faith journeys of countless people throughout history. There are dry periods in the spiritual life when a sense of meaning, happiness, and God seems to vanish. In such moments life lays its heavy hand on people in so many different ways, and they end up having to carry the burdens of suffering, tragedy, depression, and broken relationships. The terrifying wall of silence that greets one's cries of anguish in such moments seems to justify C. S. Lewis's view that, compared with the sense of desolation which accompanies the existential tragedies of human living, the intellectual arguments against the existence of God are easily answered.[69]

The human spirit wants to know if there is any significance to the seemingly futile experience through which one is living. Is there any meaning to life? Is there any point in going on? Is there a God? The anguish of life is a universal human experience, and the history of philosophy and theology suggests that it is not easy to offer a coherent explanation in the face of such suffering. Indeed, the best response is usually some version of the very humble truth that we can never fully know, for there is no response that is neat, tidy, and intellectually compelling. Faced with existential angst, it is rarely, if ever,

---

[68] *Lunacy and Letters*, http://209.236.72.127/wordpress/?page_id=1124 .

[69] *The Problem of Pain* and *A Grief Observed* are two works in which Lewis writes in very different ways of the problem of evil and suffering from the Christian perspective. The former is a more philosophical treatment, while the latter is written from within the crucible of personal grief: a tortured time lived through by Lewis after the death of his wife from cancer.

humanly acceptable or pastorally effective to provide neat philosophical and theological answers.

Instead, it is probably wiser, as well as a more urgent require-ment, to accompany a person through the journey of suffering. Filling the experience of pain with human presence is an argu-ably more adequate response to the problem of evil. Indeed, in his poem "A Cloud Was on the Minds of Men," dedicated to his friend E. C. Bentley, we have already seen that Chesterton found the presence of Bentley to be the one thing he remem-bered years after the darkness, doubts, and moods of his own journey.

Chesterton knew that experiences of darkness are terrifying, potentially very damaging, and that they can keep a person imprisoned in a lonely world. However he was also aware that they possess an ability to transform a person's understanding of self, world, and God, purging unworthy images and providing wisdom for the continuing journey.

So can we glean any insights from Chesterton for the faith journey about coping with darkness or with the unsteadiness of the light we perceive? We note three areas in which Chesterton provides a wisdom that helps us to keep walking when the light has been eclipsed. The first area is connected somewhat with what we looked at in the last section: the darkness of sorrow which comes when the human spirit is weighed down by the bur-dens of life; the second area is the darkness that is to be found at the very heart of faith, which is an act through which one places one's trust in a God who is the transcendent ground of all that is and who is, therefore, by his very nature, non-obvious; and the third may be connected to the first and second, at least in part: the normality of darkness along certain stretches of the road of everyday living, a darkness which comes from human doubts, sulks, and moods, and which can impact the imagination.

2.1 The Darkness of Sorrow

First of all, Chesterton knew the darkness of the sad or tired self, resulting from suffering and sorrow. The sustained period of confusion at the Slade had led him to flirt with various philosophical interpretations of life, notably the pessimistic solipsism fashionable at the time, and to consider acting out some of their concomitant moral temptations in fantasy, if not in actuality. Chesterton noticed that this period of extreme doubt about the worth of everything led to a profound sadness, desperation, and world-weariness, which in turn fed his doubt and sense of desperation. Later, having emerged from the darkness, he realized that his interpretations of reality had not been accurate while he was walking in the dark, and he knew that he had needed to wait for the light that followed on from a renewed sense of wonder. He also knew that finding a space in which to talk through one's struggles can often be the threshold to perceiving more clearly the light of the spiritual dawn.

Perhaps nowhere does Chesterton explore the themes of the darkness of sadness and sorrow with more insight than in his "Introduction to the Book of Job." The Book of Job was one of Chesterton's favorite parts of Scripture, and in his short introduction he explores how Job faces the perennial questions of human suffering and God's existence, trying to make sense of the existence of God while finding himself in a situation in which he can hardly lift his head to see the world properly, so exhausted and devastated is he because of the trials and tribulations that have come upon him.

At the beginning of this classic biblical tale, God and Satan make a wager about how Job will react if he has to undergo a period of suffering. Satan, thinking that all trust in God is ultimately self-interest and can survive only as long as things are going well, bets that Job will curse God. God, on the other hand, bets that Job's faith will survive. Job is patience personified as trial after trial besets him. Eventually Job cries out in anguish, but not because he is cursing life itself:

> Job does not in any sense look at life in a gloomy way. If wishing to be happy and being quite ready to be happy constitute an optimist, Job is an optimist. He is a perplexed optimist; he is an exasperated optimist; he is an outraged and insulted optimist. He wishes the universe to justify itself, not because he wishes it to be caught out, but because he really wishes it to be justified. He demands an explanation from God, but he…does it in the spirit in which a wife might demand an explanation from her husband whom she really respected. He remonstrates with his Maker because he is proud of his Maker. He even speaks of the Almighty as his enemy, but he never doubts, at the back of his mind, that his enemy has some kind of a case which he does not understand.[70]

Here we see one of Chesterton's favorite themes: romance, the unpredictability of stories, which underlines the mystery and open-endedness of life. He had written in *Heretics* that "romance is the deepest thing in life, romance is deeper even than reality…[and though] life may sometimes appear…as a book of science …[or] a book of metaphysics…life is always a novel… our existence is still a story."[71] Job wants to believe that there is a purpose to the open-endedness of life and still wants to believe in the goodness of existence and God.

> "Oh, that mine adversary had written a book!" It never really occurs to him that it could possibly be a bad book. He is anxious to be convinced, that is, he thinks that God could convince him. In short,

---

[70] "Introduction to the Book of Job," in *Prophet of Orthodoxy: The Wisdom of G. K. Chesterton*, ed. R. Sparkes, 187-8. Hereafter, *Intro. to Job*. Some parts of this work are missing from the passages selected by Sparkes and so where those parts are referred to, online versions have been used.

[71] *Heretics*, 143.

we may say again that if the word optimist means anything (which I doubt) Job is an optimist.[72]

Job's friends, his "comforters," visit him in order to be with him during his trials but, after sitting in silence for a week, they begin to offer theological interpretations of his afflictions and of his responses to their interpretations. Chesterton calls them "the mechanical and supercilious comforters of Job" and "pessimists." Why pessimists, when Job's comforters are so often portrayed as the optimists who help him to look on the bright side and seek to offer some human explanation of things? "Again, if the word pessimist means anything (which I doubt) the comforters of Job may be called pessimists rather than optimists. All that they really believe is not that God is good but that God is so strong that it is much more judicious to call Him good." The comforters insist that "everything in the universe fits into everything else: as if there were anything comforting about a number of nasty things all fitting into each other."[73]

These comforters demonstrate some of the pastoral ineffectiveness of cocksure theological certainty in the face of suffering. Their commonsense attitudes—they believe that human beings deny how truly sinful they are and deserve their afflictions on account of that sinfulness, and contend that divine justice will not be cheated by the denial and secret transgressions of human beings—sound hollow and unworthy of both Job and God, when heard against the existential cries of their friend. The Book of Job satirizes the images of God and human beings put forward by poorer forms of theology and seeks instead truer images: what image of God can we have in a world in which darkness and suffering abound? God wins his bet with Satan,

---

[72] "Intro. to Job," 188.

[73] Ibid.

because Job refuses to curse. However, pointing out that he had always lived his own life with compassion for those who suffer, Job reaches that point that most of us reach: he wants some answers from God.

God finally emerges, therefore, from the heart of the tempest in order to speak, but not to answer Job's questions. There is no mention of guilt, innocence, suffering, or compassion. Instead, for three whole chapters God asks his own questions, covering the range of the mysteries of creation and the human place within it: "Where were you when I laid the earth's foundations?"[74] "Have you been shown the gates of Death?"[75] What is remarkable is that Job is satisfied by the fact that God does not offer him a series of answers, but instead puts to him a series of questions. As Chesterton puts it:

> Job was comfortless before the speech of Jehovah and is comforted after it. He has been told nothing, but he feels the terrible and tingling atmosphere of something which is too good to be told. The refusal of God to explain His design is itself a burning hint of His design. The riddles of God are more satisfying than the solutions of man.[76]

Job's comforters had been convinced that everything in the world can be explained. Similarly the mechanical and materialist optimist "endeavours to justify the universe avowedly upon the ground that it is a rational and consecutive pattern. He points out that the fine thing about the world is that it can all be explained."[77] However, God's questions to Job imply that it cannot be, at least from the human vantage point. There are other questions which need answering:

---

[74] Job 38:4.

[75] Job 38:17.

[76] "Intro. to Job", 190.

[77] "Introduction to the Book of Job", http://www.gkc.org.uk/gkc/books/job.html.

The whole question in which the existence of religion is involved is whether, while we have feelings about the catastrophic, we are or are not to have feelings about the normal; that, while we curse our luck for a house on fire, we are to thank anything for a house. If we come upon a dead man, we start back in horror. Are we not to start with any generous emotion when we come upon a living man, that far greater mystery?[78]

As we shall see, to lament the reality of evil and suffering in the world inevitably leads to the question of the notion of good in the world, the distinction between good and evil, and the fact that human notions of justice are inadequate in the search for answers to the problem of suffering. God's questions imply that the cosmos is a much stranger place than Job had ever conceived, and this comforts Job:

There is one central conception of the Book of Job which literally makes it immortal...That is the conception that the universe, if it is to be admired, is to be admired for its strangeness and not for its rationality, for its splendid unreason, and not for its reason. Job's friends attempt to comfort him with philosophical optimism, like the intellectuals of the eighteenth century. Job tried to comfort himself with philosophical pessimism, like the intellectuals of the nineteenth century. But God comforts Job with indecipherable mystery, and for the first time Job is comforted.[79]

God's questions move Job to a place in which he perceives the inadequacy of his images of God, glimpses the utterly different nature of God, the otherness or holiness of God and, in his rejoicing in such mystery or unreason, he is mocking and undermining a typically modern axiom:

---

[78] "The Philosophy of Gratitude," *Daily News*, 20th June 1903, *The Chesterton Review* 27 (3), 2001, 294.

[79] "Leviathan and the Hook," *The Speaker*, 9th September 1905, cited in *TTFT*, 62.

> A more trivial poet would have made God enter in order to answer
> the questions…In this drama of scepticism God Himself takes up the
> role of sceptic. He asks of Job the question that any criminal accused
> by Job would be most entitled to ask. He asks Job who he is. And
> Job…comes to the conclusion that he does not know.[80]

Chesterton is pointing out that answers to the human "why?"
have been replaced by answers about what existence is and
who God is. God is utterly Other and utterly Present. Job had
disproven Satan's cynicism about the nature of religious faith
by continuing to trust God throughout his agonies and by continuing to remain in relationship with God. God remained other and distant, but Job has now come to realize that in his spirit,
an expression of which was his original quest for answers to the
mystery and riddle of existence, there is an abiding presence of
the God he has always trusted, and this realization transforms
him, satisfies him, and allows him to go on living.

After his trials and anguished cries and questions, a new
wavelength is reached by Job, where his image of God is radically different. The God who is radically Other is also radically
present in suffering, in a logic that is more in tune with that
found in a loving relationship, rather than in some philosophical or theological logic of rationality. "Job puts forward a note of
interrogation; God answers with a note of exclamation. Instead
of proving to Job that it is an inexplicable world, He insists
that it is a much stranger world than Job ever thought it was."[81]
It is a world of paradox (a theme we shall take up more fully
in our next chapter), and it is the great merit of the Book of
Job that it reveals this. "Every great literature has always been
allegorical—allegorical of some view of the universe. The Iliad
is only great because all life is a battle…the Book of Job because

---

[80] *Intro. to Job*, 188-9.

[81] Ibid., http://www.gkc.org.uk/gkc/books/job.html

all life is a riddle."[82] The Book of Job tells us that human beings are better nourished by paradoxes:

> [T]he tradition of Israel…had one of the colossal corner-stones of the world: the Book of Job…[which] avowedly only answers mystery with mystery. Job is comforted with riddles; but he is comforted…For when he who doubts can only say, "I do not understand," it is true that he who knows can only reply or repeat "You do not understand." And under that rebuke there is always a sudden hope in the heart; and the sense of something that would be worth understanding.[83]

We have seen that for Chesterton, God's questions are more satisfying than human solutions, and for him the great merit of the Book of Job is that it does not end in a way that is conventionally satisfying.

The Book of Job reaffirms mystery and the romantic possibility of open-endedness that was so central to existence for Chesterton. He believed that Christianity and, later in his life, Catholic Christianity, were by far the truest truth available, but they were also romances, stories in which the participants were persons with free will granted by the God who had loved them into existence. So there were different possible alternative endings to the story, just as he pointed out in the eighth chapter of *Orthodoxy*:

> So Christian morals have always said to the man, not that he would lose his soul, but that he must take care that he didn't. In Christian morals, in short, it is wicked to call a man "damned": but it is strictly religious and philosophic to call him damnable.[84]

For Chesterton life and religion pose questions that are not always answered, and with some issues death alone is the moment of truth. He stated that the big difference between

---

Christianity and "the thousand transcendental schools of to-day" and all ancient paganisms or gnostic movements, is that the latter involved an enlightening initiation for the select few, while in the case of the former, "the Christian mysteries are so far democratic that nobody understands them at all."[85] While this is a characteristically Chestertonian witticism, it certainly offers us a reminder that the theologian will never solve mystery, even if she sheds welcome light upon it.

The unfathomable sense of mystery to be found in the Judeo-Christian tradition, and the need, therefore, for theological humility when exploring that mystery, increases for Chesterton when we consider that the Book of Job also assures us that that we do not suffer because of our sins or flourish because of our virtues. However, this does not mean that we can do without good, solid, academic theology. "Here in this Book the question is really asked whether God invariably punishes vice with terrestrial punishment and rewards virtue with terrestrial prosperity." At various times throughout the Church's history, one could be forgiven for thinking that the Church's answer to that question, in practice if not in theory, is "yes!" The Christian who does this has:

> ...sunk even down to the level of modern well educated society. For when once people have begun to believe that prosperity is the reward of virtue their next calamity is obvious. If prosperity is regarded as the reward of virtue it will be regarded as the symptom of virtue. Men will leave off the heavy task of making good men successful. They will adopt the easier task of making out successful men good. This, which has happened throughout modern commerce and journalism, is the ultimate Nemesis of the wicked optimism of the comforters of Job.[86]

Hence we still need good theology to clarify true from false interpretations. Church history reveals that any time the Church

---

[85] *The Common Man*, London: Sheed and Ward, 1950, 222.

[86] *Intro. to Job*, 192.

compromises in its intellectual endeavors, ecclesial life and Christian spirituality suffer the consequences. Good theology is a great corrective for the Church, without which the Church loses balance (an image reminiscent of Chesterton's image for the Church as "the heavenly chariot [which] flies thundering through the ages, the dull heresies sprawling and prostrate, the wild truth reeling but erect"[87]). If theology is to be carried out assiduously, theologians have to remain humble before the unfathomable mystery of the divine self-communication in salvation history:

> Job is not told that his misfortunes were due to his sins or a part of any plan for his improvement....It is the lesson of the whole work that man is most comforted by paradoxes; and it is by all human testimony the most reassuring. I need not suggest what a high and strange history awaited this paradox of the best man in the worst fortune. I need not say...there is one Old Testament figure who is truly a type; or say what is prefigured in the wounds of Job.[88]

The God whose paradoxes comfort Job is also the God who is crucified on Calvary. God, as he is understood by the Judeo-Christian tradition, is not always very well understood. This is something similar to what Aquinas was saying when he stated that, though God is self-evident in himself, he is not self-evident to us.[89] As we shall explore in the next chapter, this has consequences both for our theology and our notion of faith: it means that our words and imaginative constructs for God are always inadequate and in danger of becoming representative of a false god; and it means that we must never make a simple identification between our imagination, feelings, and concepts and whether or not we have faith in God: faith in God must

---

[87] *Orthodoxy*, 306.

[88] *Intro. to Job*, 192-3.

[89] See *Summa Theologiae* I, 2.

never be confused with our ability or inability to imagine God or his existence.

That God is always beyond our imaginative constructs of him is a key lesson of the Book of Job. Job's story prefigures the presence of the God who inhabits all human suffering, sadness, and fatigue on Calvary. Whatever else we might have expected from an incarnate God, we could never have expected his crucifixion:

> In every century, in this century, in the next century, the Passion is what it was in the first century, when it occurred; a thing stared at by a crowd. It remains a tragedy of the people; a crime of the people; a consolation of the people; but never merely a thing of the period.[90]

In *Orthodoxy* Chesterton makes the point that the divinity of Christ, so often dismissed by liberal thinkers, is most definitely a liberal and revolutionary idea, pointing as it does to the deep bond of human beings with the divinity. On Calvary, the Author of all not only went through agony, but also some of the doubts expressed by those who suffer, once again showing the radically different nature of the God who surpasses all human attempts to circumscribe Him with the intellect:

> Christianity is the only religion on earth that has felt that omnipotence made God incomplete. Christianity alone has felt that God, to be wholly God, must have been a rebel as well as a king. Alone of all creeds, Christianity has added courage to the virtues of the Creator. For the only courage worth calling courage must necessarily mean that the soul passes a breaking point and does not break...in that terrific tale of the Passion there is a distinct emotional suggestion that the author of all things (in some unthinkable way) went not only through agony, but through doubt. It is written, "Thou shalt not tempt the Lord thy God." No; but the Lord thy God may tempt Himself; and it seems as if this was what happened in Gethsemane. In a garden Satan tempted man: and in a garden God tempted God.

---

[90] *The Way of the Cross, Collected Works* Vol. 3, 549.

He passed in some superhuman manner through our human horror of pessimism. When the world shook and the sun was wiped out of heaven, it was not at the crucifixion, but at the cry from the cross: the cry which confessed that God was forsaken of God.[91]

For Chesterton, the same kind of doubt and revolt espoused by the free-thinking revolutionists came from the mouth of the divinity in the Christian creed. Chesterton pleads, "...let the atheists themselves choose a god. They will find only one divinity who ever uttered their isolation; only one religion in which God seemed for an instant to be an atheist."[92] Echoing Job's experiences, the figure on the cross is carried across the threshold of mystery by trusting in a relationship that helps him to survive the darkness of suffering. He invites all who find themselves in similar periods of darkness to trust that this moment will not last, and he asks them not to trust the more negative self that seems to dominate so naturally in such painful periods: the sad self, the sulking self, the anguished self, the bitter self, the unloving self. Doubts are normal. The yes of faith is sure at times, less sure at other times. It can be either yes or no during certain seasons of life; but a larger freedom of heart and a generous self-giving out of love, like that of the figure on the cross, brings the eventual victory of the yes.

As Chesterton knew from his own life, the God of the Judeo-Christian tradition does not rescue people from suffering and death, but enters into that suffering and death, shares human grief and, ultimately though not immediately, redeems that suffering, death, and grief. The fact that we cannot always make coherent sense of something like the existential agonies of suffering does not mean that there is no sense to be discovered.

---

[91] *Orthodoxy*, 343.

[92] Ibid.

The fact that we cannot adequately imagine God or understand some of the mysteries pertaining to God and the cosmos points more to the finite nature of the human mind in its wrestling with the paradoxical nature of reality than it does to the existence or otherwise of the Transcendent Source of reality.

The problem of theodicy, of reconciling suffering and the existence of God, is one of the deepest questions there is. However, as hinted at by Chesterton in his reflections on the Book of Job, it is not a question that stands in isolation, but is intimately connected to other questions about the meaning of existence. In *Orthodoxy* he takes this up again as he writes:

> If Cinderella says, "How is it that I must leave the ball at twelve?" her godmother might answer, "How is it that you are going there till twelve?" If I leave a man in my will ten talking elephants and a hundred winged horses, he cannot complain if the conditions partake of the slight eccentricity of the gift. He must not look a winged horse in the mouth. And it seemed to me that existence was itself so very eccentric a legacy that I could not complain of not understanding the limitations of the vision when I did not understand the vision they limited. The frame was no stranger than the picture.[93]

Chesterton believes, then, that the profound question of theodicy is preceded by an even profounder question: the problem of existence and its goodness. As C. S. Lewis said, we only have some notion of a crooked line if we already hold some notion of a straight line. With what are we comparing this cosmos when we call it cruel, unjust and evil?[94] Or, as Chesterton puts it so brilliantly,

> There is at the back of all our lives an abyss of light, more blinding and unfathomable than any abyss of darkness; and it is the abyss of actuality, of existence, of the fact that things truly are, and that we

---

[93] Ibid., 260.

[94] C. S. Lewis, *Mere Christianity*, 41-2.

ourselves are incredibly and sometimes incredulously real. It is the fundamental fact of being, as against not being; it is unthinkable, yet we cannot unthink it, though we may sometimes be unthinking about it; unthinking and especially unthanking. For he who has realized this reality knows that it does outweigh, literally to infinity, all lesser regrets or arguments for negation, and that under all our grumblings there is a subconscious substance of gratitude.[95]

Darkness has to be seen against the ultimate background of light. Evil and suffering are indeed problems for the theist, but here we may recall Newman's observation that "ten thousand difficulties do not make one doubt, as I understand the subject; difficulty and doubt are incommensurate."[96] Thomas Dubay notes helpfully that,

> Many of us assume that difficulties necessarily create doubts. They need not. A doubt is a suspension of judgment: I do not know if A is B. A difficulty can be concerned with a certain judgment and not in the least damage it: I am sure C is D (a certain judgment) but I do not see how they fit together (a difficulty). An example from physics may help. Light is a plain fact. But thus far physicists cannot reconcile its wave characteristics with its quanta of energy characteristics. Wisely they do no deny either set of truths even though they do not see how they can be fitted together. Surely they are not stupidly going to deny the light.[97]

A difficulty is a limitation on our knowledge: it is a situation we do not yet understand, and sometimes it is something we may never understand. We shall see in the next chapter that for Chesterton the cosmos is full of mysteries and full of paradox, and that the inability of the finite human mind to see how mysteries are joined together does not imply the invalidity of a certain conclusion. As Job discovered when God finally came

---

[95] *Chaucer*, 36-7.

[96] *Apologia pro Vita Sua*, 317.

[97] *Faith and Certitude*, San Francisco: Ignatius Press, 1985, 83.

to speak with him, our inability to perceive the mystery of how terrible evils and a loving God can be put together does not mean that they cannot be so reconciled—any more than the human inability to grasp the wave and quanta characteristics of light disproves the reality of both of those characteristics and the existence of light.

> We saw earlier in this chapter that Chesterton believes that, "The whole question in which the existence of religion is involved is whether, while we have feelings about the catastrophic, we are or are not to have feelings about the normal."[98] By seeing the abyss of darkness against the abyss of light, Chesterton is saying that evil and suffering cannot be problems without some acknowledgement of the existence of God. In a cosmos without God, there is only the brute fact of the absurdity of existence. There is no such thing as the "problem" of evil, merely the existence of it. An ultimately meaningless cosmos requires no explanation. For there to be a "problem" with evil, there has to be a means of gauging what is better and what is worse—in other words, a way of judging the good and that which deviates from the good. There is no such good in an ultimately absurd universe. Furthermore, to claim that things ought to be better in the cosmos is to argue that we know how a perfect cosmos ought to be set up. It is at that point that God asks us, as He asked Job, where we were when He laid the foundations of the world.

To be caught in the grip of suffering and the trials of life in this cosmos does not make it easy to hold such a Chestertonian perspective. Tiredness, sadness, or world-weariness usually distorts our judgment, and what is needed is a patience that waits for the morning, which always follows even the darkest of nights. With sufficient patience, our better self—more positive, more hopeful, more generous and more willing to acknowledge and to trust in the goodness of reality—can survive, and

---

[98] "The Philosophy of Gratitude," *Daily News*, 20th June 1903, *The Chesterton Review* 27 (3), 2001, 294.

our lesser self—negative, sceptical, cynical, and full of doubts and the need to control—moves into the background (even if something of the same flux between the two selves is a lifelong struggle and adventure). The God of Christian revelation offers us the opportunity to move into relationship with him and to trust in the love and goodness of the Creator who is responsible for the gift of the creation.

2.2 THE DARKNESS OF FAITH

The *Catechism of the Catholic Church*, recalling the teaching of both Aquinas and the First Vatican Council[99] that faith is, paradoxically, both certain yet dark, reminds us that, "Now, however, 'we walk by faith, not by sight';[100] we perceive God as 'in a mirror, dimly' and only 'in part.'"[101] "Even though enlightened by him in whom it believes, faith is often lived in darkness and can be put to the test."[102] Chesterton knew that at times an unavoidable darkness lies at the very heart of the type of knowledge that faith is. "[Hamlet's faith is such that] though he cannot see the world is good, yet certainly it is good...though he cannot see man as the image of God, yet certainly he is the image of God."[103] If faith is certain, it is not going to be a certainty that involves some utterly compelling evidence for God.

In a culture like that of the contemporary West, many people voice their doubts about the existence of God on the basis of some form of two of the great strands that underpin atheistic

---

[99] See *Dei Filius* 3, DS 3008-10; *Summa Theologiae* II-II 171, 5, obj. 3.

[100] 2 Corinthians 5:7.

[101] 1 Corinthians 13:12.

[102] *Catechism of the Catholic Church*, 164.

[103] OH.

thought: empiricist materialism, which automatically excludes from consideration any notion of the spiritual or of transcendent mystery, because these are impossible to apprehend using the normal sense apparatus through which so much of our experience in this world comes; and a psychological theory that views religious faith as born of groundless human desires and hopes for fulfillment.

Chesterton fought against both of these reductionisms of faith all his life. The starting point of his argument against such partial visions of reality was the need to be humble before the immensity of reality: "…if a man would be making his world large, he must be making himself small."[104] One of the problems with some exponents of modern thought, as far as Chesterton could see, was that they did not have the antecedent humility required to let reality reveal itself in all its glorious and multifaceted complexity, which meant that they did not see it properly:

> Looking down on things may be a delightful experience, only there is nothing, from a mountain to a cabbage, that is really seen when it is seen from a balloon. The philosopher of the ego sees everything, no doubt, from a high and rarefied heaven; only he sees everything foreshortened or deformed.[105]

In an essay entitled "In Defence of Humility," Chesterton notes that, since one can see only small things from the peak of one's arrogance, it is better to cultivate the virtue of "Humility…the art of reducing ourselves to a point…to a thing with no size at all, so that to it all the cosmic things are what they really are—of immeasurable stature."[106]

---

[104] *Orthodoxy*, 234.

[105] *The Defendant*, 59.

[106] Ibid., 60.

Chesterton is proposing here a certain anthropology that prepares the way for faith: as we shall see in the next chapter, when we look at his very first Ethic of Elfland, there has to be a humble disposition in a person or culture, a disposition whose absence he found alarming in the Edwardian period. In this respect there are echoes of Newman here (with whose task while writing the *Apologia* Chesterton finds similarities in writing *Orthodoxy*, as he states in the Preface to the latter). In an exchange of correspondence with his brother, Charles, over the latter's atheism, Newman wrote, "you are not in a state of mind to listen to argument of any kind" and that kind of unbelief can often arise "from a fault of the heart and not of the intellect."[107]

Newman felt that the spiritual and psychological dispositions of an individual can make him more or less open to the possibility of religious faith. He believed that mere argumentation in apologetics was limited if it paid no attention to what today we might speak of as pre-conceptual zones of reflection. Before we can speak of our explicit beliefs and the reasons why we hold them, we need to consider our fundamental attitudes or dispositions, which determine the antecedent probability (or otherwise) of faith. Newman realized that a person's inner disposition determines so much of what is seen when one tries to interpret religious questions. Precisely because it neglected this key element of interiority, Newman had distanced himself from the Oxford apologetical school of evidentialism, which sought to convince others of the existence of God largely (though not exclusively) through extrinsic arguments.

Chesterton, who also insisted on the need for humility if one is to read the cosmos correctly, was also unimpressed by

---

[107] John Henry Newman, *Letters and Diaries*, Vol. I, ed. I. Ker & T. Gornall, Oxford, 1978, 212-226.

contemporary apologetics. "I never read a line of Christian apologetics. I read as little as I can of them now."[108] As we shall see in our final chapter, by accepting the grounds and terms of debate from the dominant empiricist and materialistic scientific ideology of the day, seeking to "prove" the existence of God by some appeal to external evidence, while ignoring the essential interiority required for approaching faith, the Christian apologetics which Chesterton dismissed had been reduced to some quest for pseudo-objectivity and had become a shadow of the rich self that it had been for much of the Church's theological history.

As we have already seen in Chapter I of this book, in the second chapter of *Orthodoxy*, where Chesterton describes the rationalist Maniac who is too proud to acknowledge the complex inter-relatedness of reality, Chesterton stated that one can only find truth with logic if one has first found truth without logic. Reason has to be humble, because it is rooted in assumptions, which are acts of faith, about the nature of reality. Chesterton knew all too well that the nature of the knowledge or certainty that comes from faith is not the type that is found by empirical science.

No one can make an argument for God's existence that would compel others to believe in God in the same way that they would believe something based on the evidence of scientific or mathematical reasoning. The "proofs" of Aquinas, Descartes, Spinoza, and Leibniz are indicators of some important insights about the existence of God, but they can never be overwhelming evidence of that existence. Though such proofs have a certain usefulness in apologetics, God rarely becomes part of a person's life as the conclusion of a blindingly clever

---

[108] *Orthodoxy*, 288.

argument. To demand such a proof for the reality of God is to equate the real—what is—with the empirically verifiable, to forget that there are other dimensions of reality (unlike Chesterton's "mystic") and to set out on a faith journey that is destined for failure because its point of departure is misguided.

In *Orthodoxy* Chesterton pointed out that reality is neither perfectly reasonable nor unreasonable. It is "nearly reasonable, but not quite. Life is not an illogicality; yet it is a trap for logicians."[109] When Descartes established his basic principle for any attempt to understand anything—"In order to arrive at the knowledge of all things...never to accept anything as true unless I know from evidence that it is so"—he was putting forward an idea with which Chesterton would have had no disagreement. However, when Descartes defined as reliable evidence "Only that which presents itself so clearly and distinctly in my mind that I can have no occasion to doubt it,"[110] he was unwittingly giving birth to an intellectual attitude that has reigned ever since, and against which Chesterton inveighed all his life: the attitude that bows before nothing but that which compels assent, which is usually only that which is capable of being proved by scientific experiment. It is toward this exclusivist notion of evidence and truth that Chesterton's hostility is displayed. Those who insist on submitting reality to a merely empirical analysis will be caught in the trap for logicians that the complex world sets.

For Chesterton what we would today term scientism seeks to reduce the whole of reality to its own favorite, pre-selected bits: "Common things are never commonplace. And in the last analysis most common things will be found to be highly

---

[109] Ibid., 285.

[110] Descartes, R., *Discourse on the Method*, trans. Donald A. Cress, Indianapolis: Hackett Publishing, 1999, 16.

complicated."[111] The reductionist tendency is a disingenuous analysis of the complexity of reality:

> Some men of science do indeed get over the difficulty by dealing only with the easy part of [reality]: thus, they will call first love the instinct of sex, and the awe of death the instinct of self-preservation. But this is only getting over the difficulty of describing peacock green by calling it blue. There is blue in it.[112]

Scientism selects a naïve empiricist philosophy as the foundation of its methodology when analyzing the cosmos, without acknowledging the way in which it has to rely on other fields of knowledge. The natural sciences rely on methods of apprehending truth which are not merely empirical, but do not acknowledge this indebtedness. Science is, ultimately, a set of quantitative correlations of quantitatively specified data of observation and, in order to be this, it has to presuppose philosophy. Of course, scientific reason, if accurate, is valid, but it is not the only kind of valid reasoning.

There are so many philosophical presuppositions that underpin the empirical scientific method—non-contradiction; validity; truth; meaning; value (which underpins the scientific community's demand that scientists report data truthfully and share it generously with colleagues in the common search for truth); purpose; obligation; the uniformity of matter throughout the universe; the fact that matter can neither come into nor go out of existence at will; that separate human minds operate along essentially the same lines; that nature works in the simplest way; that there is some correlation among the human senses, the mind, and reality ("It is idle to talk always of the alternative of reason and faith. Reason is itself a matter of faith.

---

[111] *What's Wrong with the World*, 68.

[112] Ibid.

It is an act of faith to assert that our thoughts have any relation to reality at all"[113]).

All of these have to be assumed before science can start its tasks, but none of these are themselves empirical phenomena, and so are unable to be submitted to scientific verification. Those who say that nothing can be known by human reason except through the means and intellectual equipment of science are, in the very act of speaking, going beyond the remit of science itself. It would seem, then, that a close inspection of science itself teaches us that the cosmos is a playground in which science is only one of the many adventures we may enjoy. If one takes seriously Chesterton's remark that, "Science must not impose any philosophy, any more than the telephone must tell us what to say,"[114] one may safely assume that he would deem it more reasonable and more honest if science were to acknowledge its indebtedness to philosophy and other disciplines of knowledge, rather than making unsupported philosophical claims about the nature of the universe, the possibility of the supernatural, the transcendent and life beyond the grave, all of which go beyond the scope of its own competence.

Chesterton saw no conflict between science and religion and none of the schizophrenic understanding of truth that can be seen by extremists on both sides of that false opposition. The true Christian approach to reading reality sees the need for both science and religion, which was the approach of Thomas Aquinas and not that of Siger of Brabant:

> Siger of Brabant said this: that the Church must be right theologically, but she can be wrong scientifically. There are two truths; the truth of the supernatural world, and the truth of the natural world, which

---

[113] *Orthodoxy*, 236.

[114] "Science: Pro and Con," *Illustrated London News*, 9th October 1909, *Collected Works*, Vol. 28, 406.

contradicts the supernatural world…It was not two ways of finding the same truth; it was an untruthful way of pretending that there are two truths…St. Thomas was willing to allow the one truth to be approached by two paths [of faith and reason] precisely because he was sure there was only one truth. Because the Faith was the one truth, nothing discovered in nature could ultimately contradict the Faith. Because the faith was the one truth, nothing really deduced from the Faith could ultimately contradict the facts.[115]

There is one truth about the cosmos, and all academic disciplines must be free to pursue that truth in their legitimate fields of research and then pool their insights. What irritated Chesterton was the way in which the dominant modern worldview of scientism excluded from the conversation from the outset the contribution of faith:

…science [cannot] forbid men to believe in something which science does not profess to investigate. Science is the study of the admitted laws of existence; it cannot prove a universal negative about whether those laws could ever be suspended by something admittedly above them…the visible order of nature follows a certain course if there is nothing behind it to stop it. But that fact throws no sort of light on whether there is anything behind it to stop it. That is a question of philosophy or metaphysics and not of material science.[116]

Chesterton was a supremely rational person and he did not wish to rebel against reason, but to dispute with those scientists who, unaware of the fiduciary foundations of science, wished to limit reality to that which could be explored by their truncated version of rationalist dogmatism.

Like Newman before him in the Victorian period, Chesterton was not alarmed by Darwinian theories. "Development is the unfolding of all the consequences and applications of an idea; but of something that is there, not of something that is not

[115] Saint.Thomas Aquinas, 92-3.

[116] The Thing: Why I Am A Catholic, 296.

there. In this sense the Catholic Church is the one Christian body that has always believed in Evolution."[117] This harmonizes with Chesterton's view of life as a journey in which we develop. Certainly he believed that there could be no such thing as development without a truth toward which we were growing: "As enunciated today 'progress' is simply a comparative of which we have not yet settled the superlative…Nobody has any business to use the word 'progress' unless he has a definite creed and a cast-iron code of morals."[118] But when we develop we grow from what has gone before, retaining all that is good in it, but moving on to a deeper vision or appreciation of it: "… real development is not leaving things behind, as on a road, but drawing life from them, as from a root."[119] For this reason, therefore, although it is correct to explore (as we shall in Chapter IV) the importance of dogma in Chesterton's thought, it is dangerously one-sided to view him as championing merely a doctrinal theology of faith.

When in *Orthodoxy* Chesterton criticizes the materialistic worldview of the Maniac, he does so because the cosmos in which we live is more, much more, than that to which scientism would reduce it. Human beings have to live life based on unfounded "certitudes" or "truths." One cannot prove one's love for the beloved. One cannot prove that priesthood or marriage is one's vocation in life. One cannot prove that the plane on which one is travelling will not fall out of the sky. Scientism is by definition reductionist since it holds that only the methods, categories, and objects of interest of the natural sciences can constitute a way of coming to know the truth about the world.

---

[117] "Roman Catholicism," *An Outline of Christianity*, ed. A. S. Peake, 1926, cited in *TTFT*, 118.

[118] *Heretics*, 52-3.

[119] *The Victorian Age in Literature*, 6.

It therefore loses its way in the quest to give a full account of reality and, therefore, God.

One does not come to know one's wife, let alone God, in the same way that one knows the truth that water boils at 100 degrees Celsius, or the truth of Pythagoras' Theorem, or a geographical truth such as "Rome is the capital of Italy." To argue for the existence of God with a detached, "objective" mind, as if God were something that could be put under a microscope, in a test tube, or connected to electrodes and measured in a scientific laboratory, is to set out on a quest that will ultimately prove to be unsuccessful, even if it unearths useful pointers along the way. God is the transcendent ground and source of all that is, ipsum Esse subsistens, not one being among many, and so He remains inaccessible to the senses.

Chesterton's notion of truth is something slippery and elusive:

> Truth seems to me to be a condition of the soul; possible in a German professor and also in a Sussex peasant. A man seeking after truth… appears to me like a man setting out with a knapsack and an Alpine-stock to discover his own sense of gravity…It is possible to teach truth only in such things as arithmetic…But if we wish to teach anything to our children beyond these things, uncontested truth is impossible. If we are content with teaching such things as that a giraffe is a mammal or that three feet make one yard, then of course these things can be taught exactly; and in that case we are independent of all doubt and all controversy, of all philosophy, theology, ethics or aesthetics…But if we have the least notion of teaching him such things as history and philosophy, religion or ethics, art or literature, let us abandon altogether the notion that we can tell him the truth, in the complete and real sense.[120]

The nature of religious truth, especially the truth of the existence of God, is not, therefore, something scientific or mathematical.

---

[120] "A Plea for Partial Historians," *Lunacy and Letters*, cited in *TTFT*, 67.

Whereas some human convictions can be proved mathematically or logically (4+3=7; the whole is greater than the part; a married man has a wife), and some can be proved scientifically (salt is made up of a sodium ion and a chloride ion), other convictions—the types which give human existence meaning, direction, and importance—cannot be "proved" in this way. Among such convictions could be listed the widespread notion that justice should prevail among human beings, or the belief that rape is wrong. The fact that they cannot be "proved" scientifically or logically does not mean that they are unreasonable convictions. Belief in God, then, is such a conviction: it is a condition of the soul and requires a much more personal understanding of truth, an approach that involves the whole of a person, rather than the intellect alone (even if the latter is involved).

In a way that is analogous to the relationship between two friends or lovers, coming to knowledge of God involves a personal trust, a personal risk, and a commitment to move oneself to a place in which one is then better able to perceive and come to know God. If a man finds himself attracted to or curious about a woman, he may observe her, ask her friends about her, and do some research and find out where she lives or works. However, he will never know her intimately—he will never know her heart—until he sits down with her and listens to her as she opens her heart to him. When she discloses her heart to him, he is then faced with a personal decision: does he believe her or not? If all the man wants to do is control the situation with aggressive questions and an aggressive rationalism, then he may know a lot about her, but he will never know her. He may be an acquaintance of the woman, but he will never fall in love. In interpersonal relationships one cannot remain outside as an impartial spectator.

Faith knowledge, dark yet certain, is more like this sort of interpersonal knowledge, the knowledge between friends or lovers, than the knowledge of the empirical natural sciences. We can know a lot about God, but the final surrender of faith is a surrender to a person on the far side of reason. Questions and the workings of reason are essential in the journey toward God, lest faith become mere superstition; but faith is ultimately suprarational, a surrender to a personal reality that I cannot control aggressively, but which attracts and beguiles me from the other side of reason.

As we shall see later, when we discuss more fully his assessment of the materialist assumptions which underpinned so much of the natural sciences of the day, Chesterton thought that a different wavelength was needed to perceive their shortcomings. Indeed, for Chesterton unbelief had much to do with a failure in imagination: "Men will not believe because they will not broaden their minds."[121] The alternative wavelength required for faith is nourished by the imagination and a sense of wonder:

> All that new culture [informed by the empiricist-materialistic or scientistic mindset] was very clean and very vacuous. There was nothing in it to make common life interesting; that could only be done by making common things interesting. And that can be done by imagination but not by invention; by festivals, traditions, images, legends, patron-saints or household-gods; but not by gadgets.[122]

The wavelength that is informed by imagination speaks to those depths of the human person that are more than rational, though not irrational; they speak to the very heart of what it is to be a human being. Chesterton says repeatedly in *Orthodoxy* that logic and reason are necessary but insufficient for the

---

[121] *Saint Francis of Assisi*, 16.

[122] *G. K.'s Weekly*, 13 December 1934, cited in *TTFT*, 132.

adventure of life in this cosmos. He would certainly have agreed with Pascal that, when it comes to religious faith, "Le coeur a ses raisons, que la raison ne connait point; on le sait en mille choses."[123] It is a characteristic misunderstanding of modern thought that to follow one's heart is to be ruled by mere emotion, or something that is entirely divorced from reason, and so to end up with either only simple truths or even falsehoods. As we shall see in the next chapter, however, for Chesterton the truth is complex, and at its heart lies paradox. Following the heart leads us to multi-layered truths, the complexities of truth, because the heart, ever-humble before reality, approaches the world informed by both reason and imagination. As Newman said, "The heart is commonly reached, not through the reason, but through the imagination...Persons influence us, voices melt us, looks subdue us, deeds inflame us."[124]

So is it possible to move away from the desperate, and ultimately doomed, search to find watertight proof for the existence of God, toward an intelligent and imaginative engagement with a complex world that could yield reasons of the heart that support belief in God? Can we move from an attitude that moves us from being a merely external observer and judge of all that we survey; through a more humble openness to the richness of the world before us, nourishing our previously held truths with further insights, adding to them, stretching them, abandoning them if necessary; and eventually reaching that level of Chestertonian wonder at the sheer gift of the complex and astonishing reality which has been entrusted to us?

---

[123] B. Pascal, *Pensées*, 277. "The heart has its reasons, of which reason knows nothing. We feel it in a thousand things." (My translation).

[124] J. H. Newman, *Discussions and Arguments*, 1882, 293. Newman was here quoting, some three decades after first writing them, his own words from his *Essay in Aid of a Grammar of Assent*, 89.

Again we arrive at the same point as before: the awakening of wonder. Something has to be roused up within a person before she can truly set out on the journey that leads to God: that something is the imagination. The imagination is not the same thing as the imaginary—a faith that is rooted in images is not to be confused with a faith that is untrue because it is merely a fantastic fiction—but the imagination is crucial in coming to faith, because it is the capacity to shape our interpretations of the world by images, stories, and metaphors. Indeed, Chesterton said that "all descriptions of the creating and sustaining principle in things must be metaphorical, because they must be verbal."[125] As Jesus showed us himself, images, stories, and metaphors are the only means we have for speaking of the God who is the ineffable, transcendent Other.

There has been an enormous amount of attention placed on the links between imagination and theology in the last few decades.[126] In the next chapter we shall explore more fully some of the insights that Chesterton had into human imagination but, given this recently sharpened theological focus on the subject, it is appropriate to say a brief word about some key Chestertonian insights in this regard. Chesterton knew that imagination was a complex subject and one that could never be exhaustively treated. When he used words like *poet*, *poetic*, *artist*, and *artistic*, Chesterton was also including words like *imaginative* and the *imagination*. To his mind, whereas a mathematician can explain why an answer is exactly right, the lover of poetry can never fully explain why a word or image is exactly right. In a piece on Samuel Taylor Coleridge,

---

[125] *Orthodoxy*, 281.

[126] For an excellent overview of these links and a bibliography of relevant literature, see http://www.st-andrews.ac.uk/itia/reading/imagination.html .

Chesterton said that, whereas the poet rides the air on imagination alone, with wings and no feet, "almost all that has been attempted, in the way of analyzing those imaginative laws, has been done by some metaphysician, who has feet and no wings."[127]

Chesterton, however, was both poet and metaphysician and had plenty of interesting insights to share on this topic. For the purposes of our present chapter, we underline once again the key Chestertonian emphasis in *Orthodoxy* on the importance of the imagination, or the poetic, for balanced and sane human living. Ever the defender of reason, he also pointed out the limits of reason. "The madman is not the man who has lost his reason. The madman is the man who has lost everything except his reason."[128] Though human beings are rational creatures, it is unhealthy to neglect the other dimensions that constitute a human being:

> Poetry is sane because it floats easily in an infinite sea; reason seeks to cross the infinite sea and so make it finite....The poet only asks to get his head into the heavens. It is the logician who seeks to get the heavens into his head. And it is his head that splits.[129]

Art, freedom, affectivity, and so many other elements are needed for a balanced and healthy human existence. Logic is of real value to the person who seeks to converse about existence, but only if imagination is also used in our explorations of the gift of the cosmos that stares us in the face:

> A great deal is said in these days about the value or valuelessness of logic. In the main, indeed, logic is not a productive tool so much as a weapon of defence. A man building up an intellectual system has

---

[127] "On S.T.C.," *As I Was Saying*, New York: Books for Libraries Press, 1966, 87-88.

[128] *Orthodoxy*, 222.

[129] Ibid., 220.

to build like Nehemiah, with the sword in one hand and the trowel in the other. The imagination, the constructive quality, is the trowel, and argument is the sword.[130]

Imagination is as vital as logic, because "The function of imagination is not to make strange things settled, so much as to make settled things strange; not so much to make wonders facts as to make facts wonders."[131]

There is a difference, then, between being reasonable and being a rationalist. Reason is a wonderful gift in the task of coming to understand reality, but it can only take us so far in this task and has to be supplemented by creative imagination and faith (captured by Chesterton in the word *poetry*). For Chesterton, the problem with "the [rationalist] madman" is that his view of the cosmos, his philosophy of life, is not broad enough. It makes perfect rational sense to him, but he is nevertheless wrong:

> [The madman's error lies in the fact that] his mind moves in a perfect but narrow circle. A small circle is quite as infinite as a large circle; but though it is quite as infinite, it is not so large. In the same way the insane explanation is quite as complete as the sane one, but is not so large. A bullet is quite as round as the world, but it is not the world. There is such a thing as a narrow universality; there is such a thing as a small and cramped eternity....The lunatic's theory explains a large number of things, but it does not explain them in a large way."[132]

Chesterton was doing battle with the imperialistic tendencies of the scientific rationalism of the period, where what was real was reduced to the physical and empirically measured. He was rebelling against a superficial view of reality and advocating a vision of the cosmos that was much more poetic, deep,

---

[130] *Varied Types*, 93.

[131] *The Defendant*, 37.

[132] *Orthodoxy*, 222.

multi-layered, and saturated with beauty than could ever be entertained by the merely scientific imagination. The latter type of imagination is that of a person who lives with "…a horrible clarity of detail… but not hampered by a sense of humour or charity, or by the dumb certainties of experience." Such people dwell "in the clean and well-lit prison of one idea;…sharpened to one painful point…without healthy hesitation and healthy complexity…the combination of an expansive and exhaustive reason with a contracted common sense."[133]

There are interesting resonances here with some of the recent calls from Pope Benedict XVI to broaden or enlarge the notion of rationality that is dominant in western culture at the beginning of the twenty-first century. The Pope sees the same truncated post-Enlightenment rationalism today that Chesterton perceived in Edwardian culture, perceiving also the same "wedge [driven] between truth and faith" and the identification of truth and knowledge. Benedict reminds us, however, that from a Christian perspective, the service of truth in the midst of humanity is born of a "dynamic between personal encounter, knowledge and Christian witness." Religious truth, then, "speaks to the individual in his or her entirety, inviting us to respond with our whole being."[134]

If there has been a shift of attention toward the role of imagination in theology of late, this does not mean that our theological images, which are grounded in the analogy of being (another favorite theme of Chesterton that we shall discuss in our next chapter), can ever be adequate. The fourth Lateran Council of 1215 defined dogmatically that all of our theological concepts,

---

[133] Ibid, 221, 225.

[134] http://www.vatican.va/holy_father/benedict_xvi/speeches/2008/april/documents/hf_ben-xvi_spe_20080417_cath-univ-washington_en.html [accessed 24th January 2011]

languages, and images are inadequate.[135] Although they communicate something that is true, they also communicate more
that is untrue; they tell us more of how unlike us and the rest
of creation God is, even as they tell us a little of how like us
and the rest of creation God is: similarity in difference, and
difference in similarity. The inadequacy of images, words, and
metaphors notwithstanding, they are all we have and they need
to be nourished by imagination. They help our hearts to know
things and to experience things for which we can never find full
expression. As Chesterton knew from his days at the Slade, the
imagination can provide us with a way of recovering neglected
or forgotten depths of our humanity, of paving the way for the
victory within the self of wonder and desire over dullness, in this
way reminding left-brain rationalism that there are other ways
of approaching and interpreting reality.

Although Chesterton had some very definite ideas, and
though he constantly emphasized the objectivity of the manifold parts of creation and the cosmos as a whole, I contend that
he knew as well as anyone that in theology and philosophy, as
in science, we have to develop a tolerance and appreciation of
ambiguity and that there are subjective elements that constitute
any act of knowing:

> ...it seems a somewhat wild proposition to say that we can think we
> know anything, since knowledge implies certainty and sincerity...
> Our knowledge is perpetually tricking and misleading us, [and] we
> do not know what we know, but only what we feel.[136]

Taken on its own, such a line might be interpreted as fideistic,
but the whole of his life's work can be taken as evidence to the

---

[135] DS 806: "*Inter Creatorem et creaturam non potest similitudo notari, quin inter eos maior sit dissimilitudo.*" "Between Creator and creature no similitude can be expressed without implying a greater dissimilitude." (Translation mine)

[136] *Lunacy and Letters*, cited in *TTFT*, 14.

contrary. He believed that the human mind was made for truth: "The object of opening the mind, as of opening the mouth, is to shut it again on something solid."[137] He praised the Church for being a "continuous intelligent institution that has been thinking about thinking for two thousand years."[138] However, and as we shall see later, he also knew that truth was complex and paradoxical, not simple and always obvious; reality is multicolored, not monochromatic; and no single perspective will ever suffice to describe truth and God. To equate God with one theological perspective or image,

> ...is idolatry: the preference of the incidental good over the eternal good which it symbolises. It is the employment of one example of the everlasting goodness to confound the validity of a thousand other examples. It is the elementary mathematical and moral heresy that the part is greater than the whole.[139]

While Chesterton was certain that human beings need truth and that Catholic Christianity was "the trysting place of all the truths in the world,"[140] he also knew that one had to live and feel one's way into a grasp of truth, a mixture of "healthy hesitation and healthy complexity."[141] Another reason for his love for the Book of Job, with its untidy open-endedness, was because it appealed to his notion of life as an asymptotic human quest into religious mystery. As Kevin Morris says, for Chesterton,

> ...if life, man and existence were a story, it was one told about characters; it was a drama of time, place and action, and the engine of the art was spirit, or mind and heart, emotion and psychology; and

---

[137] *Autobiography*, 230.

[138] *The Thing: Why I Am A Catholic*, 129.

[139] *Lunacy and Letters*, cited in *TTFT*, 229.

[140] *The Thing: Why I Am A Catholic*, 132.

[141] *Lunacy and Letters*, cited in *TTFT*, 14.

he was perfectly well aware that religion was to do with mental need, with inner drives which were not susceptible to dissection by the materialist's scalpel, or even by the theologian's: what the theologian did was cast light upon the mystery, not solve it; and what the dogmatist did was provide the spot-marks by which to best direct the action of the stage drama.[142]

We saw earlier in this chapter that Aquinas points out that God, the utterly ineffable one, is self-evident in himself but not self-evident to us,[143] and so it follows that theologians never understand Him too well. The good theologian is always aware of the danger of creating God in our own image and likeness.

In approaching reality, then, one must have an attitude of humility, openness, and, as far as possible (for it is impossible to achieve it to the highest degree), an absence of preconceptions, biases or fixed agendas, from either believer or unbeliever. In this way the ground is prepared for a better appreciation of the complexity of the world to be contemplated, the human being that contemplates and the God who is the transcendent source of both. The reawakening to the human leads to a richer understanding, one which refuses to identify truth with the reductionism of scientism, and which senses the different nature of faith knowledge.

Aquinas captures this difference when he calls faith knowledge an act of the intellect commanded by the will, moved by God's grace.[144] Decision is part of the journey toward this kind of religious truth. Imagination, our human capacity for images, metaphors, and stories, is what we use in so many of the ways we approach truths about the human and the divine. As said earlier, faith knowledge is a personal and non-rational, but not

---

[142] *TTFT*, 15.

[143] *ST* I, 2

[144] *ST* II-II, 2,9

irrational, kind of truth. Like the love between two people, and all answers to the deeper human questions, it can never be totally proved, and so requires trust, or Aquinas's act of the will.

Chesterton, deeply marked by the futility of the excessively analytical thinking he had done during his period of depression at the Slade, wrote poetic language and painted word pictures in order to emphasize the need for human beings to think not only with the left-side brain, with its focus on external verification, but also with the intuitive, imaginative, and personal right-side brain. He invited the people of Edwardian England to note the strangeness of reality and the richness of the God who was the source of reality. As I shall argue later, he was a man who was aware that the mature human being is someone who has passed from a naïve and uncritical stance before the cosmos, through a period of critique of the cosmos, in order to reach an attitude of post-critical wonder toward the cosmos.

2.3 THE DARKNESS OF FEELINGS AND MOODS

Thirdly, Chesterton's own words, and his ministry of communication to others, can be a useful reminder that doubts and darkness are normal experiences along certain stretches of the religious journey. Chesterton once received a letter from a young woman called Rhoda Bastable who was suffering from "spiritual growing pains" and had "expressed to him a fear that she was a hypocrite" in the Christian faith. In his gentle reply he refers to his own struggles:

> ...I have doubted if I believed anything: but I have found the trick of saying: "If I did not really believe I should not have done this work, or resisted that temptation—or even tried to resist it. My Will knows me better than my Mind does." Think about solid things outside you; especially about the most solid thing in the world—affection...I can

think at least as well as most who tell you the contrary [that faith is not about facts]: and I doubt if there is a doubt anywhere I have not entertained, examined and dismissed. I believe in God the Father Almighty, Maker of Heaven and Earth and in the other extraordinary things in that statement. I believe them more, the more I see of human experience. And when I say, "God bless you, my dear girl," I have no more doubt of Him than of you.[145]

Here Chesterton is pointing out, among other things,[146] something that pastoral accompaniment of people in their faith journeys reveals to be all too evident: that in certain moods or moments doubts can come at people from many angles, but that there are also other factors that determine whether we really believe or not.

Anything that touches on God, Christ, Church, religion, or the transcendent can seem unreal, impossible, an illusion created by the weak or inadequate for the weak and inadequate— something that is a projection of human neediness, even if communicated with wisdom and witnessed to by generous selflessness. As we shall see in our fourth chapter, the sinful nature of the Church (on which Chesterton commented several times) can be a source of deep alienation for many.

Religion, the human and structured response to the self-revealing God, while containing much that is good and life-giving, has also been a source of violence, rigidity, hostility, and exclusion—even toward religious people who have been prophets seeking to purify their own religious community and its traditions. It is hardly surprising, then, that people on the religious journey go through the darkness of doubts and pass negative judgments about the worth of religion. Why become a Christian and member of the Church or, if one is already

---

[145] M. Ward, *Return to Chesterton*, 202.

[146] We shall return to this passage later in order to uncover more of its richness.

a Christian, why stay in the Church? When Chesterton was going through his own darkness at the Slade, the doubts were particularly acute when he cut himself off from others, and the darkness began to lift when he reconnected himself to his friends.

Chesterton's experience echoes in some ways the experience of one of the patrons of all doubters, Thomas the apostle.[147] It would seem that on Easter Sunday Thomas had cut himself off from the other disciples and had decided to walk alone. He was disheartened, disillusioned, angry, and in mourning, all conditions of heart which made him hard-hearted in his questioning and closed to accepting the word of the community that proclaimed the Risen Christ. Then Christ appears to Thomas, and the latter proclaims his faith, to which Christ says, "Blessed are those who have not seen, but who have believed."[148]

In the final line of *Heretics* Chesterton alludes to this Gospel scene: "We shall be of those who have seen and yet have believed."[149] His playing with the Gospel words is done to make a point about his opposition to what he saw as the arrogant tone of the strident doubt and scepticism found in the excesses of modern thought. "The great march of mental destruction will go on. Everything will be denied."[150] Only the Christian creed will assert its belief, not only in divine things, but in earthly things:

> It is a reasonable position to deny the stones in the street; it will be a religious dogma to assert them. It is a rational thesis that we are all in a dream; it will be a mystical sanity to say that we are all awake. Fires will be kindled to testify that two and two make four. Swords will be drawn to prove that leaves are green in summer. We shall be left

---

[147] John 20:24-29

[148] John 20:29

[149] *Heretics*, 207.

[150] Ibid.

defending, not only the incredible virtues and sanities of human life, but something more incredible still, this huge impossible universe which stares us in the face. We shall fight for visible prodigies as if they were invisible. We shall look on the impossible grass and the skies with a strange courage. We shall be of those who have seen and yet have believed.[151]

In the face of such modern doubt, Chesterton maintains that we need faith to believe in the evidence of our eyes. To maintain belief in natural things, we need to believe in supernatural ones. Chesterton asserts this not as a matter of Christian dogma, but as a matter of historically observing those who deny religious belief and then try to offer a coherent explanation of why they believe in the things of this world, such as truth, the moral law, a reason to love, etc. The flip side of this helps to explain why Chesterton advises Rhoda that the immersion of self into the things of this world, especially affection and relationship, are a truer indicator of the level of our religious faith.

So often it is the case that people's lives trace a journey from a position of less mature faith, through a position of doubt or disbelief, before reaching a position of a more mature faith. Having doubts in our search for truth is nothing to be ashamed of and can actually turn out to be a stage of growth in our journey of faith. For Chesterton, it is arrogance, pride, and sulkiness that can prevent us from progressing on that journey. As Thomas sulked ("Unless I see the marks...") because he was on the outside of those who had witnessed the risen Lord, so too we can sulk and dismiss the worth of the experience of others when we feel that we have been left out of the inner circle of the privileged. Such dismissiveness of others, all too evident in the modern pride Chesterton often criticized, can lead to petulant demands for proof of the significance of what is being talked about.

---

[151] Ibid.

It is significant that Jesus offers no resistance or rebuke in the face of Thomas's petulance. Instead, he takes Thomas at his word and invites him to act with reverence before the reality that is unfolding in front of him, and also to make himself part of the community again by reconnecting with others. This reconnection with ordinary, everyday reality and relationship is precisely the invitation Chesterton extends to Rhoda, and it is an open challenge for all of us: honesty before reality and generous giving of self to others, in order to move ever more deeply into the mystery of Christ. Doubt, scepticism, agnosticism, and atheism are not a problem as long as we are ready to be humble before reality as it unfolds before us, to admit when we are wrong and, as we shall see in Chapters V and VI, give our life away to others in loving relationship. As Chesterton said,

"If I did not really believe I should not have done this work, or resisted that temptation—or even tried to resist it. My Will knows me better than my Mind does." Think about solid things outside you; especially about the most solid thing in the world—affection.[152]

God is neither angered nor threatened by honest agnosticism, providing we are attentive to what is before us, honest about our interpretations, open to changing our minds when necessary, and faithful in loving.

At the Slade, Chesterton had made life more difficult for himself by cutting himself off from others and walking alone. People who are grieving, angry, or disillusioned can tend toward self-isolation. We said earlier that pain can consume the whole body, such that there seems to be no other reality but pain. In a similar fashion, the sulking person acts with irreverence toward others and the world, dismissing everybody but self and discarding every opinion other than his

---

[152] M. Ward, *Return to Chesterton*, 202.

own. Chesterton believed that in such moments a sense of reverence needs to be discovered or re-discovered:

> It was by this deliberate idea of starting from zero, from the dark nothingness of his own deserts, that [Saint Francis of Assisi] did come to enjoy even earthly things as few people have enjoyed them... There is no way in which a man can earn a star or deserve a sunset... The less a man thinks of himself, the more he thinks of his good luck and of all the gifts of God.[153]

Humility, reducing ourselves to zero, eventually moves us to a place in which we can perceive a wisdom that is more worthy of our deepest self. Of course, and as Job showed us, patience is necessary, since we may find ourselves outside this stance of reverence for a while, but we must bear with this because the reverence that comes from humility is key to faith.

We will have occasion to explore the role of community in the forging of an agenda for apologetics today in Chapter IV. For now we can note that time away from the Church, times of doubt and darkness about Church, Christ, God, religion, may be periods of emptiness in which God works on us and brings us to growth, but such growth always points us back, renewed, stronger in faith, toward the life of community within the Church. The darkness is real when it comes, and the "yes" of faith is often mixed with "no." Much depends on where we are standing. The vision of faith, the "yes" of faith, is sometimes sure and steady, and at other times unsure. That is normal. But the "yes" can win through, and we can journey through the darkness and clouds without undue anxiety.

In the preceding section of this chapter we noted the different quality of the type of knowledge that is involved in faith because of God's ineffability and the inadequacy of our

---

[153] *Saint Francis of Assisi*, 67-8.

theological constructs. We stated that this should prevent us from ever identifying God with our theologies. Another consequence of God's non-obviousness and the tentative nature of our explorations of God is that we should not make a simple identification between our imagination or feelings and our faith. John of the Cross[154] described the dark night of the soul in which a felt sense of God disappears, leaving us feeling arid and empty. Our feelings and our imagination are devoid of a sense of God, and we are left feeling utterly dry and insecure as all consolatory feelings and images of God disappear. Agnosticism or a real sense of unbelief may take over as we no longer feel or imagine the existence of God. John of the Cross would say that what has disappeared is not God, whose existence is not dependent on an internal human barometer reading on any given day, but our feelings about God and our capacity to imagine God's reality. On certain stretches of the spiritual journey the heart, mind, and imagination may not be able to feel, think, and picture the reality of a God who is, by definition, utterly Other and ineffable, and so we are left with feelings of dryness, aridity, a sense of absence and dejection.

In Chesterton's profound and vivid image of the atheistic Christ on Calvary, we are told that:

> ...in a garden God tempted God. He passed in some superhuman manner through our human horror of pessimism. When the world shook and the sun was wiped out of heaven, it was not at the crucifixion, but at the cry from the cross: the cry which confessed that God was forsaken of God.[155]

Chesterton engages in speculative Christology when he suggests that at the moment when "God was forsaken of God," God

---

[154] See *Dark Night of the Soul*, Book II, Chapter 5, sections 5-6.

[155] *Orthodoxy*, 343.

went through his own dark night of the soul. When Jesus cried out in anguish, was he expressing feelings of emptiness at his abandonment, no longer able to imagine, feel, or perceive in any way the presence of a loving Father? In spite of such desolation Jesus did as Chesterton had advised Rhoda to do in her own darkness and doubts: he continued on the path dictated by faith, on the journey set out for him by the Father, pushing against the negative feelings brought on by the darkness and actively seeking to entrust himself to the God he could no longer sense or picture. Inside what appears to be abandonment, he trusted.

Jürgen Moltmann writes that:

> Our faith begins at the point where atheists suppose that it must end. Our faith begins with the bleakness and power which is the night of the cross, abandonment, temptation, and doubt about everything that exists! Our faith must be born where it is abandoned by all tangible reality; it must be born of nothingness, it must taste this nothingness and be given it to taste in a way no philosophy of nihilism can imagine.[156]

Here a major Protestant theologian is writing of the immense importance of the classical Protestant injunction against putting one's ultimate trust in anything other than God. At the risk of sounding a little austere and masochistic, and remaining ever-aware of the truth already voiced—that all theological commentary requires nuance lest it become more untrue than true—to maintain faith in the teeth of a total absence of feelings and images that could bolster such faith (that is to say, the reality described by John of the Cross's metaphor of the dark night of the soul) is to have real faith.

Chesterton would agree that often in life, having undertaken some of life's major commitments, a person has to pass through

---

[156] J. Moltmann, *The Crucified God*, 31-2.

dark nights, when feelings and imagination feel undernourished for the task in hand:

> In everything on this earth that is worth doing, there is a stage when
> no one would do it, except for necessity or honour...Two people must
> be tied together in order to do themselves justice; for twenty minutes
> at a dance, or for twenty years in a marriage. In both cases the point
> is, that if a man is bored in the first five minutes he must go on and
> force himself to be happy. Coercion is a kind of encouragement; and
> anarchy (or what some call liberty) is essentially oppressive, because
> it is essentially discouraging...The whole aim of marriage is to fight
> through and survive the instant when incompatibility becomes un-
> questionable. For a man and a woman, as such, are incompatible.[157]

To arrive at a more mature stage of marriage, of vocational commitment, of prayer and of faith in God, is to have journeyed
through testing periods of aridity. The darkness of faith and the
absence of feelings and images along certain stretches of the
spiritual pathway teach us, ultimately, to rely on and put our
trust in God alone, and not on the gifts of the cosmos that are
meant to be icons that open us up to God. While all things can
be used to lead us to God, in the end these things are not God.
While God may permit us to come to him in myriad ways, he
does not want us to rest in these realities, but to keep searching
for the God who is none of these, but is the *Deus semper maior*.

Such dark nights are intended to be periods of purification,
stretches along the spiritual path when we are asked to let go
of good things which have served us for a while in the spiritual
life, but which are now in danger of becoming idols and of
leading us away from a fuller grasp of truth, a fuller encounter
with reality and a more intimate knowledge of God. When
we are unable to relinquish our hold on those things that, at
a given moment, we deem essential to our relationship with

---

[157] *What's Wrong with the World*, 45-6.

God, then we are in danger of idolatry, since something less than God has taken hold of our mind, heart, soul, and strength. For Chesterton this "Madness is a preference for the symbol over that which it represents."[158] The aridity of the dark night, so austere, harsh, and utterly devoid of religiously nourishing images and feelings, is a weaning off such idols.

When in *Orthodoxy* Chesterton describes Jesus of Nazareth as the "only...divinity who ever uttered [the atheists'] isolation" and Christianity as the "only...religion in which God seemed for an instant to be an atheist,"[159] he is agreeing with Moltmann that faith begins precisely where atheism assumes it ends. In the isolation and abandonment of what seemed to be atheism, Jesus was held fast to a Father whom he could hardly imagine as real by a reality that went beyond what his feelings and imagination taught him to be true. This was true faith, as witnessed to by Jesus' actions of trustfulness.

The periodic absence of light during the journey of faith is inevitable. Faith is a relationship and, as in any relationship between two persons, it is a fragile and unsteady mix of certainty and doubts, light and darkness, strength and faltering weakness. Of course, Jesus' trust through the darkness was crowned with the light of the Resurrection. The dawn always follows the darkness. Darkness can be a purifying friend of faith and need not, ultimately, leave us unfree for faith.

---

[158] *Lunacy and Letters*, cited in *TTFT*, 229.

[159] *Orthodoxy*, 343.

3. The Effects of Culture on
Our Capacities for Faith

We saw at the beginning of this chapter that Chesterton first came to the public eye by seeking to defend human freedom against all attempts to deny, remove, or weaken that freedom. He was acutely aware that cultural forces could impact negatively on the human capacity for faith. However, as P. N. Furbank has written, Chesterton "was a refugee from the fin-de-siècle, and yet he borrowed almost all his equipment as a writer from it."[160] When in the next chapter we explore Chesterton's notion of paradox, we shall observe more clearly that, though he was horrified by so much of the moral vision of the Decadents, the literary tools that he used so ably in his career most definitely bear the stamp of that same cultural period in English history. As Aidan Nichols puts it, "Chesterton was apparently indebted for the means in which he stated his vision to those whom he regarded as its enemies or at least rivals...in the more decorous metaphor of St. Augustine, he despoiled the Egyptians of their gold and silver."[161]

If Bernard Lonergan's definition of theology as mediator "between a cultural matrix and the significance and role of religion in that matrix"[162] is true, then Chesterton's writings reveal that, for Christianity, the mediation is a mutual self-mediation between the timeless truths (about human beings and God) of the Christian tradition and the cultural matrix in which that tradition is being expressed. As Aidan Nichols says,

---

[160] P. N. Furbank, "Chesterton, the Edwardian," *G. K. Chesterton: A Centenary Appraisal*, ed. John Sullivan, London: 1974, 18.

[161] A. Nichols, "Chesterton and Modernism," *The Chesterton Review*, XV, 1-2 (1989), 170-1.

[162] *Method in Theology*, xi.

> There is an inevitable give-and-take between the culture in which the Church finds herself and the manner of her expression of the gospel which she preaches. Chesterton thus bore witness implicitly and despite himself to a truth that he would have suspected if not combatted: namely, the essential relatedness of the Church to its own age.[163]

This author agrees and holds that Chesterton was aware of both the positive and negative potential for the sharing of Christian faith that a surrounding culture could exert. Perhaps he was aware of Newman's belief that a new question needs a new answer[164] and that a consequence of this is that Christian apologetics in every age and every culture has to learn from as well as teach a culture, if it is to fashion images and languages that enable it to carry out its task of explaining, expounding and defending the Christian faith for the life of the world.

We shall see in Chapter IV, when we explore Chesterton's relationships with Shaw and Wells, and compare his friendship with Wells with Belloc's acrimonious relationship with Wells, that it would be a mistake to think of Chesterton as some dour veteran of Edwardian culture wars who was unable to appreciate anything good in the culture around him or in the people with whom he disagreed. His sense of the world as a gracious gift evoked in him a sense of humility, gratitude, and wondrous joy, and ensured that his default position vis-à-vis the world and others was one of consolation, not desolation.

Cultural critique, however, was something for which the jolly journalist became rapidly famous. John Coates[165] believes that Chesterton was intimately bound into the cultural fabric of his age by his choice of career. Coates argues that during the

---

[163] "Chesterton and Modernism," *The Chesterton Review*, XV, 1-2 (1989), 171.

[164] *Letters and Diaries*, cited in T. Merrigan, "Newman and Theological Liberalism," *Theological Studies* 66 (2005) 605-21 at 614-15.

[165] *Chesterton and the Edwardian Cultural Crisis*, Hull: University of Hull, 1984.

Edwardian period there was an anxiety among the educated classes of England and Chesterton was keenly aware of some of the snobbish consequences of this nervousness. Their disquiet arose possibly from the wider access to education that had resulted from the increasing number of people in the lower social classes who could read.

To what extent early modernist literature (understood here as a reference to literary, as opposed to theological modernism) was reclaiming the educational high ground is a subject open to debate, but it can certainly be argued that Chesterton's choice of career was heavily influenced by the early trading of blows in such cultural battles. He passionately believed in the rights of the ordinary citizen, the "man of the street," and believed that the instincts and approach to life of such ordinary people were wholesome and sensible. Chesterton believed that human lives are ultimately happy or unhappy and human institutions, both great and small, ultimately live or die, because of the degrees of truth and falsity to be found in the ideas that underpin them. The modern intellectual, the specialist, with his rationalist approach to understanding the world, was the loudest voice in the market place of ideas as Chesterton was starting out in journalism.

As we saw in his musings in chapters 2 and 3 of *Orthodoxy*, and as we have explored earlier in this chapter, for Chesterton there is much more that influences the human interpretation of reality than the left-brain rationalist approach of clear ideas. There are influences that are "mystical," right-brain, artistic, poetic, and creative, all of which affect the human knower's encounter with the external cosmos. The interpretations we have about the deeper things of life are found at the imaginative level and are not always explicitly formulated as clear ideas. To say that the way we interpret the cosmos and our place within it is found at the level of the imagination is not to say that our interpretations are fictitious. So much of what we care most deeply about—trust, love, art, music, meaning, all of those realities that are most specifically human, including religious faith—goes beyond clear verbal and conceptual formulation and has to find creative and imaginative expression. For Chesterton, the way in which human beings imagine themselves is vital for human flourishing in this world and for the journey of faith.

Here we are entering the territory of what Charles Taylor calls the "social imaginary." Taylor is a moral and political philosopher whose work on cultural history, and in particular on the historical emergence and development of modernity, sheds much light on how cultural contexts influence the potential for faith today. A little like Newman does with his understanding of spiritual and psychological dispositions, the social imaginary shifts the focus of the readiness or un-readiness for faith from explicitly thought-out ideas and ideologies to the less conscious zone of self-images and implicit self-understanding. It is "a wider grasp of our whole predicament: how we stand to each other, how we got to where we are, how we relate to other groups, and so on." The roots of the crisis of religious faith experienced in the modern age are to be found in "that largely unstructured and inarticulate understanding of our whole situation"[166]—that is to say, in the culture, which is formed by the assumptions, images of self, and sets of attitudes and values that can be acquired, transmitted, and expressed in behavior, rituals, symbols, beliefs, etc., and which end up constituting our modern identity. How we intuitively envisage ourselves is critical to the possibilities for faith at the individual and societal level.

---

[166] *Modern Social Imaginaries*, 25.

In trying to explain how we have made the transition from a world in which it was almost culturally impossible not to believe in God and spiritual realities, to a secular culture, in which belief in God and spiritual realities is just one of the worldviews which people could hold if they so wished (and which they often do not), Taylor makes a distinction between a "porous" self and a "buffered" self.[167] The porous self was much more open to the transcendent, the spiritual, and God, and understood human existence and the human search for happiness to be intimately connected to the rest of the multi-layered mystery of the cosmos and to the transcendent Creator who is the source of that cosmos. The porous self was almost powerless to stop the transcendent, spiritual, eternal, and mystical from seeping in to human consciousness.

The buffered self, on the other hand, is protected or buffered against this invasion of the spiritual and the eternal. The secular consciousness is able to shut out any notion of the mystical and the transcendent, and sees the meaning of human life and the search for human happiness to be found within the parameters of concrete existence in this world—its self-understanding or imaginary is much more horizontal than vertical, "[imagining] society horizontally unrelated to any 'high points.'"[168] In such a culture faith is rarely the result of social structures and supports, seldom an inherited faith; it will almost always be the result of a choice that is counter-cultural, akin to what Karl Rahner suggested when he stated that the West would soon reach a moment in history when a person's choice will be between being either a mystic or an unbeliever.[169] There is little doubt that the

---

[167] See C. Taylor, *A Secular Age*, 38 ff.

[168] *Modern Social Imaginaries*, 157.

[169] *Theological Investigations* Vol. VII, 15.

Chesterton who wrote that, "A dead thing can go with the stream; only a living thing can go against it"[170] would concur with both Rahner and Taylor. We shall see in our fourth chapter that Taylor applauds many of modernity's positive achievements, and is very sceptical about the long-term value of any attempt by Christian bodies to supplant the institutions of society with a new type of Christendom. However, he emphasizes "the unquiet frontiers of modernity,"[171] pointing out that glimpses of the transcendent, the spiritual, and the mysterious still manage to get through the buffers of our modern, secular consciousness, and he remains critical of some of the shadow sides of modernity, contending that its reluctance to take both transcendence and community seriously is a threat to human flourishing.

We shall see that Chesterton also believed in seeking out the good that was to be found in people and in cultures with which he was not totally sympathetic, but he was utterly certain, having lived through the Slade, that the battles for imaginations, hearts, and minds had to be fought. At the beginning of the twentieth century, the arena for this was Fleet Street. For G. K. Chesterton, the medium of the newspapers had much to contribute to the shaping of the public imagination and thereby human happiness or unhappiness, and it was in journalism that he found the vocation that allowed him to express the inner creative force that had been with him since his teenage years and his formative encounter at the Slade:

> My first impulse to write, and almost my first impulse to think, was a revolt of disgust with the Decadents and the aesthetic pessimism of the 'nineties…I thought that all the wit and wisdom in the world was banded together to slander and depress the world…then above all, everyone claiming intelligence insisted on "Art for art's sake"…I

---

[170] *The Everlasting Man*, 256.

[171] *A Secular Age*, 711 ff.

started to think it out, and the more I thought of it, the more certain I grew that the whole thing was a fallacy; that art could not exist apart from, still less in opposition to, life; especially the life of the soul which is salvation; and that great art had never been so much detached from conscience and common sense, or from what my critic would call moral earnestness.[172]

Chesterton's self-perception, then, was as a controversialist, as a man who liked a controversy, an argument, a struggle with ideas about true and false, right and wrong, and he engaged in such battles principally in the daily newspaper. We shall see in our next chapter the tools he used to influence ideas (among them paradox, images, word pictures). He thought that there was much that was wrong with the world, and that there was equally much that was wrong with the world of newspapers. "Modern man is staggering and losing his balance because he is being pelted with little pieces of alleged fact...which are native to the newspapers; and, if they turn out not to be facts that is even more native to the newspapers."[173]

The cultural resistance in which Chesterton engaged was displayed toward newspapers and any other medium that communicated modernist philosophies, and he argued that the various reigning ideologies reduced human beings and the cosmos, degraded human dignity, and slowly eroded human culture. Empiricism, materialism, rationalism, scientism and unbridled progressivism all combined to view human beings as machines or clever animals, whose well-being could be planned in a scientific way, and such pseudo-scientific claims were often the targets of Chesterton's criticism. He lamented the hostility

---

[172] "Milton and Merry England," *Fancies Versus Fads*, in *G. K. Chesterton: An Anthology*, ed. D. B. Wyndham Lewis, 142-3.

[173] *Illustrated London News*, 27th April 1923, cited in D. Ahlquist, *Common Sense 101: Lessons from G. K. Chesterton*, 68.

displayed toward religion and the transcendent in general, and Christianity in particular, and he despised the egotistical lifestyle advocated in the name of the development of the human species (as witnessed in his outspoken and courageous criticism of, among other things, British Imperialism and eugenics). He also attacked modern utopianism for the inconsistencies of its critique of Christianity and also its inability to encourage people to enjoy their life in this world:

> Even the latest Utopians, the last lingering representatives of that fated and unfortunate race, do not really promise the modern man that he shall do anything, or own anything, or in any effectual fashion be anything. They only promise that, if he keeps his eyes open, he will see something…the Universal Trust or the World State…coming in the clouds in glory. But the modern man cannot even keep his eyes open. He is too weary with toil and a long succession of unsuccessful Utopias. He has fallen asleep.[174]

The secularists ridiculed Christianity for looking to the Kingdom of God, but their unbridled optimism was itself ridiculed by Chesterton because of its insistence that the human race was marching relentlessly onwards toward some future perfection, while simultaneously ignoring the gift of the present moment.

However, if Chesterton was a great critic of the press and of the culture in which he lived, he was entitled to be, because he also loved the press and the world of Fleet Street, and so was also their greatest champion, being well aware of the capacity of the press to achieve great good in the world which he treasured as gift of God. As we have already said, although Chesterton had plenty to say about what was wrong with the world, he was not merely some sour critic of Edwardian culture; he was a man filled with wonder, joy, and gratitude at the complex and multi-faceted gift of reality, and a man who knew

---

[174] G. K.'s Weekly, 20th October 1928, cited in TTFT, 93.

how to discern and praise all that was good in the culture that surrounded him. As he said repeatedly in his book of essays, *What's Wrong with the World*, one of the main problems that we have is that "we do not ask what is right."[175]

What was right? As we shall see in our next chapter, Chesterton saw the world as the good gift of the Creator, and he believed that all the many wonderful things that go toward making up the world are essentially and eternally good gifts from God. However, he loathed the fact that these essentially good gifts had been reduced by an industrialist and capitalist cultural mindset to the level of merely utilitarian goods, and only for as long as they served these utilitarian purposes. Such a reductionist view of the cosmos and human beings has:

> ...taken what all ancient philosophers called the Good, and translated it as the Goods...They ought to have said, not "Trade is good," but "Living is Good," or "Life is good." I suppose it would be too much to expect such thoroughly respectable people to say, "God is good"; but it is really true that their conception of what is good lacks the philosophical finality that belonged to the goodness of God. When God looked on created things and saw that they were good, it meant that they were good in themselves and as they stood; but by the modern mercantile idea God would only have looked at them and seen that they were the Goods.[176]

The reduced capitalist worldview of Chesterton's (and indeed any) day undermined the dignity of the human person, reducing human beings to a function, or a resource within a market, a cog in an industrial production process, or a specimen for a more intellectual specialist to improve:

> All the flowers and birds would be ticketed with their reduced prices; all creation would be for sale or all the creatures seeking employment;

---

[175] *What's Wrong With the World*, 17.

[176] "Reflections on a Rotten Apple," *The Well and the Shallows*, 496-7.

with all the morning stars making sky-signs together and all the Sons of God shouting for jobs...The idea of a man enjoying a thing in itself, for himself, is inconceivable to them.[177]

Chesterton believed that the cosmos was a permanently good thing that came as gift to human beings from the hand of God and was something to be enjoyed in and for itself and not for how it could be manipulated to achieve other ends.

Although Chesterton denied that he was a Medievalist, i.e., a person who demonstrates a nostalgic yearning for all things Medieval and sees only value in Medieval culture, it might be argued that on occasion he exaggerated the merits of that ecclesio-centric culture. However, it would be a mistake to view Chesterton as some kind of reactionary, reacting against modern progress out of a longing for a bygone age. He seeks not to offer an apology for the past, but for human freedom and the spiritual dimensions of human beings that alone can safeguard that freedom. Freedom has to be defended against the:

...huge modern heresy of altering the human soul to fits its conditions, instead of altering human conditions to fit the human soul. If soap-boiling is really inconsistent with brotherhood, so much the worse for soap-boiling, not for brotherhood....it would be better to do without soap rather than without society.[178]

So Chesterton's cultural critique is not a defense of the past against the present, but of the dignity of the human person against all forces, past or present, which undermine that dignity. The correct Chestertonian question is the one that asks what the human being is made for, what the human being's ultimate end is, and not what can be done with human beings, or what societal function or purpose they can serve. "It is rather as if

---

[177] Ibid., 497.

[178] *What's Wrong with the World*, 80.

a nurse had tried a rather bitter food for some years on a baby, and on discovering that it was not suitable, should not throw away the food and ask for a new food, but throw the baby out of the window and ask for a new baby."[179] Within certain specified limits all the good things of the cosmos are meant to serve human dignity, and human dignity must never be the means to some other end, be that end the improvement of society or any other abstract notion.

Whenever the cosmological and anthropological become detached from the theological (and Chesterton saw the ultimate safeguard against this happening as residing in the Christian tradition, for which cosmology, anthropology, and theology are a seamless garment), a certain consequence will be that the anthropological worldview will become too narrow. Chesterton thinks that the purveyors of such an anthropology will be unaware of its narrowness and attempt to peddle their vision to others in the name of improving the lot of human beings. In his writing he constantly painted word pictures against such visions, arguing that to do so "is a question of liberty from catchwords and headlines and hypnotic repetitions and all the plutocratic platitudes imposed on us by advertisement and journalism."[180] He was all too aware of the power of the newspapers to influence culture.

> I do feel very strongly about the frivolity and irresponsibility of the press. It seems impossible to exaggerate the evil that can be done by a corrupt and unscrupulous press…it acts on the corporate national will and sways the common national decision.[181]

---

[179] "Mr. Bernard Shaw," *Heretics*, 70.

[180] Cited in *TTFT*, 49.

[181] "Prohibition and the Press," Fancies versus Fads, New York: Dodd, Mead and Co., 1923, http://www.cse.dmu.ac.uk/~mward/gkc/books/Fancies_Versis_Fads.txt [last accessed 17th January 2012].

Chesterton intended, therefore, to remain a journalist all his life, seeing it as his vocation in life to do good from Fleet Street. He had plenty to communicate, wishing to laud all that was praiseworthy in an essentially good world, and looking to warn against everything that was anthropologically reductive and therefore destructive of human happiness. His preferred method of reaching people was, from the very beginning, the essay, and some of the most memorable chapters of his books were more polished versions of essays that had first appeared in his newspaper columns. Chesterton was an essayist for most of his life, and never a mere reporter of facts. Indeed, in another example of what Aidan Nichols describes as the symbiotic, "give-and-take" nature of the relationship between evangelizer and culture, of the despoiling of Egypt of some of her treasures, it might be said that whatever else their many differences would have been, perhaps Chesterton would have at least concurred with Oscar Wilde's belief that "Truth is independent of facts always." Indeed, scribbled in one of Chesterton's notebooks, probably dated around 1910, is the following: "Not facts first, truth first."[182]

Chesterton became a journalist because he sought to reach people with the truth, by discussing what was familiar to them: that is, the ordinary and everyday experience that they knew from the newspapers and the interpretations of that experience that were proffered by Fleet Street. He always took as his journalistic point of departure precisely where people found themselves and the interpretations being set before them, and then subjected those experiences and interpretations to scrutiny. At all times he respected whatever truth was to be found

---

[182] Quoted in Pearce, *Wisdom and Innocence*, 83, and referenced as an unpublished notebook. c. 1910, G. K. Chesterton Study Centre, Bedford, UK.

in the newspapers, while also seeking to refine anything that needed either nuance or improvement and to refute anything that needed to be contradicted. His sense of democracy always regarded with suspicion the learned expert who displayed con-descension toward the ordinary experience of ordinary people, and he championed the common sense grasp on reality and happiness of the non-intellectual citizen. Chesterton was keenly aware that the learned experts and the newspapers were gradu-ally exerting a cultural influence, for better or (particularly with regard to the possibilities of religious faith) for worse, and so he wanted to add his voice to the public conversation that was taking place in Edwardian England.

For several decades Michael Paul Gallagher has explored this role that culture plays in the possibility of people com-ing to faith. He has examined cultural influences on lifestyles, believing that our capacities for faith are enhanced or di-minished more at this level than at the level of concepts and ideas. There is an "inescapable role [which] culture plays in shaping our sense of identity," as "it forms our mind-sets and heart-sets and gives us our typical way of [imagining or] in-terpreting our lives." There is a persuading element to culture as it massages us into self-interpretations. Awakening to this non-neutrality is a first step toward a Christian response to culture.[183] Chesterton was wide awake to the non-neutral-ity of the ocean of both positive and negative influences in which his contemporaries swam, to the formative capabilities of such influences on the imagination, heart, and mind, and to the consequences of those influences in terms of human happiness and unhappiness. He realized the power of the newspapers either to imprison human beings, reducing their

---

[183] *Clashing Symbols: An Introduction to Faith and Culture*, 10, 12.

habitual way of thinking about themselves and their world to ways that were unworthy of their divine origins and calling, or to liberate them, setting them free to live with a renewed sense of wonder at the adventure of life in this cosmos.

In order to communicate a message that was worthy of such wonder and of the full range of human capacities to know, Chesterton—who had been an artist from the moment he first took up pencils, crayons, and paints in the nursery, and on into his years of study at the Slade—always looked to paint word pictures in his writing, hoping to create realities that leave their imprint on the imagination that shapes our way of interpreting our sense of self and world. As we have already seen from his words in *Heretics*, although he was keenly aware of the importance of dogma, in a very real sense Chesterton was more an artist than a dogmatic thinker (even if the latter is, perhaps, the reputation he has increasingly acquired in the years since his death and one which either endears him to or alienates him from people). He used this artistic temperament that had been formed by his adventures in the late Victorian and Edwardian cultural crises to express in a fresh way the timeless wisdom of the Christian narrative:

> To the young people of my generation, G. K. C. was a kind of Christian liberator. Like a beneficent bomb, he blew out of the Church a quantity of stained glass of a very bad period, and let in gusts of fresh air, in which the dead leaves of doctrine danced with all the energy and indecorum of Our Lady's Tumbler.[184]

In Chapter III we shall explore in more detail the importance of art in Chesterton's writing. It would be correct to say that Chesterton was an artistic raconteur of stories because he saw life as a masterpiece, a story, a romance created by God, who

---

[184] D. L. Sayers, Preface to G. K. Chesterton, *The Surprise: A Play*, 5.

is the Artist, Storyteller, and Romantic Supreme: "Romance is the deepest thing in life; romance is deeper than reality" and, although "life may sometimes appear...as a book of metaphysics...life is always a novel...our existence is...a story."[185]

Although Chesterton was not a theologian in the strict academic sense of the term, he was a gifted and energetic debater of theological matters and a man who asserted the crucial importance of doctrine. However, it would be a mistake to see his only contribution to an agenda for Christian apologetics today in terms of a strictly rational approach that allows us to sweep aside with a few clever phrases all challenges to the Christian narrative. Chesterton was not a systematic thinker, nor a dogmatic theologian, but an artist: a very imaginative (if rather untidy) thinker who connected the ordinary and the everyday with the God who is their source. His habit of leaping from one subject to another means that his reader, if she is to understand Chesterton, has to make leaps with the imagination as well as the reason. He paints images with his words, pictures that require his readers to stretch an imagination that may have become dulled, drowsy, and captive to the reductionist cultural influences that surround them.

---

[185] *Heretics*, 143.

We shall see in Chapter IV that Chesterton believed that the Christian vision needs rigorous theological thought if it is to flourish, but it is equally important to stress the Chestertonian emphasis on romance, affectivity, beauty, wonder, and all the other elements that capture the human imagination. For Chesterton, the ideal apologist would be a great theologian and a great Gospel artist (and, as we shall also see, a great lover: a saint). A mature apologetics that is worthy of the name needs theological vision and rigor, as well as an affective romanticism that can capture the heart and imagination.

4. Concluding Remarks

In this chapter we have attempted to show how Chesterton's life and writings bear witness to the fact that, so often in the journey to religious faith, a first and necessary step is to become free from certain things in order then to be free for God: anthropology and theology are intimately connected in the Christian and Chestertonian vision of things. As we shall see in our subsequent chapters, although Chesterton certainly believed in employing the mind to the full in the quest for God, he also contended that a human being is more than a cool, logical, left-brain, rationalistic processor of concepts. Adopting the latter as one's approach to the cosmos can often (though not necessarily) produce an attitude that sees knowledge about this world and the big questions of reality as ways of asserting one's intellectual superiority and winning arguments.

This is a superficial disposition. It is inadequate as a stance from which to discuss anything truly worthwhile, since one of the most evident things about the cosmos for Chesterton is that the key to its mystery is not obvious. Existence is not some external textbook, waiting to be picked up and read by some clever external observer; rather, it is a paradoxical riddle, a mystery which invites human beings to participate in it and to relish that involvement. The truths we discover about the cosmos and God are born (as we shall see in Chapter VI) of what Avery Dulles calls "participatory knowledge."[186] They are not merely external truths, but also personal truths which embrace us and who we are, and they can only be seen if our disposition or initial stance is right. For Chesterton, a personal decision is required if we are to see accurately. If we make that decision, if we take that step, the cosmos opens up before us and we begin to see the rich and paradoxical nature of the mystery of reality.

Chesterton knew from experience that faith is a relationship—at times a fragile and unsteady relationship—with God. The existential darkness can be brought on by Job-like suffering (real, potentially devastating in some instances, and still the biggest question mark of all about the existence of God. That is not to say, as God reminds Job, that there are not then other problems which arise); the darkness that lies at the heart of the type of knowledge that faith provides and the shadows that feelings and moods can put on our imagination can all lead to dry periods in the spiritual life when a sense of meaning, happiness, and God seem to vanish. This may especially be the case when human beings are immersed in cultures that exert formative influences on the imagination, heart, and mind and which act like a negative magnifying glass over human existence, emphasizing some dimensions of human existence and, either implicitly or explicitly, de-emphasizing others, such that a reductionist anthropology and theology result.[187]

---

[186] *Models of Revelation*, 136 ff.

[187] In a chapter about human freedom and the capacity for God,—anthropology and theology— one might quite reasonably have inserted a section that explores some of the images of God that lie just beneath the surface in the imagination of many people today. These theistic pictures

Chesterton's whole career aimed, therefore, at doing what the apologist needs to do today: engaging people's imaginations and self-understanding; attempting to rouse people to wonder at the gift of daily life in the cosmos; striving to awaken tired, sad, or proud minds so that they can perceive the strange and polychromatic glory of existence and receive it in humility and gratitude. Chesterton knew that reason is essential to human flourishing and yet, like Newman before him, he also realized that the human person is much more than reason, and that faith is more often reached through the imagination. He communicated, therefore, in a way that appealed to the poetic, the artistic, the rational, and the many other dimensions of what constitute the human person, recognizing, like Pope Benedict XVI after him, that the reductionist, post-Enlightenment Western notion of rationality is not faithful to the complexity of human beings. A richer anthropology can lead to a greater awareness of the multi-layered texture of human existence and a sense of the different nature of faith knowledge.

Our human capacity for images, metaphors, and stories is what we employ in many of the ways that we approach truths about the interpersonal. Faith knowledge is a personal and non-rational, but not irrational, kind of truth. Like the love between two people, and as with all answers to the deeper human questions, it can never be totally proved, and so requires trust, an act of the will. Moreover, like such a relationship between two friends or lovers, coming to knowledge of God involves

---

are so often distorted, unworthy of the God of the Christian tradition, and often the result of a stunted religious development. As with so many other topics, Chesterton has plenty to say about the notion of false gods and idolatry, but I shall postpone an exploration of his wisdom in this regard until our next chapter, where it will be situated in the context of his thoughts on paradox, truth, balance, and breadth of perspective.

a personal trust, a personal risk, and a commitment to move oneself to a place in which one is then better able to perceive and come to know God.

On the other hand, an aggressive rationalism that seeks to control reality will never allow a person to move to a place in which God can be found. Such a personal disposition may permit us to know something about God, but we will never know God intimately. We will never be grasped by God and fall in love with God. In interpersonal relationships one cannot remain outside as an impartial spectator. Faith knowledge, dark yet certain, is more like this sort of interpersonal knowledge, the knowledge between friends or lovers, than the knowledge of the empirical natural sciences. We can know a lot about God, but the final surrender of faith is a surrender to a person on the far side of reason. Though reason plays an important role in coming to faith, faith is ultimately suprarational: a surrender to a personal reality that I cannot control aggressively, but which attracts and beguiles me from the far side of reason. Therefore personal decision is part of the journey toward the kind of truth that is religious, demanding the response of our whole being.

Chesterton knew that the absence of constant light for the journey of faith is inevitable because faith is a relationship, and any relationship between two persons is a fragile and un-steady mixture of emotions, feelings, and thoughts. Although the theological content of what the notion of God implies is never to be simply identified with the contents of the human imagination, since the nature of God is utterly Other. This is especially so in the Christian tradition, in which God is the abandoned one who died in darkness and questioning, there-by showing that the Christian God inhabits our darkness and brings Presence to our suffering. God thus demands a certain degree of humility of all theologians in their pronouncements, and although the existence of God is never merely to be equated with the contents of the human imagination at a given moment, because of the unsteadiness of our thoughts and feelings, Chesterton's own life showed that the dawn always follows the darkness. Darkness can be a purifying friend of faith and need not, ultimately, leave us unfree for faith. Faith is, as Chesterton put it, the ability to survive our moods.

CHAPTER III

Wonder, Paradox, and Contingency

You cannot evade the issue of God, whether you talk about pigs or the binomial theory, you are still talking about Him. Now if Christianity be…a fragment of metaphysical nonsense invented by a few people, then, of course, defending it will simply mean talking that metaphysical nonsense over and over. But if Christianity should happen to be true—then defending it may mean talking about anything or everything. Things can be irrelevant to the proposition that Christianity is false, but nothing can be irrelevant to the proposition that Christianity is true.[188]

It is impossible for anything to signify nothing.[189]

WE HAVE SEEN that at the Slade Chesterton lived through an experience of deep loneliness and depression that revealed to him an inner poverty, a lack or an absence, which served as a starting point for his journey toward faith. A positive desire (as opposed to a Feuerbachian projection of wish fulfillment) awoke him to a

---

[188] G. K. Chesterton, *Daily News*, 12th December 1903, cited in D. Ahlquist, *G. K. Chesterton: The Apostle of Common Sense*, 19.

[189] G. K. Chesterton, *A Handful of Authors*, 40.

fullness of being that he was meant to have. He displayed a certain weariness with the world that came from being told by the reigning cultural voices that the world was all there is. "The modern philosopher had told me again and again that I was in the right place, and I had still felt depressed even in acquiescence." When Chesterton had come to know the Christian creed, however, "I had heard that I was in the wrong place, and my soul sang for joy, like a bird in spring."[190] An Augustinian awakening had taken place.

Chesterton had lived through difficult times and had come to realize the importance of being as present as possible to the richness of the ordinary contours of our daily existence. We saw that he believed that human beings are in Eden still, but their eyes have changed so that they do not perceive it. As we grow away from the instinctive wonder of childhood, the heartaches, restlessness, self-obsession, pragmatism, and over-sophistication of adulthood assail us. It stands to reason for Chesterton that unhappiness and over-sophistication should go hand in hand, for "Human beings are happy so long as they retain the receptive power and the power of reaction in surprise and gratitude to something outside...a something that is present in childhood and which can still preserve and invigorate manhood."[191] He believes that ordinary, everyday reality is brimming with extraordinariness, with plenitude of meaning. He has the gift of contemplation, of being able to gaze at existence and to perceive what is inside of human experience. He would certainly have understood and appreciated the insights of Thomas Merton who wrote,

> It is enough to be, in an ordinary human mode, with one's hunger and sleep, one's cold and warmth, rising and going to bed. Putting

[190] *Orthodoxy*, 284.

[191] "If Only I Had One Sermon to Preach," *The Common Man*, 252.

on blankets and taking them off, making coffee and then drinking it. Defrosting the refrigerator, reading, meditating, working, praying. I live as my ancestors lived on this earth, until eventually I die. Amen. There is no need to make an assertion about my life, especially so about it as mine, thought doubtless it is not somebody else's. I must learn to live so as to forget program and artifice.[1]

Chesterton perceived with Merton that our ordinary lives are enough, because they contain what is timeless and eternal, because they are eternally significant, and because they are the gift of a Creator. The fact that we are of eternal significance should be enough (though often it is not) to guarantee that we do not need forever to assert ourselves and our uniqueness.

In this third chapter we are going to look at how Chesterton detects the presence of the extraordinary in the ordinary, "moments filled with eternity...moments [which] are joyful because they do not seem momentary."[2] Such moments can act as pointers to God, points of departure for the journey of faith. We shall explore the notion of paradox, which was central to so much of Chesterton's work, and which allowed him to argue for a broad apologetics, one which admits evidence for the existence of God from a variety of areas of human experience of life in the cosmos. He believed in starting out from anywhere in order to make the case for God, and was utterly opposed to the reduction of faith to a few singular perspectives, themes, or agendas (a reductionism which ultimately leads to a false god).

More specifically, this chapter of the book looks at Chesterton's "Ethics of Elfland" (Chapter 4 of *Orthodoxy*) and his exploration of both contingency and "the doctrine of conditional joy" (the latter denoting the moral law and its relationship to human flourishing). We shall see that Chesterton's

---

[1] Cited by J. H. Griffin, *Follow the Ecstasy: the hermitage years of Thomas Merton*, 26.

[2] *Heretics*, 95.

grasp of being as truth is a description of the indemonstrability of the first rational or speculative principle, and his grasp of being as good is a presentation of the indemonstrability of the first moral principle—that good is to be pursued and done and evil avoided. The chapter ends with an exploration of the importance of art in the thought of Chesterton.

Chesterton believed that fallen human beings have a habit of forgetting their greatness and the lessons of Elfland, and it was for this reason that he contended that so much of modern art had become divorced from the search for the transcendent and eternal, in favor of the ephemeral and new. The artistic faculty (which can be expressed in many ways: through painting, writing, planting a garden, bringing up children, teaching, coaching a sport, etc.) is a uniquely human quality that allows human beings a share in the creativity of God. It reminds us of our divine nature and points to the divine since, for Chesterton, "All art is born when the temporary touches the eternal."[3]

We saw in our last chapter that the cosmos is a mystery inviting human participation. An initial disposition, one which requires a personal decision, is required if we are to be more open to reading it correctly. At the beginning of this chapter, then, we are reminded again, using two pieces on Chesterton by Bernard Lonergan, that the Chestertonian point of departure which opens us up to the glorious paradoxes of a mysterious cosmos is a grateful, humble, and receptive disposition or wavelength of wonder.

---

[3] *Illustrated London News*, 15th July 1922, cited in D. Ahlquist, *Common Sense 101*, 64.

1. The Reverence of the Wondering Mind

Lonergan wrote two short pieces on Chesterton: "Gilbert Keith Chesterton"[4] and "Chesterton the Theologian?"[5] Both pieces admire the sheer wonder that lies at the root of Chesterton's thought and writings. "More than any other modern man [Chesterton] shared the fresh and fearless vitality of medieval inquisitiveness. His questions go the root of things."[6] Lonergan contends that:

> Perhaps [Chesterton's] deepest theological intuition is to be found in the most bizarre of mystery yarns. *The Man Who Was Thursday* is a labyrinth of double roles, of plots and counterplots, of aimless, painful quests, of buffoonery and high seriousness, that lures the unsuspecting reader face to face with God and the problem of evil. Chesterton now knows better, though not differently, the Man who was Sunday [God].[7]

The face of God will be uncovered in the multifaceted mystery that is human existence. Lonergan continues:

> More than critical acumen, it was a grasp of the conditions of healthy living that brought him to the Church. His ideal would be the old ideal of the universal man—the man who lives and thinks, who finds nothing so small that it fails to give him pleasure, who finds nothing so great that he may not think about it, either to question or to adore... He runs against the modern worship of science and scholarship to be the champion of plain thinking. He vindicates the plain man's right to think for himself...When he speaks it is not with a mandate from science, such as so many popularisers arrogate; it is with an appeal to the lore of human experience and to the first principles latent in daily life.

---

[4] *Collected Works of Bernard Lonergan* Vol. 20, 53-59.

[5] Ibid., 89-91.

[6] Ibid., 91.

[7] Ibid.

For Lonergan, then, Chesterton points to the ordinary and the everyday, which are not so ordinary and everyday, as the place in which God is to be found. To notice God, however, requires a certain basic disposition. Chesterton reverences the experience of ordinary people and is suspicious of the intellectual elites whose pride often prevents them having this fundamental attitude, and Lonergan concurs:

> Modern education with its pompous curricula has overemphasized the measurable part of cultural development to the neglect of purely intellectual training. The methods of physical inquiry have invaded letters in the name of scholarship to make letters not a preparation for life but a lifelong pastime.[8]

Until we are free of the need to control and manipulate reality and our knowledge of reality, until we realize that the cosmos invites us to immerse ourselves in it, to participate in it, to enjoy it, and not merely to posture as "masters of the universe" or to while away the years in disinterested speculation, then we will join the many figures who believe that "Private judgment has come to mean the intellectual's right to say what he pleases and the average man's choice to say what pleases him best." For Lonergan,

> With a happy combination of circumstances, a generous allotment of luck, and an imposing tome of pseudo-science to his credit, any clever person may command the enthusiastic support of vast numbers of men...[thereby adding to the many examples] of noble sentiment and addled thought uniting to bring forth a monstrosity.[9]

What is truly needed to see the cosmos correctly is that humility, wonder, and humor by which Chesterton "puts awe and mystery into common things...the power of wondering...that is

---

[8] Ibid., 55-6.

[9] Ibid., 56.

the root of thought [rather than] a rather insignificant certainty that puts an end to thought."[10]

> Because he had a quite brilliant mind and a great confidence that the human mind, when working properly and honestly, could reach knowledge of God, Chesterton was insistent that people observe the cosmos, think long, hard, and rationally about it, and then draw their conclusions intelligently and with integrity. Consequently, he may sometimes give the impression of being perhaps a little forceful and an overly intellectual apologist, trying to lead people to God through a cold and distant logic and an excessively evidentialist approach. This, however, would be to miss the lessons of *Orthodoxy*, in which the whole tone of Chesterton's own approach to God is one of grateful wonder at the multi-faceted gift, the adventure, that is the cosmos. The "...strongest emotion was that life was as precious as it was puzzling. It was an ecstasy because it was an adventure; it was an adventure because it was an opportunity."[11]

Certainly Chesterton believed in employing the mind to the full in the quest for God, but he thought that a human being was more than a logical processor of concepts. Adopting the latter as an approach to understanding the cosmos can often give rise to an attitude that sees knowledge as ways of asserting one's intellectual superiority and winning arguments. This is a superficial disposition and is inadequate as a stance from which to discuss anything truly worthwhile, as the most evident thing about the cosmos is that the key to its mystery is not obvious:

> We all feel the riddle of the earth without anyone to point it out. The mystery of life is the plainest part of it. The clouds and curtains of darkness, the confounding vapours, these are the daily weather of this world. Whatever else we have grown accustomed to, we have grown accustomed to the unaccountable. Every stone or flower is a

---

[10] Ibid., 57.

[11] *Orthodoxy*, 258.

hieroglyphic of which we have lost the key; with every step of our
lives we enter into the middle of some story which we are certain to
misunderstand.[12]

Without the sense of reverence that filled the awe-struck
Chesterton, then, the entry point for discussion is wrong.
Chesterton knew that when asking such questions about the
cosmos and God, we are dealing with issues that touch everything about human existence, history, the micro and the
macro. We are dealing not just with what is external to us, not
just with questions that can be assessed by some sort of "pure,"
objective, presuppositionless reason; rather, we are dealing with
that which touches everything about us and our existence in
this universe for the duration of the relatively brief period of
time which we share with others on the stage of history.

To realize this is to have the correct point of departure: a reverenced wonder that allows us to be grasped by the questions
and to make them our own. The questions are then no longer
mere problems or academic discussions, but become multi-layered mysteries that surround us and invite us to participate
in them. The cosmos is not an object that exists for the mere
amusement of some clever intellectual; it is a paradox, a riddle,
a mystery that invites human beings to participate in it and to
relish their involvement in it. As we have seen, our knowledge
of the cosmos and God is "participatory knowledge,"[13] personal
truths that embrace us and who we are, and they can be seen
only if our disposition or initial stance is right. Personal choice
is required, therefore, if we are to see accurately the paradoxical
nature of life in the cosmos.

---

[12] *William Blake*, 38.

[13] See A. Dulles, *Models of Revelation*, 136ff.

2. CHESTERTON AND PARADOX

We shall see in Chapter VI that Avery Dulles finds in Chesterton's writings the same "cumulative case method" of doing apologetics that he admires so much in Augustine, Pascal, and Newman.[14] There is a hint here that our foregoing discussion—about Chesterton's need to get free, to have the right disposition and to get in touch with his deepest hopes and inner need before setting out on the journey toward faith, to see the significance[15] of everything—is heading in the right direction. As with Newman before him, whose personal motto was *cor ad cor loquitur* and for whom "the heart is commonly reached, not through the reason, but through the imagination,"[16] there is more "heart" to Chesterton's apologetics than is often assumed. The cumulative case method relies on the notion that the best way of showing that it is not irrational or unintelligent to believe in God involves a set of convergences of various pieces of evidence to be found in the world and in the human person.[17] It states that the credibility of faith is a multi-dimensional and complex whole, and so is neither merely a heart affair (though it is partly that), nor just a head or intellectual affair (though it is partly that too): it is not, in fact, reducible to evidence from any single aspect of reality in this cosmos.

We should not be surprised to discover that Chesterton relies on many converging bits of data to make a case for God. He was a man keenly aware that reality is one, and yet at the same time complex and multi-faceted, and that the source of the unity of

---

[14] A. Dulles, *A History of Apologetics*, 293, 362.

[15] That is to say, the characteristic of acting as a sign, or pointer to something.

[16] *An Essay in Aid of a Grammar of Assent*, 89.

[17] See *Catechism of the Catholic Church*, 31.

the cosmos in all its wonderful difference was the Creator who stood behind it. Sameness in difference, the analogical or analogous nature of being is something associated with the Middle Ages and Aquinas, and Chesterton, who had a great love for both, wrote about the analogy of being early in his career:

> [H. G. Wells, whom he was critiquing at this point] must surely realize the first and simplest of the paradoxes that sit by the springs of truth. He must surely see that the fact of two things being different implies that they are similar. The hare and the tortoise may differ in the quality of swiftness, but they must agree in the quality of motion. The swiftest hare cannot be swifter than an isosceles triangle or the idea of pinkness. When we say the hare moves faster, we say that the tortoise moves. And when we say of a thing that it moves, we say, without need of other words, that there are things that do not move. And even in the act of saying that things change, we say that there is something unchangeable.[18]

These two creatures are alike in that they both move, but they are different in the speed and quality of their movement. This likeness in difference, analogy, sheds light on how changing individual beings (creatures) participate in being whose plenitude is the unchanging Creator (Subsistent Being Itself, *Ipsum Esse Subsistens*). All creatures have being (and a host of other qualities), in a way that is proportionate to and consonant with the being that they have, and God has being (and qualities) which is proportionate to and consonant with the being that God has (or, to put it better, is). As Hugh Kenner says:

> Everything that is is wrapped in the mystery of its own incommunicable individuality, and hence all things are wonderfully different; but everything that is exercises the act of existence in common with everything else, and in that sense all things are alike. Both the wonder of differentiation and the wonderful fact of existence are explained and illuminated by the Thomistic ascription of difference to the individual

---

[18] *Heretics*, 78-79.

essences of things, in proportion to which they exercise the act of existence. The grass exists grassily, the cloud cloudily; they both are, and they are both different, according to the way in which they are.[19]

Therefore, as Alison Milbank points out:

> The result of this analogical way of thinking is a world that offers a network of analogies consisting of unity with difference, and consequently an infinite opportunity for paradox. Indeed the reader of a paradox is presented with the difference between two things, and seeks for that which unites them—their relation. This relation takes him or her back beyond the two contrasted things to their cause, which is God.[20]

God, the fullness of being, is the source of all beings, who participate in the divine being. Milbank goes on to point out that, because all being is analogical, all attempts to systematize thought will have to be content to wrestle with paradoxes.[21] She quotes Kenner, according to whom the rationality that Aquinas displays in the *Summa* comes about because he wishes to "resolve the paradox created by a previous imperfect solution,"[22] and who also points out that for Chesterton and Aquinas, "the world is a baffling place, incapable of being enmeshed in a phrase or a formula."[23]

What exactly is paradox? Looking at the etymological roots, *The Concise Oxford Dictionary of Current English*[24] states that *para* is a Greek word denoting something that protects, wards off, or acts against or contrary to; and *doxa* is a Greek word for common opinion or belief. Hence a paradox is a belief that

---

[19] *Paradox in Chesterton*, 30.

[20] *Chesterton and Tolkien as Theologians: The Fantasy of the Real*, 91.

[21] Ibid., 91-92.

[22] Ibid, 92.

[23] Hugh Kenner, *op. cit.*, 21.

[24] 741-2.

is remarkable, uncommon, or unexpected, going against the common opinion, or a "seemingly absurd though perhaps actually well-founded statement." Dale Ahlquist notes a second meaning, which "is the notion of the proposition that seems to contradict itself: two statements that are both true, but absolutely contradict one another."[25] Both the Judeo-Christian scriptures and the Chestertonian literary corpus are full of paradox. "A Virgin shall give birth."[26] "Blessed are those who are persecuted."[27] "[T]he self is more distant than any star."[28] "The mere pursuit of health always leads to something unhealthy."[29]

Much has been written both for and against Chesterton's abundant use of paradox. Very early on in his career he was criticized for what seemed to some as merely an unnecessary and extravagant verbal fireworks display. "Paradox ought to be used like onions to season the salad. Mr. Chesterton's salad is all onions. Paradox has been defined as 'truth standing on her head to attract attention.' Mr. Chesterton makes truth cut her throat to attract attention."[30]

It is certainly true that for many Victorians, Gilbert and Sullivan among them,[31] paradox was a clever game in which the participating speakers tried to outdo each other in the ostentatiousness of their choice of words, with little regard for the truth or otherwise of what was being expressed. Perhaps

---

[25] *Common Sense 101: Lessons from G. K. Chesterton*, 44.

[26] Isaiah 7:14.

[27] Matthew 5:11.

[28] *Orthodoxy*, 257.

[29] Ibid., 280.

[30] Cited in M. Ward, *GKC*, 113.

[31] See *Pirates of Penzance*, 1879, "A paradox, a paradox, a most ingenious paradox,," http://math.boisestate.edu/gas/pirates/web_op/pirates18.html [last accessed 17th January 2012].

the most famous players of this game were Oscar Wilde and the Decadents, who have been described by Aidan Nichol as "hierophants of a shimmering wit divorced from truth by the simple declaration 'art for art's sake.'"

Nichols says that, "Association with the decadents...did nothing to assist Chesterton's reputation as a serious philosopher, much less as a theologian."[32] Although Chesterton himself was aware of the risks of excessive use of paradox—"Critics were almost entirely complimentary to what they were pleased to call my brilliant paradoxes; until they discovered I really meant what I said"[33]—Chesterton had little time for the showmanship of Wilde and his companions. "I know of nothing so contemptible as a mere paradox; a mere ingenious defence of the indefensible...It is as easy as lying because it is lying."[34] The usefulness of rhetorical paradox lay not in its ability to display one's intelligence, but in its ability to express metaphysical paradox, which was something fundamental to the nature of reality.

It is entirely understandable, of course, that Chesterton's style of writing is not to everyone's taste. His customary forms of expression, which worked well in the world of journalistic headlines, may appear to some a little repetitive and tiresome if one reads him for any length of time. Chesterton was forever trying to get at the foundations or heart of things, and so he has a tendency to cut away the inessential. However, he always lets things be what they are, in all their glorious complexity. While it is true that he often used paradox as a tool to turn the status quo upside down with a few choice words—which is an

---

[32] G. K. Chesterton: Theologian, 89-90.

[33] Autobiography, 180.

[34] Orthodoxy, 213.

ideal tactic for a journalist with limited column inches. He believed that a truth was no less true or rational merely because it was expressed in a form that was more poetic than prosaic. Unlike some users of rhetorical paradox, Chesterton did not wish to show off with his words; he wished to use them to communicate meaning in a culture in which the masses were being bombarded by ideas. If his choice of expression could convey that meaning more strikingly, so much the better.

If Chesterton did not always succeed in convincing his addressees that his words were not mere rhetoric, he did manage to communicate the complexity, mystery, and indeed the paradoxical nature of the cosmos itself. As Maisie Ward explains, for Chesterton paradox was more than mere literary preference (which is rhetorical paradox); it was something that had to be used because it reflected the analogical nature of reality itself: "...it is God, not I, should have the credit for it."[35] This is metaphysical paradox.

For Chesterton, "Thinking means connecting things"[36] or, as Kierkegaard puts it, "The requirement of existence [is] to put things together," and the real difficulty of human existence "consists precisely in putting differences together."[37] As the latter part of Kierkegaard's observations suggests, sometimes when we are trying to make connections in life, things don't connect. There is a contradiction, a discontinuity, or an opposition. Instead of trying to remove the contradiction, "It is only the Mystic, the man who accepts the contradictions who can laugh and walk easily through the world."[38] This man:

---

[35] M. Ward, *GKC*, 113.

[36] *Orthodoxy*, 238.

[37] Soren Kierkegaard, *Concluding Unscientific Postscript*, 473, 448-449.

[38] G. K. Chesterton, *The Blatchford Controversies*, 384.

...has always cared for truth more than consistency. If he saw two truths that seemed to contradict each other, he would take the two truths and the contradiction along with them. His spiritual sight is stereoscopic, like his physical sight; he sees two different pictures at once, and yet sees all the better for that...It is exactly this balance of apparent contradictions that has been the whole buoyancy of the healthy man. The whole secret of mysticism is this: that man can understand everything by the help of what he does not understand. The morbid logician seeks to make everything lucid, and succeeds only in making everything mysterious. The mystic allows one thing to be mysterious and everything else becomes lucid.[39]

By allowing reality to be itself, to receive and respect its complexity, by not trying to master or manipulate it, we are more able to perceive the truth about reality. Again we are reminded here of Kierkegaard, who says that truth can be a stumbling block for the merely clever, because of its paradoxical nature.[40] Chesterton's use of paradox, then, is in harmony with what Kenner and Milbank perceive about systematic thinking: it was a way of expressing a neglected or under-emphasized truth or part of a truth.

What it amounted to roughly was this: paradox must be of the nature of things because of God's infinity and the limitations of the world and of man's mind. To us limited beings God can express His idea only in fragments. We can bring together apparent contradictions in those fragments whereby a greater truth is suggested. If we do this in a sudden or incongruous manner we startle the unprepared and arouse the cry of paradox. But if we will not do it, we shall miss a great deal of truth.[41]

---

[39] *Orthodoxy*, 230-1.

[40] *Concluding Unscientific Postscript*, 203-4.

[41] M. Ward, *Gilbert Keith Chesterton*, Harmondsworth: Penguin, 1958, 113. In my opinion there are links here with Bernard Lonergan's epistemological-metaphysical notions of higher and lower viewpoints, which may be worth fuller exploration. See *Insight*, 13-19, and *Method in Theology*, 288.

For Chesterton, then, as for Kierkegaard before him, the sane mind that approximates to the truth is the one that is humble enough to grasp that reality is a complex mystery which can only be disclosed to limited human capacities very gradually. We recall from our last chapter that he sees truth as a condition of the soul and something that involves us in a quest, like an adventurer setting out with map, compass, and food and drink in a rucksack. Truth is paradoxical, utterly strange, such that "Whatever may be the meaning of faith, it must always mean a certainty about something we cannot prove."[42] The things that make humans human and human life worth living require that "a man must take what is called a leap in the dark, as he does when he is married or when he dies, or when he is born, or when he does almost anything else that is important."[43]

In the sixth chapter of *Orthodoxy*, entitled "The Paradoxes of Christianity," Chesterton discusses further the connection between sanity and the acceptance of paradox. He notes the ability of the Church to hold in tension the merits of what appear to be opposites. Noting the criticisms that Christianity drew from its detractors, Chesterton wondered how it could be that a single church, movement, or philosophy could contain in itself so many mutually contradictory sources of contention:

> For not only (as I understood) had Christianity the most flaming vic-
> es, but it had apparently a mystical talent for combining vices which
> seemed inconsistent with each other. It was attacked on all sides and
> for all contradictory reasons. No sooner had one rationalist demon-
> strated that it was too far to the east than another demonstrated with
> equal clearness that it was much too far to the west. No sooner had
> my indignation died down at its angular and aggressive squareness

---

[42] *Heretics*, 127.

[43] *A Handful of Authors*, 29.

than I was called up again to notice and condemn its enervating and sensual roundness.[44]

Some people criticized the Christian creed for being too morbid and miserable, others for being too happy in the face of life's hardships. One person called it a nightmare, another described it as a fool's paradise. One person lamented that the Church had contempt for women's intellect, while another sneered that only women went to Church. One charge was that the Church was too ascetical, another that it was too full of pomp and ritual:

This puzzled me; the charges seemed inconsistent. Christianity could not at once be the black mask on a white world, and also the white mask on a black world. The state of the Christian could not be at once so comfortable that he was a coward to cling to it, and so uncomfortable that he was a fool to stand it… It looked not so much as if Christianity was bad enough to include any vices, but rather as if any stick was good enough to beat Christianity with.[45]

In his own spiritual and intellectual journey, Chesterton saw no need to rush either to affirm or deny the contradictory charges made against Christianity. However he did begin to wonder if the problem might lie, not with Christianity, but with its opponents:

And then in a quiet hour a strange thought struck me like a still thunderbolt. There had suddenly come into my mind another explanation. Suppose we heard an unknown man spoken of by many men. Suppose we were puzzled to hear that some men said he was too tall and some too short; some objected to his fatness, some lamented his leanness; some thought him too dark, and some too fair. One explanation (as has been already admitted) would be that he might be an odd shape. But there is another explanation. He might be the right shape. Outrageously tall men might feel him to be short. Very short men might feel him to be tall. Old bucks who are growing

---

stout might consider him insufficiently filled out; old beaux who were growing thin might feel that he expanded beyond the narrow lines of elegance…Perhaps (in short) this extraordinary thing is really the ordinary thing; at least the normal thing, the center. Perhaps, after all, it is Christianity that is sane and all its critics that are mad—in various ways.[46]

While he praises here the Church's sanity, Chesterton knew that criticism of the Church is sometimes justifiable. History serves as a perennial reminder that the Church must never be thought of as the Kingdom fully present, and that the Church must be *ecclesia semper reformanda*, and therefore open to critique. So it might be pertinent to add a qualification here: although the Church's theology can indeed on occasion be narrow and monochromatic, nevertheless Chesterton asserts that when it is at its best, when it is being faithful to its own mission to teach the truth, the Church fully allows reality to speak in all its broad, glorious, and multi-colored complexity.

The Church, then, is not meant to be some drab, boring, sensible, temperate, respectable, middle of the road mean to all positions. Rather, the Church is that reality which is able to bring together the insights and truths of those positions that appear to be opposites and to make sense out of them. The Church allows opposites to be what they are in themselves, but also shows how they can coexist, finding a balance that leads to sanity. It finds a way of combining the passion of opposing positions without either contradicting its own message or compromising the passion:

All sane men can see that sanity is some kind of equilibrium; that one may be mad and eat too much, or mad and eat too little. Some moderns have indeed appeared with vague versions of progress and

---

[46] Ibid., 294-5.

evolution which seeks to destroy the *meson* or balance of Aristotle.[47]
They seem to suggest that we are meant to starve progressively, or to
go on eating larger and larger breakfasts every morning for ever. But
the great truism of the *meson* remains for all thinking men, and these
people have not upset any balance except their own. But granted
that we have all to keep a balance, the real interest comes in with
the question of how that balance can be kept. That was the problem
which Paganism tried to solve: that was the problem which I think
Christianity solved and solved in a very strange way.[48]

For example, a Christian is able to be proud of being the greatest of all creatures, while also being ashamed at falling from
the greatness of that position as the only creature that sins. As
a creature of the Creator, the Christian can agree with Hamlet
who, as we have already seen, writes: "How infinite in faculty...
this quintessence of dust." The human being is a child of God,
and so everything; yet completely dependent on God, and so
by her own merits she is utterly nothing. Christian paradox
allows two conflicting truths to be held at full strength.

This paradox is not something that belongs to Christianity
as a possession but, rather, Christianity merely reflects the
paradoxical nature of reality. Christianity's ability to perceive
paradox at the heart of reality permits human beings to avoid
the excesses of extreme pride and extreme self-loathing, while
still retaining the passionate feelings of elation at being a
child of God and shame at being a rebellious child of God. If
Aristotle's golden mean thought that virtue was to be found
in balance, Christianity said that the equilibrium was to be
found in the conflict born of two apparently contradictory
passions:

---

[47] A reference to the Aristotelian notion of the golden mean in virtue ethics: see *Nicomachean Ethics* II, 6-7.

[48] *Orthodoxy*, 296-7.

Courage is almost a contradiction in terms. It means a strong desire to live taking the form of a readiness to die. "He that will lose his life, the same shall save it," is not a piece of mysticism for saints and heroes. It is a piece of everyday advice for sailors or mountaineers. It might be printed in an Alpine guide or a drill book. This paradox is the whole principle of courage; even of quite earthly or quite brutal courage. A man cut off by the sea may save his life if he will risk it on the precipice. He can only get away from death by continually stepping within an inch of it. A soldier surrounded by enemies, if he is to cut his way out, needs to combine a strong desire for living with a strange carelessness about dying.[49]

Similarly, whereas a merely rational approach hints that it might be acceptable to forgive a person for his moderate transgressions against others, Christianity insists that all sin—great, small, politically incorrect or otherwise—must be detested, but the sinner must be loved.

Chesterton points out that the criticisms of the Christian creed contain some truth, but that they fall short as full explanations of the ultimate truth of things because they fail to allow for paradox. They are unable to grasp the truth in the position that stands opposite to their own:

Thus, the double charges of the secularists, though throwing nothing but darkness and confusion on themselves, throw a real light on the faith. It is true that the historic Church has at once recognized celibacy and recognized the family; has at once (if one may put it so) been fiercely for having children and fiercely for not having children. It has kept them side by side like two strong colours, red and white, like the red and white upon the shield of St. George. It has always had a healthy hatred of pink. It hates that combination of two colours which is the feeble expedient of the philosophers. It hates that evolution of black into white which is tantamount to a dirty grey. In fact, the whole theory of the Church on virginity might be symbolized in the statement that white is a colour: not merely the absence of a colour. All that I am urging here can be expressed by

---

[49] Ibid., 297.

saying that Christianity sought in most of these cases to keep two colours coexistent but pure.[50]

For Chesterton, paradox is not a feeble compromise between two opposing ideas, a middle ground that is neither one nor the other, a pink that is neither red nor white. Nor is it a synthesis, or sheer contradiction or oxymoron, although, as Ahlquist points out, these (and many compromises, hybrids, or utterances of nonsense) "point to the paradox, because each of these others attempts to deal with contradiction, and contradiction is the essence of the paradox."[51] Indeed, for Chesterton, "...by paradox we mean the truth inherent in a contradiction...[in a paradox] the two opposite cords of truth become entangled in an inextricable knot...[a] knot which ties safely together the whole bundle of human life."[52] This ability to let opposites coexist is seen by Chesterton as characteristic of the prophet who says that the lion will lie down with the lamb. Although it is often assumed that this meant that the lion would become lamb-like,

> ...that is brutal annexation and imperialism on the part of the lamb. That is simply the lamb absorbing the lion instead of the lion eating the lamb. The real problem is—Can the lion lie down with the lamb and still retain his royal ferocity? That is the problem the Church attempted; that is the miracle she achieved.[53]

The perspicacity that discerns paradox at the heart of things, which allows opposites to exist together at full strength, but also to contribute to an equilibrium of sanity, is what Chesterton refers to in the sixth chapter of *Orthodoxy* as:

---

[50] Ibid., 301-2.

[51] *Common Sense 101*, 47.

[52] *George Bernard Shaw*, 173-7.

[53] *Orthodoxy*, 303.

...guessing the hidden eccentricities of life. This is knowing that a man's heart is to the left and not in the middle. This is knowing not only that the earth is round, but knowing exactly where it is flat. Christian doctrine detected the oddities of life. It not only discovered the law, but it foresaw the exceptions. Those underrate Christianity who say that it discovered mercy; any one might discover mercy. In fact everyone did. But to discover a plan for being merciful and also severe—that was to anticipate a strange need of human nature.[54]

Chesterton had a huge admiration for some of the elements of pagan antiquity and applauded the Aristotelian golden mean as an attempt to achieve human balance and health. Chesterton believed that Christianity perfected this attempt, in that Christianity's ability to allow for the paradox of letting opposites coexist liberates human beings from the tendency of pagan ethics to make human living a long, dull, passionless process of calculation. Christianity (when at its best) is meant to set passions free and limit them only inasmuch as they threaten to destroy the healthy balance of human sanity. Opposites are meant to create a harmonious balance: man and woman in the sacramental union of marriage; positive and negative forces forming the nucleus of the atom; reward and sanction contributing to the rounded education of the child; light and darkness helping the human eye to see; every embrace containing some element of loneliness, or some sense of distance or separation from the person that one is embracing. This balance at the heart of a healthy life is what Chesterton calls Christian orthodoxy.

> This was the big fact about Christian ethics; the discovery of the new balance. Paganism had been like a pillar of marble, upright because proportioned with symmetry. Christianity was like a huge and ragged and romantic rock, which, though it sways on its pedestal at a touch, yet, because its exaggerated excrescences exactly balance each other,

---

[54] Ibid., 303.

is enthroned there for a thousand years. In a Gothic cathedral the columns were all different, but they were all necessary. Every support seemed an accidental and fantastic support; every buttress was a flying buttress. So in Christendom apparent accidents balanced.[55]

The similarities and dissimilarities between the pagan and Christian worldviews are an important Chestertonian theme, as we shall see shortly. But when Chesterton writes that the Catholic Church is "the trysting place of all the truths in the world,"[56] perhaps one of the things that are implicit in this is that the Church's theology and apologetics need to be roomy enough to hold in tension all the paradoxes that reveal this multi-faceted thing we know as reality. It is not that we cannot make definite claims about truth, but that the truth will always be richer and more paradoxical than our limited minds can grasp at given moments in our journey. As noted earlier, the Church defined dogmatically[57] at Lateran IV in 1215 that all of our theological images and words are more inadequate than adequate. So we have to be humble in our theological language and images and open to anything that could refine and add to our theology and our apologetics, whatever its source.

Chesterton's own explorations in the world of pagan antiquity taught him to savor what he found there, to delight in its many good things, to puzzle long and hard while there over the questions that arose in his mind (especially about that world's inability to satisfy him) and to journey with openness and honesty wherever his questions took him. Chesterton invites all who would seek the face of the God of Christian revelation

---

[55] Ibid.

[56] *Why I Am a Catholic, Collected Works* Vol. 3, 132.

[57] "...no similarity can be said to hold between Creator and creature which does not imply a greater dissimilarity between the two." (DS806) (translation mine)

to remain open to being surprised by each other's insights: a fundamental requirement for exploring reality and truth is a readiness both to teach and to learn. He also invites them to enjoy and stay with their questions, to let these become real questions that are important to them, before searching for answers within the long tradition of theological reflection that has sought to translate God's self-revelation for the concrete here-and-now.

---

3. WHEN THE PART IS GREATER THAN THE WHOLE: *Chesterton and False Gods*

In his Notebook, started in 1894 and added to periodically over the course of the next five years, Chesterton wrote, "Woe unto them that keep a God like a silk hat, that believe not in God, but in a God."[58] Another entry says, "There is one kind of infidelity blacker than all infidelities/worse than any blow of secularist, pessimist, atheist/it is that of those persons who regard God as an old institution."[59] These quotes seem to suggest that the youthful Chesterton was aware of a common feature of human existence, even among religious people: the tendency to fashion false gods or idols.

The lessons of history teach us that every heresy is simply a truth only half-spoken; it is a part of the truth that has been allowed to become so big and important that it distorts a fuller picture of the truth. A heresy prevents those who believe it from perceiving other truths that are necessary for a fuller appreciation of the overall truth. Too much weight placed on one part of the truth has resulted in an imbalance. Therefore,

---

[58] Ward, *GKC*, 45.

[59] Ibid., 49.

in the context of discussing the breadth of Chesterton's thought and its emphasis on the need for equilibrium if one is to grasp the paradoxical truths of reality, it seems appropriate to say a brief word about the encounter with sub-Christian gods as one makes the journey toward faith in the God who is revealed in Christ, since false gods can often be the result of theological imbalance.

Chesterton wrote:

> Madness is a preference for the symbol over that which it represents. The most obvious example is the religious maniac, in whom the worship of Christianity involves the negation of all those ideas of integrity and mercy for which Christianity stands…This is the great sin of idolatry, against which religion has so constantly warned us.[60]

Here Chesterton is reminding us that one of the most common signs that a person has a false god is when John's statement that "God is love"[61] is not the dominant hermeneutic in that person's religious thinking. "A religion is dead when it has ceased to dwell on the positive and happy side of its visions, and thinks only of the stern or punitive side."[62] When a hypersensitive, overly scrupulous conscience or controlling voice is forever reminding us not to break God's rules, where God is a grumpy old grandfather figure who sulks at our moral failures, then we have forgotten John's other reminder that, "In love there is no room for fear, but perfect love drives out fear."[63] When the voice that speaks to us deep in our heart is not a stiller, calmer, less shrill, less hysterical, and less controlling voice, coaxing even

---

[60] "Lunacy and Letters," *Lunacy and Letters*, cited in *TTFT*, 229.

[61] 1 John 4:8.

[62] "Nothing but Negative Morality," *Illustrated London News*, 1st October 1932, *Collected Works* Vol. 36, 152.

[63] 1 John 4:18.

as it challenges us, then it is a sub-Christian voice. As we shall explore more fully later in this chapter, the Christian God is the God who does not stop loving us because of the countless false starts we make in life, who invites us to relish our place in the unfolding story of the cosmos and to enjoy co-creating our role in that romance.

It would be a sub-Christian mistake of the equal and opposite kind, however, to think of God as some sort of senile old man who absent-mindedly smiles on us whatever we do with our life. If the Christian is sure that God is always on our side and always sure of God's love, she also remembers that "Love is not blind... Love is bound; and the more it is bound the less it is blind."[64] Because we share this cosmos with other creatures, there is a moral law written into reality. "There is no such thing as a condition of complete emancipation...In moral matters...there is no lawlessness, there is only a free choice between limitations."[65]

As we shall see, a truly Christian understanding of God means accepting him as the Creator who sets our limits as creatures. We are to share the world with our fellow creatures, and to live out that condition of creatureliness with gratitude and a spirit of receptivity, not with a manipulative, grasping and ungrateful spirit. The grateful spirit will be evident from the way we live: we are invited by the Christian God to enjoy scenery and sunsets, to be attentive to the way we speak, not to possess others as means to our own ends, to pour out our lives for others, and to live out an authentically human existence for the sake of the happiness of others, thereby ensuring our own deepest joy as a by-product.

---

[64] *Orthodoxy*, 274.

[65] "The Fallacy of Freedom," *Daily News*, 21st December 1905, http://www.personal.reading. ac.uk/~spsolley/GKC/Chesterton_selections.html#fallacy [last accessed 22nd January 2012].

In *Orthodoxy* Chesterton says, "The perfect happiness of men on the earth (if it ever comes) will not be a flat and solid thing, like the satisfaction of animals. It will be an exact and perilous balance; like that of a desperate romance."[66] Health, sanity, and happiness are a complex business in a complex world. Chesterton notes that:

> The modern world is not evil; in some ways the modern world is far too good. It is full of wild and wasted virtues. When a religious scheme is shattered (as Christianity was shattered at the Reformation), it is not merely the vices that are let loose. The vices are, indeed, let loose, and they wander and do damage. But the virtues are let loose also; and the virtues wander more wildly, and the virtues do more terrible damage. The modern world is full of the old Christian virtues gone mad. The virtues have gone mad because they have been isolated from each other and are wandering alone. Thus some scientists care for truth; and their truth is pitiless. Thus some humanitarians only care for pity; and their pity (I am sorry to say) is often untruthful.[67]

Here we note that Chesterton sees and praises all that is good and virtuous in the cultural mindset of his day, while at the same time noting that these virtues have become separated and therefore unbalanced because the vision that glued them together has become blurred. We have already noted that balance is vital if we are to appreciate as much as possible the truths of a paradoxical world, and we have commented on how all theological words and images cannot do justice to the reality of God. It would seem, then, that equilibrium is equally required if we are not fall into some unworthy image of God:

> ...Idolatry exists wherever the thing which originally gave us happiness becomes at last more important than happiness itself...This is idolatry: the preference for the incidental good over the eternal

---

[66] *Orthodoxy*, 318.

[67] *Orthodoxy*, 233.

good which it symbolizes. It is the employment of one example of the everlasting goodness to confound the validity of a thousand other examples. It is the elementary mathematical and moral heresy that the part is greater than the whole.[68]

A Christian vision of God never prefers truth to compassion, or compassion to truth, but sees that the fact that God is love means that both are necessary components of a healthy human and Christian existence; similarly, forgiveness and moral challenge are both gifts of the living God, and other pairs of what seem to be opposite goods or values can be combined paradoxically to reveal something of the face of God in a person's life: the aesthetic with poverty or simplicity of lifestyle; the intellectual with the affective; the beauty and energy of the young disciple with the wisdom and discipline of the elder; institutional structure with prophecy; the sense of identity that comes from belonging to one's group with the need to reach out beyond one's group to those who are different; personal morality and social justice. To prefer one good over another is to bow down before a false god; it is to tame the living God and to turn him into a "silk hat" or "old institution," an idol that is no greater than our own shrunken imagination. Even the things of religion—theology, liturgy, pastoral programs, social justice causes, moral causes, all of which are good things in themselves—are themselves only means to the end of deeper relationship with God. When they become anything other than that (for example the means to the end of pursuing a career, or fame, or an ecclesial or academic promotion), then we are bowing down before a false god in the name of the living God.

In the final section of his book on Shaw, Chesterton examines

---

[68] "Lunacy and Letters," *Lunacy and Letters*, cited in *TTFT*, 229.

the agnostic philosophy of his friend and criticizes him for an impoverished understanding of the very notion of God:

> I must frankly say that Bernard Shaw always seems to me to use the word God not only without any idea of what it means, but without one moment's thought about what it could possibly mean. He said to some atheist, "Never believe in a God that you cannot improve on." The atheist (being a sound theologian) naturally replied that one should not believe in a God whom one could improve on; as that would show that he was not God. In the same style in *Major Barbara* the heroine ends by suggesting that she will serve God without personal hope, so that she may owe nothing to God and He owe everything to her. It does not seem to strike her that if God owes everything to her He is not God. These things affect me merely as tedious perversions of a phrase. It is as if you said, "I will never have a father unless I have begotten him."[69]

Chapter IV examines this passage further to see what value it holds for the apologist who seeks to understand the various types of atheism that may be found in any culture. In the present chapter we note two sub-Christian notions of divinity with which Shaw seems to be operating in Chesterton's view. Firstly, the god rejected by Shaw is a divinity who is not as intelligent as human beings. He does not really grasp the complexity of the cosmos. Shaw does not give God credit for being as bright as he himself is.

Secondly, Major Barbara's is a Promethean divinity, possibly the most common false god worshipped by believers and rejected by unbelievers: a god who is threatened by and in competition with human beings. This divinity is petty and threatened by human intelligence, powers, and creativity, and he does not permit us to steal his fire. The heroine of Major Barbara rebels against the notion of a God who would demand that she recognize her indebtedness to Him. Such a divine being could

---

[69] Cited in *TTFT*, 191-2.

only be a tyrant and stand in opposition to human dignity. The God that many believers place their faith in is often this type of threatened and defensive God.

The temptation to bow down before idols of our own making is an abiding danger due to our tendency to forget the ineffability of God. In one of his notebooks Newman reminds us that all of our thoughts and imaginative constructs about God have to be necessarily provisional, if we are to avoid idolatry:

> We can only speak of Him, whom we reason about but have not seen, in the terms of our experience. When we reflect on Him and put into words our thoughts about Him, we are forced to transfer to a new meaning ready-made words, which primarily belong to objects of time and place. We are aware, while we do so, that they are inadequate. We can only remedy their insufficiency by confessing it. We can do no more than put ourselves on the guard as to our own proceeding, and protest against it, while we do adhere to it. We can only set right one error of expression by another. By this method of antagonism we steady our minds, not so as to reach their object, but to point them in the right direction; as in an algebraical process we might add and subtract in series, approximating little by little, by saying and unsaying, to a positive result.[70]

Nicholas Lash agrees with Newman that all the things we say of God need to be correctively unsaid, that "speaking appropriately of God is well nigh impossible" and yet, "on the other hand...learning to speak appropriately of God is a not unimportant part of what it is to learn to be a creature."[71] The truly Christian imagination knows, therefore, that although we can never fully imagine or express God, we must nevertheless always endeavor to do so, and with all of the means at our disposal. This, I maintain, is what Chesterton was seeking to do when he constantly encouraged others to advert to the

---

[70] *The Theological Papers of John Henry Newman on Faith and Certainty*, 102.

[71] *Theology for Pilgrims*, 8.

wonders of the cosmos and to allow reality to speak in all its glorious paradox.

4. TEN THOUSAND REASONS: *the Breadth of Chesterton*

Since his vision of reality is that of a glorious, paradoxical, multicolored and complex gift from the Creator, Chesterton is not easily labeled as a religious thinker. As we shall explore at greater length in the next chapter, he saw the Church at its best as a living tradition which conserves and embodies truth and love, being open to embracing all that is good, true and beautiful in the world, learning from the world, as well as teaching it, and allowing its core teachings to develop over the centuries. "To become a Catholic is not to leave off thinking, but to learn how to think. It is so in exactly the same sense in which to recover from palsy is not to leave off moving but to learn how to move."[72] That is why Chesterton himself has an outlook that is broad, as well as deep.

Chesterton said, "A man is not really convinced of a philosophic theory when he finds that something proves it. He is only really convinced when he finds that everything proves it."[73] That does not make offering an apologetics for faith easy because, as we see from the epigraph at the beginning of this chapter, defending faith may mean talking about anything or everything. As far as Chesterton was concerned, nothing is irrelevant to Christian faith, and so a discussion of anything in the cosmos may lead to God if conducted honestly and with integrity:

---

[72] *The Catholic Church and Conversion, Collected Works* Vol. 3, 106.

[73] *Orthodoxy*, 287.

> The difficulty of explaining why I am a Catholic is that there are ten thousand reasons all amounting to one reason: that Catholicism is true. I could write ten thousand separate sentences each beginning with the words, "The Catholic Church is the only thing that..."[74]

Of these ten thousand reasons, Chesterton knew that many of them were the full flourishing of the various elements of truth, goodness, and beauty that he had first come across in pagan antiquity. Chesterton's education as a child and an adolescent had put him in touch with the classical Greco-Roman world, and he knew the many wonders and beauties of paganism. "I think I am the sort of man who came to Christ from Pan and Dionysus and not from Luther or Laud; that the conversion I understand is that of the pagan and not the Puritan."[75] Although eventually Chesterton perceived that the inordinate expressions of paganism did not ultimately serve human dignity, the poetry of Walt Whitman had initially nourished Chesterton's fascination with the pagan worship of the world.

Chesterton always sought to keep the positive elements of paganism alive in people's minds, while at the same time tirelessly pointing out that paganism was incomplete as an interpretation of the world. If Chesterton was eventually able to write that "Pagans were wiser than paganism; that is why the pagans became Christians,"[76] he nevertheless believed that pagans were to some degree wise; if he reminded an increasingly pagan 1920s Western culture that "Neo-pagans have sometimes forgotten, when they set out to do everything that the old pagans did, that the final thing that the old pagans did was

---

[74] *The Thing: Why I Am a Catholic*, 127.

[75] *The Catholic Church and Conversion*, 108.

[76] *Saint Francis of Assisi*, 21.

to get christened,"[77] he also told the world that there was plenty
to be found in the ancient world that would not be to the taste
of the neo-pagans:

> The New Paganism is no longer new, and it never at any time bore the
> smallest resemblance to Paganism…The term "pagan" is continually
> used in fiction and light literature as meaning a man without any reli-
> gion whereas a pagan was generally a man with about half a dozen…
> Pagans are depicted as above all things inebriate and lawless, whereas
> they were above all things reasonable and respectable.[78]

We shall see in our next chapter that Chesterton perceived the
entry of the figure of Christ into human history as a unique
irruption that changed forever the relationship between a humanity that had painstakingly searched for meaning, truth,
goodness, and beauty, and the God who is the source and fullness of all these things; however, in this present chapter we shall
be reminded by Chesterton that it was the same Holy Spirit—
binding Father and Eternal Word—who was the seed of Christ's
conception in a woman's womb who was also at work sowing
seeds of the Word in the hearts and minds of human beings
long before the figure of Christ came into the world. Though
Christianity is the corrective for the excesses of paganism, the
path of Chesterton's life led to the Church because he eventually
saw, like Francis and Aquinas before him, that the Church was
the trysting place of all truths, and was broad enough to let
pagan truths flourish and be perfected.

Chesterton, therefore, had no time for a colorless, puritanical type of Christianity that dismissed paganism simply because it was pagan. "The primary fact about Christianity and

---

[77] "The Return of the Pagan Gods," *Illustrated London News*, 20th March 1926, *Collected Works*
Vol. 34, 64.

[78] *Heretics*, 122.

Paganism is that one came after the other."[79] Because of this temporal arrangement by divine providence, Chesterton saw the Christian creed as the fulfillment of the elements of the religious traditions of humanity throughout history:

> Nobody ever disputed that humanity was human before it was Christian; and no Church manufactured the legs with which men walked or danced, either in a pilgrimage or a ballet...What can really be maintained, so as to carry not a little conviction, is this: that where such a Church has existed it has preserved not only the processions but the dances; not only the cathedral but the carnival.[80]

Human beings had been searching for the divine long before Christianity's formal appearance on the planet, and the Church, when functioning at its best, has always honored that search and preserved from that deeply human quest all those elements of truth that were to find their fulfillment in Christ. In the face of Blatchford's criticisms of Christianity that it shared so much in common with paganism, Chesterton replied:

> Mr. Blatchford and his school point out that there are many myths parallel to the Christian story; that there were pagan Christs and Red Indian Incarnations, and Patagonian Crucifixions, for all I know or care. But does not Mr. Blatchford see on the other side of this fact? If the Christian God really made the human race, would not the human race tend to rumours and perversions of the Christian God? ...If we are so made that a Son of God must deliver us, is it odd that Patagonians should dream of a Son of God?[81]

We find echoes of this same insight three decades later in a conversation between J.R.R. Tolkien and C.S. Lewis, both of whom were highly influenced by Chesterton. Lewis tells how, on the eve of his conversion to theism, Tolkien explained to

---

[79] Ibid., 123.

[80] *The Superstition of Divorce*, CW Vol. 4, 264.

[81] *The Blatchford Controversies*, 375.

him that myths are not mere lies because human beings are not ultimately "liars." The human use of imagination to construct myths in order to express truth—mythopoeia—was part of the divine self-expression, the expression of truth, under the impulse of the Holy Spirit.[82] As God had helped human beings express truth in pagan imagery and poetry, so he had also done the same thing in Christianity, with the exception that in the latter he used "real people and actual history." For Lewis, then, what Christianity showed was how "Myth Became Fact."[83]

While acknowledging, then, the necessity of a critical and corrective faculty in the Church's stance toward paganism, Chesterton insists with Lewis that those who would set Christianity and paganism in total opposition to each other "miss the point" that was grasped by Francis of Assisi (inspired as he was by Ovid) and by Aquinas, who drew inspiration from Aristotle and other pagan thinkers.

> St. Francis was becoming more like Christ, and not merely more like Buddha, when he considered the lilies of the field or the fowls of the air; and St. Thomas was becoming more of a Christian, not merely more of an Aristotelian, when he insisted that God and the image of God had come in contact through matter with a material world. These saints were, in the most exact sense of the term, Humanists; because they were insisting on the immense importance of the human being in the theological scheme of things.[84]

Although he was not slow to critique the godless ideas and movements within a culture that led to human unhappiness, particularly for the voiceless and marginalized, Chesterton belonged to a Church that understood grace to perfect nature,

---

[82] See H. Carpenter, *The Inklings: C. S. Lewis, J. R. R. Tolkien, Charles Williams, and their Friends*, especially 33-45.

[83] C. S. Lewis, "Myth Became Fact," *God in the Dock: Essays in Theology*.

[84] *Saint Thomas Aquinas: The Dumb Ox*, 36.

and he knew how to recognize the *Logos spermatikos* in people who thought differently from him and in strange philosophies of life. He believed that Christian faith completes all natural human yearnings and that anything that is truly human and humanizing is not out of place in the Church, even if it will only receive its completion within Christianity. It was for this reason that he said that if he ever left the Church,

> The best I could hope for would be to wander away into the woods and become…a pagan, in the mood to cry out that some particular mountain peak or flowering fruit tree was sacred and a thing to be worshipped. That at least would be beginning all over again; but it would bring me back to the same problem in the end. If it was reasonable to have a sacred tree it was not unreasonable to have a sacred crucifix.[85]

Therefore the conversation between Church and culture has to be a constant dialogue. When, during the period of his engagement to Frances, Chesterton wrote to her that they should certainly "have bad things in our dwelling and make them good things. I shall have no objection to your having an occasional dragon to dinner, or a penitent Griffin to sleep in the spare bed,"[86] he could almost have been reminding the Church that it has nothing to fear from dialogue with any culture, pagan or otherwise. We shall see in our next chapter that Chesterton put this theory into practice in his own life, forging deep and lasting friendships with people such as Shaw and Wells, with whom he had very little in common in terms of philosophical outlook.

By lauding the attempts made by Francis, Aquinas, and other Christians to value the good in non-Christian positions and bring them to their fullness in Christ, Chesterton's thought shares some elements in common with that of Karl Rahner. Just

---

[85] *The Catholic Church and Conversion*, 108.

[86] Ward, *GKC*, 72.

as Chesterton had confessed in *Orthodoxy* that he read very little of the apologetics of his day, so unimpressive did he find it, so too Rahner felt that the language and preaching of the Church needed to be expressed with a new imagination and creativity in a new cultural situation. Rahner did not believe that the traditional content of faith had changed; however, he did believe that the context for making a decision to embrace Christian faith had changed.

The old, pre-modern culture in which the Christian faith had been born and established had collapsed and, in this new cultural milieu, if the Church merely sought to repeat old theological propositions, without in any way seeking to build bridges between these and the questions, searching, and hungers of the people who found themselves in this new cultural environment, the project was doomed to fail. As a man steeped in Catholic tradition, Rahner did not wish to weaken that tradition by his change of emphasis; on the contrary, he looked to strengthen it by putting it in conversation with the inner life of the people who were struggling to find a pathway to faith in a more complex and questioning world.

Rahner's approach to making sense of faith was more anthropological, starting "from below," even if he always maintained that this anthropological adventure was to be understood in the light of God's grace and, ultimately, in the light of the Gospel of Christ. He contended that the Holy Spirit, the gift of God, is already at work in the heart of every human being, and that there is therefore no such thing as an ungraced human being. God offers his grace, the self-communication of his love and mystery, to each and every human being, because God's will is that all people be saved. The Spirit is at work in human hearts, in the drama of everyday, concrete human existence in this world, such that human hearts are drawn toward the God who is the Creator, source, and final resting place of all people. Human hearts, by God's grace, are open and oriented to the divine mystery. Of course, the self-communication of God's love and mystery is also at work in what the Christian tradition calls salvation history: the long story of biblical revelation, which is the traditional path of Christian faith as communicated through the Scriptures, preaching, the sacraments, and all the other elements that constitute the life of the Church. This is the privileged and what Rahner terms the "categorical" road to faith.

There is, however, a more hidden, less public arena in which people live out a more implicit faith: for Rahner, each time a human being seeks love and truth, each time a woman faces trials with courage, each time a man obeys his conscience, then that person is open in self-transcendence. This can only happen because of the impulse of the Spirit of God: it is an experience of the grace of God at work, without the preaching and categories of the Christian Gospel having come into play. In this way the Holy Spirit can be at work in all persons and cultures long before any awareness of the Gospel has reached the person. When a person lives these experiences of self-transcendence, this is an "unthematic" or "transcendental" way of responding to God's self-communication, self-revelation or self-giving.

These unrecognized promptings of the Spirit of God, whereby people's lives encounter God in a usually unrecognized way, lead to an implicit, unthematic faith; whereas the recognized promptings of the Spirit of God in the life of the Church lead to an explicit, categorical faith. Another way of differentiating these two is to say that the transcendental is what is lived out implicitly and the categorical is what is expressed explicitly. Just as there is many a believer in God whose life can contradict their faith in God, there is many an atheist whose life can contradict their belief that there is no God.[87]

The phrase for which Rahner is perhaps most famous (or infamous, depending on the degree of appreciation one has for him or the phrase itself) is that of the "anonymous Christian":

> We prefer the terminology according to which a man is called an "anonymous Christian" who on the one hand has de facto accepted of his freedom this gracious self-offering on God's part through faith, hope and love, while on the other hand he is absolutely not yet a Christian at the social level (through baptism and membership of the Church) or in the sense of having consciously objectified his Christianity to himself in his own mind (by explicit Christian faith resulting from having hearkened to the explicit Christian message). We might therefore put it as follows: the "anonymous Christian" in our sense of the term is the pagan after the beginning of the Christian mission, who lives in the state of God's grace through faith, hope and love, yet who has no explicit knowledge of the fact that his life is orientated in grace-given salvation to Jesus Christ.[88]

Rahner saw that the use of the term was problematic and indicated that he would use another if a suitable one could be found, but he insisted on the reality that stood behind whichever form of words was used:

> ...the theory [of anonymous Christianity] arose from two facts: first, the possibility of supernatural salvation and of corresponding faith which must be granted to non-Christians, even if they never become Christian; and secondly, that salvation cannot be gained without reference to God and Christ, since it must in its origin, history and fulfilment be a theistic and Christian salvation.[89]

---

[87] For a more detailed investigation of this brief summary of Rahner's vision, see K. Rahner, "Chapter V: The History of Salvation and Revelation," *Foundations of Christian Faith*, New York: Crossroad, 1978, 138-175.

[88] *Theological Investigations* Vol. XIV, 283.

[89] *Theological Investigations* Vol. XVI, 218.

Rahner says that the reality of salvation for non-Christians can only be avoided if one adopts the pessimism of the past and consigns them to hell or limbo for eternity, or if one maintains that salvation is granted only in terms of human respectability without reference to God or Christ, or if one ignores the relationship between Christ and these people, which is to ignore the universal character of Christ's redemptive action. Essentially, Rahner is maintaining both God's universal salvific will and the identity of Christ as the only savior of all people. This means that all non-Christians who are saved must be saved by the grace of Christ at work in their lives without their realizing it; that is, by anonymous Christianity.

Rahner states that psychology—depth psychology and an analysis of human knowledge and freedom—teaches us that people are not always aware of the full implications of their thoughts and actions:

> Is it surprising that in certain circumstances the real situation and the basic self-understanding of a person may be grasped more clearly by someone else than by the person himself, who may in fact strongly resist the other's interpretation? This fact must be accepted; it cannot be avoided or explained away, since it frequently happens that one man interprets another differently from the latter's own reading of himself.[90]

Nicholas Lash recalls how J.R.R. Tolkien "pointed out to a mutual friend that many basic, fundamental English words which now sound like abstract nouns originally expressed relationship and activity. Truth, for example, is the same word as troth, a pledge or promise."[91] Noting that "the meaning of believe

---

[90] Ibid., 219.

[91] *Theology for Pilgrims*, 22.

has undergone a shift similar to that which…saw truth emerge from troth: a shift from pledge or promise to expression of opinion,"[92] he argues that "if a theist is someone who believes in God, and an atheist someone who does not, then there must be two kinds of theism and two kinds of atheism, corresponding to the two senses of belief."

Lash locates in these distinctions the ambiguities that Rahner has in mind, when Rahner writes that "theism can be the mask of a concealed atheism and vice versa, and…in this sense ultimately no one can say of himself whether he believes in God or not."[93] Lash, in harmony with Rahner's observations that another person may in actual fact have grasped the reality of our situation better than we have, and that this has consequences for the issue of belief in God, wisely perceives that, "We know what our opinions are, but none of us is so self-transparent as to know quite where, in fact, our hearts are set."[94]

The Second Vatican Council's Dogmatic Constitution on the Church, *Lumen gentium*, states that:

> Those also can attain to salvation who, through no fault of their own, do not know the Gospel of Christ or his Church, yet sincerely seek God and, moved by grace, strive by their deeds to do his will as it is known to them through the dictates of conscience.[95]

Rahner saw in this the possibility that all human beings, "whatever their externally verifiable attitudes and beliefs," could "live in a subjective state of freedom from serious sin."[96] While at

---

[92] Ibid., 34. See also W. C. Smith, *Faith and Belief*, Princeton, NJ: Princeton University Press, 1979.

[93] "Observations on the Doctrine of God in Catholic Dogmatics," *Theological Investigations* Vol. IX, 127-144; 140.

[94] Lash, *op. cit..*, 34.

[95] *Lumen gentium* 16.

[96] *Theological Investigations* Vol. XVI, 202.

no point compromising on the status of Christ as the only and universal savior, and the need therefore to proclaim the Gospel unceasingly, Rahner adopted an anthropologically maximalist position that comes close to Chesterton's embracing of much that is of value in paganism. By seeking to put the Church into dialogue with all that is good, true, and beautiful in a culture, Chesterton implicitly criticizes the puritanical critique of paganism. Chesterton calls the puritan's denunciation of pagan pleasures a mistake, albeit "a highly credible mistake,"[97] since it noted the debilitating effect on humanity of some of the inordinate expressions of those pleasures.

Chesterton sees puritans as heirs to the theological inheritance of the Manicheans, who thought of the physical world as evil. He sees the puritan as someone who would rather worship God in a barn than a cathedral, for the perverse reason that the cathedral is beautiful. The puritan can worship God with his brain, but must not worship God with his body, passions, habits or gestures. He is a "man whose mind had no holidays."[98]

Chesterton viewed Shaw's psychological puritanism as the main reason why he was far too serious about everything (he said that Shaw was "the most savagely serious man of his time," who even took his own jokes seriously) and, echoing the criticisms he had made four years previously in a newspaper column, Chesterton quotes Shaw's opinions about Shakespeare as evidence of this:

> His misunderstanding of Shakespeare arose largely from the fact that he is a Puritan, while Shakespeare was spiritually a Catholic. The former is always screwing himself up to see the truth; the latter is

---

[97] *William Blake*, 48.

[98] *George Bernard Shaw*, 33.

often content that truth is there. The Puritan is only strong enough to stiffen; the Catholic is strong enough to relax.[99]

Orthodox Christianity, when operating at its best, is able to relax, to enjoy the good things of this world, without seeing the constant need for censorship. Of course good things can be misused and abused by human beings, but the fault lies in the human being, not the thing, which in itself is good. Chesterton said that it made as much sense to talk of the "Problem of Drink—as if drink could be a problem"—as to talk of "the practice of wife-beating as the Problem of Pokers."[100] Paganism worships the good things of this world, while puritanism, reacting against paganism, avoids those good things; ironically, both miss the very point of good things, which is to point to their Creator.

In discerning the need for balance between the extremes of paganism and puritanism, we are reminded again of Chesterton's vivid image of:

> ...the thrilling romance of *Orthodoxy*. People have fallen into a foolish habit of speaking of orthodoxy as something heavy, humdrum, and safe. There never was anything so perilous or so exciting as orthodoxy. It was sanity: and to be sane is more dramatic than to be mad. It was the equilibrium of a man behind madly rushing horses, seeming to stoop this way and to sway that, yet in every attitude having the grace of statuary and the accuracy of arithmetic. The Church in its early days went fierce and fast with any warhorse; yet it is utterly unhistoric to say that she merely went mad along one idea, like a vulgar fanaticism. She swerved to left and right, so exactly as to avoid enormous obstacles.[101]

---

[99] Ibid., 98.

[100] "Humanitarianism and Strength," cited in R. Sparkes, *Prophet of Orthodoxy: The Wisdom of G. K. Chesterton*, 125.

[101] *Orthodoxy*, 305.

As we saw earlier in this chapter, in this strange and wonderful cosmos, human health and happiness depend on the equilibrium that comes from letting good things be in tension with each other. In our next chapter we shall see how Chesterton believes that, if such poise is to be maintained, there is a need for doctrine and a teaching Church, but for the remainder of this chapter we shall explore a few of those Chestertonian good things which need to be kept in tension, and all of which point to God. Chesterton believed that the Church does not ask the person that seeks to make sense of the cosmos to avoid the good things to be found in that cosmos in order to embrace Christianity. On the contrary, the Church "is a house with a hundred gates; and no two men enter at exactly the same angle" and Chesterton's own angle of entry "was at least as much Agnostic as Anglican."[102]

5. ORTHODOXY: *Starting Anywhere*

Maisie Ward describes how, "Gilbert said once he was willing to start anywhere and develop from anything the whole of his philosophy."[103] Chesterton's understanding of the link between the goodness of the world and the Church, between paganism and Christianity and between nature and grace, and his capacity to perceive the paradoxical nature of reality, meant that in his writing he was able to make the most astonishing connections between things and ideas. The issues he discusses in print and in debate are vast in number and bewilderingly different in nature. The very quality for which he praises Dickens's writing is something found in abundance in Chesterton himself:

---

[102] *The Catholic Church and Conversion*, 72.

[103] *GKC*, 196.

A man who deals in harmonies, who only matches stars with angels, or lambs with spring flowers, he indeed may be frivolous; for he is taking one mood at a time, and perhaps forgetting each mood as it passes. But a man who ventures to combine an angel and an octopus must have some serious view of the universe...the mark of the thoughtful writer is its apparent diversity.[104]

The myriad subjects on which Chesterton discourses, therefore, are all ways of accessing the central treasure trove of beliefs which he professes and which were expressed in *Orthodoxy*.

It is the over-abundant evidence of the concrete, everyday world and its simple, primordial lessons, its first principles, which led Chesterton to embrace Christianity:

It is very hard for a man to defend anything of which he is entirely convinced. It is comparatively easy when he is only partially convinced. He is partially convinced because he has found this or that proof of the thing, and he can expound it. But a man is not really convinced of a philosophic theory when he finds that something proves it. He is only really convinced when he finds that everything proves it. And the more converging reasons he finds pointing to this conviction, the more bewildered he is if asked suddenly to sum them up. Thus, if one asked an ordinary intelligent man, on the spur of the moment, "Why do you prefer civilization to savagery?" he would look wildly round at object after object, and would only be able to answer vaguely, "Why, there is that bookcase...and the coals in the coal-scuttle...and pianos...and policemen." The whole case for civilization is that the case for it is complex. It has done so many things. But that very multiplicity of proof which ought to make reply overwhelming makes reply impossible.[105]

Chesterton's work consisted in his pointing to innumerable bits of evidence, all of which converge to convince him of "the largest idea of all [which] is the idea of the fatherhood that

---

[104] Ibid., 134.

[105] *Orthodoxy*, 287.

makes the whole world one."[106] Chesterton's apologetics, there-fore, is a matter of cumulative convergences. The references in Orthodoxy to "the dumb certainties of experience"[107] and the nuggets of wisdom concerning first principles, along with his appraisal of the life and work of Charles Dickens, also support this interpretation:

> The thing that cannot be defined is the first thing; the primary fact. It is our arms and legs, our pots and pans, that are indefinable. The indefinable is the indisputable. The man next door is indefinable, because he is too actual to be defined. And there are some to whom spiritual things have the same fierce and practical proximity; some to whom God is too actual to be defined...The word that has no definition is the word that has no substitute...Precisely because the word is indefinable, the word is indispensable.[108]

Just as one can begin with any object and illustrate the reality of being, so one can select anything as a point of departure and end up arriving at the faith of the Church:

> There is, therefore, about all complete conviction a kind of huge helplessness. The belief is so big that it takes a long time to get it into action. And this hesitation chiefly arises, oddly enough, from an indifference about where one should begin. All roads lead to Rome; which is one reason why many people never get there. In the case of this defence of the Christian conviction I confess that I would as soon begin the argument with one thing as another; I would begin it with a turnip or a taximeter cab.[109]

He truly believes that one can start anywhere and find God; that "You cannot evade the issue of God, whether you talk about pigs or the binomial theory" and that "defending [Christianity]

---

[106] The Everlasting Man, 95.

[107] Orthodoxy, 221.

[108] Charles Dickens, 3.

[109] Orthodoxy, 287.

may mean talking about anything or everything."[110] However, remembering the days of his youthful agnosticism at the Slade, Chesterton was aware that several factors—the pressures of the surrounding culture which pushed him toward narcissism, a materialistic and scientistic epistemology, deep scepticism, solipsism, and the sense of restlessness and desperation that these caused in him—conspire to leave human beings with the feeling that ordinary, everyday experience is merely secular and has no reference to the transcendent at all. For this reason, though the evidence for God is everywhere, "it takes a long time to get [belief] into action." The things that seem ordinary and humdrum to us are the very things about which we are mistaken, for they point beyond themselves to the extraordinary and the special, but often we do not have the necessary disposition to see this.

Chesterton describes in Orthodoxy how his own spiritual journey, trying to make sense of the cosmos, had seen him go off course. He had been something akin to an Englishman landing on what he thought was a South Sea island, only to discover that it was England all along:

> I did, like all the other solemn little boys, try to be in advance of the age...And I found that I was eighteen hundred years behind it...When I fancied that I stood alone I really was in the ridiculous position of being backed up by all Christendom...I did try to found a heresy of my own; and when I had put the last touches to it, I discovered that it was orthodoxy.[111]

He discovered that the very things that we take for granted all along are the very things that will lead us home if we follow them:

---

[110] Daily News, 12th December 1903, cited in D. Ahlquist, *G. K. Chesterton: The Apostle of Common Sense*, 19.

[111] *Orthodoxy*, 214.

Whatever it is that we are all looking for, I fancy that it is really quite close…Always the kingdom of Heaven is "at hand"…so I for one should never be astonished if the next twist of a street led me to the heart of that maze in which all the mystics are lost.[112]

That is why he always writes with the intention of getting us to notice the everyday realities that surround us, with a spirit of wonder, awe, and gratitude.

When he wrote *Manalive*, which was published in 1912, four years after *Orthodoxy*, Chesterton's intention was to get those who read this novel to do precisely what they did when they read *Orthodoxy*: to look at common things in an uncommon way; to look at familiar things in such a way that they became unfamiliar. Just as Chesterton described himself in *Orthodoxy* as a man who set out on a voyage and ended up appreciating the ordinary in a totally new and wonder-filled way, so in *Manalive* the main character, Innocent Smith, often walks around his house in order to see his home regularly from a new angle, and also leaves his home in order to walk around the world and arrive back at home with new eyes that are full of appreciation for home. He regularly looks at his wife as if for the first time, aware that she, their home, all the things that they have in their life, and indeed life itself are all unmerited gifts, the proper response to which should be wonder, gratitude and respect. Innocent (but not naïve) is a name chosen to reflect the type of person who possesses these fundamental attitudes toward existence; Smith is a name chosen as representative of an ordinary, everyday human being (possibly not an intellectual or academic specialist).

Smith shoots guns at academic professors, not in order to kill them, but to rouse them with a start into realizing the

---

[112] "A Glimpse of My Country," *Tremendous Trifles*, 105.

preciousness of the sheer gift of life. He laments that such intellectuals are not alive enough to fear death and says, "that [although] there should be priests to remind men that they will one day die...at certain strange epochs it is necessary to have another kind of priest, called poets, actually to remind men that they are not dead yet."[113] For Innocent Smith the world is sacramental: it is full of signs, it points beyond itself and is therefore loaded with significance. As we shall see, this meaningfulness is described in the fourth chapter of *Orthodoxy* as central to the Ethics of Elfland.

The same sacramental understanding of the cosmos—real and very much there, yet symbolic and pointing to an invisible reality that is personal—is grasped by Gabriel Syme, the poet and undercover detective in another of Chesterton's novels, *The Man Who Was Thursday*:

> "Listen to me," cried Syme with extraordinary emphasis. "Shall I tell you the secret of the whole world? It is that we have only known the back of the world. We see everything from behind, and it looks brutal. That is not a tree, but the back of a tree. That is not a cloud, but the back of a cloud. Cannot you see that everything is stooping and hiding a face? If we could only get round in front..."[114]

Syme, like Smith, wishes to rouse the world to being truly contemplative, to what Chesterton refers to in *Orthodoxy* as being a mystic,[115] to being wide awake to all that is there to be perceived in our human experience. When it does that, the world will see, "not the creature-without-the-creator, or the creator-without-the-creature, but the

---

[113] *Manalive*, Rockville, MD: Serenity Publishers, 2009, 107.

[114] *The Man Who was Thursday: A Nightmare*, 123.

[115] *Orthodoxy*, 230-1.

creature-and-the-creator-in-the-cosmological relationship."[116]
The world will recognize its contingency, which is to recognize
God.

Let's look at Chesterton's account of how he himself recognized the fact of contingency, see examples from his writings of his evidence for contingency, and also revisit what he considers to be the obstacles that block us from perceiving contingency and the role of the artistic or poetic imagination in removing some of those blockages.

5.1 ELFLAND AND CHESTERTON'S RECOGNITION OF CONTINGENCY

In the fourth chapter of *Orthodoxy*, entitled "The Ethics of Elfland," Chesterton says:

> Tradition means giving votes to the most obscure of all classes, our ancestors. It is the democracy of the dead. Tradition refuses to submit to the small and arrogant oligarchy of those who merely happen to be walking about. All democrats object to men being disqualified by accident of birth; tradition objects to their being disqualified by the accident of death."[117]

Chesterton was always more predisposed toward tradition and the insights of what C. S. Lewis was later to refer to as "the solid folk,"[118] the unscientific majority, rather than toward the latest intellectual ideas of the specialist oligarchies:

> I have always been more inclined to believe the ruck of hard-working people than to believe that special and troublesome literary class to which I belong. I prefer even the fancies and prejudices of the

---

[116] See Austin Farrer, *Finite and Infinite: A Philosophical Essay*, 16ff. and 45ff.

[117] *Orthodoxy*, 251.

[118] See C. S. Lewis, "In Praise of Solid People," *Spirits in Bondage*, part II, poem XXIV, in *Poems: The Collected Poems of C. S. Lewis*, edited by Walter Hooper, 199.

people who see life from the inside to the clearest demonstration of
the people who see life from the outside. I would always trust the old
wives' fables against the old maids' facts.[119]

Perhaps in reaction to the marked tendency among the
Edwardian intellectual elite to disregard the insights of the past,
Chesterton always emphasized the wealth of wisdom that could
be gleaned from tradition, and he says that his view of the
cosmos consists of the few general ideas that he "learnt in the
nursery...I shall roughly synthesize them, summing up my personal philosophy or natural religion; then I shall describe my
startling discovery that the whole thing had been discovered
before. It had been discovered by Christianity."[120]

These few general ideas were set down in fairy tales and repeated through the generations, not because they never happened in reality, but because they always happen over and over
again in the reality of people's lives. They are the stories of normal people, the common folk, in ordinary situations: tales of love
and hate, passion and self-sacrifice, courage and rescue, knight
and dragon, good and evil. Although Chesterton could teach his
reader about particular lessons in the fairy tales—for example,
Beauty and the Beast teaches us that something must be loved
before it is lovable—he says, "I am not concerned with any of the
separate statutes of elfland...I am concerned with a certain way
of looking at life, which was created in me by the fairy tales, but
has since been meekly ratified by the mere facts."[121] The lessons
which these tales offer are referred to by Chesterton as "The
Ethics of Elfland," and they formed his personal philosophy
and led him to discover the Christian faith that harbored and

---

[119] *Orthodoxy*, 251-2.

[120] Ibid., 252.

[121] Ibid., 253.

protected them. We will see how Chesterton arrived at these Ethics and their inner meaning; for now we can summarize them, as he does at the end of Orthodoxy's fourth chapter.[122]

First, there is no necessary explanation and connection between realities in Elfland. The world does not explain itself. Something or somebody has to explain it to us. So it is an astonishing thing that Elfland exists at all, and a cause of wonder and gratitude. Second, the beauty, wonder, and magic of the cosmos, of Elfland, repeat themselves over and over. When apples fall to the ground, when suns rise and set, when eggs turn to birds, and when trees produce fruit, they point beyond themselves. They mean something, they signify something, and if they mean something, there must be something or somebody to which they point (either that or the realities within Elfland are deceptive and the people to be found there behave in a self-contradictory manner). There has to be somebody to mean the meaning, which means that there is something personal at work in the world.

Third— even though there are exceptions to the rule (such as dragons)—the design of the world, of Elfland, is beautiful. Fourth, since Elfland is gift, utterly unsolicited and unmerited, so it imposes on us a debt of gratitude, a debt paid by humility and self-control in the face of the limits of Elfland: "we should thank God for beer and Burgundy by not drinking too much of them." Obedience is owed to whatever made us. And finally, there is a sense that all that we have around us in Elfland was "a remnant to be stored and held sacred out of some primordial ruin," as Robinson Crusoe and his ordinary, everyday goods were treasures from a shipwreck.[123] Chesterton says:

---

[122] Ibid., 268.

[123] Ibid., 268.

These are my ultimate attitudes toward life; the soil for the seeds of doctrine. These in some dark way I thought before I could write, and felt before I could think...All this I felt and the age gave me no encouragement to feel it. And all this time I had not even thought of Christian theology.[124]

How did he arrive at these Ethics of Elfland? As we have already seen, having insisted earlier in *Orthodoxy* on the need for creative imagination and faith for a balanced personality, Chesterton points out that reason is itself an act of faith:

It is idle to talk always of the alternative of reason and faith. Reason is itself a matter of faith. It is an act of faith to assert that our thoughts have any relation to reality at all. If you are merely a sceptic, you must sooner or later ask yourself the question, "Why should anything go right; even observation and deduction? Why should not good logic be as misleading as bad logic? They are both movements in the brain of a bewildered ape?" The young sceptic says, "I have a right to think for myself." But the old sceptic, the complete sceptic, says, "I have no right to think for myself. I have no right to think at all."[125]

Thought, logic, and all argument rest on an act of faith, which is a trust that the mind can know the reality beyond itself in some way, and that logic will always give valid answers from true premises. This is unproved and unprovable, and yet absolutely essential if the world is going to function. Total scepticism makes life unlivable: "There is a thought that stops thought. That is the only thought that ought to be stopped."[126] Here Chesterton is continuing with the same kind of criticism of the reigning philosophical ideas that he displayed in *Heretics*, critiquing the contradistinction so often made between religious and scientific interpretations of the cosmos.

---

[124] Ibid.

[125] Ibid., 236.

[126] Ibid.

Far from being mutually exclusive, reason relies on faith. As we shall argue more fully in the next two chapters, critique of some of the inconsistencies, superficialities of thought and downright silliness that occur in any culture are part of the apologist's task.

C. S. Lewis echoes this assessment of scepticism:

> Can we carry through to the end the view that human thought is merely human: that it is simply a zoological fact about homo sapiens that he thinks in a certain way: that it in no way reflects (though no doubt it results from) non-human or universal reality? The moment we ask this question, we receive a check. We are at this very point asking whether a certain view of human thought is true. And the view in question is just the view that human thought is not true, not a reflection of reality. And this view is itself a thought. In other words, we are asking, 'Is the thought that no thoughts are true, itself true?' If we answer Yes, we contradict ourselves. For if all thoughts are untrue then this thought is untrue.

There cannot be such a thing as total scepticism, or we have to make an exception even as we assert our scepticism, "just as the man who warns the newcomer 'Don't trust anyone in this office' always expects you to trust him at that moment."[127] Lewis and Chesterton both show the incoherence of total scepticism. Chesterton also points out to us that, whereas the rationalistic maniac thinks he has worked out the foundations of a cosmos using his reason, foundations that turn out to be without foundation, the sceptic thinks that there can be no deduction of first principles and that we cannot know anything at all. Both rationalist and sceptic (for different reasons) do not like the fact that to start thinking at all we have to trust the reality that stands before us.

Chesterton had penned a newspaper article entitled

---

[127] C. S. Lewis, "De Futilitate," *Christian Reflections*, 84.

"Philosophy for the School Room" a year before Orthodoxy
was published, in which he makes the same point:

> What modern people want to be made to understand is simply that
> all argument begins with an assumption; that is, with something
> that you do not doubt. You can, of course, if you like, doubt the
> assumption at the beginning of your argument, but in that case you
> are beginning a different argument with another assumption at the
> beginning of it. Every argument begins with an infallible dogma, and
> that infallible dogma can only be disputed by falling back on some
> other infallible dogma; you can never prove your first statement or it
> would not be your first. All this is the alphabet of thinking.[128]

There are many things which are unproved and unprovable,
among them the notion that both the self and the cosmos are
real, the notion that one ought to obey one's conscience, the
notion that human beings have universal rights, the notion that
certain courses of action are right and certain courses of action
wrong, and the notion that human beings are free and responsible for their actions. Chesterton is saying that ultimately one
cannot prove this, but it is a reasonable assumption without
which reality simply does not work. He is claiming that to do
any thinking at all requires a non-rational assent to the reality
that is in front of us, which is not the same thing as saying that
it is an irrational assent. Randall Paine argues:

> Trying to systematically and rationally arrive at a first principle [of
> thought] is precisely the topsy-turvy ruse Chesterton is rebuking.
> Although one can reflect on one's principles and present them in an
> orderly and methodical way, it is in no way a demonstration of them
> to do this, except in the primitive, etymological sense of "showing"
> them to be there.[129]

Instead of rationally arriving at these principles, "They can

---

[128] Daily News, June 22 1907,

[129] Op. cit. 91.

only be defended indirectly, and in one of three ways": the arguments of those who deny such principles can be rationally refuted (as demonstrated by both Chesterton and Lewis above); the inner coherence of the principles can be shown through illustration; or the psychology of their genesis can be scrutinized and described. But to prove them, one would need recourse to some higher tribunal of evidence than theirs,[130] in which case, in Chesterton's words, "you are beginning a different argument with another assumption at the beginning of it," or "falling back on some other infallible dogma." Chesterton was aware that "all the sceptics of our time are sceptics at different degrees of the dissolution of scepticism."[131] The sceptic tells us what she does not believe, and so the Christian apologist needs to work out what the sceptic does believe. "Before arguing, we want to know what we need not argue about."[132] Everyone reasonably believes that certain things are true, while realizing that these beliefs cannot be proved by science or by logic. Faith, believing that certain things are true, is part of what it means to be a limited human being living in this cosmos. Fiduciary commitments are part and parcel of any interpretation of the world, religious or otherwise.

Reason, then, cannot be the foundation of reason. In a very real sense, a human being finds himself already in the middle of the drama of life long before his reason starts to perform its functions. Reason is aroused when the external world meets something mysterious and primordial in the heart and soul of a human being. This mysterious something is activated and

---

[130] Ibid.

[131] "Philosophy for the Schoolroom" *Daily News*, 22nd June 1907, http://www.cse.dmu.ac.uk/~mward/gkc/books/philosophy.html [last accessed 24th January 2012].

[132] Ibid.

at work long before human beings learn how to reason. This mysterious, indefinable something, is our first consciousness of ens or being: it is the beautifully expressed, "There is an Is!" that appears in Chesterton's work on Aquinas.[133] Chesterton says that what is essential in Aquinas:

> ...is the intense rightness of his sense of the relation between the mind and the real thing outside the mind...In other words, the essence of the Thomistic common sense is that two agencies are at work; reality and the recognition of reality; and their meeting is a sort of marriage.[134]

Where modern philosophers go wrong, according to Chesterton, is in seeing "the main metaphysical question [as being] whether we can prove that the primary act of recognition of any reality is real." Chesterton insists that the answer to that most modern of questions has to be yes, otherwise we can "never answer any question, never ask any question, never even exist intellectually, to answer or to ask." The fundamental sceptic cannot be consistent and thoroughgoing in his scepticism: he has to "first deny everything and then admit something, if for the sake of argument." Drawing on personal experience, Chesterton uses the example of the solipsist who never seems to realize that if his philosophy is true, "there obviously [are] no other philosophers to profess it." To the modern's question whether there is anything, the common sense philosophy of Aquinas answers in the affirmative, for "if [Aquinas] began by answering 'No,' it would not be the beginning, but the end...Either there is no philosophy, no philosophers, no thinkers, no thought, no anything; or else there is a real bridge between the mind and reality."[135]

---

[133] *Saint Thomas Aquinas: The Dumb Ox*, 166.

[134] Ibid., 182-4.

[135] Ibid., 147-9.

Once human beings have bowed before the reality of being, then the real world that Chesterton inhabits, Elfland, is found to be full of the rationality and logic which Chesterton wishes to preserve, rather than demolish:

> For instance, if the Ugly Sisters are older than Cinderella, it is (in an iron and awful sense) necessary that Cinderella is younger than the Ugly Sisters. There is no getting out of it…If Jack is the son of a miller, a miller is the father of Jack. Cold reason decrees it from her awful throne: and we in fairyland submit.

However, even if logic obtains there, Elfland contains much more than mere logic:

> But as I put my head over the hedge of the elves and began to take notice of the natural world, I observed an extraordinary thing. I observed that learned men in spectacles were talking of the actual things that happened—dawn and death and so on—as if they were rational and inevitable. They talked as if the fact that trees bears fruit was just as necessary as the fact that two and one trees make three. But it is not. There is an enormous difference by the test of fairyland; which is the test of the imagination. You cannot imagine two and one not making three. But you can easily imagine trees not growing fruit; you can imagine them growing golden candlesticks or tigers hanging on by the tail…We have always in our fairy tales kept this sharp distinction between the science of mental relations, in which there really are laws, and the science of physical facts, in which there are no laws, but only weird repetitions. We believe in bodily miracles, but not in mental impossibilities.[136]

Once again, Chesterton is reiterating his insistence on the importance of imagination if one is to know reality on a more than superficial level, an importance which we shall explore later. Fairyland is too rich to be described in terms of mere logic. To see the sheer miraculousness of the fact that there is something rather than nothing requires a quality of mind that

---

[136] *Orthodoxy*, 253-4.

moves a human being beyond the internal relations of science and logic. In his first book of essays Chesterton wrote that, "It is a monotonous memory which keeps us in the main from seeing things as splendid as they are."[137] As we have seen, he informs us that his intention is to use his whole vocation as a writer to:

> ...provide that longest and strangest telescope—the telescope through which we could see the star upon which we dwelt. For the mind and eyes of the average man this world is as lost as Eden and as sunken as Atlantis...[And Chesterton's vocation is to help his readers and his listeners to rediscover their vision because] Most probably we are in Eden still. It is only our eyes that have changed.[138]

There is no need to flee some platonic imperfect world of sensibility because the real and wonderful world of Elfland is here already, in this realm. If we find life dull and stupid, then Chesterton contends that, as was the case in his Slade period, the problem is likely to be with us and our way of looking at the world, rather than with the world itself. Chesterton reminds us that the first and main ethic or lesson of Elfland is something that we should never forget, but in fact often do, that our world might have been quite different and is, therefore, quite magical precisely in the way that it is. It is this world, in actual fact, which is wild, surprising, unpredictable, unnecessary and magical.

Although Elfland is full of logic and rational necessity, nevertheless (and this is the point at which Chesterton believes that many modern thinkers make their biggest mistake—an error which is a serious impediment to the recognition of contingency) all of this comes to us in a world that is utterly unnecessary. In a very real sense the things of Elfland are the way they are

---

[137] *The Defendant*, 7.

[138] Ibid., 9-10.

because they are, to use the word Chesterton heard repeatedly in the fairy tales of his childhood, "magic."[139] The world is utterly gratuitous gift. "If you refuse to accept this principle as a gift, but want first to establish the giver logically by means of the as yet unreceived gift, you will end up by losing both."[140] If the chapter entitled "The Suicide of Thought" taught us that embracing rationalism and scepticism both lead to losing the gift of Fairyland, the first of that strange but wonderful country's ethics teach us that we regain it (as had Chesterton during the Slade years) by recovering the sense of wonder of the child, by being astonished that the logic and necessity of Elfland only come to us in an Elfand that is utterly non-necessary, gratuitous gift. Furthermore, the remaining ethics of Elfland teach us how to nourish the gift.

Though they are accounts of ordinary, everyday things, children love to hear the fairytales of Elfland again and again because they find them astonishing. Drawing on the experience of his childhood, Chesterton spent his whole career pointing out why this is so. The sense of gratitude within Chesterton for the miraculous gift of existence, and his instinct for the "there-ness" of reality, had been part of him since his days in the nursery. This fundamental sense of a given affirmed absolutely was strengthened by his later study of Aquinas. On the question of what a child sees when it looks out upon a lawn, all sorts of answers have been given throughout the history of philosophy, from green mists to parts of the child's own mind. Chesterton is thrilled to discover that Aquinas intervenes in this "nursery quarrel" and declares that the child is aware of ens.

The child knows that something is something. Chesterton

---

[139] *Orthodoxy*, 255.

[140] R. Paine, *The Universe and Mr. Chesterton*, 96.

says that perhaps it would be best to say emphatically "(with a blow on the table), 'There is an is!'" One has to submit to being as truth before one can do anything else in reality. Chesterton sees this affirmation "as the sharp point of reality" upon which the whole cosmic system of Christianity is built. As consequences of this primary affirmation, Chesterton traces the emergence of the law of non-contradiction, questions of truth and falsity and "the everlasting duel between Yes and No."[141]

How do other philosophies go wrong? Problems arise after the initial judgment of fact. Because on closer inspection the reality affirmed may be seen to change, or its qualities may be relative, or it may appear to be in constant movement, or it may even vanish altogether, to some this experience may then appear to justify scepticism. Thus some philosophers lose hold of their primary affirmation (of being) and begin to think that all is flux, or relative; they might even doubt that there is anything to know other than the self (one of the thoughts that most tormented Chesterton himself in his youth). In Chesterton's words, "they took away the number they first thought of."[142] It is fatal to go back on that first affirmation of fact, of reality, of being. Clearly this first affirmation is obviously not everything, but it is the sine qua non, the beginning of the journey, toward further intelligibility.

There is a remarkable similarity here between the way Chesterton approaches this central affirmation and Bernard Lonergan's much fuller treatment of what he refers to as the "virtually unconditioned."[143] For Lonergan, when we say that

---

[141] *Saint Thomas Aquinas: The Dumb Ox*, 167.

[142] Ibid., 169.

[143] *Insight: A Study of Human Understanding*, 279-347. Every effort has been made by the author, without success, to trace the source that is the inspiration of the present paragraph. He recalls a link being made between Lonergan and Chesterton in a Philosophy postgraduate seminar

something exists or is, the existence which is posited is absolute, since the affirmation of existence utterly excludes non-existence. It might not have been the case, and so is a conditioned existence, but it is a conditioned existence whose conditions for existence have all been met, and so it exists as a virtually unconditioned. Lonergan here examines the first principle of affirmation, as Chesterton calls it. The basis of all our knowing is not something necessary, but contingent fact. The facts we affirm are established upon a basis of sense experience, intelligent insight, and rational affirmation. We move toward a conclusion from the presentation of data, through inquiry ("What is this?" "Is it grass?" "Is it a book?"), toward a rational affirmation of fact ("Yes, it is grass." "Yes, it is a book."). A fact is virtually unconditioned—this is grass, this is a book. It might not have been; it might have been different from what it is. But as affirmed as grass or a book, it possesses conditional necessity.

As Chesterton can see, it is necessary to stay with one's first principle of "This is something," or Lonergan's virtually unconditioned fact. For Lonergan we may have an unrestricted desire to know, but at this given moment our inquiry is about grass or books. For both Lonergan and Chesterton there may be a million questions to be asked about these items and about the cosmos as a whole, but here and now our inquiry is limited, as is our judgment. Before we can ask or know all these other things, we must know that the thing before us is grass or a book. Chesterton then goes on to say: "I begin by the grass to be bound again to the Lord." This is another way of expressing the Chestertonian principle that one can start anywhere within the experience of the given and arrive at God.

---

at the PUG during the academic year 1999-2000, and was so impressed by the points made that they have been committed to memory and are reproduced here. He would be delighted to receive any information about the original source.

Nicholas Lash maintains that acknowledgement of our radical contingency, of our (and the whole of creation's) utter dependency on the Creator, is essential for coming to know God:

> Learning to use the word 'God' well, learning to speak appropriately of God, is a matter of learning that we are creatures and that all things are created, and created out of nothing. And learning this takes time. In fact, it took the Jewish and then the Christian tradition many centuries. The story of this learning process simply is the history of Jewish and Christian doctrines of God. Moreover there is a sense in which each generation, and indeed each individual, has to take the time to learn this for themselves; has to grow, or fail to grow, into some understanding of what it means to be, in every fibre of one's being, absolutely dependent on the mystery that we call God.[144]

This understanding of God, the belief in this God, is not the same thing as the notion that "'belief in God' is a matter of supposing there to be, over and above the familiar world we know, one more large or powerful fact or thing, for the existence of which there is no evidence whatsoever."[145] Rahner points out:

> that God really does not exist who operates and functions as an individual existent alongside other existents, and who would thus be a member of the larger household of all reality. Anyone in search of such a God is searching for a false God. Both atheism and a more naive form of theism labour under the same false notion of God, only the former denies it while the latter believes that it can make sense of it.[146]

For Rahner, as Chesterton himself had perceived, to utter the word "God" brings a person "face to face with the single whole of reality" and "the single whole of his own existence."[147] To speak of God is to speak of everything (including ourselves)

---

[144] Op. cit., 25.

[145] Ibid., 20.

[146] Foundations of Christian Faith, 63.

[147] Ibid., 47.

in absolute dependence. That is why Chesterton believed that one could start anywhere in the cosmos, in which all existents are contingent, and end up having to deal with God.

Robert Barron sees a skewed understanding of the relationship between the creation and the Creator as leading to the "centuries-long and terribly unproductive" battle between modernity and Christianity, which was at root a dispute between modernity and an impoverished form of nominalist Christianity. In an attempt to make the esse of God more immediately intelligible, Duns Scotus opted for a univocal conception of being, which saw God and creatures as sharing the same metaphysical category, the genus of "being."

Aquinas's analogical conception of being, grasped so brilliantly and expressed so pithily by Chesterton, holds that God is the sheer act of "to be" itself, *ipsum esse subsistens*, is the act through which all creatures exist, and can therefore be placed in no genus whatsoever. The meaning of "to be" with regard to God and to creatures must be analogous, with God as primary analogue and creatures secondary. God will always remain mysterious to us since our frame of reference to God is always in this secondary, analogous, creaturely mode of existence toward God's primary way of existing. "We may say that God exists, but we're not quite sure what we mean when we say it; the 'cash value' of the claim that God exists is that there is a finally mysterious source of the to-be of finite things."

With Scotus's shift toward a univocal conception of being, and the consequent rejection of an analogical notion of being, Barron sees the end of the participation of creatures in the divine esse of the Creator, and its replacement with a schema that sees them as existing side by side in the same genus of being. Furthermore, creatures are no longer essentially related, but are isolated and self-contained individual entities with nothing in common to relate them to each other or to the God who is also an isolated and self-contained entity.

> "A consequence of this conception is that God and finite things have to be rivals, since their individualities are contrastive and mutually exclusive. Just as a chair is itself precisely in the measure that it is no other creaturely thing, so God is himself only inasmuch as he stands over and against the world he has made, and vice versa."[148]

We shall return to the theme of the uneasy relationship between modernity and Christianity in our final chapter, and we shall see if Chesterton's notion of God can bring any healing to the wounds that the two have inflicted on each other.

Barron's vision is steeped in the thought of Aquinas, and the fourth chapter of *Orthodoxy* captures very well the heart of the central Thomistic insight that this cosmos does not explain itself, but is constituted in relationship with God as the primary analogue of being. It is a wonderful thing to grasp the insights of science, logic, and the intricate details of how this cosmos works; it is something even more wonderful, in Chesterton's mind, to stand back and wonder why this cosmos, this existence, is here at all. To have this sense of wonder is to be ready to let the fact of contingency act as a signpost to God:

> St. Thomas maintains that the ordinary thing at any moment is something; but it is not everything that it could be. There is a fullness of being, in which it could be everything that it can be. Thus, while most sages come at last to nothing but naked change, he comes to the ultimate thing that is unchangeable, because it is all the other things at once. While they describe a change that is really a change in nothing, he describes a changelessness which includes the changes of everything. Things change because they are not complete; but their reality can only be explained as part of something that is complete. It is God…The defect we see, in what is, is simply that it is not all that it is. God is more actual even than man; more actual even than matter;

---

[148] *The Priority of Christ: towards a postliberal Catholicism*, 12-16.

for God with all His powers at every instant is immortally in action.[149]

The Thomistic theism which Chesterton here expresses so succinctly states that at every moment of existence all beings are actively being maintained in existence by God. The act of creation by the Creator is an act that has no past, present or future tenses. It is an ongoing and eternal act of creation which means that all concretely existing beings in the cosmos are breathed into existence and kept in existence by God. Not to recognize the fact of this contingency and the reality of the Ultimate Being is not to be gazing at the cosmos with the correct eyes. If a human being does not perceive the reality of God, it is not because God does not exist, but because there is something amiss with human perception.

Chesterton sees this same lack of perception and this inability to grasp the consequences of the notion of contingency in those who would claim that evolutionary theory disproves the existence of God:

> ...there is always something really unthinkable about the whole evolutionary cosmos...because it is really something coming out of nothing; an ever-increasing flood of water pouring out of an empty jug...The world does not explain itself and cannot do so merely by continuing to expand itself...It is absurd for the Evolutionist to complain that it is unthinkable for an admittedly unthinkable God to make everything out of nothing; and then pretend that it is more thinkable that nothing should turn itself into everything...change is not mere change, but is the unfolding of something; and if it is thus unfolded, though the unfolding takes twelve million years, it must be there already. In other words [evolutionists] agree with Aquinas that there is everywhere potentiality that has not reached its end in act. But if it is a definite potentiality, and if it can only end in a definite act, why then there is a Great being, in whom all potentialities exist as a plan of action. In other words, it is impossible even to say that

---

[149] *Saint Thomas Aquinas: The Dumb Ox*, 168-9.

the change is for the better, unless the best exists somewhere, both before and after the change.[150]

As we saw in our last chapter, because Chesterton maintained that, "Development is the unfolding of all the consequences and applications of an idea; but of something that is there, not of something that is not there,"[151] there was no real conflict between evolutionary theory and the Christian theology of Creation. Chesterton saw quite clearly that, "Evolution as an explanation…of the cause of living things is still faced with the problem of producing rabbits out of an empty hat; a process commonly involving some hint of design."[152] To talk, as evolutionists often do, of "the purpose of nature" is a discussion about a personal act. For Chesterton, "To talk of the purpose of Nature…is believing in a goddess because you are too skeptical to believe in a god."[153] But for Chesterton, "Nature is not our mother: Nature is our sister. We can be proud of her beauty, since we have the same father."[154]

The importance of Chesterton's cosmological vision shows real insight into what science is and what science cannot be, according to Stanley Jaki.[155] A distinguished professor of physics and author of many books about theology, the philosophy of science, and the overlap of these academic disciplines, Jaki points out that when an office block is constructed, scaffolding and cranes dominate the scene.[156] When a scientific theory is

---

[150] Ibid., 173-5.

[151] "Roman Catholicism," *An Outline of Christianity*, ed. A. S. Peake, 1926, cited in *TTFT*, 118.

[152] *Chaucer*, 186.

[153] *The Superstition of Divorce*, CW Vol. 4, 253.

[154] *Orthodoxy*, 317.

[155] *Chesterton: A Seer of Science*, Pinckney, Michigan: Real View Books, 2001.

[156] *Means to Message: A Treatise on Truth*, Grand Rapids: William B. Eerdsman, 1999, 49-52.

being constructed, non-scientific considerations which provide the philosophical foundations and scaffolding are traceable everywhere. When the office block is complete, the scaffolding is removed and the cranes moved elsewhere, but there remains a vast amount of matter—foundations, walls, roof, interior design.

When a major scientific theory is complete, however, the opposite happens: there remains nothing in it that has contact with the material. The building is a complex set of equations, existing independently from all the philosophical assumptions that helped construct it. Even letters within the formula are merely reference points to correlate quantitative data. Science has to be about the physical. But the question is: does mathematical formalism justify this grounding in the physical, or does the justification lie in something else?

For Jaki, the latter option has to be the case. As an illustration of this, Jaki points to Niels Bohr's postulation of his idea of complementarity: as we saw in Chapter II, some experiments in atomic physics demand an approach that understands matter as particles, while other experiments demand that matter be understood as waves. But the ultimate difference between the two perspectives lies in a mutual incommensurability of two mathematical formalisms. It is similar to concluding that, because a circle cannot be squared, everything is at one moment a square and at another moment a circle. But the main problem with Bohr's understanding (useful as it is), as far as a Chestertonian perspective is concerned, is that it evades questions about reality itself. Any assertion about complementary aspects entails the question: of what are they aspects? There may be disparity between my two cheeks, but I must ultimately admit that cheeks make sense only if they inhere in a face. But Bohr's philosophy prohibits such an inference—one may speak only of the aspects, and not of whether these aspects belong to anything at all. The edifice of exact science as a conceptual structure of quantitative ideas cannot provide the material reality on which its equations are supposed to work. Jaki maintains that this is why it is seized upon by idealists, paradigmatists, and all who scoff at realism.

Here Jaki expresses very eloquently the point that Chesterton makes in the Ethics of Elfland and which he views as an enormous weakness in modern thought—the fact that so much of what passes itself as modern science has not made itself sure of the very first step it takes, which is to register the existence of a reality on which it is to carry out its clever work. In other words, it has not acknowledged being. It has not made the deep bow to the cosmos which is necessary before proceeding to explore it. Jaki points out that when Wittgenstein wrote at the beginning of the Tractatus[157] that, "The world is everything that is the case," it had to be true that the world was no less a real thing than the copy of the Tractatus which was the very means by which Wittgenstein communicated his message about the world to that world. An unconditional acknowledgement of reality happens in the very first sentence of Wittgenstein's book.[158]

Similarly, no scientist, nor any modern philosopher or academic, can make assertions about their work until they have first declared their intellectual surrender to reality. Unless they do so, they will have no right to use any means to carry their message to the world. The use of means such as books, journals, instruments, telescopes, and test tubes, obliges the

---

[157] Ludwig Wittgenstein, *Tractatus Logico-Philosophicus*, London: Routledge & Kegan Paul, 1951, p. 31.

[158] Jaki, *Means to Message*, 15.

scientist to recognize the objective truth of means—otherwise he cannot pass from (as the title of Jaki's book puts it) means to message. Even if he denies this truth, his denial is an act of communication, an implicit falling back on objective means by which alone other scientists can be instructed. In other words, the scientist commits himself to realism, a philosophical position which is not empirically verifiable. In doing this, the scientist himself, it would seem, teaches us that the cosmos is a playground in which science is only one of the adventures we can enjoy.

Chesterton did indeed see the cosmos as a playground, a place in which there was no absolute necessity in sunrise and sunset, or the falling of apples to the ground:

> Now, the mere repetition made the things to me rather more weird than more rational. It was as if, having seen a curiously shaped nose in the street and dismissed it as an accident, I had then seen six other noses of the same astonishing shape. I should have fancied for a moment that it must be some local secret society. So one elephant having a trunk was odd; but all elephants having trunks looked like a plot…the repetition in Nature seemed sometimes to be an excited repetition, like that of an angry schoolmaster saying the same thing over and over again…the crowded stars seemed bent upon being understood. The sun would make me see him if he rose a thousand times. The recurrences of the universe rose to the maddening rhythm of an incantation, and I began to see an idea.[159]

This idea was that repetition may go on and on out of mere choice. Not only was the world a miraculous and wonderful gift, but it was also a gift full of repetitions which science, stepping beyond its remit, called laws. For science there can only be mere repetitions, but to use the word "law" is to imply that there is a lawgiver, who puts these repetitions there by choice. So the Giver is also a Lawgiver:

---

[159] *Orthodoxy*, 262-3.

I had always vaguely felt facts to be miracles in the sense that they are wonderful: now I began to think them miracles in the stricter sense that they were wilful. I mean that they were, or might be, repeated exercises of some will. In short, I had always believed that the world involved magic: now I thought that perhaps it involved a magician. And this pointed a profound emotion always present and sub-conscious; that this world of ours has some purpose; and if there is a purpose, there is a person. I had always felt life first as a story: and if there is a story there is a story-teller.[160]

Here Chesterton is pointing out that to talk of repetitions as laws of the cosmos is to invoke the notion of something personal. The magic implied a personal magician with free will, which implies that there is purpose or meaning in the cosmos. The wonders of the cosmos point to meaning. The cosmos has significance. It means something. If it means something, then there must be something personal behind the meaning which intends that meaning. It is from this personal something, which transcends the gift of the cosmos, that all notions of personal action get their own meaning. That is why "atheism is abnormality...It is the reversal of a subconscious assumption in the soul; the sense that there is a meaning and a direction in the world that it sees."[161] For Chesterton, everyone has a sense of ultimate reality, an ultimate interpretation of the worth of life; whether they formulate it explicitly or not, they act out of it. Elfland offers many instances of people speaking and behaving in ways that seem to contradict their stated beliefs: they invest their lives, their words and their actions with an ultimate sense of truth and value, even as they deny the significance of the discussion about ultimate reality.

When Chesterton says that "thanks are the highest form

---

[160] Ibid., 264.

[161] *The Everlasting Man*, 162.

of thought,"[162] he is saying that the most basic knowledge of God is worship, which is the recognition of contingency, of the mystery of the dependence of everything. Rahner, too, says that "we are coming to the innermost center of the Christian understanding of existence when we say: Man is the event of a free, unmerited and forgiving, and absolute self-communication of God."[163] Creation is the act of God's self-communication with creatures, the sharing of the divine self. Human beings are that part of the creation which can be aware of the divine self-communication or self-sharing. Recognition of that self-communication—the human act of saying yes to that divine sharing, the human act of sharing in God's yes to humanity—is the act of faith. Part of what Rahner means by his distinction between transcendental and categorical faith is that human beings can say yes to God's self-communication and self-sharing in different ways and with different degrees of awareness. Similarly, when Chesterton posits the relationship between the Creator who is the giver of the gift of creation and human beings who are the conscious part of that creation, he is not only saying that human beings may start anywhere in Elfland and end up having to deal with the God who is the plenitude of meaning toward which everything that is meaningful points; he is also maintaining that, even if they forget or remain unconscious of the God who is the other pole of their most fundamental relationship, human beings still implicitly respond to God by the way they respond to the gifts provided by God. This is especially the case when it comes to the gift of other people: the way we treat others constitutes the moral law.

---

[162] *A Short History of England*, 43.

[163] *Foundations of Christian Faith*, 116.

5.2 THE DOCTRINE OF CONDITIONAL
JOY: *the Moral Law and Happiness*

We have seen that the point of departure for Chesterton's journey toward faith was found in the feelings of loneliness, boredom, and despair that he knew during his time at the Slade.
This started him off on a journey in search of a remedy. Years
later he believed that in a world in which there is scant or no
reference at all to the transcendent ground of all meaning and
values, things would not ultimately turn out well. A painful
personal struggle was the first insight that nudged him toward
God, while the second was born of a wonder-filled curiosity
about the contingent cosmos, giving birth to "a fierce pleasure
in things being themselves...the wetness of water, the fieriness of fire, the steeliness of steel, the unutterable muddiness
of mud."[164]

These two insights are connected. Chesterton says that
Elfland teaches us that, if we are to see and understand the
beauty of the cosmos around us, we must be humble enough to
accept it as sheer gift, as unnecessary and utterly contingent, as
what Rahner calls the gracious divine self-communication. We
must have the wavelength or disposition of grateful receptivity.
The human being in the world is already in medias res, and
must nod his head in the evident face of being, ens, before going on to do other clever things in the world, such as counting
apples, rivers, or giants, and working out whether one should
eat apples, drink wine, or kill giants. In Paine's words:

> The universe was there first and we cannot, we may not, postpone our
> lives till we have figured that out. Other things we may, to a certain
> extent, scrutinize and know with precision and exactitude. But all this
> is based on reason's modest acknowledgement of its prior situation in

---

[164] Ward, *GKC*, 79.

a world of wonder. This was the first lesson of fairyland.[165]

Having relinquished the need to be in control of the cosmos by having accepted the gift of being, Chesterton then moves on to "the second great principle of the fairy philosophy," a principle that combines the two insights above:

> For the pleasure of pedantry I will call it the Doctrine of Conditional Joy...according to the elfin ethics all virtue is in an "if." The note of the fairy utterance always is, "You may live in a palace of gold and sapphire, if you do not say the word 'cow,'" or "You may live happily with the King's daughter, if you do not show her an onion." The vision always hangs upon a veto. All the dizzy and colossal things conceded depend upon one small thing withheld. All the wild and whirling things that are let loose depend upon the one thing that is forbidden.[166]

Paine points out that, just as the "blaze and blur" of the first intellectual grasp of being as truth is Chesterton's brilliant description of the indemonstrability of the first rational or speculative principle, so "the 'incomprehensible condition' of the will's first contact with being as good, is likewise a presentation of the indemonstrability of the first moral principle,"[167] something not easily understood by rational principles:

> ...the true citizen of fairyland is obeying something he does not understand at all. In the fairy tale an incomprehensible happiness rests upon an incomprehensible condition. A box is opened and all evils fly out. A word is forgotten, and cities perish. A lamp is lit, and love flies away. A flower is plucked, and human lives are forfeited. An apple is eaten, and the hope of God is gone.[168]

---

[165] *Op. cit.*,106.

[166] *Orthodoxy*, 258.

[167] *Op. cit.*, 107

[168] *Orthodoxy*, 259.

Bonum est faciendum et prosequendum, et malum vitandum.[169]
For Chesterton the goodness of being is—like the truth of being—absolute, a first principle. Like the "is-ness" (which he
interprets as Aquinas's "there is an is-ness") of being, so too the
"ought-ness" of being is without rational explanation. "The idea
of choice is an absolute and no one can really get behind it."[170]
There is no way to get beneath or behind the moral principle.
Morality or ethics offers a third Chestertonian signpost to God
which unites the first two: the desire for what we seek, and the
nature of a contingent world that points beyond itself to the
grounding of all being, truth, and meaning, come together in
that it is only in obedience to the truth of the moral law—that
is to say, it is only in fulfilling the "if"—that we will find joy.

The fundamental principle behind all moral action (for it is
apparent to all people that the actions which they perform are
perceived to be a good to be pursued, even if those actions are
not truly good in themselves) is that what is done is something
that does not have to be done, since human beings are free
agents, but is something that has to be done if the happiness of
the moral agent is to be increased. "Cinderella received a coach
out of wonderland and a coachman out of nowhere, but she
received a command...that she should be back by twelve."[171] As
with the fundamental principle of the truth of being, at which
children wonder and rejoice, so with the fundamental principle
of the goodness of being and its precarious nature and relationship to joy: children seem to grasp it much more easily. "Stand
on a crack and you'll marry a rat and the devil will come to
your wedding!" is an old warning from this author's childhood

---

[169] Thomas Aquinas, *Summa Theologiae* I-II, 94, 2

[170] *All I Survey*, 104.

[171] *Orthodoxy*, 259.

which captures well the fragility of joyful living in Elfland:

> [Cinderella] had a glass slipper; and it cannot be a coincidence that glass is so common a substance in folk-lore. This princess lives in a glass castle, that princess on a glass hill; this one sees all things in a mirror; they may all live in glass houses if they will not throw stones. For this thin glitter of glass everywhere is the expression of the fact that the happiness is bright but brittle, like the substance most easily smashed by a housemaid or a cat. And this fairy-tale sentiment also sank into me and became my sentiment towards the whole world. I felt and feel that life itself is as bright as the diamond, but as brittle as the window-pane; and when the heavens were compared to the terrible crystal I can remember a shudder. I was afraid that God would drop the cosmos with a crash.[172]

But the condition for everything not smashing into a million pieces is obeying the command:

> Remember, however, that to be breakable is not the same as to be perishable. Strike a glass, and it will not endure an instant; simply do not strike it, and it will endure a thousand years. Such, it seemed, was the joy of man, either in elfland or on earth; the happiness depended on not doing something which you could at any moment do and which, very often, it was not obvious why you should not do.[173]

At this point in Chapter IV of *Orthodoxy* Chesterton remembers the insight he had had about the truth of being—that to see the truth of being, you have first to receive it as gift, and only then can you have it and explore it as a possession, in accordance with its own nature. Similarly, to want the good, to perceive the goodness of being, you must first accept it as a gift from a giver, and only then can you have it and desire it as a possession, in accordance with its own nature. There is a personal intention behind the good: the source of all that is good. The lawgiver stands behind the law. For Chesterton (even

---

[172] Ibid, 259-60.

[173] Ibid, 260.

if the reasons behind them are not always easily grasped), the rules and regulations of Elfland:

> ...did not seem unjust. If the miller's third son said to the fairy, "Explain why I must not stand on my head in the fairy palace," the other might fairly reply, "Well, if it comes to that, explain the fairy palace." If Cinderella says, "How is it that I must leave the ball at twelve?" her godmother might answer, "How is it that you are going there till twelve?" If I leave a man in my will ten talking elephants and a hundred winged horses, he cannot complain if the conditions partake of the slight eccentricity of the gift. He must not look a winged horse in the mouth. And it seemed to me that existence was itself so very eccentric a legacy that I could not complain of not understanding the limitations of the vision when I did not understand the vision they limited. The frame was no stranger than the picture.[174]

Paine maintains that the two fundamental principles which underpin Chesterton's Ethics of Elfland—the truth of being and the goodness of being—are rooted "in a fundamental attitude of humility." However, he maintains that:

> Being and first principles are evident to the mind—there is no darkness about it at all. It is just that we are quite able (even in sophisticated philosophical form) to mix ourselves up to such a degree that we think they are not evident (all the time using them in the attempt to discredit them).[175]

There are, of course, many examples of our confusion about first principles and our incoherent attempt to discredit them. Many people, while rejecting or postponing belief in God or any other absolute, live by normative ideals and ideologies— moral, humanitarian, political, educational, aesthetic—which are invested with values just as binding and non-negotiable as those with religious justifications. People live, if not theoretically then certainly practically, with absolutes (and, as will be

---

[174] Ibid.

[175] Op. cit., 108.

stated later, practical absolutes are arguably more important in the Christian vision of things). These are but a few of the abundant contradictions of Elfland.

Rather than being merely an act of faith, then, the apprehension of being and the first principles of the truth and goodness of being:

> ...is an act of high-noon intellectual vision. The "faith" and "belief" Chesterton spoke of [earlier in *Orthodoxy*, when he maintained that it is an act of faith that our thoughts have any contact with reality at all] is only regarding the sceptic's curious and prying question: "How do you know that your mind's report of evidence can be trusted to begin with?" Again, we cannot get behind this, so we must answer: The report can be trusted because the evidence, though in the mind, is not really of it...we know the world to be true because it has come into our mind and we, in turn, have gone out into the world and found the two to agree. On the witness of the two the evidence stands. If this does not satisfy the skeptic, he can join Descartes, Kant, and Husserl in their endless search of proof for principles, like men insisting on having a thing photographed before daring to look at it. Chesterton stands rather with Aristotle, who insists that "each of the first principles should command belief in and by itself."[176]

Existence and all the constituent parts of existence, including truth and falsehood and the good and the bad, cannot have any ultimate significance unless these point in some way to some absolute. Bertrand Russell, in a famous debate with Frederick Copleston, acknowledged the coherence of this theistic position, before rapidly adding that the cosmos is a brute fact which is ultimately meaningless. Russell's position, which seeks to pronounce on the truth about the cosmos and the implicit moral duty to tell that truth to others, would be incoherent to Chesterton.

In the seventh chapter of *Orthodoxy* Chesterton offers

---

[176] Ibid., 108-9.

further examples of such contradictions when he examines some features of the notion of progress, which is a concept implicit in any worldview that commends truth and goodness. He begins by explaining how the notion of progress, embraced with great zeal by the various forms of evolutionary thought that were on offer in the Edwardian ideological marketplace, implies some sort of standard or gauge of value toward which progress is being made (or away from which regress can be measured). This gauge cannot be found in nature:

> ...for the simple reason that (except for some human or divine theory), there is no principle in nature. For instance, the cheap anti-democrat of to-day will tell you solemnly that there is no equality in nature. He is right, but he does not see the logical addendum. There is no equality in nature; also there is no inequality in nature. Inequality, as much as equality, implies a standard of value. To read aristocracy into the anarchy of animals is just as sentimental as to read democracy into it. Both aristocracy and democracy are human ideals: the one saying that all men are valuable, the other that some men are more valuable. But nature does not say that cats are more valuable than mice; nature makes no remark on the subject. She does not even say that the cat is enviable or the mouse pitiable. We think the cat superior because we have (or most of us have) a particular philosophy to the effect that life is better than death. But if the mouse were a German pessimist mouse, he might not think that the cat had beaten him at all. He might think he had beaten the cat by getting to the grave first. Or he might feel that he had actually inflicted frightful punishment on the cat by keeping him alive...You cannot even say that there is victory or superiority in nature unless you have some doctrine about what things are superior. You cannot even say that the cat scores unless there is a system of scoring. You cannot even say that the cat gets the best of it unless there is some best to be got.[177]

In this vision of things, nature says nothing at all about good or bad, higher or lower, superior or inferior. It just is—a sheer

---

[177] *Orthodoxy*, 307-8.

brute fact (as stated by Russell). Rather, human beings come along and read a standard into nature, interpret nature with a philosophy of life, and say that life is good or bad, better or worse, in accordance with that standard. There is also another group of modern thinkers who say that progress means that the world is moving toward what they desire it to be. Chesterton does not necessarily agree with the goal they have in mind, but he commends the consistency of their thought, in that they see progress as a passage toward some definite point, or goal or state of affairs. These are the only sensible people in his opinion:

> This is the only really healthy way to work with the word evolution: to work for what you want, and to call that evolution. The only intelligible sense that progress or advance can have is that there is a definite vision, and that we wish to make the whole world like that vision.[178]

Chesterton points out that the evolutionary vision implies that what we have is not a world, but the material for a world, and this is a vision with which the Christian creed would concur:

> God has given us not so much the colours of a picture as the colours of a palette. But he has also given us a subject, a model, a fixed vision. We must be clear about what we want to paint. This adds a further principle to our previous list of principles. We have said we must be fond of this world, even in order to change it. We now add that we must be fond of another world (real or imaginary) in order to have something to change it to.[179]

That is to say, there must be a fixed goal, a sure origin, an abiding rule or model, a permanent (i.e., eternal and transcendent) point of reference, according to which all progress, reformation, or revolution takes place. However, one of the major problems with modern thinkers in Chesterton's opinion was that they believed that the goal should change; however, if the goal or

---

[178] Ibid., 310.

[179] Ibid.

vision changes, progress does not take place. All previous work carried out to achieve one goal counts for nothing if a new goal is set.[180] Or, as C. S. Lewis points out, if the railway station is moving, one could never state that the train is either getting closer or moving further away.[181] To talk of approximation is to talk of something moving toward a fixed point:

> Now here comes in the whole collapse and huge blunder of our age. We have mixed up two different things, two opposite things. Progress should mean that we are always changing the world to suit the vision. Progress does mean (just now) that we are always changing the vision. It should mean that we are slow but sure in bringing justice and mercy among men: it does mean that we are very swift in doubting the desirability of justice and mercy: a wild page from any Prussian sophist makes men doubt it. Progress should mean that we are always walking toward the New Jerusalem. It does mean that the New Jerusalem is always walking away from us. We are not altering the real to suit the ideal. We are altering the ideal: it is easier.[182]

Rather than change human behavior to suit the goal of human living, the goals of human living are changed to justify human behavior. The great irony of this situation, in which it is not people's behavior that changes, but the moral standard against which that behavior is measured, is that the only thing that results is the maintenance of the status quo:

> But the man we see every day—the worker in Mr. Gradgrind's factory, the little clerk in Mr. Gradgrind's office—he is too mentally worried to believe in freedom. He is kept quiet with revolutionary literature. He is calmed and kept in his place by a constant succession of wild

---

[180] In human affairs, when the vision changes the cultural life changes. As I sit here writing this book, a general election approaches in the United Kingdom and the British government is desperately trying to pass legislation that will ensure that, should it lose the next election, some of the major goals it has pursued in its term of office cannot be removed or undone by a new government.

[181] "The Poison of Subjectivism," *Christian Reflections*, 103.

[182] *Orthodoxy*, 310.

philosophies. He is a Marxian one day, a Nietzscheite the next day, a Superman (probably) the next day; and a slave every day. The only thing that remains after all the philosophies is the factory. The only man who gains by all the philosophies is Gradgrind. It would be worth his while to keep his commercial helotry supplied with sceptical literature. And now I come to think of it, of course, Gradgrind is famous for giving libraries. He shows his sense. All modern books are on his side. As long as the vision of heaven is always changing, the vision of earth will be exactly the same. No ideal will remain long enough to be realized, or even partly realized. The modern young man will never change his environment; for he will always change his mind.[183]

If progress is something about which human beings cannot agree, then nobody knows how to work toward it, and the only people who benefit are those with a vested interest in the way things already are. The first requirement for progress, then, is that there must be a fixed standard of the ideal toward which progress is directed.

> Whistler used to make many rapid studies of a sitter; it did not matter if he tore up twenty portraits. But it would matter if he looked up twenty times, and each time saw a new person sitting placidly for his portrait. So it does not matter (comparatively speaking) how often humanity fails to imitate its ideal; for then all its old failures are fruitful. But it does frightfully matter how often humanity changes its ideal; for then all its old failures are fruitless.[184]

If individuals or communities are to make moral progress, there must be a transcendent and fixed source of moral goodness.

A second feature of progress in Chesterton's view is that the goal of it, its fixed reference point, must not be something simple, or mono-dimensional, but something composite and complex. If the former, then the whole process might be impersonal;

---

[183] Ibid., 312-3.

[184] Ibid., 313.

but if the latter, the process must surely be personal:

> The only arresting point is this: that if we suppose improvement to
> be natural, it must be fairly simple. The world might conceivably be
> working towards one consummation, but hardly towards any particu-
> lar arrangement of many qualities. To take our original simile: Nature
> by herself may be growing more blue; that is, a process so simple
> that it might be impersonal. But Nature cannot be making a careful
> picture made of many picked colours, unless Nature is personal. If
> the end of the world were mere darkness or mere light it might come
> as slowly and inevitably as dusk or dawn. But if the end of the world
> is to be a piece of elaborate and artistic chiaroscuro, then there must
> be design in it, either human or divine. The world, through mere
> time, might grow black like an old picture, or white like an old coat;
> but if it is turned into a particular piece of black and white art—then
> there is an artist.[185]

What human beings tend to want is not a simple, uniform happiness, but a complex and multifaceted happiness. "The perfect
happiness of men on earth (if it ever comes) will not be a flat
and solid thing, like the satisfaction of animals. It will be an
exact and perilous balance; like that of a desperate romance."[186]
Human beings do not want a merely natural drift toward longer
and longer noses, such as one might imagine could be provided by simple biological processes. Rather, humans want a
nose long enough to make a face interesting. "But we cannot
imagine a mere biological trend towards producing interesting
faces; because an interesting face is one particular arrangement
of eyes, nose, and mouth, in a most complex relation to each
other. Proportion cannot be a drift: it is either an accident or
a design."[187]

Human needs are complex, not the same as those of mere

---

[185] Ibid., 315-6.

[186] Ibid., 318.

[187] Ibid., 317-8.

animals, and not satisfied by the merely logical. For this reason human improvement involves a delicate balance of various qualities. As we saw earlier in this chapter, people should neither worship nature, like the pagans, nor flee from it, like puritans. Humans should revere nature, like a sister, a theme to which Chesterton was to return in his work on Francis of Assisi. Various attitudes and qualities should be carefully opposed and taken for what they are, without letting either have total control in such a way that they upset the equilibrium of a healthy human life. If nature is only capable of producing simple changes, then such a combination of needs can only be designed and met by a person, for "only a mind can place the exact proportions of a composite happiness":[188]

> This, then, is our second requirement for the ideal of progress. First, it must be fixed; second, it must be composite. It must not (if it is to satisfy our souls) be the mere victory of some one thing swallowing up everything else, love or pride or peace or adventure; it must be a definite picture composed of these elements in their best proportion and relation…If the beatification of the world is a mere work of nature, then it must be as simple as the freezing of the world, or the burning up of the world. But if the beatification of the world is not a work of nature but a work of art, then it involves an artist…only a personal God can possibly be leading you (if, indeed, you are being led) to a city with just streets and architectural proportions, a city in which each of you can contribute exactly the right amount of your own colour to the many coloured coat of Joseph.[189]

If there is any ultimate meaning to morality, if the deeply ingrained human habit of obeying the moral sense, the "ought" which one experiences deep within, is to have any ultimate significance, if the human practice of pursuing the good and avoiding the bad (however we interpret these in terms of

---

[188] Ibid., 319.

[189] Ibid.

content) is to be in any way coherent and meaningful, then there must be a person to intend that meaning. There must be a Significance or a Signified pointed to by the signs; a Reality who is at the same time also the Ultimate Signifier, the one who gives the complex gift of Elfland to those who dwell there, the laws for dealing with each other there and the law of joy that follows on from those laws:

> Twice again, therefore, Christianity had come in with the exact an-
> swer that I required. I had said, "The ideal must be fixed," and the
> Church had answered, "Mine is literally fixed, for it existed before
> anything else." I said secondly, "It must be artistically combined, like
> a picture"; and the Church answered, "Mine is quite literally a picture,
> for I know who painted it."[190]

The third and final mark of any understanding of true progress is that by leaving human affairs alone, they have a tendency to change and decay:

> We have remarked that one reason offered for being a progressive
> is that things naturally tend to grow better. But the only real reason
> for being a progressive is that things naturally tend to grow worse.
> The corruption in things is not only the best argument for being
> progressive; it is also the only argument against being conservative.
> The conservative theory would really be quite sweeping and unan-
> swerable if it were not for this one fact. But all conservatism is based
> upon the idea that if you leave things alone you leave them as they
> are. But you do not. If you leave a thing alone you leave it to a torrent
> of change. If you leave a white post alone it will soon be a black post.
> If you particularly want it to be white you must be always painting it
> again; that is, you must be always having a revolution.[191]

All human institutions, the Church included, grow old very quickly and we have to be unceasingly vigilant to prevent them corrupting. If things really stayed as they were, or if they

---

[190] Ibid.

[191] Ibid., 319-20.

improved, there would be no need for intervention. The true progressive knows that, given the state of fallen human nature, things must change if they are not to decline:

> Briefly, if you want the old white post you must have a new white post. But this which is true even of inanimate things is in a quite special and terrible sense true of all human things. An almost unnatural vigilance is really required of the citizen because of the horrible rapidity with which human institutions grow old.[192]

The person of true vision, who seeks real progress, is constantly attentive to human affairs and:

> ...must always be on the lookout for every privilege being abused, for every working right becoming a wrong. In this matter I am entirely on the side of the revolutionists. They are really right to be always suspecting human institutions; they are right not to put their trust in princes nor in any child of man. The chieftain chosen to be the friend of the people becomes the enemy of the people; the newspaper started to tell the truth now exists to prevent the truth being told.[193]

Once more Chesterton discovered that a deeply felt instinct—in this case the need to be ever vigilant in order to make sure that the good remains good—was also understood and expressed by Christianity, which constantly reminded people of a strange human leaning toward selfishness and so urged people to wrestle with their temptations:

> Christianity spoke again and said: "I have always maintained that men were naturally backsliders; that human virtue tended of its own nature to rust or to rot; I have always said that human beings as such go wrong, especially happy human beings, especially proud and prosperous human beings. This eternal revolution, this suspicion sustained through centuries, you (being a vague modern) call the doctrine of progress. If you were a philosopher you would call it, as I do, the doctrine of original sin. You may call it the cosmic advance

---

[192] Ibid., 320.

[193] Ibid., 321.

as much as you like; I call it what it is—the Fall."[194]

What Christianity calls the fallen human condition, a proclivity for self-centeredness and for not being what we are intended to be, is not grounds for being pessimistic about the human race. On the contrary, Chesterton saw it as:

> ...not only the only enlightening, but the only encouraging view of life...It refers evil back to the wrong use of the will, and thus declares that it can be righted by the right use of the will...happiness is not only a hope, but also in some strange manner a memory; and that we are all kings in exile.[195]

Happiness is the goal for which our hearts are made and the wrong use of the will—sin—itself provides a sign of this. When human hearts use free will to pursue the wrong goals, when they disobey the moral law laid down by the Moral Lawgiver, they are acting in a way that goes against their original nature, the nature intended by the Creator. They miss the goal[196] of human living as prescribed by the Creator. As we shall see shortly, this unnatural behavior ends in human unhappiness. For Chesterton the evidence for the fallen nature of human beings can be found merely by looking at the streets[197] and by observing everyday human behavior:

> The main point is that the Fall...is embodied in the common language talked on the top of an omnibus. Anybody might say, "Very

---

[194] Ibid.

[195] *The Thing: Why I Am a Catholic*, 311-12.

[196] Interestingly (as pointed out in our last chapter, when we discussed the notion of sin as the human tendency to forget who we are) *hamartia*, the New Testament word for "sin," is a concept image taken from the ancient world of sport, denoting the idea of a goal or target to be aimed at. The implication, then, is that by sinning human beings miss the goal of the fullness of their humanity as intended by God. Sin is a failure to be the human being fully alive that Irenaeus sees as the glorification of the Creator (*Adversus Haereses*, IV. xx. 7).

[197] *Orthodoxy*, 217.

few men are really manly." Nobody would say, "Very few whales are really whaley." If you wanted to dissuade a man from drinking his tenth whisky you would slap him on the back and say, "Be a man." No one who wished to dissuade a crocodile from eating his tenth explorer would slap it on the back and say, "Be a crocodile." For we have no notion of a perfect crocodile; no allegory of a whale expelled from his whaley Eden.[198]

Human beings can become more or less human by obeying or disobeying the moral law. Unlike other species, human beings can choose whether or not to act in conformity with their nature. In the Summa[199] Aquinas considers whether the word "God" denotes a nature or an operation—that is to say, a noun or a verb. Although he tends toward the substantival use of the word, he insists on retaining the tension between the two since, unlike creatures, whose identity and activity can be distinguished, the distinction between who God is and what God does cannot be made. The divine mystery is the giving, uttering, and breathing that God is said to be and do. If we recall our insight from earlier in this chapter, taken from Rahner, that human existence is what happens when God freely communicates Himself, then it follows that human beings are expressions of the self-giving nature that God is.

It also follows that the more we mirror God's self-giving, we become simultaneously more human and more divine. Jesus of Nazareth is the only utterly human being there has ever been, the only utterly perfect human response to God's self-giving. It follows that it is the saint, not the sinner, who is more human. When human beings choose not to obey the moral law, then, the unhappiness that follows on from an unnatural state of affairs is the result. However, instead of remedying this state

---

[198] *The Blatchford Controversies*, 385.

[199] *Summa Theologiae*, Ia, 13.8.

of affairs, this wrong use of the will, by means of the right use of the will, human beings often continue to sink further into the mire, chasing the wrong objects to satiate their desire for happiness:

> There comes an hour in the afternoon when the child is tired of 'pretending'; when he is weary of being a robber or a Red Indian. It is then that he torments the cat. There comes a time in the routine of an ordered civilization when the man is tired at playing at mythology and pretending that a tree is a maiden or that the moon made love to a man. The effect of this staleness is the same everywhere; it is seen in all drug-taking and dram-drinking and every form of the tendency to increase the dose. Men seek stranger sins or more startling obscenities as stimulants to their jaded senses. They seek after mad oriental religions for the same reason. They try to stab their nerves to life, if it were with the knives of the priests of Baal. They are walking in their sleep and try to wake themselves up with nightmares.[200]

Any addict would probably realize that excess is a substitute for joy. Addiction—to alcohol, food, sex, electronic gadgets, shopping, power, influence, and all manner of finite objects of desire—controls and enslaves a person and causes her to increase the dosage in order to bring deadened appetites to life. (Or, as the poet Ernest Dowson put it, "I cried for madder music and for stronger wine."[201]) As a person seeks legitimate goods but in excessive measures unworthy of human nature, he becomes less than human, and the original good that was sought in the object of desire no longer brings enjoyment; on the contrary, a deep sense of boredom and even despair can overtake the person who is driven to possess such goods. Then she is driven to increasingly extreme measures (tormenting the cat) in order to find the joy that she seeks:

---

[200] *The Everlasting Man*, 159.

[201] "Non sum qualis eram bonae sub regno Cynarae," https://www.theguardian.com/books/booksblog/2011/mar/14/non-sum-qualis-cynarae-dowson. [Last accessed 4.18.17]

The sound rule in the matter would appear to be like many other sound rules—a paradox. Drink because you are happy, but never because you are miserable. Never drink when you are wretched without it, or you will be like the grey-faced gin-drinker in the slum; but drink when you would be happy without it, and you will be like the laughing peasant of Italy. Never drink because you need it, for this is rational drinking, and the way to death and hell. But drink because you do not need it, for this is irrational drinking, and the ancient health of the world.[202]

The things of the cosmos are given by the Creator as gifts to be enjoyed, and the enjoyment of them leads to health and joy and points beyond the gifts to their Giver. Misuse, on the other hand, results in misery and disaster. As we shall see also in our next chapter, the moral law, as with all boundaries pertaining to human coexistence, is there to protect human flourishing.

The misery and lack of wholeness that follow on from compulsive behavior can only be rectified by disciplined habits, by an asceticism that trains a person to live a more measured human existence. So our capacity to enjoy life has to be trained. The "Doctrine of Conditional Joy" says that joy comes after we have fulfilled the condition, after we have obeyed the "if" of the moral law as prescribed by the Moral Lawgiver. As Chesterton puts it succinctly: "we should thank God for beer and Burgundy by not drinking too much of them. We owe[d]…an obedience to whatever made us."[203] Here we perceive once again the recurring Chestertonian theme of humble gratitude, in a spirit of receptivity, for the good gifts contained in the world.

As long as we receive the cosmos with gratitude we will find happiness; but the moment we seize or take the cosmos for

---

[202] *Heretics*, 92.

[203] *Orthodoxy*, 268.

our own amusement, as if we were the center of the cosmos and free to do with it as we like, instead of a recipient of its goodness and subject to the inner laws set out by its Creator, then we will encounter misery. The Creator does not impose the moral law as if it were some arbitrary decision taken on a bad day when he was in a bad mood, merely to stop human beings enjoying themselves; rather, the moral law is the very condition of human joy and enjoyment, something inherent to love itself, inherent to the nature of the cosmos as gift. In a cosmos created and given out of love, the contours of reality are love-shaped and only by deeply respecting these contours can things ever turn out well for human beings.

We have seen that during his time at the Slade Chesterton had searched for a philosophy of life that would aid him in his struggles with both solipsism and moral temptation. Starting from within his pain and unhappiness, and from a belief in the worthiness of trying to resolve that struggle, he discovered the search for the good, the voice of conscience, as a road to God. By experiencing his own (potential or actual) inner moral fragility and reflecting upon the cosmological consequences of that, he discovered an inner, non-rationalistic (albeit perfectly reasonable) way of listening to reality. To wrestle with choices between good and bad, to listen to the voice of conscience within, and to live with the happy or unhappy consequences of one's choices, is to move beyond the merely rational and to engage with reality in a different way.

Just as the ethics of Elfland state that the truth of God can never be demonstrated to the proud rationalist, so the promptings of conscience can never be proved in an utterly compelling way. Conscience is more like an invitation to listen to the cosmos with reverence and respect, to receive it as gift and not to manipulate it as something owed. It points to something deeper, inviting us either to trust or doubt the ultimate significance of the cosmos. It is the same kind of moral trust that is required when one loves or trusts somebody.

If Chesterton's own struggles with moral conscience were more individualistic in tone at their beginnings, by following this thread of experience toward the Giver of the moral law he was moved toward the world of others as he became the voice of the voiceless through his writing and speaking. Defending the ability of human beings to make free choices about moral decisions—"Was there not once a thing, a church, that taught us we were free in our souls?"[204]—he defended the poor, roused by Blatchford's association of behavior with environment, saying that a poor environment inevitably produced bad people. In an article entitled "The Eternal Heroism of the Slums," Chesterton tore into "this association of vice with poverty, the vilest and the oldest and the dirtiest of all the stories that insolence has ever flung against the poor."[205]

The journey of conscience leads to a God who is not just one's own individual God, but also the God of all others creatures and all creation. Therefore, as we shall see in our next chapter, this is a God who wants the individual to translate his moral instinct into a life of self-giving that makes a difference to the world of others. These whispers of conscience that move us beyond self to our neighbor find echoes in the global justice, solidarity, and stewardship of creation that are so readily displayed by postmodern culture a century later. The move toward a more just and democratic world is certainly a good thing. If postmodernity feels summoned to live out this more compassionate vision, Chesterton would invite them to ponder the fact that,

---

[204] *The Blatchford Controversies*, 395.

[205] Ward, *GKC*, 144.

historically, "[Human beings] gained their morality by guarding their religion...Anarchy was evil because it endangered the sanctity. And only when they made a holy day for God did they find they had made a holiday for men."[206] Arguing that, "There is no basis for democracy except in a dogma about the divine origin of man,"[207] his question would be: from where, therefore, does this admirable summons to solidarity arise?

5.3 THE QUALITIES OF THE GIFT: *the Main Philosophical Points of the Ethics of Elfland*

Chesterton's feelings toward the universe were not that it was some vast, sprawling, faceless, impersonal thing, but that it was cozy, lovely, and personal:

> A man chooses to have an emotion about the largeness of the world; why should he not choose to have an emotion about its smallness? It happened that I had that emotion. When one is fond of anything one addresses it by diminutives...[Materialists] professed that the universe was one coherent thing; but they were not fond of the universe. But I was frightfully fond of the universe and wanted to address it by a diminutive. [Materialists] showed only a dreary waste; but I felt a sort of sacred thrift. For economy is far more romantic than extravagance. To them stars were an unending income of halfpence; but I felt about the golden sun and the silver moon as a schoolboy feels if he has one sovereign and one shilling.[208]

Once again we are reminded of Chesterton's abiding sense of the magical and priceless nature of the ordinary and the everyday. Once more we realize that for him, life is "not only a pleasure but a kind of eccentric privilege." The two sexes, the hills, the trees, the plants and the Matterhorn, and everything

---

[206] *Orthodoxy*, 271.

[207] *What I Saw in America*, 261.

[208] *Orthodoxy*, 266-7.

else in the cosmos were precious jewels to be treasured from the wreckage of non-being. "This cosmos is indeed without peer and without price: for there cannot be another one."[209] Instead of the vast, endless, and dreary empty spaces of an infinite cosmos, Chesterton's image is of a cozy, personal gift full of infinite wonders to be explored.

The fourth chapter of *Orthodoxy* ends with a summary of the Ethics of Elfland which "in some dark way [Chesterton] thought before [he] could write, and felt before [he] could think."[210] These were listed earlier in this chapter, so here let us simply draw out the main philosophical points which were to become "the soil for the seeds of doctrine." The cosmos does not explain itself, it is "magic," no matter how vast and sprawling it proves to be, and no matter how far science goes toward explaining its secrets. The cosmos has qualities which human beings have a tendency to forget. The cosmos has something personal both in it and behind or beyond it, and is a gift like a work of art: it is a person-to-person gift and communication. Human beings should be grateful to the giver of the gift, and the best way to show gratitude is to enjoy the gift, which can only be done if one respects the law of the giver, inherent in the gift. "The proper form of thanks to [the giver] is some form of humility and restraint...we should thank God for beer and burgundy by not drinking too much of them...we also owe[d] an obedience to whatever made us." So the personal gift of freedom is to be used by submitting it in obedience to the laws of Elfland, for therein lies human happiness. Finally, "all good was a remnant to be stored and held sacred out of some primordial ruin. Man had saved his good as Crusoe saved his goods: he

---

[209] Ibid., 268.

[210] Ibid., 268.

had saved them from a wreck."[211]

I believe that Chesterton's "Ethics of Elfland" was the soil in which grew his theological vision of life as a constant religious experience. He himself lived, and he believed that all reality lives, in the presence of God. He saw Elfland, created reality, as pointing to and revealing the divine reality, the Creator God who is its source. As we saw earlier in this chapter, when he places his vision of the cosmos in the mouth of Syme, for Chesterton everything can be a sign and sacrament, if only we have eyes to see. Chesterton saw that there is a totality, an all-determining reality, which grounds everything that we experience in his cosmos. In experiencing glimpses of this divine reality, in and through the experiences that we have in this cosmos, we also experience ourselves as contingent beings in a relationship with this God and as beings who are related to other beings that are dependent on this God. The "root horror" experienced by Gabriel Syme was:

> ...isolation, and there are no words to express the abyss between isolation and having one ally. It may be conceded to the mathematicians that four is twice two. But two is not twice one; two is two thousand times one. That is why, in spite of a hundred disadvantages, the world will always return to monogamy.[212]

In solitude, in recognizing ourselves as separate creations, we are opened up to the possibility of relationship, of interpersonal communion with creatures similar to ourselves. Chesterton saw himself as a human being in radical need, but also as one who trusted that, underneath, or behind, or at the heart of

---

[211] Ibid.

[212] *The Man Who Was Thursday*, 549.

everything, the cosmos makes sense—it has a principle of unity which grounds the worth of human existence. Ultimately, all dragons and evil dwarves notwithstanding, Elfland is a friendly place, and human beings are called to be friendly too.

Chesterton, it seems to me, aligns himself in some respects with the likes of Karl Rahner[213] and other theologians[214] who view the fundamental dynamism of the human spirit as offering the conditions for the possibility of religious experience. Every human experience reveals its openness to the infinite and offers in a dim, implicit, and unconscious way the God who is later experienced in a more illuminated, explicit, and conscious way. At the Slade Chesterton stared meaninglessness, despair, loneliness, and possibly the prospect of death by his own hand fully in the face; in his *Autobiography* he claimed that he held onto religion by one thin thread of thanks, by a burst of gratitude at the gift of existence.

It is easy to see how Chesterton's personal journey fits the description offered by Gerald O'Collins, when the latter expands the emphasis of some theologians on the dynamism of the human spirit toward the infinite to include "our drive toward the fullness of life, meaning/truth, and love. Spontaneously we seek to escape from death, absurdity and isolation. We long to live, to see the basic meaning and truth of things, and to love and be loved."[215] O'Collins goes on to cite the transcendental therapy of Karlfried Graf Dürckheim,

...who studied situations in which human beings felt threatened by

---

[213] See *Foundations of Christian Faith*, 19-23, 31-5, 51-71.

[214] Wolfhart Pannenberg writes: "we experience simultaneously the Infinite that lies within finite things and the finite that is its manifestation"; "the confused intuition of the Infinite, which lies, prethematically, at the basis of all human consciousness, is already in truth a mode of the presence of God" (*Metaphysics and the Idea of God*, 25, 29).

[215] *Rethinking Fundamental Theology*, 54.

death in its various forms, became overwhelmed by a sense of injustice and meaningless absurdity, and were abandoned, cruelly treated, and hated. Then they could be given life, experience a deeper order and meaning in things, and know themselves to be the object of generous love. These experiences made people long even more for some experience of life, meaning, and love that would change everything.[216]

We recall again here that after his own dark period at the Slade, Chesterton wrote to his friend Bentley:

> Inwardly speaking I have had a funny time. A meaningless fit of depression, taking the form of certain absurd psychological worries, came upon me, and instead of dismissing it and talking to people, I had it out and went very far into the abysses indeed. The result was that I found that things, when examined, necessarily spelt such a mystically satisfactory state of things, that without getting back to earth, I saw lots that made me certain it is all right. The vision is fading into common day now, and I am glad. It is embarrassing talking to God face to face, as a man speaketh to a friend.[217]

Alluding to the experience of the Lord which Moses had in Exodus 33, Chesterton saw the whole period—of darkness and the subsequent realization of the goodness and giftedness of all created reality—as an encounter with God, after which never again is there a record of Chesterton falling into despair and helplessness. His life's work sought to articulate this sense of the goodness of created reality. He was able to write in the *Autobiography* that:

> At the back of our brains, so to speak, there was [subsequent to the Slade] a forgotten blaze or burst of astonishment at our own existence. The object of the artistic and spiritual life was to dig for this submerged sunrise of wonder; so that a man might suddenly understand that he was alive, and be happy.[218]

---

[216] Ibid., n. 20

[217] W. Oddie, *CRO*, 124.

[218] *Autobiography*, 92.

For Chesterton, trained as an artist (though it is open to conjecture precisely how much a man of his natural ability was able to learn at the Slade), there is a direct link between the artistic imagination and a healthy spirituality.

---

6. ART: *Remembering that We Have Forgotten the Qualities of the Gift*

We have seen that Chesterton believes that the child's grasp of ens, of being, of the fact that "There is an is," is the foundation of all his subsequent thoughts. That grasp has to be there in order that any other thought can take place. Once that grasp is there, an awareness of the contingent nature of reality follows, at least in an ideal situation, when all is as it should be and the mind is working properly. However, very often the mind is not working properly and the situation is some distance from being ideal. As we have already seen, many things can conspire to leave us unfree for faith and prevent us from viewing reality in all its complexity and beauty.

So often to the adult mind nothing is more humdrum than everyday reality. However, says Chesterton, to the little child reality is not humdrum. It only becomes humdrum as the child grows a little bit older and more sophisticated. Why does the smaller child love the element of surprise in the fairy tales? Is it because he does not yet know enough about life, has not yet experienced enough of this world to become disillusioned and disavowed of the magic of Elfland? No, replies Chesterton:

> This elementary wonder...is not a mere fancy derived from the fairy tales; on the contrary, all the fire of the fairy tales is derived from this. Just as we all like love tales because there is an instinct of sex, we all like astonishing tales because they touch the nerve of the ancient

instinct of astonishment.[219]

There is something primordial about the sense of awe in human beings. When we are very young, says Chesterton,

> …we do not need fairy tales, we only need tales. Mere life is interesting enough. A child of seven is excited by being told that Tommy opened a door and saw a dragon. But a child of three is excited by being told that Tommy opened a door… even nursery tales only echo an almost pre-natal leap of interest and amazement. These tales say that apples were golden only to refresh the forgotten moment when we found that they were green. They make rivers run with wine only to make us remember, for one wild moment, that they run with water…All that we call common sense and rationality and practicality and positivism only means that for certain dead levels of our life we forget that we have forgotten. [220]

Existence itself, the fact that anything is at all, is, or should be, the first cause of wonder. But we forget this because of the rote nature of everyday living as we grow up.

> "All that we call spirit and art and ecstasy only means that for one awful instant we remember that we forget."[221]

Although the native human instinct for wonder can get dulled and damaged with living in the world, artistic, ecstatic, still, and silent moments can become deeply prayerful encounters—another way of listening to and interpreting reality. They can awaken us to appreciate the nature of the cosmos as sheer contingent and unnecessary gift. They then carry out on us a healing effect, offering us space to bring us to an awareness of our true selves and our place in a bigger picture, in a shared and contingent cosmos.

---

[219] *Orthodoxy*, 256-7.

[220] Ibid, 257.

[221] Ibid.

Fairy tales, art and other human experiences do not, for Chesterton, only provide us with raw material on which to reflect rationally and scientifically; they have a remedial function, reminding us of who we are.[222] In fact for Chesterton the whole purpose and value in art is to awaken and keep alive in human beings the sense of wonder. "The success of any work of art is achieved when we say of any subject, a tree or a cloud or a human character, 'I have seen that a thousand times and I never saw it before.'"[223] Chesterton believes that art and the power of the imagination can heal us, renew our way of seeing and help us to regain the humility and gratitude that are needed to perceive the cosmos as it is.

That an artistic imagination and sensibility are necessary to know the deeper truths about life was a major theme in Chesterton. He believed that we are all in need of what Aidan Nichols calls "a kind of therapy of perception."[224] Nichols continues:

> What Chesterton admires in an artist or writer is, often enough, the ability to cleanse the inner eye from the filming effects of excessive familiarity or of cultural distortion so that our perceptual limits may approximate more fully to those of integral nature. This is essentially the basis for his veneration of Blake: admitting that the sentimental classicism of Blake's rival, Thomas Stothard, was sometimes more finely executed in strictly painterly terms than Blake's own work, Chesterton adds that this argument reflects "the duel between the artist who has the higher and harder ambition to be man—that is, an archangel."[225]

---

[222] In Plato's *Republic* it is worth noting in this regard that the verbal arts and mathematics are part of a young man's education only after years of studying music, poetry, dance, and observation of the stars.

[223] *The Thing: Why I Am a Catholic*, 173.

[224] *A Grammar of Consent*, 169.

[225] Ibid., 170.

Nichols sees Chesterton as belonging to that long line of thinkers, from Plato to Kierkegaard, which regards rhetoric and creative use of the imagination as vital for removing certain obstacles to insight. Rational statement alone of the issue under discussion is not always sufficient if people are to see the truth. While for many people there may be both an element of attraction and repulsion about Chesterton's use of humor, paradox, and other stylistic features, C. S. Lewis thought that Chesterton's playfulness and humor arose naturally as he gazed at reality, and were not merely a question of stylistic affectation: "The humour is inseparable from the argument. It is [as Aristotle taught]…the "bloom" on dialectic itself."[226] It is the mark of the artist.

Chesterton's training in art did indeed serve him well, for this artist turned writer wrote visually, creating an almost verbal impressionism. Although he wrote about innumerable things in his career, art was a theme he returned to again and again. Da Vinci, Michelangelo, Raphael, Giotto, Botticelli, G. F. Watts, and many other artists were all treated in his writings over the years. Art was something that characterized human beings uniquely for Chesterton: "Art is the signature of man."[227] When it came to defining what he meant by art, Chesterton, as with so many topics he treats, does not give only one simple answer that excludes other insights:

> All the very great classics of art are a rebuke to extravagance not in one direction but in all directions. The figure of a Greek Venus is a rebuke to the fat women of Rubens and also a rebuke to the thin women of Aubrey Beardsley…This is perhaps the test of a very great work of classic creation, that it can be attacked on inconsistent grounds, and that it attacks its enemies on inconsistent grounds. Here is a broad

---

[226] *Surprised by Joy*, 153.

[227] *The Everlasting Man*, 34.

and simple test. If you hear a thing being accused of being too tall
and too short, too red and too green, too bad in one way and too bad
also in the opposite way, then you may be sure that it is very good.[228]

As when discussing all subjects, Chesterton seeks to defend
truths that are being attacked from many angles and to maintain that delicate balance of truth that makes it seem to some
that he is being contradictory, when he is actually respecting
the deeply paradoxical nature of truth.

One of Chesterton's main criticisms of much of modern art
was that it had abandoned the transcendent and eternal, and
gone frantically in search of the transient and the new. As one
art movement gained ascendancy over another, Chesterton said
that it was:

> ...just as if one controversialist were called a Thursdayite, and the oth-
> er completely eclipsed him by being called a Fridayite...The notion
> that every generation proves the last generation worthless, and is in
> its turn proved worthless by the next generation, is an everlasting
> vision of worthlessness.[229]

Art had become more and more divorced from the quest for
the eternal in direct proportion to the degree to which it had
been left in the hands of the experts:

> The tragedy of humanity has been the separation of art from the peo-
> ple. Indeed, it is a queer fact that the same progressives who insist that
> government shall be democratic often insists that art must be [elitist],
> and "the public," which is a god when they are talking about votes,
> becomes a brute when they are talking about books and pictures.[230]

Art belonged to the common people and everyone can be an

---

[228] "The Macbeths," in *The Spice of Life*, ed. Dorothy Collins, 43.

[229] "Are the Artists Going Mad?" *Century Magazine*, December 1922, cited in D. Ahlquist, *Common Sense 101*, 57.

[230] Ibid., 58.

artist, even if not everyone is equally talented as a painter, a sculptor, a poet, or a writer.

For Chesterton the creation of a work of art is a divine act, a share in the creative nature of God and a faculty which only the human being possesses. It was not a monkey that painted in the prehistoric caves.[231] As Chesterton points out in *The Everlasting Man*, the origins of our species are shrouded in mystery. However, paleontology sees no gradual transition from the absence of tools to their appearance in history. For paleontologists, the human being remains an animal very different from all others, none of which are known to have made and used implements (and an ever-wider and more complex variety of them).

We are creatures that create. Our ancestors first created tools and then used them to display their artwork by covering the walls of their caves with paintings of animals. The apparatus which they had made with their own hands were made for a purpose—indeed, to express that same purpose symbolically. To say, as we have already seen that Chesterton did, that "art is the signature of man," is to express clearly the uniqueness of human beings as creatures that make tools and use them to create symbols. Human beings are beings with a message to communicate: they ascribe meaning and purpose to existence. It is here that Chesterton sees the origin of art—"all art is religious."[232] "All art is born when the temporary touches the eternal."[233] All art is an attempt to ascribe an interpretation to existence. True art always points to the nature of the cosmos as being something full of meaning.

In Chapter 5 of *Orthodoxy* Chesterton makes the connection

---

[231] See *The Everlasting Man*, 33-4.

[232] *ILN*, 15 July 1922, cited in D. Ahlquist, *Common Sense 101*, 63.

[233] Ibid., 64.

between art and creation. Pointing out that the notion of creation is at the heart of Christian theology, he says:

> ...the root phrase for all Christian theism was this, that God was a creator, as an artist is a creator. A poet is so separate from his poem that he himself speaks of it as a little thing he has "thrown off." Even in giving it forth he has flung it away. This principle that all creation and procreation is a breaking off is at least as consistent through the cosmos as the evolutionary principle that all growth is a branching out. A woman loses a child even in having a child. All creation is separation. Birth is as solemn a parting as death.[234]

The transcendence of the Christian Creator is like the separation of Artist from artifact, Poet from poem. The poem is the purposeful and homely place that the Poet has created for human beings. We should feel at home here, but without feeling at home. We must be in the world but not of the world. We should love the world, but not worship it, since it is a world that has gone wrong:

> According to most philosophers, God in making the world enslaved it. According to Christianity, in making it, He set it free. God had written, not so much a poem, but rather a play; a play he had planned as perfect, but which had necessarily been left to human actors and stage-managers, who had since made a great mess of it.[235]

The world, then, is our home, given to us as the gift of the Creator, and we have our role in that world. Once the bit of the puzzle that is the Christian notion of creation had fallen into place, the other pieces rapidly followed for Chesterton:

> And then followed an experience impossible to describe. It was as if I had been blundering about since my birth with two huge and unmanageable machines, of different shapes and without apparent connection—the world and the Christian tradition. I had found this

---

[234] *Orthodoxy*, 281.

[235] Ibid., 281-2.

hole in the world: the fact that one must somehow find a way of loving the world without trusting it; somehow one must love the word
without being worldly. I found this projecting feature of Christian
theology, like a sort of hard spike, the dogmatic insistence that God
was personal, and had made a world separate from Himself. The spike
of dogma fitted exactly into the hole in the world—it had evidently
been meant to go there—and then the strange thing began to happen.
When once these two parts of the two machines had come together,
one after another, all the other parts fitted and fell in with an eerie
exactitude. I could hear bolt after bolt over all the machinery falling
into its place with a kind of click of relief. Having got one part right,
all the other parts were repeating that rectitude, as clock after clock
strikes noon. Instinct after instinct was answered by doctrine after
doctrine.[236]

All of the instincts that Chesterton had had, as described in the
Ethics of Elfland, were embodied by the truths of Christianity.
He was correct in supposing that roses were red or elephants
have trunks by choice: the divine choice. He was right to suppose that human joy is conditional, since this is what the doctrine of the Fall states. The suspicion he had held since being a
boy that the cosmos was not vast and unfriendly, but snug and
small, made perfect sense because all works of art are small in
the sight of the artist. Even the notion:

> that somehow good was not merely a tool to be used, but a relic
> to be guarded, like the goods from Crusoe's ship—even that had
> been the wild whisper of something originally wise, for, according to
> Christianity, we were indeed the survivors of a wreck, the crew of a
> golden ship that had gone down before the beginning of the world.[237]

Good was something logically inexplicable and placed within
the very contours of the cosmos by its Creator. Human beings
are to seek and guard the good:

---

[236] Ibid., 282-3.

[237] Ibid., 283.

> The principle of progress in which all sane men believe is mainly this: that we are engaged and ought to be engaged in a persistent effort to change the external world into the image of something that is within ourselves; to turn what is, as far as we are concerned, a chaos into what shall be, as far as we are concerned, a cosmos. God did not give us a universe, but rather the materials of a universe. The world is not a picture, it is a palette…Heaven gave us this splendid chaos of colours and materials. Heaven gave us a few instinctive rules of practice and caution corresponding to "do not put the brush in the mouth." And Heaven gave us a vision…It may be that we shall never reach perfection, but we may continue to approach it. But even if we only approach it, we must believe that it exists, we must believe that there is some incomprehensible statement of what it is and where it is.[238]

Conscience, then, is the eternal summons to share in the work of the Creator, to co-create a work of art.

In order to see such intimate links between religion and art, Chesterton thinks that the imagination is necessary. Morris argues that Chesterton values imagination as the Romantics had valued it, as a cognitive power, a power of insight into hidden realities and the divine power of creativity. That is why he saw one of the constituents of religion as a "tendency to break out into colours and symbols, to do wild and beautiful things with flowers and garments," and why he lamented that this tendency had become separated from religion and was now known as "art."[239] One of the reasons he loved Francis so much was because of his romantic imagination, seeing him as "primarily a poet," who called fire his brother and water his sister, using an imaginative cognition that saw life as an interrelated whole, in which spirit and matter were connected, as the former tried to discern meaning in the latter. Art was able to explore this meaning in matter: art was a playground in which to enjoy the

---

[238] *Daily News*, 15th September 1906, in Morris, *TTFL*, 137.

[239] *The Truest Fairy Tale*, 46.

exploration of the cosmos.

For Chesterton, then, there is no such thing as Oscar Wilde's art for art's sake. "Philosophy is always present in a work of art."[240] And the true artist is driven by an ache to find a philosophy, to discover meaning, to transcend time and touch the eternal, to find some sense in the things around him, using his images and his creativity to show us the shadows of the eternal things that he perceives dimly through the veil of the temporary: "something behind the clouds or within the trees; and he believes that the pursuit of beauty is the way to find it; that imagination is a sort of incantation that can call it up."[241] Deep within the artist, whether recognized or not, there is an eternal hunger. "A man cannot have the energy to produce good art without having the energy to pass beyond it. A small artist is content with art; a great artist is content with nothing except everything."[242] The best artist, therefore, is the one who follows the hunger for something more. Even bad art is an attempt to make a statement about meaning and an attempt to capture forever in a single moment something which is at once eternal and ephemeral.

Chesterton says that a revival of interest in art:

...does not lie in increasing the number of artists who can startle us with complex things, but by increasing the number of people who can be startled by common things. It lies in restoring relish and receptivity to human society; and that is another question and a more important one...It not only means making more Giottos, but also

---

[240] *Illustrated London News*, 15 June 1929, cited in D. Ahlquist, *Common Sense 101*, 61.

[241] *The Everlasting Man*, 105.

[242] *Heretics*, 198.

making more shepherds.[243]

Once again wonder, receptivity, gratitude, and a refusal
to be cynical, grasping, and manipulative, are vital to the
Chestertonian understanding of art. These come together to
constitute a predisposition that better fits a person to appreciate art and the eternal. Perhaps in a postmodern culture in
which there seems to be a surge of popular interest in art, the
apologist might discern signs of an increase in wonder and a
humbler spiritual search for meaning and the transcendent,
and therefore a possible openness to the message of the Artist
that is Christ, who is himself the artistic self-expression of God.
Perhaps there is a corresponding need for poetic apologists in
such a culture, Gospel artists who can awaken all that is sleeping and highest within the surrounding culture, and who are
able to express themselves creatively and imaginatively, such
that the human imagination is better able to discern what is
already there to be seen before its eyes.

Chesterton offers the example of himself in this regard. He
saw his own vocation as a writer in such artistic terms. "I do
propose to strike wherever possible this note of what is new and
strange, and for that reason the style even on so serious a subject may sometimes be deliberately grotesque and fanciful."[244]
Like the Romantics, he saw himself as both sage and artist. He
was a controversialist and rhetorician who often spoke sug-
gestively rather than definitively, even if his conclusions may
sound too definite for some people. Like Dickens, his great
literary hero, he wrote and conveyed his meaning by painting caricatures. He exaggerated for effect and regularly made

[243] "Are the Artists Going Mad?" *Century Magazine*, December 1922, cited in D. Ahlquist,
Common Sense 101, 59.

[244] *The Everlasting Man*, 18.

lateral-thinking connections between unlike realities: "There are…certain real advantages in pictorial symbols, and one of them is that everything that is pictorial suggests, without naming and defining. There is a road from the eye to the heart that does not go through the intellect."

His imagery always aimed at rousing sleeping spirits to action. "The supreme and most poetical value of all poetry is this, that in poetry, as in music, a note is struck which expresses beyond the power of rational statement, a condition of mind, and all actions arise from a condition of mind."[245] His dexterity with symbol, metaphor, analogy, and paradox made a virtue out of necessity, because it is ultimately impossible to describe the deeper things in life and God by any other means: "all descriptions of the creating and sustaining principle in things must be metaphorical, because they must be verbal."[246]

Chesterton would have agreed with C. S. Lewis, who wrote that:

> The man who wishes to speak to the uneducated in English must learn their language. It is not enough that he should abstain from using what he regards as 'hard words.' He must discover empirically what words exist in the language of his audience and what they mean in that language.[247]

Chesterton was aware of the powerful potential of words to capture the human imagination. He analyzed the verbal manipulations, illogicalities, and non sequiturs that were regularly peddled in the newspapers, literature, and theatre of the day, aware of the fascination that forms of expression can exert upon us, aware that a surrounding culture can transmit massaging

---

[245] *Robert Browning*, 185.

[246] *Orthodoxy*, 281.

[247] "God in the Dock," *God in the Dock: Essays in Theology*, 98.

messages. He saw one of the Church's roles as being the guardian of all values and, therefore, the guardian of the value of words,[248] which was "a question of liberty from catchwords and headlines and hypnotic repetitions and all the plutocratic platitudes imposed on us by advertisement and journalism."[249]

However, while such artistic and intellectual brilliance might have led to some degree of pride in the weaker among us, it is often said of Chesterton that one of his most striking features was his unassuming humility and self-effacement, which were not poses but his truest self. He took himself very lightly indeed. He saw his own artistic task in this world as akin to that of the priest. "The preaching friar puts his sermon into popular language, the missionary fills his sermon with anecdotes and even jokes, because he is thinking of his mission and not himself."[250] He admitted he had firm opinions, pointed out "the meaningless affectation of impartiality" and maintained that "It is impossible for any man to state what he believes as if he did not believe it";[251] and yet he referred to himself as nothing more than a journalist throughout his life and kept his writings and the fame that accompanied them strictly in perspective.

The true artist, the authentic human being, is, for Chesterton, humble because she knows her place in creation: the humbler she is, the greater she is:

> Progress is superiority to oneself, and it is stopped dead by superiority to others...The more we attempt to analyse that strange element of wonder, which is the soul of all the arts, the more we shall see that it must depend on some subordination of the self to a glory existing

---

[248] *The Thing: Why I Am a Catholic*, 261.

[249] Ibid., 265.

[250] *The Well and the Shallows*, 350.

[251] *An Outline of Christianity*, http://www.gkc.org.uk/gkc/books/upon-this-rock.html [last accessed 31st January 2012].

beyond it, and even in spite of it. Man always feels as a creature
when he acts as a creator. When he carves a cathedral, it is to make
a monster that can swallow him.[252]

For Chesterton, the cultivation of a creative spirit, giving ourselves over to creativity, means using our own blessings and
capacities in order to build rather than destroy; it entails recognizing and appreciating those same creative capacities and abilities in others. The only alternative to this is to cultivate a sense
of personal inadequacy and to suffer the jealousies, pettiness
and resentment that follow on from this. We either become an
artist, contributing to the work of art that is the cosmos and
regarding appreciatively the artwork of others in that cosmos,
or else we become destructive, critical, bitter, and petty. Art is a
reminder that human beings are part of a whole, a reality, which
is much greater than themselves, but which is also a reality that
invites them to play their part in contributing to the beauty of
the whole. In their contribution, in their creativity, in seeking
the truth and expressing it in the good life, human beings find
their own joy.

There are echoes in von Balthasar of the themes we have
looked at in this chapter: the need for humility to interpret
reality correctly; art and its remedial function; and the notion
of the cosmos and human existence as works of art. Balthasar
rejected the idea that we arrive at religious faith through two
successive stages of inquiry, the first being rational and the second religious. He maintains that to see life properly there has
to be a central trust that remains open to mystery, a disposition
that gives priority to love over knowledge.[253] Truth is more than
a thing to be grasped and mastered, for Balthasar; it is a person,

---

[252] *Irish Impressions, Collected Works* Vol. 20, 183-4.

[253] *Theo-Logic* I, 261.

the person of Christ, and therefore truth is something we enter into through relationship. We need to "learn to see again, which is to say, to experience the total otherness of Christ as the outshining of God's sublimity and glory."[254] With a line that would have pleased Chesterton immensely, Cardinal Ratzinger, in his homily at Balthasar's funeral in 1988, quoted a line from Augustine which he believed grasped the Swiss theologian's main focus: "Our entire task in this life...consists in healing the eyes of the heart so they may be able to see God."[255]

Balthasar, like Chesterton, recognizes that God's revelation is something like a great work of art: it attracts us. However, this revelation does not remain at the level of mere cozy attraction. We are also invited to respond in love to the self-communication or self-bestowal in love that constitute the gift of God. When we perceive that love is "the core of everything,"[256] that "the very existence of truth, of eternal truth, is grounded in love,"[257] then we are called to move beyond ourselves and to engage our freedom in the loving service of others so that individuals and societies are transformed.[258] The divine self-communication which comes in countless ways through the manifold treasures of creation and which is seen in its fullness in Christ is utterly contingent and freely given gift, given out of love, which invites us to respond in love toward its other recipients.

---

[254] Ibid., 20.

[255] *Communio* 15 (Winter 1988), 512.

[256] *The Glory of the Lord* Vol. VII, 19.

[257] *Theo-Logic* I, 272.

[258] *Theo-Drama* Vol. I, 15-17.

7. Concluding Remarks

According to Chesterton, to be filled with gratitude and humility before the gift of reality is to possess a basic disposition or stance on life that enables a person to be more receptive of the richness of life. When the cosmos and human existence in the cosmos are received as gift, one is more able to see them correctly and to discover the treasures they contain. On the contrary, when one tries to grasp and manipulate the world, understanding it as something owed to human beings and ours by right, one can neither understand nor enjoy properly what life has to offer. Lonergan perceived that for Chesterton the face of God is hidden in everyday existence, and the spirit of gratitude and receptivity is the condition for perceiving that face.

Any agenda for apologetics in a secular culture, therefore, needs to help people to interpret their ordinary lives as gift, and not as something owed or expected. Everything that we have—our loved ones, sexuality, food, drink, our careers, our gifts, the material things in our life, the breath in our bodies, and life itself—is contingent gift, utterly unnecessary. To recognize this and be grateful for it is the first step on the road to God for Chesterton. To take for granted anything that is actually gift in our life, to perceive something as a mere satellite to our own existence, is an enormous impediment to perceiving the Giver of the gift. Conversely, to begin to perceive, no matter how dimly, the fragile, precious, and contingent nature of all that we have as sheer gift is to ready ourselves for the gift of God's self-disclosure.

We noted that Dulles sees Chesterton's approach to doing apologetics as involving the cumulative case method that is found in Augustine, Pascal, and Newman. Chapter II revealed that Chesterton's own life showed that there is often a need to get free from something—an image, a vision of self or universe that is often conditioned by many cultural and personal factors—before one can set out on the path to God. We saw in this third chapter that early on in his career Chesterton wrote about the analogy of being. He perceived the world as a network of analogies consisting of unity with difference, and consequently an infinite opportunity for paradox. Paradox presents a difference between two things, and seeks for the relation which unites them. This relation takes us back beyond the two contrasted things to their cause, which is God, the fullness of being and the source of all beings who participate in the divine being. Because all being is analogical, all attempts to systematize thought, as Aquinas and Kierkegaard also realized, will have to be content to wrestle with paradoxes. The world is incapable of being encapsulated in a system or formula, which has implications for the way that the Church does all her theology and apologetics.

Chesterton's understanding of reality and truth as paradoxical meant that he was utterly opposed to any form of reductionism, an over-simplistic analysis which does not allow the cosmos to speak in all its multi-colored and glorious complexity. For Chesterton, therefore, when the Church is at its best and being faithful to her mission to speak the truth, she will bring together the insights and truths of those positions which appear to be opposites and make sense out of them. The Church allows opposites to be what they are in themselves, and also shows how they can coexist, finding a balance that leads to sanity. As the trysting place of all truths, the Church has to find a way of combining the truth of opposing positions without either contradicting its own message or compromising the truths of the opposing positions.

Any Chestertonian notion of apologetics, therefore, may never be reduced to an approach that permits only a few select bits of evidence when making the case for the existence of God. The cumulative case method relies on the idea that the best way of showing that it is not irrational or unintelligent to believe in God involves a set of convergences of various pieces of evidence to be found in the world and in the human person. For Chesterton, since reality is a multi-dimensional and complex whole, evidence for God, the Creator of reality and the Giver of the gift of reality, can come from many sources, and so apologetics can never be either merely a heart affair or merely an intellectual affair. The Church's theology and apologetics need to be roomy enough to hold in tension all the paradoxes that reveal the Source of the multi-faceted gift that the cosmos and human life within it are. It is not so much that we cannot make definite claims about truth but, as Lateran IV noted, the truth will always be richer and more paradoxical than our limited minds, images, and expressions can grasp and express at a given moment. Apologetics and all branches of theological exploration have to be humble and open to refinement through dialogue.

The Christian creed's ability to allow for paradox permits opposites to coexist and creates a harmonious balance out of them, and what Chesterton understands by Christian orthodoxy is this ability to set free the various dimensions of reality in order to be what they truly are, and to limit them only in so far as they might destroy the healthy and precarious equilibrium of human sanity and flourishing. Theological health and sanity become unbalanced when one aspect of God, one part of the truth about God, becomes over-emphasized to the detriment of another part of that truth. When the part becomes greater than the whole, a whole procession of sub-Christian idols result. To believe that God prefers truth to compassion, or compassion to truth, is to place one's trust in an idol; to believe that the beauty and energy of youth speak more to us of the divine than the wisdom and restraint of old age, or vice versa, is to bow down before a false divinity. The ineffability of God should keep us humble in our theological endeavors, and yet we must theologize, for it is part of what it means to be a creature to strive always to speak of God with all the means at our disposal—which for Chesterton means nothing less than the whole cosmos.

That is why he believed that one cannot evade the issue of God. Since everything in being, from pigs to the binomial theory, has God as its ultimate source, talking about anything means talking about God. Nothing is irrelevant to the Christian faith, and an honest and open discussion about anything can shed light on the mystery of God. For Chesterton, therefore, any healthy apologetics must be prepared to talk about anything. It must constantly put the Christian tradition in dialogue with the world, just as Christianity embraced all that was good in the old paganism of antiquity, while at the same time be able to refine and correct its inordinate expressions and errors.

As we shall see again in the next chapter, any healthy apologetics must enter into the thrilling adventure that is true dialogue between the Christian tradition and the many cultures of the world. The Church will thereby pledge itself to a perilous balancing act: she will follow the example of Karl Rahner, seeking to discern the seeds of the Word and the presence of the Spirit in the movements and opinions of the cultures of the world, while simultaneously proclaiming the Christ as the Word made flesh and the one to whom the Spirit always leads, and therefore at times offering refinements and corrections to some of those movements and opinions. The attempt to carry off this demanding and exhilarating equilibrium is the thrilling romance of Christian orthodoxy.

In *Orthodoxy* Chesterton describes how he himself became a Christian because of the abundant evidence provided by the cosmos. The various bits of evidence converged to convince him of the fatherhood that makes the whole world one. Although several factors can conspire to make us unaware of that transcendent underpinning of reality, we have looked in this chapter how Chesterton describes in *Orthodoxy*, and specifically in "The Ethics of Elfland," how he himself became aware of God through the facts of contingency and morality. Since the whole tone of Chesterton's wondering about Elfland is rooted in a spirit of awe and gratitude for the gift of a cosmos, acquired after a long Augustinian inner struggle, one could not accuse him in *Orthodoxy* of advocating a cold, distant, rationalistic, theistic approach to arguing for the existence of God. Filled with an inner disposition of humility, wonder, and gratitude, he had the simple and fundamental realization that "this world does not explain itself."[259]

Noting the scoffing of some of the scientists of the day at the claims of faith, Chesterton points out the unproved and unprovable assumptions on which all thought, logic, and argument depend: that the human mind can know reality beyond itself in some way, and that logic will always give valid answers from true premises. These acts of faith are absolutely necessary if the world is going to function. This readiness to critique cultural assumptions and thought processes are a necessary part of the apologist's task at any moment in history.

Human reason is stirred when the cosmos meets something mysterious and primordial in the heart and soul of a human being. This mysterious something—which is the first

---

[259] *Orthodoxy*, 268.

consciousness of being—is activated a long time before human beings learn how to reason. To submit to being, to receive it as utterly unnecessary and wonderful gift, is the first and necessary step before any other rational and scientific endeavor can occur in the cosmos which, as Jaki points out, is the very thing that modern philosophy refuses to do. One has to first receive the gift of being as truth before one can proceed to enjoy as many human adventures as one likes.

Chesterton invites us to let go of mere cleverness and to enter a deeper level of questioning and wondering. It is the difference between asking "How?" and asking "Why?" Chesterton explored in his work on Aquinas the many ways in which modern philosophy becomes confused by refusing to bow first before the gift of being, and by confusing "how" with "why." To acknowledge the priority of being is to acknowledge one's own contingency and the contingency of the whole cosmos, which is, in the thought of Lash and Rahner, to acknowledge oneself as creature before the Creator. The finite, contingent, and incomplete things of the cosmos change and can only be explained as part of something that is complete and does not change. The things of the cosmos are simply not all that they can be. Chesterton perceives that at every moment of their existence, all contingent beings are actively being maintained in existence by God, *ipsum esse subsistens*.

Chesterton also notes that the strange phenomena of the cosmos (such as sunsets, or birds being born from eggs) repeat themselves again and again, and he says that to understand the repetition of these phenomena as laws implies a Lawgiver. With its own conceptual framework and methodology, science can only describe these phenomena as repetitions. To use the word "law" is to introduce another factor: it is to say that there is something personal at work in the cosmos.

The things and events of the cosmos imply a Person with free will, which implies purpose or meaning. The cosmos has significance; it points to something; it means something and, if it means something, then there must be something personal behind the meaning which intends that meaning. Since most people operate in life as if there is meaning, everyone has a sense of ultimate reality, an ultimate interpretation of the worth of life; whether they formulate it explicitly or not, they act out of it.

Elfland offers many instances of people speaking and behaving in ways that seem to contradict their stated beliefs: atheists invest their lives, their words, and their actions with a sense of proximate truth and value, even as they deny the ultimate significance of reality. Although this may seem incoherent from a Christian perspective, nevertheless Rahner shows us that we could interpret this more positively—as an implicit and unconscious response to the plurality of ways in which the gift of the Creator's self-communication is mediated.

This implicit response to God is seen especially in the way human beings treat one another. Chesterton's notion of the doctrine of conditional joy says that only by obeying certain rules—which one does not have to obey since one is free—can one live joyfully in the world. One is free and one has to make choices, and these choices are linked to human happiness and unhappiness. Just as Chesterton says that one has to submit to being as truth before one can do anything else in the cosmos, which is a description of the indemonstrability of the first rational or speculative principle, so one has to submit to being as good before making choices to act in this way or that way, which is a presentation of the indemonstrability of the first practical or moral principle.

The pursuit of the good and the avoidance of evil is an acknowledgement of the first and indemonstrable principle of the goodness of being, and so morality or ethics offers a third Chestertonian signpost to God, uniting the first two that we have already seen: that is to say, there is a coming together of the inner desire which pushed Chesterton outwards to find what he was seeking, and the external, utterly contingent world which points beyond itself to the grounding of all being, truth, and meaning. They come together since it is only in obedience to the rules of the pre-existing reality—the truth of the moral law—that human beings can live joyfully.

In order to see the truth of being you have first to receive it as gift, and only then can you have and explore it properly. Similarly, to want the good, to perceive the goodness of being, you must first accept it as a gift from a giver, and only then can you have it and desire it properly. There is a personal intention behind the goodness of being, a Person who is the source of all that is good. Again, the Lawgiver stands behind the law. The notion of a personal principle grounding the moral law is further demonstrated by Chesterton in Orthodoxy when he explores the ideas of progress in general, moral revolution, and moral progress, the link between moral progress and human happiness, and the eternal vigilance that is required (because of human proclivity to sin) to ensure that human beings keep pursuing the good and continue thereby to flourish. The humble and grateful person shows her gratitude to God for the gift of reality by enjoying the gift in accordance with God's dictates (which is the moral law). Obedience to the moral law is the very condition of human flourishing and joy, whereas disobedience is the precursor to human misery.

By reflecting on his own unhappiness and believing in the worthiness of trying to resolve that unhappiness, Chesterton set out on a quest to discover the good, which led him to discover the voice of conscience as a doorway to God. He realized that

that this inner way of reflecting on the world was a foundational, pre-rationalistic way of tuning in to reality. To wrestle with the free choice between good and bad and to face the joy or misery that ensues from making that choice is to engage with reality in another way, beyond the merely rational. Conscience is an invitation to listen to the cosmos with reverence and respect, in a spirit of receptivity, and not to view the world as something owed to oneself. It is a silent summons either to trust or doubt the ultimate significance of the cosmos—a similar kind of choice to that which one faces when choosing whether or not to trust a person.

Any apologetics today has to take seriously and commend the very real and concerted efforts that unbelievers make to live the good life, acknowledging and praising such efforts to make the world a place of human flourishing, while also engaging in patient and respectful dialogue with these people in order to help them uncover the philosophical foundations of their moral endeavors.

The ethics of Elfland captures the fundamental experience of contingency, which Chesterton saw as the principle of unity of all reality and the link with its transcendent source. All aspects of reality point to the Creator God. We get glimpses of the Creator through the multiple and paradoxical aspects of creation. In solitude, in recognizing ourselves as separate parts of a creation which we intuit to be one, we are opened up to the possibility of relationship with creatures similar to ourselves. Chesterton saw that the cosmos has a fundamental principle of unity that grounds the worth of human existence. He knew from his own spiritual journey that life in the cosmos opens up onto the infinite and offers in a dim, implicit and unconscious way the God who can be later experienced in a more illuminated, explicit and conscious way.

A perennial task for apologetics, therefore, is always to build bridges between the explicit that is Christian revelation and the questions, adventures, movements, and actions of concrete individuals and peoples and the cultures these generate, which may contain much that Christianity would approve and which would imply the presence of the Spirit. Apologists must be confident that the Spirit slowly changes hearts and molds human responses, in order to forge a more humane culture in which people can flourish, while at the same time remaining ever-confident, as well as gentle and respectful of people's struggles, of the power of the Christian message to shed the fullness of divine light on all human quests, yearnings, and aspirations.

Finally, this chapter explores the importance of art and imagination in the thought of Chesterton. Since human beings have a habit of forgetting their greatness and the lessons of Elfland, Chesterton believed that much of modern art had become divorced from the search for the transcendent, eternal, and permanent, in favor of the ephemeral, transient, and novel. However, the true function of art is remedial, for the artistic imagination and the ability to be creative are uniquely human qualities which help us to recall who we are—creatures who seek meaning in the world around us and who express that meaning.

Art also reminds us that human creativity is a share in divine creativity. Art points to our divine origin and goal, and is born where the temporary touches the eternal. The apologist can learn from Chesterton that art will always be an essential part of human life, a means of expressing and communicating outlooks on life and the world. Apologetics needs to engage and stir the human imagination in order to arouse in it the gift of wonder and to help people see human life as a work of art in which human beings are co-creators with the Supreme

Artist, summoned to that task by conscience and the moral law. Wonder, receptivity, gratitude and a refusal to be cynical, grasping and manipulative, come together to constitute a predisposition that better fits a person to appreciate both art and the eternal.

Perhaps in a postmodern culture in which the perennial human fascination with art shows no signs of being diminished, and in which there is a more global sense of human solidarity, the apologist might be able to discern signs of an increase in wonder, a humble spiritual search for meaning and the transcendent, a greater compassion, and therefore a possible openness to the message of the Artist that is Christ, who is himself the artistic self-expression of God. Perhaps there is also a need for poetic apologists in such a culture, Gospel artists who can awaken all that is highest and best in the surrounding culture, such that the human imagination is better able to see what is already out there before its eyes.

CHAPTER IV

Community and Church
in the Search for God

Anyone who says "I love God" and hates his brother is a liar, since no one who fails to love the brother whom he can see can love God whom he has not seen.[260]

We make our friends; we make our enemies; but God makes our next-door neighbour.[261]

THE CARTESIAN COGITO that was arguably the point of departure for the whole modern project seems to imply that we humans do our thinking in total isolation. However, we learn to communicate—with ourselves and with others—from others. We learn to think and to talk in community of life with others. To neglect the crucial role of family, community, and other people in life is to imagine that every human being that comes into this world is condemned to some

---

[260] 1 John 4:20

[261] *Heretics*, 139-40.

sort of lonely Cartesian project of discovering the meaning of life alone. On the contrary, human beings are made for relationship and therefore long for real community. However, as the citations at the head of this chapter indicate, it is a continual struggle to build and live in real community. Almost instinctively we sense that the normal source and place of nurture for Christian faith is the community of the Church. It is also one of its abiding fruits; but it comes with shadows and struggles. In this chapter, then, we shall explore some of the facets of companionship in the adventure of searching for the face of God.

We shall explore some of the friendships in Chesterton's life, harvesting from them some features that are useful for creating an agenda of apologetics today. We shall see Chesterton's thoughts on what he perceived to be happening to human togetherness in the industrial culture produced by modernity. We shall note how Chesterton viewed the Church as the graced, yet fragile, community of faith, capable of being at the same time both a vehicle of grace and sin. We will also look at some aspects of the Church's task of theological reflection: how theology strives to make the concrete and definite self-revelation of the God who comes in search of human beings in Christ both a coherent and livable reality in every age and culture; we shall explore how the Church has to mediate God's self-communication in the varied circumstances of the people of each generation, learning to discern their questions, hopes and aspirations and discerning where the gift of the Spirit, which is also God's self-communication, is already present in their search for God; and we shall note how the Church's theology has to be a dialogue between Peter and Pan: encouraging, discerning, and prophetic, carried out in a tone marked by humility and love, and seeking to enable human beings to flourish by avoiding the equal and opposite dangers of disintegration and petrification.

1. Chesterton and Friends

Aristotle said that friendship was to be held in higher esteem than either justice or honor.[1] Chesterton, in spite of being one of the most forthright speakers of his day and a man seemingly forever embroiled in some sort of controversy or other, had an enormous gift for friendship. "In the tradition of Catholic apologetics, no one was as concurrently friendly and fervent as Mr. Gilbert Keith Chesterton."[2] He believed that "the principal problem with a quarrel is that it interrupts an argument"[3] and, as we shall see in more detail, among his closest friends could be numbered some of his most ideologically opposed sparring partners, figures like George Bernard Shaw and H. G. Wells. We also noted in Chapter I that, aside from Frances, who has been described by Nancy Carpentier Brown as "the woman who was Chesterton,"[4] Chesterton's closest friend was probably Belloc. In this section, therefore, I propose to explore in brief Chesterton's friendships with his wife, Belloc, and Shaw, to see what light they shed on the forging of an agenda for apologetics today.

1.1 Frances Chesterton

We noted in Chapter I how Frances's happiness and personal witness as a Christian left a deep impression on her husband.

---

[1] See the *Nicomachean Ethics*, Books VIII-IX, for his discussion of friendship.

[2] D. Fagerberg, *The Size of Chesterton's Catholicism*, Notre Dame, IN: University of Notre Dame Press, 1998, 1.

[3] *Autobiography*, 200.

[4] "Frances Chesterton," http://uncommonsense.libsyn.com/us-34-frances-chesterton. In fact, Brown has published a biography of Frances with that title, the result of exciting new research on this most private and hidden of figures from Chesterton's life.

Her influence on him was incalculable. When Chesterton was writing his autobiography toward the end of his life, the figure of Frances is conspicuous by her absence: out of humility she had asked him not to mention her, which must have been difficult. No mean intellect herself, she had written poetry all her life and has a prize-winning carol, "How Far is It to Bethlehem?" in the *Oxford Book of Carols*. More importantly, Frances was the most important presence in Chesterton's life, truly his other half, as he became a world-famous writer. Though he knew better than anyone her aptitudes and abilities, he also understood the silent and hidden depths of her character that had shaped the man and writer that he became.

They started their married life with virtually nothing and occasionally during the hardest times they had to rely on friends for their food (an act of charity that was reciprocated when the same friends themselves were short of life's essentials). One of their greatest sorrows was Frances's inability to have children, even after corrective surgery, and it is evident that their life together was far from idyllic:

> The fairy tales said that the prince and princess lived happily ever afterwards; and so they did. They lived happily, although it is very likely from time to time they threw the furniture at each other. Most marriages, I think, are happy marriages; but there is no such a thing as a contented marriage. The whole pleasure of marriage is that it is a perpetual crisis.[5]

For Chesterton marriage is not some panacea that protects us from the burdens of daily struggle in this world. He learned, from the mutual love and trust that he shared with his wife, that the deepest human happiness can survive suffering, moments of tragedy, and the other vicissitudes of living in community.

---

[5] *Charles Dickens*, 136.

The friendship he shared with Frances taught them both to struggle toward joy.

Although to a twenty-first century mind some of Chesterton's writings about women may seem a little strange and archaic, so worried was he about the potentially corrosive effects on the family of the rise of feminism, nevertheless to Dorothy Collins, who was Chesterton's secretary and, later, something akin to the daughter that the Chestertons never had, the insinuation that there was anything misogynistic about him was a charge to be utterly refuted:

> He had a mystical regard for women. I have even seen him rise from his chair when a young girl came into the room...His wife Frances, who was a very great friend of mine, gave him the security he needed. She was a profound character with depths of understanding and sympathy, and he was entirely dependent on her for his happiness.[6]

My own personal opinion is that Chesterton was guilty not so much of the sexism sometimes attributed to him but, on the contrary, that he could more easily be accused of idealizing women and not allowing them to take their place as the other half of the human race, and thereby sharing the same mix of virtue and vice as their male counterparts.[7]

It is well known that Chesterton was highly impractical and relied on his wife to organize him. There is the famous story of how he sent Frances a telegram which read, "Am at Market Harborough. Where ought I to be?" and there is plenty of evidence in his writings that he would agree with Collins about his total dependence on Frances. Commenting on the familiar Fleet Street portrayal of him, he warned people that they:

---

[6] J. Sullivan, ed., *G. K. Chesterton: A Centenary Appraisal*, 16.

[7] He once told a Suffragette, "The question is not whether women are good enough for votes: it is whether votes are good enough for women." *What's Wrong With the World*, 124.

…must not be misled at this stage by that Falstaffian figure in a brig-
and's hat and cloak, which has appeared in many caricatures. That
figure was a later work of art; though the artist was not merely the
caricaturist; but a lady artist touched on as lightly as possible in this
very Victorian narrative. That caricature merely commemorates what
the female genius could do with the most unpromising materials.[8]

Though here once again some may see Chesterton's claim that
woman shapes man in her own way as a sign of sexism, once
again it is arguable that this passage can be read with a hermeneutic of idealization.

Ian Ker points out that there were several people who pitied
Frances because of the burden placed on her by her unpractical
husband, citing the disgust showed by Chesterton's socialist debating partner Robert Blatchford when Frances had to go into
the rain to call a taxi for her husband. He notes how Chesterton
was a husband who could "suddenly say, 'Where is Frances? I
don't want her now, but I might want her any minute.'"[9] Freda
Spencer, one of Chesterton's secretaries, while acknowledging
how wonderfully generous and Christian he was, also said that
what "spoilt him and made life very difficult for those who had
to do with him, was his utter abhorrence of anything approaching discipline, restraint or order," which placed a great strain
on Frances.[10]

Others, such as Cecil Chesterton, the latter's wife Ada, and
the wife of Hilaire Belloc, Elodie, expressed in varying degrees
the opinion that Chesterton was perhaps a little henpecked by
a wife who always got her own way and made all the major
decisions, such as where they lived and where they took their
holidays. It is more than likely that, as happens so often in

---

[8] *Autobiography*, 137.

[9] I. Ker, *GKC*, 160-1.

[10] Ibid., 363.

real companionship, the actual truth consists in some blend of these opinions but, of course, no couple could possibly stay together for forty years without offering each other deep mutual help and support. Indeed, Chesterton wrote to his priest friend, Father John O'Connor, expressing his amazement that:

> One of the mysteries of Marriage (which must be a Sacrament and an extraordinary one too) is that a man evidently useless like me can yet become at certain instances indispensable. And the further oddity (which I invite you to explain on mystical grounds) is that he never feels so small as when he really knows that he is necessary.[11]

Whatever the relative degree of dependence of each on the other, we saw in our first chapter that it is clear that Chesterton was deeply marked by the fact that his wife not only professed a Christian faith, but also practiced it with joy as a high Anglican. His attitude toward the institutions of Christianity matured after Frances came into his life, and *The Ballad of the White Horse* was dedicated to the woman "Who brought the cross to me."[12] He idolized his wife and, if she had not forbidden him to mention her in his autobiography, it is possible that the book would have contained as much information about her life as his. Nearly forty years before this book, before they were married, Chesterton wrote to Frances of his love for her as a light in his heart that was never extinguished:

> …there are four lamps of thanksgiving always before him [Chesterton]. The first is for his creation out of the same earth with such a woman as you. The second is that he has not, with all his faults, "gone after strange women." This third is that he has tried to love everything alive: a dim preparation for loving you. And the fourth is—but no words can express that. Here ends my previous existence. Take it: it led me to you.[13]

---

[11] Ibid., 240-1.

[12] *Ballad of the White Horse*, xli.

[13] M. Ward, *GKC*, 77.

Chesterton was grateful for the space of mutual presence which he and Frances offered each other—a presence which exacted a price but also brought deep joy. Human happiness depends on people learning to offer each other a space of mutual presence. Chesterton and Frances learned to be there for one another down the years, loving and trusting one another in such a way that they faced the mix of life together, enjoying the adventure of joy which they co-authored through all the vicissitudes that their life brought: learning to adjust to one another in the early years together; the tragedy of being unable to have children; the deaths of siblings; the near fatal illness of Chesterton from the winter of 1914 to the spring of 1915; Chesterton's conversion to Catholicism in 1922.

All of this shared space and mutual presence freed taught them how to love. If, as we have already seen, George Bernard Shaw believed that the kinship of ideas and deep camaraderie which existed between Chesterton and Belloc justified coining the concept of the Chesterbelloc, perhaps it is left to Nancy Carpentier Brown and future researchers to show that it would be equally appropriate to write of the Chesterblogg.

As Chesterton and Frances show, the longer human beings stay together in relationship, trying to build community, the more aware they become of the tough demands of love. It is not easy to live out a life of love in community. When human beings learn, through the vicissitudes of day-to-day living, to be present to each other, they realize that fidelity and mutual respect are required to build community. Real love, true community, means being faithful to one's word, never walking away from the relationship for good (even if one occasionally needs space to breathe) and recognizing the dignity of the other person enough to allow him or her to be free and to grow in the direction that their freedom dictates. Love is about remaining faithful to that decision, that act of the will, whether or not that decision is supported by feelings of warmth. In this sense, then, one can talk of community as affording us the opportunities for self-transcendence in real commitment to one another. As we shall see in our final chapter, one of the dangers of a rationalistic and impoverished apologetics is that it can encourage people to believe in an unrelated and therefore sub-Christian deity. Dorothee Soelle, however, advocates a more concrete approach, rooted in the praxis of relationship and costly loving, to the communication of the reality of God. The constant challenge to transcend the self, which is demanded by living in relationship, can become a costly way of living that opens up a road to faith. Rather than asking, "Does God exist?" Soelle suggests that a more urgent question should be, "Does God occur also among us?" This more feminine notion of the immanence of God complements the more masculine notion of the transcendence of God, and allows us to state that God "occurs" in those places where there is evidence of that "justice and care for others without which we cannot become human."[14]

1.2 HILAIRE BELLOC

When Chesterton and Belloc first met in 1900, the latter was already a well-established writer. Chesterton said of Belloc, "What he brought into our dream was his Roman appetite for reality and for reason in action, and when he came to the door there entered with him the smell of danger."[15] Joseph Pearce sees in the words "reason in action" and "danger" the key to unlocking one of the secrets of the Chesterbelloc.[16] He believes

---

[14] *Theology for Sceptics*, 103.

[15] Ward, *GKC*, 94.

[16] J. Pearce, *Wisdom and Innocence*, 50.

that Chesterton was attracted to Belloc so intimately because the latter possessed an abundance of that love for action and adventure which the former only admired from afar:

> As he admired Frances not only for professing a faith but practicing it, so he admired Belloc not only for believing in romantic adventures but for living them out. Chesterton dreamed of the adventure, Belloc was the adventurer. Chesterton imagined the excitement of the high seas, Belloc was an accomplished sailor. Chesterton imagined the bravery of battle, Belloc had been a soldier in the French army. Chesterton imagined the exhilaration of exploring wild frontiers, Belloc had walked and hiked across the United States from the east to the west coast, discovering the "Wild West" in the 1890s. Last but not least, [at the time of their meeting] Chesterton was grappling with religious truths in the abstract while Belloc lived religious truths ritually. Quite literally, Belloc gave body to the ideas in Chesterton's head. He gave them substance.[17]

It is easy to imagine how the awkward, clumsy, quiet, and bookish Chesterton, with his unexpressed dreams of quintessentially English chivalry, would eagerly seek the company of the loud and outspoken French controversialist whose Catholicism led him into many a tight corner. From the very first they (and their wives, though without the same penchant for consuming vast amounts of alcohol displayed by their husbands) developed an intimate friendship and joie de vivre that later caused H. G. Wells to lament that, "Chesterton and Belloc have surrounded Catholicism with a kind of boozy halo."[18]

The "uproarious" nature of Belloc's company is conveyed by Chesterton's account of his meeting with the famous American author Henry James in 1908. Chesterton and Frances had rented a holiday home for a short break, and James lived next door. While visiting the Chestertons with his brother William

---

[17] Ibid., 50-51.

[18] A. Noyes, *Two Worlds for Memory*, 260.

(a pioneer in the field of psychology and pragmatic philosophy), a very serious and learned discussion was rudely interrupted by a din resembling that of "an impatient fog-horn" as Belloc gate crashed the gathering, calling for beer and bacon. Having been walking in France with a colleague from the Foreign Office, who was a Catholic from an old recusant family, the pair had run out of money and somehow, filthy, penniless, and unshaven, managed to get back to England:

> In this fashion they burst in upon the balanced tea-cup and tentative sentence of Mr. Henry James. Henry James had a name for being subtle; but I think that situation was too subtle for him. I doubt to this day whether he, of all men, did not miss the irony of the best comedy in which he ever played a part. He left America because he loved Europe, and all that was meant by England or France; the gentry, the gallantry, the tradition of lineage and locality, the life that had been lived beneath old portraits in oak-panelled rooms. And there, on the other side of the tea-table, was Europe, was the old thing that made France and England, the posterity of the English squires and the French soldiers; ragged, unshaven, shouting for beer, shameless above all shades of poverty and wealth; sprawling, indifferent, secure. And what looked across at it was still the Puritan refinement of Boston; and the space it looked across was wider than the Atlantic.[19]

It is at the very least arguable that many if not most people would think this a highly amusing narrative, but it is also worth asking to what extent Chesterton ignored, or at least glossed over, the darker underbelly of his friend's enjoyment of being cast in the role of either lovable rogue or bête noire. While there is something entirely understandable about the quiet, more pensive Chesterton's attraction to Belloc's carefree spirit, it is beyond doubt that the loud, boisterous belligerence that was habitually displayed by his companion could at times be construed as, at best, tactlessness and at worst a total lack of charity.

---

[19] *Autobiography*, 226-7.

As we shall see later in this chapter, while he was a great admirer and friend of Chesterton, H. G. Wells loathed Belloc and added himself to the long list of enemies acquired by the latter. As the Australian Catholic publisher and popular apologist Frank J. Sheed, who knew well both Belloc and Chesterton, put it, "Each had his own way of being himself, which means that they had their different ways of forcing men to listen...Belloc rude to the polite stranger, Chesterton polite to the rude stranger..."[20] He captures the essence of the two friends pithily: "Belloc went about as if he owned the earth, Chesterton as if he didn't care who owned it."[21]

Other people came to much the same conclusion when comparing the two friends. Frank Swinnerton, a contemporary of both men, made a point that must be kept very much in mind by all who would proclaim the Gospel and engage in apologetics in a secular culture:

> One reason for the love of Chesterton was that while he fought he sang lays of chivalry and in spite of all his seriousness warred against wickedness rather than a fleshly opponent, while Belloc sang only after the battle and warred against men as well as ideas.[22]

In a world and a Church in which, at times, discussion, debate and dispute can become, not a necessary part of the adventure in the search for truth but an angry and bitter polemic in which reputations, career and the caricature and denunciation of others are the guiding stars of participants, Christopher Hollis's appreciation of Chesterton's warmth and humor is timely:

> Just as General Booth refused to let the devil have all the best tunes, so Chesterton refused to let him have all the best jokes, and claimed

---

[20] F. J. Sheed, *The Church and I*, 33.

[21] Ibid.

[22] F. Swinnerton, *The Georgian Literary Scene*, 88.

that those who had the faith should also be allowed to have the fun... Belloc made jokes which were as excellent as those of Chesterton. But Belloc's jokes were all too often bitter and satiric. Their aim was to make the object of them ridiculous. He struck to wound. There was, as Chesterton himself said of him to Douglas Woodruff, a sundering quality in his controversies. Chesterton's jokes were warm jokes—the jokes of a kindly man.[23]

Belloc, however, saw it as one of his good friend's chief weaknesses that Chesterton was unable to be more wounding in his debates and polemics:

> You do not rise from the reading of one of Chesterton's appreciations with that feeling of being armed which you obtain from the great satirists and particularly from the masters of irony. He wounded none, but thus also he failed to provide weapons wherewith one may wound and kill folly. Now without wounding and killing, there is no battle; and thus, in this life, no victory; but also no peril to the soul through hatred. Of the personal advantage to himself of so great and all-pervading a charity, too much cannot be said; but I believe it to be a drag upon his chances of endurance upon paper—for what that may be worth—and it is worth nothing compared with eternal things.[24]

The different tone of the two friends' way of communicating is an important topic of discussion for a book that seeks to work toward a new vision of apologetics, and thus merits further discussion in Chapter VI. Here, however, I simply wish to point out the fact that the two constituent parts of the Chesterbelloc were very different creatures indeed. In a world that is blessed with a breathtakingly wonderful multiplicity of difference, it would be unusual if friendships were not at times forged through, rather than in spite of, difference. The many and varied contingent factors—biology, circumstance, culture, accidents, and free will—that contribute toward the formation of

---

[23] C. Hollis, *The Mind of Chesterton*, 8-9.

[24] H. Belloc, *On the Place of Gilbert Keith Chesterton in English Letters*, 80-82.

persons conspire to make us very complex individuals, and it is through the mutual interaction and influence of such individual characteristics that a more glorious adventure can take place. Uniformity of human character seems a high price to pay for the easy peace, understanding, and blandness that could result from it.

The enduring public perception of the Chesterton-Belloc friendship has been that of two halves—mere carbon copies—of a mythical creature engaged in apologetics: two chips off the same sectarian, narrowly Roman Catholic, Chesterbellocian block. This is far too simplistic an appraisal of their relationship. Some people may be of the opinion that Chesterton was unduly influenced by his friend, and that with that came an alarming narrowing of vision.[25] If as eminent a mind as C. S. Lewis can state that Belloc was "always, on the intellectual side, a disastrous influence on Chesterton,"[26] and if Frank Sheed can write that "Belloc had so much to do with the making of Chesterton, and Chesterton not much with the making of Belloc,"[27] one cannot argue to the contrary without careful consideration. However, there was to be found in Chesterton both a humility and a breadth of vision and sympathies that were not immediately apparent in Belloc.

Pearce maintains that Belloc himself would have disagreed with Sheed's assessment of their mutual influence. He quotes Belloc as considering Chesterton "a thinker so profound and so direct that he had no equal."[28] Pearce goes on to quote many

---

[25] It is beyond the scope of this book to evaluate the degree to which Belloc's own anti-Semitic views contributed to the anti-Semitism of which Chesterton is often accused, but Ker explores the question in a balanced and intelligent manner: see *GKC*, 421-4.

[26] D. J. Conlon (ed.), *G. K. Chesterton: A Half Century of Views*, 71.

[27] J. B. Morton, *Hilaire Belloc: A Memoir*, 122.

[28] H. Belloc, *On the Place of Gilbert Keith Chesterton in English Letters*, 72.

other instances of Belloc's self-effacement in the light of his friend's abilities and vision.[29] When Father John O'Connor quoted a verse of poetry to Belloc, arousing great excitement in him, and then explained that it had been penned by their friend, Belloc replied, "Ah! The Master!"[30] Belloc believed Chesterton's "Lepanto" to be the "summit of rhetorical verse in all our generation," exclaiming that "Chesterton expresses everything so much better than I do."[31] Perhaps the supreme testimony to Belloc's appreciation of his friend's abilities is found in some untitled verses he wrote. The final line referred to Chesterton as "The only man I regularly read":

> I like to read myself to sleep in Bed,
> A thing that every honest man has done
> At one time or another, it is said,
> But not as something in the usual run;
> Now I from ten years old to forty-one
> Have never missed a night; and what I need
> To buck me up is Gilbert Chesterton,
> (The only man I regularly read)...
> Prince, have you read a book called "Thoughts upon
> The Ethos of the Athanasian Creed"?
> No matter—it is not by Chesterton
> (The only man I regularly read).[32]

It is might be nearer the truth, then, to state that if, as is to be expected in a close friendship, Belloc exerted a big influence on Chesterton, it is at least equally as arguable that their friendship was mutually beneficial. Chesterton had a permanent effect on Belloc's habitual way of thinking. Belloc was an excellent historian but not really a philosopher, and he had his thought

---

[29] *Wisdom and Innocence*, 61-64.

[30] J. O'Connor, *Father Brown on Chesterton*, 112.

[31] R. Speaight, *The Life of Hilaire Belloc*, 481.

[32] M. Ward, *Return to Chesterton*, 113.

stretched (albeit insufficiently perhaps) by Chesterton's own philosophical acumen. In turn, Belloc lent Chesterton a perspective on European history that was much broader than the standard Anglocentric vision of the world afforded him by the late Victorian educational establishment, and perhaps this ultimately contributed in no small part to his decision to leave the Church of England for the Church of Rome. Belloc had a fine grasp of economics and Chesterton readily digested and promoted his friend's distributist ideas (which we shall mention in the next chapter). However, I suspect that how one views the degree of reciprocal influence between the two friends is very much dependent on one's own theological, philosophical, historical, and economic preferences, and a balanced sense of proportion has to be kept in mind.

For Pearce, the real beating heart of the Chesterbelloc is something other than the merely intellectual. Their Christian (and ultimately Catholic) faith was "the pearl of great price which neither would sacrifice for anything the world had to offer."[33] And this is where Pearce sees what many commentators do not perceive—the positive influence that Chesterton had in keeping Belloc's footsteps firm on the path toward Christ. Belloc once wrote, "By my nature, I am all sceptical and sensual—so much so as hardly to understand how others believe unseen things."[34] If Belloc was disposed to total scepticism, he looked upon Chesterton as a rock of faith in an ocean of falsehood, the one towering lighthouse he could see when the storms of doubt assailed him relentlessly. This surely begs a reappraisal both of the relative contributions each made to the Chesterbelloc, and of the extent to which Gilbert's charity

---

[33] *Wisdom and Innocence*, 63.

[34] K. G. Schmude, *Hilaire Belloc: His Life and Legacy*, 8.

COMMUNITY AND CHURCH IN THE SEARCH FOR GOD   313

and virtue, to paraphrase Belloc, "eternal things in comparison with which all else is worth nothing," were in the end the very concrete and mundane manifestations of the invisible and transcendent realm which had a purifying effect on Belloc.

There was certainly a mutual and reciprocal influence between Chesterton and Belloc, different as they were, and perhaps this is one of the great gifts of friendship. Both halves of the Chesterbelloc were aware of the preciousness of what grew between them. They helped each other to move beyond their previous vision and understanding, altering each other's vision of things in the incremental stages that mark the path of long relationships. Grateful for each other and in spite of imperfections, they sensed a goodness in each other. It might be argued from Belloc's words about Chesterton's literary legacy that Chesterton caused his friend, at least momentarily, to make a reassessment of the priorities of his life. Belloc was called, however fleetingly, beyond a smaller self and a narrower agenda, out of a lonelier vision of the cosmos, toward something greater. As was stated in Chapter II, the journey to God sometimes requires as its first step a different way of perceiving.

David Tracy wrote that perhaps the biggest challenge in a postmodern and pluralistic world is that of facing our social, political, cultural, moral, and religious differences. How do we accept the otherness of the person whose worldview is different from our own?

> For anyone in this troubled, quarrelling centre of privilege and power (and as a white, male, middle-class, American, Catholic, professor and priest I cannot pretend to be elsewhere) our deepest need, as philosophy and theology in our period show, is the drive to face otherness and difference. Those others must include all the subjugated others within Western European and North American culture, the others outside that culture, especially the poor and the oppressed now speaking clearly and forcefully, the terrifying otherness lurking

in our own psyches and cultures, the other great religions and civilizations, the differences disseminating in all the words and structures of our own Indo-European languages.[35]

In concrete relationships, however, this is far from easy. A mere glimpse at many parishes at the weekend would suffice to show that people experience great difficulties even communicating with those whose liturgical or musical tastes are different to their own. There may be a lot of Christian rhetoric about community and mutuality, but so often we are less than fully open to discovering the riches that others may bring to our life culturally, morally, intellectually, spiritually or theologically. While Chesterton and Belloc were both rooted in a strong sense of their own ideas and vision, and sought to protect the boundaries of that vision, nevertheless, through their mutual friendship, they gradually realized (albeit, perhaps, to differing degrees) that our present vision is a mere starting point. We may retain many of the values and tenets of our point of departure, but our maturity and the maturity of the world depends on moving outwards to face what is different from ourselves. One cannot live very long in this world without having to encounter that which is other to one's own perspective.

Of course, as the author of the Letter to the Hebrews reminds us,[36] being moved beyond our familiar circles may in fact be an invitation to grow more deeply in our knowledge of God. God is the Holy One, the One who is utterly "Other" to us, the Supreme Mystery who is different to all that we are. God's self-revelation may often come in the many experiences and kinds of encounter with others that may at first seem

---

[35] *On Naming the Present*, 4.

[36] Hebrews 13:2 "Do not forget to entertain strangers, for by so doing some people have entertained angels without knowing it."

strange to us. Tracy is right to point out the importance of otherness in a postmodern context. It might be said that some people feel almost overwhelmed by the plurality of ideological, political and religious options that are on view today. They may not enjoy the insecurities that often accompany, at least initially, the experience of being stretched beyond their comfort zones, especially religiously.

But Tracy is right, as were Belloc (to a lesser extent) and Chesterton (to a greater extent), to acknowledge the importance of engaging seriously with that which is different from us. This is especially the case in theological matters. We can never grasp theological truths deeply enough. God is ineffable, the Utterly Other, the Holy One. Even the Church's Spirit-filled reflection on the divine self-gift and self-revelation that took place in Jesus of Nazareth will never, this side of eternity, grasp the truths implicit in that event deeply enough. As Paul says, now we know only in part[37]—we are blessed with only partial insights into the great mysteries of God. Our theologizing, therefore, needs to be humble and we need to pledge ourselves to living in relationship with all people. We can discover more and more about the mystery of God by entering into community with that which is different to us.

1.3 GEORGE BERNARD SHAW

We saw in our opening chapter that the notion of the Chesterbelloc, which became something of an English literary-cultural institution in the first three decades of the twentieth century, was originally a creation of George Bernard Shaw. The Irishman was already a famous playwright, literary critic, and social commentator years before Chesterton's career had

---

[37] 1 Corinthians 13:12.

begun. Shaw first became aware of the man who was to become his lifelong friend and ideological opponent when he read an article by Chesterton in the Daily News.[38] Shaw wrote to Chesterton to congratulate him as a new literary figure whose star was clearly on the rise, but he received no reply. According to Shaw, they eventually met over lunch with Belloc, possibly in 1906.[39]

It is clear that they encountered each other in the media long before they met in the flesh. In his autobiography Chesterton states:

> I began arguing with Mr. Bernard Shaw in print almost as early as I began doing anything. It was about my pro-Boer sympathies in the South African War. Those who do not understand what the Fabian political philosophy was may not realize that the leading Fabians were nearly all Imperialists...even Bernard Shaw, though retaining a certain liberty to chaff everybody, was quite definitely an Imperialist, as compared with myself and my friends the pro-Boers.[40]

Shaw had parted ideological company with the radical Liberals who opposed the Boer War, citing "the inefficiency of leaving stray little States lying about in the way of great powers."[41] If Chesterton and Shaw saw political and economic realities very differently, it was merely one example of how their respective worldviews opposed each other in almost every way. Maisie Ward quotes a New York Times journalist as writing that "the

---

[38] Pearce says that the piece was a review of Scott's *Ivanhoe*, dated 10th August 1901: see *Wisdom and Innocence*, 128.

[39] As explained by Pearce, ibid., 128-9, there seems to be some element of doubt and mystery surrounding the precise date and venue of the first meeting. Lucian Oldershaw, Chesterton's brother-in-law, claimed it was the studio of Rodin in Paris, where Shaw was sitting for the sculpting of his bust.

[40] Chesterton, *Autobiography*, 231.

[41] A. Stone Dale, *The Outline of Sanity: A Life of G. K. Chesterton*, 44-5.

main meaning of Chesterton's life, aside from the religious meaning, is to be found in the running debate...with George Bernard Shaw."[42]

Chesterton's first criticisms of Shaw in the newspapers arose because of the latter's judgment that Shakespeare was overrated:

> The fault of Mr. Shaw as a philosopher or critic of life...is altogether on the side of being too grave, too stern, too fanatical, too unbending and austere. Mr. Bernard Shaw is too serious to enjoy Shakespeare. Mr. Bernard Shaw is too serious properly to enjoy life. Both these things are illogical where he is logical, chaotic where he is orderly, mystical where he is clear. In all the great Elizabethan writers there is present a certain thing which Mr. Shaw, with all his astounding abilities, does not really understand—exuberance, an outrageous excess of words, a violent physical pleasure in mere vocabulary, an animal spirit in intellectual things.[43]

The charge of over-seriousness was to be a recurring theme in their running debates for the remainder of their lives, even if, as we shall see, Chesterton was also Shaw's most loyal defender from an even greater seriousness—one with a puritanical hue, a stern and obdurate gravity that offended Chesterton's sense of wonder at the goodness of life and perceived nothing good in Shaw's agnostic humanism.

As we have already seen in our first chapter, the general public first noticed the relationship between Shaw and Chesterton when the latter teamed up with Belloc in an ongoing debate with Shaw and Wells in 1908. The yearlong argument whetted the public appetite for Chesterton's full-length work, *George Bernard Shaw*, which appeared in 1909. He began the work in the epigrammatic fashion for which he was rapidly becoming famous. "Shaw is like the Venus of Milo; all that there is of him

---

[42] *Return to Chesterton*, 5.

[43] *Daily News*, 15th April 1905, in *Collected Works*, Vol. 11, 347.

is admirable."[44] Joseph Pearce believes that this "deliberately barbed" comment subtly implies that Chesterton believed that "Shaw's sins were those of omission. The rest of the book, in chapters discussing Shaw as Irishman, Puritan, Progressive, Critic, Dramatist, and Philosopher, incisively dissects Shaw to discover what is missing."[45] Chesterton thinks that Shaw's upbringing might as easily have taken place in Wimbledon as in Ireland, for all the effect that the long traditions of his country had on him:

> In reading about his youth, one forgets that it was passed in the island which is still one flame before the altar of St. Peter and St. Patrick... It would never cross the mind of a man of the Garrison that before becoming an atheist he might stroll into one of the churches of his own country, and learn something of the philosophy that had satisfied Dante and Bossuet, Pascal and Descartes.[46]

One of the most Irish of characteristics which Shaw did not share was a fondness for alcohol. He was a teetotaler and vegetarian, and looked upon the practice of consuming alcohol with abject horror and disdain. There was more than one instance of alcoholism in the family, but perhaps the discovery of his father in a drunken state molded his generally sceptical and cynical outlook on reality more permanently than any other event in his life. Having whispered to his mother his suspicions about his father's inebriated state, his mother replied, "When is he ever anything else?" Shaw explains:

> The wrench from my childish faith in my father as perfect and omniscient to the discovery that he was a hypocrite and dipsomaniac was

---

[44] *George Bernard Shaw*, 12.

[45] *Wisdom and Innocence*, 133.

[46] *George Bernard Shaw*, 48.

so sudden and violent that it must have left its mark on me…I have never believed in anything since: then the scoffer began.[47]

Add to that the fact that he could do nothing to receive his mother's love—"she was simply not a wife or mother at all"—he gave up it up as hopeless, carrying "traces of that disillusion to the grave."[48]

If drink was an enormous skeleton in the Shaws' closet, and if Shaw was unable to follow his own advice to others—"If you cannot get rid of the family skeleton, you may as well make it dance!"[49]—it seems likely that Chesterton was sympathetic (not least of all because of his own relatively idyllic childhood) toward this intellectual opponent who, by this time, was also a close friend. Shaw could say that "fortunately I have a heart of stone: else my relations would have broken it long ago."[50]

Chesterton had that largeness of heart and generosity of spirit that permitted him to discern that the seeds of later character traits were sown in Shaw's troubled childhood in Ireland. Hence, rather than simply dismiss him as a heretical headache, as did certain Christians, Chesterton defended him and his work on many counts. "It would be untrue to say that he was a cynic; he was never a cynic, for that implies a certain corrupt fatigue about human affairs, whereas he was vibrating with virtue and energy."[51]

This desire for fairness enabled Chesterton to write that "No one ever approximately equaled Bernard Shaw in the power of

---

[47] M. Holroyd, *Bernard Shaw*, Vol. I: 1856-1898, *The Search for Love*, 15.

[48] Ibid., 16.

[49] Printed source untraced, but popularly attributed to him, e.g., http://www.wishafriend.com/quotes/georgebernardshaw/

[50] M. Holroyd, *op. cit.*, 8.

[51] *George Bernard Shaw*, 62.

finding really fresh and personal arguments for these recent schemes and creeds. No one ever came within a mile of him in the knack of actually producing a new argument for a new philosophy."[52] It led him to see that the negative criticism that Shaw poured out, although an attitude very much at odds with Chesterton's outlook, had much healthier roots than the cynicism of decadents such as Wilde or Whistler. Rather than being:

> ...another of these silent sarcastic dandies who went about with one epigram, patient and poisonous, like a bee with his one sting...They found a talkative Irishman with a kind voice...Shaw's human voice and hearty manner were so obviously more the things of a great man than the hard, gem-like brilliancy of Wilde or the careful ill-temper of Whistler.[53]

In Chesterton's opinion there was a kindness, an openness, a sincerity, and a goodness to Shaw that marked him as different from some of the other clever wordsmiths of the late Victorian period. Chesterton's ability to discern these elements of truth, goodness, and beauty in Shaw is consonant with the observation made in our last chapter: Chesterton refused to dismiss some element of paganism simply on the grounds of its being pagan. The ability to discern everything that is of value in the positions of those with whom we disagree is of vital importance for all apologists in a pluralistic culture.

The respect which Chesterton undoubtedly had for his friend did not, however, prevent him from disagreeing quite fundamentally with Shaw on several matters. The fact that Chesterton was in love with life and the concrete particular things that this world has to offer, made him almost the complete antithesis of Shaw, whom he regarded (even if preferable to the Decadents):

---

[52] Ibid., 55.

[53] Ibid., 86-7.

...as a merely destructive person. He was one whose main business was, in his own view, the pricking of illusions, the stripping away of disguises, and even the destruction of ideals. He was a sort of anti-confectioner whose whole business it was to take the gilt off the gingerbread.[54]

Chesterton believed that Shaw constantly assumed the role of critic as a result of the excessive seriousness caused by the psychological Puritanism which we have already mentioned. Because of his inability to relax and enjoy life, Shaw was "wrong about nearly all the things one learns early in life and while one is still simple."[55] Among these Chesterton lists Shaw's misunderstanding of romance, citing as evidence Shaw's portrayal of Anne, the woman who pursues and marries his hero, Tanner, in his play *Man and Superman*:

> It cannot be denied, I think, that Shaw is handicapped by his habitual hardness of touch, by his lack of sympathy with the romance of which he writes...The result is that while he makes Anne, the woman who marries his hero, a really powerful and convincing woman, he can only do it by making her a highly objectionable woman...In short, Bernard Shaw is still haunted with his old impotence of the unromantic writer; he cannot imagine the main motives of human life from the inside.[56]

Although one need not have personal experience of a given topic to contribute wisely to a discussion about it, the point Chesterton makes is a sound one: the imagination is crucial to understand the experiences and positions of others, a truth which makes serious demands on the apologist.

In the final section of his book on Shaw, in which he explores Shaw the Philosopher, Chesterton examines the agnostic

---

[54] Ibid., 63.

[55] Ibid., 186-7.

[56] Ibid., 208-9.

outlook of his friend and criticizes him for an impoverished understanding of the very notion of God. In a passage we mentioned in Chapter III of this book, he writes:

> I must frankly say that Bernard Shaw always seems to me to use the word God not only without any idea of what it means, but without one moment's thought about what it could possibly mean. He said to some atheist, "Never believe in a God that you cannot improve on." The atheist (being a sound theologian) naturally replied that one should not believe in a God whom one could improve on; as that would show that he was not God. In the same style in Major Barbara the heroine ends by suggesting that she will serve God without personal hope, so that she may owe nothing to God and He owe everything to her. It does not seem to strike her that if God owes everything to her He is not God. These things affect me merely as tedious perversions of a phrase. It is as if you said, "I will never have a father unless I have begotten him."[57]

This passage is of value for the apologist seeking to understand the various types of atheism that may be found in any culture. There will always exist various forms of intellectually thought-out atheism, in which the non-believer has reached a conclusion based on foundations which are of an empirical-materialistic nature, or one which sees religious faith as the projections of false human hopes.

However, there are also types of atheism that result from choices made by way of reaction against those experiences of life that cause the human heart and spirit to become tired, hurt, desperate, disappointed, and disillusioned. It might be argued in fact that unbelief of conscious thought is, in fact, relatively rare, and perhaps almost always affected by a disposition of heart and will. We also saw in Chapter II that a third type of unbelief may be the result of more deep-rooted cultural factors, as people are carried along by prevailing currents and

---

[57] Ibid., 191-2.

sensibilities, such that God is not so much rejected as gradually eclipsed: God is missing but not missed.

There is usually a significant degree of overlap between these families of unbelief and if Chesterton is wise enough to note that Shaw rejects notions of God which a Christian would also reject, he is also enough of a friend to discern the deep-lying roots and dispositions of Shaw's philosophical outlook. Shaw is perceived by Chesterton as being a type of the modern secular culture, in that his opinions are not so much totally wrong and dangerous, as at times confused and incomplete. Indeed Chesterton ends the book as he began it: with praise for his friend:

> ...[T]he world owes thanks to Bernard Shaw for having combined being intelligent with being intelligible...He has stood up for the fact that philosophy is not the concern of those who pass through Divinity and Greats, but of those who pass through birth and death. Nearly all the most awful and abstruse statements can be put in words of one syllable, from 'A child is born' to 'A soul is damned.' If the ordinary man may not discuss existence, why should he be asked to conduct it?...He does not think that difficult questions will be made simpler by using difficult words about them.[58]

Though he disagreed with nearly all of his answers, Chesterton the promoter of democracy was grateful to Shaw for re-popularizing the discussion of the big questions which, in more recent times, had been arrogated by the dons and the intellectual elite.

Reviewing Chesterton's book on him, Shaw wrote with great magnanimity: "This work is what everybody expected it to be: the best work of literary art I have ever provoked."[59] But he disagreed with Chesterton's portrayal of him:

---

[58] Ibid., 239, 242.

[59] *The Nation*, 25th August 1909, in D. J. Conlon, ed., *The Critical Judgements, Part I: 1900-1937*, 201.

Generally speaking, Mr. Chesterton's portrait of me has the limitations of a portrait, which is, perhaps, fortunate in some respects for the original. As a picture, in the least personal and most phenomenal sense, it is very fine indeed. As an account of my doctrine, it is either frankly deficient and uproariously careless or else recalcitrantly and... madly wrong.[60]

Shaw was always ready to engage in fierce debate with Chesterton, a willingness that lasted until the latter's death in 1936. To the charge that he was excessively grave, Shaw responded, through the mouthpiece of one of his stage characters, that Chesterton was not serious enough. Immenso Champernoon, a caricature of Chesterton in Shaw's play *Back to Methuselah*, is told by Mrs. Etteen:

> You flirt with religions, with traditions, with politics, with everything that is most sacred and important. You flirt with the church, with the Middle Ages, with the marriage question, with the Jewish question, even with the hideous cult of gluttony and drunkenness...you are not a bit in earnest.[61]

Despite such free and frank exchanges, Chesterton said of Shaw in 1912, "I believe I have two true affections—one for truth, and the other for Mr. Shaw. I follow truth with reluctance"[62] and Shaw described Chesterton to T. E. Lawrence as a man of "colossal genius."[63] Almost the total antithesis of each other physically—Shaw matchstick-thin with a long white beard and emaciated look; Chesterton the grossly overweight bon viveur—they were both world-famous in their day and each contributed to the fame of the other. As Maisie Ward writes:

---

[60] Ibid., 203.

[61] M. *Bernard Shaw, 1998-1918, Volume II: The Pursuit of Power*, London: Chatto and Windus, 1989, 215.

[62] *Everyman*, 20th December 1912, *Collected Works*, Vol. 11, 497.

[63] C. Hollis, *op. cit.* 86.

I don't think the country has appreciated sufficiently how much G. K. C. and G. B. S. contrived to make one another. Their natural opposition helped largely to make their separate reputations and their perpetual watchfulness helped to define the limits of each. Until G. K. C. turned up G. B. S. had the world of controversy to himself. But as soon as G. K. stepped into the ring he had to watch his step in a new way and make the most of his ring-craft. G. K. could always get through the old man's guard; and that made it especially exciting when they met either on the platform or in the pages of G. K.'s Weekly or the New Witness.[64]

Not just physically, but philosophically too, Shaw and Chesterton were complete opposites of each other. One was a vegetarian, the other a carnivore. One a teetotaler, the other a consumer of copious amounts of alcohol. One the cynic who believed that God was the classic Feuerbachian projection of humanity's ultimate impotence and that human beings could be sacrificed for some higher purpose such as refinement of the state, the other the defender of the supreme dignity of the human being as made in God's image, and therefore superior to all human structures and institutions.

In economics Shaw was the socialist who favored state ownership over private ownership, Chesterton the economic distributist who believed in as wide a distribution as possible of private property and loathed socialism and capitalism in equal measure. They were ideological antipodes, as Chesterton implied when he said of Shaw, "everything is wrong about him."[65]

Despite this, as Chesterton himself wrote, in the public mind Chesterton and Shaw had become almost as synonymous as Chesterton and Belloc. "They seem to suppose that I am his [Shaw's]

---

[64] *Return to Chesterton*, 224.

[65] *Autobiography*, 231.

brother or his keeper."[66] We cannot know for certain why this should be so, but perhaps it has something to do first of all with the fact that they laughed together, at each other and against themselves, and secondly, and perhaps more importantly, with the fact that Chesterton, despite thinking that almost everything was wrong about Shaw, quickly added two more words: "everything is wrong about him, except himself".[67] There was something fundamentally good about Shaw, so much so that Chesterton was also able to say of him:

> There is one fundamental truth in which I have never for a moment disagreed with him. Whatever else he is, he has never been a pessimist; or in spiritual matters a defeatist. He is at least on the side of Life, and in that sense of Birth. When the Sons of God shout for joy, merely because the creation is in being, Mr. Shaw's splendid Wagnerian shout or bellow will be mingled with my less musical but equally mystical song of praise.[68]

The striking beauty about the relationship between Shaw and Chesterton was that they had a deep and affectionate friendship that was equally as intense and real as their philosophical differences. In a world and a Church in which disagreements often lead to bitterness and partisan sectarianism, along a whole spectrum of ideological and theological lines, these two twentieth century literary figures have much to teach us. When apologists seek to give reasons for the hope that is in them, they could learn from the friendship between Chesterton and Shaw. They can remember that the energy, generosity, warmth, affection, humor, truth, and goodness that they encounter in people is an indication that Christ is already somehow present. They are reminded by these two friends and intellectual sparring partners that, while not acknowledging the existence of God, or not attending church, or pouring ridicule on the claims of

---

[66] G. K.'s Weekly, 18th April 1931, Collected Works, Vol. 11, 571.

[67] Autobiography, 231.

[68] G. K.'s Weekly, 21st March 1933, cited in J. Pearce, Wisdom and Innocence, 145.

organized religion are not themselves good things, nevertheless, people who display the fruits of the Holy Spirit are, like Shaw, not pessimistic defeatists, but are on the side of life. They are also reminded and challenged as Christians to display the same virtues and qualities themselves.

Chesterton's relationship with Shaw is a reminder to all apologists and theologians to enter into true dialogue with their partner in conversation, to listen as well as speak, to learn as well as teach. It is also a lesson in courage, for Chesterton defended Shaw from well-intentioned but narrower types of Christian. Chesterton was able to resist the prevailing errors and what we might call today the political correctness of both left and right; he stood firmly opposed to the subtle and not-so-subtle agendas of the mob.

Chesterton was able to learn from the good that he found in Shaw, without worrying about the criticism of those Christians who saw nothing of value in him; yet at the same time Chesterton remained aware that Shaw's thought was often in thrall to the relentless modern march toward utopia, and thus contained serious errors that would lead to dehumanization and the sacrificing of the weak in favor of the greater good.

Political correctness and being called names by both ends of the ideological spectrum did not concern Chesterton, and it is a lesson that the apologist does well to learn in a complex and pluralistic culture and Church. It is often necessary to be part of a movement in order to achieve certain goals, but there are also seasons in life when to do what is right, moral, and good demands that we have to be critical of that movement. Chesterton shows the apologist and the theologian that at times fidelity to the truth means that we have to carefully discern the elements of truth that are to be found in the position of those who oppose us.

History teaches us that every heresy is simply a truth only half-spoken; that every heresy is a truth held so close to the eye that it blocks out everything else; that a heresy is a truth that has become so big and important that those who hold it have let it get in the way of other truths that are of equal or greater importance. So it behooves the apologist to see if there is something that is partly true in the error of those with whom he disagrees overall, and something therefore that could be a corrective for his own position. To engage in this more nuanced type of apologetic conversation is not easily done and requires courage, because what often rapidly follows is the loss of friends, popularity, and prestige among the people with whom we usually walk.

Sometimes it is easy enough, but sometimes not, to discern who is in the right and who is in the wrong, whose opinions speak for truth, goodness, beauty, community, and human flourishing, and whose ideas will lead to error, falsehood, self-ishness, disunity, destructiveness, and dehumanization. The apologist does well today to learn from Chesterton's friendship with Shaw not to be too quick to draw the demarcation lines, nor too simplistic in the application of labels to people and their ideas, as she struggles to discern what will lead to a culture of life and what will lead to a culture of death.

In the three relationships we have just examined, there are various things that emerge. In a friendship forged over four decades as lovers and spouses, Chesterton and Frances learned how to build overall, through the ebb and flow of concrete daily living, an adventure of joy. As with any friendship, it was a struggling kind of happiness, born of faithful presence to each other.

Chesterton was attracted to Belloc because he possessed characteristics that Chesterton admired but did not possess (at least to the same degree). Although at times this admiration may have caused Chesterton to ignore or make light of some of Belloc's less attractive features, it would be a big mistake to view Chesterton as somehow being in thrall to the personality of his friend. On the contrary, Belloc was often frustrated that, given Chesterton's genius, the latter did not share his own tone and approach to debating opponents of the Christian and Catholic position. There was indeed a reciprocal influence between the two friends, something expected in any relationship that lasts decades. But Belloc readily acknowledged both an intellectual and moral debt to Chesterton, whose charity and kindness were, *sub specie aeternitatis*, much more important than winning arguments with ideological opponents. Chesterton was not slow to point out both privately and publicly what he perceived to be Shaw's philosophical shortcomings.

However, he always attempted to do this in a spirit of charity and understanding, interpreting the Shavian outpourings in the context of his friend's upbringing and cultural background, and viewing his faults as sins of omission rather than commission. Chesterton always looked for the good in Shaw, consciously trying to understand why he arrived at the positions he did. Furthermore, he often found himself in the position of defending him from well-intentioned but narrow types of Christian who saw nothing good in Shaw.

What strikes me as being common to all three friendships is the constancy displayed by the individuals involved, through the passing of the years and their growth as individuals. There is something very ordinary and everyday about the quality of what is brought to these relationships. Although no doubt there was probably some degree of emotional intensity at times in these relationships (especially the one between Chesterton and

Frances), nevertheless, it was probably true that, by turning up and being present to the friend with an everyday fidelity, all parties were nourished and grew as persons. Mutual presence down the years helped all four people grow as human beings. Community was built between them not because they were always of a common mind. Rather, faithful commitment to the friendship, patience, gentleness, and understanding in charity of the other's faults and failings, all contributed to the creation of community, beyond the instances of their natural incompatibility and difference. As Soelle might put it, God "occurs" in the midst of such a community.

2. COMMUNITY AND THE CHRISTIAN SEARCH FOR GOD

I have argued that community seems to be the birthplace and home of support for Christian faith. In a postmodern culture many question that assumption. There seems to be a clear split between spirituality and ecclesiology, between what people perceive as authentic Christian faith and the version of Christianity promulgated by the Church. Some people may be frustrated or angry at the gap between Christian belief and practice, such that they think of the members of the Church and the institutional Church itself as hypocritical, while others argue more sophisticatedly that they simply do not believe that Christ intended to found a particular religious group as the embodiment of his vision and the physical means of continuing the grace of the incarnation.

Many people today criticize ecclesiology in the name of spirituality, refusing, as they see it, to dilute their faith by associating themselves with such an imperfect body of human beings. Is this dichotomy between the individual and the communal justified in Christian living, or is it a distortion of a fuller Christian vision and in need of healing?

If the postmodern searcher is instinctively allergic to organized forms of Christian faith, nevertheless he has also happily discovered and fostered in other areas of life a sense of solidarity and mutual support (for example, with the poor and the marginalized) that had perhaps been a casualty of modernity's emphasis on the dignity of the self (which is in itself justifiable). Such a searcher often turns out to be a lonely and isolated self.

A mature Christian faith will help today's religious seeker see that without the same concrete and historical belonging to community that is being rediscovered in other spheres of existence, we all run the risk of theoretically belonging without actually belonging. We run the risk of criticizing real communities from a safe distance of non-commitment, without concretely doing anything to improve them. Christian spirituality, ultimately, is not a lonely search for what is best and most noble in oneself, but a journey with others in a community that is often just as imperfect and compromised as oneself.

The central importance of relationships (which constitute community) for Christian living is stressed by Chesterton in his discussion of the differences between Christianity and Buddhism. While he admits that there might be superficial similarities between the two religions—Christ and Buddha both heard voices from the skies and both washed feet—there are also essential differences. For the Buddhist, enlightenment is found by looking inward and finding the divinity within; the Christian seeks God outside himself, since he recognizes that human beings are not gods, but distinct creations. This vital distinction is depicted in the art of both religions:

> No two ideals could be more opposite than a Christian saint in a Gothic cathedral and a Buddhist saint in a Chinese temple. The

opposition exists at every point; but perhaps the shortest statement of it is that the Buddhist saint always has his eyes shut, while the Christian saint always has them very wide open. The Buddhist saint has a sleek and harmonious body, but his eyes are heavy and sealed with sleep. The mediaeval saint's body is wasted to its crazy bones, but his eyes are frightfully alive. There cannot be any real community of spirit between forces that produced symbols so different as that. Granted that both images are extravagances, are perversions of the pure creed, it must be a real divergence which could produce such opposite extravagances. The Buddhist is looking with a peculiar intentness inwards. The Christian is staring with a frantic intentness outwards.[69]

Despite the fact that he sought wisdom wherever it was to be found because he believed that the cosmos is one reality and that humility before that reality and in the face of all faiths and traditions is the indispensable starting point in the pursuit of truth, still Chesterton has been accused of presenting world faiths as "summary abstractions"[70] when he compares them with Christianity. In the above passage, however, in the absence of a text suggesting otherwise, it might be argued that his notion of Christian spirituality is presented in a rather abstract way. There is an absence of nuanced qualification which opens Chesterton up to the charge of neglecting the inner dimensions of concretely lived Christian spirituality.[71]

His description of the Christian saint leaves that type of spirituality looking excessively "secular," while neglecting the inner world of prayer in which the human heart meets God in an intimacy that is based upon familiarity rooted in daily, regular

---

[69] *Orthodoxy*, 336.

[70] K. L. Morris, *TTFR*, 33.

[71] Perhaps part of Chesterton's reluctance to deal with this inner aspect of the Christian spiritual life was founded on his suspicion of the uncritical acceptance of some of the rationalistic presuppositions of much of modern liberal theology during the era of Modernism in the Roman Catholic Church, and the consequent reductionistic tendencies.

contact. The Francis of Assisi whom Chesterton loved and admired so much regularly looked inwards as well as outwards (as, indeed, do all Christian saints). Francis looked inwards at the God who met him there, in order then to return to an outer world which was indeed, as Chesterton clearly grasps, distinct and other than Francis.

Once this necessary qualification is made, the point that Chesterton is making in the above passage remains valid: the Christian seeks to know and love others as others, as creatures of the God who is totally Other (the transcendent Creator), and does not merely wish to know himself, much less to know that he himself is God and is everything else, which is the position in which the Buddhist finds himself. The Christian saint gazing outwards is indicative of the otherness that the Christian seeks to know and love. The Christian knows that her fellow creatures, experienced as other than self, are rooted in the God who is Other.[72]

In Christian faith the God who is the creative source of one's own person is also the creative source of all other persons in the cosmos and, though one can meet God in the inner life of prayer, one must never forget that God is also to be found in relationship with others. There is an intimate connection, therefore, between oneself, others, and the God who is utterly Himself, utterly Other to the cosmos, and the source of all selves in that cosmos.

For Chesterton, then, Christianity constantly asserts the distinctness and interrelatedness of persons against the theological opinion (popular in Chesterton's day) that there are not really beings, but that all things and all persons, including God, are

---

[72] Chesterton explores some of the social and political consequences of the contrasting philosophical principles of East and West in books such as *What's Wrong With the World?* and *The Outline of Sanity*.

really one. Chesterton says that such a "liberal" position runs counter to many liberal ideals. For example, if everything is one, it is impossible to love, since to love is to love another self for its own sake, but there are no other selves if all is one, and any generous act toward another is only then a generous act to oneself:

> Love desires personality; therefore love desires division. It is the instinct of Christianity to be glad that God has broken the universe into little pieces, because they are living pieces. It is her instinct to say "little children love one another" rather than to tell one large person to love himself.[73]

This is why Chesterton criticized the Unitarian denial of the Christian doctrine of the Trinity. Although at pains to point out the great track record of intellectual study and social reform in the religious tradition in which he was raised as an infant and in which his father spent his whole life, he points out that the substitution of a pure monotheism for the Trinitarian doctrine is potentially dangerous for human society because it goes against the human instinct for community through relationship:

> The complex God of the Athanasian Creed may be an enigma for the intellect; but He is far less likely to gather the mystery and cruelty of a Sultan than the lonely god of Omar or Mahomet. The god who is a mere awful unity is not only a king but an Eastern king. The heart of humanity, especially of European humanity, is certainly much more satisfied by the strange hints and symbols that gather round the Trinitarian idea, the image of a council at which mercy pleads as well as justice, the conception of a sort of liberty and variety existing even in the inmost chamber of the world. For Western religion has always felt keenly the idea "it is not well for man to be alone."

The Christian idea is that it is not good for human beings to live alone because "it is not well for God to be alone."[74] Human

---

[73] *Orthodoxy*, 337.

[74] Ibid., 340.

beings are made in the image and likeness of the God who is love, who is a Trinitarian community constituted by the giving and receiving of love from all eternity. Christianity claims, not that God became love through the act of creation, at which point His creatures then became objects of the divine love, but rather, that God is love. Only by living in this image and likeness, living in a communion of life that gives and receives love, and thereby reflecting the God who is and does this from all eternity, can a human being find joy. We are separated as distinct beings in order to be reunited, not as in a soupy mixture, but as in an embrace.

For Chesterton, religions that deny the Trinity have a tendency toward violence or at least dysfunction, since they neglect the social dimension of human existence. At the same time, a Christian should remember that the Church periodically offers evidence of its own dysfunctionality. (Indeed, the Church has on occasion been no stranger to violence, thereby denying its own central dogma in praxis, if not in words).

When the Christian faith says that "God is love"[75] and that God is a Trinity of persons, what is being said is that God is a community, a family of relationships in which the participants in that community of life are constantly and eternally involved in the mutual giving and receiving of love, a reciprocity which constitutes their unity as well as their diversity. Their mutual presence to each other in loving relationship means that they do not exist as selves without each other. Furthermore, the Christian tradition, taking up and developing further the precious insight that it has received from its older Jewish sibling,[76] states that human beings are made in the image of this triune

---

[75] 1 John 4:16

[76] See Genesis 1:27

God, which means that the human person is, paradoxically, uniquely a self, but a self that only flourishes through the presence of others in relationship. To be true to our own nature, we need others. Relationship is written into our very identity.

Chesterton perceived that modernity and the industrialization, urbanization, and imperialism that went with it, made it more difficult for human beings to understand that it is of their very nature to live together and belong together. "It is not fashionable to say much nowadays of the advantages of the small community. We are told that we must go in for large empires and large ideas."[77] For Chesterton, however, the human being is formed and matures more easily when thrown into the demands of community:

> There is one advantage, however, in the small state, the city, or the village, which only the wilfully blind can overlook. The man who lives in a small community lives in a much larger world. He knows much more of the fierce varieties and uncompromising divergences of men. The reason is obvious. In a large community we can choose our companions. In a small community our companions are chosen for us.

When one lives in a community, one is forced to live side by side with others, a whole range of people, who have not been chosen by oneself. Blood, loyalty, or some other force binds the members into community. This is the difference between family and clique, or between Church and clubs of like-minded members.

> Thus in all extensive and highly civilized societies groups come into existence founded upon what is called sympathy, and shut out the real world more sharply than the gates of a monastery. There is nothing really narrow about the clan; the thing which is really narrow is the clique. The men of the clan live together because they all wear the

---

[77] *Heretics*, 136.

same tartan or are all descended from the same sacred cow; but in their souls, by the divine luck of things, there will always be more colours than in any tartan. But the men of the clique live together because they have the same kind of soul, and their narrowness is a narrowness of spiritual coherence and contentment, like that which exists in hell. A big society exists in order to form cliques. A big society is a society for the promotion of narrowness. It is a machinery for the purpose of guarding the solitary and sensitive individual from all experience of the bitter and bracing human compromises. It is, in the most literal sense of the words, a society for the prevention of Christian knowledge.[78]

In cliques people often bond on the basis of like-mindedness or sympathies of vision, real community; however, a real bond that stands the test of time is rooted in something that transcends mutual liking or like-mindedness. Even when people do not necessarily like each other all of the time, even when people are often in disagreement with one another, real depth of relationship can become a reality through the conscriptive duties of living together. Christian knowledge, Christian faith, is born and increases when one submits to the pedagogical rhythms of life within community.

In a simpler pre-modern world, the deep human need for community was more easily nourished; but a culture of individualism which invites us to imagine ourselves as self-sufficient and our relationships with each other to be rooted in personal preference and like-minded sympathy is, ironically, the very thing that threatens to make us dysfunctional and which could prevent our flourishing as individuals and as a society. This will result in "the prevention of Christian knowledge." We are prevented from knowing God when our hearts are closed to the community formed from friendship in spite of difference. We can never come to know God if we are not prepared to commit

---

[78] Ibid.

ourselves to dealing with each other throughout the changes and the messy complexities of life. However, when we begin to realize, as did Chesterton at the Slade, that we are not lonely entities trapped in some solipsistic nightmare, but are somehow connected, constituted as persons in our relationships with others, then the glimpse of a larger horizon and another presence and relationship, becomes possible.

Community can be an enormous help on the journey toward God. The re-discovery of the deep human need for relationship, belonging, and solidarity, and its concrete embodiment in new ways of living community, are among some of the most welcome aspects of postmodern culture. In spite of the understandable nervousness of some Christians about some aspects of postmodernity (for example the fact that it seems allergic to overarching narratives, truth claims, and authority, and places too much emphasis on moral autonomy and idiosyncrasy), other features of postmodernity offer renewed possibilities for Christian faith, which has never been a merely solitary journey, but a communal search for the face of God.

3. The Church as the Graced, Sinful, and Communal Search for God

The notion that Christian faith is a journey toward God undertaken with others is seen most obviously in the fact of the existence of the Church. It is in the Church that countless people, from all backgrounds, have throughout the centuries discovered friendship, strength, and nourishment for the journey of faith. As Chesterton says, the Catholic Church "is the only type of Christianity that really contains every type of man; even the respectable man,"[79] as it reaches across class and borders. The Church is the essential home and servant of faith in Christ. However in the aftermath of modernity, the search for meaning today can seem much more private and lonely. Modernity has placed great emphasis on the importance of the individual and brought about a changed context of human living that has eroded older ways of social belonging. The postmodern culture today is nervous of institutions, authority, overarching narratives of interpretation, and the very concrete claims to truth that are embodied by Christianity. If one adds to this the further complications arising from the disappointments, pain, and anger that people experience at the hands of the Church, then the relevance and importance of the Church in the journey toward God is no longer immediately obvious to people.

Although he was convinced that "If every human being lived a thousand years, every human being would end up either in utter pessimistic scepticism or in the Catholic creed,"[80] Chesterton was himself sensitive to the shortcomings of the Church and was by no means uncritical of the community that was his spiritual home for the last fourteen years of his life. Making reference to Psalm 146, he wrote that, "I am entirely on the side of the revolutionists. They are really right always to be suspecting human institutions; they are right not to put their trust in princes nor in any child of man."[81] Kevin Morris writes that,

> …it was Chesterton's personal paradox that he, a great individualist, preached conformity to Rome. His lifelong preoccupation with liberty was probably partly responsible for his long delay in becoming

---

[79] *Why I Am a Catholic*, 127.

[80] *William Blake*, 208.

[81] *Orthodoxy*, 321.

a Roman Catholic; although eventually he managed to convince himself that the Church stood for freedom more than any other institution or ideology of the time.[82]

Having embraced the Church of Rome in 1922, he wrote both of the Catholic Church's necessary and incomparable significance in bearing Christ to the world, and its faults and failings in that mission. He sought to use "that excellent method which Cardinal Newman employed when he spoke of the 'notes' of Catholicism,"[83] painting with broad brushstrokes the features of the faith which seemed most fundamental to him, rather than some of its more intricate technicalities.[84]

He was keenly aware that, "the Saints were sometimes great men when the Popes were small men,"[85] and for the first forty-eight years of his life presumably there were sufficient factors in his life that caused him to harbor doubts about the need to become Catholic: "By every instinct of my being, by every tradition of my blood, I should prefer English liberty to Latin discipline."[86]

Chesterton writes that:

...against the Church of Pio Nono the main thing to be said was that it was simply and supremely cynical; that it was...founded...on the worldly counsel to leave life as it is; that it was not the inspirer of hopes, of reward and miracle, but the enemy, the cool and skeptical enemy, of hope of any kind of description.[87]

---

[82] *TTFT*, 20-21.

[83] *Appreciations and Criticisms of the Work of Charles Dickens*, 109.

[84] He did not, for example, mention the enormously important event for the Catholic world of the 1917 Code of Canon Law.

[85] *St. Francis of Assisi*, 141.

[86] *The Resurrection of Rome, Collected Works*, Vol. 21, 433.

[87] *Robert Browning*, 142.

COMMUNITY AND CHURCH IN THE SEARCH FOR GOD

This historical tendency of the Church to get things wrong sometimes is documented in Chesterton's writings more often than is commonly assumed. For example, he laments that "the stoic philosophy and the early church discussed woman as if she were an institution, and in many cases decided to abolish her"; he disapproves of the fact that "certain historic tendencies" (such as the Augustinian and Anselmian inclinations to overemphasize the spiritual to the detriment of the physical) had "hardened into habits in many great schools and authorities" in the Church, which later had to be reformed by figures such as Francis of Assisi and Thomas Aquinas; and saw the same danger of unimaginative and hardened habits of thought threatening the Church's mission to proclaim the Gospel afresh in changing circumstances:

> I do really believe that there is a need for the restatement of religious truth; but not the statement of something quite different, which I do not believe to be true. I believe there is a very urgent need for a verbal paraphrase of many of the fundamental doctrines; simply because people have ceased to understand them as they are traditionally stated...in language that is intrinsically correct but practically misleading...We do not allow enough, in justifying the words that we speak, for the difference in the words that [the Church's addressees] hear.[88]

Chesterton used his own enormous powers of imagination to communicate deep truths in word sketches that could arouse dulled minds, and he called on the Church to do the same. If Chesterton was aware that without a vision the human person gets lost, he was also equally aware that without some engagement of the heart and imagination by that vision, nobody would even want to take a preliminary step. Hence, setting a fine example for the Church to follow, he did all that he could to bring together the intellectual and the imaginative.

---

[88] "Some of our Errors," *The Thing: Why I Am a Catholic*, 283-4.

The importance of the imagination for Chesterton is reflected in the fact that he perceived Francis of Assisi as "primarily a poet": a man who sees fire as his brother and water as his sister is a man possessed with a fertile imagination and a marvelous ability to recognize the reciprocal relationship between the human mind and matter, since there is inherent meaning in the latter and the ability to grasp that meaning in the former. All poetry and all artistic expression, which can take hold of the human imagination, can reveal the secrets of the cosmos—the secrets of religion—to human beings.

For example Chesterton believed that there was "this eternal metaphysical value in chalks and paints."[89] This understanding had an effect on the way Chesterton wrote and spoke for others. Morris notes that the Chestertonian tone is not academic, pedantic, and theorizing, but playful, epigrammatic, poetic, and whimsical. He believed that "language is not a scientific thing at all, but wholly an artistic thing,"[90] and that there were times when human beings could not always say what they meant, since reality was too rich and wonderful to be captured by human expression.

For this reason art, poetry, symbol, metaphor, gesture, ritual, color, and a whole host of other media had to be employed to communicate the mysteries of the universe and Christian faith. Although he really believed that "Theology is thought"[91] and that Christianity is a rational religion that demands that people think hard, nevertheless, if it was to be effectively communicated, something had to be done about the over-familiarity and consequent prejudice that people felt toward it. "The preaching

---

[89] "Paints in a Paint Box," *On Lying in Bed and Other Essays*, ed. A. Manguel, 59.

[90] R. Davies, "Memories of G.K.C.," *Pax*, vol. 26, no.178 (August 1936), 115.

[91] *The Everlasting Man*, 160.

friar puts his sermon into popular language, the missionary fills his sermon with anecdotes and even jokes, because he is thinking of his mission and not of himself."[92]

It might be argued that in the Church of the twenty-first century we are not lacking in good academic theology, catechesis, spirituality, and pastoral programs, and we are not without rational ideas for spreading the Gospel; however, it is at least arguable that we lack the fire, passion, imagination, artistic sensibility, and aesthetics required to capture the hearts and minds of a culture that is often bored, tired, restless, distracted, or self-preoccupied.

Chesterton knew that it was not the academic theology of Francis that moved the Church and world of his day, but his artistic imagination and holiness. The Church will always need good, corrective, academic theology, in order to help people keep their balance in a complex world and to avoid superstition and unhealthy notions of God; but it will also always need good ways of capturing the human heart and imagination through artistic expression and transparent holiness of life, lest people not be sufficiently moved to inquire about the faith. The intellect and the imagination, the mind and the heart, are both ways of coming to God, and any agenda of apologetics in a secular culture needs to address both.

Chesterton was aware of the need to recast and re-interpret the faith from age to age in various cultural circumstances, and he was critical of the Church's failure to do that at times—choosing, as it did instead, to lapse into repeating the tired old words and images that had worked on other past occasions. One therefore has to disagree with Chesterton's sister-in-law, who said that he "was so impregnated with the supernatural power of the Church

---

[92] Cited in Morris, *TTFT*, 47-8.

over her disciples, that he credited Catholics as such with an undue impeccability of motive and purpose in worldly affairs,"[93] and who portrayed Chesterton as a Catholic propagandist who approved of everything the Church said and did.

This conclusion is not faithful to the evidence. If, as we have seen, Chesterton believed that reality is much more complex than the highly selective human mind usually allows for, this applies in equal measure to the thought of Chesterton, which is very subtle. Those who seek to interpret his full vision will find that he was both critical of the Church and yet loved and was proud of it:

> So far as a man may be proud of a religion rooted in humility, I am very proud of my religion; I am especially proud of those parts of it that are most commonly called superstition. I am proud of being fettered by antiquated dogmas...it is only the reasonable dogma that lives long enough to be called antiquated. I am very proud of what people call priestcraft...Mariolatry...the mysteries of the Trinity or the Mass; I am proud of believing in the Confessional; I am proud of believing in the Papacy.[94]

Though he knew enough about human nature never to submit in blind obedience to any institution in which there was human involvement, he was a happy Catholic and he and Newman were described by Douglas Woodruff in 1942 as "the two chief apologists for Catholicism in the last hundred years in England."[95] The Catholicism he wrote about was the faith of a Church that was capable of great goodness and desperate sinfulness, for:

> ...it is part of that high inconsistency which is the fate of the Christian faith in human hands, that no man knows when the higher side of

[93] A. Chesterton, *The Chestertons*, 97.

[94] *Autobiography*, 77-8.

[95] *For Hilaire Belloc: Essays in Honour of his 71st Birthday*, ed. D. Woodruff, 37.

it will really be uppermost, if only for an instant; and that the worst ages of the Church will not do or say something, as if by accident, that is worthy of the best.[96]

The Church to which Chesterton belonged will always be capable of virtue and vice, but that is because it is made up of human beings. It is not exempt from the same temptations as the rest of the human race, an empirical observation which, for Chesterton, provides evidence in support of rather than against the Church's creed. "When the world goes wrong, it proves rather that the Church is right. The Church is justified, not because her children do not sin, but because they do."[97]

In 1907, fifteen years before he entered the Church of Rome, Chesterton wrote that,

> When people impute special vices to the Christian Church, they seem to forget entirely that the world (which is the only other thing there is) has these vices much more. The Church has been cruel; but the world has been much more cruel. The church has plotted; but the world has plotted much more. The Church has been superstitious: but it has never been so superstitious as the world is when left to itself.[98]

No institution and no individual person is immune from the temptation to sin, which is to settle for being less than human, and to forget this is the beginning of spiritual ruin, as Father Brown reminds us: "'And what is the one spiritual disease?' asked Flambeau, smiling. 'Oh, thinking one is quite well,' said [Father Brown]." [99]

The fact of the matter is that to point the finger away from one's own life to the lives of others is to miss something crucial

---

[96] *A Short History of England*, 102.

[97] *The Everlasting Man*, 10.

[98] *Illustrated London News*, 14th December 1907, *Collected Works* Vol. 27, 604.

[99] "The Eye of Apollo," *The Penguin Complete Father Brown*, 132.

about the state of the world. The centrality of this truth is captured beautifully by an insight that Chesterton offers in a response he penned to a reader who had criticized one of his articles, and written under the headline, "What is Wrong." "The answer to the question, 'What is Wrong?' is, or should be, 'I am wrong.' Until a man can give that answer his idealism is only a hobby."[100]

Chesterton's vision of the Church, and of every other human institution, is the same as that of the mixed field of the Gospel, in which wheat and weed grow side by side.[101] Any construct that contains traces of human involvement, even one whose origin is divine, will reflect on a macro-scale the private micro-struggles of the human heart, the moment-by-moment conflict between grace and sin.

For Chesterton, the problems of community can never remain at a comfortable distance from one's own life. Although one's sense of anger or shock at the sinfulness of the Church seems to echo the reactions of the Gospel laborers who are dismayed at the weed growing with the wheat, Chesterton invites us to share the wider horizon of the field's owner, and also hints that some recollection of the struggles of our own lives may be a good starting point for this movement toward greater compassion, greater awareness of how grace and sin can coexist in the same institution, and a recognition therefore of the importance of the Church in the quest for the face of God.

On one level Chesterton's understanding of the Church as a fragile, sinful yet graced community of faith, seems to imply that he would understand people's struggles, anger, and

---

[100] *Daily News*, 16th August 1905, personal collection of D. Ahlquist, President of The American Chesterton Society.

[101] Matthew 13:24-30.

disappointment with the Church. However, on another level he seems to be saying also that what is more important is to grasp that the Church is some bigger reflection of what goes on inside one's own heart as well as every other human heart. The Church may occasionally be, for a while at least, an impediment to one's growth toward faith in Christ. However, at some point in that spiritual journey, one needs to recognize that the Church is not a club for the perfect, but the sacrament of the unity of all humanity in Christ, a graced and sinful community that is composed of people who are just like oneself. To travel alone, without encouragement, wisdom, and support from community and friends in the faith, is to be involved in a lonely and dangerous quest:

> [The Church] does definitely take the responsibility of marking certain roads as leading nowhere or leading to destruction, to a blank wall, or a sheer precipice. By this means, it does prevent men from wasting their time or losing their lives upon paths that have been found futile or disastrous again and again in the past…[The church] does dogmatically defend humanity from its worst foes, those hoary and horrible and devouring monsters of the old mistakes.[102]

Life is short, and without the help of others the spiritual pilgrim can get lost and waste precious time on a private quest that neither nourishes others nor is nourished by others.

Pope Benedict XVI, when a young professor of theology at the University of Regensburg, was once asked why he remained in a sinful Church. In responding he referred to an ancient image used to describe the Church: that of moonlight. He said that the light of the moon is borrowed light. In these days, when science has permitted human beings to walk on the moon, we can think of the moon as all darkness, dust, mountain and desert, which would be a reductionist image of the moon. However,

---

[102] *Why I Am a Catholic*, 129.

the moon is much more than its surface: the moon is illuminated by the sun. Without the sun the moon would indeed be darkness; but the moon does not exist without the sun. The same is true of the Church: "In itself it is darkness, but it sends out light from another." The Church receives light from the true sun, from Jesus Christ, even though at times, especially to the media, it seems to be nothing more than dust and desert.[103]

Chesterton similarly understands the Church to be both darkness and light. He states that the Church "is the only thing that talks as if it were the truth; as if it were a real messenger refusing to tamper with a real message."[104] As we have seen, part of that message is that human beings (many of whom are members of the Church) are sinful, a fact which for Chesterton, as we have seen, proves that the Church is right, not wrong, in its teaching.

For Chesterton the Church is above all the messenger and bearer of Christ. It invites us to move away from considering ourselves as the only way of measuring meaning in life. Like Professor Ratzinger, Chesterton would say that ultimately the best reason to stay in the Church is because it helps us to find God: it makes the presence of Christ real and alive for each new moment of the history of the cosmos. The undeniable moments of sin and failure are ultimately set against and outweighed by these moments of grace, as Christ nourishes human hearts and refreshes and challenges human vision through the friendship and communal living found within the Church.

---

[103] See J. G. Roten, "Why Stay in the Church, Benedict XVI?"'s http://campus.udayton.edu/mary/benedictxvi.html [last accessed 17th February 2012].

[104] *Why I Am a Catholic*, 127.

4. The Church and Theology

In our exploration of the Ethics of Elfland, we saw the importance that tradition held for Chesterton. Chesterton said that the Catholic Church "is the one continuous intelligent institution that has been thinking about thinking for two thousand years. Its experience naturally covers nearly all experiences; and especially nearly all errors."[105] The Church seeks to nourish the members of its community by reflecting on human experience and on the long memory of the Christian tradition in order to translate and re-imagine the riches of that tradition in new cultural contexts. Thus will people be better equipped to flourish and to avoid all that would dehumanize our living together.

Recall the words of Lonergan that "A theology mediates between a cultural matrix and the significance and role of a religion in that matrix."[106] Thus, an urgent item on the Church's agenda needs to be the ongoing theological task of mediating between the meaning of the content of the Church's living tradition and what is evolving in a rapidly changing culture. This mediation requires prayerful reflection, intelligent consideration of the Word of God as it has been held in the Church's accumulated wisdom throughout the centuries, and translation into idioms that re-express the significance of faith for people who live in various different contexts today.

Accordingly, it involves finding various ways of respecting and cherishing people's questions, before connecting these with the inherited spiritual wisdom of the Church. It also requires creativity in discovering ways to touch people's hearts and imaginations with that wisdom. Of course, there may first

---

[105] Ibid., 129.

[106] *Method in Theology*, xi.

have to be some "ministry of unblocking": a removal of whatever may be deadening the innate human desire to explore and know reality, upon which the discovery and reverencing of one's questions are dependent.

We have seen from his debates with Blatchford that Chesterton had little patience with the academic specialist who sneered at those who did not possess a highbrow level of learning. However, this must not be taken to mean that Chesterton did not appreciate the need for serious thought and reflection. Although one need not be a theologian to practice the faith of the Church simply, that is not to say that the Church's faith is a simple matter. *Orthodoxy's* strikingly vivid image of the Church as the thundering chariot swerving first this way, then that, in order to avoid error and maintain the balance of truth, reveals that centuries of intellectual reflection have been required in countless cultural situations in order to allow the simple practice of the faith.

One of the benefits of belonging to the Church is that different members of the community are assigned different tasks in order to build up the community. One such task is that of doing theology, and this is a labor that is vital because "common things are never commonplace. And in the last analysis most common things will be found to be highly complicated."[107] The rest of this chapter explores how Chesterton understood the task of doing theology as fitting into the Church's notion of the common life lived together in Christ. If even common things are complicated, even more complex is the utterly unique event in history that is the life of Christ, whom Chesterton referred to as "The Everlasting Man." Reflection on this Everlasting Man, the Christ Event, constitutes the theological task and reveals

---

[107] *What's Wrong with the World?*, 68.

how theology is, in Chesterton's terminology, a complex and elaborate key that can unlock the various riddles of the cosmos. At the same time, the mystery and wonder of human existence in the cosmos and of the God revealed by Christ in the Church are never reducible to the Church's theological pronouncements, and so the theological tradition develops and unfolds throughout the movement of history by means of the dialogue between the tradition and cultures. All of this takes place, of course, in order to promote human flourishing in community.

4.1 THE EVERLASTING MAN: *the Uniqueness of Christ*

Chesterton's book *The Everlasting Man*, published in 1925, was a key moment in C. S Lewis's path to God. As the latter put it, "In reading Chesterton...I did not know what I was letting myself in for. A young man who wishes to remain a sound Atheist cannot be too careful of his reading. There are traps everywhere...God is, if I may say it, very unscrupulous."[108] However, although it proved to have great potency as a work of apologetics in Lewis's life, this work was originally written not as an explicit apologetics, but as a history of the world, penned as an alternative to the vision portrayed in H. G. Wells's popular work *The Outline of History*.

Chesterton wrote this book with the same intent as modern authors who were writing histories and other books of a scholarly nature: in order to get people to examine the subject matter of the book from the outside, fairly. He hoped that people who read the book would examine the claims of Christianity as impartially as possible (and not with "a random and illiterate heckling"), in order then to have placed enough distance

---

[108] *Surprised by Joy*, 154.

between themselves and the Church to allow for a more objective assessment. "It is exactly when the boy gets far enough off to see the giant that he sees that he really is a giant. It is exactly when we do at last see the Christian Church afar…that we see that it is really the Church of Christ."[109]

Chesterton criticized Wells's book for having inadequately treated two subjects: human beings and the human being known to history as Christ. By treating human beings as merely another species of animal, and Christ as just another type of human being, Chesterton believed that Wells had glossed over the two central events in the history he purported to describe. Chesterton had dismissed the first claim back in 1908 in the ninth chapter of *Orthodoxy*. There he had pointed out that, although the modern agnostic sees the human being as "a mere variety of the animal kingdom," quite clearly human beings are a very different sort of animal than is to be found in other species:

> If you leave off looking at books about beasts and men, if you begin to look at beasts and men then (if you have any humour or imagination, any sense of the frantic or the farcical) you will observe that the startling thing is not how like man is to the brutes, but how unlike he is. It is the monstrous scale of his divergence that requires an explanation. That man and brute are like is, in a sense, a truism; but that being so like they should then be so insanely unlike, that is the shock and the enigma.

Chesterton argues that he is not disputing that human beings and animals share several characteristics in common, but that the differences between them are of a different order completely:

> That an ape has hands is far less interesting to the philosopher than the fact that having hands he does next to nothing with them; does not play knuckle-bones or the violin; does not carve marble or carve

[109] *The Everlasting Man*, 12.

mutton...Certain modern dreamers say that ants and bees have a society superior to ours. They have, indeed, a civilization; but that very truth only reminds us that it is an inferior civilization. Who ever found an ant-hill decorated with the statues of celebrated ants? Who has seen a bee-hive carved with the images of gorgeous queens of old? No; the chasm between man and other creatures may have a natural explanation, but it is a chasm.

This theme of the vast qualitative differences between the human race and other species of the animal kingdom—the fact that "this first superficial reason for materialism is, if anything, a reason for its opposite; it is exactly where biology leaves off that all religion begins"[110]—is developed at some length seventeen years later in his Christological work.

In *The Everlasting Man* Chesterton says that if we look at the man in the cave, the caveman, the one thing we do not find is that he behaves just like any other animal. We see that he alone among the species of the planet draws pictures on the walls of his habitat. As we have already seen in Chapter III, he puts this point pithily when he says that, "Art is the signature of man."[111] Pointing out that when compared with animals, human beings have advantages and disadvantages, Chesterton observes that they cannot sleep in their own skin, nor trust their own instincts. They are creators with their hands and fingers; they use "artificial bandages called clothes" and "artificial crutches called furniture"; they are "shaken with the beautiful madness called laughter"; and they experience "the mystery of shame." In fact, "the simplest truth about man is that he is a very strange being; almost in the sense of being a stranger on the earth...He has much more of the external appearance of one bringing alien

---

[110] *Orthodoxy*, 348-9.

[111] *The Everlasting Man*, 34.

habits from another land than of a mere growth of this one."[112] To try to reduce human beings to the level of mere animals is to leave out of one's explanation traces of evidence to the contrary. "The more we really look at man as an animal, the less he will look like one."[113] Human beings constitute a species on the planet that behaves in very different ways to other species, and it is the religious instinct in human beings that lies at the root of their essential difference.

Chesterton believes that the creation of a work of art is a divine act, a share in the creativity of God and the expression of a faculty which only human beings possess. Only the members of the human species create symbols to express other realities. They use symbols to ascribe meaning and purpose to existence and the cosmos. For Chesterton all art is religious, since "The Arts exist...to show forth the glory of God...to awaken and keep alive the sense of wonder in man."[114] He maintains, contrary to the popular claims of many moderns, that it was the impulse of religion that cultivated human beings and advanced civilizations.

When, during a dispute with a politician, Chesterton was accused of resisting modern reforms and being as obscurantist as the ancient priest who probably wanted to resist the invention of the wheel, he replied that, "it was far more likely that the ancient priest made the discovery of the wheel. It is overwhelmingly probable that the ancient priest had a great deal to do with the discovery of the art of writing."[115] Because religion asks about the ultimate meaning of reality, it developed

---

[112] Ibid., 36.

[113] Ibid., 27.

[114] *The Thing: Why I am a Catholic*, 173.

[115] *The Everlasting Man*, 67.

and interpreted symbols which advanced communication and learning. A. N. Whitehead argues that it is no coincidence that science emerged in a western culture that was shaped by the Judeo-Christian tradition.[116]

Chesterton also points out that, whereas other ancient peoples combined their various pagan gods and believed in a whole panoply of divine beings, the Jewish people preserved the notion of one God who was Creator of the cosmos. "[T]he world owes God to the Jews."[117] Although the myths of ancient peoples tried to express with great creativity and imagination the human yearning for the transcendent and the eternal, these did not satisfy and, out of desperation, the societies of these ancient peoples began to decay around them. They stopped seeking the divine and started to worship idols—poor substitutes for the divine. As he points out in *Orthodoxy*,

> The only objection to Natural religion is that somehow it always becomes unnatural. A man loves Nature in the morning for her innocence and amiability, and at nightfall, if he is loving her still, it is for her darkness and her cruelty. He washes at dawn in clear water as did the Wise Man of the Stoics, yet, somehow at the dark end of the day, he is bathing in hot bull's blood, as did Julian the Apostate. The mere pursuit of health always leads to something unhealthy. Physical nature must not be made the direct object of obedience; it must be enjoyed, not worshipped.[118]

It is natural to human beings to worship, to bow before something; but when people substitute for God something less than God, things do not turn out well.

Into the midst of this situation comes the Everlasting Man, Jesus of Nazareth. Chesterton says that if people look at this

---

[116] See A. N. Whitehead, *Science and the Modern World*. New York: Simon and Schuster, 1997.

[117] *The Everlasting Man*, 95.

[118] *Orthodoxy*, 280.

event and at the Gospels that offer us our primary data about this event as fairly as possible, the one thing that they will not find is the very thing that many people often claim to find: a book of mere ethical platitudes from a moral teacher. Such reductionism of the Everlasting Man would have been anathema to Chesterton who loathed any unnecessary reduction of the beauty and complexity of reality to our own favorite and partial viewpoints.

Just as in *Orthodoxy* Chesterton had been forced to reflect on how strange must be the Christian Church if it could be criticized by so many people for so many (often conflicting) characteristics, so too Chesterton thought that, "There must surely have been something not only mysterious but many-sided about Christ if so many smaller Christs can be carved out of him."[119] But the one thing that one must not try to do is to reduce Christ merely to the level of one of these sides. Christ was never merely an ethical teacher, for his claims were much greater than that.

Although Christ was a great teacher and said many things that echo the great sages of antiquity and resonate in the mouths of many great teachers and lawgivers, nevertheless he makes Christianity unique among world religions and philosophies in that the founders of these other wisdom traditions did not claim to be God. "Mahomedans did not misunderstand Mahomet and suppose he was Allah. Jews did not misinterpret Moses and identify him with Jehovah."[120] As C. S. Lewis was to point out two decades later, "Either this man was, and is, the Son of God: or else a madman, or something worse."[121] Christianity, then, is "The Strangest Story in the World."[122]

---

[119] *The Everlasting Man*, 197.

[120] Ibid., 202.

[121] *Mere Christianity*, 52.

[122] *The Everlasting Man*, 199. This is the title of the third chapter of Part II of this book.

The unique nature of this oddest of stories strikes us even more when we discover that the Everlasting Man is executed in an obscure backwater of the Roman Empire at a certain moment in human history, and that this single historical event becomes the center of history: "the cross is the crux of the whole matter."[123] On Calvary human beings "know not what they do" and reveal that "Man could do no more. Rome and Jerusalem and Athens and everything else were going down like a sea turned into a slow cataract."[124]

Chesterton points out, then, that all of the great groups representing humanity and its achievements are present at the crucifixion scene, and that "Externally indeed the ancient world was still at its strongest." However, it is always when human beings are at their strongest "that the inmost weakness begins."[125] Chesterton reminds us, however, that the story of the Everlasting Man does not close with the tragedy and hopelessness of deicide, but with the empty tomb of God:

> On the third day the friends of Christ coming at daybreak to the place found the grave empty and the stone rolled away. In varying ways they realized the new wonder; but even they hardly realized that the world had died in the night. What they were looking at was the first day of a new creation, with a new heaven and a new earth; and in a semblance of the gardener God walked again in the garden, in the cool not of the evening but the dawn.[126]

What is revealed in the cross and resurrection is that at the heart of God lie unfathomable love and forgiveness; the Everlasting Man is the revelation of a God who continues to love human beings even when they commit terrible atrocities, with a love

---

[123] Ibid., 134.

[124] Ibid., 209-10.

[125] Ibid., 210.

[126] Ibid., 213.

that is their ultimate salvation if they so choose. In spite of all the many things that Christianity shares with other religious and wisdom traditions, herein lies the unique difference. No other tradition says that God loved the world so much that he became part of it as a human being, then died and rose again. This is an enormous and unprecedented statement, whose most sublime expression is to be found in a very concrete and particular historical event and not just in some visionary's experience or inner inspiration.

Although other faith and wisdom traditions may express beautifully the inner human desire for communion with the divine, and may be inspired and nourished by the Spirit of God, they are still essentially engaged in seeking out the face of God. Christianity makes the sui generis claim that God has sought us out and revealed his face to us in Christ, a face filled with a love that was willing to die for us in order to touch our hearts. The death and resurrection of Christ was a new beginning for humanity, and the Church was the sign and agent of this new beginning. Its message was that of a new birth, as it offered the world the Gospel which "met the [ancient instinct for the] mythological search for romance by being a story and the [ancient instinct for the] philosophical search for truth by being a true story."[127]

What emerged from the Upper Room at Pentecost was not some simple ethical society or an unworldly bunch of pitiful idealists. What emerged was a Church, to which had been granted, through the final words of the Everlasting Man who is her Lord, the keys that "could unlock the prison of the whole world; and let in the white daylight of liberty."[128] This was good

---

[127] Ibid., 248.

[128] Ibid., 214.

news, the Christian creed of the Church, a creed which was like a key in that it had a definite shape and "a rather elaborate pattern."[129] Thus Chesterton sees one of the functions of the Christian community as reflecting on the shape and pattern of the key in order to help people to live in true liberty.

4.2 Theology as a Complex and Elaborate Key

Although a detailed theological treatment of the Church as a living teacher who bears good news to the world is a worthy and essential task for the fundamental theologian, it also takes us beyond the limits of this book. However, it is interesting to note that Chesterton refers to the same theme explicitly at the beginning of *Orthodoxy*, while maintaining his own intention not to deal with it in any depth. "[These pages] are not intended to discuss the very fascinating but quite different question of what is the present seat of authority for the proclamation of [the Christian] creed." Nonetheless, it is evident from the final chapter of that book that the notion of an authoritative teacher was important to him and therefore something which in all likelihood he would have to address at some point on his spiritual journey. The liturgical and Chestertonian scholar David Fagerberg asks the readers of his work on Chesterton if they know:

> ...the optical illusion in which if one looks at black on white one sees a vase, but if one blinks and looks at white on black one sees two faces? Chesterton was sketching a vase to hold the flowers of his philosophy, and when he blinked, he saw the face of a human, ecclesial community (and it had a Roman nose).[130]

---

[129] Ibid., 215.

[130] *The Size of Chesterton's Catholicism*. Notre Dame, Ind.: University of Notre Dame Press, 1998, 184.

Although Chesterton, like Newman before him, was to offer his apologia for embracing Catholicism in his 1926 work *The Catholic Church and Conversion*, and also gave further insights into his ecclesiological thinking in *The Thing: Why I Am a Catholic* in 1929 and *The Well and the Shallows* in 1935, it might be argued that as early as 1908, when he states that "the very word 'romance' has in it the mystery and ancient meaning of Rome,"[131] Chesterton already had some sense that the Catholic Church would be the final guarantor and provider of the truth and life of adventure that he had always sought.

Whether this be true or not, in the final chapter of *Orthodoxy* Chesterton offers as another reason for accepting orthodox Christian belief the fact that people seek a living teacher. When a person such as a father, and especially a mother, consistently provides answers to one's questions, one places one's trust in that person:

> I remember with certainty this fixed psychological fact; that the very time when I was most under a woman's authority, I was most full of flame and adventure. Exactly because when my mother said that ants bit they did bite, and because snow did come in winter (as she said); therefore the whole world was to me a fairyland of wonderful fulfilments, and it was like living in some Hebraic age, when prophecy after prophecy came true. I went out as a child into the garden, and it was a terrible place to me, precisely because I had a clue to it: if I had held no clue it would not have been terrible, but tame. A mere unmeaning wilderness is not even impressive. But the garden of childhood was fascinating, exactly because everything had a fixed meaning which could be found out in its turn. Inch by inch I might discover what was the object of the ugly shape called a rake; or form some shadowy conjecture as to why my parents kept a cat.[132]

---

[131] *Orthodoxy*, 212.

[132] Ibid., 360-1.

The Church, even if it has shown itself on occasion to be as imperfect as any human mother, has also regularly proven itself to be, in regular conversation with the world, as trustworthy a teacher as any mother; and this fact should encourage the members of the Church to trust that there are further adventures and secrets not yet discovered in the cosmos to be enjoyed. The Church says that the cosmos is meaningful, and that therefore there are adventures to be enjoyed in the garden, "exactly because everything had a fixed meaning which could be found out in its turn."[133]

Of course, the Church's promulgation of the various secrets of the cosmos is no easy task. *Orthodoxy*'s image of the Church as the chariot thundering through the ages is a vivid and breathtaking reminder of the perennially difficult ecclesial undertaking of doing theology. The very notion of theological reflection can strike some people as being part of the problem with religion in general and the Church in particular. Many people long for a much simpler faith and, indeed, it is wise to acknowledge that on occasion in the Church's history certain theologies that have been held and promoted have been influenced by less worthy considerations: selfishness, fear, power, and pettiness. However, understood correctly, the Church's doctrines, dogmas, rules, and structures can be seen to come from a desire to offer a complex and complicated world the key to the door of life:

> When people complain of the religion being so early complicated with theology and things of the kind, they forget that the world had not only got into a hole, but had got into a whole maze of holes and corners. The problem itself was a complicated problem; it did not in the ordinary sense merely involve anything so simple as sin. It was also full of secrets, of unexplored and unfathomable fallacies,

---

[133] Ibid., 361.

of unconscious mental diseases, of dangers in all directions. If the faith had faced the world only with the platitudes about peace and simplicity some moralists would confine it to, it would not have had the faintest effect on that luxurious and labyrinthine lunatic asylum... it is enough to say here that there was undoubtedly much about the key that seemed complex, indeed there was only one thing about it that was simple. It opened the door.[134]

As we saw when we discussed Chesterton's attitudes toward scientism, he does not believe that reducing the complexity of reality for the purposes of a simpler analysis is a good method, since, "[T]his is only getting over the difficulty of describing peacock green by calling it blue. There is blue in it."[135]

The key entrusted by the Everlasting Man to the Church has a very definite and elaborate shape because it has to have if it is to open up the multi-faceted riddle of life. Because the world is a complex place, human beings have to do some hard thinking if they are to find happiness in it. It is native to the finite and imperfect human mind, sitting before a cosmos that is the paradox-filled gift of an infinite Creator, to discover doctrines that express the relationship between the human mind and reality:

> Man can be defined as an animal that makes dogmas. As he piles doctrine on doctrine and conclusion on conclusion in the formation of some tremendous scheme of philosophy and religion, he is, in the only legitimate sense of which the expression is capable, becoming more and more human. When he drops one doctrine after another in a refined scepticism...when, in his own imagination, he sits as God, holding no form of creed by contemplating all, then he is by that very process sinking slowly backwards...Trees have no dogmas. Turnips are singularly broad-minded.[136]

---

[134] *The Everlasting Man*, 215.

[135] *What's Wrong with the World*, 68.

[136] *Heretics*, 196-7.

Chesterton calls on human beings to allow reality to be what it is in all its beautiful complexity, to describe that reality as truthfully as possible and never to reduce this account to a partial description, for that would ultimately be a falsification. At its best the Church's theology has always tried to communicate to the world "the complete philosophy which keeps a man sane; and not some single fragment of it."[137]

As was noted above, theology and philosophy will always seem to some people an unnecessary complication of a simple faith. In Chesterton's own day there was a cry for a greatly simplified religion, one that that merely insisted on human beings loving each other. Lennon and McCartney famously maintained that all you need is love, and because Christianity holds that human beings are made in the image of the Trinitarian God, it is likely that few Christians would disagree. The difficulty arises, however, when one asks what is meant by the notion of love. Chesterton insists that because of the complex nature of moral living among human beings, to ask for a religion which tranquilly asks for love:

> ...is exactly as if somebody were to say about the science of medicine: "All I ask is Health; what could be simpler than the beautiful gift of health? Why not be content to enjoy for ever the glow of youth and the fresh enjoyment of being fit? Why study dry and dismal sciences of anatomy and physiology; why inquire about the whereabouts of obscure organs in the human body? Why pedantically distinguish between what is labelled a poison and what is labelled an antidote, when it is so simple to enjoy Health?

Would those who wish for a simplified religion say that in the pursuit of health we do not need to know the chemical composition of tablets and potions, nor wonder what dosage to take and at what intervals? Chesterton rounds off his refutation of facile over-simplifications with a ringing sense of irony:

------

[137] *The Thing: Why I Am a Catholic*, 307.

Away with your priestly apparatus of stethoscopes and clinical ther-
mometers; with your ritualistic mummery of feeling pulses, putting
out tongues, examining teeth and the rest! The god Aesculapius[138]
came on earth solely to inform us that Life is on the whole preferable
to Death; and this thought will console many dying persons unat-
tended by doctors.[139]

Chesterton's point is that, "You cannot make a success of anything, even loving, entirely without thinking."[140] The Church's
theology exists to achieve the practical goal of helping human
beings to live well: that is, to love. "When things will not work,
you must have the thinker, the man who has some doctrine
about why they work at all. It is wrong to fiddle while Rome is
burning; but it is quite right to study the theory of hydraulics
while Rome is burning."[141]

Is there anything in the traditional sources of human wisdom that can help individuals or whole cultures when human
flourishing seems to be hindered in some way? We have seen
that the autobiographical intellectual and spiritual journey
which Chesterton described in *Orthodoxy* was a quest to find
some way of solving the riddle and crisis that he felt deep
within because he experienced both a passionate love for the
cosmos, as well as a sense of despair in that cosmos. Peace came
to Chesterton in the Christian creed:

I had found this hole in the world: the fact that one must somehow
find a way of loving the world without trusting it; somehow one
must love the world without being worldly. I found this projecting
feature of Christian theology, like a sort of hard spike, the dogmatic
insistence that God was personal, and had made a world separate

---

[138] The ancient Greek god of healing and medicine

[139] *The Thing: Why I Am a Catholic*, 180-1.

[140] Ibid.

[141] *What's Wrong with the World*, 19.

from Himself. The spike of dogma fitted exactly into the hole in the world—it had evidently been meant to go there—and then the strange thing began to happen. When once these two parts of the two machines had come together, one after another, all the other parts fitted and fell in with an eerie exactitude. I could hear bolt after bolt over all the machinery falling into its place with a kind of click of re-lief...Instinct after instinct was answered by doctrine after doctrine.[142]

The notion of the Church's theological heritage fitting and filling the empty spaces of the human heart is another reminder, and one that Chesterton found rooted in his own life experience, that doctrines and dogmas are necessary means to the end of human flourishing, albeit not ends in themselves. Christians do not worship the key—they worship the Lord who gave the key in order that the world may have life to the full—but they may not throw away the key.

For Chesterton, then, the Christian creed in no way denies the good, the true, and the beautiful elements to be found in pagan worldviews, but rather saves them from their own inordinate expressions and tendencies toward desperation. Chesterton sees Christian theology as a way of ordering and systematizing religious instincts that would otherwise (and in the pagan world did in fact) cause damage. If Chesterton knows all too well the imperfections of the Church, he is still ready to defend organized religion from the charge of over-complicating things, because his knowledge of the history of pagan antiquity (many of whose instincts he perceived to be resurfacing in the excesses of modernity) led him to see very clearly the dangers of disorganized religion:

Nothing on earth needs to be organised so much as Mysticism. You say that man tends naturally to religion; he does indeed; often in the form of the human sacrifice of the temples of Sodom. Almost

---

[142] *Orthodoxy*, 282-3.

all extreme evil of that kind is mystical. The only way of keeping it healthy is to have some rules, some responsibilities, some definitions of dogma and moral function.[143]

Just as Chesterton claims that "It is always simple to fall; there is an infinity of angles at which one falls, only one at which one stands,"[144] so too he believes it is easy to be less than human, less than fully alive, because there exists a multitude of wrong ideas about the cosmos. That is why the Church makes itself "acquainted with ideas, and moves among them like a lion-tamer," whereas "The man of no ideas will find the first idea fly to his head like wine to the head of a teetotaller."[145] The Church has to discern the value of all ideas because:

> if some small mistake were made in doctrine, huge blunders might be made in human happiness. A sentence phrased wrong about the nature of symbolism would have broken all the best statues in Europe. A slip in the definitions might stop all the dances; might wither all the Christmas trees or break all the Easter eggs.[146]

Theology proper is, for Chesterton, not a question of remote figures in ivory towers debating erudite opinions about matters that bear little relevance to day-to-day life, but rather a struggle to identify, make possible, and nourish all that makes human life worth living.

If theology sets people free to enjoy life, Chesterton is also well aware that there have been tensions between theology and spirituality down the centuries. The briefest survey of history reveals that "the Saints were sometimes great men when the Popes were small men". Indeed:

---

[143] Cited in a letter in Ward, *GKC*, 370.

[144] *Orthodoxy*, 306.

[145] *Heretics*, 202.

[146] *Orthodoxy*, 305.

Saint Francis was so great and original a man that he had something in him of what makes the founder of a religion. Many of his followers were more or less ready, in their hearts, to treat him as the founder of a religion. They were willing to let the Franciscan spirit escape from Christendom as the Christian spirit had escaped from Israel. They were willing to let it eclipse Christendom as the Christian spirit had eclipsed Israel. Francis, the fire that ran through the roads of Italy, was to be the beginning of a conflagration in which the old Christian civilisation was to be consumed.[147]

The charisms of saintly people can often capture the human imagination of others and exert an utterly compelling attraction on people. This can be a force for good in the building up of the kingdom and the spread of the Gospel, but it can sometimes create problems too. It is at this point that good theology has to come in.

That was the point the Pope had to settle; whether Christendom should absorb Francis or Francis Christendom. And he decided rightly, apart from the duties of his place; for the Church could include all that was good in the Franciscans and the Franciscans could not include all that was good in the Church.[148]

Chesterton notes that Francis was a poet, "a person who could express his personality." In Chesterton's mind, a poet is made larger by his limitations—"he is what he is, not only by what he has, but in some degree by what he has not. But the limits that make the lines of such a personal portrait cannot be made the limits of all humanity." Chesterton illustrates this point by way of Francis' attitude toward books and scholarship:

He ignored and in some degree discouraged books and book-learning; and from his own point of view and that of his own work in the world he was absolutely right. The whole point of his message was to be so simple that the village idiot could understand it. The whole point of his point of view was that it looked out freshly upon a fresh

---

[147] *Saint Francis of Assisi*, 141-2.

[148] Ibid., 142.

world, that might have been made that morning. Save for the great primal things, the Creation and the Story of Eden, the first Christmas and the first Easter, the world had no history. But is it desired or desirable that the whole Catholic Church should have no history?[149]

While it is granted by God to some, such as Francis, to have a profound grasp of the bare essentials of the Christian message, to others God also gives the gift of being able to explore the riches of the complexities of the same message. No one person or group has all the charisms that are needed for the Church to exercise her ministry in the world. By grasping that truth, Chesterton believed that the Pope showed, "that great men are sometimes wrong when small men are right. And it will be found, after all, very difficult for any candid and clear-headed outsider to deny that the Pope was right, when he insisted that the world was not made only for Franciscans."[150]

Though there will be a perennial tension between individual prophetic charism and institutional Church, in true Chestertonian paradoxical fashion both need to be present for the good of the Church. If the Church were not to carry out its duty of theologizing, of translating the vision of Christ for a multitude of historical epochs and cultural contexts, it would be in danger of upsetting the delicate balance that permits humanity to flourish and of failing in its God-given mandate to serve the world in love. Even the finest theological distinctions can make a world of difference to one's vision of the world and one's consequent ways of living out that vision. There was only one letter, or one iota (to choose the word that recalls the historical event as it passed into the collective linguistic memory of the English people) of difference between the *homoousion*

---

[149] Ibid., 142-3.

[150] Ibid., 141.

and *homoiousion* positions; but of course, the same numerical degree of distinction exists between the theist and the atheist. Changing the image to one offered by the Gospel,[151] it is only by showing interest in the doctrinal seed and roots that the Church can be confident that the fruits visible in daily living will be sound.

4.3 The Movement of History and Dialogue between Church and Culture

For Chesterton, the life of the Everlasting Man is the most revolutionary event in all of human history, offering human beings a multi-faceted revelation of the heart of God that will remain forever as their abiding consolation and challenge. The theological project of the Church is to unfold gradually through the movement of history the full implications of that unique and complex revelation. To adapt the metaphor used in the previous section, the development of doctrine in the Church's theological tradition is the flowering of the Gospel seeds as the Church, filled with the Holy Spirit, slowly absorbs some of the lessons, as yet unlearned, that are contained in the revelation of Christ.

This theological concept is perhaps most famously (albeit not exclusively) associated with Newman. Unsurprisingly, given that Newman was one of his literary heroes, Chesterton himself wrote of the fecund and developmental nature of theological ideas. "It is the friction of two spiritual things, of tradition and invention, or of substance and symbol, from which the mind takes fire. The Creeds condemned as complex have something like the secret of sex; they can breed thoughts."[152]

---

[151] Matthew 7:16

[152] *The New Jerusalem, Collected Works* Vol. 20, 218.

The fruits of this fertility constitute the Church's long tradition. The development of the Church's theological vision is not a break with the original Gospel proclamation, but the full flowering of the consequences of that primordial kerygma in every age and culture:

> When we talk of a child being well-developed, we mean that he has grown bigger and stronger with his own strength; not that he is padded with borrowed pillows or walks on stilts to make him look taller. When we say that a puppy develops into a dog, we do not mean that his growth is a gradual compromise with a cat; we mean that he becomes more doggy and not less. Development is the expansion of all the possibilities and implications of a doctrine, as there is time to distinguish them and draw them out.[153]

To borrow a genetic metaphor, doctrinal development is the gradual growth to maturity of all that is contained in the Gospel's DNA.

Chesterton believed that both Francis of Assisi and Thomas Aquinas were excellent examples of how the Gospel message can respect and build on the goodness, truth, and beauty found among people and ideas who do not consider themselves to be part of the Church or its tradition. Thomas, for example, in his discussion of the importance of the body and the senses in Aristotelian epistemology, was insisting that the body was a Christian thing. "It might be a humbler or homelier thing than the Platonic mind; that is why it was Christian. St. Thomas was, if you will, taking the lower road when he walked in the steps of Aristotle. So was God, when He worked in the workshop of Joseph."[154] By being open to learning from the cultures around them, and in the face of ecclesial opposition at times, these two medieval saints also became excellent exemplars of the

---

[153] *Saint Thomas Aquinas: The Dumb Ox*, 27-8.

[154] Ibid., 42.

development of doctrine in action, and reminders of the constant need for the Church to be in open and critical dialogue
with the world.

> …[Thomas's and Francis's] tendency, humanistic and naturalistic in a
> hundred ways, was truly the development of the supreme doctrine;
> which was also the dogma of all dogmas. It is in this that the popular
> poetry of St. Francis and the almost rationalistic prose of St. Thomas
> appear most vividly as part of the same movement. They are both
> great growths of Catholic development, depending upon external
> things only as every living and growing thing depends on them; that
> is, it digests and transforms them; but continues in its own image
> and not in theirs.[155]

Both saints looked to the elements of goodness, truth, and
beauty in the world that surrounded them and used these to
nourish the Church's tradition. In this way they showed the
incarnational nature of Christianity and how the Church grows
through contact with the cultures in which it finds itself. Both
of these saints:

> …saved us from Spirituality…Perhaps it may be misunderstood if
> I say that St. Francis, for all his love of animals, saved us from be-
> ing Buddhists; and that St. Thomas, for all his love of Greek phi-
> losophy, saved us from being Platonists…They both reaffirmed the
> Incarnation, by bringing God back to earth.[156]

Clearly Chesterton's use of the word "spirituality" here intends
to communicate how some forms of Christian thought can tend
to be more dualistic, other-worldly, and platonic than the more
holistic, sacramental, or incarnational forms of spirituality to
which we have become more accustomed in recent decades.
The temptation to platonize or spiritualize the Church's theology, such that it is cut off from the culture in which that theology

---

[155] Ibid., 28.

[156] Ibid., 29.

is trying to express itself, is a perennial danger to the Church's evangelizing mission.

This was part of the reason why the apologetics dominant during Chesterton's lifetime and in the years preceding the Second Vatican Council was unsatisfactory (we recall that Chesterton remarked in *Orthodoxy* that he read as little of the contemporary apologetics as possible). Chesterton, on the other hand, as we have already seen from his correspondence with Frances during the period of their engagement, concurred with these two great Christian figures of the thirteenth century that bad (or less than ideal) things can be taken into one's domicile in order both to make them better things and to enrich one's home.

Paraphrasing Chesterton's words to his betrothed, the Church should have no objection to having an unbeliever to dinner, or a penitent (or even impenitent) heretic to sleep in the spare bed.[157] Such generous and open hospitality would not only benefit the world:

> St. Thomas, every bit as much as St. Francis, felt subconsciously that the hold of his people was slipping on the solid Catholic doctrine and discipline, worn smooth by more than thousand years of routine; and that the faith needed to be shown under a new light and dealt with from another angle...It needed something like the shrewd and homely touch of Aristotle to turn it again into a religion of common sense.[158]

At its best the Church's theological tradition tries to express all that God communicates of himself in both revelation and reason, and so the tradition has to remain ever-open to all the truths that are yet to be discovered and to use them in the service of the Gospel. Chesterton cites Aquinas's mentor

---

[157] See Ward, *GKC*, 72.

[158] *Saint Thomas Aquinas: The Dumb Ox*, 82.

Albertus Magnus as a good example of this process of learning through dialogue with the world. Albert, a great scientific mind, provided a lot of new information for the Church to reflect on. Chesterton noted first that many Scholastics used new data more as a way of teaching logic—"'If a unicorn has one horn, two unicorns have as many horns as one cow.' And that is not one inch the less a fact because the unicorn is a fable." Chesterton then said that Albert took a different route and did as Aristotle had done before him. He asked:

> "But does the unicorn only have one horn or the salamander a fire instead of a fire-side?" Doubtless when the social and geographical limits of medieval life began to allow them to search the fire for salamanders or the desert for unicorns, they had to modify many of their scientific ideas. A fact which will expose them to the very proper scorn of a generation of scientists which has just discovered that Newton is nonsense, that space is limited, and that there is no such thing as an atom.[159]

Here, Chesterton captures three contrasting attitudes toward developments in scholarship. One of them, displayed by many Scholastics, is to use new knowledge to continue to support an already existing system of thought, which is fine in itself, providing that this is the only thing for which the new knowledge can be used. The second attitude, one possessed in abundance by the scientist Albert, is to see how new knowledge can challenge and even alter philosophical and theological systems. The third attitude, and one which Chesterton associates with the haughty and arrogant disposition of some of the scientists of his own day, is one which he goes on to describe as that of "a sneer."

Chesterton points out how so many scientists forget that so much of what is claimed as human knowledge can be

[159] *Saint. Thomas Aquinas: The Dumb Ox*, 67-8.

provisional, open to being refined, deepened, or even abandoned. Seemingly blind to the fact that modern science regularly revises its own theories, ideas, and conclusions in the light of new data, Chesterton notes with irony how many scientists contemptuously find the Church's theological revisionism a source of amusement.

Echoing some of the narrow and imprisoning dispositions we saw in Chapter II, Chesterton identifies intellectual haughtiness, a lack of openness, and a vision of the growth in human knowledge as a competition to be won or lost against others who work in the same or other fields, as the very attitudes and issues that bedevil any growth to maturity in the intellectual, scientific, spiritual and theological life. "As a matter of fact, it is generally the man who is not ready to argue, who is ready to sneer. That is why, in recent literature, there has been so little argument and so much sneering."[160]Chesterton would have relished debating some of the "new atheists" of our own day, and would in fact see nothing new in the contemptuous dismissiveness displayed toward religious worldviews that are so prevalent today. For Chesterton, however, the Christian apologist must always be on guard against developing such an attitude toward his dialogue partners.

Of the saintly Aquinas he said, "There is not a single occasion in which he indulged in a sneer. His curiously simple character, his lucid but laborious intellect, could not be better summed up than by saying that he did not know how to sneer."[161] Noting that Chesterton's apologetic tone always had an "'either-or' which gave [them] their polemical force," Gabriel Daly remarks that, "It has been said of Lucien Laberthonière

---

[160] Ibid., 126.

[161] Ibid.

that he needed someone to think against. Perhaps in a sense we all do, if we are to be saved from blandness."[162] While Chesterton's style of writing and debating was often robust and uncompromising, it was also kind, humble, and humorous, and it never descended to the level of a sneering contempt for his dialogue partner. Chesterton, like the Aquinas he depicts in his volume on the saint, never saw debate and the quest for new knowledge and insight as a competition in which others were to be ridiculed or made to feel small. Perhaps this is why the atheist H. G. Wells, when asked about the company he would choose to have with him if he were a painted pagan living on a frescoed celestial ceiling, replied by choosing Chesterton over the latter's coreligionist Belloc:

> The company about me on the clouds varies greatly with the mood of the vision, but always it is in some, if not always a very obvious way, beautiful. One frequent presence is G. K. Chesterton, a joyous whirl of brushwork, appropriately garmented and crowned. When he is there, I remark the whole ceiling is by a sort of radiation convivial. We drink limitless old October from handsome flagons, and we argue mightily about Pride (his weak point) and the nature of Deity... Chesterton often—but never by any chance Belloc. Belloc I admire beyond measure, but there is a sort of partisan viciousness about Belloc that bars him from my celestial dreams. He never figures, no, not even in the remotest corner, on my ceiling.[163]

The Church does well to remember that when it enters into dialogue with the culture in which it finds itself, it is in conversation with brothers and sisters, children of the same God, and not the great unwashed, unconverted mob. As the Church seeks to evangelize the world, God can work on both dialogue

---

[162] "Apologists in the Modernist Period," *Chesterton and the Modernist Crisis*, ed. A. Nichols, Saskatoon: The Chesterton Review Press, 1990, 91-2.

[163] *New Age*, 11th January 1908, cited in J. Pearce, *Wisdom and Innocence*, 59.

partners. Although which has most to learn and which most to teach in a given situation may be a matter for conjecture, it remains certain that finite human minds which are trying to enter more fully into the Divine Mystery must always remain open to deeper insight, wherever it comes from. The Church must enter into true dialogue with others who do not share its vision. Chesterton points out that Aquinas believed that Christians must enter into the philosophy of the dialogue partner and try to understand it from the inside:

> It is no good to tell an atheist that he is an atheist; or to charge a denier of immortality with the infamy of denying it; or to imagine that one can force an opponent to admit that he is wrong, by proving he is wrong on somebody else's principles, but not on his own. After the great example of St. Thomas, the principle stands, or ought always to have stood as established; that we must either not argue with a man at all, or we must argue on his grounds and not ours. We may do other things instead of arguing, according to our views of what actions are morally permissible; but if we argue we must argue [according to Aquinas] "on the reasons and statements of the philosophers themselves."[164]

The Church exists, not primarily to defend carefully a deposit of faith that has been entrusted to it by its Lord, but in order to be food for the life of the world. Of course, as Chesterton teaches us, nourishing the world with the Gospel of life will inevitably entail protecting and expounding the Church's long theological tradition, since no kingdom can exist without boundaries. Moreover, the human flourishing which consists of a life of love needs to know what is meant by "love" which, as we have seen, necessitates a lot of careful reflection. But in attempting to delineate and carry out the Church's theological and pastoral ministry in a complex and pluralistic world, it is a question of

---

[164] *Saint Thomas Aquinas: The Dumb Ox*, 95-6.

delicately discerning which emphasis to make at what time and in what particular circumstances.

Aquinas entered into the outlooks of Greek, Jewish, and Islamic philosophers not only because he sought to bring all things under the reign of Christ, but also because he realized that the Church's tradition could gain much from their learning. As he had pointed out (in a passage quoted earlier) in opposition to Siger of Brabant during their controversy about the truths of reason and the truths of faith, there were not two truths, but only one:

> Siger of Brabant said this: that the church must be right theologically, but she can be wrong scientifically. There are two truths: the truth of the supernatural world, and the truth of the natural world, which contradicts the supernatural world…In other words, Siger of Brabant split the human head in two…and he declared that a man has two minds, with one of which he must entirely believe and with the other may utterly disbelieve…[This] was the assassination of Thomism. It was not two ways of finding the same truth; it was an untruthful way of pretending that there are two truths…St. Thomas was willing to allow the one truth to be approached by two paths, precisely because he was sure there was only one truth. Because the Faith was the one truth, nothing discovered in nature could ultimately contradict the Faith. Because the Faith was the one truth, nothing really deduced from the Faith could ultimately contradict the facts.[165]

A Christian faith worthy of the name must be open to all truth and must be a mature faith—one that is not shy of the world's complexities. The Church's tradition gives us tested religious and moral roots and nourishment; but if the Church is to remain ever open to further maturity, that tradition must be prepared to engage with cultures and with all that is strange, new and "other."

The Thomistic medieval spirit admired so much by Chesterton displayed a "faith in receptiveness, and in respect

---

[165] Ibid., 92-3.

for things outside oneself...[It] loved its part in life as a part, not a whole; its charter for it came from something else...and Benedictus benedicat is very precisely the motto of the earliest medievalism." For Chesterton, since Christianity holds that "everything is blessed from beyond,"[166] Christian tradition must allow itself to be stretched by encounter with that which is new and which may at first seem foreign to it. Apologetics must by its very nature remain in conversation with that which is other.

Of course, throughout its long history of encounter with that which is new and strange, the Church has learned that not every dialogue partner, or certainly not at least every constituent element of a dialogue partner's outlook, is always true, good, beautiful, and life-giving. Consequently the Church's tradition contains many guidelines and maps that are useful for avoiding dangers, and which warn us to be mindful of what we experience and how we experience it. Chesterton says, "The Catholic Church is the only thing that saves a man from the degrading slavery of being a child of his age."[167] He warns us that:

> Nine out of ten of what we call new ideas are simply old mistakes. The Catholic Church has for one of her chief duties that of preventing people from making those old mistakes; from making them over and over again forever, as people always do if they are left to themselves... The Catholic Church carries a sort of map of the mind which looks like a map of a maze, but which is in fact a guide to the maze...Its experience naturally covers nearly all experiences; and especially nearly all errors. The result is a map in which all the blind alleys and bad roads are clearly marked, all the ways that have been shown to be worthless by the best of all evidence: the evidence of those who have gone down them.

---

[166] *A Short History of England*, 43-6.

[167] *The Catholic Church and Conversion, Collected Works* Vol. 3, 110.

Precisely because human beings do not live for a thousand years, because life is short and because searching down blind alleys can be a lonely and time-consuming affair, the Church's tradition "does prevent men from wasting their time or losing their lives upon paths that have been found futile or disastrous again and again in the past."[168] Sometimes what is new and strange can be so novel or powerful that it can overwhelm us and thereby corrode our faith and capacities for living well. At the same time, however, Chesterton believes that we must not make the opposite error either. We do not serve well the purposes of the Gospel when we see the world and its thought, art and cultural expressions merely as potential or actual threats to the faith of the Church.

As Chesterton did with Shaw and Wells, we must assume that the encounter with what is different from us may in some way improve us, give us something to think about and learn from, something that can enrich us and our faith, even if we cannot completely agree with it. We must be prudent and critical, yet also open. The Gospel needs protection and boundaries, but it also needs and energy and openness to the new, lest its richness and expression not be communicated to the world because of that petrified fear and an unwillingness to take risks, which were contradicted so courageously by Aquinas.

Chesterton makes any abstract discussion of this need for openness much more specific and personal, when he writes of his own need to remain as open to learning about the wisdom of the Church's tradition as he was to discovering the mysteries of life through his mother's teaching when he was a child:

> So, since I have accepted Christendom as a mother and not merely as a chance example, I have found Europe and the world once more like

---

[168] *The Thing: Why I am a Catholic*, 129.

the little garden where I stared at the symbolic shapes of cat and rake; I look at everything with the old elvish ignorance and expectancy. This or that rite or doctrine may look as ugly and extraordinary as a rake; but I have found by experience that such things end somehow in grass and flowers. A clergyman may be apparently as useless as a cat, but he is also as fascinating, for there must be some strange reason for his existence.[169]

Although he could not always claim to understand the Church's teaching, he found that often there is contained within it some deep and traditional wisdom that has long been thought to benefit the human race:

> I give one instance out of a hundred; I have not myself any instinctive kinship with that enthusiasm for physical virginity, which has certainly been a note of historic Christianity. But when I look not at myself but at the world, I perceive that this enthusiasm is not only a note of Christianity, but a note of Paganism, a note of high human nature in many spheres. The Greeks felt virginity when they carved Artemis, the Romans when they robed the vestals, the worst and wildest of the great Elizabethan playwrights clung to the literal purity of a woman as to the central pillar of the world…With all this human experience, allied with the Christian authority, I simply conclude that I am wrong, and the church right; or rather that I am defective, while the church is universal.[170]

The truth, then, is forever beyond us, and we all need to be stretched in order to know it better, since life is a mysterious and complex gift from a God who has communicated himself to us in many ways, and definitively in Jesus of Nazareth. God remains ineffable and sends the Church the gift of the Spirit in order that it may be immersed ever more fully into the mystery of God's self-revelation, the divine self-communication, in Christ. The human experience of the mystery of life and the

---

[169] *Orthodoxy*, 361.

[170] Ibid.

Church's experience of the mystery of the divine self-giving are always richer and will always transcend the human capacity to conceptualize, imagine, and express them.

This is one of the more positive reasons for the many disputes that take place within the same Church. "[I]f anyone doubts that there is such a thing as Catholic liberty, I think it can do no harm to let him realize that there is such a thing as Catholic controversy; I mean controversy between Catholics." If Hilaire Belloc pronounces on some issue as a Catholic, it does not necessarily follow that his coreligionists will concur:

> On the contrary, each would say something quite different. It is not that they need agree with him; but that he need not agree with them... Catholics know the two or three transcendental truths on which they do agree; and take rather a pleasure in disagreeing on everything else.[171]

Faith in God is not a narrowing of the mind or spirit, but something which stretches human beings beyond the limited self into the worlds and perspectives of others. It is the opening up of the human spirit to a cosmos and a God that enlightens and surprises. It calls all apologists to display an attitude of humility before life and learning:

> It takes all sorts to make a church; she does not ask me to be celibate. But the fact that I have no appreciation of the celibates, I accept like the fact that I have no ear for music. The best human experience is against me, as it is on the subject of Bach. Celibacy is one flower in my father's garden, of which I have not been told the sweet or terrible name. But I may be told it any day.[172]

Chesterton knew that he and all finite, creaturely members of the human species had to remain forever open to learning

---

[171] *The Thing: Why I Am a Catholic*, 265.

[172] *Orthodoxy*, 361.

about life and God. He also knew from personal experience that the impetus and motivation for such learning can be found both inside and outside the Church. Furthermore, sustained reflection does not end once one enters the Church. "To become a Catholic is not to leave off thinking, but to learn how to think."[173] The gifts that have been given to the Church in the divine self-communication that constitutes Christian revelation impose on the Church the never-ending (this side of the *Parousia*) theological tasks of contemplating and translating that revelation for the present moment.

When the Church faithfully expounds its understanding of Christian revelation in new cultural contexts and historical moments, it shows itself to be not some mummified dead body of traditionalism, worshipping a bygone age and fearful of what will come next in the movement of history but, on the contrary, a living tradition:

> The Church in its practical relation to my soul is a living teacher, not a dead one. It not only taught me yesterday, but will almost certainly teach me tomorrow…The person who lives in contact with what he believes to be a living Church is a person always expecting to meet Plato and Shakespeare tomorrow at breakfast. He is always expecting to see some truth he has not seen before.[174]

The Church, at its best, is the guardian of living doctrines, lessons from the past that have served human happiness well and that will help to keep people alive, colorful, energetic, and happy in the future too. Even before he entered the Church of Rome, Chesterton knew that by putting the great tradition in dialogue with the very real, concrete, and definite present moment, the Church was being faithful to Newman's vision of

---

[173] *The Catholic Church and Conversion*, 106.

[174] *Orthodoxy*, 359-60.

the development of doctrine and was creating a space within which new treasures could be added to that tradition:

> A man who is always going back and picking to pieces his own first principles may be having an amusing time but he is not developing as Newman understood development. Newman meant that if you wanted a tree to grow you must plant it finally under some definite spot. It may be (I do not know and I do not care) that Catholic Christianity is just now passing through one of its numberless periods of undue repression and silence. But I do know this, that when the great flowers break forth again, the new epics and the new arts, they will break out on the ancient and living tree.[175]

Tradition, therefore, is not a concept that signifies what some strands of modern thought in Chesterton's (and our own) day understood it to mean: a dirty word, to be avoided at all costs, because it stands in the way of human flourishing and progress. On the contrary, it is only by being rooted in the wisdom of the Church's living tradition, which links one generation of believers with the next, that authentic development in the present cultural context can take place and the next generation of believers be prepared for their own Christian adventure. Chesterton said, "I think I am the sort of man who came to Christ from Pan and Dionysus and not from Luther or Laud; that the conversion I understand is that of the pagan and not the Puritan."[176]

If one remembers that Pan was an important figure in 19th century Romanticism and 20th century neo-paganism, and if one understands at least some of the 21st century postmodern sensibilities as born of some of the same disillusionment with the modern project and the same spiritual hungers, it might be argued that if the Church's tradition today is to engage in

---

[175] Cited in Ward, *GKC*, 138.

[176] *The Catholic Church and Conversion*, 108.

cross-cultural conversation, then Peter has to be in dialogue with Pan. We shall take up this theme again in our final chapter.

4.4 THEOLOGICAL DOCTRINE: *the Walls of the Human Playground*

Several times in the unfolding of this book we have seen the great value that Chesterton placed on tradition. Nowhere is this illustrated more clearly than in a famous passage in which Chesterton asks us to consider a scenario in which a reformer or revolutionary comes across a gate or a fence in the middle of a road:

> The more modern type of reformer goes gaily up to it and says, "I don't see the use of this; let us clear it away." To which the more intelligent type of reformer will do well to answer: "If you don't see the use of it, I certainly won't let you clear it away. Go away and think. Then, when you can come back and tell me that you do see the use of it, I may allow you to destroy it."

Chesterton says that when faced with any human institution (and we could insert here any example we like—a church, a group of people, a building, a moral code, or a teaching), the reformer first needs to ask how its original existence came about:

> If he knows how it arose, and what purposes it was supposed to serve, he may really be able to say that they were bad purposes, or that they have since become bad purposes, or that they are purposes which are no longer served. But if he simply stares at the thing as a senseless monstrosity that has somehow sprung up in his path, it is he and not the traditionalist who is suffering from an illusion.[177]

Applying this to the wisdom, customs and doctrines that have emerged from the Church's tradition of theological reflection, Chesterton sees these as ways of protecting human flourishing and happiness. He wishes to contradict those who hold:

---

[177] *The Thing: Why I Am a Catholic*, 157.

...the view that priests darken and embitter the world. I look at the world and simply discover that they don't. Those countries in Europe which are still influenced by priests, are exactly the countries where there is still singing and dancing and coloured dresses and art in the open-air. Catholic doctrine and discipline may be walls; but they are the walls of a playground.[178]

Doctrines are the boundaries laid down by Christianity, establishing "a rule and order, [and] the chief aim of that order was to give room for good things to run wild."[179] Once again highlighting the continuity and discontinuity between the pagan worldview and the Christian creed, Chesterton stresses that:

Christianity is the only frame which has preserved the pleasure of Paganism. We might fancy some children playing on the flat grassy top of some tall island in the sea. So long as there was a wall round the cliff's edge they could fling themselves into every frantic game and make the place the noisiest of nurseries. But the walls were knocked down, leaving the naked peril of the precipice. They did not fall over; but when their friends returned to them they were all huddled in terror in the center of the island; and their song had ceased.[180]

This is a typically Chestertonian paradox: the things which are commonly assumed to suppress human freedom, creativity and self-expression—doctrines, dogmas, rules, rubrics, and all the other components of tradition—are in actual fact the very things which guarantee those human values.

In the second chapter of *Orthodoxy* Chesterton had maintained that "man can understand everything by the help of what he does not understand...The mystic allows one thing to be mysterious, and everything else becomes lucid."[181] In bowing

---

[178] *Orthodoxy*, 350.

[179] Ibid., 300.

[180] Ibid., 350.

[181] Ibid., 231.

before the gift of the evidence offered by reality, rather than by refusing to do so and remaining forever trapped within the loneliness of solipsism, Chesterton had discovered that there are many adventures to be enjoyed in the cosmos. Now, in the closing pages of the same work, he relates that he had also discovered that "something [God] we have never in any full sense known [because of our fallen human nature], is not only better than ourselves, but even more natural to us than ourselves."[182] In answer to the question, "What is the fall?" Chesterton says, "with complete sincerity, 'That whatever I am, I am not myself.'"[183] That is why moral laws exist in Elfland. In Elfland he had been taught that,

> "You may live happily with the King's daughter, if you do not show her an onion." The vision always hangs upon a veto. All the dizzy and colossal things conceded depend upon one small thing withheld. All the wild and whirling things that are let loose depend upon one thing that is forbidden.[184]

The moral law exists in Elfland in order that the fallen inhabitants of that kingdom could enjoy life. Now, as Orthodoxy draws to a close, Chesterton tells of his discovery that,

> The unpopular parts of Christianity turn out when examined to be the very props of the people. The outer ring of Christianity is a rigid guard of ethical abnegations and professional priests; but inside that inhuman guard you will find the old human life dancing like children, and drinking wine like men; for Christianity is the only frame for pagan freedom. But in the modern philosophy the case is opposite; it is its outer ring that is obviously artistic and emancipated; its despair is within.[185]

---

[182] Ibid., 363.

[183] Ibid.

[184] Ibid., 258.

[185] Ibid., 362.

By explaining how boundaries permit a space within which good things can be thoroughly enjoyed, Chesterton is making explicit something that he sensed both in his childhood and in his understanding of art: that limits and lines are fun and give rise to creative beauty:

> It is plain on the face of the facts that the child is positively in love with limits. He uses his imagination to invent imaginary limits. The nurse and the governess have never told him that it is his moral duty to step on alternate paving-stones. He deliberately deprives this world of half its paving-stones, in order to exult in a challenge that he has offered to himself…[Chesterton exulted in the fact that he could] divide and subdivide, into these happy prisons, the house in which I was quite free to run wild…This game of self-limitation is one of the secret pleasures of life.[186]

As the Ethics of Elfland already taught us, reality is full of limits, and human happiness and fullness are contingent upon learning to accept that fundamental fact. As any true artist knows, to deal with the real is to deal with limits and boundaries:

> [I]t is impossible to be an artist and not care for laws and limits. Art is limitation; the essence of every picture is the frame…The moment you step into the world of facts, you step into a world of limits…Do not free a camel of the burden of his hump: you may be freeing him from being a camel.[187]

Any act of human creativity, be it a scientific theory or a doctoral thesis, requires a framework and delimitations if it is to find proper expression. This also applies to the gradual and lifelong works of art that are our relationships, our marriages, and our life of community. On the moral level, "every act of

---

[186] *Autobiography*, 106-7.

[187] *Orthodoxy*, 243.

will is an act of self-limitation."[188] Every human choice implies many renunciations.

To choose to marry one woman is to delimit the possibility of marrying the 3.25 billion other women in the world. To choose to live in Rome is to choose not to live in London, New York, or Tokyo. To opt for one career seriously limits the potential to pursue other careers. Finite human beings do not have unlimited potentialities, but must make specific choices out of several possible options in order to build something lasting and worthwhile:

> God is that which can make something out of nothing. Man (it may truly be said) is that which can make something out of anything. In other words, while the joy of God be unlimited creation, the special joy of man is limited creation, the combination of creation with limits. Man's pleasure, therefore, is to possess conditions, but also to be partly possessed by them; to be half-controlled by the flute he plays or by the field he digs. The excitement is to get the utmost out of given conditions; the conditions will stretch, but not indefinitely.[189]

Choices—difficult choices—have to be made if human beings are to create something worthwhile and have any chance of finding joy. "I could never conceive or tolerate any Utopia which did not leave me the liberty for which I chiefly care, the liberty to bind myself."[190] For Chesterton, choice and adventure—choice and romance—are intimately connected. Reflecting on the metaphysics of this he says, "complete anarchy would not merely make it impossible to have any discipline or fidelity; it would also make it impossible to have any fun."[191] No romance, no adventure, and no fun could ever begin without a commitment or obligation of some sort.

---

[188] Ibid.

[189] *What's Wrong with the World?* 41.

[190] *Orthodoxy*, 328.

[191] Ibid.

In his doctoral dissertation, eventually published as *Geist in Welt*[192] in 1939, Karl Rahner refers to human beings as spirit in the world. We are enfleshed spirit, not spirit and body, or body and soul, but both together, integrated in the one person that each of us is. None of us has a choice about being spiritual, so none of us has a choice about having a spirituality. We all have one, either a life-giving one or a destructive one. In the Phaedrus, Plato says that we are fired with a madness that comes from the gods (*theia mania*): we are built too big for this world.[193]

Christianity agrees that we are built in the *imago Dei*, with all that this entails for concrete existence and, as we recall from our second chapter, Augustine reminds us that our hearts are restless in this world as they seek their eternal rest in God. We are infinite spirits living in a finite world. As Rahner puts it, it is "myopic [to believe] that there is some 'happiness' or other in this world outside tranquilly accepting that here [in this life] all symphonies remain unfinished."[194] We are constituted by God in such a way that we are too great for this world, since our hearts are made for union with all that is, and yet in this life our hearts meet finite and mortal realities.

To be restless, therefore, is part of what it means to be human. All of us possess this madness from the gods, and we have to find a way of negotiating that. We do not in this world have the sense that we possess all that we need for fulfillment. As Chesterton puts it, "This world is too small for the soul of

---

[192] See K. Rahner, *Spirit in the World*, foreword by J.B. Metz, London: Continuum, 1995.

[193] See 243e-245c. For a Christian understanding of this Platonic doctrine, see J. Pieper, *Divine Madness: Plato's Case Against Secular Humanism*.

[194] *Servants of the Lord*, 152.

man."[195] We all seek "that home behind home for which we are all homesick."[196] Hence to be an enfleshed spirit is not about serenely choosing certain religious or spiritual activities, like whether or not we will go to church, or whether or not we will pray; it is something far more basic to our humanity than that. Long before we do anything explicitly religious at all, we have to do something about the fact that we have been constituted by the Creator as made for another world that transcends the cosmos; that a divine energy drives us or burns within us, such that "since the end of Eden, the very sky is not large enough for lovers."[197]

The Church's theological traditions, doctrines, dogmas, and rules are boundaries or limits which seek to help human beings make choices and live life in such a way that they can handle the divine energy within without getting damaged by its power. Contrary to the opinion of many people, the Church's teachings are there so that human beings can flourish, such that their time here on Earth becomes life-giving and not destructive, and brings deep-seated joy, not misery, to them and those around them. Chesterton puts before us the image of those people who think the opposite—who understand the Church as negative and foreboding—and describes them as people who look at:

> ...the convert entering with bowed head a sort of small temple which they are convinced is fitted up inside like a prison, if not a torture-chamber. But all they really know about it is that he has passed through a door. They do not know that he has not gone into the inner darkness, but out into the broad daylight...[The Catholic] does not want to go into a larger room, because he does not know

[195] "If Don John of Austria had Married Mary Queen of Scots," in *The Common Man*, cited in Morris, *TTFR*, 56.

[196] *The New Jerusalem, Collected Works* Vol. 20, 222.

[197] "If Don John of Austria had Married Mary Queen of Scots," in *The Common Man*, cited in Morris, *TTFR*, 56.

of any larger room to go into. He knows of a larger number of much smaller rooms, each of which is labelled as being very large; but he is quite sure he would be cramped in any of them.[198]

Chesterton here uses the image of smaller rooms both to describe other churches and ecclesial bodies, but clearly his vision of the Church as the trysting place of all truths would also imply that the rooms stand for all ideas and values which need to be connected with other ideas and values. As Chesterton said, embracing the Church's way of life has as one of its chief effects that of stepping into a larger, not more cramped space, even though at first glance this does not seem to be the case:

> [Just before deciding whether to join the church or not] the convert often feels as if he were looking through a leper's window. He is looking through a little crack or crooked hole that seems to grow smaller as he stares at it; but it is an opening that looks toward the Altar. Only, when he has entered the Church, he finds that the Church is much larger inside than it is outside. He has left behind him the lop-sidedness of lepers' windows and even in a sense the narrowness of Gothic doors; and he is under vast domes as open as the Renaissance and as universal as the Republic of the world.[199]

We are built for another world, but live within this one; built with a divine fire, a burning desire for infinite union and joy, and yet confined to living one vocation, with one person or set of persons, in one place, at a given moment in history. Elfland, and the living community of believers known as the Church, both teach us that to embrace reality means that our infinite desire is limited by finite choices. To accept this fact is to begin to ease, at least in part, this congenital restlessness, so that the divine fire does not damage us. It is then we will stop demanding that our spouse, our job, our Church or community, our bishop

---

[198] *The Catholic Church and Conversion, Collected Works* Vol. 3, 107.

[199] *The Catholic Church and Conversion, Collected Works* Vol. 3, 94.

or religious superior, our vocation, our holidays, and whatever other gift we have in our life, give us something which, by their very nature, they cannot give: pure joy, or what Rahner would refer to as the finished symphony. Mature love, as opposed to an immature floating or uncommitted "love" (a contradiction in terms for Chesterton who believes that "Love is not blind; that is the last thing that it is. Love is bound; and the more it is bound the less it is blind"[200]), implies painful renunciations. We shall return in more detail to this truth in our next chapter.

For now we observe that doctrines circumscribe, but in so doing they nourish human joy. Accordingly, the Church's theology needs to be in touch with the color, joy, humor, and energy that follow from the divine energy and fire within human beings who are made in the image of God. The apologist needs to be aware that the Church's theological doctrines are the walls of a human playground and permit those within to fling themselves into every frantic game of life, thereby preserving the true pleasures of paganism, while avoiding its dangers and inordinate expressions, which ultimately lead only to sadness and ruin.

---

5. Concluding Remarks

This chapter has explored how Christian faith is a journey undertaken with others. We started by looking at some of the friendships in Chesterton's life. We saw that in the relationship between Chesterton and Frances, community was not built up merely because they shared the same home, table, or bed. Community was the result of a shared space of mutual presence in which, through the ups and downs of life in this world, they struggled together to build an adventure of joy.

---

[200] *Orthodoxy*, 274.

We saw that Belloc and Chesterton were aware of their differences and also of the gifts they contributed to each other. By inspecting the reactions to the debating style of these two famous speakers, we noted how tone may be vitally important in any conversation between the apologist and the surrounding culture.

This importance is also underlined by a perusal of the relationship between Chesterton and Shaw. While Chesterton never held back in any debate with Shaw, he always sought the good in Shaw and in his opinions, and regularly pointed them out to well-intentioned but narrower types of Christians who could find in Shaw nothing but danger and hostility to the Christian faith. Chesterton was able to put the views of Shaw in the context of the personality that had been influenced and disappointed by his upbringing, thus revealing the importance for the apologist of being able to discern a bigger picture or wider horizon when dialoguing with a person who does not share the Christian faith. The problem as understood and formulated by that person is not always the only element in the equation of the unbelief, but may be symptomatic of a deeper confusion, a frustrated or undernourished hunger for meaning and, ultimately, a blocked disposition for God. It is essential, therefore, that the apologist be able to transpose the dialogue into these broader horizons of vision.

From the point of view of community what was common to all three friendships was that they were very ordinary and very "everyday" in nature. Sheer mutual presence down the years helped all four people grow as human beings. Community was built in these relationships not because the friends necessarily agreed on certain things. Although there were some shared outlooks and approaches, there were also enormous differences of opinion and tone. At various times one or both parties to the relationship were able to display constancy, patience, gentleness, an ability to bear the other's faults and failings, and charity; and the ability to do this forged real relationship and community, beyond incompatibility and difference. These qualities allow people to be faithful to community, even when the journey seems all uphill.

From the Christian perspective, human beings are made for community because they are made in the image of the triune God, and avoiding relationship means acting against human nature. Modernity and the industrialization and individualism that followed from it made discovering and building human togetherness more difficult. This in turn made the possibilities of finding and living Christian faith more difficult. If people will not commit themselves to each other in lasting relationship, throughout the messiness and complexity of life, the face of God becomes less easy to discern. In spite of its self-proclaimed understanding of human meaning as atomized, postmodernity's rediscovery of the need for human solidarity and mutual concern offers renewed hope for the possibilities of faith, since the human journey toward God is never a solitary one.

The Church is the place above all others in this world where faith is born and where we find nourishment and community on our adventure toward God. The world could never have known Christian faith nor even heard of Christ without the Church who keeps the memory of Christ quite literally alive, and embodies the presence of Christ in our wounded world. In spite of postmodernity's advocacy of solidarity and support, it is not easy in an individualistic and suspicious culture to speak of the importance and relevance of the Church. However, any apologetics that seeks to be credible to the biblical record, in which Christ identifies himself with this struggling, graced, sinful, and weak community, has to be able to articulate a humble explanation of the need for the Church.

The Church claims to be the sign and agent of the very concrete and definitive self-giving of God in Jesus of Nazareth, a definiteness that can be another cause of nervousness and hostility for the postmodern person. The long history of God's self-revelation to humanity, which culminated in the Everlasting Man, and the translation of that revelation for the many and varied situations in which people find themselves in the numerous cultures and movements of history down to our own day, constitutes the tradition of the Church's theological reflection. Peter needs to be in constant dialogue with Pan if he is to mediate God's meaning for a new generation of searchers.

The Church can discern where the Spirit of God is already at work in the hungers and quests of a culture, and help the people of that culture to see that the Spirit who is active within them leads to Christ. The Spirit can gently help them see that their quest could become lonely and fruitless without the nourishing wisdom of a community that has behind it a long history of reflecting on human and divine realities. If postmodern seekers find all this a little too definite and authoritative, if they are not yet ready to embrace the gift of God in Christ, then perhaps honest responses to the promptings of the Spirit in other areas of experience—which we will explore in the next two chapters—will help prepare them for this fuller surprise of the Everlasting Man.

Chesterton says that the Church's doctrines and dogmas are the walls around a playground: they are there to help human beings flourish and enjoy life in this cosmos. God's grace is so abundant that honest seekers outside the Church will certainly be flourishing in myriad ways, even if they are unaware that it is by the Spirit of the risen Christ that they do so. The divine energy that burns within human beings who are made in the image of God finds expression in many ways in the world.

That energy needs careful handling, however, and the signposts of doctrine marking the well-trodden paths of destructive behavior and errors of thinking are fruits of the Church's perennial theological labor. They guard against the self-ruination and disintegration that follow on from not handling the divine fire within with reverence and prudence.

The Church's tradition helps people to think things through and serves as a constant reminder not to ignore the wise warnings of the history of human experience. Nevertheless, it seems important to end this chapter by emphasizing once more that the Church's theology must also remain ever-vigilant against shutting itself off from the world, for that would be to reduce itself to a merely internal or "in-house" conversation that would be out of touch with cultural realities, the concrete lives of people and their honest searching and aspirations. If that were to happen the Church's tradition would lose all its potential to be nourishment for the life of the world; it would become ossified, colorless, bland, and devoid of energy, and it would lead, not to moral irresponsibility and the personal disintegration of human beings, but to the equal and opposite error of an overly cautious and joyless frigidity before God's gift of life in the cosmos.

CHAPTER V

Doing the Truth in the
Romance of the Ordinary

St. Francis really meant it when he said he had found the secret of
life in being the servant and the secondary figure.[201]

…it is true to say with St. Irenaeus, "ubi ecclesia ibi Spiritus," but it
would not be true to say, "where the Church is not, neither is the
Spirit there." The operations of the Holy Ghost have always pervaded
the whole race of men from the beginning, and they are now in full
activity even among those who are without the Church.[202]

WE HAVE SEEN THAT CHESTERTON did not believe
that we could truly begin to appreciate and enjoy
the gift that is life in this cosmos without a certain
prior disposition of humility and gratitude, and without a recognition of the contingency of being. We have also learned that
one of the recurrent themes of his work was that of romance:
because human beings are free, their existence in this cosmos

---

[201] *St. Francis of Assisi*, 62.

[202] G. O'Collins, *Rethinking Fundamental Theology*, 316.

is an unpredictable and open-ended story in which they choose whether or not to conform their liberty to choosing the good.

Conscience is the summons to receive the gift of the cosmos and others with gratitude and respect, and not to consider them as owed or mere satellites to one's own existence. In the Chestertonian vision the "secular," the ordinary and the everyday, the non-intense and the humdrum events of existence in this world are anything but ordinary, if only we have the eyes to see it. "Ordinary" life is in fact a romance, a drama, and a threshold to be crossed by the way we employ our freedom. That crossing leads to an encounter with mystery and a gentler wisdom, and it opens us up to the possibility of perceiving the Giver of the gift.

This chapter briefly revisits Chesterton's contemplative, almost mystical insight that the deepest nature of the ordinary and the routine is laden with mystery, and we shall learn how the experience of pain or loss is often the harsh reality that rouses us to become alive to this truth. We examine human pride—the notion that we are self-sufficient and existentially, if not theoretically, unaware of our need for the redemption offered by Christ and appropriated through our relationships with others. We first need a humble recognition before we can be ready to receive the fullness of the Gospel. The virtues of humility and humor are essential in this regard, and we shall see some of Chesterton's insights on them.

Although Chesterton (probably because of what the Slade taught him about the risks of excessive introspection) displayed a certain nervousness about the turn to the subject that was evident in some Modernist theologians, he was aware, nonetheless, that it is only by the grateful, thinking, willing, choosing, and loving human subject that the gifts of the cosmos and the Creator could be received. For Chesterton God is both transcendent and immanent and, with the help of Rahner, O'Collins, von Balthasar, and Lonergan, we shall articulate how an appreciation of this transcendence and immanence is necessary for a healthy Christian theology of God and an adequate understanding of the demands of Christian living.

Chesterton, like any other human being, was involved in the struggle to learn to cooperate with the promptings of the Spirit, which is a slow and costly shaping and transformation in the romance of daily life, as people are gradually moved from selfishness and toward the gift of self in relationship. The Christian life entails a long journey of conformity to the essential content of the self-revelation of God, which is a life given over to and lived for the other in self-sacrificial love. We are called to become ever more what God created us to be: images of the triune divinity, persons baptized gradually into selflessness and the building of community through a unity of difference.

Chesterton believes that the family is the ideal place for learning this painful and lifelong lesson of self-gift, and also, therefore, the ideal preparation for living in any human institution. He believed that in the family, through the rhythms of the relationships of communal life, we are broken out of self-preoccupation and immersed into the world of others. The costliness of genuine love, as opposed to its cheaper, counterfeit versions, is explored first of all through Chesterton's advocacy of the poor and then by an examination of some of his insights into the figures of Saint Francis of Assisi and Peter Pan, which are supplemented by a few images taken from the Gospels.

So, we see that the romance of the ordinary is an invitation to accept that life is a gift, a mystery to be lived and enjoyed rather than a possession to be grasped and manipulated, and that we are invited to cross the threshold of mystery in order to share the gift of life with others whom we encounter (especially the marginalized and wounded). In that light we will ask whether this "performative" notion of faith[1] helps us be more ready to accept the reality of God. Does the credibility of Christian faith follow on from its livability? Does love offer us the correct lens through which to view life and perceive God, the giver of life?

1. THE FRAGILE TREASURE OF THE ORDINARY

In his work on Aquinas, Chesterton criticizes (with possibly a hint of exaggeration) the unfolding theological history of Eastern Christianity.

> …Eastern Christianity flattened everything, as it flattened the faces of the images into icons…The Greek element in Christian theology tended more and more to be a sort of dried up Platonism; a thing of diagrams and abstractions; to the last indeed noble abstractions, but not sufficiently touched by that great thing that is by definition almost the opposite of abstractions: Incarnation. Their Logos was the Word; but not the Word made Flesh.[2]

The doctrine of the Incarnation is the "opposite of abstractions": through it God takes on flesh, the Creator becomes part of the creation, the spiritual becomes secular. It is the concrete, definite, particular, historical, and secular nature of the claims made by Christianity whose consequences are also mirrored in the sacramental nature of the Church, which have scandalized particular groups of people at various times in history. Heaven has descended into the world of matter; the supreme spiritual power is now operating by the machinery of matter, dealing miraculously with the bodies and souls of men. It blesses all the five senses; as the senses of the body are blessed at a Catholic christening. It blesses even material gifts and keepsakes, as with relics or rosaries. It works through water or oil or bread or wine…The Incarnation is as much a part of that idea as the Mass;… and the Mass is as much a part of that idea as the Incarnation. A

---

[1] A phrase of Pope Benedict XVI.

[2] *Saint Thomas Aquinas: The Dumb Ox*, 83.

Puritan may think it blasphemous that God should become a wafer. A Moslem thinks it blasphemous that God should become a workman in Galilee.[3]

This radical challenge of concreteness and specificity from the heart of the Christian creed still causes no small measure of discomfort today, and not only for the postmodern mindset's suspicion of authority, overarching narratives, and specific claims to either partial or definitive truth and meaning. Even committed Christian believers can show themselves reluctant to think of God's self-communication as something that occurs here and now, in community, in the Church, in the complex lives of human beings who have the capacity for great goodness and great sinfulness, and in the flow of the ordinary and the everyday of our humdrum lives.

For Chesterton, however, God is neither a God of rare experiences nor an absentee cosmic landlord. We said in our second chapter that one of the most distinctive features of Chesterton is that he sees differently; he looks at reality with different eyes. He was able to see how tremendous were things commonly perceived as mere trifles. He saw the world through eyes of gratitude: he was grateful that anything existed at all; he rejoiced that this particular universe, not some other possible cosmos, was the gift we have been given; and he accepted in humility that he had been allowed to play a part in it and find it an endless source of wonder and joy. This wonder led him to discover many pearls of wisdom and their transcendent source, the highest wisdom of all, the Giver of the gift, God. It also led him to embrace the Church as a present and living teacher, a way of discovering more wisdom in a pilgrimage toward wisdom and holiness that had started many years before.

---

[3] *The Thing: Why I Am a Catholic*, 258-9.

Chesterton joins the rest of the cosmos in singing the praises of the Creator through the sheer fact of his own existence. Chesterton states that long before he "had anything worth calling a religion,"

> I had...a notion about that point at which extremes meet, and the most common thing becomes a public and mystical thing. I did not want so much to alter the place and use of things as to weight them with a new dimension; to deepen them by going down to the potential nothing; to lift them to infinity by measuring from zero. The most logical form of this is in thanks to a Creator...such praises could never raise too high; because they could not even reach the height of our own thanks for unthinkable existence, or horror of more unthinkable non-existence. And the commonest things, as much as the most complex, could thus leap up like fountains of praise.[4]

In a very real sense, Chesterton's heart rejoiced at the common, humdrum realities of daily living, including the gift of his own life. He saw the ordinary and the everyday as the epiphany of God, the source of all being. Logic, science and the various disciplines of knowledge are wonderful, but if they do not somehow provoke in us a sense of this primordial wonder at the origins of the gift of the cosmos, then we have missed something of their beauty.

> [A person] sees more of the things themselves when he sees more of their origin; for their origin is a part of them and indeed the most important part of them. Thus they become more extraordinary by being explained. He has more wonder at them, but less fear of them; for a thing is really wonderful when it is significant and not when it is insignificant.[5]

For Chesterton, the whole cosmos, in all its parts, great and small, speaks of God.

---

[4] *G. K.'s Weekly*, 6ᵗʰ December 1934, cited in Ward, *GKC*, 392.

[5] *Saint Francis of Assisi*, 68.

The mystic is not a man who reverences large things so much as a man who reverences small ones, who reduces himself to a point, without parts or magnitude, so that to him the grass is really a forest and the grasshopper a dragon. Little things please great minds.[6]

It might be said that Chesterton's heart was that of a contemplative, someone fully awake and aware. His way of seeing was that of someone tuned in to the deepest implications of reality. His faith was nourished by an awareness of the God of the bits and pieces, the God of the ordinary, the everyday and the secular, and he rejoiced in that. He offers us a Christian spirituality of down-to-earth living as he points out to us the hidden spiritual depths of things and the humility, gratitude and deep-seated joy that follow on from that realization.

For Chesterton, precisely because Elfland taught him that there is nothing necessary and therefore nothing ordinary about reality, that it is sheer miraculous gift whose miraculous nature may only dawn upon us after staring at it a thousand and one times, so the ordinary and the everyday, the humdrum routine, is ultimately the deepest source of joy and meaning. Ordinary life is a treasure that often goes unappreciated. Although at times it is only a crisis in life—pain, illness, suffering, loss, death—that helps us to realize this, the people and the objects of our concrete existence root us in the real and the precious.

A fierce sense of the value of things lies at the heart…of tragedy; for if lives were not valuable, tragedies would not be tragic…It may be that this is indeed the whole meaning of death; that heaven, knowing how we tire of our toys, forces us to hold this life on a frail and romantic tenure.[7]

---

[6] "The Little Things", *The Speaker*, 15th December 1900, cited in *TTFT*, 153.

[7] "The Poetic Quality in Liberalism," *The Independent Review*, February 1905, cited in *TTFT*, 167.

Sometimes the ordinary may need to be threatened or taken away before we appreciate its worth. "The way to love anything is to realize that it might be lost."[8] For Chesterton, "It is the point of all deprivation that it sharpens the idea of value; and, perhaps, this is, after all, the reason of the riddle of death."[9] The spiritual life often attests to the truth that, so often, we have to be brought to our knees before we learn real wisdom.

2. PRIDE, HUMILITY, AND HUMOR

In C. S. Lewis's work of allegorical fiction *The Pilgrim's Regress*, in which the pilgrim sets out with a guide in pursuit of wisdom through the philosophical landscape, before arriving at Christianity, the pilgrim asks his guide at one point of the journey, "And what is this valley called?" His companion replies, "We call it now simply Wisdom's valley: but the oldest maps mark it as the Valley of Humiliation."[10] It is a truth of the human condition that human beings often have to be humbled before becoming wise, which may be why Chesterton describes himself at the beginning of *Orthodoxy* as a disoriented and humbled seafarer, a man who only eventually found his way in life, once he had had the humility to acknowledge that his own maps and schemes were not up to the task.

In our earlier discussion of the sinfulness of the Church we saw that Chesterton puts into the mouth of Father Brown a great truth. In response to Flambeau's question "And what is the one spiritual disease?" he replies, "Oh, thinking one is quite

---

[8] *Tremendous Trifles*, 23.

[9] "On Being Moved," *Lunacy and Letters*, cited in *TTFT*, 167.

[10] C. S. Lewis, *The Pilgrim's Regress: An Allegorical Apology for Christianity, Reason and Romanticism*, London: Fount, 1977, 159.

well."[11] Chesterton advocates that we concern ourselves with our own faults and sinfulness: "The answer to the question, 'What is Wrong?' is, or should be, 'I am wrong.' Until a man can give that answer his idealism is only a hobby."[12] Rather than spend our time pointing out the defects of others, the wise person is the humble and grateful person, aware that all she possesses is gift of God.

> The instinct of the human soul perceives that a fool may be permitted to praise himself, but that a wise man ought to praise God. A man who really has a head with brains in it ought to know that this head has been gratuitously clapped on top of him like a new hat…[All is grace of God and no one has the right to be proud since we are all] the acceptors of some beautiful accident.[13]

For Chesterton, the Christian Gospel is the great love story of the Everlasting Man coming as one of the human race, the gift of God's self-communication whose essence is love, and who calls us to communion in love with him and each other. The distinctive feature of Christianity is not our quest for God, but God's search for us—"it is not we who loved God, but God loved us and sent his Son."[14] It follows that "we too should love one another."[15]

This is the grittier side of the Christian message: Elfland teaches us that our love for God is often expressed indirectly, through the love we give to others in the cosmos which we share as creatures loved into existence by God's abundance. If

[11] "The Eye of Apollo,," *The Penguin Complete Father Brown*, 132.

[12] *Daily News*, 16th August 1905, personal collection of D. Ahlquist, President of The American Chesterton Society.

[13] "The True Vanity of Vanities," *G. K. Chesterton: The Apostle and Wild Ducks*, cited in *TTFT*, 227.

[14] 1 John 4:10

[15] 1 John 4:11

the totality of the Gospel message consisted of the fact that God loves us, then it might be possible to stay within a self-satisfied comfort zone in which all was right with the world. Christ challenges us, however, to rise up with gutsy realism in order to love the world in all its mess and woundedness.

Chesterton often writes of the reality of sin—our poverty of response to the demanding invitation of Christ to bear responsibility for others and our world. It is tempting to shy away from this more demanding side of Christian revelation. If at times we are afraid of the more humbling demand of acknowledging our failure, worse still, and indeed even more dangerous, is the fact that often we do not even perceive our failure.

We see again and again in the pages of the Gospel, in Jesus' dealings with the Pharisees and religious leaders for example, illustrations of the truth articulated above by Father Brown: that if we are to be led by the Everlasting Man from emptiness to fullness, some sort of admission of our need is first required.

> The highest thing in the world is goodness. It is so high that, fortunately, the great majority of people who have it are horribly frightened of it, and keep their own virtue as they would keep some sort of wild horse or griffin. But every now and then there do appear people who are good and who know they are good, and who are proud of being good…These are the people whom Jesus Christ could hardly forbear to scourge. This is…the whole subtlety of the sin of pride; all other sins attack men when they are weak and weary; but this attacks when men are happy and valuable and nearer to all the virtues.[16]

The conflict between human pride (in the sense of "thinking one is quite well") and the realization of our essential human poverty and need of God—at the personal or the cultural level—is often the vital precursor to a growth toward a more mature

---

[16] "The True Vanity of Vanities," G. K. Chesterton: The Apostle and Wild Ducks, cited in TTFT, 227.

Christian faith. In an essay called "The Divine Detective" in *A Miscellany of Men*, Chesterton writes, "Rien comprendre est rien pardoner": to understand nothing is to forgive nothing. Forgiveness implies being aware of that which needs to be forgiven. Referring to a play by a Rann Kennedy, entitled *The Servant in the House*, Chesterton points out how in this play Christ comes to pardon evil, not ignore it. He knows well the people to whom he brings salvation. The two main characters in the play

> …are a popular and strenuous vicar and his fashionable and forcible wife. It would have been no good to tell these people that they had some good in them for that is what they were telling themselves all day long. They had to be reminded that they had some bad in them—instinctive idolatries and silent treasons which they always tried to forget.

Or, as Chesterton concludes in the final line of the essay, "the proud have secrets that…need to be detected before they are forgiven."[17] Whenever Jesus displays the anger in the Gospels to which Chesterton refers in this passage, it is because religious people's self-satisfaction has impeded a growth toward the life, freedom, and love that true religion brings. They have replaced these with a false religion, "instinctive idolatries," which destroy, imprison, trap and dehumanize. The real love revealed in Christ is a disturbing, provocative, and uncomfortable love, shattering the self-satisfied illusions of those "who are proud of being good."

The shattering of the illusions of smug religious self-satisfaction is a theme in the writings of Flannery O'Connor. She often pointed out (sometimes quite abruptly and forcefully) the hidden influence of pride that is at work in all people's lives.

---

[17] "The Divine Detective," *A Miscellany of Men*, 239-40.

Everybody is in need, and everyone is poor before the fullness of the gift that is Christ. One of O'Connor's charisms was to be able to write in such a way that she helped disclose to people the many ways in which they avoided their own spiritual poverty. "Smugness is the great Catholic sin. I find it in myself,"[18] she said. She sought to make people aware of their very real existential emptiness and to prepare them to be filled with the Holy Spirit, who can mold them for a life of generous love. In a real sense, the way in which she described one of her stories was emblematic of so much of her work: "It's not so much a story of conversion as of self-knowledge, which I suppose has to be the first step in conversion."[19] Her intention was not so much to unfold the riches of Christ for people, but more to prepare the way for him through a John the Baptist-like ministry, by shocking them into seeing their need for the Gospel. Her *praeparatio evangelica* aimed at reconfiguring the imagination of the smug and self-satisfied person (whether religious or not) for the strangeness of Christ.

Both Chesterton and O'Connor defended and made use of the grotesque in art in order to bring home to people their need of the Gospel. Although for Chesterton grotesque was a way of conveying the idea of vitality and energy, more importantly with regard to the theme we are discussing here, "To present a matter in a grotesque manner does certainly tend to touch the nerve of surprise."[20] Similarly O'Connor refers to her own way of writing as Southern Grotesque, "a realism which does not hesitate to distort appearances in order to show a hidden

[18] *Collected Works*, ed. S. Fitzgerald, 983.

[19] Ibid., 1076.

[20] *Robert Browning*, 241.

truth."[21] The hidden truth of revelation will remain hidden from us unless some explosive shock or surprise shatters our complacency. "Redemption is meaningless unless there is cause for it in the actual life we live, and for the last few centuries there has been operating in our culture the secular belief that there is no such cause."[22]

Returning to a theme that we explored in Chapter II, when our images of self are inaccurate or at least undernourished, our capacities for imagining God also suffer. Our smug self-satisfaction has to be disturbed in such a way that we are left with no opportunity for half-measures and hiding places, for only then can we be ready for the Gospel fullness of a life that is lived in love because it is nourished by Eternal Love. O'Connor's humorous and shocking fiction aims at breaking us in order to make us more receptive to the ways of grace. Chesterton too, ever since the days of the Slade, was wary of the dangers of making the ego the measure of reality, as he expressed so cogently in the second chapter of *Orthodoxy*, entitled "The Maniac." "The men who really believe in themselves are all in lunatic asylums…[Over the cell of such a man] shall be written, with dreadful truth, 'He believes in himself.'"[23] Such a man needs a dose of humor and humility.

We noted in the last chapter that one of the criticisms that Chesterton made of Shaw was that he was too serious about life. Perhaps Shaw needed a touch more of the humour that was to be found in both Chesterton and Flannery O'Connor, in order that a more human flavour of humility could be added to his undoubted wit. Ian Ker has offered some fascinating insights into

---

[21] *Mystery and Manners: Occasional Prose*, eds. S. & R. Fitzgerald, 179.

[22] Ibid., 33.

[23] *Orthodoxy*, 216, 229.

the role of humour and humility in the holiness of Chesterton.[24] He points out that for Chesterton, "all animals except man are serious,"[25] that "man is the only creature who does laugh"[26] and that "Alone among the animals, he is shaken with the beautiful madness called laughter."[27] Although, as James Martin says,

> some anthropologists and biologists who study the behavior of higher primates might quibble…chimpanzees, for example, seem to 'laugh' and enjoy playing with one another—few people would argue with the proposition that a sense of humor is a necessary part of being a fully alive, emotionally mature, psychologically healthy human being.[28]

Ker points out that Chesterton sees as highly significant the uniquely human (pace Martin) characteristic of laughter: it points beyond itself to the God in whose image Christianity claims human beings are made. Chesterton "knew there can be laughter/On the secret face of God."[29] Ker says, "A humourless Christianity was for Chesterton a defective Christianity. Because it was a 'universal' religion it was both a 'serious' religion but also because 'universal'…full of comic things.'"[30] Chesterton says that, "It is the test of a responsible religion…whether it can take examples from pots and pans and boots and butter-tubs…It is the test of a good religion whether you can joke about it."[31]

---

[24] See I. Ker, "Humour and Holiness in Chesterton," in *The Holiness of G. K. Chesterton*, ed. W. Oddie, 36-53. Some of the points I make here are based on these pages.

[25] *The Uses of Diversity: A Book of Essays*, 1.

[26] *Fancies Versus Fads*, 122.

[27] *The Everlasting Man*, 36.

[28] *Between Heaven and Mirth: why joy, humour and laughter are the heart of the spiritual life*. 57.

[29] "The Fish," in *The Wild Knight and Other Poems*, 24.

[30] I. Ker, "Humour and Holiness in Chesterton," 42.

[31] *Collected Works*, Vol. 27, 205-6. Martin, *op. cit.*, argues that humour, laughter and joy are at the heart of a healthy Christianity, and that their absence is the sign of a dysfunctional religion.

To Chesterton, humour is not the opposite of seriousness, but of solemnity. Funny is not the opposite of serious, but of not funny. If one cannot joke about sacred subjects, "one must not jest at all," as "there are no subjects that are not sacred subjects. Every instant of human life is awful…Life is too uniformly serious not to be joked about…You can be a great deal too solemn about Christianity to be a good Christian."[32] So to be serious about the gift of life is to be humorous, and a humourless Christianity was a Christianity that was too solemn about the great gift of the cosmos, and therefore a flawed Christianity. For Ker, Chesterton "really does believe that comic dialogue is a more powerful apologetic for the Catholic Church than any amount of more formal theological apologetics."[33] Although one need not be totally convinced that Ker is correct in identifying humour as the most important feature of Chesterton's notion of apologetics, it was certainly central to the Chestertonian vision and anything that can make God and the things of God seem more interesting, colorful, engaging and life-enhancing have to be given serious consideration by apologists. All too rarely do Christian apologists talk of a God who is the source of all humour, wit, creativity, life, color, energy and anything else that is good and life-giving. As we saw in Chapter III, for Chesterton all good things come from God, but rarely does a Christian apologetics conceptualize that in a way that is meaningful for contemporary culture. If we find traces of humor and comedy in the things of this world, how much more will we find them in the God who is the source of all that is good?

In Chesterton's opinion there is a vital connection between humor and its cognate, humility. Though Chesterton saw that

---

[32] *Lunacy and Letters*, ed. Dorothy Collins, 95-7.

[33] I. Ker, "Humour and Holiness in Chesterton," 44.

most of the Christian virtues were also pagan virtues, the one exception was humility. "Upon one point and one point only, was there really a moral revolution that broke the back of human history. And that was upon the point of Humility."[34] Whenever humility is seen not as virtue but as vice, joy is replaced by the pagan insistence upon self-assertion.[35] For Chesterton, "Joking is undignified; that is why it is good for one's soul"[36] and "No man has ever laughed at anything till he has laughed at himself."[37] Laughter "makes men forget themselves in the presence of something greater than themselves"[38] and is the "chief antidote to pride."[39] Without laughter there is no joy, "no strong sense of an unuttered joy" without "a hearty laugh."[40]

The themes of laughter ("mirth"), joy and sorrow, and their relative degrees of presence in Christianity and paganism, are discussed in the closing paragraphs of *Orthodoxy*. There Chesterton points out that so often "It is said that Paganism is a religion of joy and Christianity of sorrow; it would be just as easy to prove that Paganism is pure sorrow and Christianity pure joy. Such conflicts mean nothing and lead nowhere." This is because any human life will contain some mixture of the two, but "the only matter of interest is the manner in which the two things are balanced or divided." Christianity recognizes that the true state of human beings is one of joy, while grief or sorrow is transitory. The pagans of antiquity, whose

---

[34] *Collected Works* Vol. 5, 655.

[35] *The Defendant*, 57.

[36] *Alarms and Discursions*, 200.

[37] *Collected Works* Vol. 29, 546.

[38] *The Common Man*, 158.

[39] *The Spice of Life and Other Essays*, ed, D. Collins, 29.

[40] *Collected Works* Vol. 27, 151-2.

gods were despotic and fates deadly, were joyous about the small and trivial things in life and terrified about the big things (something which they hold in common with the exponents of an unbridled modernity, according to Chesterton). However,

> it is not native to man to be so. Man is more himself, man is more manlike, when joy is the fundamental thing in him, and grief the superficial. Melancholy should be an innocent interlude, a tender and fugitive frame of mind; praise should be the permanent pulsation of the soul. Pessimism is at best an emotional half-holiday; joy is the uproarious labour by which all things live.[41]

The Christian might know grief in life, but he knows that his life is gift from God, that he is in God's hand, and that God's plans for him are his eternal joy and well-being, when all manner of thing will be well. "Joy ought to be expansive; but for the agnostic it must be contracted, it must cling to one corner of the world. Grief ought to be a concentration; but for the agnostic its desolation is spread through an unthinkable eternity. This is what I call being born upside down." There is a world of difference between a philosophy of life that sees the world as significant, as pointing to the ultimate meaningfulness of reality, and a philosophy that sees everything as ultimately absurd. In the former, humility and humour ought to abound, while in the latter self-assertion and solemnity are more likely. Any attempt to muster up joy in a meaningless cosmos is precisely that—a human attempt to stave off the ultimate absurdity of it all by superficial attempts at diversion.

> Christianity satisfies suddenly and perfectly man's ancestral instinct for being the right way up; satisfies it supremely in this; that by its creed joy becomes something gigantic and sadness something special and small. The vault above us is not deaf because the universe is an idiot; the silence is not the heartless silence of an endless and aimless

---

[41] *Orthodoxy*, 364.

world. Rather the silence around us is a small and pitiful stillness like the prompt stillness in a sick-room. We are perhaps permitted tragedy as a sort of merciful comedy: because the frantic energy of divine things would knock us down like a drunken farce. We can take our own tears more lightly than we could take the tremendous levities of the angels. So we sit perhaps in a starry chamber of silence, while the laughter of the heavens is too loud for us to hear.[42]

Clearly Chesterton is not saying that suffering, tragedy, and sadness do not exist and are not keenly felt. He is not advocating an inhuman denial of the harsh realities of existence in this cosmos. Rather he is calling our attention to something deeper and more abiding. It is easy to be happy when the cosmos seems to be on our side; but joy is something deeper and more real than happiness. Joy is a virtue that is rooted in the knowledge that we and the whole cosmos are loved by God. This knowledge is a cause for rejoicing even when life is hard. Suffering brings unhappiness, and we are right to be sad about suffering; but suffering is not the last word. Chesterton is advocating a contemplative awareness of the deepest nature of the cosmos—that it is loving gift of the Creator. This prayerful noticing of the world makes it easier to perceive our blessings.

In one of the most famous paragraphs he ever wrote, Chesterton points out that the suspicion or instinct he had learned from the experience of life in this world—that joy is more fundamental to human beings than sadness—was something that finds its roots in the eternal joy that is to be found at the heart of the divinity.

Joy, which was the small publicity of the pagan, is the gigantic secret of the Christian…The tremendous figure which fills the Gospels towers in this respect, as in every other, above all the thinkers who ever thought themselves tall. His pathos was natural, almost casual.

---

[42] Ibid., 365.

The Stoics, ancient and modern, were proud of concealing their tears. He never concealed His tears; He showed them plainly on His open face at any daily sight, such as the far sight of His native city. Yet He concealed something...I say it with reverence; there was in that shattering personality a thread that must be called shyness. There was something that He hid from all men when He went up a mountain to pray...There was some one thing that was too great for God to show us when He walked upon our earth; and I have sometimes fancied that it was His mirth.[43]

For Chesterton mirth is at the heart of the divine life. The Chestertonian Heaven is not a joyless, heavy and grey affair, but joyful, light, fun and colorful. Humour and lightness of being are ordinary human glimpses of our eternal destiny for Chesterton. It is only a counterfeit Christianity that suggests otherwise. True religion, leading to sanity, receives the gift of life, is humble and grateful in the face of that gift, and laughs and rejoices in the gift.

It is absolutely useless and absurd to tell a man that he must not joke about sacred subjects...because there are no subjects that are not sacred subjects...in anything that does cover the whole of your life—in your philosophy and your religion—you must have mirth. If you do not have mirth you will certainly have madness.[44]

Here again then, as in Chapters II and III, we see Chesterton's insistence on the link between humour, humility, balanced sanity and joy. Modernity has many wonderful insights to offer to the world, but its excesses are in danger of leading us to the solemn and insane position of seeing ourselves as the center of the universe. When that happens human community is in danger because, as the myths of the pagan gods warn us, rival divinities, competing centers of the universe, do not tolerate

---

[43] Ibid., 365-6.

[44] *Lunacy and Letters*, 95.

each other too easily. They jostle for position, outmanoeuvre and even eliminate each other. As Chesterton was starting out in his career, Nietzsche was coming to the end of his life in an asylum, and his works were becoming ever more popular among the literati of London, such that H. G. Wells wrote of the "gall-stones of vicious, helpless and pauper masses," and the "swarms of black, and brown, and dirty-white, and yellow people, who do not come into the new needs of efficiency."[45] Throughout his career Chesterton responded to this solemn, joyless and ruthless shadow-side of modernity with a cry for humility and humor: virtues which help human beings to ap-preciate the drama of the ordinary, to perceive themselves as invited to take part in a cosmic romance that is a gift from a giver, and virtues which help them restore their "ancestral instinct for being the right way up."[46]

Of course, an aggressively predisposed atheist might proclaim the self-evident obviousness of the modern project and ridicule any suggestion that the world is anything more than what is pre-sented to the senses. However, there may be other unbelievers who display a greater willingness to admit that there might be more to reality than meets the eye and the senses, and who may therefore be open to the possibility of honest inquiry among the bits and pieces of human experience for traces of the transcen-dent. They might find in Chesterton a friend who encourages them to set out on the spiritual quests and adventures that are to be found everywhere in the romance of Elfland.

> Whatever it is that we are all looking for, I fancy that it is really quite close…Always the Kingdom of Heaven is "at hand"…So I for one

---

[45] *Anticipations of the Reaction of Mechanical and Scientific Progress upon Human Life and Thought*, 87, 342.

[46] *Orthodoxy*, 365.

should never be astonished if the next twist of a street led me to the heart of that maze in which all the mystics are lost.[47]

For Chesterton, people bump into God all the time in the guise of their ordinary experience, but they do not call him God. Chesterton encourages us to be open to the religious dimensions of our ordinary experience, and especially, as we shall see, to the divine presence in human beings who are the "million masks of God."[48] He draws our attention to our submerged and hidden spiritual depths and our potential greatness, and points out that to notice these will lead to joy. The Chestertonian counsel is not to try to make God present, but to make ourselves present to God by trying to be present to the richness with which our ordinary, everyday experience is laden. It is not that the spiritual, the religious and the mystical are not here; it is more the case that so often we are not here—not present to life and to others.

The Chestertonian ability to see God in the ordinary and the everyday finds parallels, as we have already seen, in the work of Karl Rahner. He too insists that the experience of God is not to be thought of merely in terms of rare experiences, but as grounded in the depths of the ordinary flow of living.

> Have we ever kept silent, despite the urge to defend ourselves, when we were being unfairly treated? Have we ever forgiven another even though we gained nothing by it and our forgiveness was accepted as quite natural? Have we ever made a sacrifice without receiving any thanks or acknowledgment, without even feeling any inward satisfaction? Have we ever decided to do a thing simply for the sake of conscience, knowing that we must bear sole responsibility for our decision without being able to explain it to anyone?...If we can find such experiences in our life, then we have had that very experience of the

---

47 "A Glimpse of My Country," *Tremendous Trifles*, 195.

48 "Gold Leaves," *The Wild Knight and Other Poems*, 25.

Spirit...the experience of the Eternal, the experience that the Spirit
is something more than and different from a part of this world..."[49]

In such ordinary moments Rahner insists that we experience
God, even if God remains unacknowledged in these encounters. In the depths of human existence we either welcome
truth and love, or we refuse them. If the general flow of the gift
of one's life is toward opening up in surrender to knowledge,
learning, truth, wisdom and especially to selfless love, then
this is an experience of God. For Rahner, though he never
for one moment denies the utter transcendence of God, our
life history is the history of our encounter with the Spirit of
God: the humdrum is the romance of our cooperation with
or rejection of the Spirit who was promised to us as another
advocate, as that Spirit of truth who would gently and gradually help us uncover the fullness of the meaning of the self-gift
of God in Christ.[50]

Like Chesterton, Rahner believed that the Kingdom of God
was at hand. We experience God in the contingency of the
cosmos and know that there is a deeper grounding to the reality
in which we find ourselves. Our everyday life is the theatre in
which the drama of a moment-by-moment choice is acted out.
It is a lifelong tussle in which we sometimes choose to fulfill all
God's hopes and desires for us, while at other times we refuse
to do this. We have seen that since God has loved us, we too
should love one another.[51] While believers know, however imperfectly, both loves, and struggle to find images, languages and
actions that can make these loves known in our world, unbelievers too can carry out the essential task of living the second

[49] "Can God be Experienced?," *Do You Believe in God?* tr. R. Strachan, 112-3.

[50] John 14:16, 26.

[51] 1 John 4:11

love, even if the surprise of the first love remains concealed from them for a variety of reasons. When an unbeliever loves, this is a grace-filled response to what Gerald O'Collins refers to as "the universal, dynamic presence of [the risen] Christ and his Holy Spirit. That presence touches everyone and all cultures and religions."[52] O'Collins points out that he dislikes the negative implication of labels such as "non-Christians" and "non-evangelized" and prefers instead to refer to non-Christian people, of other religions or none, as "God's other peoples."[53] Applying this terminology to Rahner's work, in exploring the presence of the Holy Spirit among God's other peoples (especially unbelievers), Rahner shows himself to be one of the great theologians of the immanence of God.

In the last chapter we noted Chesterton's discussion of some of the differences between Christianity and Buddhism, and the question of God's immanence was raised in the context of asking whether or not Chesterton gives sufficient emphasis to the role of the inner life of prayer, where the human heart meets God in rooted, regular contact. In *Orthodoxy* Chesterton wrote:

> By insisting on the immanence of God we get introspection, self-isolation, quietism, social indifference—Tibet. By insisting specially on the transcendence of God we get wonder, curiosity, moral and political adventure, righteous indignation—Christendom. Insisting that God is inside man, man is always inside himself. By insisting that God transcends man, man has transcended himself.[54]

Gabriel Daly sees this tendency in Chesterton to set transcendence and immanence in opposition to each other as a mistake, and one that is rooted in his forceful apologetic approach.

---

[52] *Rethinking Fundamental Theology*, 293.

[53] Ibid.

[54] *Orthodoxy*, 339-40.

The pity is that Chesterton should have thought it necessary to choose transcendence over immanence. Today most Christian apologists would argue for the necessity of maintaining the two in dialectical tension. It was, however, the "either-or" which gave Chesterton's writings their polemical force.[55]

It is true that Chesterton's way of writing and debating was often direct and provocative, confronting head-on the address-ees whose ideas had moved him to a response. In the above passage it is arguable that this forthrightness was because of the real dangers he perceived in excessive introspection, which he had known first-hand while at the Slade. This in turn made him very wary of anything that over-emphasized a turn to the subject, and we have noted more than once his suspicion of the Modernist theologians. However we recall from Chapter II the importance of the human subject for Chesterton. He believed that "faith in [one]self [is] the first condition of all faith. If a man does not enjoy himself whom he has seen, how shall he enjoy God whom he has not seen? To the great poet, as to the child, there is no hard-and-fast line drawn between the ego and the Cosmos."[56] Chesterton knew that the cosmos is not some object that stands "out there" unrelated to human beings: it is only to the receptive, perceiving, thinking, willing, choosing, loving human subject that the secrets of the cosmos and the Creator could be revealed.

This same interplay between the subjective and objective dimensions of Christianity is to be found in the writings of Hans Urs von Balthasar. Von Balthasar is often celebrated, quite rightly, as a great theologian of the "otherness" of Christ and of the unique nature of Christian revelation. He was keenly aware of the distinction between the objective otherness of God and

---

[55] "Apologists in the Modernist Period," *Chesterton and the Modernist Crisis*, ed. A. Nichols, 91.

[56] "Victor Hugo," *A Handful of Authors*, 41-2.

the world, between God's self-communication in revelation and the subjective explorations of the human mind that tries to make sense of that revelation. Balthasar could very easily be called upon to support various Chestertonian stances, such as his vision (seen in our last chapter) of the uniqueness of the Everlasting Man and the need to bow before the utterly transcendent other-ness of God:

> The quality of "being-in-itself" which belongs to the beautiful, the demand the beautiful makes to be allowed to be what it is, the demand, therefore, that we renounce our attempts to control and manipulate it, in order to be truly happy by enjoying it: all of this is, in the natural realm, the foundation and foreshadowing of what in the realm of revelation and grace will be the attitude of faith.[57]

There are clear echoes here of some of Chesterton's insights. When von Balthasar writes that we must "learn to see again, which is to say, to experience the total otherness of Christ as the outshining of God's sublimity and glory,"[58] we are not that far from Chesterton's way of seeing the Everlasting Man as the figure who is the key to history and to the gift of the cosmos. Chesterton's constant post-Slade refrain was that we need to get ourselves out of the way if we are to perceive the true beauty of the world and its Creator. Like Chesterton, Balthasar sensed that human fullness comes as gift from God in Christ, not from striving with all the intellectual might of modernity. For Balathasar, as for Chesterton, although human beings are *capax Dei*, they are filled to the point of overflowing by the fullness that is Jesus, who has ontological priority and in whom all creation holds together.[59] This is why Balthasar constantly

---

[57] *The Glory of the Lord*, I, 153.

[58] *Theo-Logic*, I, *The Truth of the World*, 20.

[59] See Colossians 1:15-19.

wishes to keep focusing our theological attention on the *concretissimus* that is Christ.[60]

However, as we have seen, it was only very gradually that Chesterton came to perceive Christ as this fullness of meaning and as the key to the cosmos. If Chesterton did not believe that the human subject is the measure of knowledge of the objective cosmos and if he held that the object must in some sense reveal itself in order to be known, nevertheless he also knew that the object still needs a subject in order to perceive its unfolding. So too with von Balthasar. Just as the child only comes to know himself in the smile of his mother, so:

> a revelocentric approach is not a merely "from above" approach. Just because Jesus Christ is the measure of our knowledge of God, does not mean that Christ himself does not appropriate humanity's search for God. Again, it is on account of, and not in spite of, his Christocentrism and revelocentrism that Balthasar will insist upon defending the proper autonomy and integrity of humanity's natural search for God.[61]

There are other strands, then, of Balthasar's thought, which do not always receive as much attention as his Christocentric emphases. One such thread is that he also sees faith as something fleshed out in the drama of everyday living. If we see our encounter with Christ merely as a meeting with beauty (the theological aesthetics for which Balthasar is possibly most famous), this might leave us thinking that faith is a cozy, almost New Age-like thing: something that exists merely to make us feel good about ourselves and our life in the world. In the Theo-Drama, however, Balthasar is at pains to state that Christian faith is not just about the contemplation of God's glory and beauty as revealed in Christ: it is also a call to discipleship of

---

[60] *Explorations in Theology*, Vol. I, *The Word Made Flesh*, 162.

[61] R. Howsare, *Balthasar: A Guide for the Perplexed*, 66.

the Lord whose glory is revealed as the Crucified One. Faith is a slow, daily and lifelong erosion of selfishness as we are called to conform our freedom and our choices to the way of love that is revealed in the Crucified God. We have to appropriate God's self-revelation in Christ at the heart of our everyday human experience, and "no one is enraptured without returning, from this encounter, with a personal mission".[62]

The appropriation of the divine self-revelation in daily living is a reminder also of one of the central insights of Bernard Lonergan. The Canadian Jesuit maintains that conversion is central to Christian faith and religious experience. Lonergan, himself a huge admirer of Chesterton as we saw in Chapter III, offers a list of precepts which help fulfill the "demands of the human spirit" and which in some ways mirror Chesterton's own spiritual and intellectual journey. Lonergan says that we have to "be attentive, be intelligent, be reasonable, be responsible, be in love".[63] In Lonergan's vision human beings flourish (or wither) by: attending (or not attending) to the full range of their experience; by seeking (or fleeing) insights that integrate that experience; by arriving at truth (or falsehood) about reality; by living out commitments based on that truth (or falsehood); and then, through doing all of this, one finally arrives (or does not arrive) at the "complete self-transcendence" of a "deep-set joy" through being in love with God. Chesterton's radically joyful new way of seeing the cosmos after his long intellectual and spiritual journey, as expressed in *Orthodoxy* and in the Autobiography, is what Lonergan means when he says that the convert apprehends differently because he has become different.[64]

---

[62] *Theo-Drama*, II, 31.

[63] *Method in Theology*, 268.

[64] B. J. F. Lonergan, "Theology in Its New Context," *A Second Collection*, 66.

For Lonergan theology has entered a new stage in its history and, instead of being a deductive science resting solely on truths taken from scripture and ecclesial documents, it is now largely an empirical discipline, using data from the subject who reflects on religious experience and on the process which he is undergoing and which we call conversion: "As conversion is basic to Christian living, so an objectification of conversion provides theology with its foundations."[65] This final, contemplative stage, however, is something reached only through the daily struggle for authenticity. As Avery Dulles points out in an article which links fundamental theology with conversion, "conversion is a continuous process demanded at every stage of the Christian life, and…fundamental theology is therefore of existential import to all believers."[66] Because of Dulles' reminder[67] that no Christian ever totally and securely possesses the faith, it is vital to hold together the dual insights of von Balthasar: faith is both a gift to behold and a challenge to be lived.

Chesterton also manages to keep in tension this connection between theology and morality. "Only where death and eternity are intensely present can human beings feel their fellowship. Once the divine darkness against which we stand is really dismissed from the mind…the differences between human beings become overpoweringly plain."[68] Only a common divine origin guarantees fraternity between fellow creatures. Remove God and there is no longer anything to bind human beings together:

---

[65] *Method in Theology*, 130.

[66] "Fundamental Theology and the Dynamics of Conversion," *The Thomist*, April 1981, 177.

[67] Ibid.

[68] *The Victorian Age in Literature*, 30.

[A good social order cannot be achieved by] a mere improvement in social machinery…I think it happens only when there is a strong sense of duty and dignity implanted in people, not by any government or even any school, but by something which they recognize as making a secret call upon a solitary soul.[69]

Human community will only ever be achieved, for Chesterton, when human beings realize that the voice of conscience is a summons to recognize their divine origins and to treat their fellow human beings accordingly. "Charity, as applied to humanity, means a more or less mystical realization of the value and even the virtue of humanity; even if it be hidden virtue… The Christian has to use his brain to see the hidden good of humanity…To see good is to see God."[70] To live a life of Christian faith is slowly to become conformed to the essential content of the self-revelation of God, which is a life that is given to and lived for the other in self-sacrificial love. Only by being converted and willing to pay the price of love will community be constructed. Chesterton wrote in one of his poems, "God! shall we ever honour what we are…?"[71] We have seen that Chesterton repeatedly pointed out the human tendency to forget our origins, and so it follows that human beings regularly forget to treat one another in a humane fashion. The process of conversion is costly and painfully slow.

---

[69] "On the Next Hundred Years," *Avowals and Denials*, cited in *TTFT*, 148.

[70] "Reflections on Charity," *The Listener*, 4th January 1933, unpublished collection of Dale Ahlquist, President of The American Chesterton Society.

[71] "King's Cross Station," *The Wild Knight and Other Poems*, 39.

3. JUSTICE AND SERVICE OF THE OTHER: *The Costly Decision to Love and Build Community*

At the beginning of Chapter IV we learned that Chesterton believed that the Scriptures command us to love our neighbors and to love our enemies probably because they are usually the same people! We also saw in the same chapter that he knew from his own experience that a good and happy marriage is not the same thing as a panacea for all of life's problems or an insurance policy against the troubles, problems, disagreements and arguments that are marks of any human relationship. Chesterton knew that because we have little choice about the people we have to deal with on a daily basis, and because even in the friendships and relationships we choose for ourselves there exist the complications that arise because of free will and human imperfections (including our own), so building and remaining in community is no easy task.

Freda Spencer worked for a while as a secretary to Chesterton and pointed out that Chesterton had the same mixture of weaknesses and strengths as any human being. While he displayed "a curious, unusual kind of self-indulgent selfishness that went back to his childhood and the permissive parents who had spoiled him and his brother," he was also filled with enormous generosity and selflessness. Spencer "marvelled at the amount of time and effort he could expend on 'giving pleasure and amusement to entirely unimportant people', endowing 'the trivialities of life' with 'a richness and importance which was essentially Christian' and enlivening the daily routine with so much 'fun and laughter'. On the other side of Chesterton's weakness then, there was "the immense good nature, the humility, the humour."[72]

---

[72] Ker, *GKC*, 363.

In the drama of the ordinary and the everyday Chesterton had to be molded by the Spirit into a man who gave himself for others. The daily breaking and shaping of the individual—out of egocentric isolation, pride, self-preoccupation and self-sufficiency, into a person constituted by relationship, and the community that arises through the unity of difference that comes from transparent selfless loving—is a laborious process.

Chesterton could be both magnanimous (especially toward those of lower social status or intelligence) and pusillanimous. He had weaknesses, but he was aware that Christian faith invited him to reclaim his true greatness, to recognize what was best and most honourable inside him, and to share it with others in relationship. The only way to become fully human is to be immersed in the daily give and take of life in community, and especially to give of oneself for those deemed insignificant or expendable by a culture.

3.1 The Family and Advocacy
of the Marginalized

In *Heretics*, in a chapter entitled "On Certain Modern Writers and the Institution of the Family," Chesterton defends the importance of the community of the family as the ultimate human institution and the basic unit of all institutions and society:

> It is a good thing for a man to live in a family for the same reason that it is a good thing for a man to be besieged in a city. It is a good thing for a man to live in a family in the same sense that it is a beautiful and delightful thing for a man to be snowed up in a street. They all force him to realise that life is not a thing from outside, but a thing from inside.[73]

---

[73] *Heretics*, 141.

The truly human life does not depend on outer circumstances but on the inner resources which shape one's responses in all situations. Whether one lives in a family, a religious community or a marriage, the same rhythms of human community (which make life "a thing from inside") will be found. "Aunt Elizabeth is unreasonable, like mankind. Papa is excitable, like mankind. Our youngest brother is mischievous, like mankind. Grandpa is stupid, like the world." The world is simply a community which, though numerically containing more members, nevertheless is no more dramatic than the community into which we were born biologically:

> Those who wish, rightly or wrongly, to step out of all this [the family], do definitely wish to step out into a narrower world. They are dismayed and terrified by the largeness of the family...I do not say, for a moment, that the flight to this narrower life may not be the right thing for the individual, any more than I say the thing about flight into a monastery. But I do say that anything is bad and artificial which tends to make these people succumb to the strange delusion that they are stepping into a world which is actually larger and more varied than their own. The best way that a man could test his readiness to encounter the common variety of mankind would be to climb down a chimney into any house at random, and get on as well as possible with the people inside. And that is essentially what each one of us did on the day that he was born.[74]

Chesterton views the ability to live in the ordinary, humdrum reality of a family as ideal preparation for living in any other institution. The rhythms of life in the family—with its give and take, pluses and minuses, virtues and vices, joys and sorrows—are ideal training for living in any group of human beings.

Living in community teaches us that the choice is between committing oneself to life with others amidst imperfection, sin, compromise, and selfishness, or not committing oneself at all.

---

[74] Ibid., 142.

There is no such thing as the ideal community. Wherever one lives, one will discover that to live out one's nature as a person made in the image of God, to commit oneself to live in relationship with others and build up community, is a costly commitment. Though the price is high, it has to be paid if human beings are to find joy. To pledge oneself to live for others in relationship in the family is the supreme adventure of being born, as "we step into a world which is incalculable, into a world which has its own strange laws, into a world which could do without us, into a world that we have not made. In other words, when we step into the family we step into a fairy-tale." Life in community is a daily romance, a repeated story, and "In the fiery alphabet of every sunset is written, 'to be continued in our next.'"[75]

The sense of our mutual connectedness was vital to Chesterton's vision, and the daily attempt to build community lay at the heart of his work. For Chesterton the basic unit of society was the family, and it was his desire to help others share his vision of community and the fraternity that exists between all people that caused him to remain a journalist all his life. Throughout his life Frances, Shaw, and many other friends and supporters pleaded with Chesterton to leave behind the world of journalism in order to take up the culturally more respectable career of the novelist and playwright. However, the man who wrote literally hundreds of thousands of words on criticism, poetry, philosophy, theology, fiction, history, politics and other topics, said that, "among many more abject reasons for not being able to be a novelist, is the fact that I have always been and presumably always shall be a journalist."[76]

---

[75] Ibid., 143.

[76] *Autobiography*, 298.

As we saw in Chapter I, Aidan Mackey believed that to ask Chesterton to be otherwise, to be a mere literary star, would be to ask him not to be G. K. Chesterton. He thought of himself as a man of the newspapers, primarily because it was his best way of making a daily contribution to the common good of the human family. He concerned himself with the ideas and events of the day in which he was writing, aware that ideas were important, since the various ways in which the world imagines or understands itself have practical consequences for that world: it is not long before the way in which human beings perceive themselves and their place in the cosmos becomes reflected in the way in which they act in the world.

Chesterton believed that human institutions, great and small, ultimately live or die, and human lives are ultimately happy or unhappy, because of the degree of truth and falsehood to be found in the ideas and images that underpin them. Chesterton thought of his career as a vocation, since he thought that the classical missionary has the right idea:

> [The missionary] is the last representative left of the idea of changing a community from the inside: of changing it by changing the minds of its citizens. Or, rather (to preserve free will, the only basis of political freedom), to get the citizens themselves to change their minds… Missionaries do try to alter society from the inside; while all statesmen and sociologists, reactionary and revolutionary, old-fashioned and new-fashioned, try to change it from the outside.[77]

He believed that ideas and images had to be engaged with in their own arena and, at the beginning of the twentieth century, with the relatively recent phenomenon of mass literacy, this arena was Fleet Street. For Chesterton, the medium of the newspapers had much to contribute to human happiness or unhappiness, and it was through journalism that he sought to

---

[77]The *Illustrated London News* 30th March 1912, *Collected Works* Vol. 29, 265-6.

express the gratitude and joy that had been his since the Slade period. Journalism was his vocation, allowing him to make a gift to the world of his grateful vision of the cosmos. In this sense, then, journalism was quite literally a medium through which Chesterton tried to serve the world in love. It was his contribution to sustaining the joyful living of the wider human community.

Chesterton had a special regard and love for the poor, and his journalism was marked by a special desire to serve the cause of the marginalized. His writing is shot through with his attempt to fight against systemic injustice and to promote the cause of true equality. Chesterton wrote of Aquinas that he "had from the first that full and final test of a truly orthodox Catholicity: the impetuous, impatient, intolerant passion for the poor; and even that readiness to be rather a nuisance to the rich, out of a hunger to feed the hungry."[78] Chesterton could just as easily have been saying that of himself. He wrote that "If the Church exists ten million years hence, amid alien costumes and incredible architecture, I know that it will still put the oppression of the poor among the five sins, crying aloud for vengeance."[79] He thought of the poor as "jewels of God,"[80] and Ker notes that Chesterton was incapable of refusing beggars.[81]

The Chestertonian corpus abounds with examples of his defense of those whom modernity deemed to be unimportant non-persons on the margins of society. We have given hints of this position in his debate with Blatchford. Among the many

---

[78] *Saint Thomas Aquinas: The Dumb Ox*, 130.

[79] *The Church Socialist Quarterly*, cited in *TTFT*, 217.

[80] "The Giant," *Tremendous Trifles*, 59.

[81] I. Ker, *GKC*, 262.

reasons he offers for his love of Dickens, he lists the fact that Dickens despised the patronizing attitude of the powerful toward the poor:

> It was a vague and vulgar Benthamism with a rollicking Tory touch in it. It explained to the poor their duties with a cold and coarse philanthropy unendurable by any free man. It also had at its command a kind of brutal banter, a loud good-humour…[Dickens] fell furiously on all their ideas: the cheap advice to live cheaply, the base advice to live basely, above all, the preposterous primary assumption that the rich are to advise the poor and not the poor the rich.[82]

The subtle, or at time not so subtle, superiority complex displayed by the rich toward the poor is almost the total antithesis of the attitude of the saint. "The one thing which separates a saint from ordinary men is his readiness to be one with ordinary men…a saint is long past any desire for distinction; he is the only sort of superior man who has never been a superior person."[83]

Though he was at one time a member of the Liberal Party and campaigned on their behalf, what he witnessed of the party when it was in power caused him to leave it. Politically Chesterton is not easily labeled as he criticizes all politics that undermine the dignity of human beings, especially the marginalized. Both the eager, energetic progressive, whom he calls Hudge, and the resistant conservative, whom he calls Gudge, are his targets. Both of them have the wrong conception of the poor: "[A]ll evil began with some attempt at superiority; some moment when…the very skies were cracked across like a mirror, because there was a sneer in Heaven."[84]

Both the progressive and the conservative sneer in very subtle ways at poor people, and refuse to grant them the full

---

[82] *Chesterton on Dickens, Collected Works* Vol. 15, 137-9.

[83] *Saint Thomas Aquinas: The Dumb Ox*, 120.

[84] "If I Only Had One Sermon to Preach," *On Lying in Bed and Other Essays*, 507.

dignity of personhood. Hudge wants to get the poor out of the slums and put them in tenement flats, while Gudge wants to convince the poor that the slums and their foul conditions are not really too bad at the end of the day. Chesterton believes that in actual fact Hudge and Gudge have a secret agreement with one another. Gudge wants cheap labor from an abundance of workers who simply do what they are told. Hudge advocates docility, pacifism, teetotalism, and the liberation of women from the repressive constraints of the family so that they can then take up their place in the factory. Chesterton's concern was not to advance a political agenda, but to promote the dignity and worth of "the mass of the common people." Of these people he says:

> Caught in the trap of a terrible industrial machinery, harried by a shameful economic cruelty, surrounded with an ugliness and desolation never endured before among men, stunted by a stupid and provincial religion, or by a more stupid and more provincial irreligion, the poor are still by far the sanest, jolliest, and most reliable part of the community.[85]

It was because of his love for the marginalized that Chesterton trained his journalistic guns on both socialism and capitalism: big government and big business. The exponents of socialism saw it as their task to improve the lot of the poor. However, despite their "common ground of anti-selfish collectivism," Chesterton did not "agree with those who hold that modern socialism is an exact counterpart or fulfillment of the socialism of Christianity:"

> The modern socialist regards Communism as a distant panacea for society, the Christian regarded it as an immediate and difficult regeneration of himself; the modern socialist reviles…society for not

---

[85] "Why I Am Not a Socialist," *The New Age*, 4th January 1908, 190, http://dl.lib.brown.edu/pdfs/1140813731375533.pdf. [last accessed 9th March 2012].

adopting it, the early Christian concentrated his thoughts on the problem of his own fitness and unfitness to adopt it; to the modern socialist it is a theory, to the early Christian it was a call; modern socialism says, "Elaborate a broad, noble and workable system and submit it to the progressive intellect of society." Early Christianity said, "Sell all thou hast and give to the poor."…For three characteristics at least the Galilean programme makes more provision: humility, activity, cheerfulness, the real triad of Christian virtues.[86]

He believed that the poor despised socialism because it set itself against what the poor loved most: "the privacy of homes, the control of one's own children, the minding of one's business." Chesterton had little time for either socialism or capitalism because he believed passionately in democracy and the right of every human being to do certain things for himself, without the interference of others, which is the meaning of one of his most quoted lines: "if a thing is worth doing, it is worth doing badly."[87] There is an abundance of example to choose from: choosing a career or vocation, choosing a spouse, blowing one's nose, taking a shower and raising one's children.

Whereas Chesterton saw socialism as something that a few rich, powerful intellectuals wanted to impose on the poor, thereby meddling with democratic rights and the welfare of the family, he also viewed capitalism's desire to grasp more and more property and capital for a few powerful individuals or groups as working against the common good and the family. "It is the negation of property that the Duke of Westminster should own whole streets and squares of London; just as it would be the negation of marriage if he had all living women in one great harem."[88] Capitalism was:

[86] M. Ward, GKC, 58-9.

[87] What's Wrong with the World? 175.

[88] "Why I Am Not a Socialist," The New Age, 4th January 1908, 190, http://dl.lib.brown.edu/

at war with the family, for the same reason which has led to its being at war with the Trade Union…Capitalism believes in collectivism for itself and individualism for its enemies. It desires its victims to be individuals, or…atoms…If there be any bond,…if there be any class loyalty or domestic discipline, by which the poor can help the poor, these emancipators will certainly strive to loosen that bond or lift that discipline in the most liberal fashion. The masters of modern plutocracy know what they are about…A very profound and precise instinct has led them to single out the human household as the chief obstacle to their inhuman progress. Without the family, we are helpless before the state.[89]

Catholic social teaching has long since proclaimed the family as the basic unit of society, and Chesterton knew that both capitalists and socialists alike wanted to break up this fundamental unit in order to yield weaker, cheaper, and more docile fodder for the workplace and other modern schemes.

We see here how Chesterton believed that criticism of the reigning systems and ideologies is a necessary part of the Christian agenda. Chesterton, who was a man who insisted on the need for doctrine, personal piety, and Church membership, was not content to preach half a Gospel. He also insisted on the need to engage with justice issues and to point out where the poor and the marginalized were helpless pawns in modernity's relentless search for greater wealth and efficiency. He criticized both left and right in their undermining of the rights and welfare of the poor. Only by caring for the marginalized will the true health of a culture ever be safeguarded. The way a culture treats its weakest members is an index of the health or otherwise of that culture.

Chesterton's writings remind us that the Christian apologist always has to be ready to proclaim this and to confront injustice,

---

pdfs/1140813731375533.pdf. [last accessed 9th March 2012].

[89] *The Superstition of Divorce*, cited in Morris, TTFR, 215-6.

marginalization, and the manipulation of human beings for economic or other ends. Part of any apologetics in any age has to be the reminder that the Kingdom of God is a new reality and the Church therefore has to be an alternative community that, when necessary, is unafraid to criticize the systems and worldviews that reign in the world.

The industrially induced poverty loathed by his hero Dickens was no less despised by Chesterton himself. The nineteenth-century free-market economists of the Manchester School, personified by Dickens as Mr. Gradgrind, regarded the hunger and misery of the poor as necessary evils if the rich were to maintain their affluence. Russell Sparkes notes that:

> Although Chesterton knew little economics [although he did gain some knowledge from Belloc], insight told him that the world had shifted from the political economy of Adam Smith, based on morality and the sense of a small community where the butcher and the baker had to face their customers anew each day. In theory it had been replaced by the idea of the iron laws of economics, essentially the mathematical calculus applying the utilitarian philosophy of Jeremy Bentham, by such as J. S. Mill and David Ricardo. In practice this meant that Big Business was given a free rein, so that the isolated individual was left facing huge industrial combines. GKC wanted to get back to the moral economics of Adam Smith, and the way to do this was to distribute as much property as possible to as many people as possible. From the mid-1920s GK's Weekly became a manifesto for this Distributist philosophy...[which was] an attempt to put catholic social teaching into practical effect, and many of its ideas reappeared in the 1970s when Fritz Schumacher rediscovered that Small is Beautiful.[90]

It would take us beyond both the scope of this book and the capabilities of its author to explore more fully the merits and

---

[90] *Prophet of Orthodoxy: The Wisdom of G. K. Chesterton*, 69-70.

demerits of Chesterton's distributist economic theory.[91] My main intention here is to concur with Sparkes that its roots are to be found in Catholic social teaching, which Chesterton's love for the poor and desire to alleviate the misery of their condition caused him to embrace enthusiastically. Chesterton writes:

> Most of us [distributists] began to realise that socialism was not inevitable; that it was not really popular; that it was not the only way, or even the right way, of restoring the rights of the poor. We have come to the conclusion that the obvious cure for private property being given to the few is to see that it is given to the many; not to see that it is taken away from everybody or given in trust to the dear good politicians. Then, having discovered that fact as a fact, we look back at Leo XIII and discover in his old and dated document, of which we took no notice at the time, that he was saying then exactly what we are saying now.[92]

Chesterton, then, is again demonstrating that an essential part of the Christian agenda, as emphasized by the Pope, is to address the specifics of injustice.

Chesterton's word *distributism* comes from the Leonine phrase "distributive justice." "Among the many and grave duties of rulers who would do their best for the people, the first and chief is to act with strict justice—with that justice which is called distributive—toward each and every class alike."[93] Leo says that "since the end of society is to make men better, the chief good that society can possess is virtue." However, political

---

[91] He discusses his ideas in books such as *What's Wrong With the World* and *The Outline of Sanity*. For a good and succinct summary of some of its key ideas, see Ker, *GKC*, 553-561 and Ahlquist, *G. K. Chesterton: The Apostle of Common Sense*, 44-54, 126-138. The ideas of both of these authors inform my work here.

[92] *The Catholic Church and Conversion, Collected Works*, Vol. 3, 114. Chesterton refers to Leo XIII's encyclical *Rerum novarum* of 1891, which described the plight of workers as similar to that of slaves and proposed that property be more equitably shared among them.

[93] *Rerum novarum* 33, Encyclical Letter on Capital and Labour, http://www.vatican.va/holy_father/leo_xiii/encyclicals/documents/hf_l-xiii_enc_15051891_rerum-novarum_en.html [last accessed 16th august 2011].

rulers have a duty to ensure a well-constituted body politic that can "see to the provision of those material and external helps 'the use of which is necessary to virtuous action.'"[94]

Because the wealth of the state comes from the sweat of the brow of its workers, the interests of the poorer classes have to be safeguarded out of justice, "so that they who contribute so largely to the advantage of the community may themselves share in the benefits which they create."[95] For the Pope, the "great labour question cannot be solved save by assuming as a principle that private ownership must be held sacred and inviolable. The law, therefore, should favor ownership, and its policy should be to induce as many as possible of the people to become owners." This will produce three main benefits in Leo's view: firstly, "property will certainly become more equitably divided;" secondly, there will be a:

> ...great abundance of the fruits of the earth. Men always work harder and more readily when they work on that which belongs to them; nay, they learn to love the very soil that yields in response to the labour of their hands, not only food to eat, but an abundance of good things for themselves and those that are dear to them.

Thirdly, "men would cling to the country in which they were born, for no one would exchange his country for a foreign land if his own afforded him the means of living a decent and happy life."[96]

Leo XIII saw the intimate links that exist between property and justice, and between the well-being of the poorer classes and the moral well-being of the state. In a very real

---

[94] *Rerum novarum* 34 [Pope Leo is citing Aquinas, *On the Governance of Rulers*, 1, 15 (*Opera omnia*, ed. *Vives*, Vol. 27, p. 356)].

[95] Ibid.

[96] *Rerum novarum*, 47.

and concrete sense, the health of the state and the individual person is displayed by the way in which these treat the weakest people in their midst. We noted above that it was his love for democracy and the rights of the ordinary person that caused Chesterton's distrust of both capitalism and socialism. We can add here another reason why he did not trust either economic system:

> A pickpocket is obviously a champion of private enterprise. But it would perhaps be an exaggeration to say that a pickpocket is a champion of private property. The point about Capitalism and Commercialism, as conducted of late, is that they have really preached the extension of business rather than the preservation of belongings; and at best have tried to disguise the pickpocket with some of the virtues of the pirate. The point about Communism is that it only reforms the pickpocket by forbidding pockets…The capitalist system, good or bad, right or wrong, rests upon two ideas: that the rich will always be rich enough to hire the poor; and the poor will always be poor enough to want to be hired.[97]

Neither economic system encouraged small-scale property, the lack of which, in Chesterton's mind, undermined the dignity and freedom of people, especially the poor.

We see further confirmation here of the Chestertonian emphasis in *Orthodoxy* on the need for proper balance or proportion in order to permit human flourishing. He is not denying that producing and consuming are important, but he is denying that mere exchange, as witnessed for example when a capitalist society puts undue emphasis on trade for trade's sake, leads to imbalance and human misery.

Society becomes fragmented, and people have no sense of contentment in what they are living for. Proper balance is needed. "The aim of human polity is human happiness…There is

---

[97] *The Outline of Sanity, Collected Works* Vol. 5, 41; 57-8.

no obligation on us to be richer, or busier, or more efficient, or more productive, or more progressive, or in any way worldlier or wealthier, if it does not make us happier."[98] Or, in the words of Jesus, what does it profit a man to win the whole world and lose his very soul? What can be offered in exchange for one's self?[99]

Pope Leo XIII and Chesterton join that long line of prophetic figures in the Judeo-Christian tradition who measure the quality of a person's or nation's faith by the quality of mercy and justice they bring into the world. Chesterton sees an intimate link between the way the marginalized non-persons of a culture—the widows, strangers, and orphans,[100] the hungry, the thirsty, the naked, the sick, the lonely, the imprisoned,[101] the poor, the people living in slums, the unborn, the disabled, the unattractive, the unintelligent—are treated and a way that is pleasing to God.

We saw in our third chapter that Chesterton saw this world as sheer gratuitous gift of God, and that human beings show their gratitude for the gift by enjoying it through obedience to its laws, as set by God. Basic to these laws of the lawgiver is to recognize the other, one's fellow creature, as an equal heir to the gift of creation, as a child of the same God, as one's brother or sister:

> When we say that all pennies are equal, we do not mean that they all look exactly the same. We mean that they are absolutely equal in their one absolute character...They are coins of a certain value...It may be put symbolically, and even mystically, by saying that they all bear

---

[98] Ibid., 145.

[99] Matthew 16:26

[100] Among several other verses of Scripture, see Exodus 22:21-24; Deuteronomy 10:18; 24:17-18; Psalm 10:1; Isaiah 58:1-10.

[101] Matthew 25: 31-46.

the image of the King. And...it is also the most practical summary of equality that all men bear the image of the King of Kings.

Since all are equal in dignity, all have both the same rights as well as duties:

> This idea had long underlain Christianity...a dogma of equal duties implies that of equal rights. I know of no Christian authority that would not admit that it is as wicked to murder a poor man as a rich man...The idea of the equality of men is in substance simply the idea of the importance of man.[102]

Here we have another example of Chesterton's insistence that the Church's theological rigor is on the side of human flourishing. "If we wish to protect the poor we shall be in favour of fixed rules and clear dogmas. The rules of a club are occasionally in favour of the poor member. The drift of a club is always in favour of the rich one."[103] All systems, the Church included, need prophetic reminders of their duty to the marginalized.

Although the media and culture at large today are often hostile toward religion in general and Catholic Christianity in particular, it is important to remember that, from the pharisaic features and legalistic structures of the Temple religion of Jesus' day, to the peddling of the Gospel on television or the manipulation of religion for political ends today, Mammon has always been able to enlist religious people in his service. In Chapter II we talked of the effects of the surrounding culture on our capacities for faith; we need to have a few healthy suspicions (without lapsing into an aggressive and ultimately destructive cynicism) of the systems that are enthroned in society. Christianity can never be just one more consumer choice on the shopping list of human needs. At times it has to be strongly countercultural

---

[102] *A Short History of England*, 147-8.

[103] *Orthodoxy*, 346.

because, as we shall now see, it entails a close discipleship of Christ that is not merely about subscribing to truth, but is also the incarnation of a life of concrete love.

The Church's teachings call us to uphold justice for all and to promote the dignity of all members of society, even those despised by a culture, since all people are heirs to the Kingdom and God's promises. The Kingdom of God, an alternative vision of community, is built up by confronting the particular and concrete instances of injustice in the world.

Every human being, then, is called to move beyond her own private needs and agenda into the world of others, in order to help heal the wounds that are formed when individuals and whole categories of people are relegated to the status of non-persons. To make this move is to grow up. We shall now see that, according to Chesterton, Francis of Assisi had grasped that the secret of life, the secret of human maturity, was to give oneself over in service of others. Francis was willing to pay the price of human maturity in a way that Peter Pan, the boy who never grew up, was not.

3.2 FRANCIS OF ASSISI AND PETER PAN:
Loving Service as the Secret of Life

Chesterton writes, "[L]ong ago in those days of boyhood my fancy first caught fire with the glory of Francis of Assisi."[104] Francis had always been a vital part of the formation of the Chestertonian imagination. Indeed Chesterton believed that "St. Francis…had that liberating and humanising effect upon religion; though perhaps rather on the imagination than the intellect."[105] If in physical appearance the abstemious, peniten-

---

[104] *Saint Francis of Assisi*, 8.

[105] *Saint Thomas Aquinas: The Dumb Ox*, 34.

tial, and emaciated Francis probably had more in common with Shaw than with the overweight bon viveur that was Chesterton, the equally exuberant nature of Francis, as expressed in his Canticle of the Sun, is not in essence that different from that of the man who wrote that "the object of the artistic and spiritual life was to dig for this submerged sunrise of wonder; so that a man sitting in a chair might suddenly understand that he was alive and actually be happy."[106]

Chesterton always felt that knowing something of the Franciscan spirit—allowing Francis to capture one's imagination and to shape the way one perceived one's life and the purpose of religion—might help a person to travel along the same road on which Chesterton himself had journeyed. That was a path out of the despair induced by the excesses of a lopsided and proud modernity, and into the joy, laughter, romance, and generosity of a Christian orthodoxy properly understood.

In the context of a discussion about why Francis referred to his companions as jongleurs, or minstrels, Chesterton praised Francis for seeing the connections among service, freedom, and joy:

> Of the two minstrels or entertainers, the jester was presumably the servant or at least the secondary figure. St. Francis really meant what he said when he said he had found the secret of life in being the servant and the secondary figure. There was to be found ultimately in such service a freedom almost amounting to frivolity. It was comparable to the condition of the jongleur because it almost amounted to frivolity. The jester could be free when the knight was rigid; and it was possible to be a jester in the service which is perfect freedom.[107]

Central to any discovery of human maturity and joy is the willingness to make of one's life an act of service to the other,

---

[106] *Autobiography*, 92.

[107] *Saint Francis of Assisi*, 62.

because this connects with the ultimate meaning or purpose of life as imagined by the Giver of life. C. S. Lewis wrote that "The hardness of God is kinder than the softness of men and His compulsion is our liberation."[108]

When we looked at the doctrine of conditional joy in Chapter III, we saw that the moral rules of Elfland are not put there in some arbitrary way by God as the condition to be met before God reluctantly and begrudgingly permits human beings to have a good time. God does not meanly demand that we go to bed early if we are to enjoy ourselves in the morning. Rather, going to bed early and getting a good night's sleep constitute the very ontological conditions necessary to the experience of running around joyfully in the park at ten o'clock tomorrow.

A disordered will cannot by the very nature of things enjoy itself, and if a person's will does not seek to live life as poured out for the other, then it cannot reflect the Trinitarian God in whose image that person is made, and that person cannot be who he is and cannot find joy. "Keeping to one woman is a small price for so much as seeing one woman."[109] There is a price to be paid for anything precious, but this price is not some random, capricious prerequisite, but part of the very constitution of reality and the only way to enjoy reality.

We noted in the last chapter that Rahner says that there is no finished symphony in this world, and that all experiences of joy, meaning, and fulfillment are partial. It is not surprising, therefore, that it is not always easy to find happiness this side of the grave. Human beings often misunderstand the nature of true happiness and look for it in the wrong places. A superficial understanding of happiness might lead us to think that

---

[108] *Surprised by Joy*, 183.

[109] *Orthodoxy*, 261.

wealth, pleasure, and the absence of difficulties and tensions constitute a happy life.

We saw in his analysis of capitalism that Chesterton denies that there is any necessary relationship between wealth and happiness. It might equally be said that there is no necessary connection between difficulties and unhappiness. The real question we should be asking ourselves is whether we are connecting our life to its ultimate purpose. Francis knew that he and all human beings were caught up in a story, a drama, or a romance that had been unfolding since the world began. That story had an author who "illustrates and illuminates all things."[110] Since this was so, "all these things that God had given [were] something…precious and unique."[111]

Chesterton contends that when we discover with Francis that we are part of a cosmic romance, we must seek out the will or intentions of the author in our regard; we will then discover with Francis that the secret of life is to seek to make of one's life a gift of self for others, who have also been willed into existence by the same God: we are to be the servant of others, the secondary figure, the one who centers one's life on others, rather than the one on whom life has to center. To find that we are creatures of a Creator is:

> …the discovery of an infinite debt. It may seem a paradox to say that a man may be transported with joy to discover that he is in debt. But this is only because in commercial cases the creditor does not generally share the transports of joy; especially when the debt is by hypothesis infinite and therefore unrecoverable. But here…the parallel of a natural love-story of the nobler sort disposes of the difficulty in a flash. There the infinite creditor does share the joy of the infinite debtor; for indeed they are both debtors and creditors.

---

[110] *Saint Francis of Assisi*, 68.

[111] Ibid., 81.

THE SCRAPPY EVANGELIST

In other words debt and dependence do become pleasures in the presence of unspoilt love.[112]

We are key figures in a love story, as we are willed into existence by the love of God and are then granted the dignity of freedom of response. Chesterton situates this passage in a section of his work on Francis in which he discusses the common misunderstanding of asceticism as something miserable and harsh. On the contrary, says Chesterton, the asceticism of Francis is the natural response of anyone who is in love. The person who realizes that he is part of this dramatic cosmic romance will use his freedom in order to respond with gratitude by loving the Creator and his fellow creatures:

> It is the highest and holiest of the paradoxes that the man who really knows he cannot pay his debt will be forever paying it. He will be forever giving back what he cannot give back, and cannot be expected to give back. He will always be throwing things away into a bottomless pit of unfathomable thanks…A man must have magnanimity of surrender, of which he commonly catches a glimpse in first love, like a glimpse of our lost Eden.[113]

In first love we discern a hint of the truth that our life's task in Elfland is to learn to give, and that this is the best response for the gift of life. In the words of the famous prayer that is attributed to the saint from Assisi, if we seek to console rather than be consoled, to understand rather than be understood, to love rather than be loved, then we shall discover that in so giving ourselves away we shall find our very selves and receive all that we need. The gift of self to others does not destine us for a life of morbid masochism but for a life of frivolity and freedom, even if it is not inconsistent with pain, worries, disappointments,

---

[112] Ibid., 72.

[113] Ibid.

heartaches, and the many other problems that arise from living in a fallen world.

Our freedom is a freedom to be for others. Selfishly guarding our freedom leads ultimately to sadness, whereas giving it away in obedience to the rhythms of the loving service of others is to employ our freedom correctly. Immaturity perceives freedom as being free from constraint, whereas maturity views freedom as being free for loving. As we have seen, true freedom lies in conforming one's will to the good. The good that the will desires is to be found in the moral law; good is to be done and pursued and evil is to be avoided, and to do so brings joy.

Francis knew the costliness of the decision to conform one's freedom to the task of loving others:

> He was riding listlessly in some wayside place, apparently in the open country, when he saw a figure coming along the road toward him and halted; for he saw it was a leper. And he knew instantly that his courage was challenged, not as the world challenges, but as one would challenge who knew the secrets of the heart of a man.

Francis was full of the courage of the soldier, but here a different sort of steel was required:

> What he saw advancing was not the banner and spears of Perugia, from which it never occurred to him to shrink; nor the armies that fought for the crown of Sicily, of which he had always thought as a courageous man thinks of mere vulgar danger. Francis Bernadone saw his fear coming up the road towards him; the fear that comes from within and not without; though it stood white and horrible in the sunlight. For once in the long rush of his life his soul must have stood still. Then he sprang from his horse, knowing nothing between stillness and swiftness, and rushed on the leper and threw his arms around him. It was the beginning of a long vocation of ministry among many lepers, for whom he did many services; to this man he gave what money he could and mounted and rode on.[114]

---

[114] Ibid., 42-3.

The bravery required to live differently is a demand made by the Gospel of Christ, and it was something that had already been embraced by Francis even before he made the decision to renounce the worldly goods that had been bestowed on him by his father. While a prisoner of war Francis showed the same ability to behave in a deeply countercultural way, regardless of how it made him look in the eyes of others, by displaying kindness and friendship to all, even one of the prisoners who was despised by the other inmates in the dungeon:

> [I]t seems most probable that there had been some tale of treason or cowardice about the disaster; for we are told that there was one of the captives with whom his fellow-prisoners flatly refused to associate even in prison; and when this happens in such circumstances, it is generally because the military blame for the surrender is thrown on some individual. Anyhow...Francis, we are told, moved among his captive companions with all his characteristic courtesy and even conviviality, "liberal and hilarious" as somebody said of him, resolved to keep up their spirits and his own. And when he came across the mysterious outcast, traitor or coward or whatever he was called, he simply treated him exactly like all the rest, neither with coldness or compassion, but with the same unaffected gaiety and good fellowship...All those limits in good fellowship and good form, all those landmarks of social life that divide the tolerable and the intolerable, all those social scruples and conventional conditions that are normal and even noble in ordinary men, all those things that hold many decent societies together, could never hold this man at all.[115]

Francis was able to serve the marginalized without alienating himself from those who were doing the marginalizing. The tone of his countercultural conduct was such that he managed to maintain the difficult but necessary balance of remaining in warm relationships with as many parties as possible. Significantly—and here Chesterton was another prime example

---

[115] Ibid., 37-8.

of the same virtue—Francis displayed a deep civility toward those with whom he found himself in disagreement. "He had acted out of an unconscious largeness, or in the fine medieval phrase largesse, within himself."[116]

Taking a stance against prevailing attitudes will inevitably bring criticism and even enemies, and Francis's stance meant that family and ecclesial figures distanced themselves from him, but Francis was ready to pay the price demanded by the loving service of others, while doing his utmost to be generous and warm to all. Like the Chesterton who had admired him from boyhood, the saint of Assisi was a fine example of the magnanimity required to conduct apologetics in a pluralistic world and Church.

Chesterton believed that for "…this great mystic his religion was not a thing like a theory but a thing like a love-affair."[117] Francis did not view Christianity as a clever word-game or a mere philosophy of life to which we subscribe. It is more like a love affair, a handing over of our lives in love to others, which is a costly romance. This theme of the costliness of love, and the fact that the paying of this price is the only way to reach human maturity, is dealt with in one of Chesterton's newspaper columns, where he writes of the unsatisfactory ending to the famous work penned by his friend J. M. Barrie, *Peter Pan*:

[Peter] is represented as a sort of everlasting elf, a child who never changes age after age, but who in this story falls in love with a little girl [Wendy] who is a normal person. He is given his choice between becoming normal with her or remaining immortal without her, and either choice might have been made a fine and effective thing. He might have said that he was a god—that he loved all, but could not live for any; that he belonged not to them but to multitudes of unborn

---

[116] Ibid., 38.

[117] Ibid., 8.

babes. Or he might have chosen love, with the inevitable result of love, which is incarnation; and the inevitable result of incarnation, which is crucifixion—yes, if it were only crucifixion by becoming a clerk in a bank and growing old. But it was the fork of the road; and even in fairyland you cannot walk down two roads at once. The one real fault of sentimentalism in this fairy play is the compromise that is ultimately made, whereby he shall go free forever, but meet his human friend once a year. Like most practical compromises, it is the most unpractical of all possible courses of action. Even the baby in that nursery could have seen that Wendy would be ninety in no time, after what would appear to her immortal lover a mere idle half-hour.[118]

This passage consciously makes use of several Christian themes: incarnation, choice, crucifixion, love. We saw in Chapter III that Chesterton was grateful to both Pan and Peter, Paganism and the Church. He saw the Church as the fulfillment and purification of the goodness, truth, and beauty which he had discovered outside the Church. In the above passage Chesterton indicates that the problem with Peter Pan is that he never really grows up because he refuses to do what everyone has to do in order to mature: he does not make a choice founded on love and does not live with the consequences—at times painful—of that choice. Life in this cosmos involves making choices and, as we have seen already, all choice implies limitation. We cannot have it all ways in fairyland. To constantly value the possible over the actual, not to make the choice, to attempt to have it all ways, in the end proves impractical and ruins the opportunities to find joy that do exist in fairyland.

Malcolm Muggeridge once wrote that, "Every happening, great and small...is a parable whereby God speaks to us; and

[118] *Illustrated London News*, 20th August 1927, from the private unpublished collection of Dale Ahlquist, President of the American Chesterton Society.

the art of life is to get the message."[119] Like Chesterton, he believed that "the material universe is, as it were, a message in code from God, which mystics, artists and scientists strive to crack, sometimes with a measure of success, but to which Christ provides the key."[120] Ultimately, Christian revelation says that love is the message. Love is the only question on the final exam paper or, as John of the Cross puts it: "When evening comes, you will be examined in love."[121]

Chesterton notes that Peter Pan chose to remain free forever, but did not realize that in fairyland true freedom is found in making the choice to love in an incarnate form. The question put to the citizens of fairyland is: did they become, during their time in that land, mirrors of that selfless giving that is the very nature of the Creator of that land? Did they permit themselves to be cracked open sufficiently by life, by the poor, the naked, the hungry, the thirsty, the sick, the lonely, the imprisoned, the depressed, and the devastated in order to allow God's compassion to be seen in the world?

Did they allow persons and events to be the conduits of the grace of the Spirit, enabling the Spirit to chip away at the pride and self-sufficiency that are to be found at times within the inhabitants of fairyland? At times such "attitude erosion"—that slow wearing away of the selfish encrustations that have accumulated through the years—is too slow. Still, if they enter into the give-and-take, the constant demands of love, the need for communication and searing honesty, the lack of a hiding place from the demands of others, the constant interruptions of their

---

[119] *Christ and the Media.* https://books.google.com/books?isbn=1573832529. [Last accessed 4.19.17]

[120] *The Very Best of Malcolm Muggeridge*, ed. I. Hunter, 211.

[121] *Sayings of Light and Love*, in *The Collected Works of Saint John of the Cross*, eds. O. Rodriguez and K. Kavanaugh, saying number 57, p.90.

unchallenged agendas that are occasioned by life in community, then they will recognize God's promptings, the promptings of grace, trying to break them from their own projects and schedules, in order to move them into the agenda and greater project of love. Like Francis, they will discover that they will forever want to pay back the eternal debt that they cannot pay.

The Christian journey is a long journey of discovery in which we are to unearth, like Francis of Assisi and the other saints who have gone before us, the secret of life, which is the concrete service in love of the person who stands before us in life at a given moment. Francis of Assisi:

> ...was a Lover. He was a lover of God and he was really and truly a lover of men; possibly a much rarer mystical vocation. A lover of men is very nearly the opposite of a philanthropist...A philanthropist may be said to love anthropoids. But as St. Francis did not love humanity but men, so he did not love Christianity but Christ. Say, if you think so, that he was a lunatic loving an imaginary person; but an imaginary person, not an imaginary idea.[122]

Francis thus understood the Christian life to be the incarnation of love in daily living rather than the intellectual assent to a theory or set of propositions. Francis dealt, not with generalities and abstractions, but with concrete specifics in relationships:

> To him a man was always a man and did not disappear in a dense crowd any more than in a desert. He honoured all men; that is, he not only loved but respected them all...from the Pope to the beggar, from the sultan of Syria in his pavilion to the ragged robbers crawling out of the wood, there was never a man who looked into those brown burning eyes without being certain that Francis Bernardone was really interested in him; in his own inner individual life from the cradle to the grave; that he himself was being valued and taken seriously, and not merely added to the spoils of some social policy or the names in some clerical document.

---

[122] *Saint Francis of Assisi*, 7.

What Francis always saw before him was not the "many-headed beast [of the mob]. He only saw the image of God multiplied but never monotonous."[123] If he did see a mob, it was "a mob of kings,"[124] since each of them bore the image of the King of kings. This was why he served them.

3.3 SOME LIGHTS FROM C. S. LEWIS AND THE GOSPELS

Although it might be argued that C. S. Lewis has a sterner, more puritanical tone at times than Chesterton, both Lewis and the Gospels shed some useful light on the Chestertonian themes of love, the costliness of love, and love as the path to human maturity. In his biography of C. S. Lewis,[125] A. N. Wilson describes how Lewis's routine as an Oxford don, preparing classes and writing books, was regularly interrupted by the domestic chores and the burden of caring for Janie King Moore, the elderly mother of a deceased friend. Lewis's brother Warnie lamented the demands made on Lewis's time and energy, believing that these humdrum distractions deprived the world of many wonderful works from the pen of his brother. This daily cross had been laid on Lewis's shoulders because of his fidelity to a promise made to a friend in the trenches of the Great War when they were discussing the possibility of either of them dying. He gave his word to care for his friend's mother in the event of his friend's not returning home.

Equally important, he carried out his obligation in a generous spirit. He also interpreted the interruptions of his agenda in a very different manner from his brother.[126] Lewis believed

---

[123] Ibid., 88.

[124] Ibid., 89.

[125] See especially *C. S. Lewis: A Biography*, 92-5.

[126] It is also a matter of conjecture whether Lewis and Moore had been lovers at some point,

that rote duty and routine domesticity kept him grounded and in touch with the realities of daily living in ways from which perhaps other members of academia were sheltered. This in turn afforded him certain insights that he harvested and turned into sources of wisdom for his readers.

In his poem "As The Ruin Falls," written to his wife Joy after her untimely death from cancer, Lewis reminds us how easily we can lull ourselves into believing that we are loving somebody, when all we are really doing is serving ourselves and our conscious or unconscious, private, unchallenged agendas:

> All this is flashy rhetoric about loving you.
> I never had a selfless thought since I was born.
> I am mercenary and self-seeking through and through:
> I want God, you, all friends, merely to serve my turn.
> Peace, reassurance, pleasure, are the goals I seek,
> I cannot crawl one inch outside my proper skin:
> I talk of love—a scholar's parrot may talk Greek –
> But, self-imprisoned, always end where I begin.[127]

With acute honesty and painful self-knowledge, Lewis is able to discern the difference between real, costly love, which puts the needs of the beloved before one's own, and the feather-bedding of one's own agendas in the name of love. There are echoes here of the subtle selfishness discerned by Chesterton in the treatment of Wendy by Peter Pan. Because he wishes to "walk down two roads at once," Peter refuses to pay the price of love in fairyland, refuses the cross laid on his shoulders by the demands to choose a concrete way of loving in the real world, and so ends up making both himself and Wendy unhappy.

This is an instance of what Lewis refers to as mere talk of love. Wendy knew in her own sadness that talking of love and loving

---

which may have contributed to the sense of obligation experienced by Lewis.

[127] C. S. Lewis, "As the Ruin Falls," *Poems: The Collected Poems of C. S. Lewis*, ed. W. Hooper, 123.

in reality are very different things, just as knowing about God and knowing God and creedal Christianity and performative Christianity are very different realities. What shocks Lewis into realizing the distinction are the illness and impending death of his beloved:

> Only that now you have taught me (but how late) my lack.
> I see the chasm. And everything you are was making
> My heart into a bridge by which I might get back
> From exile and grow man. And now the bridge is breaking.
> For this I bless you as the ruin falls. The pains
> You give me are more precious than all other gains.[128]

The crucifixion which Lewis experienced because of the daily demands of living in relationship and building community with his wife slowly broke him from the exile of self-centerdness. As Flannery O'Connor dragged her characters into reality by shocking them out of their complacency, so Lewis needed a horrific jolt before he recognized his inner poverty or "lack." "God whispers to us in our pleasures, speaks to us in our conscience, but shouts in our pains: It is His megaphone to rouse a deaf world."[129] The experience of living in community with his wife, especially as she moved toward death (when the bridge was breaking), was the bridge that led Lewis back from the exile of a life lived out of harmony with what he was called to be, to that place where he was able to "grow man." To pay the costly price of love, to act in conformity with our truest nature as made in the image of the triune God, is to grow up, to become mature, and the crucifixion involved in that journey is the greatest of all possible blessings. To conform one's freedom to obeying the moral law of Elfland is to learn how truly to enjoy

---

[128] Ibid., 124.

[129] *The Problem of Pain*, 74.

Elfland. Since the whole cosmos is, for Chesterton, the gift of the God who is a unity of loving relationships, a gift given by God in love to creatures who are made in the image of God, then to discern God's purposes, to discover and live out the truth of who we are in God's eyes, is the path to true wisdom, maturity, and joy.

As might be expected, the Scriptures bear abundant witness to this truth. At the Last Supper Jesus' command to the disciples is to "Do this in memory of me."[130] The "this" which is denoted is the whole way of loving that is embodied in what might be called the Eucharistic way of living that became incarnate in Christ: a life rooted in gratitude to God, expressed through the laying down of one's life for others. We are commanded to enact in our own daily reality the whole self-gift of Christ in love, strengthened by him and by his gift of self to us, especially in the Eucharist.

In John's Gospel[131] the evangelist reminds us that the washing of feet—the concrete gestures of loving service of others, the payment of the price of love—are the only way to blessedness, to our deepest joy. "Now that you know this, blessed are you if you act accordingly." It takes a long time to learn that human joy depends on learning to love, for this is our true nature. This is how human beings have been created by God. If the human person seeks to act out of harmony with that reality, then things turn out badly. After washing their feet Jesus asks the disciples if they understand what he has just done for them; but for human beings it takes time, often a lifetime, for the message to sink in that life is about learning to love.

---

[130] Luke 22:19; 1 Corinthians 11:25.

[131] John 13:17.

In another scene from the end of John's Gospel,[132] when Jesus commissions Peter to feed his sheep after the Resurrection, we see that the very lesson that Chesterton knew that Peter Pan did not learn was put into words for another Peter by Jesus himself. "When you were young you put on your own belt and walked where you liked; but when you grow old you will stretch out your hands and somebody else will put a belt round you and take you where you would rather not go." When we are immature, we believe that freedom means being "free from": free to do whatever we like. However, growing up into human maturity requires that we learn that the real lesson of life is learning to hand over our freedom to the demands and crucifixions of real love.

We are to learn, however painfully, that we are to give ourselves for the others who are in our life—and this real love involves, more often than not, no longer putting on our own belt, but having a belt put on us by those we have in our life and by the circumstances in which we find ourselves. Being bound in this way will often take us to places where we would rather not go. Real love costs because community living makes demands on human freedom. Maturity involves submitting our freedom to the demands and rhythms of community willingly, out of love, rather than conscriptively and in a spirit of resentment.

Lewis wrote that it is our deepest nature to love, and that to seek to protect oneself by refusing to face up to the costliness of love would be to act against our nature. We are to use our freedom to act in harmony with who we are:

> There is no safe investment. To love at all is to be vulnerable. Love anything, and your heart will certainly be wrung and possibly be

---

[132] John 21:15-23.

broken. If you want to make sure of keeping it intact, you must give your heart to no one, not even to an animal. Wrap it carefully round with hobbies and little luxuries; avoid all entanglements; lock it up safe in the casket or coffin of your selfishness.

We are to be under no illusions about love. It is not some comfortable, nice, warm woolly sentiment. Real love is costly, and we are free to choose whether or not we will pay the price:

> But in that casket [of selfishness, having decided against paying the price]—safe, dark, motionless, airless—[the heart] will change. It will not be broken; it will become unbreakable, impenetrable, irredeemable. The alternative to tragedy, or at least to the risk of tragedy, is damnation. The only place outside Heaven where you can be perfectly safe from the all the dangers and perturbations of love is Hell.

To refuse to love is to enclose oneself in a freely chosen, self-sufficient world in which one believes that one has no need of other people, which Lewis describes as hell. We see here that the Christian vision is the total antithesis of the famous line of Sartre: "L'enfer, c'est les autres."[133] The Christian notion of Hell is not other people, but rather the absence of other people from one's life and the refusal to deal with other people in the complexities of daily reality:

> I believe that the most lawless and inordinate loves are less contrary to God's will than a self-invited and self-protective lovelessness...Christ did not teach and suffer that we might become, even in the natural loves, more careful of our own happiness...We shall draw nearer to God not by trying to avoid the sufferings inherent in all loves, but by accepting them and offering them to Him; throwing away all defensive armour. If our hearts need to be broken, and if He chooses this as the way in which they should break, so be it.[134]

We get a sense here of why Christ became so angry with the

[133] *Huis-clos*, ed. K. Gore, 6.

[134] *The Four Loves*, 111-112.

smugness of Pharisaism: it enabled the exponents of smug, self-satisfied religion to avoid the demands of self-gift. Christ's intention is that we learn to love, to lay down our lives for those we have in our lives, in order to become who we really are at our deepest level, persons made in the image of the triune God, persons made for community by the giving and receiving of love in relationship. Even imperfect attempts to do so are more pleasing to God than an unwillingness to try.

Though love is costly and sometimes painful, it is far better for the human heart in the long run to submit itself to this pedagogy. We have to risk learning to love or else live in a hell of our own making, a self-enclosed world, where we refuse depth and entanglement because it might hurt. Like Flannery O'Connor, Lewis believes that Christ prefers to break us from a mere existence or half-life which is rooted in an attitude that is proud and self-sufficient and neither gives to nor receives from others, so that we can be free for a fuller life of love.

We might recall here a point from Chapter IV, that theology, at its best, exists in order to allow human beings to flourish and live joyful lives, which is to remember who they are. The Christian creed challenges us to leave behind the half-life, the mere existence, the floating or drifting of a life without commitments in love, in order to embrace the cross of living for others, for therein lies the deepest joy of all. To do this is to reflect the Trinitarian God in whose image we are made and to whom the ancient doctrines of the Church point:

> If there is one question which the enlightened and liberal have the habit of deriding and holding up as a dreadful example of barren dogma and senseless sectarian strife, it is this Athanasian question of the Co-Eternity of the Divine Son. On the other hand, if there is one thing that the same liberals offer us as a piece of pure and simple Christianity, untroubled by doctrinal disputes, it is the single sentence, "God is love." Yet the two statements are almost identical;

at least one is very nearly nonsense without the other. The barren dogma is only the logical way of stating the beautiful sentiment.[135]

Dogmas are not clever word games that belong to the academy, but the unfolding in time of the full implications of the DNA written into the heart of the self-gift of God in the revelation of Jesus of Nazareth:

> For if there be a beginning without beginning, existing before all things, was He loving when there was nothing to be loved? If through that unthinkable eternity He is lonely, what is the meaning of saying He is love? The only justification of such a mystery is the mystical conception that in His own nature there was something analogous to self-expression; something of what begets and beholds what it has begotten…It was emphatically [Athanasius] who really was fighting for a God of Love against a God of colourless and remote cosmic control; the God of the stoics and the agnostics. He was fighting for that very balance of beautiful interdependence and intimacy, in the very Trinity of the Divine Nature, that draws our hearts to the Trinity of the Holy Family. His dogma…turns even God into a Holy Family.[136]

The doctrine of the Trinity explains why human beings yearn for relationship, love, community, and family. They are made in the image of that triune family. It also explains why Chesterton fought to defend these things all his life and why any apologetics needs to reverence the rhythms of self-gift in love, wherever these are to be found. Ultimately human beings are not fooled: they recognize the Spirit wherever it manifests itself, and in spite of the words that they explicitly state to each other. The fruits of the Spirit speak more clearly than any of the sounds that are formed by our mouths.

---

[135] *The Everlasting Man*, 227.

[136] Ibid., 228.

4. LOVE, LIVE-ABILITY, AND CREDIBILITY[137]

In his book on Shaw Chesterton wrote of his subject, "In a sweeter and more solid civilization he would have been a great saint,"[138] and when H. G. Wells was seriously ill, he wrote to Chesterton and said, "If after all my Atheology turns out wrong and your Theology right I feel I shall always be able to pass into Heaven (if I want to) as a friend of G.K.C.'s. Bless you." To this Chesterton replied:

> If I turn out to be right, you will triumph, not by being a friend of mine, but by being a friend of Man, by having done a thousand things for men like me in every way from imagination to criticism. The thought of the vast variety of that work, and how it ranges from towering visions to tiny pricks of humour, overwhelmed me suddenly in retrospect; and I felt we have none of us ever said enough... Thanking you again a thousand times for your letter...and everything else. Yours always, G. K. Chesterton.[139]

Here, in his acknowledgement of the virtues of two men whose ideas he most vehemently opposed,[140] we discern that although Chesterton believed that ideas really do matter, that thinking correctly is important and that doctrines and dogmas are vital if we are to think correctly, he also believed that people with rather odd and incorrect ideas (often because of the influence of the surrounding culture) can still find salvation because they have one or two good ideas, especially about love and

---

[137] Parts of the following two pages are based on an article written by the author of this book. See P. Rowan, "G. K. Chesterton and the 'Court of the Gentiles' (3)," *The Pastoral Review* 6 (6), 2010, 59-65.

[138] *George Bernard Shaw*, 11-12.

[139] M. Ward, *GKC*, 370-1.

[140] Shaw and Wells both displayed a willingness to sacrifice the individual person and particular nations in favour of the greater good of the whole or for Empire. They also supported Eugenics. Chesterton clashed with both of them on these and countless other issues.

the service of others. In the charity and altruism displayed by Shaw and Wells, Chesterton heard faint echoes of those who, in Mt 25:31-46 and Mt 7:21, do the will of the Father without knowing it and who enter the Kingdom of Heaven by doing the will of the Father, without necessarily saying "Lord, Lord!"

Chesterton once received a letter from his wife's cousin, Rhoda Bastable, a young woman who had been a bridesmaid at their wedding, who was suffering from "spiritual growing pains" and who had "expressed to him a fear that she was a hypocrite" in the Christian faith. Chesterton gently replied with a reference to his own struggles:

> ...I have doubted if I believed anything: but I have found the trick of saying: "If I did not really believe I should not have done this work, or resisted that temptation—or even tried to resist it. My Will knows me better than my Mind does." Think about solid things outside you; especially about the most solid thing in the world—affection."[141]

For Chesterton the solidity of our love is the truest measure of where we are in relationship to the will of God, a thought that would later be expressed by Karl Rahner: "The Christian knows that love alone is the highest light of knowledge."[142] Central to Rahner's notion of the anonymous Christian is the idea that a person's love for the person in front of him is love for God:

> ...the two [great commandments of love of God and neighbour] together are valid in the Synoptic tradition as the life-giving (Lk 10:28) epitome of the Old Testament revelation in the scriptures and the prophets (Mt 22:40), greater than which there is nothing (Mk 12:31). Furthermore in this Synoptic theology of love, it certainly must not be overlooked that in the eschatological discourses about Judgement, love of neighbour is given in St Matthew as the only explicit standard by which man will be judged (Mt 25:34-46).

---

[141] Letter cited in M. Ward, *Return to Chesterton*, 202.

[142] *Theological Investigations* Vol. 6, 41.

Such love of neighbor does not take place without God's grace but, on the contrary, "whenever there is an absolutely moral commitment of a positive kind in the world and within the present economy of salvation, there takes place also a saving event, faith, hope and charity, an act of divinising grace."[143] Rooted, concrete, specific acts of love are the very mark of God's presence, the presence of the Holy Spirit in the person who is doing the loving.

We recall that Chesterton regularly pointed out to several of Shaw's critics that, though they disagreed on many issues, nevertheless he believed there to be so much goodness present in Shaw. If God's grace is required to be a good person, is it too much to suggest that Chesterton discerned the presence of the Holy Spirit in his friend? Gerald O'Collins writes:

> For those who challenge the presence of the spirit in the life of all human beings, the short answer, at least for those who accept Christ's universal presence, might be: the presence of the Spirit accompanies and enacts the presence of the risen Christ which is a universal presence. Since the co-Sender of the Spirit (the risen Christ) is always inseparably there with the Sent (the Holy Spirit) and since Christ is present everywhere and in every human life, the Spirit must also be present everywhere and in every human life. People do not have to be aware of living in the presence of Christ and the Holy Spirit for this to be the case. Being present does not as such imply being known to be present.[144]

Calling on Luke,[145] O'Collins notes that the Spirit does indeed call all people into the Church community, but he also enlists

---

[143] Ibid., 238-9.

[144] *Rethinking Fundamental Theology*, 311-12.

[145] Acts 2:5-11

Luke again[146] and Paul[147] to show that the "invisible mission of the Spirit extends far beyond the visible members of the Church to be powerfully present in the whole of creation."[148] He goes on to quote the passage of "Ambrosiaster": "whatever truth is said by anyone whosoever is said by the Holy Spirit." He goes on to point out, in slightly modified form—"everything that is true, no matter by whom it is said, is from the Holy Spirit"[149]— that "this expression turns up eighteen times in the works of Thomas Aquinas."

By noting that John Paul II gave it a fresh twist by saying that all authentic prayer can go up to God anywhere (a belief which the Pope made incarnate by praying with members of God's other peoples in Assisi in 1986), O'Collins says, "For good measure [John Paul] added that the Spirit is 'mysteriously present in the heart of every person.'"[150] O'Collins finds this papal teaching helpful and illuminating in a pluralistic world and a genuine development of Lucan and Pauline teaching.

He also believes that the New Testament teaching is further developed by the same Pope in Redemptoris Missio. Though the Spirit is present "in a special way in the Church and her members," the "presence and activity" of the same Spirit are "universal...The Second Vatican Council recalls that the Spirit is at work in the heart of every person, through the 'seeds of the Word,' to be found in human initiatives—including religious ones—and in mankind's efforts to attain truth, goodness and

---

[146] Acts 10:1-11:18

[147] Romans 2:14-16

[148] Op. cit., 313.

[149] In Epistolam S. Pauli ad Corinthios Primam, 12. 3; PL 17, col. 243B, cited in Rethinking Fundamental Theology, 314, n.24.

[150] Rethinking Fundamental Theology, 314.

God himself."[151] For O'Collins, the universal presence of the Holy Spirit "presupposes a rich view of the nature of personal presence." It is not a question of total presence or complete absence: personal presence can assume many forms and levels of intensity:

> To be sure, the Spirit is present in a special and intense way within the Christian Church. But that does not allow us to say: 'outside the Church there is no Holy Spirit.' There is no such thing as being 'outside the Holy Spirit'...Where there is the kingdom of God, there is the Spirit...[152]

Certainly an inspection of the friendships between Chesterton and Shaw and Chesterton and Wells would indicate that he discerned much in them that would resonate with this notion of the presence in them of the Spirit. It is also possible to cite various witnesses throughout Christian history to this conviction of the universal presence of the Holy Spirit, among them Justin Martyr, Augustine of Hippo and Aquinas,[153] but O'Collins is happy to cite the Archbishop of Westminster, Henry Edward Cardinal Manning, himself a robust and faithful guardian of the Church's tradition, who wrote in 1875,

> ...it is true to say with St. Irenaeus, 'ubi ecclesia ibi Spiritus,' but it would not be true to say, 'where the Church is not, neither is the Spirit there.' The operations of the Holy Ghost have always pervaded the whole race of men from the beginning, and they are now in full activity even among those who are without the Church.[154]

Such a line would have pleased Chesterton, who had a special

---

[151] Ibid., 315.

[152] Ibid., 316.

[153] See F. Sullivan, *Salvation Outside the Church? Tracing the History of the Catholic Response*, 14-16, 28-43; 47-62; 165.

[154] O'Collins, *Rethinking Fundamental Theology*, 316.

reverence for Manning, having been greatly impressed by him when he saw him as a boy out walking with his father on Kensington High Street in London and particularly admiring him for his battles on behalf of the poor and the rights of workers. It is at the very least arguable, therefore, that where the "race of men" is seen to be building the Kingdom of God through community, through the gift of self to others in love and in the service of justice, there the Spirit of God is at work in the heart and life of those who spend themselves in this way. To borrow from and adapt Ambrosiaster and Aquinas, every truly authentic act of gift of self in loving service of the other, no matter by whom it is carried out, is from the Holy Spirit.

Of course, as we have seen, Chesterton, the champion of paradox, railed against any attempt to reduce the complexities of reality and the complexities of Christian orthodoxy. Consequently, it is imperative that we do not reduce the multiple treasures of the Gospel message to our own favorite bits. Truth can never be divorced from love, nor love from truth. The choice is never truth or love, but both truth and love. Love is never mere fuzzy sentimentality. As Pope Benedict puts it:

> ...only in truth can charity be authentically lived. Truth is the light that gives meaning and value to charity...Without truth, charity degenerates into sentimentality. Love becomes an empty shell, to be filled in an arbitrary way. In a culture without truth, this is the fatal risk facing love. It falls prey to contingent subjective emotions and opinions, the word "love" is abused and distorted, to the point where it comes to mean the opposite.[155]

Were Chesterton around today, having lamented modernity's separation of the virtues in Chapter 3 of *Orthodoxy*, it is more than arguable that he would urge us not to allow ourselves to be defined by labels such as "left" or "right," "conservative"

---

[155] *Caritas in Veritate*, 3.

or "liberal," and "traditionalist" or "progressive," but to move beyond the limitations of such slogans, which are always reductionistic and never do justice to the beauty and complexity of Gospel truth and love. We must be ready to see many sides of an issue, as did Chesterton when he criticized both Hudge and Gudge for their different ways of being indifferent to the needy persons before them.

In criticizing socialism and capitalism, however, Chesterton bore witness to something vital: although the Gospel message is multifaceted and complex, which means that the Church must forever in its theology explore the riches of that message and proclaim the results of its explorations to the world in order that the world might flourish, nevertheless the basic truth of the Gospel revelation is that we were created by Love, for Love. Hudge and Gudge neither grasp nor live out this basic truth by ignoring the needs of the poor. Christianity is founded on an interpersonal encounter with Love and is meant to overflow into interpersonal encounters in love.

As Pope Benedict said in his first encyclical, "Being Christian is not the result of an ethical choice or a lofty idea, but the encounter with an event, a person, which gives life a new horizon and a decisive direction."[156] By analysing the concepts of "ascending love," Eros, and "descending love," Agape, Benedict goes on to stress the point which, as we saw above, he would later repeat in *Spe Salvi*: that all love is from God, but that the authentic love that is shaped by Christian faith (agape) is not easy and must be learned though the cross:

> Two things emerge clearly...First, there is a certain relationship between love and the Divine: love promises infinity, eternity—a reality far greater and totally other than our everyday existence. Yet we have

---

[156] *Deus Caritas Est*, 1.

also seen that the way to attain this goal is not simply by submitting to instinct. Purification and growth in maturity are called for; and these also pass through the path of renunciation.[157]

As does Chesterton in his analysis of the ending of *Peter Pan*, Benedict teaches us that the only way to human maturity, and the very nature of true love, as opposed to its pale counterfeits, is through the humdrum daily crucifixion that finds us in the home, the bank, the factory, and the school. Christian living is above all a way of enfleshing discipleship of the Lord who came not to be served but to serve.[158] While Pope Benedict was still Cardinal Ratzinger, he said in a lecture that was part of a conference to mark the 70th birthday of Johann Baptist Metz, "the question of God is finally not a theoretical question, but rather the question of the praxis of one's life,"[159] which is like Chesterton's insight that Francis's religion was a love affair. The strong note of social concern that marked the work of Metz is also to be found in Pope Benedict's third encyclical, *Caritas in Veritate*, but even before that, in his second encyclical *Spe Salvi* he writes that:

> …the Christian message was not only "informative" but "performative." That means: the Gospel is not merely a communication of things that can be known—it is one that makes things happen and is life-changing…The one who has hope lives differently.[160]

The decision whether or not to live love concretely is the ultimate criterion for evaluating the quality of faith and the worth of a human life, as indicated by Matthew 25: 31-46. There is a

---

[157] Ibid., 5.

[158] Mark 10:45.

[159] *The End of Time? The Provocation of Talking About God*, with J. B. Metz et al., ed. J. M. Ashley, 25.

[160] *Spe Salvi*, 2.

vast difference between the "Lord, Lord" religion of Matthew 7:21 and Benedict's costly vision of performative faith, which flows from the vision of faith depicted in the Parable of the Sheep and Goats.

This may be the reason why, in *Orthodoxy*, Chesterton, almost in anticipation of Rahner and von Balthasar, was able to write that, "To hope for all souls is imperative; and it is quite tenable that their salvation is inevitable."[161] This idea is in tension with his firm belief that life is a romance or story, which necessarily entailed the possibility that a human life could end in damnation. (Chesterton always hotly contested the Calvinist position that human freedom is ultimately sacrificed on the altar of predestination, and so the tension is even more marked.)

For many people in our culture faith without love is a scandal, justifiably so, since love is the organizing principle of life for Christians; but when people see the transparent generosity of saintly lives lived out in concrete love, the imaginations and hearts of even our own confused culture are moved to sense the possibility of a different wavelength and a broader horizon. There are whispers from another world, a different way of viewing things. Whenever human beings live in a way that bears witness to the fundamental and inalienable equality between all human beings, whenever they reach out to serve the needs of others, especially the most marginalized, even the most cynical and world-weary heart can be moved to wonder.

Chesterton did not imagine faith to be merely a question of truth for the mind (even if he did view "theology as simply thought applied to religion"[162]), but a commitment to live as Jesus did, in love for others and as exemplified in the transparent

---

[161] *Orthodoxy*, 341.

[162] *The New Jerusalem, Collected Works* Vol. 20, 276.

love of the saints such as Francis, for whom religion was also less of a theory and more of a love-affair. Love is the religious vocation in its essence, and the call of every human being. The commonly held view is that if a person understands faith better, he can begin to live it better. Perhaps Chesterton would enjoy the paradox involved when one suggests that perhaps true wisdom lies in reversing this: if a person lives faith as love, she will come to understand it more. Credibility follows on from livability. As Lonergan said, we have to stand within reality and the depths of love's experiences if we are to perceive and understand:

> It is as though a room were filled with music though one can have no sure knowledge of its source. There is in the world, as it were, a charged field of love and meaning; here and there it reaches a notable intensity; but it is ever unobtrusive, hidden, inviting each of us to join. And join we must if we are to perceive it, for our perceiving is through our own loving.[163]

Newman would say, "We believe because we love"[164] and argues that:

> We are Christ's, not by faith merely, nor by works merely, but by love; not by hating the world, nor by hating sin, nor by venturing for the world to come, nor by calmness, nor by magnanimity—though we must do and be all this; and if we have love in perfection we shall— but it is love makes faith, not faith love.[165]

Wittgenstein would argue that, "Only love can believe the Resurrection. Or: it is love that believes the Resurrection."[166]

---

[163] *Method in Theology*, 1972, 290.

[164] "Sermon 12," *Fifteen Sermons Preached Before the University of Oxford, Between A.D. 1826 and 1843*, 236.

[165] Sermon XXI "Faith and Love," "Parochial and Plain Sermons Vol. IV," *John Henry Newman: Selected Sermons*, ed. and introd. by I. Ker and pref. by H. Chadwick, 269.

[166] *Lectures on Ethics, Culture and Value*, ed. G. H. von Wright, tr. P. Winch, 77.

When Aquinas stated, *"ubi amor, ibi oculus,"*[167] he was saying that love is the correct lens through which to see life and to perceive God: little acts of concrete love sensitize the human heart more to the presence of the God of the ordinary and the everyday. Love offers a different perspective: it is the eye of love, love as the lens and filter on life, which sensitizes the human heart to the presence of the God of love, who is the source, goal, and eternal backdrop of the romance of human existence and human community.

Our final chapter looks at both the modern and Christian notions of God. We shall see that the Christian God is a family of co-inherent and subsistent relationships, each of which empties itself for the other in the mutual indwelling that characterizes love. The Christian notion of relationship is not, as Aristotle's *Organon* contended, something accidental, but essential and foundational to reality. Since God is love and relationships, rather than monolithic power, the creation of the cosmos and human beings comes about, as Chesterton perceived, through sheer gift: through a non-manipulative, non-threatening, and non-coercive act of selfless generosity. The human dignity and freedom which are, quite rightly, cherished by modernity, are not in competition with the Christian God but, on the contrary, can only be vouchsafed by relationship with this God who holds all contingent reality in being.

---

5. Concluding Remarks

For Chesterton, gratitude for the gifts of a cosmos and the life to enjoy it is the seedbed of all virtue. To be humble enough to

---

[167] Josef Pieper explains the use of this maxim by St. Thomas Aquinas, *Commentary on the Sentences* 3, d. 35, 1, 2, 1, while explaining that it comes from Richard of St. Victor. (*Faith, Hope and Love*, tr. Sr. M. F. McCarthy, San Francisco: Ignatius, 1986, 6.)

recognize the blessing of one's creatureliness and to be thankful for this "infinite debt" is the fuel that drives us toward the love of one's fellow creatures, to share with them the gift of the cosmos in accordance with the will of the Creator. The ordinary and the everyday might not have been, and so they are precious, full of beauty and majesty and a source of primordial awe, wonder, and deep-seated joy for Chesterton.

Often, of course, in the rhythms of daily existence we can fail to be aware of this. Fatigue, restlessness, boredom, and the endless quest for what we think is still missing from our happiness—the particular element of experience in this cosmos which we believe will bring us consummate joy—trick us into believing that real life, real joy, and real fulfillment are to be found wherever right now we are not. We are unable to perceive that life, love, joy, meaning, God, and all else that we seek are already present, even if we are not present to them. They don't have to be sought out; we merely have to notice, to advert to our experience. Sometimes we have to be jolted, shocked into noticing what is already there. Perhaps, Chesterton muses, this is the meaning of death. Heaven knows how we want to hang on to our toys, the *divertissement* of which Pascal spoke. Perhaps "The way to love anything is to realize that it might be lost."[168]

The painful explosion that brings us to our senses puts us in our place, not in the sense of degrading us, but of allowing us to understand or see our real status in the universe, and to appreciate the true preciousness of both ourselves and that universe. We are the children of God: our existence is sheer gift of God, and so we are utterly contingent beings and have nothing of which to boast; and yet we are called into existence by the love of God, are called to the eternal life of loving relationship

---

[168] *Tremendous Trifles*, 23.

with Him and each other, and so have everything to boast of, because our boast is in Christ.

Humility, which consists of maintaining in harmony these two truths—knowing our place as creature and our destiny as beloved child of God—is the seedbed of other virtues. It rouses us to an awareness of our need and inner poverty before the fullness that is Christ. Humor is its cousin, and is a uniquely human characteristic that points to God and helps us see that, though life and all that life contains, such as religion, are serious, they must never be solemn. Mirth is central to the life of Heaven in Chesterton's mind. We must take life, but not ourselves or our religion, too seriously. If we will not be humble, something needs to happen to make us so. Only the shock or explosion of being humbled introduces us to our need of redemption and tills the soil in which can grow the seed of the fuller vision of the Gospel. Humility, humor, and joy are uniquely human qualities and point to God.

Chesterton asks us to advert to our ordinary experience since God waits for us there, especially in the people we meet who are the "million masks of God." God is not a deistic absentee cosmic landlord, but the God of the ordinary and the everyday. Christ promises us another advocate to be with us, to shape us and mold us in the drama of daily choices. We saw that this notion of the abiding presence of the Spirit leading us ever more deeply into religious conversion, into truth and love, is the immanent presence of the God who is also transcendent. This dialectic of immanence and transcendence is central to the thought of Rahner, von Balthasar, O'Collins, and Lonergan. Dulles concurs that we have to allow ourselves to be fashioned daily in our subjectivity, which is the costly conversion that constitutes the fundamental religious call to love, to build community.

This call to love is costly. There was a deep-seated goodness and kindness to Chesterton, but he experienced some of the same struggles as the rest of us with the journey of conversion. The movement from a life that sees the world as centered on oneself to a life that is focused on others is a slow and difficult one. According to Chesterton, nothing prepares us better for that conversion than the experience of living in a family. The rhythms of family life, with its inherent instances of give and take, with its uneven mix of positives and negatives, virtues and vices, joys and sorrows, beauty and blemishes, good times and dysfunctional moments, constitute a sound formation for community living of any kind. The family prepares us for life in any institution, since we learn there that there is no such thing as perfect community in this world. The choice is between choosing to love and build community among people who are as imperfect and compromised as oneself, or choosing not to love at all.

Journalism was Chesterton's main public way of giving himself over to loving service of the world. He had a special respect and love for the poor and the marginalized. He defended their dignity and their rights in the newspapers and in public debate against the exponents of the relentless march of modern progress, who viewed the poor only as a means of increasing the wealth of the affluent or the industrial efficiency of the state. Chesterton's advocacy of the poor is seen in his attempt to spread Belloc's distributist economic theory, which was itself rooted in Catholic social teaching.

Chesterton became part of the long list of prophetic voices in the Judeo-Christian tradition who have been willing to serve the marginalized of society. He thought that the Church would still be condemning the sin of injustice toward the poor in a thousand years' time, since Christian faith places on our shoulders a responsibility for the marginalized dismissed as "non-persons" by a given culture. Christianity is not therefore merely something that exists to make us feel good about ourselves and our world. If we are aware that life and the cosmos are a gift that comes to us out of the generous love of God, we are to learn also that with that gift comes the burden of caring for others, especially the weak and wounded of our world. If we are loved, we must rise out of our comfort zone in order to show a gritty love to others.

Francis of Assisi, who had fascinated Chesterton since his earliest years, embodied the realization that the gift of God's love, the gift of creation and life, impose on us the duty of loving the world. Chesterton believed that Francis knew that the secret of life lay in being a servant and secondary figure, and that putting this into practice set him free and brought great joy. The saint from Umbria knew that to be granted the blessing of life imposes on us an infinite debt, which we can never repay but should constantly try to repay by giving the gift of our life away in service of others.

For Francis, Christian faith was less of a theory to be subscribed to than a love affair to be embodied in daily living, and he was willing to attempt to do this in all that he did. Francis's way of being countercultural was, like Chesterton's, marked by kindness, civility, and magnanimity. Both these men are a challenge to all who would be apologists in a pluralistic culture to display the same largesse and to endeavor to be, as far as possible, on good terms with all, and not bitter toward those with whom they find themselves in disagreement.

We noted that the figure of Peter Pan turns out in the end to be a deep disappointment for Chesterton. The elf refuses to choose a concrete way of embodying love, thereby disobeying one of several rules that govern true love in Fairyland: concrete love requires choice, and choice involves limitation. Even in Fairyland one cannot travel down two paths at the same time. Peter refuses to choose, opting instead for the compromise of the "best of both worlds."

However, since this is impossible in Fairyland, and even though Peter does indeed avoid the crucifixion of growing old and living in the humdrum routine with Wendy—which is the price to be paid for that particular choice—he also has to carry the cross of missing out on the joy of a life with Wendy and of watching her grow old without him. By refusing to make a choice for love one way or the other, Peter Pan never grows up.

Another Peter is told that doing merely what one likes and when one likes is a sign of immaturity, whereas the maturity of the passing years means that somebody else binds us and takes us where we would rather not go; thus is he taught that there is a world of difference between feather-bedding our own agendas in Christ's or love's name and living out an authentic Christian love that mirrors the self-gift of the Trinity by truly seeking the good of the other.

Finally, we wondered whether the selfless love of others might offer a lens, a perspective on life, through which to view daily existence. By saying yes to others in love, are we saying yes to Someone else who has already said yes to us? When Newman writes that, "We believe because we love" or, as Jesus puts it, "whoever does the truth comes out into the light,"[169] it is a lovely reversal of the notion that if we understand Christian faith, we will live it better.

In harmony with the discoveries made in Chapter II and in our reading of Flannery O'Connor, it is not our cleverness or our self-sufficiency that readies us for God, but our willingness

---

[169] John 3:21.

to become followers of Christ by becoming vulnerable for others, by becoming food for the life of the world, by nourishing and strengthening with love those whom we encounter in daily living.

What consequences this holds for our attempts to forge a new agenda for apologetics today will be discussed in our final chapter. Since the God of G. K. Chesterton shares, as we have seen, his own esse and maintains all of contingent reality in being through participation in his own "to be," then all of contingent reality is constituted by its link with God. In our final chapter, then, we shall see that authentic human flourishing need not feel threatened by the Christian God who is essentially relationship, community, and selfless gift of love.

CHAPTER VI

Scrappy Evidence and Apologetics Today

I believe in [Christianity] quite rationally upon the evidence. But the evidence in my case, as in that of the intelligent agnostic, is not really in this or that alleged demonstration; it is in an enormous accumulation of small but unanimous facts. The secularist is not to be blamed because his objections to Christianity are miscellaneous and even scrappy; it is precisely such scrappy evidence that does convince the mind. I mean that a man may well be less convinced of a philosophy from four books, than from one book, one battle, one landscape, and one old friend. The very fact that the things are of different kinds increases the importance of the fact that they all point to one conclusion.[170]

Whatever it is that we are all looking for, I fancy that it is really quite close...Always the kingdom of Heaven is "at hand"...so I for one should never be astonished if the next twist of a street led me to the heart of that maze in which all the mystics are lost.[171]

TWENTY-FIRST CENTURY Western culture is a complex mixture of modernity, postmodernity, and a yearning for some of the spiritual and communal dimensions of

---

[170] *Orthodoxy*, 348.

[171] G. K. Chesterton, "A Glimpse of My Country," *Tremendous Trifles*, 105.

existence that are associated with an earlier, premodern period. In this final chapter we shall attempt to draw together some of the strands of wisdom offered by Chesterton in order to discern what a contemporary apologetics, fit for purpose in such a complex culture, might look like. As the passage from the final chapter of *Orthodoxy* cited above indicates, Chesterton believes that signs of evidence for the existence of God are many and varied, and it is the accumulation of these—the cumulative case approach to arguing for the existence of God—that is most convincing. What bits of evidence are to be found, then, in Chesterton's life and writings?

First, let's set a brief historical context for the status of apologetics today, how it fell out of fashion in the recent past, but also how it re-emerged as a strong and fruitful theological discipline in a postmodern culture toward the end of the twentieth century and at the turn of the new millennium. This is underlined by a consideration of Pope Benedict XVI's call for the Church to open up a Court of the Gentiles in order to dialogue with those who do not share the Church's faith: to put the wisdom of the Church in conversation with the aspirations and movements of a Western culture that is searching to interpret existence.

We saw in Chapter III that Chesterton believed that he "came to Christ from Pan and Dionysus…that the conversion [he] understand[s] is that of the pagan and not the Puritan."[172] Recalling that Pan was an important figure in 19th-century Romanticism and 20th century neo-paganism, one might wonder whether some of the 21st century's postmodern sensibilities are born of the same mix of disillusionment with rationalism and a yearning for the emotional and spiritual dimensions of existence which gave rise to these earlier cultural phenomena.

---

[172] *The Catholic Church and Conversion, Collected Works* Vol. 3, 108.

After exploring, therefore, whether it is possible for the Court of the Gentiles to put Peter in dialogue with Pan, the chapter then explores some of the "scrappy" bits of evidence for God that have been gleaned from Chesterton which might, when taken together, generate a cumulative persuasiveness that appeals in a holistic way to the whole person. Given the "scrappy" nature of the evidence, it's worth summarizing what else this chapter will cover.

We will see how Chesterton insists that we need to reacquire the virtue of humility, develop the ability to look at the familiar as if it were unfamiliar again, become free of the cultural shackles of modernity in order to recognize the unacknowledged hungers within, and develop the childlike wonder that sets us on the spiritual preambles of faith. We will explore the importance of finding community, friendship, and support, and of using the tried and tested wisdom of a Church that mirrors some of the same strengths and weaknesses that we find in ourselves.

We will recognize the need to wonder intelligently about the cosmos and to ponder its multi-faceted and paradoxical complexity, with imagination and intellectual rigor. We will see that a culturally attuned apologetics must maintain an openness and willingness to learn through crosscultural conversations with all parties, and we will also recall that at all times faith has to be humble, since its conversations about God are always provisional and essentially apophatic in nature.

We will learn the value of daily prayerful pondering of the depths of reality, which is always "other" to us, and will learn especially to value the "other" people with whom we share the gift of the cosmos. However, we will also discover that we must rise from this contemplative consideration of others in order to enter and heal their world with love. All of these pieces of evidence provide insights and wisdom about basic dimensions of the humanum, and they all serve to liberate human beings at the level of disposition, as the Holy Spirit works within us in order better to prepare us for the surprise and the shock of the utterly unique revelation of Christ, Chesterton's Everlasting Man. If the definitive and particular nature of the content of Christian faith seems a little too certain and neat for the typically postmodern searcher, then perhaps the Spirit-led cultivation of other postmodern sensibilities—such as humility, recognition of others, and solidarity with others, especially the marginalized and the needy—can better prepare our culture for the recognition of the shockingly different revelation of God in Christ.

---

1. Apologetics Before and Since Vatican II: *a Context for Learning from Chesterton*

Essentially apologetics exists to offer reasons for believing the Christian proclamation and to defend that Gospel from the various criticisms and objections that arise at different times in different cultures. It can help those who believe the Christian Gospel to wrestle with their struggles, and it can assist unbelievers with their doubts and hesitations (recognizing that the line between believer and unbeliever is not always neatly demarcated). Though it can never hope to offer simple, irresistible arguments that prove beyond all shadow of a doubt that God exists and that atheists are wrong not to believe, apologetics can offer good reasons for the reliability of the Christian message and coherent signs or indications that it is neither irrational nor unintelligent to entrust oneself to Christ.

In his magisterial work on the history of apologetics, Avery Dulles devotes just under a third of the book to the developments that took place in the twentieth century.[1] He points out that until the Enlightenment apologists spoke from a stable platform of official Christianity, seeking to refute their adversaries and convince them of their errors. With the advent of modernity and the rise of deism, idealism, and liberalism, things become a lot more complex, such that:

> By the beginning of the twentieth century it is possible to speak of two basic types of apologetics: a defensive type that seeks to argue unbelievers into submission to the faith as traditionally understood and a revisionist type that seeks to forge a new synthesis between religious and secular knowledge.[2]

Dulles goes on to say that the types of apologetics that were developed in the twentieth century ended up becoming hotly disputed topics within the various Christian churches themselves. It is not my intention here to offer a detailed survey of Catholic Modernism, Protestant Liberalism, or any of the other ideas that emerged from this historical context. I wish instead to offer a brief contextualization of where apologetics is today and why Chesterton can help it in its task.[3]

In recent times this ancient and venerable tradition of theological reflection had fallen out of fashion, but it now seems to be making a revival. Apologetics—which as a term still jars against the ears of some people, because of its perceived undertones of polemic, excessive defensiveness, traditionalism, pride, superficial rationalism, and even sacred dishonesty—had been reduced, in the years preceding the Second Vatican Council, to a very pale shadow of its former self.

---

[1] A. Dulles, *A History of Apologetics*, 271-367.

[2] Ibid., 271.

[3] In his recent work on apologetics, Professor Alistair McGrath, President of the Oxford Centre of Christian Apologetics, places a quote from Chesterton on the first page of the introduction. See A. McGrath, *Mere Apologetics: how to help seekers and skeptics find faith*, 11.

In 1930 Henri de Lubac highlighted some of the shortcomings of this reductionist approach to the discipline,[4] saying that apologetics had been divorced from its great heritage (a tradition that contained the treasures of the insights of Augustine of Hippo, Pascal, and Newman, among others, with their emphasis on personal disposition and the subjective dimensions of the act of faith in the adventure of human life) by forgetting that spirituality and the inner life are critical parts of the journey to God at all times, perhaps especially in its early stages. By uncritically accepting the presuppositions of the positivistic and rationalistic versions of modernity (which Chesterton regularly railed against), the Church's dogmatic theologians gave apologists the impossible task of offering scientific proofs of the Christian Gospel to unbelievers.

Michael Buckley has criticized the apologists of the Enlightenment period for their insistence on divorcing apologetics from other theological disciplines, for forgetting that Christ is "the principal evidence for the reality of God"[5] and for allowing itself to be reduced to a philosophy that accepted the impersonal and mechanistic terms of debate from its atheistic interlocutors. One might argue that this was somewhat understandable, given that apologists were keen to show that they had grasped the importance of engaging with modernity using its own prized asset of reasonable argument.

Nevertheless the imaginative, relational, and affective dimensions of the movement toward faith were a casualty of this move toward the merely logical, and apologetics ended up defending an impoverished type of theism, seeking only to argue that there was an ultimate explanation for the universe. It forgot

---

[4] H. de Lubac, "Apologétique et théologie," *Nouvelle Revue Théologique*, Vol. 57 (1930), 361-378.

[5] M. J. Buckley, *The Origins of Modern Atheism*, 41.

that historically it had been a truly dialogical, crosscultural, and frontier discipline of theological exploration which regularly intersected with spirituality, conversion, and the religious experience rooted in an encounter with the person of Christ.

If one adds to this reductive approach the fact that the Second Vatican Council, albeit justifiably, called on the insights of Catholic scholarship from the decades immediately prior to the Council in order to take "for granted the universal distribution of grace" and to prefer "a confident, appealing, and irenic presentation of Catholic doctrine rather than an attempt to prove its truth," in a way that "tended to undermine the polemic spirit that had animated the apologetics of the past,"[6] it is understandable that some people remain unconvinced about the value of apologetics.

However, Dulles also explains that in the years since the Council there has been a sustained debate about the worth of apologetics.[7] He reminds us that the Council itself, though preferring dialogue to debate and though encouraging the Church to seek common ground with proponents of other traditions and world views, still referred to some apologetic themes, such as when in Gaudium et spes it holds before humanity "Jesus Christ as the key to the meaning of the world and its history (GS 10)[8] and as casting light on the riddles of sorrow and death (GS 22)."[9]

Dulles sketches out for us some of the great figures and themes in the post-conciliar debate about apologetics (a detailed treatment of which would be beyond the limits of this

---

[6] A. Dulles, *A History of Apologetics*, 325-6.

[7] Ibid., 326-345.

[8] These words bear a notable resemblance to one of Chesterton's major themes in *The Everlasting Man*.

[9] Ibid.

book), and offers a re-assessment of: the value of this ancient discipline for today's world; its method; its place in the relatively recent discipline of Fundamental Theology; the importance of the dynamism of the human subject toward mystery; the importance of the luminous object of the Gospel figure of Christ; and the significance of the strong re-emergence of apologetics toward the end of the twentieth century and at the turn of the new millennium.[10]

There is no such thing as a timeless and classical way of doing apologetics, since it must always look to build bridges between the Gospel and specific historical and cultural contexts. It is widely recognized that at the beginning of the twenty-first century we live in a postmodern context. It is important to add here, then, a brief word about the concept of postmodernity. Alistair McGrath locates the appearance of the term postmodernism around 1971, initially as a reference to a new architectural style, but then as a concept rapidly attaching itself to the world of ideas, art, literature, and social issues. Postmodernity became synonymous with the notion that the proud project of "modernity [with its key ideas of the centrality of human beings and the inevitability of progress] had failed and needed to be corrected." Postmodernity does not pit itself against the modern: its supporters view it "not as a rejection of every aspect of modernity, but...as an attempt to combine the best of the modern world with the best elements of classical traditions and eliminate the undesirable aspects of both."[11]

---

[10] Dulles lists as key names in this period of reflection figures such as Verweyen, Werbick, Geffré, Theobald, Pie i Ninot, Colombo, Fisichella, Sequeri, Giussani, John Paul II, as well as a whole host of American Catholic apologists, such as Tacelli, Kreeft, Scott and Kimberley Hahn, and Novak.

[11] *Mere Apologetics: how to help seekers and skeptics find faith*, 29-30.

McGrath says that although postmodernity has been criticized for its eclecticism and intellectual shallowness, its proponents claim that they want "to move society and thought
forward in a way that utilizes the best insights of the past but is
not trapped by it." They aim to fight against the totalizing uni-
formitarianism advocated by so many systems that were born
in the modern period. Such uniformity is viewed by postmodernity as a power game in which those in power or authority
manipulate and control other people.

By rejecting the modern demand for such uniformity and
for metanarratives (a comprehensive explanation of experience
and history), postmodernity rejects the insistence that there
is only one way of interpreting the world, one way of thinking and one way of behaving, advocating instead difference,
diversity, and pluralism. However, McGrath points out that
the postmodern worldview has its own metanarratives which
have become the reigning orthodoxy in parts of contemporary
Western culture: for example, the insistence that all interpretations of reality are of equal value. It seems almost a matter of
basic common sense that one can argue against this claim by
pointing out that there are clearly several readings of the world
that are highly incompatible.

McGrath argues that, instead of seeing it as a threat to
Christian faith, it might be better to understand the postmodern moment simply as the cultural context in which Christianity
is to be preached today and therefore (as with any cultural
setting in the history of the Church) as an unavoidable reality
that offers both challenges and opportunities for apologists.[12]
The issue then is whether a culturally attuned apologetics can
discern the chief characteristics of the postmodern mood and

---

[12] Ibid., 30-31.

then go on to use that knowledge in order to engage with the historical epoch in which the Church lives her faith today.

While acknowledging that it is very difficult to try to define postmodernity (its own leading representatives vary significantly in their understandings of it), McGrath,[13] drawing on the work of Kevin Vanhoozer,[14] tries to capture its essence using four criticisms that it makes of modernity. Firstly, the modern worship of reason (which also underpinned the type of apologetics that was carried out in the modern period) is viewed with suspicion. There is not just one type of rationality but many, and the enthroned rationalism of the modernity that had been excited by the empirical and instrumentalist approach of the natural sciences has been replaced by a more contextual and perspectival approach. For this reason postmodernity is attracted to stories and images (narratives), but always with the proviso that none of them can ever offer a universal explanation of reality.

Secondly, and as a consequence of this perspectivalism, the notion of universal truth is also looked at askance by the postmodern. There is a shyness and even hostility about truth claims, especially because historically these have been used to serve other, less honorable agendas. So a deconstructionist relativism has replaced a rationally ordered reality.

Thirdly, postmodernity is sceptical about the possibility of recounting a universal version of history, and of the possibility of human beings shaping history according to their projects and goals. The universal and totalizing significance of the metanarrative of Jesus Christ is a casualty in this postmodern vision.

---

[13] Ibid., 33-34.

[14] "Theology and the Condition of Postmodernity," *The Cambridge Companion to Postmodern Theology*, ed. K. Vanhoozer, 3-24.

Consequently (Vanhoozer's fourth point), postmodernity maintains that there is no way of knowing one's own history and no way of narrating one's own identity. Any attempt to understand the individual is doomed to failure, and the modern Western emphasis on the sovereign, individual human subject, self-consciousness, and personality is countered by a radical scepticism about what human identity is.

No doubt much more could be added to this sketch of McGrath's analysis of the postmodern. For example, postmodernity also stirs distant memories of Wilde and the Decadent worldview that was dominant during Chesterton's time at the Slade, because of the way it seeks to assert its independence of the moral systems of the past through hedonistic and aesthetic expressions of autonomy.

At the same time, however, and almost in contradiction of this, there are postmodern tendencies to insist on the interconnectedness of human beings because of a new global consciousness, and a concomitant sense of solidarity and mutual moral obligations (in contradistinction to the lonely isolationism of modernity). One might argue that this notion of a global village would appeal to Chesterton who, as we saw in Chapter III, loathed the notion of thinking of the cosmos as some vast, sprawling, and impersonal thing, instead preferring to see it as personal and cozy:

> A man chooses to have an emotion about the largeness of the world; why should he not choose to have an emotion about its smallness? It happened that I had that emotion. When one is fond of anything one addresses it by diminutives...[Materialists] professed that the universe was one coherent thing; but they were not fond of the universe. But I was frightfully fond of the universe and wanted to address it by a diminutive...I felt about the golden sun and the silver moon as a

schoolboy feels if he has one sovereign and one shilling.[15]

The postmodern searcher is more interested in embodied, "livable" forms of truth which are visible expressions of this compassionate human solidarity, rather than in mere abstract "explanations" of truth. We have made several references to the postmodern distrust of institutions throughout this book, which is linked to the suspicion of the manipulative tendencies indicated above.

This distrust of rationalism opens up the postmodern mindset to right-hand brain and more holistic ways of seeking to engage with reality, and it also leads postmodernity to celebrate randomness, art, aesthetic play, and leisure much more than did the economically obsessed and supremely efficient modern culture, for which the plant always had to run.

Finally, postmodernity has a strange ambiguity about God, or at least about the spiritual dimensions of existence. Some representatives of postmodern thought still uncritically assume the modern assumptions that the claims of religion were nothing more than superstition and that to deal with the immanent here-and-now is self-evidently more important than to reflect on the transcendent. Nevertheless, the number of self-help and alternative spirituality books on the market clearly show that there has also been a renewed recognition that perhaps modernity was a little premature in its celebration of the death of God and its heralding of the dissolution of the eternal backdrop to existence in the cosmos.

From the point of view of Christian apologetics, then, the present cultural context offers both challenge and opportunity. Chesterton can help us to rise to the challenge and embrace the opportunity. If apologetics is not divorced from its deeper,

---

[15] *Orthodoxy*, 266-7.

more spiritual roots, if it retains the humility required for living in this paradoxical cosmos and for engaging in theological reflection, and if it displays a polite and charitable tone, then apologetics can still be a fruitful field for fundamental theology. It also needs an intellectual robustness and commitment vital in today's pluralistic (and sometimes hostile) postmodern culture. It might be argued that Pope Benedict XVI expressed the need for such a renewed vision of apologetics just a few years ago.

2. THE COURT OF THE GENTILES: *Peter in Dialogue with Pan*[16]

On 21st December 2009, as is the custom, Pope Benedict XVI used his annual "Address to the Roman Curia and Papal Representatives for the Traditional Exchange of Christmas Greetings" to describe some of the key moments in the life of the Church and the world in the previous year.[17] After referring in his speech to the end of the Pauline Year, the beginning of the Year for Priests and his Trip to Africa, Pope Benedict moved on to express something of the joy and gratitude he had experienced because of his visit to the Czech Republic.

Noting how he had always been told that this country was a nation composed largely of agnostics and atheists, the Holy Father expressed his joyful surprise at what he encountered there: cordiality; friendliness; joyful faith among those present at the liturgical celebrations over which he presided; a real attempt on the part of the Academy and the world of high culture

---

[16] Some parts of this section have been published by this author and are reproduced here with kind permission of Rev. Professor Michael Hayes, editor of *The Pastoral Review*. See P. Rowan, "G. K. Chesterton and the 'Court of the Gentiles' (1)," *The Pastoral Review* 6 (4), 2010, 53-7.

[17] References to this address are taken from www.vatican.va/.../Benedict xvi/.../2009/december/.../hf ben-xvi spe 20091221 curia-auguri en.html [accessed 31st March 2009]

to listen attentively to his words; and great courtesy extended by the state authorities, who did everything in their power to ensure the success of the Pope's visit.

Rather than then moving on to talk of the beauty of that country and its testimonies to Christian culture, Benedict preferred instead to highlight as "most important the fact that we, as believers, must have at heart even those people who consider themselves agnostics or atheists."

Talk of a New Evangelization, part of our habitual ecclesial language since the time of Paul VI, and a recurring theme in the pontificates of both John Paul II and Benedict XVI, can be, according to the latter, a discourse that seems rather alarming to some agnostics and atheists. "When we speak of a new evangelization these people are perhaps taken aback." With a phrase that ought to have fascinating consequences for the Church's vision of how it engages in both evangelization and the apologetics that is part of that evangelizing mission, the Pope warns us that these people, "do not want to see themselves as an object of mission or to give up their freedom of thought and will."

Autonomy and the freedom not to conform—either to modernity's obsession with the western values of rationalism, science, technology, and globalization, or to the antimodern worship of traditionalism (as distinct from the real treasures of a living tradition)—are precious qualities for a postmodern culture which remains suspicious of the historically attested manipulative tendencies of institutions and the exaggerated claims of modernity. The Pope is right to point out that nobody likes to feel that they are but a means to somebody else's ends, even if that somebody claims to be the bearer of good news.

The first sentence of the first chapter of the Catechism of the Catholic Church reminds us that, "The desire for God is written in the human heart."[18] That line chimes with Chesterton's delight in discovering that when he found out that Earth was not his true home, that he was in the wrong place, as he puts it in *Orthodoxy*, "my soul sang for joy, like a bird in spring."[19] In a similar vein, Benedict notes that "the question of God remains present even for [atheists and agnostics], even if they cannot believe in the concrete nature of his concern for us." Referring to his address at the Collège des Bernardins in Paris in 2008, he asserts his belief that it was the quest for God that brought Western monasticism, and consequently Western culture, into being. Then, with words that are of immense significance for all who seek to forge a new apologetics and to establish a true humanism within a complex world, Benedict says that,

> *As the first step of evangelization* we must seek to keep this quest alive; we must be concerned that human beings do not set aside the question of God, but rather see it as an essential question for their lives. We must make sure that they are open to this question and to the yearning concealed within it. (Italics mine)

"As the first step of evangelization": as we saw in Chapter II, there is a "pre-religion" or a *praeparatio evangelica* that must take place today, one which is sensitive to the needs of people who are swimming in an ocean of cultural influences. Before we can launch into programs of apologetics, evangelization and catechesis, long before issues of creed, code, and cult are on the ecclesial menu, the Pope advocates that we try to get people to advert to the question of God. That means putting them in touch with the human adventure of their hungers, yearnings, and desires.

---

[18] *Catechism of the Catholic Church*, 27.

[19] *Orthodoxy*, 284.

Apologists are to help people recognize and nurture their questions and longing. Chesterton's hungers had been eclipsed by the cultural pressures at the close of the nineteenth century; nevertheless he knew that he had a deep desire or yearning for something, a yearning which Christian faith claims is ultimately grounded in the fact that we have been created by God for relationship with God.

This is just one instance of what Charles Taylor refers to as "the unquiet frontiers of modernity."[20] Desire seems to be one of those strange, distinctive, "other-worldly" characteristics that seem to be part and parcel of the constitution of human beings. However much religious knowledge we impart to others, however much content is assimilated on the level of understanding by others (faith as *fides quae*), it may never add up to a decision on their part to say "yes!" to God, to make a personal commitment (faith as *fides qua*). Perhaps at best it can move to one side some of the obstacles to that yes. Perhaps then we can remove some of the blockages to a recognition of desire.

As we have seen, the first words of Bernard Lonergan's *Method in Theology* state that, "A theology mediates between a cultural matrix and the significance and role of a religion in that matrix."[21] If that is so, then all who are involved in apologetics today need in some way to mediate between the content of the Church's living tradition and what is evolving in a rapidly changing culture. The Church's recent Pontiff-Pastor-Theologian seems to be indicating that, in the present cultural context, what is clear is that bridge-building—preparing the spiritual dispositions (a sort of postmodern preambula fidei) for a possible Gospel faith—is a vital prerequisite to any

---

[20] *A Secular Age*, 711 ff.

[21] Lonergan, B. *Method in Theology*, xi.

communication of the meaning of faith.

So accustomed are we today to media sound bites, which often, in the name of analysis, end up reducing the complexity of personalities, events, and reality to a few sensationalized, digestible, or marketable elements, we may have missed here the hope-filled vision that the Pope often offers. (After all, he is often caricatured as a dour and hardened Augustinian veteran of the culture wars). The Pope knows that because it is part of human nature to seek the face of the Divine Mystery, true and open dialogue between the Church and cultures will always remain a possibility.

As Chesterton himself demonstrated in his openness to the presence of goodness and truth in the likes of Shaw and Wells, the true and effective apologist today cannot possess a closed, un-nuanced and entrenched ghetto mindset; she must have the courage to recognize that the Risen Christ is Lord of history and Lord of the cosmos, and that the Holy Spirit is therefore at work in people and cultures. Cultures, then, are neither completely cultures of death, nor totally cultures of life: they contain elements of both. Today's apologist needs to be both Gospel artist and cultural critic.

Chesterton, the supporter of the poor and the marginalized, the critic of the Boer War and other government policies of his day, and the gifted crafter of works such as *The Everlasting Man*, teaches us that the creation of a contemporary and culturally attuned apologetics requires courage and imagination.

Apologetics today is called to forge new languages and create images that reach and nourish the human heart, which is, by its nature, open to the divine. It has to show the typically Chestertonian ability to discern the complexities of contemporary culture, by remaining open to all that is true, good, beautiful, and humanizing, and also ever alert to, critical of, and resistant to the dehumanizing and anti-Gospel values that lurk and persuade in any culture.

In saying that the Church must hold close to its heart those who cannot bring themselves to profess belief in God, Pope Benedict is reminded of Jesus' interpretation of Isaiah's call for the Temple to be a house of prayer for all the nations:

> Jesus was thinking of the so-called "Court of the Gentiles" which he cleared of extraneous affairs so that it could be a free space for the Gentiles who wished to pray there to the one God, even if they could not take part in the mystery for whose service the inner part of the Temple was reserved. A place of prayer for all the peoples: by this he was thinking of people who know God, so to speak, only from afar; who are dissatisfied with their own gods, rites and myths; who desire the Pure and the Great, even if God remains for them the "unknown God." (cf. Acts 17: 23)

Benedict suggests that those committed to the New Evangelization need to be able to identify what might be perceived as "extraneous" in the first step of evangelization today, and to help provide a space for people in our complex culture, so that those who sense their need and incompleteness can somehow connect with the God they do not know:

> I think that today too the Church should open a sort of "Court of the Gentiles" in which people might in some way latch on to God, without knowing him and before gaining access to his mystery, at whose service the inner life of the Church stands. Today, in addition to interreligious dialogue, there should be a dialogue with those to whom religion is something foreign, to whom God is unknown and who nevertheless do not want to be left merely Godless, but rather to draw near to him, albeit as the Unknown.

In response to the Pope's call, on 25th February 2010, Archbishop Gianfranco Ravasi, President of the Pontifical Council for Culture, announced the launching of a foundation called "The Courtyard of the Gentiles," one of whose aims, he said, was "to create a network of agnostic or atheistic people who accept dialogue and enter as members into the foundation and, as such, into our dicastery." Ravasi also stated the further intentions of starting relations with atheistic organisations, studying the "spiritual place" of non-believers and "developing themes of rapport between religion, society, peace and nature."[22]

It is evident here that there are some differences between apologetics as it is usually understood and the vision of the Courtyard of the Gentiles. Apologetics is traditionally conceived of as a theological discipline that seeks both to offer unbelievers (in their doubts) and believers (in their struggles) evidence of the reasonableness of the Christian proclamation, and to defend Christianity from the various objections and critiques that arise against it.

Although the Courtyard of the Gentiles will certainly provide plenty of occasions for apologists to engage in theological and philosophical conversation and debate, its initial conception might be more accurately regarded as a sign of the Church's commitment to humble, respectful, and charitable dialogue between believers and unbelievers, and an invitation to other parties to pledge themselves in a similar fashion. The Court is a recognition on the part of the Church that all parties in a complex and all-too-often polarized secular culture need to be involved in conversation with each other, in order better to be able to carry the tensions of that culture and in order to bring healing and human flourishing to a needy world.

Church history offers us an excellent example of a cross-cultural adventurer in Saint Thomas Aquinas, and it might

---

[22]http://www.catholicnewsagency.com/news/atheists_invited_to_join_vatican_council_for_outreach_initiative/ [last accessed 28th February 2012].

be argued that Chesterton, Thomas's devotee and biographer, is also a bridge-builder between diverse cultural viewpoints. There are several features of Chesterton's life that harmonize with the vision of dialogue between believers and unbelievers which is implicit in Pope Benedict's vision of the Courtyard.

Hermeneutics teaches us that we approach no document without presuppositions of interpretation, and we have forever been disavowed of the claim to complete neutrality: politics, football, situations in the workplace, and any aspect of reality, theology included, are all filtered. Perhaps we all have our cherished bits of a theologian, taking the bits we like and ignoring the bits we do not like, and this sometimes happens with Chesterton.[23]

Specifically, Chesterton was not slow to critique a culture when he deemed it necessary. However, some strands of Christian thought (in much the same way as has happened with C. S. Lewis) see this as the only or principal value of Chesterton for apologetics or the New Evangelization. But to think this is to succumb to the narrowness of vision, the reductionism of the richness of reality, against which Chesterton argued all his life.

Certainly the ability to critique a culture is an important lesson we can learn and apply in our own day from Chesterton. Chesterton always sided with the little ones and the marginalized, and we too need to be the voice of those who have no voice, those whom our culture deems expendable as it attempts to forget and scapegoat all who don't measure up to its own reductionist criteria of what is good, true, and beautiful. However, there is more, much more, to Chesterton that might be of use to those who do apologetics in the age of the Court of the Gentiles.

---

[23] As has been apparent throughout this book, it is my contention that even if he was not in the strictest academic sense a theologian, only a prig would claim that so much of Chesterton's writing was not in its intent a work of theology.

For example, Avery Dulles finds in Chesterton's writings the same cumulative case method of doing apologetics that is to be found in Augustine, Pascal, and Newman.[24] This type of apologetics relies on the notion that there is "an enormous accumulation of small but unanimous facts."[25] The best way of showing that it is not irrational or unintelligent to believe in God involves a set of convergences of various pieces of evidence to be found in the world and in the human person.[26] Chesterton contends that, "The very fact that the things are of different kinds increases the importance of the fact that they all point to one conclusion."[27]

Chapter III discussed how Chesterton perceived the world as a network of analogies consisting of unity with difference and consequently highly paradoxical. He perceived the relation that links the two different things that stand in an analogical relationship as grounded in the God who is the source of all beings. Because all being is analogical, all attempts to systematize thought, as Aquinas and Kierkegaard also realized, will have to be content to wrestle with paradoxes. The world is incapable of being encapsulated in a system or formula, which grounds Chesterton's belief that reality is not able to be reduced simplistically.

Reality is one, yet mysterious, complex, and wonderful in the Chestertonian vision, and so Christian apologetics should remain open to discovering evidence for the existence of God from the astonishingly multi-faceted dimensions of existence in this cosmos: "if Christianity should happen to be true—then

---

[24] A. Dulles, *A History of Apologetics*, 293, 362.

[25] *Orthodoxy*, 348.

[26] See *Catechism of the Catholic Church* 31.

[27] *Orthodoxy*, 348.

defending it may mean talking about anything or everything."[28]

At the same time, of course, Chesterton recognizes that there are many objections to Christianity. In *Orthodoxy* he maintains that he believes in Christianity, "'For the same reason that an intelligent agnostic disbelieves in Christianity.' I believe in it quite rationally upon the evidence."[29] Acknowledging that "scrappy" bits of evidence—"one book, one battle, one landscape, and one old friend"[30]—may convince the mind of both believer and unbeliever, he goes on to point out, in an entertaining evaluation of two "triads of doubt,"[31] how his interpretation of the scraps of evidence is very different to that of the agnostic.

The very pieces of evidence that cause the doubter not to believe—the similarities between the human species and other species of the animal kingdom; that religion arose out of darkness and fear and that society has since improved that condition by outgrowing religion; that religion produces joyless cultures; that Jesus was a meek, weak, and docile character; that Christianity flourished in the dark ages of ignorance, which is the period to which the Church wants to drag us back; and that religious people are superstitious, impractical, and behind the times—are refuted one by one by Chesterton.

He points out what he was to explore brilliantly two decades later in *The Everlasting Man*, "not how like man is to the brutes, but how unlike he is."[32] He outlines how of primordial times "History says nothing; and legends all say that the earth was

---

[28] *Daily News*, 12th December 1903, cited in D. Ahlquist, *G. K. Chesterton: The Apostle of Common Sense*, 19.

[29] *Orthodoxy*, 348.

[30] Ibid.

[31] Ibid., 354.

[32] Ibid., 348.

kinder in its earliest time. There is no tradition of progress; but the whole human race has the tradition of a Fall." He explains how "Those countries which are still influenced by priests are exactly the countries where there is still singing and dancing and coloured dresses and art in the open air. Catholic doctrine and discipline...are the walls of a playground."[33]

Having combed the Gospel details to show how Christ was anything but "sheepish and unworldly,"[34] having explained how the Church "was the one path across the Dark Ages that was not dark," [35] and having used the Irish as an example of a "people, whom we call priest-ridden, [but] who are the only Britons who will not be squire-ridden," Chesterton is satisfied that he has responded to this "second trinity of objections."[36] He then asks the doubter:

> "What is this incomparable energy which appears first on one walking the earth like a living judgment and this energy which can die with a dying civilization and yet force it to a resurrection from the dead; this energy which last of all can inflame a bankrupt peasantry with so fixed a faith in justice that they get what they ask, while others go empty away; so that the most helpless island of the Empire can actually help itself?[37]

This same ninth chapter of *Orthodoxy* lists a whole host of other doubts, issues and objections against the truth claims of the Christian Gospel, and Chesterton replies, "When I look at these various anti-Christian truths, I simply discover that none of them are true. I discover that the true tide and force of all the

---

[33] Ibid., 350.

[34] Ibid., 351.

[35] Ibid., 352.

[36] Ibid., 353.

[37] Ibid., 353.

facts flows the other way."[38] Chesterton deals with "such typical triads of doubt in order to convey the main contention—that my own case for Christianity is rational; but it is not simple. It is an accumulation of varied facts, like the attitude of the ordinary agnostic. But the ordinary agnostic has got all his facts wrong."[39]

Here we see Chesterton undertaking the classical twofold task of apologetics in an imaginative manner: the justification of Christian faith and its defense against the objections to it that emerge in various historical and cultural contexts. Apologetics seeks to engage with a culture's struggles with Christian faith by celebrating the imaginative and intellectual richness and depth of the Gospel vision, hoping thereby to help existing believers in their struggles and to remove obstacles on the path toward faith for unbelievers.

The characteristically Chestertonian generosity that is displayed in seeking common ground with those of other viewpoints, his belief that apologetics entails talking about anything and everything, and his courageous and imaginative intelligence when engaging the narrowness of vision that sometimes sets itself against the Christian Gospel all indicate that the Jolly Journalist can help us re-imagine apologetics in order to meet the needs of today's complex culture. He can help us forge a new agenda for apologetics that is in harmony with Pope Benedict's vision for the Court of the Gentiles, and in the remainder of this chapter we shall analyze some of the specifics of this.

More generally, it can be said that Chesterton's apologetic approach displays a willingness to admit evidence from many areas of human experience in this cosmos, as well as a rigorous degree of reflection and intellectual content on that evidence in

---

[38] Ibid., 348.

[39] Ibid., 354.

the cultural milieu of today. In this way Chesterton offers a rich soil in which to nourish the seeds of hope and humanity that are found in contemporary cultures. He also provides a way of challenging and purifying some of the sub-Christian images of God in our culture today, some of the cultural superficialities and silliness and dehumanizing tendencies, especially by drawing with imagination and creativity on some of the Church's wisdom from the ages.

3. CULTURAL PRESSURES AND CHILDLIKE SPIRITUAL PREAMBLES OF FAITH

In the opening chapter of *Orthodoxy*, Chesterton writes that we need the "life of practical romance…the combination of something that is strange with something that is secure. We need so to view the world as to combine an idea of wonder and an idea of welcome."[40] We need the unfamiliar familiar—to see the life that we have been given in such a way that we are "happy in this wonderland without once being merely comfortable."[41]

The main question posed and answered by the Ethics of Elfland is: why is there something rather than nothing? The answer is that reality is sheer gift. "We must answer that it is magic. It is not a 'law,' for we do not understand its general formula. It is not a necessity, for though we can count on it happening practically, we have no right to say that it must always happen."[42] Reality does not explain itself: it is "magic," no matter how vast and sprawling it proves to be, and no matter how far science goes toward explaining its secrets.

---

[40] *Orthodoxy*, 213.

[41] Ibid.

[42] Ibid., 255.

It has something personal in it and behind or beyond it, and it is an interpersonal gift and communication. However, as the Pope intimates when he talks of the Church's responsibility to help people get free from extraneous things in order to create a space for their encounter with God, many people are blocked from perceiving the transcendent personal God that stands behind reality.

Chapter II noted how Chesterton's struggles at the Slade School of Art and his writings bear witness to the fact that so often in the journey toward religious faith, a first and necessary step is to become free from certain things in order then to be free for God. Indeed, we also saw there how Chesterton believed that, "Men will not believe because they will not broaden their minds."[43] Reflection on the things of faith is not always easy because of the cultural pressures toward unbelief, which can narrow the imagination and self-understanding of people. An increasingly secular context has made it more difficult for people to grow toward mature and adult faith decisions, and a contemporary apologetics has to be able to supply people with some scaffolding of support so that they can recognize some of the hidden, and not so hidden, influences that impact on human freedom.

The factors involved in such support include:

• A discernment of the effect that changes in society can have on the possibilities of religious faith; some awareness of the impact that inner dramas have on the decision for or against faith;

• Some understanding of the philosophical and theological issues involved in some of the great debates between atheistic and theistic positions;

• And the serious exploration of the very nature of faith knowledge itself and its kinship with other forms of knowledge, as a decision

---

[43] *Saint Francis of Assisi*, 16.

taken partly in trust and partly in darkness.

Putting such pastoral strategies on the agenda of apologetics today might help people in their struggle to make sense of faith in a secular culture. They can at least be brought to the threshold of liberation from certain culturally induced shackles.

Chesterton, like Newman before him and Flannery O'Connor after him, recognized that a certain personal disposition is required before we can be ready to perceive God. For him, it is the virtue of humility that opens a person up to great vistas. The person who recognizes that all is gift is ready to enjoy the gift more fully. What Chesterton appreciated above all about Francis of Assisi (alluding to a famous work by Newman) may be applied in equal measure to himself: "If another great man wrote a grammar of assent, he may well be said to have written a grammar of acceptance; a grammar of gratitude."[44] Chesterton, like Francis before him, "understood down to its very depths the theory of thanks."[45]

The whole cosmos and our part in it are sheer gratuitous gift of God, and the recognition of this prepares one to see reality more clearly. This is why Chesterton contends that if we believe that a person who bows his head in order to enter the Church does so out of "a sort of claustrophobia," then we are mistaken—the real fear of such a person is that of agoraphobia. We have not realized that to stoop one's head in order to be open enough to enter the zone of faith is to open oneself up to "the forum…the market-place…the open spaces and the colossal public buildings."[46] The wavelength of humility does not mean that a person "has gone into the inner darkness [of the Church],

_____

[44] Ibid., 147.

[45] Ibid.

[46] *The Well and the Shallows, Collected Works* Vol. 3, 451-2.

but out into the broad daylight."[47]

Although Chesterton certainly believed in employing all the powers of the mind when attempting to decipher the riddle of the cosmos, he thinks that in order to do this one has to accept that human beings are constituted in such a way that they are more than dispassionate, objective, rationalistic processors of data. Not to accept this is to reduce the complexity of human beings and the cosmos in which they find themselves, which leads to a stunted epistemology and an attitude that can come to see knowledge merely as a way of winning cold, logical arguments.

This attitude will not do for Chesterton since, as we have already witnessed, one of the most evident things for him about the cosmos is that it is not some objective external textbook, waiting to be picked up and read by some clever external observer; rather, it is a riddle, a paradoxical and mysterious network of relationships between realities that participate in being. Among these beings are numbered the strange creatures called human beings, who are invited to become conscious of their participation in the mystery and relish their involvement.

When human beings accept this invitation, they discover truths about the cosmos and the God who is the source of that cosmos, in instances of what Avery Dulles calls "participatory knowledge."[48] These are not merely external truths, but also personal truths which embrace us and who we are, and they can only be seen if our disposition or initial stance is right.

For Chesterton, a personal decision is required if we are to see accurately. If we make that decision, if we take the necessary step of participating, the cosmos opens up before us and we begin to see the rich and paradoxical nature of the mystery of

---

[47] Ibid.

[48] *Models of Revelation*, 136 ff.

reality. As Dulles explains,[49] because to be human is to be incarnate spirit and to be related to the reality around us through the body, it is only by turning to the realities of the world that we get some notion of the transcendent. There has to be some earthly mediation, some sacramental medium, of the divine. We know, and we grow in our accumulation of knowledge, by living in and being committed to the cosmos and what we know about it—not by artificially standing outside our cosmos and knowledge and neutrally observing them. It is from a perspective, a vantage point, that we see truth.

No human group or individual can claim to have an objective "God's-eye" perspective on things; no one can have an objective, comprehensive and exhaustive grasp of the all-encompassing cosmos, for the simple reason that they are all part of it. To claim otherwise is to claim to be God. We can no more grasp or be totally objective about reality than the fish can about the ocean that sustains it, or the individual can about the person she is. We are unable to adopt a position outside ourselves in order to grasp ourselves in our totality as persons (which is why self-knowledge will always remain precarious and require eternal vigilance); so too we are unable to adopt a position outside our relationships with others and outside the cosmos in such a way that will permit us to get them in total focus.

This does not imply, however, that the knowledge of self, others, and the cosmos is a complete illusion. It is philosophically incoherent to say that we do not possess knowledge of realities about which we can and do know so much. In the perennial human quest for understanding, we do in fact grasp countless insights about reality (even if this never adds up to exhaustive comprehension of reality). Our understanding of reality,

---

[49] Ibid.

however, comes not only from detailed, objective, rational knowledge, but also from knowledge of a different type, which Aquinas says "is based on a certain natural affinity with the things about which, as it happens, we have to form judgments."[50]

Knowledge about the cosmos, then—especially the knowledge that is a guide to daily living and is in that sense practical and requires a natural affinity or connatural knowledge—is not limited to the rational, left-brain kind associated with the natural sciences. Faithful spouses who have been together for forty years know about chastity and love—this is not an attempt at patronizing or edification.

Or to choose another area, boxers or golfers know their sport. Only the narrow kind of rationalist so regularly criticized by Chesterton would claim that they did not know, merely on the grounds that they had not studied the physiology of the human body or the physics involved in throwing a left hook or swinging a nine iron. Detailed, objective, articulate knowledge of every kind is dependent on and is in itself an instance of participatory, connatural knowledge. We know ourselves in the same way, not by regarding ourselves as an object, but by inhabiting who we are as a subject and identifying this with the knowing self.

Such indwelling, participatory knowledge is the way we know our family, our culture, our Church and, for Chesterton, our cosmos. The whole gift of the cosmos acts as symbol, as magical symbol, beckoning us to explore its meaning. The cosmos means something, it signifies or points to something, and if it means something, then there must be something or somebody to which it points. The Ethics of Elfland says that there has to be somebody to mean the meaning inherent in Elfland, which means that there is something personal at work

---

[50] *Summa Theologiae*, II-II, 45, 2.

in the world. As Dulles says:

> A symbol is never a sheer object. It speaks to us only insofar as it lures us to recognize ourselves within the universe of meaning and value which it opens up to us. As Nathan Mitchell says, '...every symbol deals with a new discovery and every symbol is an open-ended action, not a closed-off object. By engaging in symbols, by inhabiting their environment, people discover new horizons for life, new values and motivation.[51]

For Chesterton, reality is an open-ended mystery to whose secrets we begin to gain access when we humbly recognize it as such. For all of the wonderful things that the modern project has yielded, it is the tendency of some of its proponents to seek to dominate and master reality—arrogantly and without the humble recognition that the cosmos is gift—which draws such harsh criticism from Chesterton. He says that the gift of the cosmos speaks to us of the Giver of the gift: "Whatever it is that we are all looking for, I fancy that it is really quite close... Always the kingdom of Heaven is 'at hand'...so I for one should never be astonished if the next twist of a street led me to the heart of that maze in which all the mystics are lost."[52] He also reminds us, however, that the condition of seeing the magic of Fairyland is to have the heart of the child in the nursery: "Unless you become like a little child you will not enter the Kingdom of Heaven."[53]

The whole of Chesterton's career aimed at opening people's eyes to the fact that the ordinary and the everyday are the theatre, the drama, or the romance in which we are put in touch with the divine and, in order to have our eyes opened to this, we are required to attain the heart of a child: humble, filled with

---

[51] *Models of Revelation*, 136.

[52] G. K. Chesterton, "A Glimpse of My Country," *Tremendous Trifles*, 105.

[53] Matthew 18:3.

wonder, childlike (as opposed to childish). For the child, if not damaged and dragged into adulthood prematurely, everything is wonderful, a cause of wonder: there is, for the child, a sense in which everything is miraculous.

"Our cynical indifference is an illusion; it is the greatest of all illusions; the illusion of familiarity."[54] For Chesterton, there is nothing ordinary in reality, but there are plenty of people who have grown over-accustomed to reality—so used to the cosmos that they have become over-familiar with and contemptuous of it. One example will suffice here: if only we have the eyes to see, if only we possess the requisite humble predisposition, we will grasp that there is something magical about the seemingly tedious and humdrum task of tapping at a computer while writing a book about Chesterton. That phenomenon requires magic, for it depends upon an interlacing of wondrous facts, such as: the existence of a cosmos, the emergence of life within that cosmos, the evolution of human beings and the emergence of symbol, language, and speech; the invention of parchment, pen, ink and the custom of using scribes to note things down for posterity; this of course has led to the cultural practice of collecting books in monasteries and in universities, and the historical events of the development of the printing press and the marketing of books.

We have not even scratched the surface of the technological revolutions of the twentieth and twenty-first centuries, especially in Information Technology and the Internet. With all that going on, it would not be too much to say that the whole of Western history has played a major part of the humdrum event of a writer sitting at his desk working on a book.

Chesterton would see no exaggeration here. It is because we

---

[54] *The Everlasting Man*, 154.

have become over-familiar with things and therefore unable to see their true nature, that Chesterton states at the beginning of The Everlasting Man that it would be better for those without faith "to see the whole [Christian] thing as something belonging to another continent, or to another planet."[55] With Christianity:

> ...when its fundamentals are doubted, as at present, we must try to recover the candour and wonder of the child; the unspoilt realism and objectivity of innocence...we must try at least to shake off the cloud of mere custom and see the thing as new by seeing it as unnatural. Things that may well be familiar so long as familiarity breeds affection had much better become unfamiliar when familiarity breeds contempt.[56]

The apologetic approach Chesterton commends to us, then, is to "invoke the most wild and soaring of imagination; the imagination that can see what is there."[57]

Returning again to the traditional theological distinction between two types of faith, we can say that beliefs (*fides quae*) can be taught, but the decision to say yes to God (*fides qua*) cannot be programmed.[58] However much religious knowledge we impart to others, and whatever the extent to which it is assimilated on the level of understanding by others, it may never add up to faith, to saying yes to God in a personal, existential commitment. In the present cultural context, what is clear is that preparing the spiritual dispositions for a possible faith (*preambula fidei*) is a vital prerequisite to any communication

---

[55] Ibid., 11.

[56] Ibid., 14.

[57] Ibid.

[58] Perhaps a sporting comparison may be employed here: the author recalls French football manager Gérard Houllier in 2001, while coach at Liverpool F.C., saying that success in football can be prepared for, but never programmed.

of the meaning of faith.

For Chesterton, any discussion about the existence of God has to start from a sense of amazement that we, or the cosmos, are here at all. Waking up to the surprise of our own existence is the beginning and basis for all considered reflections about God. We and all things are magical realities rescued from the wreck of non-being: we are all entities that might not have been and for which we should therefore be grateful. Chesterton says that it is always wise to remind ourselves that, like the goods that Robinson Crusoe saved from his wreck, we are great might-not-have-beens!

When we awake to the miracle of our own existence, the existence of God and the working out of ultimate meaning are no longer merely academic problems, but rather an overwhelming question, a mystery of which we too are a precious part. We cannot stand outside the mystery as a cold observer. Where we stand influences what we see, just as standing inside the church looking out helps us to see the glorious color in the stained glass windows, whereas standing outside the church looking in does not yield such a vision.

Perhaps today, then, the tentative and humble attempt to forge a new agenda for apologetics needs to consider recasting the cold, rational methods of convincing others of the "proofs" of God's existence. Instead it might, for example, try to find ways of awakening the capacity for wonder in a secular culture, by reflecting carefully on the images and language that the Church uses in order to help people engage intelligently with their lives, their loves, their struggles, their desires and longing to connect, their sexuality, their hunger for justice, solidarity, and community, their belief in morality, their failure, their suffering, their mortality, their fascination with beauty and with art. (Chesterton believed art to be something that could help us to "say of any subject, a tree or a cloud or a human character, 'I have seen that a thousand times and I never saw it before.'"[59])

Such intelligent wondering on these manifold aspects of human reality in a secular age would be instances of what, as we have already seen, Charles Taylor refers to as the "unquiet frontiers of modernity."[60] A culturally attuned apologetics will try to get people to recognize their quests and their longing which, though dulled at times by cultural factors, will re-emerge eventually because ultimately they cannot be fulfilled by anything or anyone other than God. Desire is a deeply existential piece of evidence for the existence of God. Such desire is a good example of what Charles Taylor refers to as "the unquiet frontiers of modernity."[61] The restlessness and dissatisfaction we experience with the things of this world point us beyond this world to our true homeland, and so we will never be finally purely secular, or at home in this world.

For Chesterton, as for Christ, the way to become more sensitive to this deeper reality is to become childlike. The childlike heart is fresh, receptive, full of wonder and respect, and does not yet contain the hardness and cynicism that eat away inside us because of wound, or sin, or what the harshness of life does to us. The child's heart is one that still trusts in goodness.

But it is both impossible and undesirable that as adults we should possess the pre-critical naivety of a child. We learn in time that life is tough and that we can be hurt by people and by life, just as we learn that we also can hurt others. We have to learn that we don't always live happily ever after, and that things

---

[59] *The Thing: Why I Am a Catholic*, 173.

[60] Chapter 19, "Unquiet Frontiers of Modernity," *A Secular Age*, 711 ff.

[61] *A Secular Age*, 711 ff.

do not always go according to plan. To deny the harshness of the cosmos would be to possess a pre-critical and childish naivety, and would be something which we need to grow out of as we learn to criticize life.

However, if maturity requires that we leave behind the naivety of childhood, there also comes a point at which human maturity demands that we do not remain merely at the level of such post-naïve criticism, thinking that such sophisticated critique is to be equated with maturity. This would be the mistake of the blooming, but not yet fully mature, adolescent, who often asserts his identity by idiosyncratic contrariness. Further development requires that we move on toward acquiring a second, post-critical naivety.

While learning and knowledge are not bad things, they can become so if they are absolutized, since they sometimes then lead to arrogance, disdain, and cynicism about life and the opinions of others. If we can retain our knowledge and our critical faculties, and at the same time develop a post-critical and post-sophisticated naivety that recognizes all of life as magical gift—if we can assume the wonder-filled heart of a child, which is not the same as returning to the pre-critical naivety of childhood—then we will see that, in spite of everything, despite having had our innocence removed and despite being threatened by the dragons and witches of Elfland, Elfland is still good, life is still good, and all is still gift. This childlike quality of grateful wonder was something Chesterton retained all his life, as captured in one of his poems:

> When all my days are ending
> And I have no song to sing
> I think that I shall not be too old
> To stare at everything;
> As I stared once at a nursery door
> Or a tall tree and a swing...

Strange crawling carpets of the grass,
Wide window of the sky:
So in this perilous grace of God
With all my sins go I:
And things grow new though I grow old,
Though I grow old and die.[62]

The Church always has to be sensitive to the fact that in a given cultural climate, there may be forces or pressures that can narrow human vision, reduce self-understanding, and block a sense of wonder, such that human life seems to be no more than "one damned thing after another," and a maelstrom of immediate preoccupations. In a secular culture of baffling complexity and powerful superficial stimulations, people are often locked into a certain consciousness that makes them less able to perceive God.

We saw in Chapter II that faith is a dark type of knowledge that always surpasses the modern obsession with clarity of concepts and words. If we add to this the sense that at times there is a great chasm between the language, images, and world of Christian faith and the Church, and the world of the ordinary and the everyday, then it is not surprising that faith seems unreal for people today.

Just as, perhaps, in the past there was a superficial, conventional, and shallow belief in God—people went to church or belonged to the Church out of cultural convention—so too, perhaps, today there is a superficial, conventional, and shallow unbelief. Whereas the cultural tide was such that people drifted in one direction in the past, now they drift in the other direction. When Chesterton writes that, "A dead thing can go with

---

[62] "A Second Childhood," *The Ballad of St. Barbara and Other Verses*, London: Cecil Palmer, 1922, 40, 42.

the stream; only a living thing can go against it,"[63] apologetics is being reminded that the cultural indifference to faith that is so prevalent today is a challenge to create languages and images that can help people move beyond convention to conviction and commitment.

In a world of culturally induced unbelief, atheism is not, as is so often thought, a result of human maturity and the fact that we have finally managed to throw off the yoke of superstition and ignorance which religion laid on us for so long. Rather it is as more often a consequence of the opposite: unbelief may arise because we question too little, we wonder too little, we reduce reality too simplistically, and our explorations do not go far or deep enough. In his speech for the canceled visit to La Sapienza University in Rome in January 2008, Pope Benedict pointed out that it is the task of both philosophy and theology:

> ...to be custodians of sensibility to the truth, not to allow man to be distracted from his search for the truth. Yet how could [they] measure up to this task? This is a question which must be constantly worked at, and is never asked and answered once and for all. So, at this point, I cannot offer a satisfactory answer either, but only an invitation to continue exploring the question—exploring in company with the great minds throughout history that have grappled and researched, engaging with their answers and their passion for the truth that invariably points beyond each individual answer.[64]

Just as he did in his references to the Court of the Gentiles, here Pope Benedict is indicating that one of the tasks of the university, and of the faculties of philosophy and theology, is to protect the questions of a searching postmodern culture, which

---

[63] *The Everlasting Man*, 256.

[64] "Lecture by the Holy Father Pope Benedict XVI at the University of Rome 'La Sapienza'" Thursday 17th January 2008, http://www.vatican.va/holy_father/benedict_xvi/speeches/2008/january/documents/hf_ben-xvi_spe_20080117_la-sapienza_en.html [accessed 18th April 2012].

is attracted to images and narratives. When apologists enter the Court of the Gentiles, there has to be a deep sensitivity to the fact that cultural blockages and obstacles shape people and the communities in which they live, such that their self-images become under-nourished. The Church, therefore, must also go on to show a willingness to discover what images and stories— Chesterton's notion of romance—can reawaken human wonder and hope in such situations.

4. Faith as Traveling Together in a Blemished but Wise Church

We saw in Chapter IV that Chesterton believed that human life and Christian faith are both journeys undertaken with others. The romance of which Chesterton regularly writes involves a sense that life in the cosmos is a shared drama in which a certain number of people, believer and unbeliever alike, stand together on the stage of world history at any given moment. It is this same sense of a shared world that inspires the vision of the Court of the Gentiles. Believer and unbeliever are coheirs to the phenomenon of life in the cosmos. The desire to sit down together and discuss interpretations of that phenomenon is itself recognition of human community and shared concerns.

Chesterton's friendships with Frances, Belloc, and Shaw are reminders to Christian apologists that joyful community is built through sharing a forum or space of mutual presence, throughout the ebb and flow of the different experiences and visions of the meaning of life on this planet. For Chesterton, "There is nothing really narrow about the clan; the thing which is really narrow is the clique."[65] Community is born when we

---

[65] *Heretics*, 136.

move beyond the notion of the like-minded clique to realize that we are a clan, a family invited to share the cosmos and brothers and sisters of a common God for whom the differences, gifts, agreements, and disagreements are all part of the romance that forge community. Community grows not because people necessarily always see eye to eye on certain things.

Of course, it has to be recognized that so often the sheer hard work, pain, sacrifice, and disappointments which we encounter in building and maintaining community can leave us discouraged, even bitterly disappointed. From a Christian perspective, however, since human beings are made for community because they are made in the image of the Trinitarian God, to avoid the demands of community is to act against one's own nature, which in turn makes the possibility of finding and living Christian faith more difficult. If people will not commit themselves to each other in lasting relationship throughout the messiness and disappointments of life, the face of God becomes less easy to discern. In spite of its insistence that human meaning is always provisional and uncertain, postmodernity's rediscovery of the need for human solidarity and mutual concern offers renewed hope for the possibilities of faith, since the human journey toward God is never a solitary one.

In a postmodern culture allergic to institutions and their overarching historical narratives, however, it is not always easy to offer an apology for the Church. The blemishes of a sinful Church are a painful subject for many people today, and there is also a more general suspicion and scepticism displayed toward institutions and authority. We saw in Chapter IV that Chesterton was not slow to criticize the Church when required. For example:

...against the Church of Pio Nono the main thing to be said was that

AND APOLOGETICS TODAY

it was simply and supremely cynical; that it was…founded…on the worldly counsel to leave life as it is; that it was not the inspirer of hopes, of reward and miracle, but the enemy, the cool and skeptical enemy, of hope of any kind of description.[66]

Chesterton stated that he was "entirely on the side of the revolutionists. They are really right always to be suspecting human institutions; they are right not to put their trust in princes nor in any child of man."[67] Chesterton would think that a postmodern suspicion of the Church is somewhat justified because of the sinfulness of the human condition.

However, hand in hand with this justification of one postmodern claim goes the contradiction of another postmodern tenet—about the Church's theological claims. "When the world goes wrong, it proves rather that the Church is right. The Church is justified, not because her children do not sin, but because they do."[68] From a Chestertonian perspective, then, postmodernity is both right and wrong about the Church: while we must never simplistically identify Church membership with Christian faith, nevertheless the Church contains much wisdom about the human condition in this world and remains the essential home and servant of faith in the Christ who is the revelation to humanity of both God and the human person. Christianity is both theology and anthropology.

For Chesterton, the Church is not some institution founded on a Nietzchean vision of power or perfection:

The things that have been founded on the fancy of the Superman have died with the dying civilisations which alone have given them birth. When Christ at a symbolic moment was establishing his great

---

[66] *Robert Browning*, 142.

[67] *Orthodoxy*, 321.

[68] *The Everlasting Man*, 10.

society, He chose for its corner-stone neither the brilliant Paul nor the mystic John, but a shuffler, a snob, a coward—in a word, a man. And upon this rock He has built His Church, and the gates of Hell have not prevailed against it.[69]

The Church, like any group of human beings, is not neatly divided into simplistic categories of "saints" and "sinners"; rather, it is a group of people who are sometimes good and sometimes bad, sometimes loving, sometimes sinful. The Church, like any other family, government or institution, has betrayed its own principles many times in history. In Chapter IV we witnessed how Chesterton points out that sinfulness is part of the life of the Church, but that the world beyond the Church need not feel smug about that: "The Church has been cruel; but the world has been much more cruel. The Church has plotted; but the world has plotted much more. The Church has been superstitious: but it has never been so superstitious as the world is when left to itself."[70]

A culturally attuned apologetics needs to acknowledge with total honesty the blemishes of the Church; but it must also be able to articulate the ways in which the Church has served and continues to serve the world with its wisdom. "How can we say that the Church wishes to bring us back into the Dark Ages? The Church was the only thing that ever brought us out of them."[71] The foundation of the universities and the immense body of scholarship left behind by the likes of Aquinas, who acted as a bridge between the wisdom of antiquity and the modern period, flatly contradicts the commonly voiced opinion that the Church has always been some reactionary force

---

[69] *Heretics*, 70.

[70] *Illustrated London News*, 14th December 1907, *Collected Works* 27:604.

[71] *Orthodoxy*, 352.

for obscurantism and ignorance. Apologists can also point to many other historical examples of how the Church has served the world in love.

This brings us to a final, more personal truth, and one that Chesterton clearly perceives. The reason that all of these imperfections exist in the world—in the Church, in our families, in our workplace, in governments and political institutions, in the police and in every group of human beings—is because all of these bodies are not some amorphous, abstract and faceless mass. Rather, institutions are composed of individuals—real, living, breathing people, who sometimes choose to love and sometimes refuse to love. It is the battles of individual human hearts and lives that are reflected in the Church. As Chesterton put it, "In one sense, and that the eternal sense, the thing is plain. The answer to the question, 'What is Wrong?' is, or should be, 'I am wrong.' Until a man can give that answer his idealism is only a hobby."[72]

Any apology for the Church must clearly indicate that the fault line between love and selfishness, and grace and sin, runs through the heart of every person and that consequently any project to improve the world must start out from this recognition. It is important to note, of course, that an apologetics which voices this truth should not seek to excuse or condone the Church's sinfulness.

On the contrary, for anyone who loves the Church, its sins must always be pointed out, dealt with, and corrected. However, it is equally essential to recognize that the faults of the Church and the world are the faults of each one of us. The obstacles to a better world—to the building of the Kingdom of God from

---

[72] *Daily News*, 16th August 1905, personal collection of D. Ahlquist, President of The American Chesterton Society.

a Christian perspective—are to be found in our own hearts, or—better—my heart. The Church remains, in spite of all its blemishes and sinfulness, a source of immense wisdom, light, strength, and love. A good apologetics in a postmodern culture will be able to help people see that the recognition of these qualities is a sign of maturity and truthfulness.

Any apologetics that seeks to be credible to the biblical record, in which Christ identifies himself with this struggling, graced, sinful, and weak community, has to show an ability to offer a humble argument for the need for the Church, as well as a willingness to see the need for its own regular repentance and conversion. Apologists must help those who struggle with the Church realize that their voice and their concerns are being heard. Apologists may need to be unafraid to acknowledge that the human rhythms involved in faith development may necessitate people spending time away from the Church, if the Church has become an obstacle to Christian growth.

In the end, however, a culturally attuned apologetics will also need to say that the human heart searching for Christ will get lost and lonely without the Church, without the wisdom of the ages expressed through the Church's tradition and without the friendships that are forged on the journey of faith. These constitute positive reasons for becoming part of and remaining in the Church, all of which amount to saying: in the Church we truly find the face of God, however imperfectly. We now turn to some of the specific ways in which the Church does this.

5. THINKING FAITH: *Questioning and Reflecting on the Cosmos*

We have noted throughout these chapters that for Chesterton the quest for God cannot successfully begin by means of a typically modern, disinterested, "geometric" approach that is hoping to unearth some impossible certainty about the existence of God. Rather, a more fruitful point of departure is the core experience of wonder at the fact that we find ourselves and everything else in existence at all. The journey to faith so often gets under way because of a sheer gratitude-filled astonishment that anything "is," and that the person doing the seeking also "is." An awareness that existence is "not only a pleasure but a kind of eccentric privilege," and that "This cosmos is indeed without peer and without price: for there cannot be another one"[73] may lead us to begin to perceive something akin to Pascal's "reasons of the heart" in the quest for faith. Without this point of departure the Church's doctrines and traditional statements of faith may seem mere concepts, both unreal and irrelevant.

However, while statements of faith without experiential roots can be one-sided and ineffectual, so too human experiences, without the understanding that can come from the doctrines of the Church's tradition that help interpret them, will fade ultimately into insignificance. If God is the source of every good, then both experience and doctrine will reveal something of the face of God. That is to say, both a lived curiosity, born of wonder, and the wisdom of the ages, harvested from the concrete experiences of countless people and then handed on to those who came after them via the Church's tradition, will help people in their faith journeys.

---

[73] Ibid., 268.

Chesterton believed in using the human mind to the full in seeking answers to the important questions about life and God. He also maintained that we do not have to reinvent the wheel for the road of life, nor have we to cast aside the traditional and trusted maps for the journey on that road. In Chapter III, having noted that Chesterton claimed that he became a Christian because Christianity confirmed and illuminated with its doctrines the abundant evidence for the existence of God which he had already discovered for himself in his personal experience, we concentrated on two pointers for the existence of God which Chesterton discerned in a wonder-filled and paradoxical cosmos: contingency and morality. His Ethics of Elfland was rooted in a spirit of awe and gratitude for the gift of a cosmos, a spirit acquired after a long Augustinian inner struggle, and which boiled down to the fundamental realization that "this world does not explain itself."[74]

For Chesterton, honest reflection will acknowledge the fiduciary foundations—the unproved and unprovable assumptions—on which all thought, logic, and argument depend: several prior acts of faith are required if the world is going to function at all. (One example: the notion that there is a link between human thought processes and reality.) Human reason is only aroused once something mysterious and primordial in it—the consciousness of being—encounters reality. To submit to being, which is there long before we learn how to reason about it (which is to say that we find ourselves in medias res long before we begin to inquire into and interpret reality) is to receive it as utterly unnecessary, contingent gift, and this is the first necessary step before any other rational and scientific endeavor can occur in the cosmos. A human being finds herself

[74] *Orthodoxy*, 268.

already in the middle of the drama of life long before her reason starts to perform rationally.

In other words, rationality only comes into play after there is a meeting between the external world and the mysterious and primordial consciousness of ens or being in the human heart or soul. Rather than accepting that reality and the recognition of reality meet in the human observer, the typically modern philosopher asks whether we can ever really know reality. However, if the answer to that question is no, then we will "never answer any question, never ask any question, never even exist intellectually, to answer or to ask." The choice is stark: "Either there is no philosophy, no philosophers, no thinkers, no thought, no anything; or else there is a real bridge between the mind and reality."[75]

One has first to receive the gift of being as truth before one can proceed to enjoy as many human adventures as one likes, whether these be scientific, artistic, or of any other nature. Chesterton is advocating the abandonment of the mere pursuit of cleverness in order to enter a deeper level of questioning and wondering. It is the difference between asking "How?" and asking "Why?"

Chesterton's study on Aquinas shows how modern philosophy can go astray when it refuses to bow first before the gift of being, by confusing the questions of "how" and "why." To acknowledge the priority of being is to acknowledge one's own contingency and the contingency of the whole cosmos, which is to acknowledge oneself as creature before the Creator. The finite, contingent and incomplete things of the cosmos change and can only be explained as part of something that is complete and does not change. The things of the cosmos and the cosmos

---

[75] Ibid., 147-9.

itself are simply not all that they can be. Chesterton perceives that at every moment of their existence, all contingent beings are actively being maintained in existence by God, *ipsum esse subsistens*. It is this same recognition, of course, which led Chesterton's hero Aquinas to explore ways of arguing for the existence of God.

Chesterton also notes that the strange and varied phenomena of the cosmos (such as sunsets, or eggs turning into chickens) repeat themselves again and again. Although science refers to these repetitions as laws, this is for Chesterton an illicit move. Science may only use the word repetition according to its own conceptual framework, since the use of the word "law" implies a Lawgiver: that is to say, it introduces a personal factor, by implying that there is something personal at work in the cosmos, which is to go beyond the methodology of the natural sciences.

Chesterton agrees, however, that it is factually correct to speak of laws, and that the things and events of the cosmos do indeed point to a Person with free will, which also implies purpose or meaning. The cosmos does in truth have significance, according to Chesterton: it points to something; it means something and, if it means something, then there must be something personal behind the meaning which intends that meaning. This is why Chesterton says that when asked why things are the way they are in Fairyland, "We must answer that it is magic."[76]

Most people operate in life as if there is meaning to life, and so most people have a sense of ultimate reality, an ultimate interpretation of the worth of life; whether they formulate it explicitly or not, they act out of it. Elfland offers many instances of people speaking and behaving in ways that seem to contradict their stated beliefs. One of these ways is in the human

---

[76] *Orthodoxy*, 255.

discernment of "the good"—or morality. As Chesterton commented about a conversation he had had during his struggles at the Slade, when his interlocutor had said to him that, "Good and evil, truth and falsehood, folly and wisdom are only aspects of the same upward movement of the universe," even if one cannot discern any difference between good or bad, or true and false, the question still has to be asked: "what is the difference between up and down?"[77]

Nihilistic atheists may invest their lives, words, and actions with a sense of proximate truth and value, even as they deny the ultimate significance of reality. All human beings, whatever their formulations about the ultimate significance of life in the cosmos, live with purposes or teleologies (be they related to morals, the family, the workplace and career, politics, aesthetics, education, sex, etc.) which motivate them, get them out of bed in the morning and provide anchors in meaning. To do this is to understand one's life as related to some absolute. Feuerbach and Marx have pointed out that, although we naturally act every day with some reference to an absolute, this does not necessarily imply that some absolute exists.

However, this is to miss an important point: what is being maintained by people of faith against such a projectionist theory is not that we need or want a God, and so in accordance with that desire act as though there were one; rather, we function naturally or spontaneously as human beings in this cosmos in a way that indicates that somehow, unthematically, we have already apprehended the existence of that God. The real questions, then, are whether an objective morality can be sustained coherently without a transcendent Creator God, and whether the clearly observed presence of moral principles in the world

[77] *Autobiography*, 159.

point to an ultimate meaning to the cosmos? Does a theistic or an atheistic worldview offer the better foundation for the ultimate and binding nature of the phenomenon of morality?

Even if the atheist does not see the incoherence between positing the ultimately significant nature of morality in an ultimately absurd cosmos, Karl Rahner uses the notions of the categorical/thematic and the transcendental/unthematic in order to elucidate more positive ways of interpreting this contradiction from a Christian perspective—that is, as an implicit and unconscious response to the plurality of ways in which the gift of the Creator's self-communication is mediated.

Rahner sees the implicit responses to God on the part of both unbeliever and believer alike as being evidenced especially in the ways in which human beings treat one another. If we recall Chesterton's notion of the doctrine of conditional joy, which says that it is only by obeying certain rules (which one does not have to obey, since one is free) that one can live joyfully in the world, we see that Rahner and Chesterton are saying the same thing. Chesterton holds that the choices we make with our freedom are intimately related to happiness and unhappiness. We recall that:

> ...according to the elfin ethics all virtue is in an "if." The note of the fairy utterance always is, "You may live in a palace of gold and sapphire, if you do not say the word 'cow,'" or "You may live happily with the King's daughter, if you do not show her an onion." The vision always hangs upon a veto.[78]

We saw in Chapter III that he believed that just as one has to submit to being as truth before exploring the multi-faceted nature of being scientifically, artistically, or in any other way, so one has to submit to being as good before making choices

---

[78] *Orthodoxy*, 258.

to act in this way or that way. The pursuit of the good and the avoidance of evil is an acknowledgement of the first and unprovable principle of the goodness of being.

Morality, or ethics, offers a third Chestertonian signpost to God which unites the first two: the desire for what we seek, and the nature of a contingent world that points beyond itself to the grounding of all being, truth, and meaning, come together in that it is only in obedience to the truth, to the moral law—that is to say, it is only in fulfilling the "if"—that we will be happy. In this sense, then, he is saying the same thing as Rahner. For Rahner,

> The moral law as such…is not a limitation of freedom, since it does after all presuppose freedom of its very nature and turns to it (since it is fulfilled only when it is obeyed freely), and since it orientates freedom to its own essential goal, viz. the true achievement of the person. The law (qua liberating law of freedom) can do this, to be sure, only if it is more than a merely destructive demand which provokes guilt, i.e., in so far as it is not a demand made on the powerless from without but the imperative expression of a power from within which is granted to the person in the concrete order of salvation only by the pneuma of God.[79]

Conscience is an inner spiritual power whose origin is found in God, but the moral law to which the human person is summoned to submit his conscience is not some external and arbitrary command that stands as a negative or threatening force, somehow in competition with the human person; rather, it is the very sine qua non of the flourishing and dignity of the human person.

For Chesterton, morality unites the Augustinian inner desires of human beings, who are driven outside of themselves by eros to find what it is that they seek, and the external, utterly

---

[79] *Theological Investigations*, Vol. II, 249.

contingent world, which points beyond itself to the God who is the grounding of all being, truth, and meaning. Internal human desire and the external world meet in the voice of moral conscience, since it is only in obedience to the rules of the pre-existent reality—the truth of the moral law—that human beings can live joyfully.

For Chesterton, then, just as one has first to receive being as gift if one is to see the truth of it, and only then can one explore it properly. So to want some good, to perceive the goodness of being, one must first accept it as a gift from a giver, and only then can one have it and desire it properly. There is a personal intention behind the goodness of being—a Person who is the source of all that is good. The Lawgiver stands behind the law.

Chesterton then goes on in *Orthodoxy* to discuss some of the implications of the notion of a personal principle grounding the moral law. He shows how the existence of a Moral Absolute is the necessary condition for progress in general, moral revolution and moral progress, the link between moral progress and human happiness, and the eternal vigilance that is required (because of the human proclivity to sin) to ensure that human beings keep pursuing the good and thereby continue to flourish.

Having reflected on his own unhappiness and believing in the worthiness of trying to resolve that unhappiness, Chesterton set out on a quest to discover the good, which led him to discover the voice of conscience as a doorway to God. He realized that this internal way of reflecting on the world was a foundational, pre-rationalistic way of tuning in to reality. To wrestle with the free choice between good and bad, and to face the joy or misery that ensues from making that choice, is to engage with reality in another way, beyond the merely rational.

Conscience is, therefore, an invitation to listen to the cosmos once again with reverence and respect, in a spirit of receptivity, and not to view the world as something owed to oneself and the lives of others as mere satellites to one's own existence. The whispers of conscience constitute a gentle but insistent question, which we need to answer for ourselves: do we trust or doubt the ultimate significance of the cosmos?

Perhaps a contemporary apologetics could learn from Chesterton that the Church needs to take seriously and support the efforts of unbelievers to make the world a place in which all that is good, true, beautiful, noble, and truly human can flourish, and at the same time also engage in patient, humble, and respectful conversation with unbelievers, in order that they may better elucidate the philosophical foundations of their virtuous efforts on behalf of the world.

Of course, there is a long Church tradition of hard, intelligent thinking about the various problems and riddles of reality. Throughout its history, when at its best, the Church has a long and impressive record of mediating between the Gospel and the specific needs of the people of the world. Later in this chapter we shall look at the very specific and concrete nature of the Christian proclamation, which is that the Word of God became flesh in the Everlasting Man, the historical figure of Jesus of Nazareth.

This is a claim that causes no small degree of nervousness and even hostility in a postmodern culture. For the moment we shall remind ourselves that in a complex world the apologist has a duty to reflect seriously on ways of making the faith credible, thereby addressing both the difficulties of believers and the objections or doubts of unbelievers, and that the Church's treasure chest of wisdom is an essential tool in that task.

Chesterton is not slow to warn the Church against closing itself to dialogue with the world, lest its theology become too narrow, and he knows that sin can affect the Church and its theology as it does any institution. Nonetheless, he maintains that the Church's traditions, teachings, and structures are born of the desire to offer to the world the key of Christ, who opens the door of life. The key of the Gospel, like any key, has to be elaborate because the world is a labyrinth of mysteries and complex riddles.

The only simple thing about the key is that it opens the door. It is natural to human beings to discover doctrines that express the relationship between the finite human mind and reality, which is full of paradox, since it is the gift of an infinite Creator. A human being "can be defined as an animal that makes dogmas."[80] So the Church's theological task is to harvest true dogmas and make them accessible for the world, thereby offering people "the complete philosophy which keeps a man sane; and not some single fragment of it."[81]

The Church, like Chesterton himself, holds together paradoxes, holding in tension multiple goods, which can be a source of confusion and irritation for those who wish to reduce the complexity of reality. In a culture driven by sound bites or clichés, the publication of a phrase such as, "The Church is opposed to X" will attract more readers or hits on the internet than the more truthful phrase, "The Church is opposed to X, if X is considered in isolation from Y and Z." Maintaining X, Y, and Z in equilibrium is what Chesterton refers to as the thrill of orthodoxy.

Of course, this is hard work and, as in Western culture today, so in Chesterton's day—people yearned for a simplified philanthropic religion that insisted merely on human beings loving each other. Chesterton, however, reminds us that, "You cannot make a success of anything, even loving, entirely without

---

[80] *Heretics*, 196-7.

[81] *The Thing: Why I Am a Catholic, Collected Works* Vol. 3, 307.

thinking."[82] The Church's theology exists to achieve the practical goal of helping human beings to live well; that is, to love. "When things will not work, you must have the thinker, the man who has some doctrine about why they work at all. It is wrong to fiddle while Rome is burning; but it is quite right to study the theory of hydraulics while Rome is burning."[83]

Theology is a way of reflecting on the Christ who is the door to life, both here and hereafter; one of the tasks of theology at its best is to be a means to the end of human flourishing. The Church's theology, and the apologist who is part of the Church's theological enterprise, must be in dialogue with other worldviews in order to learn about anything that is good, true, and beautiful, since all of this comes from the hand of God. In doing this work, apologetics will be able to help coordinate all that is good, true, and beautiful, placing it in a matrix with the other instances of the good, true, and the beautiful that constitute the Church's tradition. Apologetics can thus help save what has been found outside the Church from the historically attested pagan tendency toward self-destruction.

Though he knew about the danger of traditionalism and ossification in organized religion, Chesterton's impressive familiarity with the history of paganism in antiquity made him even more worried about disorganized religion! "Nothing on earth needs to be organised so much as Mysticism...The only way of keeping it healthy is to have some rules, some responsibilities, some definitions of dogma and moral function."[84]

The Church's theology is complex because, just as "It is always simple to fall; there is an infinity of angles at which one

---

[82] Ibid.

[83] *What's Wrong with the World*, 19.

[84] Cited in a letter in Ward, *GKC*, 370.

falls, only one at which one stands."[85] So too, Chesterton contends, it is very easy to be less than human, less than fully alive, because there are endless incorrect ideas about the cosmos. For this reason the Church makes itself "acquainted with ideas, and moves among them like a lion-tamer," whereas, "The man of no ideas will find the first idea fly to his head like wine to the head of a teetotaller."[86]

The Church has to discern the value of all ideas because:

> …if some small mistake were made in doctrine, huge blunders might be made in human happiness. A sentence phrased wrong about the nature of symbolism would have broken all the best statues in Europe. A slip in the definitions might stop all the dances; might wither all the Christmas trees or break all the Easter eggs.[87]

Theology, then, is not about being clever and splitting academic hairs about things that are irrelevant to most people's lives; rather, it consists of the complex task of unpacking the Gospel message of Christ and letting his light shine on our lives and his wisdom nourish our hearts so that human life is something worth living. The Church's tradition is there to help people to live life to the full. "Catholic doctrine and discipline may be walls; but they are the walls of a playground."[88] The walls are there to protect "a rule and order, [and] the chief aim of that order [i]s to give room for good things to run wild."[89]

Using a favorite theme of his—the continuity and discontinuity between the pagan worldview and the Christian creed—Chesterton stresses that:

---

[85] *Orthodoxy*, 306.

[86] *Heretics*, 202.

[87] *Orthodoxy*, 305.

[88] *Orthodoxy*, 350.

[89] Ibid., 300.

Christianity is the only frame which has preserved the pleasure of Paganism. We might fancy some children playing on the flat grassy top of some tall island in the sea. So long as there was a wall round the cliff's edge they could fling themselves into every frantic game and make the place the noisiest of nurseries. But the walls were knocked down, leaving the naked peril of the precipice. They did not fall over; but when their friends returned to them they were all huddled in terror in the centre of the island; and their song had ceased.[90]

Paradoxically, the theological task that is sometimes assumed to be an ecclesial way of suppressing human freedom, creativity, and self-expression, is more often than not the very thing that guarantee those human values.

In Chapter III we saw that Chesterton believed that tradition was the democracy of the dead; it is the refusal to give a voice only to those who happen to be alive and walking the Earth today. We also saw in the fourth chapter that he thought that, "The Catholic Church is the only thing that saves a man from the degrading slavery of being a child of his age."[91] He looks upon the Church's perennial task of theological reflection as providing a map that prevents "people from making old mistakes; from making them over and over again forever, as people always do if they are left to themselves."

Chesterton reminds us that any apologetics must proclaim that people can learn from the past in order to translate God's message, meaning, and love for human beings in a variety of cultural and personal situations here and now, in the present. Precisely because human beings do not live for a thousand years, because life is short and because searching down blind alleys can be a lonely, time-consuming and dangerous affair, the Church's tradition "does prevent men from wasting their time

---

[90] Ibid., 350.

[91] *The Catholic Church and Conversion*, Collected Works Vol. 3, 110.

or losing their lives upon paths that have been found futile or disastrous again and again in the past."[92]

Sometimes what is new and strange can be so novel or powerful that it can overwhelm us and thereby corrode our faith and capacities for living well. The Church can help people from wandering in lonely isolation into mistakes and the difficulties and debilitating situations that can arise from those errors:

> We awake at our birth staring at a very funny place. After serious examination of it we receive two fairly definite impressions; the first, delight, and the second fear. The first leads us to dance and kick about in the sunlight; the second leads us not to do it too much for fear we should get sunstroke. The first leads us, that is to say, to institute festivals and so create art. The second leads us to institute rules and so create morality. One tells us that the praise of the Lord is the beginning of art, the other, that the fear of the Lord is the beginning of wisdom. And in the days of religion…these two things, however exaggerated in one direction or another, were still parts of a whole.[93]

The Church's doctrines and dogmas are indeed the walls around a playground: they are there to help human beings flourish and enjoy life in this cosmos. God's grace is so abundant that honest seekers outside the Church will certainly discover that they will be able to flourish in myriad ways, even if they are unaware that it is by the Spirit of the risen Christ that they do so. The signposts of doctrine that mark the well-trodden paths of destructive behavior and errors of thinking demonstrate one of the perennial tasks of the Church's theological tradition—that of guarding against the self-ruination and disintegration that follow on from not thinking things through and from ignoring the wise warnings of the history of human experience.

---

[92] *The Thing: Why I am a Catholic, Collected Works* Vol. 3, 129.

[93] *Daily News*, 1st August 1903, cited in *TTFT*, 238.

Still, the Church's theology must also constantly guard against shutting itself off from the world, reducing itself to a merely internal or "in-house" conversation that is out of touch with cultural realities, the concrete lives of people, and their honest searching and aspirations. Then the Church's tradition would lose all its potential to be nourishment for the life of the world—it would become ossified, colorless, bland, devoid of energy, and it would lead, not to moral irresponsibility and the personal disintegration of human beings, but to the equal and opposite error of an overly cautious and joyless frigidity toward God's gift of life. It is to that concern that we now turn.

6. HUMBLE FAITH: *Dialogue of Church with Culture and the Provisional Nature of the Expressions of Faith*

The Ethics of Elfland captures the fundamental experience of contingency, which Chesterton saw as the principle of unity of all reality and the link between that reality and its transcendent source. All aspects of reality point to the Creator God. We get glimpses of the Creator through the multiple and paradoxical aspects of creation. In solitude, in recognizing ourselves as separate parts of a creation which we intuit to be one, we are opened up to the possibility of relationship with creatures similar to ourselves and with the Creator who is the source of all creatures.

Chesterton saw that the cosmos has a fundamental principle of unity that grounds the worth of human existence. He knew from his own spiritual journey that life in the cosmos opens up onto the infinite and offers in a dim, implicit way, hints of the God who can later be experienced in a more illuminated, explicit, and conscious way.

A perennial task for apologetics, then, is to build bridges between the explicit heart of Christian revelation and the questions, adventures, movements, and actions of concrete individuals and peoples and their cultures, which may contain much that Christianity would approve of and which would imply the presence of the Holy Spirit. Apologists must be confident that the Spirit can slowly change hearts and mold human responses, in order to forge a more humane culture in which people can flourish. At the same time apologists must remain ever-confident (as well as humble, gentle, and respectful of people's struggles) of the power of the Christian message to shed the fullness of divine light on human yearnings and aspirations.

Chesterton believed that the Church is the bearer of the Gospel key that unlocks the mystery of the cosmos. Nevertheless he also believed that the Church cannot afford to assume with arrogance that it has everything to teach the world, but nothing to learn from the world. The Church, must always, as Pope Benedict's notion of the Court of the Gentiles recognizes, remain in continual dialogue with a postmodern world, discerning cultures and historical moments and movements in the light of Christ.[94]

The Gospel will always be, to some degree, countercultural. The Church must always have more than a few healthy suspicions of the reigning kingdoms and ideologies of this world, since it has "always maintained that men were naturally backsliders; that human virtue tended of its own nature to rust or to rot...especially proud and prosperous human beings."[95]

---

[94] *Gaudium et spes* 44 is particularly strong on this, pointing out that the Church, as well as having much to offer to the world, also benefits greatly itself from the world and the authentic cultural developments of humanity.

[95] *Orthodoxy*, 321.

But we do not serve well the proclamation of the Gospel and the building up of the Kingdom of God when we gaze upon the world in a spirit of desolation—with disappointed, harsh, and constantly condemning eyes. To identify that the world contains bits of a culture of death is one thing—indeed, to discern and name all that is contrary to the spirit of the Gospel is part of the apologist's task—but to look upon cultural movements and expressions with unremitting disillusionment, as if they were nothing but potential or actual threats to the faith of the Church, is contrary to the spirit of the Gospel and the longstanding tradition of the Church to discern the seeds of the Word and the movements of the Spirit in a cosmos in which Christ is risen and reigning. The world and its cultures, therefore, can provide the Church with many potential aids in the task of translating the Gospel message for contemporary contexts.

Consequently a healthy apologetics must always prayerfully reflect on how best to incarnate God's living, healing, saving, and loving Word for a complex world, and how to act as a bridge between the Gospel message and a whole range of cultural realities and present moments. If the Gospel is to be translated for the here and now, the apologist will do well to recognize that there exists a plurality of "nows" in our world and in people's complex daily realities.

A contemporary apologetics has to encourage people— as does the Pope in the invitation he extended to people to sit down together in the Court of the Gentiles, and as does Chesterton in his relationships with Shaw, Belloc, and others— to cherish their questions and adventures, to widen their horizons, to not reduce the richness of reality, and to follow with honesty the natural human yearning for truth and the eros of the human spirit for knowledge. By urging the Church not to see unbelievers as objects of the Church's mission, apologists are reminded that people who doubt need space before their own hungers and questions can become real and living issues. Only in this way will they ever become ready to hear anything that the Church has to say to them.

One of Chesterton's poems describes human beings as "The million masks of God." In contrast to the less mature spirit, which seeks the divine in what is extraordinary and exotic, Chesterton stresses that the mature human being knows that God is to be found in the ordinary and the everyday, especially the people around us: "now a great thing in the street/Seems any human nod/Where shift in strange democracy/The million masks of God."[96]

Anything that is truly human can be the bearer of the divine for Chesterton. The Letter to the Hebrews[97] invites us to remain open to the fact that God, the Holy One, the utterly Other, may wish to speak to us and draw us into his mystery through that which is strange, different, foreign, and other to us. Because God is infinite mystery and because the human mind is finite and limited and has to struggle with paradox, God will always surpass all human attempts to grasp God and the divine ways. Expecting, therefore, to find glimpses of God where we least expect them is very much part of the Chestertonian understanding of Christian paradox.

When Chesterton counsels us against taking things for granted and when he warns us that familiarity is an illusion, this has important consequences not only for rediscovering a deep sense of primordial wonder before reality, but also for the apologist in her task of exploring and expounding the things

---

[96] "Gold Leaves," *The Wild Knight and Other Poems*, 25.

[97] Hebrews 13:2

of God in a postmodern world that is suspicious of rationalist metanarratives. If God is the holy one, the utterly other, it follows that theologians must always retain a certain humility when treating the divine mysteries.

In Chapter II we looked at the darkness of the type of knowledge provided by faith, through the story of Job and his overly confident theological comforters, and the pronouncements of Lateran IV. Faith and our expressions of it must necessarily always be fragile and provisional, at least in the face of what we will know of God when we see Him face to face.

Apophatic theology enjoys a longstanding and deserved place in the tradition of the Church's reflection. All of our pronouncements about God need to be offered with a certain restraint and humility. For Chesterton, as for Kierkegaard before him, the sane mind that approximates to the truth is the one that is humble enough to grasp that reality, and to grasp the God who is the transcendent source of reality. These are complex mysteries which can only be disclosed to limited human capacities very gradually.

As the parables of Jesus intimate, God can never be captured or exhausted through the categories that human beings use to describe things; however, they are all we have when trying to communicate something of God, and so we have to use them. Ultimately, as Job discovered, one of the major problems with trying to reduce God to human categories and not allowing God to be God, always beyond human imagination, is that He becomes a God not worth believing in. A contemporary apologetics will have to remain in conversation with all interlocutors and in contact with all dimensions of a paradoxical world, ever open to discovering glimpses of the divine mystery, wherever they emerge.

A humble apologetics that is aware that we always see God as through a glass darkly[98] will also know that a consequence of this is that, in the dialogue between belief and unbelief, relationship with the dialogue partner and the tone of the conversation are every bit as important (or even more important) as the content of the conversation. In a world and a Church in which disagreements often lead to bitterness and partisan sectarianism, along many ideological and theological lines, a striking lesson from the relationship between Chesterton and Shaw is that they had a deep and affectionate friendship that was just as intense and real as the divergence of their worldviews. They laughed together, at themselves (a quality not always evident in theological, philosophical, and other academic circles) and at each other. We have seen how strikingly different they were in so many physical and philosophical ways but, in spite of their disagreement on nearly everything, Chesterton was still able to say of his friend, "everything is wrong about him except himself."[99]

Though he never hesitated to pick apart their ideas, Chesterton often defended Shaw and Wells from the attacks of well-intentioned but excessively narrow Christians, who saw these two freethinkers as dangerous threats to the Gospel. Like Francis of Assisi in conversation with the unpopular prisoner in his cell, Chesterton's counterculturalism was kind and generous in spirit, and he challenges all apologists in a pluralistic culture to display the same charity, lack of bitterness, and magnanimity. He regularly remarked on the genius of his interlocutors. He was always intent on discerning and praising all that was good and worthy of praise in the positions of those with whom he

---

[98] 1 Corinthians 13:12.

[99] *Autobiography*, 231.

debated and ultimately disagreed, before moving on to indicate where he felt their position was lacking in some aspect or other.

For this and many other reasons he was regarded with great affection by almost of all his debating partners which, as we have noted, could not be said of Belloc, whose own approach to defending the Catholic faith was always more prickly and bellicose in tone. As Wells once wrote in the pages of the *New Witness:* "I love G. K. C. and I hate the Catholicism of Belloc and Rome."[100]

Another useful pointer which Chesterton offers to the contemporary apologist, and one which is again in harmony with the spirit of the Court of the Gentiles, is that he must have a generous and wise enough spirit to perceive that there may always be a bigger picture, a broader horizon or a submerged landscape behind or underneath the position of unbelief. There are many types of unbelief whose causes are also multiple. Furthermore, faith is developmental and there are stages in the growth of faith.

Chesterton arrived at his own Christian (and ultimately Catholic) position by a rather circuitous route, and so he was always sympathetic toward those who struggled to bend the knee in faith. Faith is developmental, and there may be hidden factors behind people's reluctance or refusal to make the act of faith. Chesterton knew from personal experience what James Fowler[101] later wrote about: that faith goes through periods of development and maturity, and that people are not always ripe for the next step toward a more mature faith. Chesterton reverenced the struggles of people's quests, seeing them as spiritual

---

[100] Cited in I. Ker, *GKC*, 498.

[101] See *Stages of Faith: the psychology of human development and the quest for meaning.* London: HarperCollins, 1995.

adventures lived in the midst of all sorts of contingent events and factors. This led him to be wise and generous enough in dialogue to perceive that there may have been other factors contributing to the stated position of his dialogue partner.

We witnessed in Chapter IV the way in which he was able both to criticize the excessive seriousness of Shaw, and contextualize it in the struggles of his childhood and youth. Although he believed that Shaw was the perennial critic, forever taking the gilt off the gingerbread, he placed such characteristics in the context of his childhood and also defended Shaw from the charge of being a cynic who was tired with life; on the contrary, he declared Shaw as being on the side of life—full of goodness and energy.

We also saw that, for all his early vehement criticism of Oscar Wilde, largely because of the perilous situation in which Chesterton found himself while at the Slade, when Decadence and Aestheticism were still a cultural force, his tone toward Wilde mellowed over the years as he saw that Wilde "desired all beautiful things—even God."[102] Chesterton eventually saw Wilde's philosophy of life as being set in the context of an internal spiritual struggle and tried to interpret his outlook with a maximum of generosity.

The apologist needs to remember, therefore, one of the golden rules of pastoral care: if the client says that the problem is "x," then although that understanding of the situation needs to be respected and worked with as a point of departure, at the same time, there needs to be an awareness that every human being is partially sighted, has blind spots of interpretation, perhaps especially in self-knowledge, and so the issue as it is first presented might not necessarily be the whole picture.

---

[102] GKC, "Oscar Wilde," *A Handful of Authors*, 146.

If this is the case with addiction, abuse, or even ordinary, everyday matters such as the tale of a family conflict, it can be equally true with faith or the lack of it. A hostile or confrontational tone toward religion is sometimes the tip of an iceberg of other submerged issues: confusion, especially in a postmodern culture that questions traditional wisdom and overarching narratives, and anger and boredom, born of a fruitless search for identity, roots, security, meaning, and ultimately, therefore, for God.

What the apologist's dialogue partner formulates in discussion may in fact be symptomatic of a deeper confusion, a frustrated or undernourished hunger for meaning and, ultimately, a blocked disposition for God. It is essential, therefore, that the apologist be able to transpose the dialogue into broader horizons of vision. The contemporary apologist, coming from the inner heart of the Temple to sit in the Court of the Gentiles will have to be:

- Generous and respectful enough to listen to the story as it is told by the representatives of contemporary Gentile cultures;

- Able to hear those interpretations; accepting of the moods of his dialogue partners;

- Wise enough to broaden the agenda and keep in mind a bigger picture that will be composed of other factors;

- And imaginative enough to reconfigure the issues discussed against that broader, richer, and more complex human horizon.

This approach would commit a contemporary apologetics to displaying sensitivity to the developmental nature of faith over time. It would also permit apologetics to be realistic about the limitations of the Church in its approaches to communicating the Gospel and translating the wisdom of the Church's tradition for now. It would also remain hopeful about future possibilities for faith in the lives of the dialogue partners, even if, for the time being, that potential faith commitment looks a long way off.

To give some concrete examples of what is meant here, a child or adolescent cannot be expected to reach a stage of faith that is really firm and lived out. He is still being pulled this way and that in the adventure (at times exhilarating, at times painful and unnerving) of growth toward early adulthood, as he seeks to discover who he is, what he values and what he seeks. The same might be said—though clearly for very different reasons—of someone who has suffered abuse at the hands of some member of the Church.

People of all ages and stages of development emerge from faith as non-existent, as embryonic, or as convention, to a mature faith as owned and lived conviction, at different stages of their life—stages which are contingent upon the experiences of life. The move from faith as inheritance to faith as one's birthright as a child of God takes place at different times and in different ways for different people.

Pope Benedict seeks to ensure that atheists do not feel pressured by the Church into giving up their freedom of thought and will, and into becoming objects of the Church's mission. He pleads with the Church to make sure that unbelievers do not set aside the question of God, but remain open to it and the eros it conceals, and he urges the contemporary apologist to remember that faith is developmental and that apologetic programs must not be put before personal circumstances. The apologist must always reverence the human person and the unique journey that has helped to form that person.

As Pope Benedict seems to have intuited, people will not hear what the Church has to say unless the relationship it has with them is right. Unless the people of our culture sense that the Church has them "at heart," they will feel themselves to be mere objects of the Church's mission. People rarely change unless first they feel loved and respected. Also, unless we assume, as does the Pope and as did Chesterton, that in some sense God is already present and at work in the hearts of our dialogue partners because they have already started their journey toward truth, beauty, and goodness, then dialogue will not be dialogue, but mere patronizing and a pausing for breath before becoming a program that aims at instructing the ignorant.

Sometimes discussion and dispute turn out to be not so much a part of the quest to discover truth, but an occasion for angry and partisan polemic motivated by other, less honorable concerns. Perhaps a renewed appreciation of Chesterton's warmth, humor, magnanimity, and openness to all that is good in the culture around us are timely and apposite for the type of apologetics in which the Court seeks to engage.

The Church claims to be the sign and agent of the very concrete and definitive self-giving of God in Jesus of Nazareth, a definiteness which can be off-putting for the postmodern searcher. The long history of God's self-revelation to humanity, culminating in the Everlasting Man, and the translation of that revelation for the many and varied situations in which people find themselves in the numerous cultures and movements of history down to our own day, constitutes the tradition of the Church's theological reflection.

Peter needs to be in constant dialogue with Pan if he is to mediate God's meaning for a new generation of searchers. The Church can discern where the Spirit of God is already at work in the hungers and quests of a culture, and help the people of that culture see that the Spirit active within them and in their noble human efforts always leads to Christ.

The Spirit can gently help them see that their quest could

become lonely and fruitless without the nourishing wisdom of a community that has behind it a long history of reflecting on human and divine realities. Postmodern seekers may find all this a little too definite, particular, universal, and authoritative, if they are not yet ready to embrace the gift of God in Christ, who is the embodiment of the love of the God who comes in search of his people. In that case, perhaps, honest responses to the promptings of the Spirit in other areas of experience can help prepare them for the fuller surprise of the Everlasting Man.

---

7. Liberty—but with Equality and Fraternity: *Daily Self-Transcendence*

In Chapter IV we observed the contrast made in Chapter Eight of *Orthodoxy* between the Buddhist saint and the Christian saint. Buddhist enlightenment is found when the seeker journeys inward, with eyes closed, to discover that enlightenment lies within; whereas the Christian, with eyes wide open, seeks God outside himself, since he recognizes that human beings are not gods, but distinct entities within the creation. The comment was made that perhaps Chesterton is here presenting Christian spirituality in a rather abstract way, not totally consonant with the realities of practical Christian prayer.

The example of Francis of Assisi was put forward as an alternative to this understanding of Christian spirituality, since he was a Christian saint who had both an inner life of prayer and an outer life of engagement with the world and, furthermore, the latter was rooted in and arose out of the former. The lack of nuance in Chesterton's caricature leaves him exposed to the charge that his experience during the Slade years left him somewhat fearful of excessive introspection and the inner life.

However, it is also possible to argue that Chesterton did

indeed foster an inner life of prayer and contemplation by his lifelong insistence that we transcend the ego in order to advert to what is there to be noticed in reality, and thereby enjoy it:

> Now, the psychological discovery is merely this, that whereas it had been supposed that the fullest possible enjoyment is to be found by extending our ego to infinity, the truth is that the fullest possible enjoyment is to be found by reducing our ego to zero. Humility is the thing which is for ever renewing the earth and the stars...The curse that came before history has laid on us all a tendency to be weary of wonders. If we saw the sun for the first time it would be the most fearful and beautiful of meteors. Now that we see it for the hundredth time we call it, in the hideous and blasphemous phrase of Wordsworth, "the light of common day."
>
> It is the lack of humility that makes us undervalue reality and demand what reality cannot give. "We are inclined to increase our claims. We are inclined to demand six suns, to demand a blue sun, to demand a green sun." The virtue of humility is the condition for all enjoyment.
>
> Humility is perpetually putting us back in the primal darkness. There all light is lightning, startling and instantaneous. Until we understand that original dark, in which we have neither sight nor expectation, we can give no hearty and childlike praise to the splendid sensationalism of things.[103]

We have seen again and again that Chesterton constantly drew people's attention to neglected dimensions of reality. He asked people to contemplate, as far as is possible, what is there in reality, and not to be selective and reductive. In this sense it is possible to conceive of this human adventure in growing awareness of the mysterious depths of reality as Chestertonian prayer, at least in its earliest stages (for as we shall see shortly, prayer is also much more than a heightened sensitivity to mystery). In a secular culture in which people's attention span so often

---

[103] *Heretics*, 128.

gets scattered due to preoccupations, busyness, self-absorption, restlessness, and other cultural forces, we can remain unaware of our enormous human potential for mystery, and of the fact that it is in the mysterious depths of experience that God waits for us. In the context of a discussion on pride and the quest for its antidote, W. H. Auden echoes much that is to be found in Chesterton's insistence that we change our eyesight and shift the focus away from the self, so as to be more able to appreciate the depths of what stands before us:

> ...[M]an has been endowed with the capacity for prayer, an activity which is not to be confined to prayer in the narrow religious sense of the word. To pray is to pay attention or, shall we say, to "listen" to someone or something other than oneself. Whenever a man so concentrates his attention—be it on a landscape, or a poem or a geometrical problem or an idol or the True God—that he completely forgets his own ego and desires in listening to what the other has to say to him, he is praying...As Ortega y Gasset said: "Tell me to what you pay attention, and I will tell you who you are." The primary task of the schoolteacher is to teach children, in a secular context, the technique of prayer.[104]

Of course, in a contemporary secular culture that seeks to keep all of us regularly on the move, spaces of silence will be required if we are to find thresholds of freedom and become more able to wonder at life. Such spaces are essential if we are to discover the deeper quality of life. Quiet moments can prepare us to enter more fully into life and into perceiving the other. One can see why Auden and Chesterton locate the beginnings of prayer, the journey toward God, in little ordinary and everyday acts of contemplation of that which is "other" than oneself—one of the goals of prayer is daily to become ever more aware of the fundamental reality that we are loved by the Holy One, the

---

[104] Cited in A. C. Kirsch, *Auden and Christianity*, 159.

utterly Other who has called us into existence out of sheer love.

However, as necessary as is the need for quiet contemplation, we saw above that Chesterton's distinction between the Christian and Buddhist contemplative, even if a little overstated, captures something important, especially in a postmodern world that is fond of inner journeys and the discovery of spaces for healing. Even if the Christian shares much in common with the Buddhist or the postmodern person seeking a different, more spiritual quality of life, he also contends that prayer is much more than a quest for self-fulfillment and inner harmony.

The Christian is turned outwards to the world of others and rises from prayer to bring Christ's healing love to the world, and especially to the wounded and marginalized of that world. To become aware of the Other who grounds all of reality and who has given us the gift of life in the cosmos is also to be aware that that Other calls on us to share love with those others in our life who are co-recipients with us of the gift of life in the cosmos. As we saw in Chapter V, we become disciples of Christ by becoming vulnerable for others, by becoming food for the life of the world, and by nourishing in love those whom we encounter in daily living.

Chesterton emphasized that before we criticize others for their failings we must advert to our own—"The answer to the question, 'What is Wrong?' is, or should be, 'I am wrong.' Until a man can give that answer his idealism is only a hobby."[105] In that same letter he outlined a major criticism of the modern worldview that seeks self-fulfillment without consideration of duty toward others. First of all he observes that all religious traditions contain some blend of rights and obligations:

---

[105] *Daily News*, 16th August 1905, personal collection of D. Ahlquist, President of The American Chesterton Society.

Every religion; every philosophy as fierce and popular as a religion, can be regarded either as a thing that binds or a thing that loosens. A convert to Islam (say) can regard himself as one who must no longer drink wine; or he can regard himself as one who need no longer sacrifice to expensive idols. A man passing from the early Hebrew atmosphere to the Christian would find himself suddenly free to marry a foreign wife, but also suddenly and startlingly restricted in the number of foreign wives. It is self-evident, that is, that there is no deliverance which does not bring new duties. It is, I suppose, also pretty evident that a religion which boasted only of its liberties would go to pieces. Christianity, for instance, would hardly have eclipsed Judaism if Christians had only sat in the middle of the road ostentatiously eating pork.[106]

The problem with the unfettered modern outlook for Chesterton is that it wants to celebrate the rights of the individual or of particular groups, without acknowledging that all people have rights:

Now to me, the devastating weakness of our time, the sin of the 19th century, was primarily this: that we chose to interpret the Revolution as a mere emancipation... Instead of the right-mindedness of the Republican stoics, we have the "broadmindedness" of Liberal Imperialists. We have taken Liberty, because it is fun; we have left Equality and Fraternity, because they are duties and a nuisance. ... Democracy, in losing the austerity of youth and its dogmas, has lost all; it tends to be a mere debauch of mental self-indulgence, since by a corrupt and loathsome change, Liberalism has become liberality.[107]

This critique of the excesses of the modern project confirms what we saw in earlier: for Chesterton, we are free in order that we may choose the good that we ought to do, and are only truly free when we do that; that is to say, we are free to the degree in which we transcend the self in order to obey the moral law by loving others. This sits easily with the social conscience,

---

[106] Ibid.

[107] Ibid.

connectedness, and desire to belong that are to be found in this postmodern moment (especially among the younger generation). There is a new sense of solidarity with the poor, the marginalized and the wounded of the world, a renewed vigor to enter into the struggles of the world and a desire to work for peace: how might life be lived as a generous, concrete, and lasting response to the needs of the world?

By responding with generosity to this Chestertonian call to notice and serve others who share this cosmos with us, we discover that coincidentally, or as a by-product of our response, we too flourish. We find our own deepest needs met and our own joy fulfilled in the service of the other. To remain faithful to the call to serve others is lifelong and costly, but certainly worthwhile.

This call of conscience—to transcend the ego in order to live for others—allows God to come into view. God is the source of the call to live this shared life with generosity; He is the one who sustains this desire to live generously; and He is the one who helps us to overcome despair at the sheer enormousness of the task and strengthens us so that we can keep going and help others and ourselves to flourish.

The God who is the creative source of one's own person is also the creative source of all other persons in the cosmos. Therefore, although one can indeed meet God in the inner life of prayer, one must never forget that God is also to be found in loving relationship with others. Any apologetics must always insist, therefore, on the intimate connection between the immanence of God in the depths of oneself and the presence of God in that which is other to oneself, for the transcendent God who is utterly Himself, utterly Other to the cosmos, is the source of all selves in that cosmos.

8. THE EVERLASTING MAN: *the Spirit Leads Always to Christ*

Chesterton's book The Everlasting Man was written as a response to H. G. Wells's popular The Outline of History. Although Chesterton appreciated many of the qualities of his friend Wells, nevertheless he criticized this particular work for its inability to grasp the sheer qualitative differences between the various species of the animal kingdom and the human species, and between the members of the human species and Christ, the Everlasting Man.

There is a similar leap to be found in the radically scandalous claim that lies at the heart of the Gospel: God is not merely a transcendent possibility that human beings may seek out to fulfill their aspirations and desires—though he is that too—but is also a scandalously concrete, historical, and incarnate eternal reality come in search of us. God's search for human beings is the long story of the gift of the divine self-communication in history: through creation; through the promptings of his Spirit in human hearts at all times and in all places, helping us to find the truth, goodness, and beauty that it is native to the human spirit to seek; in his long loving relationship with the people of Israel; and supremely in his definitive self-gift in the historical figure of Jesus of Nazareth and the outpouring of the Spirit in the Church until Christ comes again. We noted how Chesterton's emphasis on the shockingly different nature of the content of the Christian proclamation made him a forerunner of the likes of von Balthasar.

If Christian revelation seems a little too definite and particular for a postmodern culture fond of promoting the journey but not the arrival, and in which many relish the pursuit but not the discovery, then it may be reassuring to the Christian to discover that it was ever thus. Since the days of antiquity there has been a constant human temptation to spiritualize God, to reverse the Incarnation, to claim that God, being a purely spiritual being, cannot have anything to do with matter, the things of the cosmos, human beings and particularity:

> It is the mark of a false religion that it is always trying to express concrete facts as abstract…The test of true religion is that its energy drives exactly the other way; it is always trying to make men feel truths as facts; always trying to make abstract things as plain and solid as concrete things.[108]

This same nervousness about concretizing, demystifying, and domesticating God remains widespread in a secular culture which avoids organized religion, but at the same time retains a curiosity about the richer, more spiritual dimensions of existence that were ignored and ridiculed by the excessive strands of modernity.

Christianity is the culmination of an increasingly concretizing trajectory which starts with the Jewish monotheism that sets them apart from other peoples of the ancient world—"[T]he world owes God to the Jews."[109] Christianity thus insists that the truth is that "deity or sanctity has attached to matter or entered the world of the senses."[110] The particularity of the Christian proclamation—far too definite for some—is that with the birth of Christ:

> …the whole universe had been turned inside out…All the eyes of wonder and worship which had been turned outwards to the largest thing were now turned inward to the smallest…God who had been

---

[108] "The Appetite of Earth," in *Alarms and Discursions*, cited in *TTFT*, 83.

[109] *The Everlasting Man*, 95.

[110] *St. Thomas Aquinas*, 42.

only a circumference was seen as a centre; and a centre is infinitely small.[111]

The utterly unique nature of this oddest of stories strikes us even more when we discover that the Everlasting Man—the God whose face is sought by human beings, but who in fact comes to seek them out—is executed in an obscure backwater of the Roman Empire at a certain moment in human history, in a single, particular, historical event which becomes the fulcrum of history: "the cross is the crux of the whole matter."[112]

There are many ways in which we express our native desire to seek the face of God and, as we have seen, Chesterton points out that all of the great groups representing humanity and the highpoints of its achievements (Rome, Jerusalem, and Athens) are present at the crucifixion scene.[113] However, we are reminded by Chesterton that "the whole subtlety of the sin of pride...[is that] this attacks when men are happy and valuable and nearer to all the virtues."[114]

Both he and Flannery O'Connor insisted that human beings need to recognize the fact of their essential poverty and their need of salvation before they can be ready for the surprise of Christ. Rome, an international civilization, which "stood for a heroism which was the nearest that any pagan ever came to chivalry," went to her doom because:

"Scepticism ha[d] eaten away even the confident sanity of the conquerors of the world. He who is enthroned to say what is justice can only ask: 'What is truth?' So in that drama which decided the

---

[111] *The Everlasting Man*, 172.

[112] Ibid., 134.

[113] Ibid., 209-10.

[114] "The True Vanity of Vanities," *G. K. Chesterton: The Apostle and Wild Ducks*, cited in *TTFT*, 227.

whole fate of antiquity, one of the central figures is fixed in what seems the reverse of his true role. Rome was almost another name for responsibility. Yet he stands for ever as a sort of rocking statue of the irresponsible. Man could do no more."[115]

The Jewish priests of a true monotheism are also present: "that pure and original truth that was behind all the mythologies like the sky behind the clouds. It was the most important truth in the world; and even that could not save the world." At the time of the crucifixion, "Externally indeed the ancient world was still at its strongest." However, it is always when human beings are at their strongest "that the inmost weakness begins."[116] It is when human beings are filled with pride and blind to their essential poverty that they are at their most dangerous.

It might be argued that what Chesterton sees as "The most deadly moral danger in my experience of mankind: the danger of egoism and spiritual pride"[117] is exemplified most terrifyingly of all by the crucifixion of the Everlasting Man. The best that humanity had to offer could not save itself. As Chesterton puts it in his history of England, "Even good government was not good enough to know God among the thieves."[118]

However, we have seen that Chesterton reminds us that this terrible tale of the Everlasting Man does not end in tragedy, but with an empty tomb in a garden early at dawn, on what "was the first day of a new creation, with a new heaven and a new earth; and in a semblance of the gardener God walked again in the garden, in the cool not of the evening but the dawn."[119]

---

[115] *The Everlasting Man*, 210.

[116] Ibid.

[117] "On Preaching," *Come to Think of It*, cited in *TTFT*, 225.

[118] *A Short History of England*, 9.

[119] *The Everlasting Man.*, 213.

The human tendency to fall flat on its face, the fact that Calvary bore testimony to "the great historical truth of the time; that the world could not save itself. Man could do no more. Rome and Jerusalem and Athens and everything else were going down like a sea turned into a slow cataract."[120]

This was all evidence of the heart of the Gospel message, that salvation comes from without. Christianity proclaims that all is grace, all is gift, and that the cosmos is ultimately, therefore, a friendly place. Human beings have to surrender themselves to love, truth, forgiveness and fidelity because in the end, the Ultimate Mystery, the God who is the transcendent source of the cosmos, came to reveal his face in that cosmos, and it was a face shining with these and other such qualities.

Perhaps for many postmodern searchers this story sounds too good to be true. Of course, this is precisely the point of the shockingly unique nature of the Gospel revealed in the cross and resurrection of Christ: it does indeed sound almost too good to be true—and yet nevertheless is true—that at the heart of the Godhead lie not the cruel, despotic, anthropomorphic tendencies of the pagan divinities, but the utterly unfathomable self-giving love. The cosmos is ultimately on the side of human beings: it is a friendly place, for it was conceived by Love, out of love and for Love.

Jesus of Nazareth, the Everlasting Man, is the revelation of a God who continues to love human beings in spite of everything. The God who loved them into existence offers them a love that is their ultimate healing and salvation, should they choose to open themselves to it. In spite of all the many things that Christianity shares with other religious and wisdom traditions, herein lies the essential difference: no other tradition says that God loved

---

[120] Ibid., 210.

the world so much that he became part of it as a human being, then died and rose again as the vindicating sign of that love and as the invitation to human beings to wager their life on that love. This is an enormous, unprecedented and sui generis claim.

It is important to realize, then, that the Christian vision understands this self-gift of God in Christ not just as something that happened in history two millennia ago, but also as a gift of powerful transformation in the present. The Gospel events took place at a certain moment in history, certainly, but the Holy Spirit, the gift of the Father and the Son, rewrites those events in people's lives today and in every age.

We have seen that the human search for the face of God invites us to recognize various thresholds. We are summoned to notice certain things about life and about ourselves, which offer us bits of evidence or pointers toward the reasonableness of belief in God, even if they could never amount to a watertight proof (which no worldview could ever be, resting as they all do on fiduciary commitments). We are called to notice:

- That we can be unfree in many ways;

- That pride and a lack of humility can leave us unable to perceive so much of the richness of existence and the God who underpins existence;

- That we have deep desires which nothing in this world seems to satisfy;

- That reality is complex, paradoxical and wonderful, and that reflection on it points to its being contingent and the gift of the Creator;

- That we have within us a quiet but insistent voice which indicates certain courses of action to be right and others to be wrong;

- That we are relational beings, constituted in such a way that we need others as companions on the journey through life;

- That there is a treasure trove of collective human and ecclesial wisdom for the adventure of travelling together;

Finally, we are called to live out a slow and lifelong struggle of conversion (honoring our insights about the binding nature of conscience), which recognizes others, their inherent value, and the fact that we are called to heal the world in love, especially in those places where people's dignity is not being upheld and their voices unheard.

The Christian claim is that God, in Christ, invites us to cross those thresholds and to recognize that they have been various types of summonses into relationship with the God who seeks loving relationship with us, a desire that is expressed most fully in Christ. God says yes to humanity in Christ, and invites us to say yes back with lives of committed, if unsteady love. This is how human beings find fullness of life.

However, Chesterton's claim that human fullness comes from gift of God in Christ—and not as the result of the intellectual or spiritual striving of human beings—may be a little too much to accept right now for some of the participants in the gathering in the Courtyard of the Gentiles. Perhaps, then, a contemporary apologetics can place at their disposal some of the other lights that we have discussed in this book.

The hesitant, the doubtful, and the unbelieving may take some comfort from the fact that all theological formulations and images are necessarily provisional in nature. The Church does not see the Answer to the riddle of the cosmos—Jesus Christ, the Word made Flesh, the Everlasting Man—as the end of all questions. The theological unpacking of this Eternal Answer in every age and culture is a duty to be carried out by the Church in every age. Furthermore a childlike (albeit not childish) disposition, a poverty of spirit that in wonder acknowledges the mysterious nature of reality, an intellectual humility that is able to perceive with Chesterton that "all things grow young though we grow old and die," will help the postmodern pilgrim to embrace meaning wherever it discloses itself.

In this way he may be more open to a possible recognition of the figure of Christ, however fragmentary, clouded, and tentative the Gospel message may appear. This recognition will be facilitated in a particularly powerful way by the removal of self from the center of the cosmos, by the erosion of ego in self-transcendence, through the daily dying that is required for the gift of self to others in love. When Chesterton wrote that, "He who has been a servant/Knows more than priests and kings,"[121] he reminded us that to serve others in love is to begin to perceive something important about reality: as Francis had grasped, the secret of life lies in being the servant and the secondary figure.[122] Chesterton writes:

> It was by this deliberate idea of starting from zero, from the dark nothingness of his own deserts, that [Saint Francis of Assisi] did come to enjoy even earthly things as few people have enjoyed them... There is no way in which a man can earn a star or deserve a sunset... The less a man thinks of himself, the more he thinks of his good luck and of all the gifts of God.[123]

Humility, reducing ourselves to zero, eventually moves us to a place in which we can perceive a wisdom that is more worthy of our deepest self.

Since Jesus is the incarnation of the self-gift of God in love to his creatures, which is the overflowing into time and space of the divine self-giving which has been going on in the Trinitarian community from all eternity, then perhaps whenever and wherever that self-giving is mirrored in relationships

---

[121] *The Ballad of the White Horse*, 80.

[122] *Saint Francis of Assisi*, 62.

[123] *Saint Francis of Assisi*, 67-8.

in this world, we are given a glimpse, however imperfect, of the face of God. To that theme we now turn.

---

9. "My will knows me better than my mind does": *Peter and Peter Pan*

We saw above that Chesterton can help the postmodern pilgrim to transcend the ego by noticing the various "others" who exist in our world. One of the more positive aspects of postmodernity is its rediscovery of the human need for solidarity and community, after the long and lonely isolation experienced by the modern subject. Chesterton can help the Church's apologists to tap into postmodern sensibilities by fostering the contemporary curiosity about the spiritual dimensions of reality, its sense that the modern notion of rationality is a narrow or reductive road to knowledge, and its deep hunger for a sense of togetherness.

These sensitivities come together in the distinction Chesterton makes between the Buddhist and Christian contemplative. Prayer is stunted and incomplete if it remains at the level of a quest for harmony among the self, the divine, and the cosmos. True harmony with the cosmos and true self-fulfillment is reached only if one rises from contemplative prayer to transcend the self by serving in love the others with whom one shares the cosmos, especially the wounded and the marginalized. Liberty always comes with equality and fraternity. One is truly free from a Chestertonian perspective when one uses one's freedom to love the others that have been given to us by God.

In Chapter V we saw that Chesterton prayed in one of his poems: "God! Shall we ever honour what we are…?"[124] To

---

[124] "King's Cross Station," *The Collected Poems of G. K. Chesterton*, cited in Morris, 135.

choose to love, to act in conformity with our deepest nature as creatures made in the image of God, is a daily battle and a lifelong process of conversion, the same struggle which we witnessed in some of Chesterton's unthinking little acts of self-ishness toward Frances.

To live a life of Christian faith is slowly to become conformed to the essential content of the self-revelation of God, which is a life given over to and lived for the other in self-sacrificial love. For Chesterton, wherever love is, there we see the face of God: "To see good is to see God."[125] God is not some absentee deistic cosmic landlord, but the God who waits for us in the people of our daily lives, who are the "million masks of God." As the Gospel reminds us, Christ is as close as the nearest needy person.[126] However, Chesterton maintains that perceiving God in others is not an easy thing to do:

> There is a fashionable way of talking about "seeing good in everybody," as if it were quite an easy thing, achieved by anybody who is easy-going. But that is not seeing good or seeing anything. To see good is to see God; and seeing God is not a casual affair; a very paradoxical homily has even required for it a certain purity of heart.[127]

In order to live the slow, costly, and ongoing experience of conversion, then, we need help:

> We have to look at men in a certain light in order to love them all; and the most agnostic of us know that it is not exactly identical with the light of common day. But the mystery is immediately explained when we turn towards that light itself; which is the light that lighteth every man that cometh into the world. Ordinary men find it difficult to love

---

[125] "Reflections on Charity," *The Listener*, 4th January 1933, *The Chesterton Review* 21 (4), 1995, 443.

[126] Matthew 25: 31-46

[127] Ibid. The purity of heart reference is from John 1:9.

ordinary men; at least in an ordinary way. But ordinary men can love the love of ordinary men. They can love the lover of ordinary men, who loves them in an extraordinary way…Men can admire perfect charity before they practise even imperfect charity; and that is by far the most practical way of getting them to practice it.[128]

It is the grace of Christ, brought by another Advocate, the Spirit promised by Christ and who is the bond between Christ and the Father, who shapes us in the drama of the daily choices that constitute the purity of heart that helps us see God. This is the immanent presence of the transcendent God who fashions us in our subjectivity and leads us ever more deeply into the fundamental religious call to love.

The commitment to others in love is another dimension—perhaps the most important of all—of a healthy and culturally attuned contemporary apologetics. If an older type of more geometric, cosmological, and theistic apologetics tended to argue toward an unrelated, deistic, and therefore sub-Christian God, it was because it had forgotten that for so many people the journey to God begins with the daily humdrum practicalities of living for others with generosity. The transcendence of the ego and the move into the world of others is made incarnate in this life of service. As we saw in the fifth chapter, for Chesterton nothing teaches us this lesson more clearly than the experience of living in "the clan"—in the family or community. The give-and-take rhythms of community life force us to choose between loving the imperfect and not loving at all.

Turning aside from his relationships with family and friends, the more public dimension of Chesterton's service of others was carried out through his chosen career. He regularly wrote on behalf of the poor, the weak, the marginalized and

---

[128] "Utopias," *G.K.C. as M.C.*, cited in *TTFT*, 150.

those classed as non-persons or necessary sacrifices in the relentless march of modernity toward the next utopia. To become aware of God's generous love for us imposes on us the burden of displaying a gritty love that cares for the wounded and voiceless of the world.

However demanding that love turns out to be, Chesterton knew that Francis of Assisi was right when he said that the secret of life, freedom, and joy lay in being the servant and the secondary figure. Chesterton intuited that the Franciscan spirit saw life as a gift to be given to others: Christianity is less a theory to be embraced, than a love affair to be lived out in ordinary life; not so much a set of ideas and concepts to be clarified, as a leper to be embraced.

When the postmodern searcher—who harbors doubts about the truth of the Christian narrative, but also longs to see embodied truth in praxis—sees the concrete witness of believers who are "doing the truth" in loving service, transforming their own hearts and the pages of history by sharing in Christ's plan to build up the Kingdom of God, then perhaps her own path to God may begin to be less cluttered with obstacles. Though a contemporary apologetics in a pluralistic and at times hostile world has to be concerned with arguments about the existence of God, it must never forget that perhaps the more urgent issue is how to find ways of allowing God's life to be seen flowing through people's lives in today's world.

Perhaps the Gospel will be more credible when it becomes more visible in Christian lives that are lived out in love—perhaps some of the old apologetic discussion about credibility will be strengthened when apologetics enters into postmodern discussions about the "livability" of faith. As Pope Benedict XVI puts it, "the Christian message [i]s not only "informative" but "performative"…the Gospel is not merely a communication of things that can be known—it is one that makes things happen and is life-changing."[129]

The mature person chooses the concrete path of incarnate love, with all its limitations, and does not float between various options in an immature and non-committal way. Peter Pan, the boy who never grew up, did not learn the lesson taught to Simon Peter: human maturity comes when one allows oneself to be bound by the ties and demands of love, when one uses one's freedom to submit to the love of others, and thereby mirrors the mutual self-gift and outpouring of the persons of the Trinity.

Aquinas's contention is that, "ubi amor, ibi oculus"[130]: love is the correct filter through which to see reality and perceive God. Acts of ordinary, everyday love prepare the human spirit to perceive more easily the God of love. By saying yes to others in love, we say yes to the One who has already said yes to us by loving us into existence. When John's Gospel says that, "Whoever does the truth comes into the light,"[131] it is a reversal of the notion widespread in a culture obsessed with clear concepts and precise knowledge, that if we understand Christian faith, we will live it better.

Perhaps credibility follows on from livability, and not the other way round? In harmony with our discoveries in Chapter II and in the writings of Flannery O'Connor, it is not our cleverness and our self-sufficiency that ready us for God; it is our willingness to become vulnerable for others in love that prepares us for grace and vision, and that makes us followers

---

[129] *Spe Salvi*, n.2.

[130] Josef Pieper explains the use of this maxim by St. Thomas Aquinas, *Commentary on the Sentences* 3, d. 35, 1, 2, 1, while explaining that it comes from Richard of St. Victor. (*Faith, Hope and Love*, tr. Sr. M. F. McCarthy, San Francisco: Ignatius, 1986, 6.)

[131] John 3:21

of Christ.

We have seen that in his book on Shaw Chesterton wrote of his friend that, given different cultural circumstances, "he would have been a great saint."[132] We know that on the question of Wells's eternal salvation in the light of his "Atheology" and when asked whether or not his friendship with Chesterton would be of any use at the eternal judgment seat, Chesterton replied that Wells would "triumph, not by being a friend of mine, but by being a friend of Man, by having done a thousand things for men like me in every way."[133] Here we see that, although Chesterton believed that ideas really do matter, that thinking correctly is important, and that intellectual rigor and doctrines are essential elements of apologetics, nevertheless even people with erroneous philosophies (for various reasons) can still find salvation if they have the right philosophy about love and the service of others.

As Chesterton pointed out to Rhoda Bastable, the real test of faith comes in the way one lives one's life:

> I have doubted if I believed anything: but I have found the trick of saying: "If I did not really believe I should not have done this work, or resisted that temptation—or even tried to resist it. My Will knows me better than my Mind does." Think about solid things outside you; especially about the most solid thing in the world—affection.[134]

Here we are reminded of the importance of the recovery of affectivity, conversion, and praxis in the faith journey, as underlined by (among others) the likes of Rahner, Soelle, Ratzinger, Lonergan and von Balthasar.[135] Chesterton takes his place

---

[132] *George Bernard Shaw*, 11-12.

[133] M. Ward, *GKC*, 370-1.

[134] Letter, cited in M. Ward, *Return to Chesterton*, 202.

[135] Lonergan, for example, states that authentic objectivity, contact with the real, is a function of

568 THE SCRAPPY EVANGELIST

alongside these figures, offering an important reminder to the apologist who is in dialogue with unbelievers that today, as in any other period in history, the deepest refusal of God takes place not in people's confused interpretations of life, but in their refusal to love.

10. CONCLUDING REMARKS

The concluding remarks for this chapter briefly reiterate the chapter's discoveries.

This chapter has attempted to draw out from the other chapters of the book what Chesterton has to contribute toward a new agenda for apologetics in the twenty-first century. It was noted that in recent Church history the ancient theological discipline of apologetics had fallen on hard times, but enjoyed something of a revival at the close of the twentieth and beginning of the twenty-first centuries. Pope Benedict XVI has called for a Court of the Gentiles in which the Church can humbly enter into dialogue with those who do not share the Church's faith and who do not wish to be objects of the Church's mission, but who are nevertheless striving to make sense of existence. We have seen that Chesterton perceived his own conversion as a coming "to Christ from Pan and Dionysus" and so the conversion he really grasped was "that of the pagan and not the Puritan."[136] We noted that postmodernity shares some of the same disillusionment with rationalism and the same yearning for the emotional and spiritual dimensions of existence which gave rise to the Romanticism

---

properly constituted subjectivity (the converted mind). The poorly operating mind is one that is preoccupied with self and which has thereby lost contact with the world. See "Understanding and Being," *The Collected Works of Bernard Lonergan*, vol. 5, 173-4.

[136] *The Catholic Church and Conversion, Collected Works* Vol. 3, 108.

and neo-paganism that were cultural forces in Chesterton's day. Exploring other dimensions of the postmodern mindset, we concluded that postmodernity is a contemporary context that offers both challenges and opportunities for a culturally attuned apologetics.

Chesterton helps us rise to meet those challenges in several ways. His life teaches us that we have to get free of the shackles of an exaggerated and overstated modernity if we are to recover the wonder, humility, and gratitude which are the essential starting points for the realization that the cosmos and our place in it are sheer gift and that they offer pointers toward the satisfaction of our deepest yearnings. Intelligent and grateful wonder about the gift reveals a mysterious world full of paradox, and this summons us to a humble but rigorous intellectual contemplation of the multi-faceted mystery.

We discover the silent but insistent whispers of conscience, which is a sign that there is a criterion that stands above and beyond the human practice of seeking "the good." This criterion is the foundation of the moral law and the judge of what is good and bad. Conscience is also a hint that we are relational beings who share life with others, who need others and need love. The appeal to the universal human practice of morality is also an indication that faith, though it involves a rational assent to certain truths, is always much more than that—it is a relational and communal reality.

The God who comes in search of human beings in so many ways, and above all in Christ, is not some impersonal force, but a Person who gives himself in gift, and calls us to do the same for each other. We will never discover our own deepest peace until we learn to live in relationship with the God who is both our Creator and our final resting place. This relationship begins here in this world through the relationships we live with others. The Christian faith sheds light on this task, and so it is essential that we do not discard the maps left to us by those who have gone before us.

Community, companionship, and shared wisdom within the Church help us avoid loneliness and wrong turnings on the road. Humility and an awareness of the great tradition of apophatic theology will help all who would speak for the Church in the Court of the Gentiles to remain open to dialogue with all parties and open to the discovery of wisdom, wherever it may come from. Prayerful contemplation of the depths of the gift of the cosmos—which is always "other" to us—and especially of the other people who share that cosmos with us, helps us better to appreciate its value and their dignity. Prayerful contemplation, therefore, though rich and rewarding, should never leave us seeking mere consolation and a spiritual "feel good" factor about ourselves and the world in which we live; rather, it should rouse us to enter the world of others with love and healing.

All of these pieces of evidence provide insights and wisdom about basic dimensions of what it is to be a human being in this cosmos. They are thresholds, all of which serve to liberate human beings at the level of disposition, inviting them to cross those thresholds and to recognize the Holy Spirit at work within our lives today. In this way we are better prepared to recognize the unique revelation of God in Christ.

If the definitive and universal nature of the Gospel jars against postmodern ears, then perhaps the Spirit-prompted cultivation of other postmodern sensibilities—such as humility, a sense of the transcendent, the recognition of the dignity of others and above all that loving solidarity with others (especially the marginalized and the needy) which is the mirroring of the self-gift of God—can better prepare the searchers of our own day for a moment of recognition at some point on their journey: that it is the very same Spirit who authored the Gospel events two thousand years ago.

Conclusion

Apologetics has a more modest task. It seeks to show why it is reasonable, with the help of grace, to accept God's word as it comes to us through Scripture and the Church…If they wish to avoid false trails, apologists will seek wisdom from the past and will profit from the giants who have gone before them. While recognizing that apologetics is neither a necessary nor a sufficient condition for the saving act of faith, they will cultivate the discipline for its ability to challenge unbelief and remove obstacles to faith itself.[137]

I believe in [Christianity] quite rationally upon the evidence. But the evidence…is not really in this or that alleged demonstration; it is in an enormous accumulation of small but unanimous facts…it is precisely such scrappy evidence that does convince the mind. I mean that a man may well be less convinced of a philosophy from four books, than from one book, one battle, one landscape, and one old friend. The very fact that the things are of different kinds increases the importance of the fact that they all point to one conclusion.[138]

1. Spiritual and Existential Preambles of Faith

Apologetics has the same task today that it has always had: to offer reasons for Christian faith—that is to say, to offer signs which indicate that it is neither irrational nor unintelligent to

---

[137] A. Dulles, *A History of Apologetics*, 367.

[138] *Orthodoxy*, 348.

embrace the Gospel—and to defend that faith against the objections or criticisms which emerge in different cultures at various moments in history. Apologists are reminded by 1 Peter 3:15 that this double challenge also imposes on them the duty of carrying it out in a spirit of reverence, gentleness, and respect. A biblically sound apologetics has to be humble enough to recognize that, though the knowledge that comes from faith is true and sure, it is also, nevertheless, always dark. This means therefore that, as with any other philosophy or interpretation of life (all of which rest on certain fiduciary commitments), Christian claims about the existence of God can never be "proved"—if by "proofs" we mean the offering of a few simple, conclusive and winning arguments which any atheist would be stupid to reject.

The existence of God is not a mathematical or scientific problem to be solved by a detached and personally uninvolved mind. The question of God is always something that involves the whole human person who has become conscious of dwelling in the cosmos. It is consequently as much a question about who we are as it is about whether God exists and who He is. There are both subjective and objective elements to the type of reflection about the question of God that is the stuff of apologetics. For this reason there is no such thing as a perfect, perennial, ahistorical or (at the risk of using an oxymoron) "platonic" model of apologetics: apologetics at its best must always be a discipline that builds bridges between the claims of the Gospel and the questions and quests (or romances, to use the Chestertonian term) of particular, concrete, and culturally and historically contextualized people.

In recent Church history, in order to assert itself against modernity's criticisms of the faith, apologetics unwittingly ended up allowing itself to be reduced to a poorer, extrinsicist caricature of the rich and ancient discipline that it had been at other times in Church history. These apologists accepted that the likes of Descartes and the other key figures of modernity were right to see truth as some kind of pure, abstract truth that could be proved by detached logic, and they forgot that faith is necessarily an interior journey on the part of the human subject who has been summoned into relationship with God through the person of Christ.

So the proponents of this impoverished version of apologetics also accepted the rationalist, positivist, and mechanistic terms of debate that had been set by the modern critics of faith. Consequently, the apologist became not so much the defender of Christian truth as the defender of theism. Possibly because of the nervousness provoked within ecclesial life by the crisis of modernism, some of the more interior and subjective elements that had traditionally been part of the explorations of apologetics were neglected (such as relationship with the person of Christ and the lifelong and costly struggle of conversion that this encounter implies).

Ironically, by trying to offer a more "traditional" apologetics to the criticisms voiced by modernity, apologists had in fact condemned apologetics to being perceived as irrelevant precisely because they had neglected some of the strengths (i.e., the more subjective and personal elements) of the great apologetic tradition.

However, in the closing decades of the twentieth century and in the first decade of the new millennium Christian apologetics enjoyed something of a second spring. Pope Benedict pledged the Church to an engagement with its contemporaries in "a sort of 'Court of the Gentiles.'"[139] This is a space in which

---

[139] http://www.catholicnewsagency.com/news/atheists_invited_to_join_vatican_council_for_outreach_initiative/ [last accessed 28th February 2012].

the Church can humbly and respectfully enter into dialogue with those who do not share the Church's faith. Although such people do not wish to become what the Pope refers to as objects of the Church's mission, nevertheless they are looking to make sense of human existence. Having observed that Chesterton himself came "to Christ from Pan and Dionysus" and that the conversion he understood best was "that of the pagan and not the Puritan,"[140] we have been able to hope that the Court will facilitate a fruitful relationship between Peter and Pan in a postmodern setting which offers both challenges and opportunities to those looking to forge a culturally attuned apologetics.

Twenty-first century postmodern Western culture is a complex mixture of modernity and a yearning for some of the more spiritual dimensions of existence that can be associated with the premodern period (but which actually belong to every period, since they are constitutive of human nature). One need not necessarily describe oneself as a postmodernist to recognize that at the beginning of the twenty-first century we are living a historical moment in which there is a lot of scepticism about the powers and effectiveness of reason, such that people are more likely to be persuaded about Christian faith by approaches that appeal to the heart, or the whole person.

It is part of the argument of this book therefore, that if apologetics seeks to reach the typical nonbeliever of today, it needs a different initial agenda that can:

- Appeal to the more holistic sensibilities of postmodernity;

- Operate not so much on the level of rational proofs as of spiritual dispositions;

---

[140] *The Catholic Church and Conversion, Collected Works* Vol. 3, 108.

- Offer "reasons of the heart of which reason knows nothing"[141] in order to go beyond the more mathematical, geometric, or logical type of God defended by the merely theistic approach underpinning some of the more recent apologetic approaches.

It may be more difficult for Peter to attract the twenty-first century incarnation of Pan to the Court of the Gentiles to engage in intelligent conversation about God and faith—Pan is no longer so much the self-assured and rationalistic atheist of the past, even if we have had ample evidence with the New Atheism of recent years that this type of nonbeliever is unlikely ever to disappear completely. Rather, he is the comfortable (often philosophically or existentially unreflective) person who sees no need for a God who seems unreal or irrelevant.

Because this type of unbelief is more existential than properly thought through, the ways of raising the issue of God with such a person need to be, initially at least, more spiritual and existential than rational and intellectual. Such spiritual and existential preambles of faith could aim at shifting the attitudes of the unbeliever of today, so that he can get free of the culturally imposed notions of what is normal or acceptable in the discussion about God, meaning, and existence.

On many levels Chesterton is a worthy patron for this new apologetics in a new cultural context. Chesterton's life and writings disclose that often in the journey to religious faith, a first and necessary step is to become free from certain things in order then to be free for faith: anthropology and theology are intimately connected in Chesterton's vision of reality. Though Chesterton was a keen and brilliant advocate of reason, the Slade taught him to resist mere rationalism all his life.

Contrary to the claims of the excessive strands of modern thought, he believed a human being to be more than a logical

---

[141] Pascal, *Pensées*, 277

processor of concepts. Like Aquinas before him—who saw faith knowledge as an act of the intellect commanded by the will, moved by God's grace.[142] Chesterton knew that thinking can only take us part of the way toward God.

Faith knowledge is partly understanding and partly personal decision. As Chesterton knew from the Slade experience, various cultural and existential factors can have an impact on this decision. The seemingly omnipresent assumption of our own day that the scientific worldview is the sole criterion of truth is an example of the way in which such cultural factors—some hidden and some more obvious—can affect the human imagination and affect our self-understanding.

Chesterton criticizes the materialistic reductionism of what we now call scientism as an unbalanced and not fully thought through type of reflection, carried out by a person who can only entertain one idea at a time. It might be added that the scientistic mind cannot distinguish between the words "How?" and "Why?": science can find answers to the former, but other disciplines of knowledge are needed to find answers to the latter. The Chestertonian vision of the cosmos is much richer than that to which scientism would reduce the world.

Like Newman before him, Chesterton offers many examples of how we have to live life on unfounded "certitudes" or "truths"—such as the truth that our beloved loves us. To argue for the existence of God with a detached, "objective" mind—as if God were something that could be put under a microscope or in a test tube—is to set out on a quest that will ultimately prove to be unsuccessful, even if it unearths useful truths along the way.

God is the transcendent ground and source of all that is, and so remains inaccessible to the senses. We can know a lot about

---

[142] *Summa Theologiae* II-II, 2,9

God and so questions and the workings of reason are essential in the journey toward God, lest faith become mere superstition; but the final decision for faith is a surrender to a person on the far side of reason. Faith is ultimately suprarational, a surrender to a personal reality that the human subject cannot aggressively control, but who attracts and beguiles me from the other side of reason.

Turning from the cultural to the more personal or existential factors that can affect the decision for faith, Chesterton also knew from experience that faith is often a fragile and unsteady relationship with God. His explorations of the Book of Job were occasions to reflect on the darkness that lies at the heart of the type of knowledge that faith provides, and on the shadows that can come from the impact that feelings and moods have on our imagination. When people's imaginations are influenced largely by pain, a negative magnifying glass is held over human life and people can become less ready to perceive the real God. Some dimensions of human existence become emphasized and others, either implicitly or explicitly, are neglected. The resulting reductionist anthropology once again leaves people unfree for faith.

Chesterton's writings, like those of Flannery O'Connor, warn against pride as an enormous impediment to perceiving God. Chesterton sees the main obstacle to belief in God as coming from an excessive rationalism that can lead to intellectual pride. Such a predominant attitude tends to view discussion about existence, meaning, love, and God as ways of winning debates and asserting one's intellectual superiority. This superficial disposition is unworthy as a stance from which to discuss anything truly worthwhile in life.

Truth, meaning, love, freedom, and other such personal truths embrace us and who we are, and we can only begin to engage with them properly if our disposition or initial perspective is right. A decision to have a certain wonder-filled reverence or respect for these interpersonal issues is required, an attitude which takes us deeper than the superficial level of cleverness. For Chesterton, then, this personal decision frees us enough to perceive more accurately: the cosmos opens up before us and we begin to see the rich and paradoxical nature of the mystery of reality.

Chesterton saw life in the cosmos as a network of analogies consisting of unity with difference, and consequently an infinite opportunity for paradox. God, the fullness of being and the source of all beings who participate in being, is the relation, sought out by paradox, which unites two different things. Because all being is analogical, all attempts to systematize thought will have to be content to wrestle with paradoxes. This led Chesterton to be utterly opposed to any form of reductionism, since this does not allow the cosmos to speak in all its multicolored and glorious complexity. Both willful manipulation due to human pride and unwitting oversimplification due to ignorance can lead to reductionism.

Chesterton saw idolatry as the reductionism of the richness of God to human attempts to control or understand that which is ineffable: "It is the elementary mathematical and moral heresy that the part is greater than the whole."[143] Chesterton sees one of the Church's tasks as being the bringing together of the insights and truths of several positions which appear to be opposites in order to make sense out of them. The Church allows opposites to be what they are in themselves, and also shows how they can coexist, finding the balance of orthodoxy that leads to sanity. Believing the Church to be the trysting

---

[143] "Lunacy and Letters," *Lunacy and Letters*, cited in *TTFT*, 229.

place of all truths, Chesterton says that the Church has to find a way of combining the truth of opposing positions without contradicting its own message or compromising the truths contained in those positions.

Any Chestertonian notion of apologetics, therefore, may never be reduced to an approach that permits only a few select bits of evidence when making the case for the existence of God. Chesterton suggests that perhaps the best approach to doing apologetics involves a logic of convergences: "a man may well be less convinced of a philosophy from four books, than from one book, one battle, one landscape, and one old friend." The varied nature of the signs or scraps of evidence "increases the importance of the fact that they all point to one conclusion."[144] As we have seen, for Chesterton talk of God may mean that we end up discussing anything. He had ten thousand reasons why he was a Catholic, all of which amounted to the fact that Catholicism was true. The different natures of the types of evidence for God make the existence of God all the more convincing.

Chesterton's whole career, therefore, aimed at doing what the apologist urgently needs to do today:

Fostering a childlike attitude of recognition that can liberate people at their deepest human levels;

Looking to critique all that would dehumanize or reduce people and the beautiful complexity of the gift of existence;

And encouraging people to notice the multiple signs that point to God.

The attention to the more subjective and personal elements of faith that we glean from his life and work do not lead to a woolly, totally subjectivist or relativist approach to doing

---

[144] *Orthodoxy*, 348.

apologetics; still less do they minimize the importance of the rigorous and energetic objective thinking that is required for a healthy apologetics (and for which Chesterton is perhaps particularly famous). Chesterton can teach us, rather, to set this objective reflection in a richer, less monochromatic context than modernity does. He looks to free the human mind so that it is less cramped in its exploration and evaluation of the cosmos, and therefore more able to harvest the various bits of evidence for the God who stands behind the cosmos.

He offers us good foundations for a pastoral apologetics that can overlap with spirituality, evangelization, and other theological disciplines. He liberates us from all that would back us into a cramped or narrow vision of reality, so that we can recast in a twenty-first century context some of the great riches of the apologetic tradition. He shows us that it is the humble, grateful, and receptive human mind—which only starts to reflect on the meaning of life when it is already in medias res—which better perceives the wonderful and paradoxical nature of the gift of the cosmos.

Such a mind, seeing existence not as something to be manipulated but received as essential gift, gazes at the gift with wonder, gratitude, and an appreciation of the contingency of the gift. Any renewed agenda for apologetics in a secular culture today, therefore, needs to help people to cultivate the child inside the adult: to interpret their ordinary lives with wonder as contingent gift, rather than as something owed or expected. Everything that we have is utterly unnecessary, and to recognize this and be grateful for it is the first step on the road to the gift of God's self-disclosure.

Chesterton, then, helps us to discern the disposition of the culture and the various Pans who are influenced by that culture; and once this is done he helps us to gather the books, the battles, the landscapes and the old friends: that is to say, through a logic of convergences he shows us how to gather the various scraps of evidence for God from the multiple dimensions of the wondrous and paradoxical gift of human existence in the cosmos.

2. A Book, a Battle, a Landscape and an Old Friend: *Gathering the Scraps*

2.1 Faith and the Heart's Desire

The first sign or piece of evidence pointing to God comes from Augustinian desires of the heart. "The modern philosopher had told me again and again that I was in the right place, and I had still felt depressed even in acquiescence. But I had heard that I was in the wrong place, and my soul sang for joy, like a bird in spring."[145] The agony of Chesterton's dissatisfaction and deep unhappiness at the Slade became the existential impetus for him to begin to see life positively and as being rooted ultimately in the good.

The primordial sense of wonder at and gratitude for the adventure of life that he had known as a child were the "thin thread of thanks" that helped him to survive the Slade and he began to wonder whether there was meaning to life and what the final end of human beings was. The wonderful things of this cosmos did not satiate his desire, but stirred it up and caused him to conclude that the human person has somehow got lost and "been a tramp since Eden." He contends that, "Man has always been looking for [his true] home... [but under the cultural influence of modern scepticism]. For the first time in history he begins to really doubt the object of his wanderings on the earth. He has

---

145 Ibid., 284.

always lost his way; but now he has lost his address."[146]

This eternal longing can be satisfied to a limited extent by loving relationships, but only because these are the best way of sharing in a greater loving relationship. Human hungers or desire are an invitation beyond time and space to a transcendent and eternal hope. Eros is a pointer toward the possibility of God. Like a pulley dragging Chesterton's spirit down on one side, his inability to feel at home in the world was the impetus that simultaneously lifted his spirit toward new possibilities of faith. He felt a sense of awe-filled wonder as he sensed that he was in relationship with something bigger and beyond himself.

Chesterton's belief in another world was a consequence of his deep-seated and long-held conviction that existence is good. He did not seek another world because—as the modern scoffers taunted—the weakness of religious people compels them to escape the meaninglessness and imperfection of this world. What Chesterton sought was the ultimate foundations of the positive longing and hopes that emerged from within.

2.2 FAITH AS A COMMUNAL SEARCH

Another piece of the jigsaw puzzle of faith comes from the experience of making the pilgrimage through life together. Traveling with believing friends in the community of the Church is a vital part of the journey toward God. The more excessive strands of modernity are wrong to insist that the search for truth is a lonely individual quest. It is a shared adventure, in which the individual subject learns about language, thought, truth and meaning from others. Mutual presence to each other in the daily rub of living together breaks us out of the narrowness of the clique in order to become a

---

[146] *What's Wrong with the World?*, 53.

community—members of a family who share the cosmos as a gift offered to all of us.

As all members of a family or community know, living together is not easy. However, we are made for community because we are made in the image of the Trinitarian God, and so to avoid the demands of community is to act against one's own nature. The face of God becomes less easy to discern without some form of concrete commitment to living in relationships. Despite the retreat into the lonely self that was witnessed in modernity, and in spite of the postmodern claim that human meaning is always provisional, atomized, and uncertain, the more recent postmodern rediscovery of the need for human solidarity and mutual concern offers renewed hope for the possibilities of faith, since the human journey toward God is never a solitary one.

Of course, it is not always easy to offer an apologetics for the Church in a postmodern culture that is allergic to institutions and their overarching historical narratives, especially in an age more aware than ever of corporate blemishes in general and ecclesial sins in particular. Chesterton teaches apologists to be forthright about the faults of the Church, reminding them that the revolutionists are right never to put their trust in any child of man. However if backsliding and sin are perennial human weaknesses, he says that this actually proves the truth of the Gospel message. The Church is the sign and continuing mediation of the very concrete and definitive self-giving of God in Jesus of Nazareth.

The long story of God's self-revelation to humanity, which culminated in the Everlasting Man, and the translation of that revelation for the many and varied situations in which people find themselves in the movements of history down to our own day, constitutes the tradition of the Church's theological reflection. That tradition contains essential wisdom about both the human condition in the cosmos and the God who reveals Himself to His creatures. The Church remains the essential home and servant of faith in the God revealed in Christ, offering a long-term and historically attested perspective, and helping people to avoid becoming slaves of their own age and cultures.

If a culturally attuned apologetics needs to acknowledge with total honesty the faults and failing of the Church, it must also be able to articulate the ways in which the Church has served and continues to serve the world with its wisdom. The apologist also needs to be able to articulate for people the fact that this mixture of grace and sin in the Church is a mirroring of the battles of individual human hearts and lives. As Chesterton puts it, "The answer to the question, 'What is Wrong?' is, or should be, 'I am wrong.' Until a man can give that answer his idealism is only a hobby."[147]

Apologetics needs to help members of the Church and those outside the Church face with honesty and maturity the fact that the fault line between love and sin runs through the heart of every person and that consequently any project to improve the world must start with this recognition. To put it as personally as possible, the faults of the Church are my own faults (even the phrase "our faults" seems to imply mitigating circumstances that can absolve me to some extent of personal blame).

While recognizing that sometimes the Church can be an obstacle to growth and that the human rhythms involved in faith development may necessitate people spending time away from the Church, in the end a biblically sound and culturally sensitive

---

[147] *Daily News*, 16th August 1905, personal collection of D. Ahlquist, President of The American Chesterton Society.

apologetics has to argue the case for the existence of the Church with whom Christ identifies himself in the Scriptures. It must constantly call the Church to regular repentance and conversion. Apologists must help those who struggle with the Church realize that their voice is heard. Ultimately, however, the human heart searching for God will get lost and lonely without the Church that is the ongoing presence of Christ, without the wisdom of the ages expressed in that Church's tradition and without the friendships that are forged by life together on the journey. In the Church we truly, if imperfectly, see the face of God.

2.3 THINKING FAITH

Chesterton sees another piece of evidence for the existence of God lying in the sheer contingency of existence in the cosmos. The various scraps of evidence to be found in the cosmos converged to convince him of "the fatherhood that makes the whole world one."[148] Filled with an inner disposition of humility, wonder, and gratitude, he had the simple and fundamental realization that "this world does not explain itself."[149]

Chesterton points out the unproved and unprovable assumptions, or fiduciary commitments, on which all thought, logic, argument, and science depend, thereby indicating an ability to critique cultural assumptions and engage intelligently with objections to the faith that are an essential part of apologetics. In doing so, Chesterton shows that the critical faculties of reason are stirred when the external reality of the cosmos meets something mysterious and primordial in the heart and soul of a human being. This mysterious something he describes

---

[148] *The Everlasting Man*, 95

[149] *Orthodoxy*, 268.

as the first consciousness of being, and it is activated a long time before human beings learn how to reason properly.

To submit to being in this way, to receive it as utterly unnecessary and wonderfully contingent gift, is the first and necessary step before any ratiocination can take place. To acknowledge the priority of being is to acknowledge one's own contingency and the contingency of the whole cosmos, which is to acknowledge oneself as creature before the Creator. The finite, contingent, and incomplete things of the cosmos change and can only be explained as part of something that is complete and does not change. The things of the cosmos are simply not all that they can be.

Chesterton perceives that at every moment of their existence, all contingent beings are actively being maintained in existence by God, *ipsum esse subsistens*. Chesterton also notes that the phenomena of the cosmos (such as sunsets, or birds being hatched from eggs) occur repeatedly. To refer to these repetitions as laws is to take a step outside the methodology of the natural sciences: it is to imply that there is something personal, a Somebody, at work in the cosmos. It is to imply a lawgiver and purpose or meaning in the cosmos. The whole of reality, therefore, has significance, or sign value: it points to something. It means something and, if it means something, then there must be something personal behind the meaning which intends that meaning.

Just as Chesterton says that one has to submit to being as truth before one can reflect rationally on the cosmos, so one has to submit to being as good before making choices to act in this way or that way. The good is what one desires and the pursuit of the good, and the avoidance of evil is an acknowledgement of the first and indemonstrable principle of the goodness of being.

Morality, or the experience of conscience, thus offers a third Chestertonian testimony to God, uniting the first two that we have already seen: that is to say, there is a coming together of the inner desire which pushed Chesterton outwards to find what he was seeking, and the external and utterly contingent world which points beyond itself to the grounding of all being, truth, and meaning. They come together since it is only in obedience to the rules of the pre-existing reality—the truth of the moral law—that human beings can live joyfully, as they share in the way of living that is decreed by the Creator.

The human heart desires unity with the Love that is the transcendent source and grounding of all truth, goodness, and beauty. Because this longing is ultimately a longing for unity with the God who is subsistent love, this eternal longing can be satisfied to a limited extent by entering into the ways of love here and now in this life, which is to obey the moral law.

We have seen that in order to see the truth of being, you have first to receive it as gift; only then can you have and explore it properly. In the same way, in order to want the good, to perceive the goodness of being, you must first accept it as a gift from a giver, and only then can you have it and desire it properly. There is a personal intention behind the goodness of being, a Person who is the source of all that is good: the Lawgiver stands behind the law.

The absolute nature of that which underpins the moral law is further demonstrated by Chesterton in *Orthodoxy* when he explores the ideas of progress in general, moral revolution, and moral progress—all of which require a perfect standard or gauge of measurement. Chesterton argues that the humble and grateful person shows her gratitude to God for the gift of reality by enjoying the gift in accordance with God's dictates in the moral law. Obedience to the moral law is the very condition of human flourishing and joy, whereas disobedience is the precursor to human misery.

Reflection on human existence in the cosmos, such as that which takes place in "The Ethics of Elfland," captures the fundamental experience of contingency which Chesterton saw as the principle of unity of all reality and the link with its transcendent source. All aspects of reality point to the Creator God. We get glimpses of the Creator through the multiple and paradoxical aspects of creation. In solitude, in recognizing ourselves as separate parts of a creation which we intuit to be one, we are opened up to the possibility of relationship with creatures similar to ourselves. Chesterton saw that the cosmos has a fundamental principle of unity that grounds the worth of human existence. He knew from his own spiritual journey that life in the cosmos opens up onto the infinite and offers in a dim, implicit, and unconscious way the God who can be later experienced in a more illuminated, explicit, and conscious way.

2.4 HUMBLE FAITH

Chesterton believes that reflection on the various dimensions of human life in the cosmos opens out onto the infinite and unearths scraps of evidence for the existence of the God who grounds the ultimate intelligibility and value of reality. These scraps of evidence are ways in which God communicates Himself and can prepare us to receive Him explicitly and consciously later on in our life's journey.

Apologetics always has to be bridge-building, therefore, putting into conversation the heart of Christian revelation and the quests, questions, movements, deeds, and expressions of people and cultures. This has to be done in a spirit of consolation—with a confidence that the Holy Spirit is at work in the

movements of history, molding responses and forming hearts
and cultures to make them more in tune with the Gospel.

Though the Church is the bearer of the Gospel key that unlocks the mystery of the cosmos, Church history reveals that
the Church cannot afford to assume that it has nothing to learn
from the world. Therefore, it must remain in continual dialogue today with a postmodern world, discerning in the light
of Christ what is happening through events in the world and
through the movements and cultures that are being forged in
the world. The Gospel is often countercultural, and the Church
must identify the reigning kingdoms and ideologies that are
enemies of the Kingdom of God; but even if the world does
not share the totality of the Church's vision, the Church must
also identify the seeds of the Word and the movements of the
Spirit in the world, in order that it might better translate the
Gospel for multiple contemporary contexts.

In a postmodern culture the Church's apologists have to
encourage people to nurse and cherish their questions and
their quests; to avoid reductionisms of all hues and shades;
and to follow the desire for truth, meaning, and goodness that
is native to the human spirit. They must remain open to being
surprised where God's Spirit is at work, as well as ever-con-
scious that God's transcendence and ineffability render all
theological expression imperfect and inadequate to the task of
describing the divine glory. The apophatic nature of theology
should encourage a certain humility and reticence on the part
of the apologist and it can provide common ground with the
postmodern searcher who is nervous about truth claims that
sound too confident.

For Chesterton, the sane mind that approximates to the
truth is the one that is humble enough to grasp that both reality and the God who is the transcendent source of reality are

complex mysteries, which can be disclosed to limited human capacities only very gradually. The Christian needs to be able to live in the midst of mystery, doubt, darkness, and uncertainty. Faith knowledge is dark as well as sure, and both natures of that knowledge need to be honored. A postmodern apologetics that recognizes this fact may provide a useful starting point for dialogue in the Court of the Gentiles, and apologists will always look to remain in conversation with all parties in a world that is full of paradox and which discloses the divine mystery in myriad ways.

A humble apologetics, aware that we on earth see God as through a glass darkly,[150] also knows that, in the dialogue between belief and unbelief, relationship with the dialogue partner and the tone of the conversation are just as important as the content of the conversation. The deep friendship between Chesterton and Shaw is a shining example of the incarnation of this principle. Though he was quick to debate and disagree in the strongest possible terms with Shaw, Chesterton constantly pointed out the good in his friend to the excessively narrow type of Christian who attacked him.

Chesterton's way of being countercultural was always marked by charity and generosity of spirit. He was always ready to honor the truth in the position of those against whom he marched, and he looked to understand the more personal, existential reasons for the position of unbelief held by a person. He teaches the apologist to broaden the agenda of unbelief and to be aware that there may often be a whole submerged existential landscape of reasons beneath the surface of a person's atheism.

Faith is developmental, and a culturally attuned apologist will need to sit with the Pans of the twenty-first century and

---

[150] 1 Corinthians 13:12.

listen to their reasons for unbelief. He will use these as the point of departure for discussion, while bearing in mind that there may often be a broader and more complex horizon against which these need to be set. Apologetics needs to be realistic about its own limitations, sensitive to the developmental nature of faith, and faithful to carrying out its own task, all the while trusting that there will be future possibilities for faith in a person's journey. The apologist that Pope Benedict has in mind for today's work must always reverence the human person and the unique journey that has helped to form that person, and never see him merely as an object of the Church's mission.

2.5 FAITH AS EGO-EROSION

Chesterton constantly calls us to notice the cosmos, to avoid reductionism, and, as far as possible, to contemplate what is there to be contemplated, without being selective. A vital element for the achievement of this is humility—the removal of the ego from the center of reality—so that we can wonder at and be grateful for the gift of a cosmos and the breath in our bodies that allows us to enjoy the gift. Although Chesterton is notoriously reticent about his own prayer life, it is arguable that his fostering of human awareness of the mysterious depths of reality can be interpreted as a growth in prayer.

The busyness and preoccupations of daily living in a secular culture can block people from attending to their native capacity for mystery and their ability to perceive God's presence in the humdrum ordinary and everyday. The Chestertonian incitement to notice that which is "other" is the beginning of prayer, since prayer is the gradual learning of the lesson that we have been loved into existence by the utterly Other—the Holy One.

As a glance at the Spirituality and Self-help shelves of most

Western bookshops will confirm, this longing for a different quality of life—richer, less rushed, more silent, and opening onto dimensions of existence that have been more recently ignored—is a striking feature of postmodern culture. There is potential here for dialogue in the Court of the Gentiles.

However, even if Christian prayer can bring (arid periods notwithstanding) a certain peace and fulfillment, that is not its ultimate purpose. Prayer is much more than a quest for inner harmony. Prayer is the placing of oneself in the presence of the Other who grounds all of reality and who calls us to share reality with all the "others" in our world. Christian prayer nourishes us so that we can rise from prayer to turn to the world of others and bring Christ's love and healing to that world. Christian prayer is not about having our needs met (even though that may happen); it is a slow learning to relax into the love of God, and to pay the costly price of bearing that love to others.

Authentic Christianity does indeed bring the liberty for which modernity longs, but it says that the condition of true liberty is living out equality and fraternity. Christianity involves learning daily to transcend the self and to allow one's ego to be eroded by placing one's freedom at the service of those others who are one's co-heirs to the gift of life in the cosmos. As Chesterton pointed out in the Ethics of Elfland, we are free in order that we may choose the good that we ought to do, and are only truly free when we do that; that is to say, we are free and flourish to the degree to which we transcend the self in order to obey the moral law by loving others.

In the Court of the Gentiles apologists may be encouraged by the social conscience, connectedness, and sense of solidarity with the marginalized today, especially present among the younger postmodern generation, and questions that could bear fruit might be: how might life be lived as a generous, concrete, and lasting response to the needs of the world, and what are the ultimate foundations of this social concern?

2.6 Faith in the Everlasting Man

We have said that faith knowledge is different from scientific or mathematical knowledge and is more like the knowing that exists between lovers or friends. It is an interpersonal love that involves a combination of understanding and deciding. Human reflection on existence in the cosmos only takes us part of the way toward God, who, as the Church's theological tradition makes clear, always remains the Mystery partly beyond human thought. By trying to gather strands of evidence for God by thinking about Him, the possibility of opting to believe may become attractive.

However, the heart of the Christian Gospel is that the true and living God is a God of love and relationship, who comes in search of his creatures in many different ways, but above all in His Son, Jesus of Nazareth. This is the scandalously unique claim of Christianity and, in order to accept this claim, a different logic needs to be operative. The human search for God may unearth various signs that can be gathered and arranged in such a way that they make sense and are in harmony with the deepest longings, reflections, intuitions, and practices of humanity.

Human beings may follow the promptings of the Spirit within, pushing them toward lives of generous self-gift and respect for others. This then constitutes a threshold that needs to be crossed: it is the invitation to believe and to entrust one's life to God. This is the difference between thinking about God (itself a Spirit-prompted act and a form of divine self-gift) and surrendering oneself to the fullness of the revelation of God.

The surrender of faith is the human subject's hesitant, at times faltering "yes" of faith to God's "yes" of love to him. It is a human response that is, once again, not merely a matter of the head and abstract reasoning; it is an existential yes, lived out in a whole attitude of humble recognition toward life, and above all in the concrete decision to love.

2.7 PERFORMATIVE FAITH

Pope Benedict XVI says that, "the Christian message [i]s not only "informative" but "performative"…the Gospel is not merely a communication of things that can be known—it is one that makes things happen and is life-changing."[151] We can point to many signs of God's existence, all of which possess a certain usefulness. However, as Avery Dulles says in the citation at the beginning of this Conclusion, these never amount to faith in God. If faith is a yes to the God who has already said the yes of love to us, our response is not merely at the level of concepts, ideas or propositions, but is rooted in a whole loving attitude to concrete existence. As Chesterton said in reference to Francis of Assisi's life, faith is less a theory to be understood than a love affair to be lived out—a leper to be embraced. When a human being chooses to love others, when she chooses the daily path of incarnate love, with all its limitations and imperfections, and does not float between various options in an immature and noncommittal way, she is more ready to understand God's love.

Postmodernity is hesitant to accept truth claims, but it longs to see solidarity in praxis; whenever, therefore, Christians do the truth in generous self-emptying love, when faith is performative and transformative of lives and cultures, then perhaps the possibility of discerning the face of the kenotic God will

---

[151] *Spe Salvi*, n.2.

become more possible. If Aquinas is right in claiming that, "*ubi amor, ibi oculus*,"[152] if love is the correct filter through which to see reality and perceive God, then acts of ordinary, everyday generous love might prepare the human spirit to perceive more easily the God of love.

It might even be argued that a more urgent agenda for apologetics today, then, is finding ways to embody Christian generosity in concrete ways. Perhaps for the postmodern culture credibility will more easily follow on from livability. As Chesterton regularly points out, it is not our cleverness and our self-sufficiency that ready us for God; it is the erosion of our ego that prepares us to see properly. To wash the feet of others, to lay down our lives for them, is what makes us followers of Christ.

We have seen that Chesterton once assured the atheist H. G. Wells that if the theistic interpretation of the cosmos turned out to be the correct reading, then Wells would still "triumph...by being a friend of Man, by having done a thousand things for men like me in every way".[153] The love of others is the surest indicator of a life pleasing to God and the truest criterion for evaluating the worth of a human life. Today, as in any other day, if faith does not make a difference in the struggle to heal the world with love, then it is not authentic Christian faith. Any renewed apologetics needs to recognize, therefore, that the most dangerous sort of unbelief is to be found not in explicit formulations about the meaning of human existence in the cosmos, but in the concrete refusal to love here and now in that cosmos.

---

[152] Josef Pieper explains the use of this maxim by St. Thomas Aquinas, *Commentary on the Sentences* 3, d. 35, 1, 2, 1, while explaining that it comes from Richard of St. Victor (*Faith, Hope and Love*, tr. Sr. M. F. McCarthy, San Francisco: Ignatius, 1986, 6).

[153] M. Ward, *GKC*, 370-1.

Bibliography

The project of publishing in a uniform series the Collected Works of G. K. Chesterton was begun in 1986 by Ignatius Press of San Francisco. A list of the individual works and contributions of Chesterton, in accordance with their original date and place of publication, can be found in the following, which remain the benchmark for locating original sources in Chesterton Studies:

Sullivan, John. *G. K. Chesterton: A Bibliography, with an Essay on Books by G. K. Chesterton and an Epitaph by Walter de la Mare.* University of London Press, 1958.

———. *Chesterton Continued: A Bibliographical Supplement.* Hodder and Stoughton, 1968.

The New Jerusalem Bible. Darton, Longman & Todd, 1990.

Sykes, J. B. *The Concise Oxford Dictionary of Current English Usage.* 7th ed., Oxford UP, 1982.

Ahlquist, Dale. www.reesnet.com/Denver-Chesterton.../ChestertonAndKierkegaard. Accessed 18 Feb. 2012.

———. *G. K. Chesterton: The Apostle of Common Sense.* Ignatius Press, 2003.

———. *Common Sense 101: Lessons from G. K. Chesterton*. Ignatius Press, 2006.

———. President of The American Chesterton Society, private collection of hitherto unpublished Chesterton pieces, generously made available to the author of this book.

Anscombe, Elizabeth. M. Geach and L. Gormally, eds. "What Is It to Believe Someone?" *Faith in a Hard Ground: Essays on Religion, Philosophy and Ethics*. Imprint Academic, 2005, pp. 1-10.

Appleyard, Bryan. *Understanding the Present: Science and the Soul of Modern Man*. Picador, 1993.

Aquinas, Thomas. *Summa Theologiae*. Blackfriars, 1963.

Aristotle. *The Nicomachean Ethics*. Translated by J. A. K Thomson. Revised with notes and appendices by H. Tredennick. Penguin, 2004.

Arts, Herwig. *Faith and Unbelief, Uncertainty and Atheism*. The Liturgical Press, 1992.

Augustine of Hippo. *The Confessions of St. Augustine*. Fontana, 1963.

Bacik, James J. *Apologetics and the Eclipse of Mystery: Mystagogy according to Karl Rahner*. UNDP, 1980.

Barron, Robert. *And Now I See: A Theology of Transformation*. Crossroad, 1998.

———. *The Strangest Way: Walking the Christian Path*. Orbis, 2002.

———. *The Priority of Christ: Towards a Postliberal Catholicism*.Brazos Press, 2007.

Bausch, William J. *Catholics in Crisis?; The Church Confronts Contemporary Challenges.* Twenty-Third Publications, 1999.

Belloc, Hillaire. *On the Place of Gilbert Keith Chesterton in English Letters.* Sheed and Ward, 1940.

Belmonte, Kevin. *Defiant Joy: The Remarkable Life and Impact of G. K. Chesterton.* Thomas Nelson Publications, 2011

Benedict XVI. *Encyclical Letter Deus Caritas Est.* Catholic Truth Society, 2006.

———. *Encyclical Letter Spe Salvi.* Catholic Truth Society, 2007.

———. "Lecture by the Holy Father Pope Benedict XVI at the University of Rome 'La Sapienza'" 17 Jan. 2008, http://www.vatican.va/holy_father/benedict_xvi/speeches/2008/january/documents/hf_ben-xvi_spe_20080117_la-sapienza_en.html. Accessed 18 April, 2012.

———. "Address to the Roman Curia and Papal Representatives for the Traditional Exchange of Christmas Greetings." www.vatican.va/.../Benedict xvi/.../2009/december/.../hf ben-xvi spe 20091221 curia-auguri en.html. Accessed 18 Feb. 2012.

———. *Encyclical Letter Caritas in Veritate.* Catholic Truth Society, 2009.

Berger, Peter L. *A Rumour of Angels: Modern Society and the Rediscovery of the Supernatural.* Penguin, 1970.

———. *Redeeming Laughter: The Comic Dimension of Human Experience.* Walter de Gruyter, 1997.

Blondel, Maurice. *Les premiers écrits de Maurice Blondel.* Presses universitaires de France, 1956. English translation in *The Letter on Apologetics and History and Dogma.* Translated by A. Dru & I. Trethowan. Holt, Rinehart & Winston, 1964.

Brown, N. C. "Frances Chesterton: A Talk Given to the Annual Conference of the American Chesterton Society, 2010." *Uncommon Sense,* http://uncommonsense.libsyn.com/us-34-frances-chesterton.

Buckley, Michael J. *The Origins of Modern Atheism.* Yale University Press.

Bull, George. "The Spirituality of G. K. Chesterton." *The Chesterton Review,* vol. 26, no. 4, 2000, pp. 455-461.

Caldecott, Stratford. "Was Chesterton a Theologian?" *The Chesterton Review,* vol. 24, no. 4, 1998, pp. 465-481.

———. "The Evangelization of Western Culture: A Starting Point?" *The Chesterton Review,* vol. 26, no. 4, 2000, pp. 463-469.

Carpenter, Humphrey. *The Inklings: C. S. Lewis, J. R. R. Tolkien, Charles Williams, and Their Friends.* Ballantine Books, 1981.

Catechism of the Catholic Church. Veritas, 1994.

"Atheists invited to join Vatican Council for Outreach Initiative." *Catholic News Agency,* http://www.catholicnewsagency.com/news/atheists_invited_to_join_vatican_council_for_outreach_initiative. Accessed 28 Feb. 2012.

Chesterton, Ada. *The Chestertons.* Chapman & Hall, 1947.

Chesterton, Frances. *Diary of Frances Chesterton 1904-1905.* Edited by Aidan Mackey, *The Chesterton Review,* vol. 25, no. 3, 1999, pp. 283-293.

Chesterton, G. K., *The Ballad of St. Barbara and Other Verses.* Cecil Palmer, 1922.

———. *The Uses of Diversity: a Book of Essays.* Methuen, 1926.

———. *An Outline of Christianity.* Methuen, 1926, http://www.gkc.org. uk/gkc/books/upon-this-rock.html. Accessed 31 Jan. 2012.

———. *All I Survey.* Dodd, Mead and Co., 1933.

———. *Chaucer.* Faber and Faber, 1934.

———. *The Common Man.* Sheed & Ward, 1950.

———. *The Surprise: A Play.* With a preface by Dorothy L. Sayers. Sheed and Ward, 1952.

———. *A Handful of Authors.* Edited by Dorothy Collins.Sheed & Ward, 1953.

———. *Saint Thomas Aquinas: The Dumb Ox.* With an appreciation by Anton C. Pegis. Doubleday, 1956.

———. *G. K. Chesterton: An Anthology.* Edited by D. B. Wyndham Lewis. Oxford University Press, 1957.

———. *Lunacy and Letters.* Edited by Dorothy Collins. Sheed and Ward, 1958.

———. *George Bernard Shaw.* The Bodley Head, 1961.

———. *The Spice of Life.* Edited by Dorothy Collins. Darwen Finlayson, 1964.

———. *As I Was Saying.* Books for Libraries Press, 1966.

———. *The Critical Judgements, Part I: 1900-1937.* Edited by D. J. Conlon. Antwerp Studies in English Literature, 1976.

———. *The Penguin Complete Father Brown.* Penguin, 1981.

———. *Collected Nonsense and Light Verse*. Edited by Marie Smith. Dodd, Mead & Co., 1987.

———. *Autobiography*. Fisher Press, 1992.

———. *The Everlasting Man*. Ignatius, 1993.

———. *A Short History of England*. Fisher Press, 1994.

———. *What's Wrong With the World?*. Ignatius Press, 1994.

———. *A Motley Wisdom: The Best of G. K. Chesterton*. Edited and with an introduction by N. Forde. Hodder & Stoughton, 1995.

———. "Reflections on Charity." *The Chesterton Review*, vol. 21, no. 4, 1995, pp. 443-9.

———. "When I Am Dead: The After Life." *The Chesterton Review*, vol. 24, no. 3, 1998, pp. 273-279.

———. *On Lying in Bed and Other Essays*. Edited by A. Manguel. Bayeux Arts Inc., 1999.

———. *William Blake*. House of Stratus, 2000.

———. "The Philosophy of Gratitude." *The Chesterton Review*, vol. 27, no. 3, 2001, pp. 293-5.

———. *The Ballad of the White Horse*. Ignatius, 2001

———. *Basil Howe: A Story of Young Love*. With an introduction by D. J. Conlon. New City Press, 2001.

———. *Saint Francis of Assisi*. With an introduction by J. F. Girzone. Doubleday, 2001.

———. *The Poet and the Lunatics*. House of Stratus, 2001.

———. *Robert Browning*. Echo Library, 2006.

———. *Varied Types*. Echo Library, 2006.

———. *Charles Dickens*. Wordsworth, 2007.

———. *Tremendous Trifles*. Cosimo Classics, 2007.

———. *Appreciations and Criticisms of the Works of Charles Dickens*. House of Stratus, 2008.

———. *The Defendant*. NuVision Publications, 2008.

———. *The Man Who Was Thursday: A Nightmare*. Arc Manor, 2008.

———. *The Victorian Age in Literature*. Echo Library, 2008.

———. "Introduction to J. H. Newman's Book." *The Chesterton Review*, vol. 35, no. 1-2, 2009, pp. 31-4.

———. *Manalive*. Serenity Publishers, 2009.

———. *The Wild Knight and Other Poems*. Wildside Press, 2009.

———. *The Wisdom of G. K. Chesterton: The Very Best Quotes, Quips and Cracks from the Pen of G. K. Chesterton*. Edited by D. Armstrong. Saint Benedict Press, 2009.

———. *A Miscellany of Men*. Forgotten Books, 2010.

———. *The Wit and Wisdom of G. K. Chesterton*. Edited and with an introduction by B. Hillier. Continuum, 2010.

———. "The Orthodoxy of Hamlet." *Lunacy and Letters*. Sheed & Ward, 1958, http://209.236.72.127/wordpress/?page_id=1124. Accessed 16 Jan. 2012.

———. "Introduction to the Book of Job." http://www.gkc.org.uk/gkc/ books/job.html. Accessed 16 Jan. 2012.

———. "The Fallacy of Freedom." *Daily News*, 21 Dec. 1905, http://
www.personal.reading.ac.uk/~spsolley/GKC/Chesterton_selections.
html#fallacy. Accessed 22 Jan. 2012.

———. "Philosophy for the Schoolroom." *Daily News*, 22 June, 1907,
http://www.cse.dmu.ac.uk/~mward/gkc/books/philosophy.html.
Accessed 24 Jan. 2012.

——— "Prohibition and the Press." *Fancies versus Fads*. Dodd, Mead and
Co., 1923, http://www.cse.dmu.ac.uk/~mward/gkc/books/Fancies_
Versis_Fads.txt. Accessed 17 Jan. 2012.

———. "Why I Am Not a Socialist." *The New Age*. 4 Jan. 1908, http://
dl.lib.brown.edu/pdfs/1140813731375533.pdf. Accessed 9 March
2012.

———. *The Collected Works of G. K. Chesterton*. Ignatius Press, 1986-
2011. Vol. 1: *Heretics, Orthodoxy*, and *The Blatchford Controversies*;
Vol. 3: *Where All Roads Lead, The Catholic Church and Conversion,
Why I Am a Catholic, The Thing: Why I Am A Catholic The Well and
the Shallows*, and *The Way of the Cross*; Vol. 4: *What's Wrong With the
World, The Superstition of Divorce*, and *Eugenics and Other Evils*; Vol.
5: *The Outline of Sanity, The End of the Armistice, Utopia of Usurers*,
and others; Vol. 6: *The Man Who Was Thursday, The Club of Queer
Trades, The Napoleon of Notting Hill*, and *The Ball and the Cross*;
Vol. 11: *Collected Plays* and *Chesterton on Shaw*; Vol. 15: *Chesterton
on Dickens*; Vol. 20: *Christendom in Dublin, Irish Impressions, The
New Jerusalem*, and *A Short History of England*; Vol. 21: *What I Saw
in America, The Resurrection of Rome*, and *Sidelights*; Vol. 27: *The
Illustrated London News 1905-1907*; Vol. 28: *Illustrated London News
1908-10*; Vol. 29: *Illustrated London News 1911-13*; Vol. 33: *Illustrated
London News 1923-25*; Vol. 34: *Illustrated London News 1926-1928*;
Vol. 36: *Illustrated London News 1932-1934*

Clark, Stephen R. L. *G. K. Chesterton: Thinking Backward, Looking Forward*. Templeton Foundation Press, 2006.

Clemens, Cyril. *Chesterton as Seen by His Contemporaries*. Haskell House, 1982.

Coates, John. *Chesterton and the Edwardian Cultural Crisis*. University of Hull, 1984.

———. "Chesterton and the Modernist Cultural Context." *Chesterton and the Modernist Crisis*. Edited by A, Nichols. The Chesterton Review Press, 1990, pp. 51-77.

———. "Commentary on the Diary of Frances Chesterton." *The Chesterton Review,* vol. 25, no. 3, 1999, pp. 294-301.

———. "Chesterton and the 'Age of Aquarius.'" *The Chesterton Review,* vol. 26, no. 1-2, 2000, pp. 29-47.

———. "Chesterton's New Style in Apologetics." *Renascence,* vol. 61, no. 4, 2009, pp. 235-51.

Conlon, D. J., ed. *G. K. Chesterton: A Half-Century of Views*. OUP, 1987.

Conway, Eamonn. *The Anonymous Christian: A Relativised Christianity*. Peter Lang, 1993.

Coren, Michael. *Gilbert: The Man who was Chesterton*. Jonathan Cape, 1989.

Crowe, Frederick. *Lonergan: Outstanding Christian Thinkers Series*. Geoffrey Chapman, 1992.

Crowther, Ian. *Chesterton*. Claridge Press, 1991.

Dale, Alzina Stone. *The Art of G. K. Chesterton*. Loyola University Press, 1985.

Daly, Gabriel. "Apologetics in the Modernist Period." *Chesterton and the Modernist Crisis*. Edited by A. Nichols. The Chesterton Review Press, 1990, pp. 79-93.

Davies, R. "Memories of G.K.C." *Pax*, vol. 26, no. 178, 1936, p. 115.

De Lubac, Henri. "Apologétique et théologie." *Nouvelle Revue Théologique.* vol. 57, 1930, pp. 361-378.

———. *The Drama of Atheist Humanism*. Translated by E. M. Riley. Sheed & Ward, 1949.

———. *The Mystery of the Supernatural*. Herder & Herder, 1967.

———. *Paradoxes of Faith*. Translated by P. Simon & S. Kreilkamp. Ignatius, 1987.

———. *More Paradoxes*. Translated by A. E. Nash. Ignatius, 2002

Deavel, David P. "An Odd Couple? A First Glance at Chesterton and Newman." *Logos: A Journal of Catholic Thought and Culture*, vol. 10, no. 1, 2007, pp. 116-135.

Denny, David M. "The Circle and the Cross." *The Chesterton Review*, vol. 26, no. 1-2, 2000, pp. 149-159.

Enchiridion Symbolorum et Declarationum de Rebus Fidei et Morum. Edited by Denzinger, H. & A. Schönmetzer. Herder, 1967.

Descartes, René. *Discourse on the Method*. Translated by Donald A. Cress. Hackett Publishing, 1999.

Dickens, Charles. *Hard Times*. Penguin, 1995.

Dubay, Thomas. *Faith and Certitude*. Ignatius Press, 1985.

———. *The Evidential Power of Beauty: Science and Theology Meet*. Ignatius, 1999.

Dulles, Avery. "Fundamental Theology and the Dynamics of Conversion." *The Thomist,* vol. 45, April 1981, pp. 175-193.

———. *Models of Revelation.* Gill & Macmillan, 1983.

———. "The Symbolic Structure of Revelation." *Theological Studies,* vol. 41, 1980, pp. 51-73.

———. *The Assurance of Things Hoped For: A Theology of Christian Faith.* Oxford University Press, 1994.

———. *The New World of Faith.* Our Sunday Visitor Publishing Division, 2000.

———. *A History of Apologetics.* Ignatius, 2005.

———. *Evangelization for the Third Millennium.* Paulist Press, 2009

Dupré, Louis. *Symbols of the Sacred.* W. B. Eerdmans, 2000.

Eberle, Gary. *The Geography of Nowhere: Finding One's Self in the Postmodern World.* Sheed & Ward, 1994.

Eco, Umberto and Martini, Carlo M. *Belief or Nonbelief: A Confrontation.* Translated by M. Procter. Continuum, 1997.

Edwards, Denis. *Human Experience of God.* Paulist, 1983.

Fagerberg, David. *The Size of Chesterton's Catholicism.* University of Notre Dame Press, 1998.

———. "Would Chesterton Be a Convert in 2000?" *Priests and People,* vol. 14, no. 1, 2000, pp. 18-22.

Farrer, Austin. *Finite and Infinite: A Philosophical Essay.* Dacre Press, 1959.

Feser, Edward. *The Last Superstition: The Refutation of the New Atheism.* Saint Augustine's Press, 2008.

Ffinch, Michael. *G. K. Chesterton: A Biography*. Weidenfeld & Nicholson, 1987.

Fiorenza, Joseph A. "The New Age and Christian Spirituality." *The Chesterton Review*, vol. 26, no. 1-2, 2000, pp. 161-163.

Flannery, Austin, ed. *Vatican Council II: The Conciliar and Postconciliar Documents* Vol. 1. Revised edition. Dominican Publications, 1988.

Flew, Antony. *There Is A God: How the World's Most Notorious Atheist Changed His Mind*. HarperCollins, 2007.

Fowler, James. *Stages of Faith: The Psychology of Human Development and the Quest for Meaning*. HarperCollins, 1995.

Gallagher, Michael. *Free to Believe: Ten Steps to Faith*. Darton, Longman and Todd, 1987.

———. "Apologetics: Towards a Different Agenda." *Priests and People*, vol. 9, no. 10, Oct. 1995, pp. 376-371

———. *Dive Deeper: The Human Poetry of Faith*. DLT, 2001.

———. *Clashing Symbols: An Introduction to Faith and Culture*. Revised, expanded, and edited. DLT, 2003.

———. *Faith Maps: Ten Religious Explorers from Newman to Joseph Ratzinger*. DLT, 2010.

Gardiner, Alfred G. *Prophets, Priests and Kings*. Alston Rivers, 1908.

Gilbert, W. S. and Sullivan, Arthur. *Pirates of Penzance*, 1879. http://math.boisestate.edu/gas/pirates/web_op/pirates18.html. Accessed 17 Jan. 2012.

Gilley, S. "Chesterton and Conversion." *Priests and People*, vol. 9, no. 10, 1995, pp. 381-386.

Giussani, Luigi. *The Religious Sense*. Translated by John Zucchi. Ignatius, 1990.

Greeley, Andrew. *The Catholic Imagination*. University of California Press, 2001.

Griffin, John Howard. *Follow the Ecstasy: The Hermitage Years of Thomas Merton*. Edited by R. Bonazzi. Orbis Books, 1993.

Hanssen, Susan E. "Dumb Ox at the Crossroads of English Catholicism: G. K. Chesterton's 'Thoughts Not In Themselves New.'" *Renascence*, vol. 62, no. 1, 2009, pp. 3-20.

Harper, Ralph. *On Presence: Variations and Reflections*. Trinity Press International, 1991.

Hetzler, Leo A., "Chesterton and the Realm of the Unconscious." *The Chesterton Review*, vol. 22, no. 3, 1996, pp. 327-335.

Hollis, Christopher *The Mind of Chesterton*. Hollis and Carter, 1970.

Holroyd, Michael. *Bernard Shaw: 1998-1918, Volume II: The Pursuit of Power*. Chatto and Windus, 1989.

———. *Bernard Shaw: 1956-1898, Volume I: The Search for Love*.Penguin, 1990.

Howsare, Rodney. *Balthasar: A Guide for the Perplexed*. T & T Clark, 2009.

Imbelli, Robert, ed. *Handing on the Faith: The Church's Mission and Challenge*. Herder & Herder, 2006.

Jaki, Stanley. "Chesterton's Landmark Year: The Blatchford-Chesterton Debate of 1903-4." *The Chesterton Review,* vol. 10, no. 4, 1984, pp. 409-423.

———. *Means to Message: A Treatise on Truth.* W. B. Eerdmans Publishing, 1999.

———. *Chesterton: A Seer of Science.* new ed., Real View Books, 2001.

John Of The Cross. *The Collected Works of Saint John of the Cross.* Edited by O. Rodriguez and K. Kavanaugh. ICS Publications, 1994.

———. *Dark Night of the Soul.* Riverhead Books, 2002.

John Paul II. *Redemptor Hominis.* Libreria Editrice Vaticana, 1979.

———. *Crossing the Threshold of Hope.* Edited by V. Messori. Translated by J. McPhee and M. McPhee. Random House, 1994.

———. *Letter to Artists,* 1999. http://www.vatican.va/holy_father/john_paul_ii/letters/documents/hf_jp-ii_let_23041999_artists_en.html. Accessed 12 Feb. 2011

Kasper, Walter. *The God of Jesus Christ.* Crossroad, 1986.

Kenner, Hugh. *Paradox in Chesterton.* Sheed & Ward, 1948.

Ker, Ian. *Healing the Wound of Humanity: The Spirituality of John Henry Newman.* DLT, 1993.

———. *John Henry Newman: A Biography.* OUP, 1988.

———. *G. K. Chesterton: A Biography.* Oxford University Press, 2011.

Kierkegaard, S. *Concluding Unscientific Postscript.* Translated by D. F. Swenson and W. Lowrie. Princeton University Press, 1968.

———. *The Sickness Unto Death.* Translated by A. Hannay. Penguin, 1989.

Kirsch, Arthur. *Auden and Christianity*. Yale University Press, 2005.

Knight, Mark. "Chesterton, Dostoevsky, and Freedom." *English Literature in Transition*, vol. 43, no. 1, 2000, pp. 37-50.

———. *Chesterton and Evil*. Fordham University Press, 2004.

Lane, Dermot A. T*he Experience of God: An Invitation to do Theology*. Veritas, 2003

Lash, Nicholas. *Theology for Pilgrims*. Darton, Longman & Todd, 2008.

Latourelle, R., & G. O'Collins, eds. *Problems and Perspectives of Fundamental Theology*. Translated by M. J. O'Connell. Paulist, 1982.

Latourelle, R., & R. Fisichella, eds. *Dictionary of Fundamental Theology*. Crossroads, 1994.

Lauer, Quentin. *G. K. Chesterton: Philosopher Without Portfolio*. Fordham University Press, 1991.

Léonard, A. *Le ragioni del credere*. iale Jaca Book SpA, 1994.

Leo XIII. *Rerum novarum*. Encyclical Letter on Capital and Labour, 1891. http://www.vatican.va/holy_father/leo_xiii/encyclicals/documents/ hf_l-xiii_enc_15051891_rerum-novarum_en.html. Accessed 16 Aug. 2011.

Lewis, C. S. *A Grief Observed*. Faber and Faber, 1966.

———. *Mere Christianity*. Fount, 1977.

———. *Surprised by Joy: The Shape of My Early Life*. Fount, 1977.

———. *The Four Loves*. Fount, 1977

———. *The Problem of Pain*. Fount, 1977.

———. *God in the Dock: Essays in Theology*. Fount, 1979.

———. *Christian Reflections*. Edited by Walter Hooper. Fount, 1981.

———. *Poems: The Collected Poems of C. S. Lewis*. Edited by Walter Hooper. Fount, 1994.

———. *The Pilgrim's Regress: An Allegorical Apology for Christianity, Reason and Romanticism*. Fount, 1977.

Lonergan, Bernard. *Insight: A Study of Human Understanding*. Longman, Greens & Co., 1958.

———. *Method in Theology*. Toronto University Press, 1990.

———. *The Collected Works of Bernard Lonergan*, vol. 5. University of Toronto Press, 1990

———. *Collected Papers*, vol. 20. Edited by R. C. Croken, R. M. Doran & H. D. Monsour. University of Toronto Press, 2007.

Mackey, Aidan. *G. K. Chesterton: A Prophet for the 21st Century*. IHS Press, 2009.

Manlove, Colin. "G. K. Chesterton and George Macdonald: Strangers and Brothers." *The Chesterton Review*, vol 27, no. 1-2, 2001, pp. 55-65.

Martin, James. *Becoming Who You Are: Insights on the True Self from Thomas Merton and Other Saints*. Hidden Spring, 2006.

———. *Between Heaven and Mirth: Why Joy, Humour and Laughter are the Heart of the Spiritual Life*. HarperOne, 2011.

Martini, Carlo M. *Cattedra dei non credenti*. Rusconi, 1992.

Mascall, E. L. *Existence and Analogy*. Darton, Longman & Todd, 1966.

Mcfague, Sallie. *Speaking in Parables: A Study in Metaphor and Theology*. SCM Press, 2002.

Mcgrath, Alister. *The Enigma of the Cross*. Hodder & Stoughton, 1987.

———. *The Twilight of Atheism*. Blackwell, 2005.

———. *Mere Apologetics: How to Help Seekers and Skeptics Find Faith*. Baker Books, 2012.

Mcgrath, Francis. *John Henry Newman: Universal Revelation*. Burns & Oates, 1997.

Medcalf, Stephen. "G. K. Chesterton: An Everlasting Writer?" *The Chesterton Review*, vol. 24, no. 4, 1998, pp. 451-463.

Merrigan, Terrence. "Newman and Theological Liberalism." *Theological Studies*, vol. 66, 2005, pp. 605-21.

Milbank, Alison. *Chesterton and Tolkien as Theologians: The Fantasy of the Real*. T & T Clark, 2008.

Moltmann, Jurgen. *The Crucified God*. Translated by R. A. Wilson and J. Bowden. SCM Press, 1974

Monk, Ray. *Wittgenstein: The Duty of Genius*. Vintage, 1991.

Moore, Sebastian. *The Inner Loneliness*. Darton, Longman & Todd, 1982.

Morris, K. L. *G. K. Chesterton: A Great Catholic*. CTS, 1994.

———, ed. *The Truest Fairy Tale: An Anthology of the Religious Writings of G. K. Chesterton*. Lutterworth Press, 2007

Morris, Thomas V., ed. *God and the Philosophers: The Reconciliation of Faith and Reason*. OUP, 1994.

———. "Fascism and British Catholic Writers 1924-1939." *The Chesterton Review*, vol. 25, no. 1-2, 1999, pp. 21-51.

Morton, J. B. *Hilaire Belloc: A Memoir*. Hollis and Carter, 1955.

Muggeridge, Malcolm. *Christ and the Media*. https://books.google.com/books?isbn=1573832529. Accessed 19 April 2017.

———. *The Very Best of Malcolm Muggeridge*. Edited by I. Hunter. Hodder & Stoughton, 1998.

Neuner, J., & J. Dupuis, eds. *The Christian Faith in the Doctrinal Documents of the Catholic Church*. Revised and Edited. Theological Publications, 1982.

Newman, John Henry. *Discussions and Arguments*. Pickering, 1882.

———. *Fifteen Sermons Preached Before the University of Oxford Between A.D. 1826 and 1843*. Longmans, Green and Co., 1909.

———. *Apologia pro Vita Sua*. Introduction by P. Hughes. Doubleday, 1956.

———. *The Theological Papers of John Henry Newman on Faith and Certainty*. Edited by J. D. Holmes. Clarendon Press, 1976.

———. *Letters and Diaries*, vol. 1. Edited by I. Ker & T. Gornall, 1978

———. *An Essay in Aid of a Grammar of Assent*. Introduction by N. Lash. University of Notre Dame Press, 1979.

———. *John Henry Newman: Selected Sermons*. Edited and Introduction by I. Ker and Preface by H. Chadwick. Paulist Press, 1994

Nichols, Aidan. "Chesterton and Modernism." *The Chesterton Review*, vol. 15, no. 1-2, 1989, pp. 157-174.

———, ed. "Chesterton and Modernism." *Chesterton and the Modernist Crisis*. The Chesterton Review Press, 1990, pp. 157-173.

———. *A Grammar of Consent: The Existence of God in Christian Tradition*. UNDP, 1991.

———. *G. K. Chesterton, Theologian.* DLT, 2009.

Norton, E. *Secularisation.* Continuum, 2002.

Novak, Michael. *Belief and Unbelief: a Philosophy of Self-Knowledge.* Transaction, 1997.

———. *No One Sees: The Dark Night of Atheists and Believers.* Doubleday, 2008.

Noyes, Alfred. *Two Worlds for Memory.* Lippincott, 1953.

O'Collins, Gerald. *Fundamental Theology.* DLT, 1981.

———. "At the origins of 'Dei Verbum," *Heythrop Journal,* vol. 26, 1985, pp. 5-13.

———. *Retrieving Fundamental Theology: The Three Styles of Contemporary Theology.* Geoffrey Chapman, 1993.

———. *Rethinking Fundamental Theology.* Oxford University Press, 2011.

O'Connor, Flannery. *Mystery and Manners: Occasional Prose.* Edited by S. & R. Fitzgerald. Faber and Faber, 1972.

———. *The Habit of Being: Letters of Flannery O'Connor.* Edited by S. Fitzgerald. Farrar, Straus and Giroux, 1988.

———. *Collected Works.* Edited by S. Fitzgerald. Literary Classics of the United States, Inc., 1988.

O'Connor, John. *Father Brown on Chesterton.* Muller, 1937.

O'Donoghue, Noel. "Chesterton and the Philosophical Imagination." *The Chesterton Review,* vol. 24, no. 1-2, 1998, pp. 63-81.

O'Donovan, L. J., & T. Howland Sanks, eds. *Faithful Witness: Foundations of Theology for Today's Church.* Geoffrey Chapman, 1989.

O'Leary, Daniel. *Begin with the Heart: Recovering a Sacramental Vision.* Columba, 2008.

O'Malley, William J. *God: The Oldest Question.* Loyola Press, 2000.

———. *Help My Unbelief.* Orbis, 2008.

Oddie, William. *Chesterton and the Romance of Orthodoxy: The Making of GKC, 1874-1908.* Oxford University Press, 2008.

———. *The Holiness of G. K. Chesterton.* Gracewing, 2010

Paine, Randall. *The Universe and Mr. Chesterton.* Sherwood, Sugden & Company, 1999.

Pannenberg, Wolfhart. *Metaphysics and the Idea of God.* Translated by Philip Clayton. Eerdmans, 1990.

Pascal, Blaise. *Pensées.* Le Livre de Poche, 1972.

Pearce, Joseph. *Wisdom and Innocence: A Life of G. K. Chesterton.* Hodder & Stoughton, 1996.

———. *Literary Converts: Spiritual Inspiration in an Age of Unbelief.* HarperCollins, 1999.

———. "Fascism and Chesterton." *The Chesterton Review,* vol. 25, no. 1-2, 1999, pp. 69-79.

———. *The Unmasking of Oscar Wilde.* Ignatius, 2005.

Peters, Thomas C. *The Christian Imagination: G. K. Chesterton on the Arts.* Ignatius, 2000.

Pieper, Josef. *Death and Immortality.* Herder and Herder, 1969.

———. *Faith, Hope and Love.* Translated by Sr. M. F. McCarthy. Ignatius, 1986.

———. *Divine Madness: Plato's Case Against Secular Humanism*. Ignatius, 1995.

Plato. *Phaedrus*. Penguin, 2005.

Quillo, Ronald. *Two Cultures of Belief: The Fallacy of Christian Certitude, a Systems Approach*. Triumph Books, 1998.

Quinn, Dermot. "Chesterton, Lewis, Tolkien and the Moral Imagination." *The Chesterton Review*, vol. 35, no. 1-2, 2009, pp. 115-123.

Radcliffe, Timothy. *What is the Point of Being a Christian?* Burns & Oates, 2005.

Rahner, Karl. *Servants of the Lord*. Burns and Oates, 1968.

———. *Do You Believe in God?* Translated by R. Strachan. Paulist, 1969.

———. *Foundations of Christian Faith: An Introduction to the Idea of Christianity*. Crossroad, 1978.

———. *Spirit in the World*. Foreword by J.B. Metz. Continuum, 1995.

———. *Theological Investigations*. Darton, Longman & Todd, 1972-1984. Vol. II, tr. K. H. Kruger; Vol. IV, tr. K. Smyth; Vol. V, tr. K. H. Kruger; Vol. VI, tr. K. H. and B. Kruger; Vol. VII, tr. D. Bourke; Vol. IX, tr. G. Harrison; Vol. XIV, tr. D. Bourke; Vol. XVI, tr. D. Morland.

Ratzinger, Joseph. *Principles of Catholic Theology: Building Stones for a Fundamental Theology*. Ignatius, 1987.

———. "Homily at the Funeral Liturgy for Hans Urs Von Balthasar." *Communio*, vol. 15, Winter 1988, pp. 512-516.

———. *The Salt of the Earth* (conversation with Peter Seewald). Ignatius, 2002.

———. *The End of Time?: The Provocation of Talking About God*. With J. B. Metz et al. Edited by J. M. Ashley. Paulist Press, 2004.

Rausch, Thomas. *Reconciling Faith and Reason: Apologists, Evangelists and Theologians in a Divided Church.* The Liturgical Press, 2000.

Rolheiser, Ronald. *The Shattered Lantern: Rediscovering the Felt Presence of God.* Hodder & Stoughton, 1994.

———, ed. *Secularity and the Gospel: Being Missionaries to Our Children.* Crossroad Publishing, 2006.

Roten, J. G. "Why Stay in the Church, Benedict XVI?" http://campus. udayton.edu/mary/benedictxvi.html. Accessed 17th February 2012.

Rowan, Paul. "G. K. Chesterton and the 'Court of the Gentiles' (1)." *The Pastoral Review,* vol. 6, no. 4, 2010, pp. 53-7.

——— "G. K. Chesterton and the 'Court of the Gentiles' (2)." *The Pastoral Review,* vol. 6, no. 5, 2010, pp. 50-55.

——— "G. K. Chesterton and the 'Court of the Gentiles' (3)." *The Pastoral Review* vol. 6, no. 6, 2010, pp. 59-65.

Sartre, Jean-Paul. *Huis-clos.* Edited by K. Gore. Methuen & Co., 1987.

Saward, John. "Chesterton and Balthasar: The Likeness is Greater." *The Chesterton Review,* vol. 22, no. 3, 1996, pp. 301-325.

Schall, James. *Schall on Chesterton: Timely Essays on Timeless Paradoxes.* Catholic University of America Press, 2000.

Schmude, Karl. *Hilaire Belloc: His Life and Legacy.* A.C.T.S Publications., 1978.

———. "G. K. Chesterton and Malcolm Muggeridge: A Balance of Opposites." *The Chesterton Review,* vol. 35, no. 3-4, 2009, pp. 577-599.

Schwartz, Adam. "Conceiving a Culture of Life in a Century of Bones: G. K. Chesterton and Malcolm Muggeridge as Social Critics." *Logos:*

A Journal of Catholic Thought and Culture , vol. 11, no. 2, 2008, pp. 50-76.

Scott, Drusilla. *Michael Polanyi.* SPCK, 1996.

Shaw, George. Bernard. *Man and Superman: a comedy and a philosophy.* The University Press, 1903.

Sheed, Frank. *The Church and I.* Sheed and Ward, 1976.

Smith, Cyprian. *The Way of Paradox: Spiritual life as Taught by Meister Eckhart.* DLT, 1987.

Smith, Wilfred. C. *Faith and Belief.* Princeton University Press, 1979.

Soelle, Dorothee. *Theology for Sceptics.* Mowbray, 1995.

Spackman, Paul. "The Poet and the Pope: G. K. Chesterton and John Paul I." *The Chesterton Review,* vol. 27, no. 3, 2001, pp. 311-315.

Sparkes, Russell. "The Recovery of the Guilds." *The Chesterton Review,* vol. 19, no. 4, 1993, pp. 499-513.

———, ed. *Prophet of Orthodoxy: The Wisdom of G. K. Chesterton.* Fount, 1997.

Speaight, Robert. *The Life of Hilaire Belloc.* Hollis and Carter, 1957.

Špidlík, T., M. Rupnik & L. Bratina, eds. *A partire dalla persona: una teologia per la nuova evangelizzazione.* Lipa, 1994.

Stackhouse JR, John G. *Humble Apologetics: Defending the Faith Today.* Oxford University Press, 2002.

Sullivan, Francis. *Salvation Outside the Church?: Tracing the History of the Catholic Response*. Geoffrey Chapman, 1992.

Sullivan, John. *G. K. Chesterton: A Centenary Appraisal, 1874-1974*. HarperCollins, 1974.

Swinnerton, Frank. *The Georgian Literary Scene*. Hutchinson, 1950.

Taylor, Charles. *Sources of the Self: The Making of the Modern Identity*. Cambridge University Press, 1989.

———. *A Catholic Modernity*. Oxford University Press, 1999.

———. *Modern Social Imaginaries*. Duke University Press, 2004.

———. *A Secular Age*. Harvard University Press, 2007.

Tillich, Paul. *Dynamics of Faith*. With an epilogue by R. N. Anshen. Harper & Row, 1957

Tracy, David. *On Naming the Present: God, Hermeneutics and Church*. Orbis, 1994.

———. *The Analogical Imagination*. Crossroad Publishing, 1998.

Valentine, Ferdinand. *Father Vincent McNabb, O.P.: The Portrait of a Great Dominican*. Burns and Oates, 1955.

Vanhoozer, Kevin. "Theology and the Condition of Postmodernity." *The Cambridge Companion to Postmodern Theology*. Edited by Kevin Vanhoozer. Cambridge University Press, 2003, pp. 3-24.

Vardy, Peter. *What is Truth?: Beyond Postmodernism and Fundamentalism*. John Hunt, 2003.

Von Balthasar, Hans Urs. *The Glory of the Lord*, Vol. I, *Seeing the Form*. T & T Clark, 1983.

———. *Theo-Drama* Vol. I, *Prologomena*. Ignatius, 1988.

———. *Explorations in Theology*, Vol. I, *The Word Made Flesh*. Ignatius, 1989.

———. *Razing the Bastions: On the Church in this Age*. Ignatius, 1993.

———. *Theo-Drama* Vol. II, *Dramatis Personae: Man in God*. Ignatius, 1993.

———. *Theo-Logic*, Vol. I, *The Truth of the World*. Translated by A. J. Walker. Ignatius, 2000.

———. *The Glory of the Lord*, Vol. VII, *Theology: A New Covenant*. Ignatius, 2003.

Ward, Keith. *God: A Guide for the Perplexed*. Oneworld Publications, 2005.

———. *Why There Almost Certainly Is a God: Doubting Dawkins*. Lion Books, 2008.

Ward, Maisie. *Return to Chesterton*. Sheed & Ward, 1952.

———. *Gilbert Keith Chesterton*. Penguin, 1958.

Wells, H. G. *Anticipations of the Reaction of Mechanical and Scientific Progress upon Human Life and Thought*. Dover Publications, 1999.

Whitehead, Alfred North. *Science and the Modern World*. Simon and Schuster, 1997.

Williams, Peter S. *I Wish I Could Believe in Meaning: A Response to Nihilism*. Damaris Publishing, 2004.

Williams, Rowan. *Dostoevsky: Language, Faith and Fiction*. Continuum, 2008.

Wills, Gary. *Chesterton: Man and Mask*. Revised, edited and with a new introduction. Doubleday, 2001.

Wilson, A. N. *C. S. Lewis: A Biography*. Flamingo, 1991.

———. *Hilaire Belloc*. Mandarin, 1997.

Wittgenstein, Ludwig. *Tractatus Logico-Philosophicus*. Routledge & Kegan Paul, 1951.

———. *Lectures on Ethics, Culture and Value*. Edited by G. H. von Wright. Translated by P. Winch. Blackwell, 1966.

Wood, Ralph C. "Hospitality as the Gift greater than Tolerance: G. K. Chesterton's The Ball and the Cross." *Logos: A Journal of Catholic Thought and Culture,* vol. 12, no. 4, 2009, pp. 158-185.

———. *Chesterton: the Nightmare Goodness of God*. Baylor University Press, 2011.

Woodhead, Linda "Convergences between Christianity and the New Age: The Turn to Life." *The Chesterton Review,* vol. 26, no. 1-2, 2000, pp. 75-93.

Woodruff, Douglas, ed. *For Hilaire Belloc: Essays in Honour of his 71st Birthday*. Sheed & Ward, 1942.

Zacharias, Ravi. *A Shattered Visage: The Challenge of Atheism*. Hodder & Stoughton, 1996.

Zalesky, Philip. "The New Age and the Search for Self-Knowledge." *The Chesterton Review,* vol. 26, no. 1-2, 2000, pp. 135-147.

Index of Names

A

Aesculapius 364
Agatha Christie 30
Ahlquist 53, 62, 63, 69, 159, 173, 176,
    184, 193, 219, 274, 275, 279,
    280, 346, 405, 425, 437, 450,
    500, 521, 551, 586, 599
Albert the Great 373
Alfred the Great 22, 99
Ambrosiaster 464, 466
Amis 30
Anscombe 600
Anselm of Canterbury 341
Appleyard 600
Aquinas 5, 7, 39, 84, 117, 123, 126,
    129, 130, 142, 182, 183, 205,
    207, 208, 229, 232, 233, 236,
    237, 238, 247, 260, 286, 290,
    341, 370, 371, 372, 373, 374,
    376, 377, 379, 400, 431, 432,
    438, 442, 464, 465, 466, 471,
    497, 499, 508, 520, 525, 555,
    566, 578, 597, 600, 603
Aristotle 191, 194, 207, 250, 273, 299,
    370, 372, 373, 471, 600
Arts 600
Athanasius 311, 334, 459
Auden 30, 550, 613
Augsutine of Hippo 600
Augustine of Hippo 5, 39, 40, 104, 153,
    174, 181, 284, 285, 289, 341,
    389, 465, 484, 495, 499, 524,
    529, 583, 609

B

Bacik 600
Balthasar 283, 399, 420, 421, 422, 424,
    473, 554, 567, 611, 620
Barrie 449
Barron 236, 237, 600

Bastable 143, 146, 147, 150, 462, 567
Bausch 601
Beardsley 273
Beatrice 17, 32, 34
Belloc 19, 20, 26, 30, 74, 154, 299, 302,
    304, 305, 306, 307, 308, 309,
    310, 311, 312, 313, 314, 315,
    316, 317, 325, 328, 344, 375,
    381, 393, 436, 474, 517, 539,
    543, 601, 615, 620, 624
Belmonte 601
Benedict XVI 12, 139, 170, 347, 348,
    400, 466, 467, 468, 480, 491,
    492, 496, 498, 502, 516, 538,
    546, 565, 568, 575, 593, 596,
    601, 620
Bentham 432, 436
Bentley 37, 43, 45, 46, 83, 108, 269
Berger 601
Blake 180, 214, 272, 339, 604
Blatchford 51, 52, 78, 79, 186, 206,
    260, 264, 302, 350, 431, 606,
    612
Blondel 5, 601
Bohr 240
Booth 308
Bossuet 318
Botticelli 55, 273
Brown 299, 304, 602
Buddha 207, 331
Bull 602

C

Caldecott 602
Carpenter 602
Cecil Chesterton 17
Champernoon 324
Chesterton
    Ada. *See* Prothero, J.K.
Chesterton, A. 602

TAN·CLASSICS

A collection of the finest literature
in the Catholic tradition.

SAINT TERESA OF AVILA

The INTERIOR CASTLE
or The MANSIONS

TAN·CLASSICS

978-0-89555-227-3

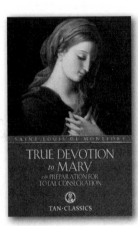

SAINT LOUIS DE MONTFORT

TRUE DEVOTION
to MARY
with PREPARATION FOR
TOTAL CONSECRATION

TAN·CLASSICS

978-0-89555-154-2

SAINT THÉRÈSE OF LI

The STORY
of a SOUL
The autobiography of the Little Flower

TAN·CLASSICS

978-0-89555-155-9

Our TAN Classics collection is a well-balanced sampling of the finest literature in the Catholic tradition.

SAINT JOHN OF THE CROSS

DARK NIGHT
of the SOUL

TAN·CLASSICS

978-0-89555-230-3

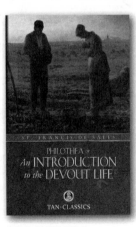

ST. FRANCIS DE SALES

PHILOTHEA *or*
An INTRODUCTION
to the DEVOUT LIFE

TAN·CLASSICS

978-0-89555-228-0

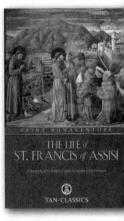

SAINT BONAVENTURE

THE LIFE *of*
ST. FRANCIS *of* ASSISI

TAN·CLASSICS

978-0-89555-151-1

TAN·BOOKS

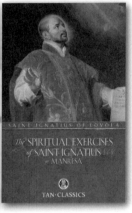

978-0-89555-153-5

978-0-89555-149-8

978-0-89555-199-3

The collection includes distinguished spiritual works of the saints, philosophical treatises and famous biographies.

978-0-89555-226-6

978-0-89555-152-8

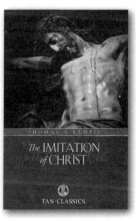

978-0-89555-225-9

Visit us at TANBooks.com

TAN·BOOKS

TAN Books is the Publisher You Can Trust With Your Faith.

TAN Books was founded in 1967 to preserve the spiritual, intellectual, and liturgical traditions of the Catholic Church. At a critical moment in history TAN kept alive the great classics of the Faith and drew many to the Church. In 2008 TAN was acquired by Saint Benedict Press. Today TAN continues to teach and defend the Faith to a new generation of readers.

TAN publishes more than 600 booklets, Bibles, and books. Popular subject areas include theology and doctrine, prayer and the supernatural, history, biography, and the lives of the saints. TAN's line of educational and homeschooling resources is featured at TANHomeschool.com.

TAN publishes under several imprints, including TAN, Neumann Press, ACS Books, and the Confraternity of the Precious Blood. Sister imprints include Saint Benedict Press, Catholic Courses, and Catholic Scripture Study.

**For more information about TAN,
or to request a free catalog, visit
TANBooks.com**

**Or call us toll-free at
(800) 437-5876**